O. HOOD PHIL...

LEADING CASES

WITHDRAWN

CONSTITUTIONAL AND

ADMINISTRATIVE LAW

AUSTRALIA AND NEW ZEALAND
The Law Book Company Ltd.
Sydney : Melbourne : Perth

CANADA AND U.S.A.
The Carswell Company Ltd.
Agincourt, Ontario

INDIA
N. M. Tripathi Private Ltd.
Bombay
and
Eastern Law House Private Ltd.
Calcutta and Delhi
M.P.P. House
Bangalore

ISRAEL
Steimatzky's Agency Ltd.
Jerusalem : Tel Aviv : Haifa

O. HOOD PHILLIPS'
LEADING CASES
IN
CONSTITUTIONAL AND
ADMINISTRATIVE LAW

Sixth Edition

BY

PAUL JACKSON
LL.D. (LIVERPOOL), B.C.L. (OXON.), M.A. (DUBLIN)
of Gray's Inn, Barrister;
Professor of Law, University of Reading

LONDON
SWEET & MAXWELL
1988

First Edition	1952
Second Edition	1957
Third Edition	1967
Fourth Edition	1973
First Impression	1978
Fifth Edition	1979
Sixth Edition	1988

Published in 1987 by
Sweet & Maxwell Limited of
11, New Fetter Lane, London
Computerset by CCI Technical Services Limited, Hitchin, Herts.
Printed and bound in Great Britain by
Richard Clay (The Chaucer Press) Limited, Bungay, Suffolk

British Library Cataloguing in Publication Data

Phillips, O. Hood (Owen Hood), *1907–1986*
O. Hood Phillips' leading cases in
constitutional and administrative law.—
6th ed.
1. Great Britain. Constitutional law
2. Great Britain. Administrative law
I. Title   II. Jackson, Paul
344.102

ISBN 0–421–40600–3

PREFACE TO THE SIXTH EDITION

In the Preface to the first edition of *Leading Cases* to appear under his own name, in 1952, Hood Phillips explained "for those interested in bibliography" that the book was a revised edition of Thomas & Hood Phillips' *Leading Cases in Constitutional Law* which had been published in 1947. *Thomas & Hood Phillips* was itself the eighth edition of Ernest C. Thomas's *Leading Cases in Constitutional Law* which had first been published in 1876. Various editions followed, under different editors. The third, in 1901, and fourth, in 1908, were by Charles L. Attenborough; the fifth, in 1924, by Hugh H.L. Bellot. The title of the book became Thomas & Bellot's *Leading Cases* for the sixth edition, in 1927, and remained the same for the seventh edition, in 1934, under E. Slade, before becoming Thomas & Hood Phillips. Early editions were little more than one hundred pages in length. The sixth edition saw a considerable increase—to over three hundred pages—occasioned, partly, by the need to take account of the constitutional issues raised by the War of 1914–18. Since then, perhaps inevitably, there has been further growth from edition to edition. Even so, new material has only been accommodated by jettisoning old: a process which has had to be ruthlessly followed in this edition where any attempt to include a reasonable selection of decisions of the last nine years has involved the deletion of nearly half of the previous text and the pruning of some of that which remains.

As in previous editions notes are kept to a minimum because it is assumed that the student reader will have to hand a copy of *O. Hood Phillips' Constitutional and Administrative Law* (7th ed.), or some other suitable textbook. In choosing cases for inclusion preference has been given to those which deal with central issues of constitutional and administrative law, preferably by reference to interesting and easily intelligible facts. Particularly in areas such as individual rights and duties, discrimination and administrative law the details of statute law and case law are dealt with well elsewhere. Similarly, the impact of European law is represented by only one recent case (*Duke* v. *Reliance Systems Ltd.*) An attempt has also been made to include cases which reflect developments after the appearance of the 7th edition of *Constitutional and Administrative Law*. For the same reason, the Crown Proceedings (Armed Forces) Act 1987 is, exceptionally, included. (In some instances developments since the appearance of the textbook are discussed in notes, following extracted cases: *e.g.*, the note to *Anns* v. *Merton L.B.C.*).

Again, as in previous decisions, the emphasis is on letting the cases speak for themselves. The introductions to the cases are not meant as headnotes containing the *rationes decidendi*. In the words of Hood Phillips, included in the preface to each of his editions of *Leading Cases*, "However skilful one may be in putting into three lines what the house of Lords takes 30 pages to say, the result is liable to mislead. The student should learn to extract the *ratio decidendi* for himself. There may be more than one in a given case. He should be aware, in particular, that it is not necessarily the statement of principle that may be contained in the judge's opinion. 'It is always a little dangerous,' as Greer L.J. said in *Monk* v. *Warbey* [1935] 1 K.B. 75, 'to pick out one or two observations from a long judgment and treat them as if they necessarily afforded the *ratio decidendi* of the case.'"

A new introductory chapter contains the lengthy judicial discussion of constitutional conventions in *Re Amendment of the Constitution of Canada*. Other extracts include judicial statements on the rule of law and the separation of powers. (The editor must not necessarily be taken to agree with the views expressed in these or other judgments included in this casebook.) There is no substantial change in the section on Parliament although recent decisions have been included where appropriate, for example, *Manuel* v. *Attorney General*. The section on the Executive includes, inevitably, *Council of Civil Service Unions* v. *Minister for the Civil Service*, as well as other recent cases on such matters as the effect of treaties on domestic law and the scope of the prerogative in relation to the police: *Ex parte Northumbria Police Authority*. The section on Administration of Justice is largely new, from the lengthy discussion in the House of Lords on the definition of a court and the scope of the law of contempt (*Attorney-General* v. *B.B.C.*) to a number of important cases on contempt, following the Contempt of Court Act 1981. In the section of Rights and Duties of the Individual attention has been devoted to questions of general principle. Freedom of Assembly and Association has, for the time being, been deleted. The earlier case law has been largely overtaken by recent legislation such as the Police and Criminal Evidence Act 1984 and the Public Order Act 1986. The detailed provisions of those Acts lie outside a book such as this and it is too early to say that they have yet produced any leading cases. Martial law, military law and the use of force by the military have been omitted because of pressure of space—as has treason. Freedom of Speech includes some judicial discussion of the importance of freedom of speech. A number of cases are included on Confidentiality, a topic which seems likely to remain an important ground for trying to limit freedom of expression in various areas. The section on Judicial Control of Public Authorities includes many new decisions beginning, inevitably, with *O'Reilly* v *Mackman*. It has also been largely re-organised to try to reflect the significance of those decisions in regard both to the grounds for judicial review and the appropriate remedies by which to challenge the acts of public bodies. There is a new section on Crown Proceedings which takes account of recent litigation such as *Trawnik* v. *Lennox* and legislation such as the Crown Proceedings (Armed Forces) Act 1987. In the sphere of remedies, *Ex parte Herbage* appears on the availability of injunctions and *Science Research Council* v. *Nasse* and *Air Canada* v. *Secretary of State for Trade* are included under the heading of Public Interest Immunity.

Although the manuscript was delivered to the publishers in March it has been possible to take account of certain later developments at proof stage.

I am indebted to Sweet and Maxwell for the preparation of the tables and index.

Acknowledgements are due to the Incorporated Council of Law Reporting in England and Wales, the Incorporated Council of Law Reporting for Northern Ireland, the Scottish Council of Law Reporting, the European Law Centre, Lloyds of London Press Ltd., and the proprietors of the *All England Law Reports*, *Simons Tax Cases*, *Lexis*, the *Times Law Reports*, the *Scots Law Times*, and the *Criminal Law Review* for permission to publish extracts from their reports; and also to the Controller of H.M. Stationery Office for permission to publish extracts from the statutes.

Paul Jackson
June 29, 1988

CONTENTS

Abbreviation
C. & A.L. is used throughout *Leading Cases* to refer to *O. Hood Phillips'
Constitutional and Administrative Law* (7th ed., 1987).

TABLE OF CASES

(References in **heavy type** indicate that a case is reported in this book)

TABLE OF STATUTES

1. INTRODUCTORY

CONSTITUTIONAL CONVENTIONS

Reference Re Amendment of the Constitution of Canada
(1982) 125 D.L.R. (3d) 1
Supreme Court of Canada

Under legislation which allowed the views of the courts to be ascertained not only on questions of law but also on non-justiciable issues, the courts of three of the provinces had been asked:

(1) whether as a matter of law the agreement of the provinces was required before the Queen could be requested to lay before the Parliament of the United Kingdom legislation to amend the Constitution of Canada (at that time contained in the British North America Act 1867, as amended);

(2) whether the agreement of the provinces was required as a matter of constitutional convention.

From the provincial courts appeal lay to the Supreme Court of Canada.

In answering the second question the Supreme Court considered at length the nature of constitutional conventions and the existence of the particular conventions alleged. This decision is not authority for the view that English Courts could engage in a similar exercise: the Supreme Court was acting under statutory provisions, which have no parallel in the United Kingdom, apart from the Judicial Committee Act 1833, s.4, which applies only to the Judicial Committee of the Privy Council. (See C. & A.L., p.296).

A majority of the Supreme Court (Laskin C.J.C., Dickson, Beetz, Estey, McIntyre, Chouinard and Lamer JJ., Martland and Ritchie JJ. dissenting) held that the consent of the provinces was not required by law.

A differently constituted majority (Martland, Ritchie, Dickson, Beetz, Chouinard and Lamer JJ., Laskin C.J.C., Estey and McIntyre JJ. dissenting) held that consent was required by convention.

The Law

LASKIN C.J.C., DICKSON BEETZ, ESTEY, MCINTYRE, CHOUINARD AND LAMER, JJ.: The proposition was advanced on behalf of the Attorney-General of Manitoba that a convention may crystallize into law and that the requirement of provincial consent to the kind of Resolution that we have here, although in origin political, has become a rule of law. (No firm position was taken on whether the consent must be that of the Governments or that of the Legislatures.)

In our view, this is not so. No instance of an explicit recognition of a convention as having matured into a rule of law was produced. The very nature of a convention, as political in inception and as depending on a consistent course of political recognition by those for whose benefit and to whose detriment (if any) the convention developed over a considerable period of time is inconsistent with its legal enforcement.

The attempted assimilation of the growth of a convention to the growth of the common law is misconceived. The latter is the product of judicial effort, based on justiciable issues which have attained legal formulation and are subject to modification and even reversal by the Courts which gave them birth when acting within their role in the State in obedience to statutes or constitutional directives. No such parental role is played by the Courts with respect to conventions.

It was urged before us that a host of cases have given legal force to conventions. This is an overdrawn proposition. One case in which direct recognition and enforcement of a convention was sought is *Madzimbamuto* v. *Lardner-Burke et al.*, [1969] 1 A.C. 645. There the Privy Council rejected the assertion that a convention formally recognized by the United Kingdom as established, namely, that it would not legislate for Southern Rhodesia on matters within the competence of the latter's Legislature without its Government's consent, could not be overridden by British legislation made applicable to Southern Rhodesia after the unilateral declaration of independence by the latter's Government. Speaking for the Privy Council, Lord Reid pointed out that although the convention was a very important one, "it had no legal effect in limiting the legal power of Parliament" (at p. 723). And, again (at the same page):

> "It is often said that it would be unconstitutional for the United Kingdom Parliament to do certain things, meaning that the moral, political and other reasons against doing them are so strong that most people would regard it as highly improper if Parliament did these things. But that does not mean that it is beyond the power of Parliament to do such things. If Parliament chose to do any of them the courts could not hold the Act of Parliament invalid. It may be that it would be unconstitutional to disregard this convention. But it may also be that the unilateral Declaration of Independence released the United Kingdom from any obligation to observe the convention. Their Lordships in declaring the law are not concerned with these matters. They are only concerned with the legal powers of Parliament."

[Their Lordships then considered and explained a number of authorities which had been cited in favour of the proposition which they here reject.]

Conventions
MARTLAND, RITCHIE, DICKSON, BEETZ, CHOUINARD AND LAMER JJ.: A substantial part of the rules of the Canadian Constitution are written. They are contained not in a single document called a Constitution but in a great variety of statutes some of which have been enacted by the Parliament of Westminster, such as the British North America Act 1867, 30 & 31 Vict., c. 3 (U.K.) (the B.N.A. Act), or by the Parliament of Canada, such as the Alberta Act 1905, 4–5 Edw. VII, c. 3 (Can.); the Saskatchewan Act 1905, 4–5 Edw. VII, c. 42 (Can.); the Senate and House of Commons Act R.S.C. 1970, c. S–8, or by the provincial Legislatures, such as the provincial electoral Acts. They are also to be found in Orders in Council like the Imperial Order in Council of May 16, 1871, admitting British Columbia into the Union, and the Imperial Order in Council of June 26, 1873, admitting Prince Edward Island into the Union.

Another part of the Constitution of Canada consists of the rules of the common law. These are rules which the Courts have developed over the centuries in the discharge of their judicial duties. An important portion of these rules concerns the prerogative of the Crown. Sections 9 and 15 of the B.N.A. Act provide:

> "9. The Executive Government and authority of and over Canada is hereby declared to continue and be vested in the Queen.

> . . . . . .

> 15. The Commander-in-chief of the Land and Naval Militia, and of all Naval and Military Forces, of and in Canada, is hereby declared to continue and be vested in the Queen."

But the Act does not otherwise say very much with respect to the elements of "Executive Government and authority" and one must look at the common law to find out what they are, apart from authority delegated to the Executive by statute.

The common law provides that the authority of the Crown includes for instance the prerogative of mercy or clemency . . . and the power to incorporate by charter so as to confer a general capacity analogous to that of a natural person. . . . The royal prerogative puts the Crown in a preferred position as a creditor . . . or with respect to the inheritance of lands for defect of heirs . . . or in relation to the ownership of precious metals and *bona vacantia*. . . . It is also under the prerogative and the common law that the Crown appoints and receives ambassadors, declares war, concludes treaties and it is in the name of the Queen that passports are issued.

Those parts of the Constitution of Canada which are composed of statutory rules and common law rules are generically referred to as the law of the Constitution. In cases of doubt or dispute, it is the function of the Courts to declare what the law is and since the law is sometimes breached, it is generally the function of the Courts to ascertain whether it has in fact been breached in specific instances and, if so, to apply such sanctions as are contemplated by the law, whether they be punitive sanctions or civil sanctions such as a declaration of nullity. Thus, when a federal or a provincial statute is found by the Courts to be in excess of the legislative competence of the Legislature which has enacted it, it is declared null and void and the Courts refuse to give effect to it. In this sense it can be said that the law of the Constitution is administered or enforced by the Courts.

But many Canadians would perhaps be surprised to learn that important parts of the Constitution of Canada, with which they are the most familiar because they are directly involved when they exercise their right to vote at federal and provincial elections, are nowhere to be found in the law of the Constitution. For instance it is a fundamental requirement of the Constitution that if the Opposition obtains the majority at the polls, the Government must tender its resignation forthwith. But fundamental as it is, this requirementof the Constitution does not form part of the law of the Constitution.

It is also a constitutional requirement that the person who is appointed Prime Minister or Premier by the Crown and who is the effective head of the Government should have the support of the elected branch of the Legislature; in practice this means in most cases the leader of the political party which has won a majority of seats at a general election. Other ministers are appointed by the Crown on the advice of the Prime Minister or Premier when he forms or reshuffles his cabinet. Ministers must continuously have the confidence of the elected branch of the Legislature, individually and collectively. Should they lose it, they must either resign or ask the Crown for a dissolution of the Legislature and the holding of a general election. Most of the powers of the Crown under the prerogative are exercised only upon the advice of the Prime Minister or the Cabinet which means that they are effectively exercised by the latter, together with the innumerable statutory powers delegated to the Crown in council.

Yet none of these essential rules of the Constitution can be said to be a law of the Constitution. It was apparently Dicey who, in the first edition of his *Law of the Constitution*, in 1885, called them "the conventions of the constitution" (W.S. Holdsworth, "The Conventions of the Eighteenth Century Constitution," 17 Iowa Law Rev. 161 (1932)), an expression which quickly became current. What Dicey described under these terms are the principles and rules of responsible government, several of which are stated above and which regulate the relations between the Crown, the Prime Minister, the Cabinet and the two Houses of Parliament. These rules developed in Great Britain by way of custom and precedent during the nineteenth century and were exported to such British colonies as were granted self-government.

Dicey first gave the impression that constitutional conventions are a peculiarly British and modern phenomenon. But he recognized in later editions that different conventions are found in other constitutions. . . .

Within the British Empire, powers of government were vested in different bodies which provided a fertile ground for the growth of new constitutional conventions unknown to Dicey whereby self-governing colonies acquired equal and independent status within the Commonwealth. Many of these culminated in the Statute of Westminster 1931, 22 Geo. V, c.4 (U.K.).

A federal constitution provides for the distribution of powers between various Legislatures and Governments and may also constitute a fertile ground for the growth of constitutional conventions between those Legislatures and Governments. It is conceivable for instance that usage and practice might give birth to conventions in Canada relating to the holding of federal-provincial conferences, the appointment of Lieutenant-Governors, the reservation and disallowance of provincial legislation. It was to this possibility that Duff C.J.C. alluded when he referred to "constitutional usage or constitutional practice" in *Reference re Power of Disallowance and Power of Reservation*, [1938] 2 D.L.R. 8 at p. 13, [1938] S.C.R. 71 at p. 78. He had previously called them "recognized constitutional conventions" in *Wilson* v. *E. & N. R. Co.* (1921), 61 D.L.R. 1 at p. 6, [1922] 1 A.C. 202 at p. 210, [1921] 3 W.W.R. 817.

The main purpose of constitutional conventions is to ensure that the legal framework of the Constitution will be operated in accordance with the prevailing constitutional values or principles of the period. For example, the constitutional value which is the pivot of the conventions stated above and relating to responsible government is the democratic principle: the powers of the State must be exercised in accordance with the wishes of the electorate; and the constitutional value or principle which anchors the conventions regulating the relationship between the members of the Commonwealth is the independence of the former British colonies.

Being based on custom and precedent, constitutional conventions are usually unwritten rules. Some of them, however, may be reduced to writing and expressed in the proceedings and documents of Imperial conferences, or in the preamble of statutes such as the Statute of Westminster 1931, or in the proceedings and documents of federal-provincial conferences. They are often referred to and recognized in statements made by members of governments.

The conventional rules of the Constitution present one striking peculiarity. In contradistinction to the laws of the Constitution, they are not enforced by the Courts. One reason for this situation is that, unlike common law rules, conventions are not judge-made rules. They are not based on judicial precedents but on precedents established by the institutions of government themselves. Nor are they in the nature of statutory commands which it is the function and duty of the Courts to obey and enforce. Furthermore, to enforce them would mean to administer some formal sanction when they are breached. But the legal system from which they are distinct does not contemplate formal sanctions for their breach.

Perhaps the main reason why conventional rules cannot be enforced by the Courts is that they are generally in conflict with the legal rules which they postulate and the Courts are bound to enforce the legal rules. The conflict is not of a type which would entail the commission of any illegality. It results from the fact that legal rules create wide powers, discretions and rights which conventions prescribe should be exercised only in a certain limited manner, if at all.

.   .   .   .   .

This conflict between convention and law which prevents the Courts from enforcing conventions also prevents conventions from crystallizing into laws, unless it be by statutory adoption.

It is because the sanctions of convention rest with institutions of government other than Courts, such as the Governor General or the Lieutenant-Governor, or the Houses of Parliament, or with public opinion and ultimately, with the electorate that it is generally said that they are political.

We respectfully adopt the definition of a convention given by the learned Chief

Justice of Manitoba, Freedman C.J.M., in the Manitoba Reference at pp. 13–4:

"What is a constitutional convention? There is a fairly lengthy literature on the subject. Although there may be shades of difference among the constitutional lawyers, political scientists and Judges who have contributed to that literature, the essential features of a convention may be set forth with some degree of confidence. Thus there is general agreement that a convention occupies a position somewhere in between a usage or custom on the one hand and a constitutional law on the other. There is general agreement that if one sought to fix that position with greater precision he would place convention nearer to law than to usage or custom. There is also general agreement that "a convention is a rule which is regarded as obligatory by the officials to whom it applies". Hogg, *Constitutional Law of Canada* (1977), p. 9. There is, if not general agreement, at least weighty authority, that the sanction for breach of a convention will be political rather than legal."

It should be borne in mind, however, that, while they are not laws, some conventions may be more important than some laws. Their importance depends on that of the value or principle which they are meant to safeguard. Also they form an integral part of the Constitution of the constitutional system. They come within the meaning of the word "Constitution" in the preamble of the British North America Act 1867:

"Whereas the Provinces of Canada, Nova Scotia, and New Brunswick have expressed their Desire to be federally united . . . with a Constitution similar in principle to that of the United Kingdom:"

That is why it is perfectly appropriate to say that to violate a convention is to do something which is unconstitutional although it entails no direct legal consequence. But the words "constitutional" and "unconstitutional" may also be used in a strict legal sense, for instance with respect to a statute which is found *ultra vires* or unconstitutional. The foregoing may perhaps be summarized in an equation: constitutional conventions plus constitutional law equal the total Constitution of the country.

. . . . .

We are not asked to hold that a convention has in effect repealed a provision of the B.N.A.Act . . . . Nor are we asked to enforce a convention. We are asked to recognize it if it exists. Courts have done this very thing many times in England and the Commonwealth to provide aid for and background to constitutional or statutory construction. Several such cases are mentioned in the reasons of the majority of this Court relating to the question whether constitutional conventions are capable of crystallizing into law.

In so recognizing conventional rules, the Courts have described them, sometimes commented upon them and given them such precision as is derived from the written form of judgment. They did not shrink from doing so on account of the political aspects of conventions, nor because of their supposed vagueness, uncertainty or flexibility.

In our view, we should not, in a constitutional reference, decline to accomplish a type of exercise that Courts have been doing of their own motion for years.

. . . . .

Requirements for establishing a convention
The requirements for establishing a convention bear some resemblance with those which apply to customary law. Precedents and usage are necessary but do not suffice. They must be normative. We adopt the following passage of Sir W. Ivor Jennings in *The Law and the Constitution*, 5th ed. (1959), p. 136:

"We have to ask ourselves three questions: first, what are the precedents; secondly, did the actors in the precedents believe that they were bound by a rule; and thirdly, is there a reason for the rule? A single precedent with a good reason may be enough to establish the rule. A whole string of precedents without such a reason will be of no avail, unless it is perfectly certain that the persons concerned regarded them as bound by it."

Note
[It is interesting in the view of the uncertainty surrounding conventions that the majority did not conclude that a convention required the consent of all the provinces but that it did require provincial consent and the proposed amendments to the construction had not received "a sufficient measure of provincial consent."

The dissenting minority took the view that the question to be answered was whether a convention existed which required the consent of all the provinces.]

LASKIN C.J.C., ESTEY AND MCINTYRE JJ.: As has been pointed out by the majority, a fundamental difference between the legal, that is the statutory and common law rules of the Constitution, and the conventional rules is that, while a breach of the legal rules, whether of statutory or common law nature, has a legal consequence in that it will be restrained by the Courts, no such sanction exists for breach or non-observance of the conventional rules. The observance of constitutional conventions depends upon the acceptance of the obligation of conformance by the actors deemed to be bound thereby. When this consideration is insufficient to compel observance no Court may enforce the convention by legal action. The sanction for non-observance of a convention is political in that disregard of a convention may lead to political defeat, to loss of office, or to other political consequences, but it will not engage the attention of the Courts which are limited to matters of law alone. Courts, however, may recognize the existence of conventions and that is what is asked of us in answering the questions. The answer, whether affirmative or negative, however, can have no legal effect, and acts performed or done in conformance with the law, even though in direct contradiction of well-established conventions, will not be enjoined or set aside by the Courts. For one of many examples of the application of this principle see: *Madzimbamuto* v. *Lardner-Burke et al.*, [1969] 1 A.C. 645. Simple convention cannot create such a power in either level of government. A Canadian convention could only be of negative effect, that is, to limit the exercise of such power. However, no limitative practice can have the effect of giving away such power where it exists in law.

There are different kinds of conventions and usages, but we are concerned here with what may be termed "constitutional" conventions or rules of the Constitution. They were described by Professor Dicey in the tenth edition of his *Law of the Constitution*, at pp. 23-4.

There can be no doubt, that a statute, by enacting the terms of a convention, could create positive law, but it is our view that it is not for the Courts to raise a convention to the status of a legal principle. As pointed out above, Courts may recognize the existence of conventions in their proper sphere. That is all that may be properly sought from the Court, ... an answer by the Court recognizing the existence of the convention or denying its existence. For the Court to postulate some other convention requiring less than unanimous provincial consent to constitutional amendments would be to go beyond the terms of the References and in so doing to answer a question not posed in the References. It would amount, in effect, to an attempt by judicial pronouncement to create an amending formula for the Canadian Constitution which, in addition to being beyond the Courts power to declare, not being raised in a question posed in any of the References before the Court, would be incomplete for failure to specify the degree or percentage of provincial consent required.

Conventions, while frequently unwritten, may none the less be reduced to writing. They may be reached by specific agreement between the parties to be bound, or they may more commonly arise from practice and usage. It is true, as well, that conventions can become law but this, in our view, would require some formal legal step such as enactment in statutory form. The Statute of Westminster 1931 (U.K.), c. 4, affords an example of the enactment of conventions concerning constitutional relations between the United Kingdom and the various Dominions. However a convention may arise or be created, the essential condition for its recognition must be that the parties concerned regard it as binding upon them. While a convention, by its very nature, will often lack the precision and clearness of expression of a law, it must be recognized, known and understood with sufficient clarity that conformance is possible and a breach of conformance immediately discernible. It must play as well a necessary constitutional role.

There are many such conventions of the Canadian Constitution and while at different periods they may have taken different forms, and while change and development have been observable and are, no doubt, continuing processes, they have been recognized none the less as rules or conventions of the Canadian Constitution, known and observed at any given time in Canadian affairs. As the reasons of the majority point out, there are many examples. The general rule that the Governor General will act only according to the advice of the Prime Minister is purely conventional and is not to be found in any legal enactment. In the same category is the rule that after a general election the Governor General will call upon the leader of the party with the greatest number of seats to form a government. The rule of responsible government that a government losing the confidence of the House of Commons must itself resign, or obtain a dissolution, the general principles of majority rule and responsible government underlying the daily workings of the institutions of the executive and legislative branches of each level of government, and a variety of other such conventional arrangements, serve as further illustrations. These rules have an historical origin and bind, and have bound, the actors in constitutional matters in Canada for generations. No one can doubt their operative force or the reality of their existence as an effective part of the Canadian Constitution. They are, none the less, conventional and, therefore, distinct from purely legal rules. They are observed without demur because all parties concerned recognize their existence and accept the obligation of observance, considering themselves to be bound. Even though it may be, as the majority of the Court has said, a matter of some surprise to many Canadians, these conventions have no legal force. They are, in short, the product of political experience, the adoption of which allows the political process to function in a way acceptable to the community.

These then are recognized conventions, they are definite, understandable and understood. They have the unquestioned acceptance not only of the actors in political affairs but of the public at large. Can it be said that any convention having such clear definition and acceptance concerning provincial participation in the amendment of the Canadian Constitution has developed? It is in the light of this comparison that the existence of any supposed constitutional convention must be considered. It is abundantly clear, in our view, that the answer must be No. The degree of provincial participation in constitutional amendments has been a subject of lasting controversy in Canadian political life for generations. It cannot be asserted, in our opinion, that any view on this subject has become so clear and so broadly accepted as to constitute a constitutional convention. It should be observed that there is a fundamental difference between the convention in the Dicey concept and the convention for which some of the Provinces here contend. The Dicey convention relates to the functioning of individuals and institutions within a parliamentary democracy in unitary form. It does not qualify or limit the authority or sovereignty of Parliament or the Crown. The convention sought to be advanced here would truncate the functioning of the executive and legislative branches at the federal level. This would impose a limitation on the sovereign body itself within the Constitution. Surely such a convention would require for its recognition, even in the non-legal, political sphere, the clearest signal from the plenary unit intended to be bound, and not simply a plea from the majority of the beneficiaries of such a convention, the provincial plenary units.

Note

See also *Attorney-General* v. *Jonathan Cape Ltd.* [1976] 1 Q.B. 752; *post* p.272, and *Air Canada* v. *Secretary of State for Trade* [1983] 2 A.C. 394, *post* p.452.

THE RULE OF LAW

Duport Steels Ltd. v. Sirs
[1980] 1 W.L.R. 142
House of Lords

The employees of the British Steel Corporation were called out on strike by their Union which was seeking an increase in pay on their behalf. In order to put pressure on the government to provide British Steel with the money necessary to pay the increase the Union called out its members who worked for privately owned steel companies. The private companies sought injunctions to restrain the Union from inducing their employees to strike. The Union successfully relied on the provisions of section 13 of the Trade Union and Labour Relations Act 1974 which protected from liability in tort acts "done by a person in contemplation or furtherance of a trade dispute."

LORD DIPLOCK: My Lords, at a time when more and more cases involve the application of legislation which gives effect to policies that are the subject of bitter public and parliamentary controversy, it cannot be too strongly emphasised that the British constitution, though largely unwritten, is firmly based upon the separation of powers; Parliament makes the law, the judiciary interpret them. When Parliament legislates to remedy what the majority of its members at the time perceive to be a defect or a lacuna in the existing law (whether it be the written law enacted by existing statutes or the unwritten common law as it has been expounded by the judges in decided cases), the role of the judiciary is confined to ascertaining from the words that Parliament has approved as expressing its intention what that intention was, and to giving effect to it. Where the meaning of the statutory words is plain and unambiguous it is not for the judges to invent fancied ambiguities as an excuse for failing to give effect to its plain meaning because they themselves consider that the consequences of doing so would be inexpedient, or even unjust or immoral. In controversial matters such as are involved in industrial relations there is room for differences of opinion as to what is expedient, what is just and what is morally justifiable. Under our constitution it is Parliament's opinion on these matters that is paramount.

A statute passed to remedy what is perceived by Parliament to be a defect in the existing law may in actual operation turn out to have injurious consequences that Parliament did not anticipate at the time the statute was passed; if it had, it would have made some provision in the Act in order to prevent them. It is at least possible that Parliament when the Acts of 1974 and 1976 were passed did not anticipate that so widespread and crippling use as has in fact occurred would be made of sympathetic withdrawals of labour and of secondary blacking and picketing in support of sectional interests able to exercise "industrial muscle." But if this be the case it is for Parliament, not for the judiciary, to decide whether any changes should be made to the law as stated in the Acts, and, if so, what are the precise limits that ought to be imposed upon the immunity from liability for torts committed in the course of taking industrial action. These are matters on which there is a wide legislative choice the exercise of which is likely to be influenced by the political complexion of the government and the state of public opinion at the time amending legislation is under consideration.

It endangers continued public confidence in the political impartiality of the judiciary, which is essential to the continuance of the rule of law, if judges, under the guise of interpretation, provide their own preferred amendments to statutes which experience of their operation has shown to have had consequences that members of the court before whom the matter comes consider to be injurious to the public interest. The frequency with which controversial legislation is amended by Parliament itself (as witness the Act of 1974 which was amended in 1975 as well as in 1976) indicates that legislation, after it has come into operation, may fail to have the beneficial effects which Parliament expected or may produce injurious results that Parliament did not anticipate. But, except by private or hybrid Bills, Parliament does not legislate for individual cases. Public Acts of Parliament are general in their application; they govern all cases falling within categories of which the definitions are to be found in the working of the statute. So in relation to section 13(1) of the Acts of 1974 and 1976, for a judge (who is always dealing with an individual case) to pose himself the question: "Can Parliament really have intended that the acts that were done in this particular case should have the benefit of the immunity?" is to risk straying beyond his constitutional role as interpreter of the enacted law and assuming a power to decide at his own discretion whether or not to apply the general law to a particular case. The legitimate questions for a judge in his role as interpreter of the enacted law are: "How has Parliament, by the words that it has used in the statute to express its intentions, denied the category of acts that are entitled to the immunity? Do the acts done in this particular case fall within that description?"

Note
Section 13 of the 1974 Act was amended by the Employment Act 1980, s.17 and the Employment Act 1982, s.19 but, as the following case shows, with little effect in terms of clarity.

Merkur Island Corporation v. Laughton
[1983] 2 A.C. 570
Court of Appeal and House of Lords

The owners of a ship sought an interlocutory injunction to restrain the International Transport Workers Federation from "blacking" the ship. Parker J. granted the injunction. Appeals by the Federation to the Court of Appeal (Sir John Donaldson M.R., O'Connor and Dillon L.JJ.) and the House of Lords (Lord Diplock, Lord Edmund-Davies, Lord Keith of Kinkel, Lord Brandon of Oakbrook and Lord Brightman) were unsuccessful. Sir John Donaldson M.R., in the Court of Appeal, and Lord Diplock, who delivered the only speech in the House of Lords, commented on the complexity of the relevant statutory provisions: Section 13 of the Trade Union and Labour Relations Act 1974, section 3(2) of the Trade Union and Labour Relations (Amendment) Act 1976 and section 17 of the Employment Act 1980.

SIR JOHN DONALDSON M.R.: At the beginning of the judgment I said that whilst I had reached the conclusion that the law was tolerably clear, the same could not be said of the way in which it was expressed. The efficacy and maintenance of the rule of law, which is the foundation of any parliamentary democracy, has at least two pre-requisites. First, people must understand that it is in their interests, as well as in that of the community as a whole, that they should live their lives in accordance with the rules and all the rules. Second, they must know what those rules are. Both are equally important and it is the second aspect of the rule of law which has caused me concern in the present case, the I.T.F. having disavowed any intention to break the law.

In industrial relations it is of vital importance that the worker on the shop floor, the shop steward, the local union official, the district officer and the equivalent levels in management should know what is and what is not "offside." And they must be able to find this out for themselves by reading plain and simple words of guidance. The judges of this court are all skilled lawyers of very considerable experience, yet it has taken us hours to ascertain what is and what is not "offside," even with the assistance of highly experienced counsel. This cannot be right.

We have had to look at three Acts of Parliament, none intelligible without the other. We have had to consider section 17 of the Act of 1980, which adopts the "flow" method of Parliamentary draftsmanship, without the benefit of a flow diagram. We have furthermore been faced with the additional complication that subsection (6) of section 17 contains definitions which distort the natural meaning of the words in the operative subsections. It was not always like this. If you doubt me, look at the comparative simplicity and clarity of Sir Mackenzie Chalmers's Sale of Goods Act 1893, his Bills of Exchange Act 1882, and his Marine Insurance Act 1906. But I do not criticise the draftsman. His instructions may well have left him no option. My plea is that Parliament, when legislating in respect of circumstances which directly affect the "man or woman in the street" or the "man or woman on the shop floor" should give as high a priority to clarity and simplicity of expression as to refinements of policy. Where possible, statutes, or complete parts of statutes, should not be amended but re-enacted in an amended form so that those concerned can read the rules in a single document. When formulating policy, ministers, of whatever political persuasion, should at all times be asking themselves and asking parliamentary counsel: "Is this concept too refined to be capable of expression in basic English? If so, is there some way in which we can modify the policy so that it can be so expressed?" Having to ask such questions would no doubt be frustrating for ministers and the legislature generally, but in my judgment this is part of the price which has to be paid if the rule of law is to be maintained.

Lord Diplock: ... One thing is plain as to the intention of Parliament in enacting s.17 of the 1980 Act; it was to impose restrictions on the circumstances in which blacking could be procured without incurring liability in tort. The only function of this House in its judicial capacity is to ascertain from the language that the draftsman used the extent of those restrictions.

My Lords, the 1974 Act and the 1980 Act, to which must now be added the Employment Act 1982, deal with industrial relations. They lay down what can and what cannot lawfully be done in connection with industrial disputes, not only as a result of decisions that are taken by the controlling body or the top officials of large trade unions or federations of trade unions like the ITF with ready and immediate access to expert legal advice, but also as a result of decisions taken by the steward on the shop floor in circumstances of urgency and under pressure from his fellow workers. I see no reason for doubting that those on whom the responsibility for deciding whether and if so what industrial action shall be taken in any given circumstances wish to obey the law, even though it be a law which they themselves dislike and hope will be changed through the operation of this country's constitutional system of parliamentary democracy. But what the law is, particularly in the field of industrial relations, ought to be plain. It should be expressed in terms that can be easily understood by those who have to apply it even at shop floor level. I echo everything that Sir John Donaldson M.R. has said in the last three paragraphs of his judgment in this case. Absence of clarity is destructive of the rule of law; it is unfair to those who wish to preserve the rule of law; it encourages those who wish to undermine it. The statutory provisions which it became necessary to piece together into a coherent whole in order to decide the stage 3 point are drafted in a manner which, having regard to their subject matter and the persons who will be called on to apply them, can in my view, only be characterised as most regrettably lacking in the requisite degree of clarity.

Note

For another aspect of the rule of law, as viewed by the judiciary, see *Francome* v. *Mirror Group Newspapers Ltd.* [1984] 1 W.L.R. 892; *infra* p. 277.

THE SEPARATION OF POWERS: THE ROLES OF PARLIAMENT
AND THE COURTS

Duport Steels Ltd. v. Sirs
[1980] 1 W.L.R. 142

See *supra*.

R. v. Her Majesty's Treasury, ex parte Smedley.
[1985] 1 Q.B. 657
Court of Appeal

The applicant sought judicial review of a draft Order in Council laid before
Parliament on the ground that it was *ultra vires* the terms of the relevant Act, the
European Communities Act 1972. Woolf J. dismissed the application. Smedley
appealed to the Court of Appeal (Sir John Donaldson M.R., Slade and Lloyd L.JJ.)

SIR JOHN DONALDSON: Mr. William Oliver Smedley, the applicant, is I am sure,
a man of many parts. Today he seeks the assistance of the court in his capacity as
Mr. Smedley, British taxpayer and elector. What troubles him is an expressed
intention by H.M. Treasury to pay the European Community a sum in excess of
£121.5 million out of the Consolidated Fund and to do so without seeking the
authority of Parliament in the form of an Appropriation Act or other similar
statute. Instead, it would seem that the Treasury proposes to operate the special
procedure provided by section 1 of the European Communities Act 1972, which
involves laying a draft Order in Council before Parliament and, if that draft Order
is approved by affirmative resolution of both Houses of Parliament and an Order
in Council is in fact made in those terms, to make the payment on the authority of
section 2(3) of that Act. [The draft Order specified as a Community Treaty an
"Undertaking" made by representatives of the member states to make payments
to the Community to finance a supplementary budget.]
    Section 1(2) of the European Communities Act 1972 defines the expressions
"the Treaties" and "the Community Treaties" as they appear in the Act. It does so
by referring to certain scheduled pre-accession treaties and to three other categories of treaty. Two of these three categories, (*a*) and (*b*), cover respectively the
United Kingdom Accession Treaty and the Council Accession Decision both of 22
January 1972. The third category is

> "any other treaty entered into by any of the Communities, with or without
> any of the member states, or entered into, as a treaty ancillary to any of the
> Treaties, by the United Kingdom."

Section 1(3) of the Act then provides:

> "If Her Majesty by Order in Council declares that a treaty specified in the
> Order is to be regarded as one of the Community Treaties as herein defined,
> the Order shall be conclusive that it is to be so regarded; but a treaty entered
> into by the United Kingdom after 22 January 1972, other than a pre-accession
> treaty to which the United Kingdom accedes on terms settled on or before
> that date, shall not be so regarded unless it is so specified, nor be so specified
> unless a draft of the Order in Council has been approved by resolution of each
> House of Parliament."

The word "treaty" as distinct from "the Treaties" is defined in section 1(4) for the
purposes of subsections (2) and (3) as including "any international agreement,
and any protocol or annex to a treaty or international agreement."
    Section 2(3) provides the Treasury with authority to charge on and issue out of
the Consolidated Fund or, as the case may be, the National Loans Fund the

amounts required to meet any Community obligation to make payments to any of the Community or member states. In this context the expression "Community obligation" means "any obligation created or arising by or under the Treaties": see Schedule 1, Pt. II.

It follows that if Her Majesty by Order in Council, the draft of which had previously been laid before and approved by resolution of each House of Parliament, were to declare that an international agreement is to be regarded as one of the Community Treaties, the Treasury would without further authority be entitled to make any payments called for by that agreement.

.   .   .   .   .

[Before considering Mr. Smedley's objections]

I think that I should say a word about the respective roles of Parliament and the courts. Although the United Kingdom has no written constitution, it is a constitutional convention of the highest importance that the legislature and the judicature are separate and independent of one another, subject to certain ultimate rights of Parliament over the judicature which are immaterial for present purposes. It therefore behoves the courts to be ever sensitive to the paramount need to refrain from trespassing upon the province of Parliament or, so far as this can be avoided, even appearing to do so. Although it is not a matter for me, I would hope and expect that Parliament would be similarly sensitive to the need to refrain from trespassing upon the province of the courts.

Against that background, it would clearly be a breach of the constitutional conventions for this court, or any court, to express a view, let alone take any action, concerning the decision to lay this draft Order in Council before Parliament or concerning the wisdom or otherwise of Parliament approving that draft. Equally, as I made clear during the course of the argument, so far as I can see there can be no possible constitutional objection to Parliament debating this draft merely because this court is seized of Mr. Smedley's complaint. The exercise upon which Parliament would be engaged and that upon which we are engaged are essentially different. That much is, I think, common ground.

However, Mr. Laws, appearing for the Treasury, took the matter a little further when he submitted that, at the present stage when no Order in Council has been or could yet be made, it is premature for the court to consider Mr. Smedley's application. There is obvious force in this submission, but it requires some further examination. It is the function of Parliament to legislate and legislation is necessarily in written form. It is the function of the courts to construe and interpret that legislation. Putting it in popular language, it is for Parliament to make the laws and for the courts to tell the nation, including members of both Houses of Parliament, what those laws mean. Furthermore, whilst Parliament is entirely independent of the courts in its freedom to enact whatever legislation it sees fit, legislation by Order in Council, statutory instrument or other subordinate means is in a quite different category, not being Parliamentary legislation. This subordinate legislation is subject to some degree of judicial control in the sense that it is within the province and authority of the courts to hold that particular examples are not authorised by statute, or as the case may be by the common law, and so are without legal force or effect.

At the present moment, there is no Order in Council to which Mr. Smedley can object as being unauthorised. All that can be said is that it seems likely that if both Houses of Parliament approve the draft Order in Council, Her Majesty will be advised to make and will make an Order in the terms of the draft, whereupon the courts would without doubt be competent to consider whether or not the Order was properly made in the sense of being *intra vires*.

In many, and possibly most, circumstances the proper course would undoubtedly be for the courts to invite the applicant to renew his application if and when an order was made, but in some circumstances an expression of view on questions of law which would arise for decision if Parliament were to approve a draft may be of service not only to the parties, but also to each House of Parliament itself. This course was adopted in *Rex* v. *Electricity Commissioners, Ex parte London Electricity Joint Committee Co. (1920) Ltd.* [1924] 1 K.B. 171. In that case an inquiry was in progress, the cost of which would have been wholly wasted if, thereafter, the Minister and Parliament had approved the scheme only to be told at that late stage that the scheme was *ultra vires.*

Similar considerations apply in the present case. It is apparent from the terms of the Undertaking that the provision of the money is considered a matter of urgency. If we defer consideration of Mr. Smedley's application until after both Houses of Parliament have considered the somewhat different question of whether each approves the draft Order in Council, we shall only have contributed an avoidable period of delay should the correct view be that an Order in Council in the terms of the draft would be valid and should only have contributed to what might be thought to be a waste of Parliamentary time if the correct view is that such an Order in Council would be invalid.

[The Master of the Rolls then turned to consider the substance of the application.]

The concept of one treaty being "ancillary" to another is not one of precision. There may be more than one view on whether a particular international agreement is or is not "ancillary." It is no doubt for this reason, amongst others, that Parliament has provided in section 1(3) of the European Communities Act 1972 for a system whereby an Order in Council shall be conclusive of what treaties are to be regarded as Community Treaties and that no treaty entered into by the United Kingdom after 22 January 1972 shall be so regarded, unless it is so characterised by an Order in Council. Furthermore, quite apart from whether a particular instrument would otherwise be regarded as "ancillary" to the Community Treaties, Parliament has retained the right to prevent it being so regarded by refusing to approve the draft Order in Council designed to achieve this result.

In that situation, the sole question for the court is whether the Order in Council, if made, would or would not be *intra vires* a the power conferred by Parliament upon those who would make it. This power does not derive from the affirmative resolution of the Houses of Parliament which, as I have explained is a power of veto. It derives from a pre-existing power to be inferred from section 1 of the Act of 1972. In accordance with familiar principles of law, that power must be assumed to be limited to making an Order in Council in relation to an agreement which *could* properly be regarded as ancillary to the Community Treaties.

And so I ask myself whether the Undertaking could be so regarded. I do not ask myself whether I would so regard it. The only real challenge, as I have explained, is based upon the submission that the Undertaking conflicts with some of the provisions of the Community Treaties. For my part I think that it may be open to doubt whether such a conflict would necessarily and in all circumstances disqualify an instrument from being regarded as ancillary to the Community Treaties. However, I do not consider that there is any such inconsistency between the Undertaking and the Treaties. As was pointed out by Lord Denning M.R. in *H. P. Bulmer Ltd.* v. *J. Bollinger S.A.* [1974] Ch. 401, 410, Community instruments are not expressed against the background of English canons of construction and should not be so construed. As I read the Community Treaties, they are designed to express principles. The relevant principle, so expressed, is that the Community budget should so far as possible, and thus usually, be entirely financed out of the Community's own resources, but this is not to say that it must in all circumstances be so financed. It is clear that in the view of the member states, unusual circumstances have arisen in 1984 which have given rise to the need for a supplementary and amending budget. A temporary departure from the guiding principle set out in the Community Treaties does not seem to me to be in any way inconsistent with the Undertaking being properly regarded as ancillary to the Community Treaties.

That objection apart, nothing could be more ancillary to the Community Treaties than the provision of funds to enable the Community to fulfil its essential functions. Accordingly I am quite unable to hold that an Order in Council in the terms of the draft would be ultra vires the order-making power. On the contrary, I think it would quite plainly be intra vires. I would dismiss the appeal.

Slade L.J. delivered a judgment agreeing in dismissing the appeal. Lloyd L.J. concurred.

Appeal dismissed.

R. v. Secretary of State for the Environment
Ex parte Nottinghamshire County Council
[1986] A.C. 240
House of Lords

The applicant councils sought to quash the decision of the Secretary of State which laid down guidance for expenditure by the local authority under the Local Government, Planning and Land Act 1980, as amended by the Local Government Finance Act 1982. Under the legislation the Secretary of State was required to submit a report containing his directions to local authorities to the House of Commons for its approval—which, in this case, he had duly done. Kennedy J. refused to quash the Secretary of State's decision but his judgment was reversed by the Court of Appeal (Lawton, Slade and Dillon L.JJ.) The Secretary of State appealed to the House of Lords (Lord Scarman, Lord Roskill, Lord Bridge of Harwich, Lord Templeman and Lord Griffiths). The local authorities had argued that in framing his guidance the Secretary of State had misinterpreted the statutory provisions and secondly, even if he complied with the statute he had exercised his powers unreasonably within the *Wednesbury* principle (see *post* p.287 *et seq.*). The House of Lord's rejected the first argument in a speech delivered by Lord Bridge of Harwich, with which his colleagues concurred. The second argument was considered at length by Lord Scarman.

LORD SCARMAN: Neither the trial judge nor the Court of Appeal accepted the second submission. But much has been made of it in the courts below and in your Lordships' House. The respondents' case is that the guidance is grossly unfair, some authorities doing disproportionately well and others being hit undeservedly hard. Your Lordships have been taken through the detail and have been invited to hold that no reasonable Secretary of State could have intended consequences so disproportionate in their impact as between different local authorities. The House is invited in its judicial capacity to infer from these consequences that the Secretary of State must have abused the power conferred upon him by the Act.

The submission raises an important question as to the limits of judicial review. We are in the field of public financial administration and we are being asked to review the exercise by the Secretary of State of an administrative discretion which inevitably requires a political judgment on his part and which cannot lead to action by him against a local authority unless that action is first approved by the House of Commons.

The Secretary of State's guidance which is challenged was included in the Rate Support Grant Report for 1985–86 which was laid before and approved by the House of Commons: no payment of grant, and no reduction in the amount of grant by the Secretary of State applying a multiplier pursuant to section 59 of the Act, can be made unless covered by the report or by a supplementary report and approved by the House of Commons. I am not surprised that the trial judge and Court of Appeal declined to intervene.

My Lords, I think that the courts below were absolutely right to decline the invitation to intervene. I can understand that there may well arise a justiciable issue as to the true construction of the words of the statute and that, if the Secretary of State has issued guidance which fails to comply with the requirement of subsection (11A) of section 59 of the Act of 1980 the guidance can be quashed. But I cannot accept that it is constitutionally appropriate, save in very exceptional circumstances, for the courts to intervene on the ground of "unreasonableness" to quash guidance framed by the Secretary of State and by necessary implication approved by the House of Commons, the guidance being concerned with the limits of public expenditure by local authorities and the incidence of the tax burden as between taxpayers and ratepayers. Unless and until a statute provides otherwise, or it is established that the Secretary of State has abused his power, these are matters of political judgment for him and for the House of Commons. They are not for the judges or your Lordships' House in its judicial capacity.

For myself, I refuse in this case to examine the detail of the guidance or its consequences. My reasons are these. Such an examination by a court would be justified only if a prima facie case were to be shown for holding that the Secretary of State had acted in bad faith, or for an improper motive, or that the consequences of his guidance were so absurd that he must have taken leave of his senses. The evidence comes nowhere near establishing any of these propositions. Nobody in the case has ever suggested bad faith on the part of the Secretary of State. Nobody suggests, nor could it be suggested in the light of the evidence as to the matters he considered before reaching his decision, that he had acted for an improper motive. Nobody now suggests that the Secretary of State failed to consult local authorities in the manner required by statute. It is plain that the timetable, to which the Secretary of State in the preparation of the guidance was required by statute and compelled by circumstance to adhere, involved him necessarily in framing guidance on the basis of the past spending record of authorities. It is recognised that the Secretary of State and his advisers were well aware that there would be inequalities in the distribution of the burden between local authorities but believed that the guidance upon which he decided would by discouraging the high spending and encouraging the low spending authorities be the best course of action in the circumstances. And, as my noble and learned friend Lord Bridge of Harwich demonstrates, it was guidance which complied with the terms of the statute. This view of the language of the statute has inevitably a significant bearing upon the conclusion of "unreasonableness" in the *Wednesbury* sense. If, as your Lordships are holding, the guidance was based on principles applicable to all authorities, the principles would have to be either a pattern of perversity or an absurdity of such proportions that the guidance could not have been framed by a bona fide exercise of political judgment on the part of the Secretary of State. And it would be necessary to find as a fact that the House of Commons had been misled: for their approval was necessary and was obtained to the action that he proposed to take to implement the guidance.

In my judgment, therefore, the courts below acted with constitutional propriety in rejecting the so-called "*Wednesbury* unreasonableness" argument in this case . . . .

The present case raises in acute form the constitutional problem of the separation of powers between Parliament, the executive, and the courts. In this case, Parliament has enacted that an executive power is not to be exercised save with the consent and approval of one of its Houses. It is true that the framing of the guidance is for the Secretary of State alone after consultation with local authorities; but he cannot act on the guidance so as to discriminate between local authorities without reporting to, and obtaining the approval of, the House of Commons. That House has therefore, a role and a responsibility not only at the legislative stage when the Act was passed but in the action to be taken by the Secretary of State in the exercise of the power conferred upon him by the legislation.

To sum it up, the levels of public expenditure and the incidence and distribution of taxation are matters for Parliament, and, within Parliament, especially for the House of Commons. If Parliament legislates, the courts have their interpretative role: they must, if called upon to do so, construe the statute. If a minister exercises a power conferred on him by the legislation, the courts can investigate whether he has abused his power. But if, as in this case, effect cannot be given to the Secretary of State's determination without the consent of the House of Commons and the House of Commons has consented, it is not open to the courts to intervene unless the minister and the House must have misconstrued the statute or the minister has—to put it bluntly—deceived the House. The courts can properly rule that a minister has acted unlawfully if he has erred in law as to the limits of his power even when his action has the approval of the House of Commons, itself acting not legislatively but within the limits set by a statute. But, if a statute, as in this case, requires the House of Commons to approve a minister's decision before he can lawfully enforce it, and if the action proposed complies with the terms of the statute (as your Lordships, I understand, are convinced that it does in the present case), it is not for the judges to say that the action has such unreasonable consequences that the guidance upon which the action is based and of which the House of Commons had notice was perverse and must be set aside. For that is a question of policy for the minister and the Commons, unless there has been bad faith or misconduct by the minister. Where Parliament has legislated that the action to be taken by the Secretary of State must, before it is taken, be approved by the House of Commons, it is no part of the judges' role to declare that the action proposed is unfair, unless it constitutes an abuse of power in the sense which I have explained; for Parliament has enacted that one of its Houses is responsible. Judicial review is a great weapon in the hands of the judges: but the judges must observe the constitutional limits set by our parliamentary system upon their exercise of this beneficent power.

2. PARLIAMENT

LEGISLATIVE SUPREMACY

Act of Parliament not Subject to Judicial Review

Pickin v. British Railways Board

[1974] A.C. 765

House of Lords

Private Acts of 1836 and 1845 provided that, if a certain branch railway line should be abandoned or given up by the promoting company, or should cease to have been used for three years, the lands acquired for the track should vest in the owners for the time being of the adjoining land. In the early 1960s the British Railways Board, in which all railways had become vested, decided to close the branch line. Its use was discontinued in stages, and the track lines were taken up in October, 1969. Meanwhile the Board promoted a private Bill before the unopposed Bill committee in Parliament with the object, *inter alia*, of cancelling the effect of such provisions in old Acts and vesting all the relevant track land in the Board from the date at which the proposed Act should come into force. The preamble recited that plans and a list of the names of the persons interested in the land had been deposited with the clerk of the county council. The Act—the British Railways Act 1968—came into force in July 1968.

Pickin, who objected to the closing of the branch line, purchased in 1969 a few feet of the adjoining land as a *locus standi*, and brought an action against the Board claiming a declaration that he was the owner of the land to mid-track, since in fact the railway had been abandoned before the date of the promotion of the British Railways Bill, and asked for the return of his land or its value. The Board denied that the railway had been abandoned before the Act of 1968 came into force, and claimed that, as under that Act the land had vested in the Board, the claim was invalid. Pickin replied that the preamble to the Act contained a false recital because no plans or list of names of the persons affected were in fact deposited with the county council; that the Board had misled Parliament by obtaining the Act *ex parte* as an unopposed Bill; and that it was therefore ineffective to deprive him of his land.

These paragraphs of Pickin's reply were struck out by the Master as frivolous, vexatious and an abuse of the process of the court. Chapman J., basing his judgment on the principle that the court could not go behind an Act of Parliament alleged to have been obtained improperly, dismissed Pickin's appeal; but the Court of Appeal (Lord Denning M.R., Edmund-Davies and John Stephenson L.JJ.) allowed his interlocutory appeal.

The House of Lords (Lord Reid, Lord Morris of Borth–y–Gest, Lord Wilberforce, Simon of Glaisdale and Lord Cross of Chelsea) now reversed the decision of the Court of Appeal and allowed the appeal by the Board.

Their Lordships took time for consideration.

LORD REID [after stating the facts, continued]: As the respondent's case developed in argument it appeared that he seeks one or other of two methods of relief against section 18. First he says that section 18 confers a benefit on the appellants and that if he can prove that Parliament was fraudulently misled into

21

enacting this benefit the court can and should disregard the section. And, secondly, he says that even if the court cannot do that and the section has taken effect, the court can on proof that Parliament was so misled nullify the resulting benefit to the appellants by requiring them to hold in trust for him the benefit which the section has given to the appellants to his detriment.

The idea that a court is entitled to disregard a provision in an Act of Parliament on any ground must seem strange and startling to anyone with any knowledge of the history and law of our constitution, but a detailed argument has been submitted to your Lordships and I must deal with it.

I must make it plain that there has been no attempt to question the general supremacy of Parliament. In earlier times many learned lawyers seem to have believed that an Act of Parliament could be disregarded in so far as it was contrary to the law of God or the law of nature or natural justice, but since the supremacy of Parliament was finally demonstrated by the Revolution of 1688 any such idea has become obsolete.

The respondent's contention is that there is a difference between a public and a private Act. There are of course great differences between the methods and procedures followed in dealing with public and private Bills, and there may be some differences in the methods of construing their provisions. But the respondent argues for a much more fundamental difference. There is little in modern authority that he can rely on. The mainstay of his argument is a decision of this House, *Mackenzie* v. *Stewart* in 1754.

The case is reported in *Morison's Dictionary of Decisions* 7443 and 15459 and in this House (1754) 1 Pat.App. 578, and a number of documents in connection with this case have been preserved. . . . At that period there were no contemporary reports of Scots appeals in this House. It would seem that quite often no other peer with legal experience sat with the Lord Chancellor and it seems to me to be probable that frequently no formal speech giving reasons was made at the conclusion of the argument. In comparatively few cases there have been preserved observations made in the House: sometimes these appear to have been observations made in the course of the argument. In the present case we have a note made by Lord Kames in his Select Decisions reported in Morrison at p. 7445 (1 Pat.App. 578, 583):

> "The Lord Chancellor, in delivering his opinion, expressed a good deal of indignation at the fraudulent means of obtaining the Act; and said, that he never would have consented to such private Acts, had he ever entertained a notion that they could be used to cover fraud."

Lord Kames' Select Decisions cover the earlier period of his long tenure of office as a judge. We do not know how he came to add this passage at the end of his report of the case in the Court of Session. He must have got it, perhaps at second hand, from someone present during the arguments: so these observations may have been made during the argument or in a speech. Lord Hardwicke was Lord Chancellor both in 1754 and in 1739 when the Act was passed, so he may have had some part in passing the Act. In any case I do not read his observations as indicating the ground of decision but rather as a comment on what took place when the Act was passed.

I must notice some other comments on the case made within a few years after its decision. Lord Elchies in an appendix to a work on tailzie says with regard to the case (No. 46): "*Vide* Lord Chancellor's speech, with the cases, by which it seems, that notwithstanding such private acts, fraud either in obtaining them, or in the execution, may be tried as well as in private contracts." Again, we do not know what information Lord Elchies had about the case. The facts must have been generally known but no detailed account of proceedings in this House would have been available.

We were also referred to some observations by the judges who took part in *Dumbarton Magistrates* v. *Glasgow Magistrates* (1771) Mor.Dic. 14769. Lord Hailes in his Reports, Vol. 1, p. 446, gives short notes of the opinions of the judges who sat with him in hearing the case. . . . .

If the decision was only as to the construction of a statutory provision that would explain why the case has received little attention in later cases. I do not think it necessary to refer to the few later references to the case which have been unearthed by the researches of counsel. And I shall not repeat what is said by my noble and learned friends about other cases relied on by the respondent. If *Mackenzie* v. *Stewart* is found to afford no support to the respondent's argument the rest of the authorities are negligible.

In my judgment the law is correctly stated by Lord Campbell in *Edinburgh and Dalkeith Railway Co.* v. *Wauchope* (1842) 8 Cl. & F. 710; 1 Bell 252. Mr. Wauchope claimed certain wayleaves. The matter was dealt with in a private Act. He appears to have maintained in the Court of Session that the provisions of that Act should not be applied because it had been passed without his having had notice as required by Standing Orders. This contention was abandoned in this House. Lord Brougham and Lord Cottenham said that want of notice was no ground for holding that the Act did not apply. Lord Campbell based his opinion on more general grounds. He said, 1 Bell 252, 278–279:

"My Lords, I think it right to say a word or two before I sit down, upon the point that has been raised with regard to an Act of Parliament being held inoperative by a court of justice because the forms, in respect of an Act of Parliament, have not been complied with. There seems great reason to believe that (sic) notion has prevailed to a considerable extent in Scotland, for we have it here brought forward as a substantive ground upon which the act of the 4th and 5th William the Fourth could not apply: the language being, that the statute of the 4th and 5th William the Fourth being a private Act, and no notice given to the pursuer of the intention to apply for an Act of Parliament, and so on. It would appear that that defence was entered into, and the fact was examined into, and an inquiry, whether notice was given to him personally, or by advertisement in the newspapers, and the Lord Ordinary, in the note which he appends to his interlocutor, gives great weight to this. The Lord Ordinary says 'he is by no means satisfied that due parliamentary notice was given to the pursuer previous to the introduction of this last Act. Undoubtedly no notice was given to him personally, nor did the public notices announce any intention to take away his existing rights. If, as the Lord Ordinary is disposed to think, these defects imply a failure to intimate the real design in view, he would be strongly inclined to hold in conformity with the principles of Donald, November 27, 1832, that rights previously established could not be taken away by a private Act, of which due notice was not given to the party meant to be injured.' Therefore, my Lord Ordinary seems to have been most distinctly of opinion, that if this Act did receive that construction, it would clearly take away the right to this tonnage from Mr. Wauchope, and would have had that effect if notice had been given to him before the Bill was introduced into the House of Commons; but that notice not having been given, it could have no such effect, and therefore the Act is wholly inoperative. I must express some surprise that such a notion should have prevailed. It seems to me there is no foundation for it whatever; all that a court of justice can look to is the parliamentary roll; they see that an Act has passed both Houses of Parliament, and that it has received the royal assent, and no court of justice can inquire into the manner in which it was introduced into Parliament, what was done previously to its being introduced, or what passed in Parliament during the various stages of its progress through both Houses of Parliament. I therefore trust that no such inquiry will

hereafter be entered into in Scotland, and that due effect will be given to
every Act of Parliament, both private as well as public, upon the just construction which appears to arise upon it."

No doubt this was *obiter* but, so far as I am aware, no one since 1842 has doubted
that it is a correct statement of the constitutional position. The function of the
court is to construe and apply the enactments of Parliament. The court has no
concern with the manner in which Parliament or its officers carrying out its
Standing Orders perform these functions. Any attempt to prove that they were
misled by fraud or otherwise would necessarily involve an inquiry into the
manner in which they had performed their functions in dealing with the Bill
which became the British Railways Act 1968.

In whatever form the respondent's case is pleaded he must prove not only that
the appellants acted fraudulently but also that their fraud caused damage to him
by causing the enactment of section 18. He could not prove that without an
examination of the manner in which the officers of Parliament dealt with the
matter. So the court would, or at least might, have to adjudicate upon that.

For a century or more both Parliament and the courts have been careful not to
act so as to cause conflict between them. Any such investigations as the respondent seeks could easily lead to such a conflict, and I would only support it if
compelled to do so by clear authority. But it appears to me that the whole trend of
authority for over a century is clearly against permitting any such investigation.

The respondent is entitledto argue that section 18 should be construed in a way
favourable to him and for that reason I have refrained from pronouncing on that
matter. But he is not entitled to go behind the Act to show that section 18 should
not be enforced. Nor is he entitled to examine proceedings in Parliament in order
to show that the appellants by fraudulently misleading Parliament caused him
loss. I am therefore clearly of opinion that this appeal should be allowed and the
judgment of Chapman J. restored.

Appeal dismissed.

Note

In so far as they refer to public Acts, the judgment of Lord Campbell in the *Wauchope* case
and the judgments in the *Pickin* case were *obiter*, but the principle that the courts cannot go
behind Acts of Parliament applies to public Acts *a fortiori* and is undoubtedly good law.

Manuel and Others v. Attorney-General
Noltcho and Others v. Attorney-General
[1983] Ch. 77
Chancery Division and Court of Appeal

The Attorney-General moved to strike out two statements of claim as disclosing no reasonable cause of action; the first (the Manuel Claim) on the ground that it challenged the validity of an Act of Parliament as ultra vires.

Sir Robert Megarry V-C: In the present case I have before me a copy of the Canada Act 1982 purporting to be published by Her Majesty's Stationery Office. After reciting the request and consent of Canada and the submission of an address to Her Majesty by the Senate and House of Commons of Canada, there are the words of enactment:

> "Be it therefore enacted by the Queen's Most Excellent Majesty, by and with the advice and consent of the Lords Spiritual and Temporal, and Commons, in this present Parliament assembled, and by the authority of the same, as follows: . . ."

There has been no suggestion that the copy before me is not a true copy of the Act itself, or that it was not passed by the House of Commons and the House of Lords, or did not receive the Royal Assent. The Act is therefore an Act of Parliament and the court cannot hold it to be invalid. The case is not one which raises any question under the Parliament Acts 1911 and 1949. It is also far removed from any case where, apart from those Acts, only one of the two Houses of Parliament had in fact passed the Bill, so that the cryptic wording of the recital was merely that it was "assented in this present Parliament," and so on: see *The Case of Heresy* (1601) 12 Co.Rep. 56, 57, 58, in relation to 5 Ric. 2, st. 2, c. 5 of 1382; *The Prince's Case* (1606) 8 Co.Rep. 1a, 20b. In the words of Lord Campbell in *Edinburgh and Dalkeith Railway Co.* v. *Wauchope* (1842) 8 Cl. & F. 710, 725:

> "All that a court of justice can do is to look to the Parliamentary roll: if from that it should appear that a bill has passed both Houses and received the Royal Assent, no court of justice can inquire into the mode in which it was introduced into Parliament, nor into what was done previous to its introduction, or what passed in Parliament during its progress in its various stages through both Houses."

In *Pickin* v. *British Railways Board* [1974] A.C. 765, 787, Lord Reid quoted this passage as it appears in Bell's Reports, and said, 1 Bell 252, 279:

> "No doubt this was obiter but, so far as I am aware, no one since 1842 has doubted that it is a correct statement of the constitutional position";

and see at pp. 790, 793, 799, 801. The Canada Act 1982 is an Act of Parliament, and sitting as a judge in an English court I owe full and dutiful obedience to that Act.

I do not think that, as a matter of law, it makes any difference if the Act in question purports to apply outside the United Kingdom. I speak not merely of statutes such as the Continental Shelf Act 1964 but also of statutes purporting to apply to other countries. If that other country is a colony, the English courts will apply the Act even if the colony is in a state of revolt against the Crown and direct enforcement of the decision may be impossible: see *Madzimbamuto* v. *Lardner-Burke* [1969] 1 A.C. 645. It matters not if a convention had grown up that the United Kingdom Parliament would not legislate for that colony without the consent of the colony. Such a convention would not limit the powers of Parliament, and if Parliament legislated in breach of the convention, "the courts could not hold the Act of Parliament invalid": see p. 723. Similarly if the other country is a foreign state which has never been British, I do not think that any English court would or could declare the Act ultra vires and void. No doubt the Act would normally be ignored by the foreign state and would not be enforced by it, but that would not invalidate the Act in this country. Those who infringed it could not claim that it was void if proceedings within the jurisdiction were taken against them. Legal validity is one thing, enforceability is another. Thus a marriage in Nevada may constitute statutory bigamy punishable in England (*Trial of Earl Russell* [1901] A.C. 446), just as acts in Germany may be punishable here as statutory treason: *Joyce* v. *Director of Public Prosecutions* [1946] A.C. 347. Parliament in fact legislates only for British subjects in this way; but if it also legislated for others, I do not see how the English courts could hold the statute void, however impossible it was to enforce it, and no matter how strong the diplomatic protests.

I do not think that countries which were once colonies but have since been granted independence are in any different position. Plainly once statute has granted independence to a country, the repeal of the statute will not make the country dependent once more; what is done is done, and is not undone by revoking the authority to do it. Heligoland did not in 1953 again become British. But if Parliament then passes an Act applying to such a country, I cannot see why that Act should not be in the same position as an Act applying to what has always been a foreign country, namely, an Act which the English courts will recognise and apply but one which the other country will in all probability ignore. . . .

I must, however, say something about the well-known statement by Viscount Sankey L.C. in *British Coal Corporation* v. *The King* [1935] A.C. 500, 520. Speaking for the Privy Council, he referred to the Statute of Westminster 1931 in relation to Canada and said that "Parliament could, as a matter of abstract law, repeal or disregard section 4 of the Statute. But that is theory and has no relation to realities." What was said by Lord Denning M.R. in *Blackburn* v. *Attorney-General* [1971] 1 W.L.R. 1037, 1040, must, I think, be read in the light of this passage, which he quoted. He referred to the Statute of Westminster 1931 as taking away the power of Parliament to legislate for the Dominions, and said:

> "Can anyone imagine that Parliament could or would reverse that Statute? Take the Acts which have granted independence to the Dominions and territories overseas. Can anyone imagine that Parliament could or would reverse those laws and take away their independence? Most clearly not. Freedom once given cannot be taken away."

I think that it is clear from the context that Lord Denning was using the word "could" in the sense of "could effectively"; I cannot read it as meaning "could as a matter of abstract law." Although it was not discussed in argument, I should observe that Parliament has now in fact repealed section 4 of the Statute of Westminster 1931, and section 7 (1) as well, so far as they apply to Canada: see Canada Act 1982, section 1, and Constitution Act 1982, Schedule, item 17.

Perhaps I may add this. I have grave doubts about the theory of the transfer of sovereignty as affecting the competence of Parliament. In my view, it is a fundamental of the English constitution that Parliament is supreme. As a matter of law the courts of England recognise Parliament as being omnipotent in all save the power to destroy its own omnipotence. Under the authority of Parliament the courts of a territory may be released from their legal duty to obey Parliament, but that does not trench on the acceptance by the English courts of all that Parliament does. Nor must validity in law be confused with practical enforceability.

[Order that the statement of claim be struck out]

On appeal

SLADE L.J. (delivering the judgment of the court)

[Referring to the submission that no Act of Parliament passed subsequently to the Statute of Westminster 1931 cannot be valid unless it complies with the conditions of the statute, his Lordship said]

This submission raises points of great interest and fundamental importance to constitutional lawyers but, for reasons which will appear, we do not find it necessary to deal with them. For the purposes of this judgment we are content to assume in favour of the plaintiffs that the first of the three propositions to which we have referred is correct, though we would emphasise that we are not purporting to decide it.

.　.　.　.　.

For the time being, therefore, let it be supposed that Parliament, in enacting the Canada Act 1982, had precisely to comply with the conditions of section 4 of the Statute of 1931, if that new Act was to be valid and effective. What then are the conditions which section 4 imposes? It is significant that, while the Preamble to the Statute of 1931 recites that

"it is in accord with the established constitutional position that no law hereafter made by the Parliament of the United Kingdom shall extend to any of the said Dominions as part of the law of that Dominion otherwise than at the request and with the consent of that Dominion: . . ."

Section 4 itself does *not* provide that no Act of the United Kingdom Parliament shall extend to a Dominion as part of the law of that Dominion unless the Dominion has *in fact* requested and consented to the enactment thereof. The condition that must be satisfied is a quite different one, namely, that it must be "expressly declared in that Act that that Dominion has requested, and consented to, the enactment thereof." Though Mr. Macdonald, as we have said, submittted that section 4 requires not only a declaration but a true declaration of a real request and consent, we are unable to read the section in that way. There is no ambiguity in the relevant words and the court would not in our opinion be justified in supplying additional words by a process of implication; it must construe and apply the words as they stand: see *Maxwell on Interpretation of Statutes*, 12th ed. (1969), p. 33 and the cases there cited. If an Act of Parliament contains an express declaration in the precise form required by section 4, such declaration is in our opinion conclusive so far as section 4 in concerned.

There was, we think, nothing unreasonable or illogical in this simple approach to the matter on the part of the legislature, in reserving to itself the sole function of deciding whether the requisite request and consent have been made and given. The present case itself provides a good illustration of the practical consequences that would have ensued, if section 4 had made an actual request and consent on the part of a Dominion a condition precedent to the validity of the relevant legislation, in such manner that the courts or anyone else would have had to look behind the relevant declaration in order to ascertain whether a statute of the United Kingdom Parliament, expressed to extend to that Dominion, was valid. There is obviously room for argument as to the identity of the representatives of the Dominion of Canada appropriate to express the relevant request and consent. Counsel for the Appellants, while firm in his submission that all legislatures of the Provinces of Canada had to join the Federal Parliament in expressing them, seemed less firm in his submission that all the Indian Nations had likewise to join. This is a point which might well involve difficult questions of Canadian constitutional law. . . . As we read the wording of section 4, it was designed to obviate the need for any further inquiries of this nature, once a statute, containing the requisite declaration, had been duly enacted by the United Kingdom Parliament. Parliament, having satisfied itself as to the request and consent, would make the declaration and that would be that.

Counsel submitted in the alternative that, even if section 4 on its proper construction does not itself bear the construction which he attributed to it, nevertheless, in view of the convention referred to in the third paragraph of the preamble, that actual request and consent of the Dominion is necessary before a law made by the United Kingdom Parliament can extend to that Dominion as part of its law. Whether or not an argument on these lines might find favour in the courts of a Dominion, it is in our opinion quite unsustainable in the courts of this country. The sole condition precedent which has to be satisfied if a law made by the United Kingdom Parliament is to extend to a Dominion as part of its law is to be found stated in the body of the Statute of 1931 itself (section 4). This court would run counter to all principles of statutory interpretation if it were to purport to vary or supplement the terms of this stated condition precedent by reference to some supposed convention, which, though referred to in the preamble, is not incorporated in the body of the Statute.

In the present instance, therefore, the only remaining question is whether it is arguable that the condition precedent specified in section 4 of the Statute of 1931 has not been complied with in relation to the Canada Act 1982. Is it arguable that it has not been "expressly declared in that Act that that Dominion has requested, and consented to, the enactment thereof"? In our judgment this proposition is not arguable, inasmuch as the preamble to the Canada Act 1982 begins with the words "Whereas Canada has requested and consented to the enactment of an Act of the Parliament of the United Kingdom to give effect to the provisions hereinafter set forth . . ."

Appeal Dismissed: petition for leave to appeal dismissed by Appeal Committee of the House of Lords.

Martin v. O'Sullivan (Inspector of Taxes)
[1982] S.T.C. 416; [1984] S.T.C. 258
High Court and Court of Appeal

The taxpayer claimed that the Social Security Act 1975, under which he had been assessed to liability for payment of Class 4 National Insurance contributions, was not a valid Act of Parliament.

NOURSE J.: . . . Mr Martin says that just prior to the second reading of the Bill which became the Social Security Act 1975 Members of Parliament changed their status for tax and National Insurance purposes from that of self-employed persons to that of employees. He then says that that means that they must have become employees of someone, and he says that they can only have become employees of the Crown. He says that since employees of the Crown cannot sit in Parliament as representatives of and agents for the people, therefore the vote on the second reading of the Bill was invalid and it never became an Act in accordance with the constitution of the land.

Even if I were to accept the whole of Mr Martin's reasoning as to the status of the members of the House of Commons at the material time—and I should like to say that I emphatically reject it—there is nevertheless a short and fundamental answer to this submission. It is that the court can only look at the Parliamentary roll. If, having done that, it sees that an Act has passed both Houses of Parliament and that it has received the Royal Assent, the court cannot inquire into the manner in which it was introduced into Parliament, what was done previously to its being introduced into Parliament or what passed in Parliament during the various stages of its progress through both Houses.

That very well established principle is taken from the speech of Lord Campbell in *Edinburgh and Dalkeith Railway Co* v. *Wauchope* (1842) 8 Cl & Fin 710, 8 ER 279. More recently, his statement of the law was expressly approved by all the members of the House of Lords in *British Railways Board* v. *Pickin* [1974] All ER 609, [1974] AC 765. It follows from the court's inability to inquire into what passed in Parliament that it cannot ask itself whether the members of one or other House were or were not disqualified in some way at the relevant time. It is therefore clear that Mr Martin's first ground of appeal fails.

STEPHENSON LJ.: This is an appeal from a judgment of Nourse J. . . . Mr Martin says that . . . the statute which provides for Class 4 contributions is invalid; that it is invalid for this remarkable reason, namely, that all members of Parliament have become employees and that disqualifies them, as I understand his argument, from passing an Act of Parliament, so that all Acts of Parliament—not only this one—which have been passed in Parliament by members now disqualified, because they are employees holding offices for profit under the Crown, should be disregarded and disobeyed and, this maximum contribution being levied under an Act of Parliament passed by members who are disqualified in that way, is invalid, and therefore the sum of £264 is not payable. Nourse J. rejected that argument. He said ([1982] STC 416 at 419):

> "Even if I were to accept the whole of Mr Martin's reasoning as to the status of the members of the House of Commons at the material time—and I should like to say that I emphatically reject it—there is nevertheless a short and fundamental answer to this submission."

And that answer is that the courts cannot look into the qualifications of members of Parliament; they simply have to be satisfied that the Act has been passed, and if the statute has been passed it is the business of the courts to see that it is complied with, and not to go behind it. An effort was made as recently as 1974 to argue that a

private Act of Parliament was invalid because of the way in which it had been
passed (see *British Railways Board* v. *Pickin* [1974] AC 765). In rejecting that
argument the House of Lords ruled completely out of court, once and for all, any
such argument as Mr Martin seeks to put forward.

Appeal dismissed.

R. v. Jordan
[1967] Crim. L.R. 483 9 J.P.Supp. 48
Divisional Court

The defendant was sentenced to 18 months' imprisonment for offences under the Race Relations Act 1965. He applied for legal aid to apply for a writ of habeas corpus on the ground that the Act was invalid as being a curtailment of free speech.

Held, dismissing the application, that Parliament was supreme and there was no power in the courts to question the validity of an Act of Parliament. The ground of the application was completely unarguable.

Parliament and the Union with Scotland

MacCormick v. The Lord Advocate
1953 S.C. 396
Court of Session First Division (Inner House)

MacCormick, Rector of Glasgow University, and Hamilton, a law student—the chairman and honorary organising secretary of the Scottish Covenant Association—presented a petition to the Court of Session against the Lord Advocate as representing Her Majesty's Ministers and Officers of State, praying for interdict (injunction) against them from publishing a Proclamation entitling Her Majesty as *inter alia* "Elizabeth the Second of the United Kingdom of Great Britain." The relief sought was a declaratory order under section 21 of the Crown Proceedings Act 1947 that the use in Her Majesty's title of the numeral II in relation to Scotland was not only inconsistent with historical fact but in contravention of Article 1 of the Treaty of Union 1707. The Lord Ordinary (Lord Guthrie) dismissed the petition on the grounds that (i) the adoption of the numeral II had been authorised by the Royal Titles Act 1953 and that an Act of Parliament of Great Britain could not be challenged in any court as being in breach of the Treaty of Union or on any other ground; (ii) the Treaty did not expressly or impliedly prohibit the use of the numeral; and (iii) the petitioners had no legal title or interest to sue.

The petitioners reclaimed (appealed). The First Division (Inner House), consisting of Lord President Cooper and Lords Carmont and Russell, after taking time for deliberation, unanimously refused the reclaiming motion (*i.e.* dismissed the appeal). Their Lordships upheld the judgment of the Lord Ordinary on grounds (ii) and (iii) above, but as regards (i) they held that as the proclamation of the Royal Titles had been made before the Royal Titles Act was passed, that Act was not relevant to the issue. This was sufficient for the decision, but the court pronounced dicta to the effect that it was not satisfied that the Royal Titles Act would have been conclusive if it had been repugnant to the Treaty, although it added that the court would have no jurisdiction to review a governmental act of this kind. The following extract from Lord Cooper's judgment deals with the question of the power of Parliament to pass legislation contrary to the expressly "fundamental" provisions of the Treaty (or Act) of Union.

LORD PRESIDENT (COOPER) [after expressing the opinion that the Royal Titles Act 1953 had no bearing on the issue, continued]: The principle of the unlimited sovereignty of Parliament is a distinctively English principle which has no counterpart in Scottish constitutional law. It derives its origin from Coke and Blackstone, and was widely popularised during the nineteenth century by Bagehot and Dicey, the latter having stated the doctrine in its classic form in his *Constitutional Law*. Considering that the Union legislation extinguished the Parliaments of Scotland and England and replaced them by a new Parliament, I have difficulty in seeing why it should have been supposed that the new Parliament of Great Britain must inherit all the peculiar characteristics of the English Parliament but none of the Scottish Parliament, as if all that happened in 1707 was that Scottish representatives were admitted to the Parliament of England. That is not what was done. Further, the Treaty and the associated legislation, by which the Parliament of Great Britain was brought into being as the successor of the separate Parliaments of Scotland and England, contain some clauses which expressly reserve to the Parliament of Great Britain powers of subsequent modification, and other clauses which either contain no such power or emphatically exclude subsequent alteration by declarations that the provision shall be fundamental and unalterable in all time coming, or declarations of a like effect. I have never been able to understand how it is possible to reconcile with elementary canons of construction the adoption by the English constitutional theorists of the same attitude to these markedly different types of provisions.

The Lord Advocate conceded this point by admitting that the Parliament of Great Britain "could not" repeal or alter such "fundamental and essential" conditions. He was doubtless influenced in making this concession by the modified views expressed by Dicey in his later work entitled *Thoughts on the Scottish Union*, from which I take this passage (pp. 252–253): "The statesmen of 1707, though giving full sovereign power to the Parliament of Great Britain, clearly believed in the possibility of creating an absolutely sovereign legislature which should yet be bound by unalterable laws." After instancing the provisions as to Presbyterian Church government in Scotland with their emphatic prohibition against alteration, the author proceeds:

> "It represents the conviction of the Parliament which passed the Act of Union that the Act for the security of the Church of Scotland ought to be morally or constitutionally unchangeable even by the British Parliament . . . A sovereign Parliament in short, though it cannot be logically bound to abstain from changing any given law, may by the fact that an Act when it was passed had been declared to be unchangeable, receive a warning that it cannot be changed without grave danger to the Constitution of the country."

I have not found in the Union legislation any provision that the Parliament of Great Britain should be "absolutely sovereign" in the sense that that Parliament should be free to alter the Treaty at will. However that may be, these passages provide a necessary corrective to the extreme formulations adopted by the Lord Ordinary, and not now supported. In the latest editions of the *Constitutional Law* the editor uneasily describes Dicey's theories as "purely lawyer's conceptions," and demonstrates how deeply later events, such as the Statute of Westminster, have encroached upon the earlier dogmas. As is well known the conflict between academic logic and political reality has been emphasised by the recent South African decision as to the effect of the Statute of Westminster (*Harris* v. *Minister of Interior*).[1]

But the petitioners have still a grave difficulty to overcome on this branch of their argument. Accepting it that there are provisions in the treaty of Union and associated legislation which are "fundamental law," and assuming for the moment that something is alleged to have been done—it matters not whether with legislative authority or not—in breach of that fundamental law, the question remains whether such a question is determinable as a justiciable issue in the courts of either Scotland or England, in the same fashion as an issue of constitutional vires would be cognisable by the Supreme Courts of the United States, or of South Africa or Australia. I reserve my opinion with regard to the provisions relating expressly to this court and to the laws "which concern private right" which are administered here. This is not such a question, but a matter of "public right" (Articles XVIII and XIX). To put the matter in another way, it is of little avail to ask whether the Parliament of Great Britain "can" do this thing or that, without going on to inquire who can stop them if they do. Any person "can" repudiate his solemn engagement but he cannot normally do so with impunity. Only two answers have suggested to this corollary to the main question. The first is the exceedingly cynical answer implied by Dicey (*Law of the Constitution*, 9th ed., p. 82) in the statement that "it would be rash of the Imperial Parliament to abolish the Scotch Courts and assimilate the law of Scotland to that of England. But no one can feel sure at what point Scottish resistance to such a change would become serious." The other answer was that nowadays there may be room for the invocation of an "advisory opinion" from the International Court of Justice. On

[1] [1952] 1 T.L.R. 1245

these matters I express no view. This at least is plain that there is neither precedent nor authority of any kind for the view that the domestic courts of either Scotland or England have jurisdiction to determine whether a governmental act of the type here in controversy is or is not conform to the provisions of a Treaty, least of all when that Treaty is one under which both Scotland and England ceased to be independent states and merged their identity in an incorporating union. From the standpoint both of constitutional law and of international law the position appears to me to be unique, and I am constrained to hold that the action as laid is incompetent in respect that it has not been shown that the Court of Session has authority to entertain the issue sought to be raised. . . .

Gibson v. The Lord Advocate
[1975] 1 C.M.L.R. 563
The Court of Session (Outer House)

A Banff fisherman sought a declarator that the opening of Scottish coastal waters to fishermen of other Community states under EEC Regulations was contrary to Article XVIII of the Act of Union 1707 which authorised the new Parliament of the United Kingdom to alter Scots law

> "with this difference betwixt the laws concerning publick right, policy, and civil government and those which concern private right, that the laws which concern publick right, policy, and civil government may be made the same throughout the whole United Kingdom; but that no alteration be made in laws which concern private right except for evident utility of the subjects within Scotland."

The Lord Ordinary (Keith) rejected the claim on the ground that while the Regulations were directly applicable they did not confer rights or impose obligations on individual citizens and operated in the realm of public not private law. His Lordship then went on to say:

There were addressed to me interesting arguments upon the question of jurisdiction and the competency of the action. These arguments raised constitutional issues of great potential importance, in particular whether the Court of Session has power to declare an Act of the United Kingdom Parliament to be void, whether an alleged discrepancy between an Act of that Parliament and the Treaty or Act of Union is a justiciable issue in this Court, and whether, with particular reference to Article XVIII of the Act of Union, this Court has power to decide whether an alteration of private law bearing to be effected by an Act of the United Kingdom Parliament is 'for the evident utility' of the subjects in Scotland. Having regard to my decision on relevancy, these are not live issues in the present case. The position was similar in *MacCormick* v. *Lord Advocate*, a case concerned with the validity of the proclamation as Queen of Her present Majesty under a title which incorporated the numeral 'Second'. The First Division held that no question properly arose concerning the validity of the Royal Titles Act 1953, but delivered certain *obiter dicta* upon the constitutional position as regards the Treaty and Act of Union. [Lord Keith then quoted passages from Lord President Cooper, *supra* at p.33, beginning "Accepting it . . ." and concluding "(Articles 18 and 19" and "From the standpoint" to "to be raised."]

Like Lord President Cooper, I prefer to reserve my opinion what the position would be if the United Kingdom Parliament passed an Act purporting to abolish the Court of Session or the Church of Scotland or to substitute English law for the whole body of Scots private law. I am, however, of opinion that the question whether a particular Act of the United Kingdom Parliament altering a particular aspect of Scots private law is or is not "for the evident utility" of the subjects within Scotland is not a justiciable issue in this Court. The making of decisions upon what must essentially be a political matter is no part of the function of the Court, and it is highly undesirable that it should be. The function of the Court is to adjudicate upon the particular rights and obligations of individual persons, natural or corporate, in relation to other persons or, in certain instances, to the State. A general inquiry into the utility of certain legislative measures asregards the population generally is quite outside its competence.

Sillars v. Smith
[1982] S.L.T. (Notes) 539
High Court of Justiciary

Four persons accused of vandalism, contrary to section 78(1) of the Criminal Justice (Scotland) Act 1980 took a preliminary plea that the Act was of no legal validity. The plea was rejected in the sheriff court and they were convicted. The accused appealed by way of stated case to the High Court on the ground that the sheriff had erred in law in rejecting their plea. The High Court (the Lord Justice-Clerk (Wheatley) Lord Hunter and Lord Dunpark) refused the appeal and delivered the following judgment:

The submission of the appellants to the sheriff was in effect that Parliament acted unlawfully in resolving that the Scotland Act 1978 (which made provision for the setting up of a Scottish Assembly with certain legislative powers) should be repealed. The Scotland Act 1978 accordingly stood with legislative effect, and the provisions thereof in relation to the legislative powers of the Assembly precluded the passing by Parliament of the Criminal Justice (Scotland) Act 1980. The purported passing of that Act therefore constituted an illegality which rendered that Act, and consequently s.78 thereof, invalid. The supremacy of Parliament was not unchallengeable in the Scottish courts, and accordingly it was competent for a Scottish court to determine that illegality and give effect to the consequences thereof by holding that a charge based on that illegal section of that illegal Act was in itself fundamentally illegal. In dismissing the plea to the competency the sheriff simply said that he rejected it upon the view that it is not competent for a court of summary criminal jurisdiction to question the validity of an Act of Parliament.

When the case came to this court on appeal the same basic arguments were presented, although they were enveloped in a variety of submissions which we do not find necessary to rehearse. As in the sheriff court the submissions were presented by the first-named appellant and adopted by the others. We go straight to the fundamental question whether the vires of an Act of Parliament which has gone through the whole Assent and been brought into operation can be competently challenged in a Scottish court. That question has been definitively answered by two Scottish cases which span over a century in time. In *The Edinburgh and Dalkeith Railway Company* v. *Wauchope* (1842) 1 Bell's App.Cas. 252 in the House of Lords Lord Campbell said at p.279:

> "All that a court of justice can look to is the parliamentary roll; they see that an act has passed both Houses of Parliament, and that it has received the royal assent, and no court of justice can enquire into the manner in which it was introduced into parliament, what was done previously to its being introduced, or that passed in parliament during the various stages of its progress through both Houses of Parliament. I therefore trust that no such enquiry will hereafter be entered into in Scotland, and that due effect will be given to every act of Parliament, both private as well as public, upon the just construction which appears to arise upon it".

In *MacCormick* v. *Lord Advocate*, 1953 S.L.T. 255; 1953 S.C. 396 Lord President Cooper said:

> "This at least is plain that there is neither precedent nor authority of any kind for the view that the domestic Courts of either Scotland or England have jurisdiction to determine whether a governmental act of the type here in controversy is or is not conform to the provisions of a Treaty".

While that was said in the context of the issue in that case it is a clear illustration of the principle enunciated by Lord Campbell (*supra*).

We are satisfied that there is sufficient in these passages alone to warrant the rebuttal of the appellants' plea to the competency, based as it is on a submission that the Act of 1980 which had gone through all the parliamentary processes and received the Royal Assent is invalid. In that situation we find it unnecessary to deal with the ancillary arguments which were adduced in purported support of that basic argument, since they fall within Lord Campbell's veto.

The question of law stated by the sheriff is: "Did I err in law in repelling the plea to the competency of the proceedings?". We answer that question in the negative and refuse the appeal.

Note
The argument that the Act of Union constitutes part of a fundamental constitutional settlement which limits the powers of Parliament has been recently restated by Sir Thomas Smith in *The Laws of Scotland, Stair Memorial Encyclopaedia* (1987), Vol. 5, paras. 345–351; reviewed: *Journal of the Law Society of Scotland* (1987), p. 409. The most convincing statement of the contrary view is to be found in C.R. Munro, *Studies in Constitutional Law* (1987), Chap. 4.

Parliament and Taxation

Bowles v. Bank of England
[1913] 1 Ch. 57
Chancery Division

On May 31, 1912, the plaintiff, Thomas Gibson Bowles, purchased £65,000 Irish Land Stock, which was transferred into his name in the books of the Bank. On this stock the dividends were payable half-yearly, on January 1 and July 1. On April 2, 1912, the Committee of the House of Commons for Ways and Means passed a resolution approving the imposition of income tax at the rate of 1s. 2d. in the pound for the financial year beginning April 6, 1912. The Finance Act embodying the resolution did not receive the Royal Assent till August 7. In the meantime, on June 26, the plaintiff issued his writ claiming an injunction to restrain the Bank of England, who were responsible under the National Debt Act 1870 for distributing the dividends on stock, from deducting the tax from the dividend payable to him in respect of the Irish Land Stock, and a declaration that they were not entitled to do so. He subsequently amended the writ and claimed £52 10s. 8d., the amount of income tax to be deducted.

PARKER J. [in the course of his judgment, said]: This question may be stated as follows: Does a resolution of the Committee of the House of Commons for Ways and Means, either alone or when adopted by the House, authorise the Crown to levy on the subject an income tax assented to by such resolution, but not yet imposed by Act of Parliament? Apart from the effect of certain provisions contained in the statutes relating to the collection of income tax, to which I shall presently refer, this question can, in my opinion, only be answered in the negative. By the statute 1 Will. & M., usually known as the Bill of Rights, it was finally settled that there could be no taxation in this country except under authority of an Act of Parliament. The Bill of Rights still remains unrepealed, and no practice or custom, however prolonged, or however acquiesced in on the part of the subject, can be relied on by the Crown as justifying any infringement of its provisions. It follows that, with regard to the powers of the Crown to levy taxation, no resolution either of the Committee for Ways and Means or of the House itself has any legal effect whatever. Such resolutions are necessitated by a Parliamentary procedure adopted with a view to the protection of the subject against the hasty imposition of taxes; and it would be strange to find them relied on as justifying the Crown in levying a tax before such tax is actually imposed by Act of Parliament. I did not, however, understand that the Attorney-General on behalf of the Crown really dissented from this position. His contention was that in the case of income tax there is statutory authority for its collection by the Crown after the resolution of the Committee of the House of Commons for Ways and Means assenting to its imposition and before the passing of the Act by which it is subsequently imposed. This contention necessitates consideration of the Acts regulating the collection of income tax, and in particular of section 30 of the Customs and Inland Revenue Act 1890. . . .

The above considerations have led me to the conclusion that the proper interpretation to be placed upon the section is to hold that, though it keeps alive the machinery of the Income Tax Acts for the purposes of all the preliminary work necessary for the collection of any income tax which may be imposed for any financial year, it does not authorise any assessment or collection of a tax not yet imposed by Parliament. I am confirmed in this opinion by the words of the section itself. Its object was stated to be the collection "in due time" of any income tax which may be imposed in any financial year, and "due time" must, I think, mean the time when the tax becomes due and payable under the Act which actually imposes it. A tax levied before the Act imposing it is passed is not, in my opinion, collected in due time within the meaning of the section, though before such Act be passed it is possible to do much preliminary work which will facilitate and expedite the collection of the tax if and when it becomes due and payable. . . .

I need only add that my decision in this case must be taken as confined to the assessment and collection of income tax not yet imposed by Act of Parliament. I have not considered the case of Customs, as to which there may be some distinction. I propose to declare that, according to the true construction of section 30 of the Customs and Inland Revenue Act 1890, the Bank were not entitled on July 1, 1912, to deduct any sum in respect of income tax for the year commencing April 6, 1912, from the dividend to which upon that date the plaintiff became entitled as the owner of £65,500 Guaranteed Two and Three-quarters per cent. Stock, and to order payment out of court to the plaintiff of £52 10s. 8d. deducted by the Bank and paid into court under my order of June 28, 1912; and the Bank must pay the plaintiff's costs of the action.

Note
This case led to the passing of the Provisional Collection of Taxes Act 1913, now superseded by the Provisional Collection of Taxes Act 1968; but the general principles that (1) a resolution of one House cannot make law, and (2) no tax may be levied by the Crown without the authority of an Act of Parliament, remain, and indeed are confirmed by the recognition of the necessity for passing the Provisional Collection of Taxes Acts.

Attorney-General v. Wilts United Dairies
(1922) 91 L.J.K.B. 897: 38 T.L.R. 781
House of Lords

The Attorney-General laid an information against Wilts United Dairies to recover the sum of £15,027 4s. 6d., being the amount of 2d. a gallon which they had agreed to pay on milk purchased by them under licence from the Food Controller. The latter had granted the licence under the Milk (Registration of Dealers) Order 1918 and the Milk (Distribution) Order 1918, made in virtue of Regulations issued under the Defence of the Realm (Consolidation) Act 1914.

Bailhache J. gave judgment for the Crown, holding there the charge for a licence was not a tax, but a valid administrative method of regulating the price of milk. The Court of Appeal reversed this decision on the ground that the charge was *ultra vires* as being a levying of money for the use of the Crown without the authority of Parliament.

The Crown now appealed to the House of Lords. Their Lordships (Lord Buckmaster, Lord Atkinson, Lord Sumner, Lord Wrenbury and Lord Sterndale) dismissed the appeal.

LORD BUCKMASTER: The question raised on this appeal is undoubtedly one of great importance, but none the less I think that it may be readily resolved.

The Food Controller, who appears here as the appellant by His Majesty's Attorney-General, purporting to exercise powers conferred upon him by statute, entered into five agreements with the respondents, by which the respondents were permitted to purchase milk within certain defined areas on terms that they should pay the sum of two pence per gallon for the privilege. The action which has resulted in this appeal was brought to recover the sums so payable, and the defence is that the Food Controller had no power whatever to impose any such condition.

The matter arises in this way. The exigencies of the war rendered necessary the control of all food supplies, and in 1916 an Act of Parliament was accordingly passed (the New Ministries and Secretaries Act 1916)[1] creating a number of new Ministries and among them was the Ministry of Food. The Minister thus created was called the "Food Controller," and section 4 of the statute established that his duty was "to regulate the supply and consumption of food in such manner as he thinks best for maintaining a proper supply of food, and to take such steps as he thinks best for encouraging the production of food"; the powers which he was to exercise for the purpose of carrying out those duties were powers which His Majesty might confer upon him by Order in Council, or such powers as might be conferred on him by Regulations under the Defence of the Realm (Consolidation) Act 1914.[2] No Order in Council has been placed before your Lordships conferring any powers beyond those which were established by the Defence of the Realm Act, but two subsections of Regulation 2F are material for the present purpose. Subsection (1) of this Regulation provided that the Food Controller might "make orders regulating, or giving directions with respect to the production, manufacture, treatment, use, consumption, transport, storage, distribution, supply, sale or purchase of, or other dealing in, or measures to be taken in relation to any article (including orders providing for the fixing of maximum and minimum prices) where it appears to him necessary or expedient to make any such order for the purpose of encouraging or maintaining the food supply of the country"; and subsection (2), that he should have power to require all persons owning any article to place the whole of the stock under his control.

The Food Controller issued various Orders by virtue of these powers. The first

[1] 6 & 7 Geo. 5, c.68.
[2] 5 Geo. 5, c. 8.

was on January 8, 1918, which provided that after certain dates which were there specified no person should deal in milk by wholesale except under licence. On October 5, 1918, a further Order was made that the Food Controller should be at liberty to "restrict or regulate the sale or delivery of milk by any person to any other person or to any place," and that directions might be given "so as to apply generally or so as to apply to any special locality, or so as to apply to any special producer, dealer or person or class of producers." The Food Controller then found that it was necessary to divide the country into certain areas for the purpose of securing an equitable distribution of milk, and these areas he fixed at three. There was the normal area, where the prices might be regarded as the normal standard prices, there was the South-West area, which comprised the counties of Somerset, Devon, Dorset and Cornwall, where the milk was two pence a gallon under the normal price, and there was the industrial area in the West Riding of Yorkshire, where the milk supply was notoriously scanty and the price was there fixed at two pence above the normal price.

Now in the ordinary course of trade there is no doubt that the prices in these different localities would have got fixed and stabilised by the ordinary play of economic and commercial relations between the several areas, but whether it was because of the impossibility of fixing the exact limits of different localities with the different prices so that one would ultimately and almost imperceptibly grade off into another—whether that was the difficulty or no—it at any rate became apparent to the Food Controller that the result of his action was that it would be open to people to use the South-West area, where the milk was cheap, for the purpose of supplying the other areas where the milk was dear, and he accordingly took steps to regulate that difficulty in the following way. In the first place he provided that no milk should be purchased within the particular area by any purchaser excepting under licence, and that no milk should be brought outside the area for distribution excepting again under licence; the respondents desiring to deal in milk, he accordingly granted them the licences which have given rise to the present dispute. One, dated April 29, 1919, gave them power to import from the South-West area to their office at Trowbridge, and the other four, granted towards the end of May 1919, were for the purpose of buying for their offices within the area in order that they might obtain the milk within that locality. The condition of the grant of each of these licences was the payment of two pence per gallon upon the milk purchased by virtue of the powers conferred.

The question before this House is not whether or not that was a wise and necessary step to take having regard to the difficulties by which the whole question of the milk supply was surrounded; the only question which we have to decide is whether there was any power conferred upon the Food Controller to do what he did. The Attorney-General has urged your Lordships to consider the extreme difficulty of the situation in which this country found itself owing to the war, and the importance of all the officials who had charge of our vital supplies being enabled to act under the powers conferred upon them without the fear of technical and vexatious objections being taken into the powers which they used. All that may be readily accepted, but it cannot possibly give to any official a right to act outside the law; nor can the law be unreasonably strained in order to legalise that which it might be perfectly reasonable should be done if in fact it was unauthorised. The real answer to such an argument is to be found in this, that in times of great national crisis Parliament should be, and generally is, in continuous session, and the powers which are required for the purpose of maintaining the integrity of the country, both economic and military, ought always to be obtained readily from loyal Houses of Parliament. The only question here is, Were such powers granted?

There are two sources from which those powers can possibly be derived. One is the Act creating the Ministry, and the other the Regulations under the Defence of the Realm Act. Neither of these either directly or, in my opinion, by inference, enabled the Food Controller to levy the payment of any sums of money from any of His Majesty's subjects. The statute of 1916 confines his duties to regulating the supply and consumption of food and taking the necessary steps for maintaining a proper supply of food. The powers so given are no doubt very extensive and very drastic, but they do not include the power of levying upon any man payment of money which the Food Controller must receive as part of a national fund and can only apply under proper sanction for national purposes. However the character of this payment may be clothed by asking your Lordships to consider the necessity for its imposition, in the end it must remain a payment which certain classes of people were called upon to make for the purpose of exercising certain privileges, and the result is that the money so raised can only be described as tax the levying of which can never be imposed upon subjects of this country by anything except plain and direct statutory means.

To my mind those reasons are sufficient for showing that the judgment of the Court of Appeal is right, and that this appeal should be dismissed with costs.

LORD ATKINSON: I concur.

LORD SUMNER: I concur.

LORD WRENBURY: I agree. The Crown in my opinion cannot here succeed except by maintaining the proposition that when statutory authority has been given to the Executive to make regulations controlling acts to be done by His Majesty's subjects, or some of them, the Minister may, without express authority so to do, demand and receive money as the price of exercising his power of control in a particular way, such money to be applied to some public purpose to be determined by the Executive. It is impossible to maintain the proposition. At any rate, in the absence of express words giving the Executive power to make such a demand, this is the assertion of a right in the Executive to impose taxation.

LORD STERNDALE: I concur.
Appeal dismissed.

Note
As a matter of interpretation this case decided that the Orders issued by the Food Controller, in so far as they charged a fee as a condition of the grant of a licence, were *ultra vires* the New Ministries and Secretaries Act 1916 and the Regulations issued under the Defence of the Realm (Consolidation) Act 1914. If the Orders had been *intra vires* the Regulations, the question would then have arisen whether the Regulations concerned were *intra vires* the Defence of the Realm Act.

Parliament *can*, of course, expressly delegate to the Executive the power to levy money; *e.g.* the Emergency Powers (Defence) Act 1939, s.2.

Parliament and Treaties

Blackburn v. Attorney-General
[1971] 1 W.L.R. 1037
Court of Appeal

See *post* p.114.

Parliament and International Law

Mortensen v. Peters
(1906) 8 F.(J.) 93
High Court of Justiciary Full Bench

Mortensen, the Danish master of a steam trawler registered in Norway, was convicted by the Sheriff Court at Dornoch of using the method of fishing known as otter trawling in a part of the Moray Firth more than one marine league from low water mark, contrary to the Herring Fishery (Scotland) Act 1889. Mortensen was fined £50, which he paid, but he appealed on the ground that, being a foreigner acting outside British territorial waters (beyond the three-mile limit), he was not subject to the jurisdiction of the Scottish court.

The High Court of Justiciary (Lord Justice General Dunedin, the Lord Justice-Clerk, Lords McLaren, Kyllachy, Stormonth-Darling, Low, Pearson, Ardwall, Dundas, Johnston, Salvesen and Mackenzie) dismissed his appeal.

THE LORD JUSTICE GENERAL: The facts of this case are that the appellent being a foreign subject, and master of a vessel registered in a foreign country, exercised the method of fishing known as otter trawling at a point within the Moray Firth, more than three miles from the shore, but to the west of a line drawn from Duncansby Head in Caithness to Rattray Point in Aberdeenshire; that being thereafter found within British territory, to wit, at Grimsby, he was summoned to the Sheriff Court at Dornoch to answer a complaint against him for having contravened the 7th section of the Herring Fishery Act 1889, and the bye-law of the Fishery Board, thereunder made, and was convicted.

It is not disputed that if the appellant had been a British subject in a British ship he would have been rightly convicted. . . .

In this court we have nothing to do with the question of whether the legislature has or has not done what foreign powers may consider a usurpation in a question with them. Neither are we a tribunal sitting to decide whether an act of the legislature is *ultra vires* as in contravention of generally acknowledged principles of international law. For us an Act of Parliament duly passed by Lords and Commons and assented to by the King, is supreme, and we are bound to give effect to its terms. The counsel for the appellant advanced the proposition that statutes creating offences must be presumed to apply (1) to British subjects; and (2) to foreign subjects in British territory; but that short of express enactment their applications should not be further extended. The appellant is admittedly not a British subject, which excludes (1): and he further argued that the *locus delicti*, being in the sea beyond the three-mile limit, was not within British territory; and that consequently the appellant was not included in the prohibition of the statute. Viewed as general propositions the two presumptions put forward by the appellant may be taken as correct. This, however, advances the matter but little, for like all presumptions they may be argued,[1] and the question remains whether they have been reargued on this occasion.

---

[1] [rebutted].

The first thing to be noted is that the prohibition here, a breach of which constitutes the offence, is not an absolute prohibition against doing a certain thing, but a prohibition against doing it in a certain place. Now, when a legislature, using words of admitted generality—"It shall not be lawful," etc., "Every person who," etc.—conditions an offence by territorial limits, it creates, I think, a very strong inference that it is, for the purpose specified, assuming a right to legislate for that territory against all persons whomsoever. This inference seems to me still further strengthened when it is obvious that the remedy to the mischief sought to be obtained by the prohibition would be either defeated or rendered less effective if all persons whomsoever were not affected by the enactment. It is obvious that the latter consideration applied in the present case. Whatever may be the views of anyone as to the propriety or expediency of stopping trawling, the enactment shows on the face of it that contemplates such stopping; and it would be most clearly ineffective to debar trawling by the British subject while the subjects of other nations were allowed so to fish.

It is said by the appellant that all this must give way to the consideration that International Law has firmly fixed that a locus such as this is beyond the limits of territorial sovereignty; and that consequently it is not to be thought that in such a place the legislature could seek to affect any but the King's subjects.

It is a trite observation that there is no such thing as a standard of International Law, extraneous to the domestic law of a kingdom, to which appeal may be made. International Law, so far as this Court is concerned, is the body of doctrine regarding the international rights and duties of states which has been adopted and made part of the law of Scotland. Now can it be said to be clear by the law of Scotland that the locus here is beyond what the legislature may assert right to affect by legislation against all whomsoever for the purpose of regulating methods of fishing?

I do not think I need say anything about what is known as the three-mile limit. It may be assumed that within the three miles the territorial sovereignty would be sufficient to cover any such legislation as the present. It is enough to say that that is not a proof of the counter proposition that outside the three miles no such result could be looked for. The locus, although outside the three-mile limit, is within the bay known as the Moray Firth, and the Moray Firth, says the respondent, is *intra fauces terræ*. Now I cannot say that there is any definition of what *fauces terræ* exactly are. But there are at least three points which go far as to show that this spot might be considered as lying therein.

First, the dicta of the Scottish Institutional Writers seem to show that it would be no usurpation, according to the law of Scotland, so to consider it.

Thus, Stair, II i. 5:

> "The vast ocean is common to all mankind as to navigation and fishing, which are the only uses thereof, because it is not capable of bounds; but when the sea is inclosed in bays, creeks, *or otherwise is capable of any bounds or meiths as within the points of such lands*, or within the view of such shores, then it may become proper, but with the reservation of passage for commerce as in the land."

And Bell, Pr. § 639: "The Sovereign . . . is proprietor of the narrow seas within cannon shot of the land, and the *firths*, gulfs, and bays around the Kingdom."

Second, the same statute puts forward claims to what are at least analogous places. If attention is paid to the Schedule appended to section 6, many places will be found far beyond the three-mile limit—*e.g.* the Firth of Clyde near its mouth. I am not ignoring that it may be said that this in one sense is proving *idem per idem*, but none the less I do not think the fact can be ignored.

Third, there are many instances to be found in decided cases where the right of a nation to legislate for waters more or less landlocked or landembraced, although beyond the three-mile limit, has been admitted.

They will be found collected in the case of the *Direct United States Cable Company* v. *Anglo-American Telegraph Company*, L.R. 2 App.Cas. 394, the bay there in question being Conception Bay, which has a width at the mouth of rather more than 20 miles.

It seems to me therefore, without laying down the proposition that the Moray Firth is for every purpose within the territorial sovereignty, it can at least be clearly said that the appellant cannot make out his proposition that it is inconceivable that the British legislature should attempt for fishery regulation to legislate against all and sundry in such a place. And if that is so, then I revert to the considerations already stated which as a matter of construction make me think that it did so legislate.

An argument was based on the terms of the North Sea Convention—which had been concluded a few years before this Act was passed, and which defines "exclusive fishery limits" in a manner which excludes part of the Moray Firth. But I do not think any argument can be drawn from that definition, for the simple reason that the Convention as a whole does not deal with the subject-matter here in question, viz:—mode of fishing.

If it had been attempted to infer from the terms of the Act a prohibition of which the effect was to give to subjects and deny to foreigners the right to fish, then the Convention might be apt to suggest an argument against such a construction. But that is not so. Subjects and foreigners are *ex hypothesi* in this manner treated alike.

I am therefore of opinion that the Conviction was right, that both questions should be answered in the affirmative and the appeal should be dismissed. . . .

LORD SALVESEN: The facts of this case have been already fully narrated. I note, however, that the appellant does not found on his nationality as a Dane. The preliminary objection which he stated to the jurisdiction of Dornoch Sheriff Court, was on the footing that he was the foreign master of a steam trawler registered in Norway; and his counsel admitted that his case falls to be treated as if his own nationality had been the same as that of the ship he commanded.

It was conceded for the Crown, and I think rightly, that if an offence is created by a Statute of the British Parliament, it will, in the ordinary case, be presumed to have no application beyond territorial waters. But as this presumption must yield to an express clause, that the Act shall apply to foreigners and British subjects alike; so I think it will yield to a clear implication to the like effect. Where a British statute prohibits a certain thing to be done within a definite geographical area, it seems to me that there is no presumption that such a prohibition shall be confirmed only to British subjects, Still more, if, on examining the subject matter of the prohibition, it is found that it will be futile or ineffectual unless its operation is generality is not capable of any limitation in favour of persons who do not ordinarily own obedience to the British Parliament. These considerations are applicable to the present case. The statutes and bye-laws contravened have, for their objects, the protection of line fishermen, and the preservation of the spawning beds of fish in the interests or supposed interests of the whole fishing community. If they were to be constructed as impliedly excepting from their scope all foreigners fishing from foreign vessels, such a construction would not merely defeat the object of the legislature, but could confer a privilege upon foreigners which was denied to British subjects. It can scarcely be supposed that a British Parliament should pass legislation which would neither have the effect of protecting line fishermen from the competition of trawlers, nor of preserving the spawning beds, but would simply place British subjects under a disability which did not extend to foreigners—in other words, create in favour of foreigners a monopoly of trawl fishing in the Moray Firth . . . .

The view which I have expressed is strengthened by a consideration of the area within which the operation of the bye-law is confined. The stretch of water known as the Moray Firth, and defined by the bye-law, is undoubtedly geographically *inter fauces terræ*; and there are many examples of States asserting exclusive jurisdiction within such areas, and of such assertion being acquiesced in by other nations. In these circumstances I think the Act, under the authority of which the bye-law in question was passed, must be treated as an assertion by the British Parliament of their right to regulate the fishing in this area, and to treat it as within the territory over which the jurisdiction of the Scottish Courts extends. The right so claimed may or may not be conceded by other Powers, but that is a matter with which this Court has no concern. We were told that the result of upholding the conviction would be to provoke reprisals by other Powers. If so, that is a matter for the Foreign Office. But it is difficult to suppose that foreign nations should object to a regulation designed for the protection of fisheries in which they all share, and which confers no exclusive privileges on British subjects. . . .

Note
Diplomatic representations were made afterwards to the Foreign Office, and the Crown remitted the fine, although it recognised that the Court was right to apply the Act of Parliament. The Trawling in Prohibited Areas Prevention Act 1909 provided that prosecutions should not be brought under the Act of 1889 for trawling outside the three-mile limit but, that fish caught by prohibited methods might not be landed or sold in the United Kingdom.

Cheney v. Conn (Inspector of Taxes)

[1968] 1 W.L.R. 242

Chancery Division

Cheney appealed against assessments to income tax and surtax on the ground that a substantial part of the tax so raised was allocated to the construction of nuclear weapons. He contended that the construction of nuclear weapons was contrary to international law which was part of the law of England, and, secondly, that it was illegal as conflicting with the Geneva Conventions which were incorporated in the Geneva Conventions Act 1957, and there was a conflict between the Geneva Conventions Act 1957 and the Finance Act 1964 under which the tax was charged.

His appeal was dismissed first by the Special Commissioners and then by Ungoed-Thomas J. on a case stated.

UNGOED-THOMAS J.: This is an appeal against an assessment to income tax under Schedule D for 1964–65 and also an assessment to surtax for 1963–64. Both these cases raise the same point. The submission is that the assessments are invalid because it is to be taken that what is collected will be, in part, applied in expenditure on the armed forces and devoted to the construction of nuclear weapons with the intention of using those weapons if certain circumstances should arise. It is conceded for the purposes of this case that a substantial part of the taxes for the years that I have mentioned was allocated to the construction of nuclear weapons. The issue therefore becomes whether the use of income tax and surtax for the construction of nuclear weapons with the intention of using them should certain circumstances arise, invalidates the assessments. . . .

The ground upon which it was said that the use of this money for the construction of nuclear weapons is illegal is that such use conflicts primarily with conventions incorporated in an Act of Parliament—and, so it was suggested, impliedly ratified by it—and also ratified by the Crown in the usual way; and also because, according to the case stated, it was contrary to international law. But the case as presented before me was tested primarily, at any rate, upon a conflict between two statutes—namely, the statute which refers to the Geneva Conventions (*i.e.* the Geneva Conventions Act 1957) and the Finance Act. Before coming to the Act of 1957 I shall deal first with the relationship of statute law to international law and international conventions.

First, International Law is part of the law of the land, but it yields to statute. That is made clear by *Inland Revenue Commissioners* v. *Collco Dealings Ltd.* where Lord Simonds[1] quoted with approval, and in accordance with the decision of the House of Lords in that case, *Maxwell on the Interpretation of Statutes*. I quote 10th ed. (1953), at p. 148: "But if the statute is unambiguous, its provisions must be followed even if they are contrary to international law." It is therefore very understandable why the taxpayer in this case relies primarily, at any rate, not upon a conflict between international law in general and the statute, but upon the conflict between the Act of 1957, and its reference to ratification, and another statute—namely, the Finance Act 1964. Secondly, conventions which are ratified by an Act of Parliament are part of the law of the land. And, thirdly, conventions which are ratified but not by an Act of Parliament, which thereby gives them statutory force, cannot prevail against a statute in unambiguous terms.

The law is thus stated in Oppenheim's *International Law*, 8th ed. (1955), at p. 924:

[1] [1962] A.C. 1, 19.

"The binding force of a treaty concerns in principle the contracting States only,
and not their subjects. As international law is primarily a law between States only
and exclusively, treaties can normally have effect upon States only. This rule can,
as has been pointed out by the Permanent Court of International Justice, be
altered by the express or implied terms of the treaty, in which case its provisions
become self-executory. Otherwise, if treaties contain provisions with regard to
rights and duties of the subjects of the contracting States, their courts, officials,
and the like, these States must take such steps as are necessary, according to their
Municipal Law, to make these provisions binding upon their subjects, courts,
officials and the like."

And at p. 40 it is said:

> "Such treaties as affect private rights and, generally, as require for their
> enforcement by English courts a modification of common law or of a statute
> must receive parliamentary assent through an enabling Act of Parliament. To
> that extent binding treaties which are part of international law do not form
> part of the law of the land unless expressly made to do so by the legislature.
> That departure from the traditional common law rule is largely due to the fact
> that, according to British constitutional law, the conclusion and ratification of
> treaties are within the prerogative of the Crown, which would otherwise be
> in a position to legislate for the subject without obtaining parliamentary
> assent." ...

The title and the preamble relied on do not make the General Convention
statute; and, therefore, except to the extent of the specific amendments to the law
made by the Act of 1957 itself, which I have mentioned and which have not been
relied on for the purposes of this case—and which, indeed, appear hardly applicable to it at all—this Act does not provide material which can be relied on as being
in conflict with the Finance Act at all. It is conceded by the Crown for the purposes
of this case, though not otherwise, that the ratification in fact took place; but it is
clear, as I have already indicated, that in so far as the ratification has taken place by
executive action and not by parliamentary action, then it yields to statute. So even
if there were a conflict between what is contained in the conventions ratified and
the Finance Act, the Finance Act, unambiguous as it is, would prevail. Therefore,
on this ground, apart from any other the taxpayer's case, in my judgment, fails.

However, I shall just mention another limb to the taxpayer's argument; namely,
that any unlawful purpose for which a statutory enactment may be made vitiates
the enforcement of that statute. As was pointed out for the Crown, if that
argument were correct it would mean that the supremacy of Parliament would, in
effect, be overruled. If the purpose to which a statute may be used is an invalid
purpose, then such remedy as there may be must be directed to dealing with that
purpose and not to invalidating the statute itself. What the statute itself enacts
cannot be unlawful, because what the statute says and provides is itself the law,
and the highest form of law that is known to this country. It is the law which
prevails over every other form of law, and it is not for the court to say that a
parliamentary enactment, the highest law in this country, is illegal. The result
therefore is that on this ground, also, the taxpayer's case fails.

I would merely add this: that references were made in the course of the
attractive arguments that were put forward for the taxpayer to the fact that the
intention that taxation was to be applied to nuclear weapons had been amply
demonstrated by Parliamentary Papers and other reliable means within Parliament itself. This, of course, is quite clear, and I have no hesitation in accepting it.
But either that is a part of the statute, or otherwise part of the law of the land, or it
is not. If it is part of a statute it is statute law and it has to be applied by this court. If
it is not, then it has no statutory effect and does not affect what is done by statute,
including the provisions of the Finance Act itself. But the true situation is that
such declarations of policy and so forth do not have statutory effect, have not the

force of the law at all, and therefore cannot affect a statute. The terms of the statute in this case are perfectly clear and binding upon the courts of this country. Appeals dismissed with costs.

Manner and Form of Legislation

Attorney-General
For New South Wales v. Trethowan
[1932] A.C. 526
Judicial Committee of the Privy Council

The Constitution Act 1902, enacted by the legislature of New South Wales, was amended in 1929 by adding section 7A, which provided that no bill for abolishing the Legislative Council (the second chamber) should be presented to the Governor for His Majesty's asset until it had been approved by a majority of the electors voting in a referendum, and that the same provision was to apply to a Bill to repeal this section.

In 1930, both Houses of the legislature passed two Bills, one to repeal section 7A and the other to abolish the Legislative Council. Two members of the Legislative Council brought an action in the Supreme Court of New South Wales against the Attorney-General for New South Wales and the President of the Legislative Council, claiming a declaration that the two Bills could not lawfully be presented to the Governor for assent until approved by the electors in accordance with section 7A of the Constitution Act, and for injunctions to restrain the presentation of the Bills. The full Court granted the declaration and the injunctions.

Leave was obtained to appeal to the High Court of Australia, limited to the questions "whether the Parliament of New South Wales has power to abolish the Legislative Council of the State, or to alter its constitution or powers, or to repeal section 7A of the Constitution Act 1902, except in the manner provided by the said section 7A." The High Court of Australia by a majority of three to two dismissed the appeal.

The grant of special leave to appeal to the Privy Council was limited to the questions above mentioned as being the subject of appeal to the High Court of Australia. The Judicial Committee of the Privy Council (Lord Sankey L.C., Lord Blanesburgh, Lord Hanworth M.R., Lord Atkin and Lord Russell of Killowen) affirmed the judgment of the High Court of Australia.

LORD SANKEY L.C. [after setting out the history of relevant legislation, said]: By the Colonial Laws Validity Act 1865, which applied generally to the colonies, and therefore to New South Wales, 'a representative legislature' was defined as follows: "representative legislature shall signify any colonial legislature which shall comprise a legislative body of which one-half are elected by inhabitants of the colony." The legislature of New South Wales has always been a representative legislature within this definition. Sect. 5 . . . of the Act [is] as follows:—

> "Section 5.—Every colonial legislature shall have and be deemed at all times to have had full power within its jurisdiction to establish Courts of Judicature, and to abolish and reconstitute the same, and to alter the constitution thereof, and to make provision for the administration of justice therein; and every representative legislature shall, in respect to the colony under its jurisdiction, have, and be deemed at all times to have had, full power to make laws respecting the constitution, powers, and procedure of such legislature; provided that such laws shall have been passed in such manner and form as may from time to time be required by any Act of Parliament, letters patent, Order in Council, or colonial law, for the time being in force in the said colony." . . .

[After reviewing the legislation, his Lordship continued]: It is now possible to state the contentions on either side.

The appellants urge: (1.) That the King, with the advice of the Legislative Council and the Legislative Assembly, had full power to enact a Bill repealing s. 7A.

(2.) That sub-s. 6 of s. 7A of the Constitution Act is void, because: (*a*) The New South Wales legislature has no power to shackle or control its successors, the New South Wales constitution being in substance an uncontrolled constitution; (*b*) It is repugnant to s. 4 of the Constitution Statute of 1855; (*c*) It is repugnant to s. 5 of the Colonial Laws Validity Act 1865.

For the respondents it was contended: (1.) That s. 7A was a valid amendment of the constitution of New South Wales, validly enacted in the manner prescribed, and was legally binding in New South Wales.

(2.) That the legislature of New South Wales was given by Imperial statutes plenary power to alter the constitution, powers and procedure of such legislature.

(3.) That when once the legislature had altered the constitution or powers and procedure, then the constitution and powers and procedure as they previously existed ceased to exist, and were replaced by the new constitution and powers.

(4.) That the only possible limitations of this plenary power were: (*a*) it must be exercised according to the manner and form prescribed by any Imperial or colonial law, and (*b*) the legislature must continue a representative legislature according to the definition of the Colonial Laws Validity Act 1865.

(5.) That the addition of s. 7A to the Constitution had the effect of: (*a*) making the legislative body consist thereafter of the King, the Legislative Council, the Assembly and the people for the purpose of the constitutional enactments therein described, or (*b*) imposing a manner and form of legislation in reference to these constitutional enactments which thereafter became binding on the legislature by virtue of the Colonial Laws Validity Act 1865, until repealed in the manner and mode prescribed.

(6.) That the power of altering the constitution conferred by s. 4 of the Constitution Statute 1855, must be read subject to the Colonial Laws Validity Act 1865, and that in particular the limitation as to manner and form prescribed by the 1865 Act must be governed by subsequent amendments to the constitution, whether purporting to be made in the earlier Act or not.

Such are the facts and such the contentions of the parties. . . .

The answer depends in their Lordships' view entirely upon a consideration of the meaning and effect of s. 5 of the Act of 1865, read in conjunction with s. 4 of the Constitution Statute, assuming that latter section still to possess some operative effect. Whatever operative effect it may still possess must, however, be governed by and be subject to such conditions as are to be found in s. 5 of the Act of 1865 in regard to the particular kind of laws within the purview of that section. Sect. 5 is therefore the master section to consider for the purpose here in hand. It will be observed that the second sentence of the section contains an enacting part with a proviso, and it was vehemently contended by the appellants that the effect of the proviso was not to cut down the operative part of the sentence, and that any construction of the words "manner and form," which are contained in the proviso, which cut down the powers previously granted was repugnant to the power so granted. In their Lordships' opinion it is impossible to read the section as if it were contained in watertight compartments. It must be read as a whole, and read as a whole the effect of the proviso is to qualify the words which immediately precede it. The powers are granted sub modo. Reading the section as a whole, it gives to the legislature of New South Wales certain powers, subject to this, that in respect of certain laws they can only become effectual provided they have been passed in such manner and form as may from time to time be required by any Act still on the statute book. Beyond that, the words "manner and form" are amply wide enough to cover an enactment providing that a Bill is to be submitted to the electors and that unless and until a majority of the electors voting approve the Bill it shall not be presented to the Governor for his Majesty's assent.

In their Lordships' opinion the legislature of New South Wales had power under s. 5 of the Act of 1865 to enact the Constitution (Legislative Council) Amendment Act 1929, and thereby to introduce s. 7A into the Constitution Act

1902. In other words, the legislature had power to alter the constitution of New South Wales by enacting that Bills relating to specified kind or kinds of legislation (e.g., abolishing the Legislative Council or altering its constitution or powers, or repealing or amending that enactment) should not be presented for the Royal assent until approved by the electors in a prescribed manner. There is here no question of repugnancy. The enactment of the Act of 1929 was simply an exercise by the legislature of New South Wales of its power (adopting the words of s. 5 of the Act of 1865) to make laws respecting the constitution, powers and procedure of the authority competent to make the laws for New South Wales.

The whole of s. 7A was competently enacted. It was *intra vires* s. 5 of the Act of 1865 and was (again adopting the words of s. 5) a colonial law for the time being in force when the Bill to repeal s. 7A was introduced into the Legislative Council.

The question then arises, could *that* Bill, a repealing Bill, after its passage through both chambers, be lawfully presented for the Royal assent without having first received the approval of the electors in the prescribed manner? In their Lordships' opinion, the Bill could not lawfully be so presented. The proviso in the second sentence of s. 5 of the Act of 1865 states a condition which must be fulfilled before the legislature can validly exercise its power to make the kind of laws which are referred to in that sentence. In order that s. 7A may be repealed (in other words, in order that *that* particular law "respecting the constitution, powers and procedure" of the legislature may be validly made) the law for that purpose must have been passed in the manner required by s. 7A, a colonial law for the time being in force in New South Wales. An attempt was made to draw some distinction between a Bill to repeal a statute and a Bill for other purposes and between "making"laws and the word in the proviso, "passed." Their Lordships feel unable to draw any such distinctions. As to the proviso they agree with the views expressed by Rich J. in the following words: "I take the word 'passed' to be equivalent to 'enacted.' The proviso is not dealing with narrow questions of parliamentary procedure"; and later in his judgment: "In my opinion the proviso to s. 5. relates to the entire process of turning a proposed law into a legislative enactment, and was intended to enjoin fulfilment of every condition and compliance with every requirement which existing legislation imposed upon the process of law making."

Again, no question of repugnancy here arises. It is only a question whether the proposed enactment is *intra vires* or *ultra vires* s. 5. A Bill, within the scope of subs. 6 of s. 7A, which received the Royal assent without having been approved by the electors in accordance with that section, would not be a valid Act of the legislature. It would be *ultra vires* s. 5 of the Act of 1865. Indeed, the presentation of the Bill to the Governor without such approval would be the commission of an unlawful act.

In the result, their Lordships are of opinion that s. 7A of the Constitution Act 1902, was valid and was in force when the two bills under consideration were passed through the Legislative Council and the Legislative Assembly. Therefore these Bills could not be presented to the Governor for His Majesty's assent unless and until a majority of the electors voting had approved them.

For these reasons, their Lordships are of opinion that the judgment of the High Court dismissing the appeal from the decree of the Supreme Court of New South Wales was right and that this appeal should be dismissed with costs. In accordance with the usual practice, the interveners will not receive any costs. They will humbly advise His Majesty accordingly.

Note

The Australian States were taken out of the definition of "Colonies" by the Statute of Westminster 1931, but their legislatures remained bound by the Colonial Laws Validity Act 1865 until the Australia Act 1986.

No argument on appeal was allowed on the question whether an injunction would lie to restrain the presentation of the Bills to the Governor. *Rediffusion (Hong Kong) Ltd.* v. *Attorney-General of Hong Kong* [1970] A.C. 1136 (P.C.) suggests that injunction would not lie, but the Act after receiving the Governor's assent would be subject to judicial review.

Trethowan's case is concerned with subordinate legislatures, and is no authority on the question whether the United Kingdom Parliament can bind itself as to the manner and form of legislation.

EUROPEAN COMMUNITIES ACT 1972 AND INTERPRETATION OF STATUTES

Duke v. Reliance Systems Ltd.

[1988] 2 W.L.R. 359

House of Lords

The appellant, Mrs. Duke, was employed by the respondent, GEC Reliance Ltd. (formerly Reliance Systems Ltd.). The policy of the respondent was to enforce the retirement of employees when they reached the pensionable age of 60 in the case of women and 65 in the case of men. In conformity with that policy the respondent ceased to employ the appellant after she attained the age of 60 and before she attained the age of 65. The appellant claimed that she was the victim of discrimination on the grounds of sex and that she was entitled to damages under the Sex Discrimination Act 1975 because the discriminatory retirement enforced on her was rendered unlawful by section 6(2) of that Act, which prohibits discrimination against a woman "by dismissing her." The respondent admitted that the appellant was discriminated against by dismissal but denied that the discriminatory dismissal was (before amendment by the Sex Discrimination Act 1986) unlawful because by section 6(4) of the Act, section 6(2) did not "apply to provision in relation to death or retirement." The appellant argued that section 6(4) only applied to discriminatory benefits provided after retirement and did not authorise discriminatory retirement ages. Alternatively, the appellant submitted section 6(4) must be construed in a sense favourable to the appellant in order to harmonise the 1975 Act with Community Law. The respondent argued that the practice of dismissing men at 65 and women at 60 was "provision in relation to" retirement and that a British court which accepted that construction was bound to give effect to it. If the dismissal of the appellant was an unlawful act of discrimination, the appellant was entitled by sections 63 to 66 of the 1975 Act to complain to an industrial tribunal and to be awarded damages on the basis that the unlawful act of discrimination must be treated as a tort. The appellant complained to an industrial tribunal, but her complaint was dismissed on the grounds that section 6(4) preserved the right of an employer to operate discriminatory ages of retirement. The decision of the industrial tribunal was upheld by the Employment Appeal Tribunal (Popplewell J., Mr. J. H. Galbraith and Mr. T. H. Jenkins) and by the Court of Appeal, (Sir John Donaldson M.R., Ralph Gibson and Bingham L.JJ.) Mrs. Duke appealed to the House of Lords (Lord Keith of Kinkel, Lord Brandon of Oakbrook, Lord Templeman, Lord Oliver of Aylmerton and Lord Goff of Chieveley).

LORD TEMPLEMAN: My Lords, this appeal raises a question of construction of an Act of the Parliament of the United Kingdom in the light of laws passed by the European Economic Community. . . .

The Equal Pay Act 1970 was passed on 29 May 1970, and, as subsequently amended, introduced into every contract of employment of a woman an equality clause whereby if the terms of her contract vary unfavourably from the terms of employment of a corresponding man, then the woman's contract shall be treated as modified so far as is necessary to eliminate that variation. By section 6(1A) an equality clause:

"(b) . . . shall not operate in relation to terms relating to death or retirement or to any provision made in connection with death or retirement."

Thus the Equal Pay Act 1970 did not prohibit an employer from contracting with men and women on terms that women must retire at the age of 60 and men at 65. The Equal Pay Act 1970 was directed to come into force on 29 December 1975 so that employers were able to adjust their contractual policies and industrial relations in the light of the requirements of the Act. The respondent's contracts with men and women did not include any term relating to retirement. Their contracts of employment were determinable at any time by notice on either side. The respondent, as a matter of policy, gave notice of determination to enforce retirement when women reached the age of 60 and when men reached the age of 65. The Equal Pay Act 1970 did not therefore apply to the retirement of the appellant. And even if the appellant had been employed under a contract which required her to retire at the age of 60, a term less favourable than a term requiring a corresponding man to retire at 65, so as to constitute discrimination under the Equal Pay Act 1970, nevertheless the discriminatory term would have been lawful by reason of section 6(1A) of the Act.

The European Communities Act 1972, passed in anticipation of the accession of the United Kingdom to the European Economic Community on 1 January 1973, accepted the supremacy of Community law under the Treaty of Rome (the E.E.C. Treaty) and allied Treaties in these terms:

> "2(1) All such rights, powers, liabilities, obligations and restrictions from time to time created by or arising by or under the Treaties, and all such remedies and procedures from time to time provided for by or under the Treaties, as in accordance with the Treaties are without further enactment to be given legal effect or used in the United Kingdom shall be recognised and available in law, and be enforced, allowed and followed accordingly; ..."

Section 2(4) provides, inter alia, that "any enactment passed or to be passed ... shall be construed and have effect subject to the foregoing provisions of this section; ...." This subsection does no more than reinforce the binding nature of legally enforceable rights and obligations imposed by appropriate Community law.

By article 5 of the E.E.C. Treaty:

> "Member states shall take all appropriate measures, whether general or particular, to ensure fulfilment of the obligation arising out of this Treaty or resulting from action taken by the institutions of the Community ...."

By a resolution dated 21 January 1974 (Official Journal 1974 No. C.13, p. 1), the Council of Ministers, one of the institutions of the Community, approved the development of a social action programme and declared its intention to adopt measures necessary to achieve, among other objects, the attainment of full and better employment in the Community and for that purpose:

> "To undertake action for the purpose of achieving equality between men and women as regards access to employment and vocational training and advancement and as regards working conditions, including pay, taking into account the important role of management and labour in this field."

This resolution was in the nature of a declaration of intent and did not impose any specific obligation on member states, although they could be expected to pursue the aims indicated by the Council in the resolution.

In September 1974 the Home Office on behalf of the United Kingdom Government published a White Paper entitled Equality for Women (Cmnd. 5724) and announced the intention of the Government to introduce a Bill providing for equal treatment of women. The White Paper made these observations about contractual and non-contractual forms of discrimination:

> "41. .... The Equal Pay Act requires equal treatment with respect to *contractual* terms and conditions of employment. The Bill will complement the Equal Pay Act by applying to *non-contractual* aspects of employment. ...
>
> "42. The Equal Pay Act does not require equal treatment as regards terms and conditions 'related to retirement, marriage and death or to any provision made in connection with retirement, marriage or death'. .... The proposed Bill will require equal treatment as regards terms and conditions relating to

marriage or any provision made in connection with marriage, and will amend the Equal Pay Act accordingly. The general exclusion of provisions relating to retirement or death (and childbirth) contained in that Act will be retained. State social security provisions are contained in separate legislation and will be dealt with together with occupational pensions schemes. . . ."

Thus the changes proposed by the Government for the Equal Pay Act 1970 did not include any change in section 6(4) but the White Paper proposed that the new Bill should contain a clause similar to section 6(4). The Bill proposed by the White Paper was intended to prohibit discrimination against women where the discrimination was not to be found in any term of a contract of employment but resulted from policies and practices in industrial relations. The Equal Pay Act and the Bill were to form part of a single code prohibiting many forms of discrimination but permitting discrimination in connection with retirement. It would not have made sense to allow by the Equal Pay Act 1970 discriminatory ages of retirement expressed in contracts of employment but to prohibit by the proposed Bill discriminatory ages of retirement which were in force by employers as a matter of policy and practice. The White Paper referred to domestic inquiries and investigations and consultations dealing with discrimination against women but did not mention Community law or intentions. But the Government must have considered that the Equal Pay Act and the proposed Bill would be consistent with the letter and spirit of Community law and Community intentions.

Article 119 of the E.E.C. Treaty, inter alia, directs that:

"Each member state shall . . . ensure and . . . maintain the application of the principle that men and women should receive equal pay for equal work."

On 10 February 1975 the Council of Ministers adopted Council Directive (75/117/E.E.C.) the Equal Pay Directive (Official Journal 1975, No. L.45, p. 19) which recited article 119 and the Council Resolution dated 21 January 1974 and called upon member states within one year to put into force laws necessary to establish the "principle of equal pay." That principle was defined to mean that "for the same work or for work to which equal value is attributed, the elimination of all discrimination on grounds of sex with regard to all aspects and conditions of remuneration." Article 119 and the Equal Pay Directive did not deal with discriminatory ages of retirement but were otherwise relevant to the Equal Pay Act 1970.

Article 189 of the E.E.C. Treaty provides inter alia:

"In order to carry out their task the Council and the Commission shall, in accordance with the provisions of this Treaty, make regulations, issue directives, take decisions, make recommendations or deliver opinions. A regulation shall have general application. It shall be binding in its entirety and directly applicable in all member states. A directive shall be binding, as to the result to be achieved, upon each member state to which it is addressed, but shall leave to the national authorities the choice of form and methods."

The Bill foreshadowed by the 1974 White Paper was introduced and was finally enacted on 12 November 1975 as the Sex Discrimination Act 1975. By section 1(1) a person discriminates against a woman if on the ground of her sex he treats her less favourably than he treats or would treat a man. Sections 6 to 21 comprising Part II of the Act deal with "Discrimination in the employment field." Section 6, so far as relevant, provides as follows:

"(1) It is unlawful for a person, in relation to employment by him . . . to discriminate against a woman—(a) in the arrangements he makes for the purpose of determining who should be offered that employment, or (b) in the terms in which he offers her that employment, or (c) by refusing or deliberately omitting to offer her that employment. (2) It is unlawful for a person, in the case of a woman employed by ... to discriminate against her—(a) in the way he affords her access to opportunities for promotion, transfer or training, or to any other benefits, facilities or services, or by refusing or deliberately omitting to afford her access to them, or (b) by dismissing her, or subjecting her to any other detriment."

Thus the respondent's policy of dismissing women at 60 and men at 65 was discriminatory within the meaning of the Act. But section 6 continued: "(4) Subsections (1)(b) and (2) do not apply to provision in relation to death or retirement." By section 82(1) "retirement" was defined to include retirement (whether voluntary or not) on grounds of age, length of service or incapacity. The Sex Discrimination Act 1975 made amendments to the Equal Pay Act 1970 consistent with the intention declared by the 1984[sic] White Paper. Both Acts were brought into force on 29 December 1975 and formed a single code dealing with discrimination against women in the field of employment whether pursuant to contract or practice. The Government and Parliament of the United Kingdom must have considered that the Equal Pay Act 1970 and the Sex Discrimination Act 1975 complied with the obligation of the United Kingdom to observe Community law and Community intentions including article 119 and the Equal Pay Directive, so far as Community law was understood in the United Kingdom and so far as Community intentions were discernible.

On 9 February 1976 the Council of Ministers adopted an Equal Treatment Directive, Council Directive (76/207/E.E.C.) (Official Journal 1976, No. L.39, p. 40), which after reciting the Council Resolution of 21 January 1974 and the Equal Pay Directive contained the following recitals setting forth some of the reasons for the adoption of the Equal Treatment Directive:

"Whereas Community action to achieve the principle of equal treatment for men and women in respect of access to employment and vocational training and promotion and in respect of other working conditions also appears to be necessary; whereas, equal treatment for male and female workers constitutes one of the objectives of the Community, in so far as the harmonisation of living and working conditions while maintaining their improvement are inter alia to be furthered; whereas the Treaty does not confer the necessary specific powers for this purpose; ..."

The Equal Treatment Directive then provided:

"Article 1.
"1. The purpose of this Directive is to put into effect in the member states the principle of equal treatment for men and women as regards access to employment, including promotion, and vocational training and as regards working conditions and, on the conditions referred to in paragraph 2, social security. This principle is hereinafter referred to as 'the principle of equal treatment.'
"2. With a view to ensuring the progressive implementation of the principle of equal treatment in matters of social security, the Council, acting on a proposal from the Commission, will adopt provisions defining its substance, its scope and the arrangements for its application
"Article 2.
"1. For the purposes of the following provisions, the principle of equal treatment shall mean that there shall be no discrimination whatsoever on grounds of sex either directly or indirectly by reference in particular to marital or family status.
"Article 5.
"1. Application of the principle of equal treatment with regard to working conditions, including the conditions governing dismissal, means that men and women shall be guaranteed the same conditions without discrimination on grounds of sex.

"*Article 9*.

"2. Member states shall put into force the laws, regulations and administrative provisions necessary in order to comply with this Directive within 30 months of its notification and shall immediately inform the Commission thereof."

In the event the time limited for compliance with the Equal Treatment Directive expired on 12 August 1978. Before that date the Government of the United Kingdom took no steps to repeal or amend section 6(1A) of the Equal Pay Act 1970 or section 6(4) of the Sex Discrimination Act 1975.

In *Roberts* v. *Cleveland Area Health Authority* [1978] I.C.R. 370, the plaintiff. Mrs. Roberts, was dismissed by the health authority pursuant to "the policy of the area health authority under which the normal retirement age for female employees was 60 whereas the normal retirement age for male employees was 65"; *per* Phillips J. in the judgment of the Employment Appeal Tribunal, at p. 371G. Mrs. Roberts claimed damages under the Sex Discrimination Act 1975 for her discriminatory dismissal. The health authority successfully pleaded that the dismissal of Mrs. Roberts was lawful under section 6(4) of the Act. The only argument of substance put before the tribunal and repeated in the course of the present appeal on behalf of the appellant was that in section 6(4) provision "in relation to death" must mean provision "consequent upon a death" and therefore provision "in relation to retirement" must be limited to provision "consequent upon retirement." Phillips J. rejected this argument. He said, at p. 374, that the word "provision" in section 6(4) is an expression intentionally wide and covers all the employer's arrangements relating to retirement including matters of policy, including the fixing of the date of retirement. He thought it likely that the draftsman

"recognised that death and retirement are in different categories in this matter, in that one cannot fix a date of death but one can fix a date of retirement; and that he had to use a form of words, in the one subsection, which was apt to cover both."

My Lords, section 6(4) makes lawful a dismissal which would otherwise be unlawful under section 6(2). The discriminatory dismissal made lawful by section 6(4) is confined to a dismissal for which provision is made in relation to retirement. If an employer dismisses a woman in order to replace her by a man, the dismissal will infringe section 6(2) and will not be saved by section 6(4). But if an employer dismisses a woman because the employer has made provision for men and women alike to retire when they reach their retirement ages, then if there are differential retirement ages, the dismissal is saved from being unlawful by section 6(4) because the dismissal is pursuant to provision relating to retirement. The respondent made provision for men and women to be dismissed when they reached the retirement age of 60 in the case of women and 65 in the case of men. If an employer does not discriminate against a woman by dismissing her but provides that her retirement benefits are to be less favourable than the benefits accorded to a man, then the employer will not be dismissing her within section 6(2) but he will be subjecting her to another detriment within section 6(2). This discriminatory detriment is also saved by section 6(4). Section 11(4) of the Sex Discrimination Act 1975 is to the like effect. That section renders it unlawful for partners, in relation to a position as partner in the firm, to discriminate against a woman:

"(*b*) in the terms on which they offer her that position, or . . . .(*d*) in a case where the woman already holds that position—(i) in the way they afford her access to any benefits, facilities or services, or by refusing or deliberately omitting to afford her access to them, or (ii) by expelling her from that position, or subjecting her to any other detriment."

But section 11(4) provides that subsection (1)(*b*) and (*d*) do not apply to provision made in relation to death or retirement.

Thus partners may lawfully offer a partnership to a woman on the terms that she will retire at 60 with power to expel her if she does not. Or if there is a partnership position which is terminable on notice, with no provision for retirement, the firm may give notice enforcing the retirement of the woman at 60 notwithstanding that men are only obliged to retire at 65. So too in the Equal Pay Act 1970 which deals with contractural obligations section 6(1A)(*b*) enables an employer to contract with men and women for retirement at different retirement ages without incurring the penalty of an equality clause. There can be no logical distinction between section 6(1A)(*b*) of the Equal Pay Act 1970, section 6(4) of the Sex Discrimination Act 1975 and section 11(4) of the latter Act; in my opinion all three subsections make lawful discriminatory retirement ages.

On 19 December 1978 the Council of Ministers adopted a Social Security Directive (79/7/E.E.C.) (Official Journal 1979, No. L.6, p. 24) which had been foreshadowed and reserved by the Equal Treatment Directive. The Social Security Directive obliged member states to put into effect equal treatment for social security within six years but by article 7:

> "7.1. This Directive shall be without prejudice to the right of member states to exclude from its scope: (a) The determination of pensionable age for the purposes of granting old age and retirement pensions and the possible consequences thereof for other benefits;" . . .

Thus Community law did not require the abrogation of British statutory retirement pension schemes whereby the pensionable age of women is 60 and the pensionable age of men is 65.

In *Roberts* v. *Cleveland Area Health Authority* [1979] 1 W.L.R. 754; [1979] I.C.R. 558 the Court of Appeal upheld the decision of the Employment Appeal Tribunal that section 6(4) of the Sex Discrimination Act 1975 allowed discriminatory retirement ages. Lawton L.J. said, at pp. 759; 566, 567;

> "My first impression was that the words 'provision in relation to death or retirement' meant 'provision about retirement.' Nothing has been said in the argument which has made me change that first impression. . . . To fix a retiring age is to make a provision in relation to retirement."

Finally, so far as English law is concerned it is material to consider the circumstances in which the Equal Pay Act 1970 and the Sex Discrimination Act 1975 were enacted. In *Roberts* v. *Cleveland Area Health Authority* [1978] I.C.R. 370, 375 Phillips J. said:

> "It is common knowledge that outside the public service, at all events, large parts of industry and commerce are organised on the basis that men and women do retire at different ages. The matter is highly controversial. There are different political and sociological views held about it; different economic views, and so on. But in 1975 it was an established fact that this was what frequently happened in practice. Furthermore, it reflects the long standing course of social legislation going back . . . 37 years to 1940, to the Old Age and Widows' Pension Act of that year. For very many years indeed, employers have made all their arrangements upon this basis. Pension funds are so organised, recruitment is so organised; and everything is organised on that basis. Obviously, in the Sex Discrimination Act 1975 there is no reason why Parliament should not, had it wished to do so, have brought all that to an end; but it seems to us largely improbable that Parliament would have brought it to an end, or would have intended to bring it to an end, at a clean sweep. The Equal Pay Act 1970 itself was given five years to be brought into operation; and when one considers the practical consequences of a reform of that character, the arrangements that would have to be made, the consultation

that would be needed, the mind boggles at the thought that it should happen overnight, between the end of one night and the beginning of the following day. . . . Furthermore it is not without relevance that other Acts such as the Equal Pay Act 1970 and the Trade Union and Labour Relations Act 1974 are in part in conformity with the view that we have indicated."

Similarly, in *Roberts* v. *Tate & Lyle Food and Distribution Ltd.* [1983] I.C.R. 521 Browne-Wilkinson J. delivering the judgment of the Employment Appeal Tribunal said, at pp. 528–529:

"We consider that the purpose of section 6(4) is fairly apparent. Parliament, in enacting the Act of 1975, was seeking to eliminate all discrimination between men and women. However, it was faced by a widespread and inherently discriminatory practice deeply embedded in the social organisation of the country, namely, the differential in retirement ages between men and women. This differential treatment was blatantly discriminatory. However, the effect of such discriminatory practice percolated throughout society. State pensions reflected the differential; the vast majority of occupational pension schemes reflected the differential; normal ages of retirement maintained the differential. Accordingly, unless all this was to be swept away, the Act had to exclude claims arising out of this inherently discriminatory practice. For this reason section 6(4) appeared in the Act."

My Lords I agree with the views expressed by Phillips J. and Browne-Wilkinson J. and would add this. If the Government had intended to sweep away the widespread practice of differential retirement ages, the 1974 White Paper would not have given a contrary assurance and if Parliament had intended to outlaw differential retirement ages section 6(4) of the Sex Discrimination Act 1975 would have been very differently worded in order to make clear the profound change which Parliament contemplated. For the reasons I have given and for the reasons advanced by the Employment Appeal Tribunal and the Court of Appeal in the judgments I have cited, I am of the opinion that the legality of discrimination between men and women with regard to retirement ages was preserved, whether as a matter of contract to which the Equal Pay Act 1970 was directed or as a matter of practice to which the Sex Discrimination Act 1975 applied.

The United Kingdom Government considered that the Equal Treatment Directive (76/207/E.E.C.) did not prohibit discriminatory ages of retirement. The argument of the Government, put forward in *Marshall* v. *Southampton and South West Hampshire Area Health Authority (Teaching)* [1986] Q.B. 401, 420 was that article 7(1) of the Social Security Directive allowed discrimination in the determination of pension age; retirement provisions were conditioned by pension age. Women retired at 60 when they qualified for a pension. Men retired at 65 because they did not reach pensionable age until then. The discrimination under Community law permitted in pensionable ages must extend to discrimination in retirement ages; pensionable ages and retirement ages ran in harness. This argument was rejected by the European Court of Justice in *Marshall's* case. The court, at p. 420, decided that:

"38. . . . article 5(1) of Council Directive (76/207/E.E.C.) must be interpreted as meaning that a general policy concerning dismissal involving the dismissal of a woman solely because she has attained the qualifying age for a state pension, which age is different under national legislation for men and for women, constitutes discrimination on grounds of sex, contrary to that Directive."

The United Kingdom, pursuant to its obligations under the E.E.C. Treaty to give effect to Community legislation as construed by the European Court of Justice and following the decision in *Marshall's* case, enacted the Sex Discrimination Act 1986 passed on 7 November 1986 and, inter alia, amended section 6(1A) of the Equal Pay Act 1970 and section 6(4) of the Sex Discrimination Act 1975 so as to render unlawful discriminatory retirement ages as between men and women. The Act of 1986 was not retrospective and does not avail the appellant.

Marshall's case decided that the Equal Treatment Directive required member states to prohibit discrimination with regard to retirement or dismissal in accordance with an employer's policy. In the present case therefore, the appellant can show that her forcible retirement before reaching the age of 65 years was discrimination contrary to the requirements of the Equal Treatment Directive. But *Marshall's* case also decided that the Equal Treatment Directive did not possess direct effect as between individuals, so that the appellant cannot claim damages against the respondent simply for breach of the Directive. In their decision the European Court of Justice said [1986] Q.B. 401, 422;

> "48. . . . according to article 189 of the E.E.C. Treaty the binding nature of a directive, which constitutes the basis for the possibility of relying on the directive before a national court, exists only in relation to 'each member state to which it is addressed.' It follows that a directive may not of itself impose obligations on an individual and that a provision of a directive may not be relied upon as such against such a person. . . ."

Nevertheless, it is now submitted that the appellant is entitled to damages from the respondent because Community law requires the Equal Pay Act enacted on 29 May 1970 and the Sex Discrimination Act enacted on 12 November 1975 to be construed in a manner which gives effect to the Equal Treatment Directive dated 9 February 1976 as construed by the European Court of Justice in *Marshall's* case published on 20 February 1986. Of course a British court will always be willing and anxious to conclude that United Kingdom law is consistent with Community law. Where an Act is passed for the purpose of giving effect to an obligation imposed by a directive or other instrument a British court will seldom encounter difficulty in concluding that the language of the Act is effective for the intended purpose. But the construction of a British Act of Parliament is a matter of judgment to be determined by British courts and to be derived from the language of the legislation considered in the light of the circumstances prevailing at the date of enactment. The circumstances in which the Equal Pay Act 1970 and the Sex Discrimination Act 1975 were enacted are set forth in the 1974 White Paper, in the judgment of Phillips J. in *Roberts* v. *Cleveland Area Health Authority* [1978] I.C.R. 370, in the judgment of Browne-Wilkinson J. in *Roberts* v. *Tate & Lyle Food and Distribution Ltd.* [1983] I.C.R. 521 and in the submission of the United Kingdom Government in *Marshall's* case [1986] Q.B. 401. The Acts were not passed to give effect to the Equal Treatment Directive and were intended to preserve discriminatory retirement ages. Proposals for the Equal Treatment Directive dated 9 February 1976 were in circulation when the Bill for the Sex Discrimination Act 1975 was under discussion but it does not appear that these proposals were understood by the British Government or the Parliament of the United Kingdom to involve the prohibition of differential retirement ages linked to differential pensionable ages.

The appellant relied on the speech of Lord Diplock in *Garland* v. *British Rail Engineering Ltd.* [1983] 2 A.C. 751, 770–771. Lord Diplock expressed the view that section 6(4) of the Sex Discrimination Act 1975 could and should be construed in the manner consistent with article 119 of the E.E.C. Treaty, the Equal Pay Directive and the Equal Treatment Directive. In *Garland's* case, following a reference to the European Court of Justice it was established that there had been discrimination contrary to article 119 which has direct effect between individuals. It was thus unnecessary to consider the effect of the Equal Treatment Directive. Lord Diplock observed, at p. 771, that:

> "even if the obligation to observe the provisions of article 119 were an obligation assumed by the United Kingdom under an ordinary international treaty or convention and there was no question of the Treaty obligation being

directly applicable as part of the law to be applied by the courts in this country without need for any further enactment, it is a principle of construction of United Kingdom statutes, now too well established to call for citation of authority, that the words of a statute passed after the Treaty has been signed and dealing with the subject matter of the international obligation of the United Kingdom, are to be construed, if they are reasonably capable of bearing such a meaning, as intended to carry out the obligation, and not to be inconsistent with it. . . . The instant appeal does not present an appropriate occasion to consider whether, having regard to the express direction as to the construction of enactments 'to be passed' which is contained in section 2(4) anything short of an express positive statement in an Act of Parliament passed after 1 January 1973, that a particular provision is intended to be made in breach of an obligation assumed by the United Kingdom under a community treaty, would justify an English court in construing that provision in a manner inconsistent with a Community treaty obligation of the United Kingdom, however wide a departure from the prima facie meaning of the language of the provision might be needed in order to achieve consistency."

On the hearing of this appeal, your Lordships have had the advantage, not available to Lord Diplock, of full argument which has satisfied me that the Sex Discrimination Act 1975 was not intended to give effect to the equal treatment Directive as subsequently construed in the *Marshall* case [1986] Q.B. 401 and that the words of section 6(4) are not reasonably capable of being limited to the meaning ascribed to them by the appellant. Section 2(4) of the European Communities Act 1972 does not in my opinion enable or constrain a British court to distort the meaning of a British statute in order to enforce against an individual a Community directive which has no direct effect between individuals. Section 2(4) applies and only applies where Community provisions are directly applicable.

The jurisdiction composition and powers of the European Court of Justice are contained in articles 164 to 188 of the E.E.C. Treaty. Those sections include the following:

"164. The Court of Justice shall ensure that in the interpretation and application of this Treaty the law is observed. . . .
"177. The Court of Justice shall have jurisdiction to give preliminary rulings concerning: (*a*) the interpretation of this Treaty; (*b*) the validity and interpretation of Acts of the institutions of the Community; (*c*) the interpretation of the statutes of bodies established by an act of the council, where those statutes so provide."

The submission that the Sex Discrimination Act 1975 must be construed in a manner which gives effect to the Equal Treatment Directive as construed by the European Court of Justice in *Marshall's* case is said to be derived from the decision of the European Court of Justice in *von Colson and Kamann* v. *Land Nordrhein-Westfalen* (Case 14–83) [1984] E.C.R. 1891, delivered on 10 April 1984. In the *von Colson* case the European Court of Justice ruled that the provisions of the Equal Treatment Directive which require equal treatment for men and women in access to employment do not require a member state to legislate so as to compel an employer to conclude a contract of employment with a woman who has been refused employment on the grounds of sex. The Directive does not specify the nature of the remedies which the member states must afford to a victim of discrimination. But the court also ruled, at p. 1910:

"3. Although [the Equal Treatment Directive] 76/207/E.E.C. for the purpose of imposing a sanction for the breach of discrimination, leaves the member states free to choose between the different solutions suitable for achieving its object, it nevertheless requires that if a member state chooses to penalise breaches of that prohibition by the award of compensation, then in order to ensure that it is effective and that it has a deterrent effect, that compensation must in any event be adequate in relation to the damage sustained and must therefore amount to more than purely nominal compensation such as, for example, the reimbursement only of the expenses incurred in connection with the application. It is for the national court to interpret and apply the legislation and adopted for the implementation of the Directive in conformity with the requirements of Community law, in so far as it is given discretion to do so under national law."

In the *von Colson* case the German court which submitted the case for a ruling asked whether it was acceptable that a woman who applied for a job and was refused because she was a woman, contrary to the intent of the Equal Treatment Directive, was only entitled under the German domestic law prohibiting such discrimination to the recovery of her expenses (if any) of her application. The German Government in making representations to the European Court expressed the view that under German law compensation for discrimination could include general damages for the loss of the job or of the opportunity to take up the job. The ruling of the European Court of Justice did not constrain the national court to construe German law in accordance with Community law but ruled that if under German law the German court possessed the power to award damages which were adequate and which fulfilled the objective of the Equal Treatment Directive then it was the duty of the German Court to act accordingly.

The *von Colson* case is no authority for the proposition that the German court was bound to invent a German law of adequate compensation if no such law existed and no authority for the proposition that a court of a member state must distort the meaning of a domestic statute so as to conform with Community law which is not directly applicable. If, following the *von Colson* case, the German court adhered to the view that under German law it possessed no discretion to award adequate compensation, it would have been the duty of the German Government in fulfilment of its obligations under the Treaty of Rome to introduce legislation or evolve some other method which would enable adequate compensation to be obtained, just as the United Kingdom Government became bound to introduce legislation to amend the Equal Pay Act 1970 and the Sex Discrimination Act 1975 in the light of *Marshall's* case. Mrs. Advocate-General Rozes in her opinion, delivered on 31 January 1984 in the *von Colson* case, said, at p. 1919:

"In proceedings under article 177 it is not for me to express a view on questions which fall exclusively within the jurisdiction of the national courts inasmuch as they concern the application of national law."

The E.E.C. Treaty does not interfere and the European Court of Justice in the *von Colson* case did not assert power to interfere with the method or result of the interpretation of national legislation by national courts.

It would be most unfair to the respondent to distort the construction of the 1975 Sex Discrimination Act in order to accommodate the 1976 Equal Treatment Directive as construed by the European Court of Justice in the 1986 *Marshall* case. As between the appellant and the respondent the Equal Treatment Directive did not have direct effect and the respondent could not reasonably be expected to reduce to precision the opaque language which constitutes both the strength and the difficulty of some Community legislation. The respondent could not reasonably be expected to appreciate the logic of Community legislators in permitting differential retirement pension ages but prohibiting differential retirement ages. The respondent is not liable to the appellant under Community law. I decline to hold that liability under British law attaches to the respondent or any other private employer to pay damages based on wages which women over 60 and under 65 did not earn before the amending Sex Discrimination Act 1986 for the first time and without retrospective effect introduced the statutory tort of operating differential retirement ages. I would dismiss this appeal.

The other members of the House concurred.

Appeal dismissed.

PARLIAMENTARY PRIVILEGE

Nature of Privilege: Authorised Publications
Stockdale v. Hansard
(1839) 9 Ad. & E. 1; 3.St.Tr.(N.S.) 723
Queen's Bench

This was the second of a series of actions brought by Stockdale against Hansard.

A medical book published by Stockdale, and found in the possession of a prisoner in Newgate, was described by two inspectors of prisons in a report to the Government as "disgusting and obscene." This report was printed and sold by the firm of Hansard by order of the House of Commons. The plaintiff brought an action for libel against Hansard.

The defendants, acting under the directions of the House of Commons, pleaded that they had printed and sold the report only in pursuance of the order of the House, that the report having been presented to and laid before the House, it became part of the proceedings of the House, and that the House had resolved (after a previous action between the same parties)

> "that the power of publishing such of its reports, votes, and proceedings as it shall deem necessary or conducive to the public interests is an essential incident to the constitutional functions of Parliament, more especially to the Commons House of Parliament as the representative portion of it."

To this the plaintiff demurred, that the known and established laws of the land cannot be superseded or altered by any resolution of the House of Commons, nor can that House by any resolution create any new privilege inconsistent with the law.

The case was argued at very great length by Sir J. Campbell, Attorney-General, for the defendants, who had been directed by the House to plead to the action merely to inform the court. The Court of Queen's Bench (Lord Denman C.J., Littledale, Patteson and Coleridge JJ.) gave judgment for the plaintiff.

LORD DENMAN C.J.: . . . The [defendants'] plea, it is contended, established a good defence to the action on various grounds.

1. The grievance complained of appears to be an act done by order of the House of Commons, a court superior to any court of law, and none of whose proceedings are to be questioned in any way. . . . It is a claim for an arbitrary power to authorise the commission of any act whatever, on behalf of a body which in the same argument is admitted not to be the supreme power in the State.

The supremacy of Parliament, the foundation on which the claim is made to rest, appears to me completely to overturn it, because the House of Commons is not Parliament, but only a co-ordinate and component part of the Parliament. That sovereign power can make and unmake the laws; but the concurrence of the three legislative estates is necessary; the resolution of any one of them cannot alter the law, or place anyone beyond its control. The proposition is therefore wholly untenable, and abhorrent to the first principles of the constitution of England.

2. The next defence involved in this plea is, that the defendants committed the grievance by order of the House of Commons in a case of privilege, and that each House of Parliament is the sole judge of its own privileges. This last proposition requires to be first considered. For, if the Attorney-General was right in contending, as he did more than once in express terms, that the House of Commons, by claiming any thing as its privilege, thereby makes it a matter of privilege, and also that its own decision upon its own claim is binding and conclusive, then plainly this court cannot proceed in any inquiry into the matter, and has nothing else to do but declare the claim well founded because it has been made.

This is the form in which I understand the Committee of a late House of Commons to have asserted the privileges of both Houses of Parliament: and we are informed that a large majority of that House adopted the assertion. It is not without the utmost respect and deference that I proceed to examine what has been promulgated by such high authority. . . .

Parliament is said to be supreme; I most fully acknowledge its supremacy. It follows, then, as before observed, that neither branch of it is supreme when acting by itself. It is also said that the privilege of each House is the privilege of the whole Parliament. In one sense I agree to this: because whatever impedes the proper action of either impedes those functions which are necessary for the performance of their joint duties. All the essential parts of a machine must be in order before it can work at all. But it by no means follows that the opinion that either House may entertain of the extent of its own privileges is correct, or its declaration of them binding. . . .

That Parliament enjoys privileges of the most important character, no person capable of the least reflection can doubt for a moment. Some are common to both Houses, some peculiar to each, all are essential to the discharge of their functions. If they were not the fruit of deliberation *in aulia regia*, they rest on the stronger ground of a necessity which became apparent at least as soon as the two Houses took their present position in the State.

Thus the privilege of having their debates unquestioned, though denied when members began to speak their minds freely in the time of Queen Elizabeth, and punished in its exercise both by that Princess and her two successors, was soon clearly perceived to be indispensable and universally acknowledged. By consequence, whatever is done within the walls of either assembly must pass without question in any other place. For speeches made in Parliament by a member to the prejudice of any other person, or hazardous to the public peace, that member enjoys complete impunity. . . . But, if the calumnious or inflammatory speeches should be reported and published, the law will attach responsibility to the publisher. . . .

The privilege of committing for contempt is inherent in every deliberative body invested with authority by the constitution. But, however flagrant the contempt, the House of Commons can only commit till the close of the existing session. Their privilege to commit is not better known than this limitation of it. . . .

Nothing is more undoubted than the exclusive privilege of the people's representatives in respect of grants of money, and the imposition of taxes. But, if their care of a branch of it should induce a vote that their messenger should forcibly enter and inspect the cellars of all residents in London possessing more than a certain income, and if some citizen bring an action of trespass, has any lawyer yet said that the Speaker's warrant would justify the breaking and entering?

. . . We were, however, pressed with numerous authorities, which were supposed to establish that questions of privilege are in no case examinable at law. [His Lordship here referred to *Thorp's Case*,[1] *Barnardiston* v. *Soame*,[2] *Alexander Murray's Case*,[3] *Brass Crosby's Case*,[4] *R.* v. *Wright (Horne Tooke's Case)*,[5] *R.* v. *Williams*,[6] *R.* v. *Dangerfield*,[7] *and Lord Shaftesbury's Case*,[8] which he considered did not sustain the Attorney-General's argument.]

But, as to these proceedings by habeas corpus, it may be enough to say that the

[1] (1452) 5 Rot.Parl. 239.
[2] (1689) 6 St.Tr. 1109.
[3] (1751) 1 Wils. 299.
[4] (1771) 3 Wils. 188.
[5] (1799) 8 T.R. 293.
[6] (1686) 13 St.Tr. 1369.
[7] (1686) 3 Mod. 68.
[8] (1677) 6 St.Tr. 1269.

present is not of that class, and that, when any such may come before us, we will deal with it as in our judgment the law may appear to require.

The Attorney-General told us of another case in point in his favour, *Burdett* v. *Abbot*.[9] We must then examine that case fully. The plaintiff committed a breach of privilege by the publication of a libel; the defendant, the Speaker, stating that fact on the face of his warrant, committed him by order of the House to prison; an action was brought for this assault and false imprisonment. Did the House of Commons threaten the plaintiff or his attorney or counsel for a contempt of their privileges? On the contrary, by an express vote they directed their highest officer to plead and submit himself to the juridiction of this court. When the suit was pending, did they entertain questions on the course of the proceedings, or resolve that they alone could define their own privileges, or declare that Judges who should presume to form an opinion at variance with theirs should be amenable to their displeasure? They suffered the cause to make the usual progress through its stages, and placed their arguments before the court. Their arguments were just; their conduct had been lawful in every respect. The court gave judgment in the Speaker's favour. The grounds of the decision were not that all acts done by their authority were beyond the reach of inquiry, or that all which they called privilege was privilege, and sacred from the intrusion of law, but that they had acted in exercise of a known and needful privilege, in strict conformity with the law. . . . The decision manifestly rests on the privilege to punish for contempt, inherent no doubt in Parliament and in each House, whether regarded in the legislative or in the judicial capacity, but which it only possesses in common with the courts of justice, and which was there exercised within the strictest bounds of common law.

This great case, solemnly argued at the bar, and on both sides with extraordinary learning and power, and in which the court evidently pursued their own inquiries in the interval between the arguments, presents a striking contrast to the rash and unmeasured language employed by former judges in *ex parte* proceedings, as writs of habeas corpus and motions for criminal information. . . .

To the assertion, that the courts have always acquiesced in the unlimited claim of privilege, I have already stated enough to authorise me in opposing the contrary assertion. [His Lordship then referred by name to many early authorities and cited with approval the judgments of Holt C.J. in *Knollys's Case* (or *Knowles's Case*)[10]; *Ashby* v. *White*[11] and *The Case of the Men of Aylesbury* (*R.* v. *Paty*).[12]]

Two admissions were made by the Attorney-General in the course of his argument here, either of which appears to me fatal to his case. He very distinctly recognised the words of Lord Mansfield,[13] that, if either House of Parliament should think fit to declare the general law, that declaration is undoubtedly to be disregarded, adding that is should be treated with contempt. . . . But, if the claim were to declare a general law, the Attorney-General agrees that no weight would belong to it. Clearly then the court must inquire whether it be a matter of privilege, or a declaration of general law: as indisputably, if it be a matter of general law, it cannot cease to be so by being invested with the imposing title of privilege.

The other concession to which I alluded is, that, when matter of privilege comes before the courts not directly but incidentally, they may, because they must, decide it. Otherwise, said the Attorney-General, there would be a failure of justice. And such has been the opinion even of those judges who have spoken

---

[9] (1811) 14 East 1.
[10] (1693) 12 St.Tr. 1167; 2 Salk, 509; 1 Ld.Raym. 10.
[11] (1704) 2 Ld.Raym. 938; 14 St.Tr. 695.
[12] (1704) 2 Ld.Raym. 1105; 14 St.Tr. 849.
[13] In the House of Lords, respecting the privileges of the other House in the Middlesex election; 16 *Parl. Hist* 653.

with the most profound veneration of privilege. The rule is difficult of application. . . .

Since, then, the courts may give judgment on matters of privilege incidentally, it is plain that they must have the means of arriving at a correct conclusion, and that they may differ from the Houses of Parliament, as Holt and the Court of Queen's Bench differed from the Lords in the *Banbury* case,[14] as he did in *Paty's* case, and as the same and many other of the judges as well as the Lords did from the Commons in the case of *Ashby* v. *White*. . . .

Before I finally take leave of this head of argument, I will dispose of the notion that the House of Commons is a separate court, having exclusive jurisdiction over the subject-matter, on which, for that reason, its adjudication must be final. The argument placed the House herein on a level with the Spiritual Court and the Court of Admiralty. Adopting this analogy, it appears to me to destroy the defence attempted to the present action. When the subject-matter falls within their jurisdiction, no doubt we cannot question their judgment; but we are now inquiring whether the subject-matter does fall within the jurisdiction of the House of Commons. It is contended that they can bring it within their jurisdiction by declaring it so. To this claim, as arising from their privileges, I have already stated my answer: it is perfectly clear that none of these courts could give themselves jurisdiction by adjudging that they enjoy it.

3. I come at length to consider whether this privilege of publication exists. The plea states the resolution of the House that all parliamentary reports printed for the use of the House should be sold to the public, and that these several papers were ordered to be printed, not however stating that they were printed for the use of the House. It then sets forth the resolution. . . .

The Attorney-General would preclude us from commencing this inquiry. . . . But, having convinced myself that the mere order of the House will not justify an act otherwise illegal, and that the simple declaration that that order is made in exercise of a privilege does not prove the privilege, it is no longer optional with me to decline or accept the office of deciding whether this privilege exists in law. . . .

The proof of this privilege was grounded on three principles—necessity—practice—universal acquiescence. If the necessity can be made out, no more need be said: it is the foundation of every privilege of Parliament, and justifies all that it requires. But the promise to produce that proof ended in complete disappointment. It consisted altogether in first adopting the doctrine of *Lake* v. *King*,[15] that printing for the use of the members is lawful, and then rejecting the limitation which restricts it to their use. . . . The case just alluded to drew a line, in the nineteenth year of Charles the Second, which has always been thought correct in law. The defendant justified the libel he had printed by pleading that it was only printed for the use of the members. Much doubt at first existed whether the justification were good in law. . . . After an advisement of many terms and even of some years, Lord Hale and the court sustained the defence, because, being necessary to their functions, it was the known course in Parliament to print for the use of members. But wherefore all this delay and doubt, if the House *then* claimed the privilege of authorising the publication of all papers before them? Or how can we believe that the defendant would not have pleaded at first that privilege, when we find that he was admitted to have acted according to the course and proceedings of Parliament, if it was then their understood right? . . .

Another ground for the necessity of publishing for sale all the papers printed by order of the House was, that members might be able to justify themselves to their constituents, when their conduct in Parliament was arraigned, appealing to documents printed by the House. This is precisely the principle denied and condemned by Lord Ellenborough and the court in *R.* v. *Creevey*,[16] a decision

[14] (1693) 12 St.Tr. 1167.
[15] (1670) 1 Saund. 131.
[16] (1813) 1 M. & S. 273.

which it may now perhaps be convenient to censure as inconsistent with privilege, but which, founded on Lord Kenyon's authority in *R. v. Lord Abingdon*,[17] has been uniformly regarded until this time as a just exposition of the law. ...

It can hardly be necessary to guard myself against being supposed to discuss the expediency of keeping the law in its present state, or introducing any and what alterations. It is no doubt susceptible of improvement: but the improvement must be a legislative act. ...

The practice, or usage, is the second ground on which the Attorney-General seeks to rest this privilege. ... But "the practice has prevailed from all time." If so, it is strange that no vestiges of it are tracked to an earlier period than 1640. ... The origin disproves the antiquity of the privilege, or its necessity for the functions of one of the three estates; no such necessity was thought of till one [the Commons] began to struggle against the other two [the King and the Lords] for an ascendancy which reduced them to nothing. True it is, the practice of so printing and publishing has proceeded with little interruption till this hour. But the question is not on the lawfulness or expediency of printing and publishing in general; it is whether any proof can be found of a practice to authorise the printing and publication of papers injurious to the character of a fellow subject. Such a privilege has never been either actually or virtually claimed by either House of Parliament. ...

The *practice* of a ruling power in the State is but a feeble proof of its legality. I know not how long the practice of raising ship-money had prevailed before the right was denied by *Hampden*; general warrants had been issued and enforced for centuries before they were questioned in actions by *Wilkes* and his associates, who, by bringing them to the test of the law, procured their condemnation and abandonment. ...

I apprehend that acquiescence in this subject proves, in the first place, too much. ... During the session, it must be remembered that privilege is more formidable than prerogative, which must avenge itself by indictment or information, involving the tedious process of law, while privilege with one voice accuses, condemns and executes. And the order to "take him," addressed to the serjeant-at-arms, may condemn the offenders to persecution and ruin. Who can wonder that early acquiescence was deemed the lesser evil, or gravely argue that it evinced a general persuasion that the privilege existed in point of law?

Besides, the acquiescence could only be that of individuals in particular hardships, brought upon themselves by the proceedings published. We have a right to suppose that a considerate discretion was fairly applied to the particular circumstances of each case; that few things of a disparaging nature were printed at all; ... that the imputations were generally true, and actions for libel would only have made them more public. ... All kinds of prudential considerations, therefore, considered to deter from legal proceedings, and will fully account for the acquiescence. ...

I am of opinion, upon the whole case, that the defence pleaded is no defence in law, and that our judgment must be for the plaintiff on this demurrer.

Judgment for the plaintiff.

---

[17] (1794) 1 Esp. N.P.C. 226.

Unauthorised Reports: Qualified Privilege
Wason v. Walter
(1868) L.R. 4 Q.B. 73
Queen's Bench

This was an action of libel against one of the proprietors of *The Times* newspaper, for publishing a report of a debate in the House of Lords in which statements had been made reflecting on the plaintiff.

There was another count in respect of a leading article in the newspaper, commenting on the charges made against the plaintiff in the course of the debate and treating them as well founded.

The action was tried before Cockburn C.J., who directed the jury that if the matter charged as a libel in the first count was a faithful and correct report of the debate, the occasion was privileged, and that as to the second count a public writer is entitled to make fair and reasonable comments on matters of public interest. The jury found for the defendant on all the counts.

A rule having been obtained for a new trial on the ground of mis-direction, it was argued before Cockburn C.J., Lush, Hannen and Hayes J.J., who discharged the rule, *i.e.* found for the defendant. The judgment of the court was delivered by Cockburn C.J.

COCKBURN C.J.: . . . It is now well established that faithful and fair reports of the proceedings of courts of justice, though the character of individuals may incidentally suffer, are privileged, and that for the publication of such reports the publishers are neither criminally nor civilly responsible. The immunity thus afforded in respect of the publication of the proceedings of courts of justice rests upon a twofold ground. In the English law of libel, malice is said to be the gist of an action for defamation. And though it is true that by malice, as necessary to give a cause of action in respect of a defamatory statement, legal and not actual malice is meant; while by legal malice, as is explained by *Bayley J.* in *Bromage* v. *Prosser*,[1] is meant no more than the wrongful intention which the law always presumes as accompanying a wrongful act, without any proof of malice in fact, yet the presumption of law may be rebutted by the circumstances under which the defamatory matter has been uttered or published; and if this should be the case, though the character of the party concerned may have suffered, no right of action will arise. "The rule," says Lord Campbell, in the case of *Taylor* v. *Hawkins*,[2] "is, that if the occasion be such as repels the presumption of malice, the communication is privileged, and the plaintiff must then, if he can, given evidence of actual malice." It is thus that, in the case of reports of the proceedings of courts of justice, though individuals may occasionally suffer from them, yet, as they are published without any reference to the individuals concerned, but soley to afford information to the public and for the benefit of society, the presumption of malice is rebutted, and such publications are held to be privileged.

The other and the broader principle on which this exception to the general law of libel is founded is, that the advantage to the community from publicity being given to the proceedings of courts of justice is so great that the occasional inconvenience to individuals arising from it must yield to the general good. It is true that, with a view to distinguish the publication of proceedings in Parliament from that of those of courts of justice, it has been said that the immunity accorded to the reports of the proceedings of courts of justice is grounded on the fact of the courts being open to the public, while the Houses of Parliament are not; as also

---

[1] (1825) 4 B. & C. 247 at p. 255.
[2] (1851) 16 Q.B. 308 at p. 321.

that, by the publication of the proceedings of the courts, the people obtain a knowledge of the law by which their dealings and conduct are to be regulated. But, in our opinion, the true ground is that given by Lawrence J. in *Rex* v. *Wright*,[3] namely, that though the publication of such proceedings may be to the disadvantage of the particular individuals concerned, yet it is of vast advantage to the public that the proceedings of courts of justice should be universally known. The general advantage to the country in having these proceedings made public more than counter-balances the inconvenience to the private persons whose conduct may be the subject of such proceedings. In *Davison* v. *Duncan*,[4] Lord Campbell says:

"A fair account of what takes place in a court of justice is privileged. The reason is, that the balance of public benefit from the publicity is great. It is of great consequence that the public should known what takes place in court, and the proceedings are under the control of the judges. The inconvenience, therefore, arising from the chance of injury to private character is infinitesimally small as compared to the convenience of publicity."

And Wightman J. says: "The only foundation for the exception is the superior benefit of the publicity of judicial proceedings, which counter-balances the injury to individuals, though that at time may be great."

Both the principles on which the exemption from legal consequences is thus extended to the publication of the proceedings of courts of justice appear to us to be applicable to the case before us. The presumption of malice is negatived in the one case, as in the other, by the fact that the publication has in view the instruction and advantage of the public, and has no particular reference to the party concerned. There is in the one case, as in the other, a preponderance of general good over partial and occasional evil. We entirely concur with Lawrence J. in *Rex* v. *Wright*, that the same reasons which apply to the reports of the proceedings in courts of justice apply also to proceedings in Parliament. It seems to us impossible to doubt that it is of paramount public and national importance that the proceedings of the Houses of Parliament shall be communicated to the public, who have the deepest interest in knowing what passes within their walls, seeing that on what is there said and done the welfare of the community depends. Where would be our confidence in the Government of the country, or in the legislature by which our laws are framed, and to whose charge the great interests of the country are committed—where would be our attachment to the constitution under which we live, if the proceedings of the great council of the realm were shrouded in secrecy, and concealed from the knowledge of the nation? How could the communications between the representatives of the people and their constituents, which are so essential to the working of the representative systems, be usefully carried on if the constituencies were kept in ignorance of what their representatives are doing? What would become of the right of petitioning on all measures pending in Parliament, the undoubted right of the subject, if the people are to be kept in ignorance of what is passing in either House? Can any man bring himself to doubt that the publicity given in modern times to what passes in Parliament is essential to the maintenance of the relations subsisting between the Government, the legislature and the country at large? . . .

Note

The matter published in *The Times* was not an *authorised report*, such as that in *Stockdale* v. *Hansard, ante*, which with the *Case of the Sheriff of Middlesex, ante*, led to the passing of the Parliamentary Papers Act 1840. *Wason* v. *Walter* is therefore not a case of parliamentary privilege, but an illustration of one of the defences ("qualified privilege") allowed by the law of tort to an action of libel.

See also *Cook* v. *Alexander* [1974] Q.B. 279. (C.A.).

---

[3] (1799) 8 Term Rep. 293 at p. 298.
[4] (1857) 7 El. & B. 229 at p. 231.

Power to Commit for Contempt

Case of the Sheriff of Middlesex
(1840) 11 Ad. & E. 273
Queen's Bench

Stockdale brought another action (the third) against Messrs. Hansard for the publication of the same report (see *Stockdale* v. *Hansard, ante*). Messrs. Hansard did not plead, and judgment went against them by default. The Sheriff of Middlesex,[1] in pursuance of a writ from the Court of Queen's Bench, levied execution upon property of the Messrs. Hansard. The House of Commons there upon committed the Sheriff for contempt. A writ of habeas corpus having been obtained, the Serjeant-at-Arms of the House of Commons made a return that he had detained the Sheriff under a warrant of commitment directed to him by the Speaker, and he set forth the warrant. That document stated that the House had resolved that the Sheriff, having been guilty of a contempt and breach of the privileges of the House, be committed to the custody of the Serjeant-at-Arms; but *it did not set forth what the contempt was*.

Upon motion to discharge the Sheriff from custody, the Court of Queen's Bench (Lord Denman C.J., Littledale, Williams and Coleridge JJ.) held that the court has no jurisdiction to interfere.

LORD DENMAN C.J.: . . . The great objection remains behind, that the facts which constitute the alleged contempt are not shown by the warrant. It may be admitted that words containing this kind of statement have appeared in most of the former cases; indeed there are few in which they have not. In the *Proceedings upon the Case of Jay and Topham*,[2] where Sir Francis Pemberton and Sir Thomas Jones were committed by the House of Commons for a judgment as just and reasonable as any ever pronounced, the resolution as to each was, that he, "giving judgment to overrule the plea to the jurisdiction of the Court of King's Bench, in the case between *Jay* and *Topham*, had broken the privileges of the House." I mention this case chiefly for the purpose of correcting a mistake of no small importance. It has been supposed that the resolution to which I referred was passed by the Convention Parliament, and had the sanction of Sir J. Holt, as one of the members: but the resolution was passed in *July* 1689; and in *April* of that year Holt was made Chief Justice of the King's Bench. In *Brass Crosby's*[3] *Sir F. Burdett's*,[4] and *Mr. Hobhouse's*[5] cases, words were used showing the nature of the contempt. In the *Earl of Shaftesbury's* case[6] the form was general: and it was held unnecessary to set out the facts on which the contempt arose. That case is open to observation on other grounds; but I think it has not been questioned on this. In *R*. v. *Paty*[7] three of the judges adopted the doctrine of that case to the extent of holding that the court could not inquire into the ground of commitment, even when expressed in the warrant. Holt C.J. differed from them on that point; but he did not question that, where the warrant omitted to state facts, the cause could not be inquired into. In *Murray's* case[8] which has often been referred to, and recognised as an authority, the warrant was in a general form.

There is, perhaps, no case in the books entitled to so great weight as *Burdett* v.

---

[1] The office was jointly held by two individuals, William Evans and John Wheelton.
[2] (1689) 12 St.Tr. 821.
[3] (1771) 2 Wm.Bl. 754.
[4] *Burdett* v. *Abbot* (1811) 14 East 1.
[5] (1820) 2 Chit.Rep. 207.
[6] (1677) 6 St.Tr. 1269.
[7] (1704) 2 Ld.Raym. 1105, 1115.
[8] (1751) 1 Wils. 299.

Abbot, from the learning of the counsel who argued and the judges who decided it, the frequent discussions which the subject under went, and the diligent endeavours made to obtain the fullest information upon it. The judgment of Lord Ellenborough there, as it bears on the point now before us, is remarkable. He says[9];

> "If a commitment appeared to be for a contempt to the House of Commons generally, I would neither in the case of that court, or of any other of the superior courts, inquire further; but if it did not profess to commit for a contempt, but for some matter appearing on the return, which could by no reasonable intendment be considered as a contempt of the court committing, but a ground of commitment palpably and evidently arbitrary, unjust, and contrary to every principle of positive law, or national[10] justice; I say, that in the case of such a commitment (if it ever should occur, but which I cannot possibly anticipate as ever likely to occur), we must look at it and act upon it as justice may require from whatever court it may profess to have proceeded."

Bayley J., as well as Lord Ellenborough, appears in that case to have been of opinion that, if particular facts are stated in the warrant, and do not bear out the commitment, the court should act upon the principle recognised by Holt C.J. in *R.* v. *Paty*; but, if the warrant merely states a contempt in general terms, the court is bound by it.

That rule was adopted by this court in *R.* v. *Hobhouse*[11]; and in the late case of *Stockdale* v. *Hansard*[12] there was not one of us who did not express himself conformably to it. In the passages which have been cited from my own judgment in that case, as showing that, if a person were committed for a contempt in trespassing upon a member's property, this court would notice the ground of committal, I always suppose that the insufficient ground should appear by the warrant. *The Earl of Shaftsbury's* case has been dwelt upon in the argument as governing the decisions of the courts on all subsequent occasions; but I think not correctly.

There is something in the nature of the Houses themselves which carried with it the authority that has been claimed; though, in discussing such questions, the last important decision is always referred to. Instances have been pointed out in which the Crown has exerted its prerogative in a manner now considered illegal, and the courts have acquiesced: but the cases are not analogous. The Crown has not rights which it can exercise otherwise than by process of law and through amenable officers: but representative bodies must necessarily vindicate their authority by means of their own; and those means lie in the process of committal for contempt. This applies not to the Houses of Parliament only, but (as was observed in *Burdett* v. *Abbot*) to the courts of justice, which, as well as the Houses, must be liable to continual obstruction and insult if they were not entrusted with such powers. It is unnecessary to discuss the question whether each House of Parliament be or be not a court; it is clear that they cannot exercise their proper functions without the power of protecting themselves against interference. The test of the authority of the House of Commons in this respect, submitted by Lord Eldon to the judges in *Burdett* v. *Abbot*, was, whether, if the Court of Common Pleas had adjudged an act to be a contempt of court, and committed for it, stating the adjudication generally, the Court of King's Bench, on a habeas corpus setting forth the warrant, would discharge the prisoner because the facts and circumstances of the contempt were not stated. A negative answer being given, Lord Eldon, with the concurrence of Lord Erskine (who had before been adverse to the

---

[9] (1811) 14 East 1, 150; see also 148.
[10] "Probably a misprint for "natural' ": note by Adolphus & Ellis.
[11] (1820) 2 Chit.Rep. 207.
[12] (1839) 9 A. & E. 1.

exercise of jurisdiction), and without a dissentient voice from the House, affirmed the judgment below. And we must presume that what any court, much more what either House of Parliament, acting on great legal authority, takes upon it to pronounce a contempt, is so.

It was urged that, this not being a criminal matter, the court was bound, by statute 56 Geo. 3, c. 100 [Habeas Corpus Act 1816], s.3, to inquire into the case on affidavit; but I think the provision cited is not applicable. On the motion for a habeas corpus there must be an affidavit from the party applying; but the return, if it discloses a sufficient answer, puts an end to the case; and I think the production of a good warrant is a sufficient answer. Seeing that, we cannot go into the question of contempt on affidavit, nor discuss the motives which may be alleged. Indeed (as the courts have said in some of the cases) it would be unseemly to suspect that a body, acting under such sanctions as a House of Parliament, would, in making its warrant, suppress facts which, if discussed, might entitle the person committed to his liberty. If they ever did so act, I am persuaded that, on further consideration, they would repudiate such a course of proceeding. What injustice might not have been committed by the ordinary courts in past times, if such a course had been recognised! as for instance, if the Recorder of London, in *Bushell's* case,[13] had, in the warrant of commitment, suppressed the fact that the jurymen were imprisoned for returning a verdict of acquittal. I am certain that such will never become the practice of any body of men amenable to public opinion.

In the present case, I am obliged to say that I find no authority under which we are entitled to discharge these gentlemen from their imprisonment.

Note
The Commons secured the passing of the Parliamentary Papers Act 1840; but the passing of this Act vindicates the correctness of *Lord* Denman's statement of the commons law in *Stockdale* v. *Hansard, ante.*

[13] Vaughan 135.

Right to Control Proceedings

Bradlaugh v. Gossett
(1884) 12 Q.B.D. 271
Queen's Bench Division

Charles Bradlaugh was elected as Member of Parliament for Northampton, but the House would not allow him to take the oath, and in July 1883 they passed a resolution: "That the Serjeant-at-Arms do exclude Mr. Bradlaugh from the House until he shall engage not further to disturb the proceedings of the House." He gave an undertaking to that effect, but was further told that he would be excluded until he engaged not to attempt to take the oath in disregard of the resolution of the House. In August 1881 Bradlaugh had tried to enter the House, but had been forcibly ejected by the Serjeant-at-Arms.

Bradlaugh now claimed an injunction to restrain the Serjeant-at-Arms (Gossett) from enforcing the order of the House, and a declaration that the order was void. The defendant pleaded that the statement of claim did not state any matter for which an action could be maintained, or ask for any relief which could be by law given in the action. The court (Lord Coleridge C.J., Stephen and Mathew JJ.) gave judgment for the defendant.

STEPHEN J.: . . . The legal question which this statement of the case appears to me to raise for our decision is this. Suppose that the House of Commons forbids one of its members to do that which an Act of Parliament requires him to do, and in order to enforce its prohibition directs its executive officer to exclude him from the House, by force if necessary is such an order one which we can declare to be void and restrain the executive officer of the House from carrying out? In my opinion, we have no such power. I think that the House of Commons is not subject to the control of Her Majesty's courts in its administration of that part of the statute law which has relation to its own internal proceedings, and that the use of such actual force as may be necessary to carry into effect such a resolution as the one before us is justifiable. . . .

The Parliamentary Oaths Act [1866] prescribes the course of proceeding to be followed on the occasion of the election of a Member of Parliament. In order to raise the question now before us, it is necessary to assume that the House of Commons has come to a resolution inconsistent with the Act; for if the resolution and the Act are not inconsistent, the plaintiff has obviously no grievance. We must, of course, face this supposition, and give our decision upon the hypothesis of its truth; but it would be indecent and improper to make the further supposition that the House of Commons deliberately and intentionally defies and breaks the statute law. The more decent, and, I may add, the more natural and probable, supposition is that, for reasons which are not before us, and which we are therefore unable to judge of, the House of Commons considers that there is no inconsistency between the Act and the resolution. They may think there is some implied exception to the Act. They may think that what the plaintiff proposes to do is not in compliance with its directions. With this we have nothing to do: but whatever may be the reasons of the House of Commons for their conduct, it would be impossible for us to do justice without hearing and considering those reasons; but it would be equally impossible for the House, with any regard for its own dignity and independence, to suffer its reasons to be laid before us for that purpose, or to accept our interpretation of law in preference to its own. It seems to follow that the House of Commons has the exclusive power of interpreting the statute so far as the regulation of its own proceedings within its own walls is concerned, and that even if that interpretation should be erroneous this court has no power to interfere with it, directly or indirectly.

This view of the matter is well illustrated by another part of the Act. By section 4 certain persons are permitted to make a declaration or affirmation instead of taking an oath. The question whether this applied to persons permitted, by 32 & 33 Vict. c. 68 [Evidence Further Amendment Act 1869], s.4, to make a promise instead of taking an oath, arise in the case of the plaintiff himself. It was considered by the House of Commons, and the House took a course which left the interpretation of the enactment to the courts. It permitted the plaintiff to make the declaration, but declared that it did not intend to interfere with his liability to the statutory penalty if he did so. He made the declaration, took his seat accordingly, and was sued for the penalty. Though the proceedings finally terminated in his favour, they established the proposition that section 4 of the Parliamentary Oaths Act did not authorise him in making a statutory declaration in lieu of taking an oath. (See *Clarke* v. *Bradlaugh*,[1] *Bradlaugh* v. *Clarke*.[2]) This case appears to me to illustrate exactly the true relation between the House of Commons and this court as regards the interpretation of statutes affecting them, and the effect of their resolutions on our proceedings.

A resolution of the House permitting Mr. Bradlaugh to take his seat on making a statutory declaration would certainly never have been interfered with by this court. If we had been moved to declare it void and to restrain Mr. Bradlaugh from taking his seat until he had taken the oath, we should undoubtedly have refused to do so. On the other hand, if the House had resolved ever so decidedly that Mr. Bradlaugh was entitled to make the statutory declaration instead of taking the oath, and had attempted by resolution or otherwise to protect him against an action for penalties, it would have been our duty to disregard such resolution, and, if an action for penalties were brought, to hear and determine it according to our own interpretation of the statute. Suppose, again, that the House had taken the view of the statute ultimately arrived at by this court, that is did not enable Mr. Bradlaugh to make the statutory promise, we should certainly not have entertained an application to declare their resolution to be void. We should have said that for the purpose of determining on a right to be exercised in the House itself, and in particular the right of sitting and voting, the House, and the House only, could interpret the statute; but that as regarded rights to be exercised out of and independently of the House, such as the right of suing for a penalty for having sat and voted, the statute must be interpreted by this court independently of the House.

[After saying that the Serjeant-at-Arms had the right to use reasonable force to exclude the plaintiff from the House, his Lordship continued]:

The only force which comes in question in this case is, such force as any private man might employ to prevent a trespass in his own land. I know of no authority for the proposition that an ordinary crime committed in the House of Commons would be withdrawn from the ordinary course of criminal justice. One of the leading authorities on the privilege of Parliament contains matter on this point which shows how careful Parliament has been to avoid even the appearance of countenancing such a doctrine. This is the case of *Sir John Elliot, Denzil Hollis and Others*, of which a complete history is given in 3 St.Tr. 294–336. In this case the defendants were convicted in 1629, on an information before the Court of King's Bench, for seditious speeches in Parliament, and also for an assault on the Speaker in the chair. They pleaded to the jurisdiction that these matters should be inquired into in Parliament and not elsewhere, and their plea was overruled. In 1666 this judgment was reversed upon writ of error—one error assigned being that the speaking of the seditious words and the assault on the Speaker were made the subject of one judgment, whereas the seditious speech, if made in Parliament, could not be inquired into out of Parliament, even if the assault upon the Speaker could be tried in the Court of King's Bench. Hence there should have been two

[1] (1881) 7 Q.B.D. 38, 61.
[2] (1883) 8 App. Cas. 354.

separate judgments. This case is the great leading authority, memorable on many grounds for the proportion that nothing said in Parliament by a member as such can be treated as an offence by the ordinary courts; but the House of Lords carefully avoided deciding the question whether the Court of King's Bench could try a member for an assault on the Speaker in the House. . . .

It is certainly true that a resolution of the House of Commons cannot alter the law. If it were ever necessary to do so, this court would assert this doctrine to the full extent to which it was asserted in *Stockdale* v. *Hansard*.[3] The statement that the resolution of the House of Commons was illegal must, I think, be assumed to be true, for the purposes of the present case. The demurrer for those purposes admits it. We decide nothing unless we decide that, even if it is illegal in the sense of being opposed to the Parliamentary Oaths Act, it does not entitle the plaintiff to the relief sought. This admission, however, must be regarded as being made for the purposes of argument only. It would, as I have already said, be wrong for us to suggest or assume that the House acted otherwise than in accordance with its own view of the law; and as we know not what that view is, nor by what arguments it is supported, we can give no opinion upon it. I do not say that the resolution of the House is the judgment of a court not subject to our revision, but it has much in common, with such a judgment. The House of Commons is not a court of justice, but the effect of its privilege to regulate its own internal concerns practically invests it with a judicial character when it has to apply to particular cases the provisions of Acts of Parliament. We must presume that it discharges this function properly and with due regard to the laws, in the making of which it has so great a share. If its determination is not in accordance with law, this resembles the case of an error by a judge whose decision is not subject to appeal. There is nothing startling in the recognition of the fact that such an error is possible. . . .

Some . . . rights are to be exercised out of Parliament, others within the walls of the House of Commons. Those which are to be exercised out of Parliament are under the protection of this court, which, as has been shown in many cases, will apply proper remedies if they are in any way invaded, and will in so doing be bound, not by resolutions of either House of Parliament, but by its own judgment as to the law of the land, of which the privileges of Parliament form a part. Others must be exercised, if at all, within the walls of the House of Commons: and it seems to me that, from the nature of the case, such rights must be dependent upon the resolutions of the House. . . .

For these reasons I am of opinion that there must be judgment for the defendant.

Judgment for the defendant.

Note

The Oaths Act 1888 (now the Oaths Act 1978) permitted affirmation in lieu of oath for all purposes where an oath is required by law.

[3] (1839) 9 Ad. & E. 1.

R. v. Graham-Campbell and others, ex parte Herbert
[1935] 1 K.B. 594
King's Bench Division

Mr. A. P. Herbert, M.P., in company with the licensee of the Dove Inn, Hammer-smith, brought some alcoholic drinks in a bar in the House of Commons. Mr. Herbert later applied to the Chief Magistrate for summonses to be directed to the members of the Kitchen Committee of the House of Commons (who controlled the arrangements in the refreshment department of the House) and the Manager of the refreshment department, for retailing intoxicating liquor which they were not licensed to sell, contrary to section 65(1) of the Licensing (Consolidation) Act 1910. The Chief Magistrate stated that he was not satisfied that he had jurisdiction to issue the summonses applied for.

Rules nisi for mandamus were granted calling on Sir Rollo Graham-Campbell (Chief Metropolitan Magistrate), the members of the Kitchen Committee and the Manager of the refreshment department to show cause why the Chief Magistrate should not hear and determine the application for the summonses, on the grounds (1) that the Chief Magistrate had erroneously held his jursidiction to be excluded by the privileges of Parliament, and (2) that he had erroneously declined jurisdiction.

The Court (Lord Hewart C.J., Avory and Swift JJ.) held that the Magistrate was justified in refusing to interfere, as the House of Commons was acting collectively in a matter falling within the ambit of its internal affairs. Avory J. considered further that it was impossible to apply to the House of Commons one provision of the Licensing (Consolidation) Act 1910 without having regard to the other provisions of that Act, the majority of which were inapplicable to the House.

LORD HEWART C.J.: ... In these cases, I am satisfied that the rules ought to be discharged. Each of the rules is a rule nisi for an order in the nature of a mandamus calling on Sir Rollo Graham-Campbell to hear and determine according to law certain summonses against members of a body called the Kitchen Committee of the House of Commons and the manager of the refreshment department of the House respectively. In my opinion, the learned Chief Magistrate came to a correct conclusion upon the quite sufficient materials before him.

I do not propose to review the long line of cases which have been cited to us. It seems to me that the authorities relied upon by the Attorney-General are much in point, in particular, *Burdett* v. *Abbot*,[1] *Stockdale* v. *Hansard*,[2] and *Bradlaugh* v. *Gossett*.[3] It was manifest to the magistrate, as well from the documents which were before him as from the argument offered to him, that he was being called upon to deal with the House of Commons, acting by means of its Kitchen Committee and the manager of there refreshment department. To pass over many authorities, I think the decision of Lord Denman C.J. in *Stockdale* v. *Hansard* is sufficient for the present purpose; in the course of his judgment he said this (9 Ad. & E. at p. 115):

"The Commons of England are not invested with more of power and dignity by their legislative character than by that which they bear as the grand inquest of the nation. All the privileges that can be required for the energetic discharge of the duties inherent in that high trust are conceded without a murmur or a doubt."

Here, as it seems to me, the learned Chief Magistrate was entitled to say upon facts which were established that, in the matters complained of, the House of

[1] (1811) 14 East 1.
[2] (1839) 9 Ad. & E. 1.
[3] (1884) 12 Q.B.D. 271.

Commons was acting collectively in a matter falling within the ambit of the internal affairs of the House; and, that being so, any tribunal might well, upon the authorities, feel a quite invincible reluctance to interfere. More than that, with the greatest respect to the observations of my illustrious predecessor, Lord Russell of Killowen C.J.,[4] it appears to me that the bulk of the provisions of the Licensing Acts are quite inapplicable to the House of Commons. It was conceded candidly enough by counsel that if there were no jurisdiction to adjudicate in a case brought against the Kitchen Committee, it followed that there was no jurisdiction to adjudicate in a case against the refreshment manager. For these reasons, I am clearly of opinion that the rules ought to be discharged.

Rules discharged.

Note
The court complimented A.P.H. and refused to grant costs to his opponents.

---

[4] In *Williamson* v. *Norris* (1899) 1 Q.B. 7, 12-13.

3. THE EXECUTIVE

THE CROWN

Town Investments v. Department of the Environment
[1978] A.C. 359
House of Lords

Orders made under the Counter-Inflation (Temporary Provisions) Act 1972 and the Counter-Inflation Act 1973 prohibited, during a "standstill" period, any increase in rent on the granting of a new lease on the determination of an existing business tenancy, which was defined as

> "... any tenancy where the property comprised in the tenancy is or includes premises which are occupied by the tenant and are so occupied for the purposes of a business carried on by him or for those and other purposes. ...; 'business' includes a trade, profession or employment and includes any activity carried on by a body of persons, whether corporate or uncorporate; ..."

Town Investments sought declaration that the legislation did not apply to leases granted by them to the Secretary of State for the Environment on the expiration of earlier leases which had been granted to the Minister of Works. (This change in title was a consequence of the Secretary of State for the Environment Order 1970, made under the Ministers of the Crown (Transfer of Functions) Act 1946. By that Order the former Ministry of Works, whose title had in 1962 been changed to that of Ministry of Public Buildings and Works, was dissolved and all the functions of the Minister of Public Buildings and Works were transferred to the Secretary of State for the Environment, to whom were also transferred all property, rights and liabilities to which that minister was entitled or subject to before the coming into operation of the Order.) Foster J. granted the declarations and his judgment was upheld by the Court of Appeal (Buckley and Lawton L.JJ. and Sir John Pennycuick.) The House of Lords (Lord Diplock, Lord Simon of Glaisdale, Lord Kilbrandon and Lord Edmund-Davies; Lord Morris of Borth-y-Gest dissenting) allowed an appeal by the Crown.

LORD DIPLOCK: ... The only issue before this House has been whether during the standstill period the premises to which this appeal relates were the subject of "business tenancies" within the meaning of the Order. This in turn depends upon the answer to three questions: (1) Who was the tenant of the premises? (2) Were the premises or any part of them occupied by the tenant? And, if so, (3) was the tenant's occupation for the purposes of a business carried on by him or for those and other purposes? ...

1. *Who was the tenant of the premises?*
In the Court of Appeal this was treated as a pure question of construction of the leases themselves, as if Her Majesty, the Minister of Works and the Secretary of State for the Environment were all persons to whose relationships to one another and to third parties the ordinary principles and concepts of private law applied. If this were right, it would involve a conflict between, on the one hand, the statement in the lease that the minister or the Secretary of State is party thereto "for and on behalf of Her Majesty" and, on the other hand, the inclusion in the definition of "the lessee" in the case of Keysign House of "his successors and assigns" and in the definition of "the tenant" in the case of 17, North Audley Street of "his assigns." This conflict was pointed out by Buckley L.J. and Sir John Pennycuick and resolved by them by holding that the tenant was the minister or

Secretary of State and not the Crown, and that the words "for and on behalf of Her
Majesty" were either a mere indication that he was acting in his corporate capacity
as minister or Secretary of State (Buckley L.J. and Sir John Pennycuick) or that he
took the leasehold interest as trustee for the Crown (Buckley L.J. and Lawton
L.J.).

My Lords, the fallacy in this argument is that it is not private law but public law
that governs the relationships between Her Majesty acting in her political capacity, the government departments among which the work of Her Majesty's
government is distributed, the ministers of the Crown in charge of the various
departments and civil servants of all grades who are employed in those departments. These relationships have in the course of centuries been transformed with
the continuous evolution of the constitution of this country from that of personal
rule by a feudal landowning monarch to the constitutional monarchy of today; but
the vocabulary used by lawyers in the field of public law has not kept pace with
this evolution and remains more apt to the constitutional realities of the Tudor or
even the Norman monarchy than to the constitutional realities of the 20th
century. To use as a metaphor the symbol of royalty, "the Crown," was no doubt a
convenient way of denoting and distinguishing the monarch when doing acts of
government in his political capacity from the monarch when doing private acts in
his personal capacity, at a period when legislative and executive powers were
exercised by him in accordance with his own will. But to continue nowadays to
speak of "the Crown" as doing legislative or executive acts of government, which,
in reality as distinct from legal fiction, are decided on and done by human beings
other than the Queen herself, involves risk of confusion. We very sensibly speak
today of legislation being made by Act of Parliament—though the preamble to
every statute still maintains the fiction that the maker was Her Majesty and that
the participation of the members of the two Houses of Parliament had been
restricted to advice and acquiescence. Where, as in the instant case, we are
concerned with the legal nature of the exercise of executive powers of government, I believe that some of the more Athanasian-like features of the debate in
your Lordships' House could have been eliminated if instead of speaking of "the
Crown" we were to speak of "the government"—a term appropriate to embrace
both collectively and individually all of the ministers of the Crown and parliamentary secretaries under whose direction the administrative work of government is carried on by the civil servants employed in the various government
departments. It is through them that the executive powers of Her Majesty's
government in the United Kingdom are exercised, sometimes in the more important administrative matters in Her Majesty's name, but most often under their
own official designation. Executive acts of government that are done by any of
them are acts done by "the Crown" in the fictional sense in which that expression
is now used in English public law.

The executive acts of government with which the instant case is concerned are
the acceptance of grants from lessors who are private subjects of the Queen of
leasehold interests in premises for use as government offices and the occupation
of the premises by civil servants employed in the work of various government
departments. The leases were executed under his official designation by the
minister of the Crown in charge of the government department to which, for
administrative and accounting purposes, there is entrusted the responsibility for
acquiring and managing accommodation for civil servants employed in other
government departments as well as that of which the minister himself is the
official head. In my opinion, the tenant was the government acting through its
appropriate member or, expressed in the term of art in public law, the tenant was
the Crown.

.   .   .   .   .

My Lords, I would not exclude the possibility that an officer of state, even though acting in his official capacity, may in some circumstances hold property subject to a trust in private law for the benefit of a subject; but clear words would be required to do this and, even where the person to be benefited is a subject, the use of the expression "in trust" to describe the capacity in which the property is granted to an officer of state is not conclusive that a trust in private law was intended; for "trust" is not a term of art in public law and when used in relation to matters which lie within the field of public law the words "in trust" may do no more than indicate the existence of a duty owed to the Crown by the officer of state, as servant of the Crown, to deal with the property for the benefit of the subject for whom it is expressed to be held in trust, such duty being enforceable administratively by disciplinary sanctions and not otherwise: *Kinloch* v. *Secretary of State for India* (1882) 7 App.Cas. 619, *per* Lord Selborne L.C., at pp. 625–626. But even if the legal relationship of trustee and cestui qui trust under a trust in private law is capable of existing between an officer of state in his official capacity and a subject, the concept of such relationship being capable of existing between him as trustee and the Crown as cestui qui trust is in my view wholly irreconcilable with the legal nature in public law of the relationship between the Crown and its servants or, in more modern parlance, the government and the ministers who form part of it.

In leases such as those that are the subject of the instant appeal where the person designated as grantee is a minister of the Crown in charge of a government department, the references to "successors and assigns" or "assigns" simpliciter as being included in the definition of "lessee" or "tenant" are explicable as referring to any other minister to whom the functions of the designated minister may be transferred under the Ministers of the Crown (Transfer of Functions) Act 1946, or otherwise, and, in the case of "assigns," also to subjects to whom the leasehold interest may be assigned. Even if they were not, I would not treat their presence in the parentheses as sufficient to displace the ordinary concepts of public law as to the relationship between the government and the ministers who form part of it.

2. *Were the premises or any part of them occupied by the tenant?*
At all relevant times the persons physically present on the premises were government servants. Expressed in the terms of art used in public law their status was that of "servants of the Crown" and of no one else. The relationship of master and servant does not exist between a minister in charge of a government department and any other government servant employed in that department in whatever grade of the civil service he may be. They are both fellow servants of the Crown. The use of the premises by government servants for government purposes thus constituted occupation of the premises by the Crown. Holding as I do that the Crown was the tenant of the premises, I would accordingly answer this question "Yes."

3. *Was the tenant's occupation for the purposes of a business carried on by him or for those and other purposes?*
The answer to this question depends upon how broad a meaning is to be ascribed to the word "business" in the definition of "business tenancy" in the two Counter-Inflation Orders.The word "business" is an etymological chameleon; it suits its meaning to the context in which it is found. It is not a term of legal art and its dictionary meanings, as Lindley L.J. pointed out in *Rolls* v. *Miller* (1884) 27 Ch.D. 71, 88, embrace "almost anything which is an occupation, as distinguished from a pleasure—anything which is an occupation or duty which requires attention is a business."

That was said by the Lord Justice in connection with the construction of a covenant in a lease against the carrying on of any trade or business on the demised premises; and ever since then there has been a consistent line of cases in which this broad meaning has been ascribed to the word "business" in the context of covenants in leases restricting the permitted user of the demised premises. It appears to me to be clear beyond argument that the use made of the premises that are the subject of the instant appeals to accommodate civil servants engaged in what consistently with common usage could be quite properly described as "government business" would constitute a breach of a covenant in a lease against permitting any business to be carried on upon the premises. The Crown or government through its servants is carrying out there a duty which requires attention.

The wide interpretation to be put upon the word "business" in restrictive covenants of this kind is dictated by the evident object of the covenants. The evident object for which powers were conferred by the Counter-Inflation Acts 1972 and 1973 to make Orders restricting increases of prices, dividends and rents was to curb inflation by preventing more money coming into circulation without any corresponding increase in production of goods or services. Separate Counter-Inflation Orders were made under the Acts, dealing respectively with business rents, agricultural rents and the rents of dwelling-houses. The mischief against which these Orders were directed did not depend upon who the tenant was or the use made of the premises by him but upon the receipt by his landlord of a greater sum of money in return for what produced no greater contribution to the national wealth that it had produced before. This would suggest that the evident object of the two Counter-Inflation (Business Rents) Orders called for a broad construction of the word "business" in the definition of the tenancies to which they applied, so as to embrace all tenancies save those which fell within the scope of one of the two other Orders dealing respectively with the rents of agricultural and residential tenancies or were excluded from the definition of "business tenancies" by express words—as were "building leases" under the 1973 Order. I would therefore hold it to be legitimate to give the word "business" in the definition of "business tenancy" in the two Orders a meaning no less wide than that which it has been interpreted as having in covenants in leases restricting the user of demised premises. This meaning is, in my view, wide enough to include the purposes for which Keysign House and 17, North Audley Street were occupied by the Crown.

I do not therefore find it necessary to rely upon any extension of the ordinary meaning of the word that may be the result of the express inclusion of "a trade, profession or employment" or of "any activity carried on by a body of persons, whether corporate or unincorporate." Nevertheless these express inclusions serve not only to underline the breadth of meaning to be given to the word "business" in the Orders but also to involve anomalies which cannot have been intended, if that word is not wide enough with or without the words of inclusion to embrace the exercise of functions of government by servants of the Crown. Functions of government in the United Kingdom are distributed, on no very consistent pattern, between the central government and local governmental and other statutory authorities comprised of bodies of persons, either corporate or unincorporate. The second part of the words of inclusion clearly embrace the activities of these authorities but not those of the Crown which is in law a corporation sole. It would be remarkable were it intended in the Order to exclude from the expression "business" an activity which would fall within it when carried on by servants of a corporation aggregate but not if carried on by servants of the Crown simply because it is a corporation sole. It may be that the reconciliation of the different phraseology used in the two parts of the inclusion clause to describe things done by or on behalf of bodies of persons and things done by or on behalf of one is to be found in the presence in the first part of the clause of the expression "employment"—a word hardly slightly less protean than "business" itself. When used in relation to a natural person "employment" seems to me to be broad enough to include anything which, in Lindley L.J.'s phrase (*Rolls* v. *Miller*, 27 Ch.D. 71, 88), is an occupation as distinguished from a pleasure, and to be understood in the same meaning as the word "activities" used in relation to bodies of persons in the second part of the inclusion clause.

. . . . .

It remains to mention two further arguments which have been advanced for excluding the business of government from the meaning of the word "business" as it is used in the Counter-Inflation Orders. The first can be disposed of shortly for only minor importance was attached to it by the Court of Appeal. It is that the definition of "business tenancy" and the inclusion clause referring to "business" were lifted by the draftsmen of the Orders from section 23(1) and (2) of the Landlord and Tenant Act 1954; and that section 56(3) of the same Act contains specific provisions applying it to tenancies "held by or on behalf of a government department" and "occupied for any purposes of a government department." In an Act which contains provisions for dealing with security of tenure of tenants of business premises by the grant of new leases and rights to compensation when a new lease could not be granted, the fact that the draftsman of the Act has thought it prudent to make specific provision as to its application to premises occupied for government purposes is a frail support for the contention that but for those specific provisions the Act would not have applied to such premises at all and therefore tenancies of them cannot have fallen within the definition of "business tenancy" in the Act, even though in the ordinary meaning of the words of the definition they would have been apt to include such tenancies. But any force that there might be in this contention is wholly lost when it is sought to use it to cut down the ordinary meaning of those words when used in other legislation passed with an entirely different object.

A matter to which all three members of the Court of Appeal appear to have attached importance was the presence of the indefinite article "a" in the reference in the definition of business tenancy to "a business carried on by him" (sc. the tenant). Both Buckley and Lawton L.JJ. were I think influenced by the conclusion they had already reached that the relevant tenant was the Secretary of State and not the Crown. They appear to have accepted that the activities of government through the various government departments might properly be described as "business," but they considered that neither that part of those activities that was carried on through a particular government department nor, it would seem, those activities as a whole could properly be described as "a business."

My Lords, it has been said that Roger Casement was hanged by a comma and (as Mr. Browne-Wilkinson has reminded us) that John Keat's mind was "snuffed out by an article." I think that in exercising the functions of government the civil servants of the Crown are all engaged in carrying on a single business on behalf of the Crown, i.e., Her Majesty's government in the United Kingdom. I do not see why the presence of an indefinite article affects the matter. I do not see why this is not *a* business carried on by the Crown on whatever premises may be used by it to accommodate civil servants employed in the various government departments, or why it is not *a* business for the purposes of which each of these premises is occupied by the Crown.

For these reasons I would allow this appeal.

LORD SIMON OF GLAISDALE: . . . Your Lordships are here concerned, not with private law, but with public, and within that with constitutional, law. In private law a phrase like "for and on behalf of" would be apt to signify agency at least, and possibly trust. Not so in public law. The distinction appears clearly from *Dunn* v. *Macdonald* [1897] 1 Q.B. 555. The question there was whether a public servant acting on behalf of the Crown was liable to the other contracting party for a breach of an implied warranty of his authority to enter into the contract. It was held in the Court of Appeal that he was not. Lopes L.J. said, at p. 557:

"... an agent acting on behalf of a government is not liable for breach of a contract made in his public capacity, even though he would by the terms of the contract be bound if it were an agency of a private nature."

In public law even a phrase like "in trust for" may not betoken at all the relationship of trustee and cestui que trust, but rather the imposition of a constitutional duty the sanction for which is political or administrative not legal (cf. Lord Selborne L.C. in *Kinloch* v. *Secretary of State for India*, 7 App.Cas. 619, 625, 626).

Nor can the first two questions be answered without also bearing in mind that your Lordships are concerned with symbolic language which cannot be understood without regard to constitutional history. The crown as an object is a piece of jewelled headgear under guard at the Tower of London. But it symbolises the powers of government which were formerly wielded by the wearer of the crown; so that by the 13th century crimes were committed not only against the king's peace but also against "his crown and dignity": *Pollock and Maitland, History of English Law*, 2nd ed. (1898), vol. I. p. 525. The term "the Crown" is therefore used in constitutional law to denote the collection of such of those powers as remain extant (the royal prerogative), together with such other powers as have been expressly conferred by statute on "the Crown."

So too "The Queen" indicates the person who by right of succession is entitled to wear the crown. But "Her Majesty" is evidently a symbolic phrase, betokening the power, the "mana," which is embodied in the person entitled to wear the crown— as "His Holiness," "His Beatitude" or "Mr. Justice" are descriptive of the power believed to inspire and characterise the person so entitled. "Her Majesty" in constitutional legal usage thus generally personifies the powers of "the Crown"—powers of the nucleus of which legally and historically are those of The Queen, but which by constitutional convention (*i.e.*, in political reality) are exercised in the name of The Queen by those who are nominally and legally her servants or agents.

The same conclusion can be reached historically. Once central government was firmly established in England, power—what in modern political science would be known as executive, judicial and legislative power—was concentrated in the King. No line was drawn at first between the private and the public business of the King. But, as the latter grew, administrative convenience called for some devolution. Offices were hived off from the King's household. There was the Chancery presided over by the Chancellor. Then there was the Private Seal office under a Keeper of the Privy Seal, and the Exchequer with a Treasurer and a Chancellor of its own. And so on. All these officials holding offices of ancient origin had their action "confined within rigid limits, expressed by the commissions by which they were appointed and the procedure which their acts must follow." The motive force behind their departments

> "was the King's command. They all existed to give effect to his will. The officials who presided over them were appointed and dismissible by him. Each was charged with the fulfilment of the royal pleasure within his own appropriate sphere."

However, for centuries thereafter the King's secretary remained within the royal household. Unlike the officials holding offices of ancient origin, the King's secretary was therefore "free to enter every new branch of royal administration as it developed." So it was that with the increase in the powers of the Crown in the 16th century the Secretary rose to the first rank among the King's servants. But under the Restoration the Secretaries (for their office was now duplicated) too became heads of departments of state, charged like the holders of the ancient offices with executing the royal will. (For the foregoing historical development, see *D. L. Keir, The Constitutional History of Modern Britain 1485–1937*, 3rd ed. (1947) pp. 16, 17, 113, 245–246, whence also came the quotations.)

With the development of modern government fresh departments were formed to be headed by ministers or by Secretaries of State. Just as all were originally appointed to carry out departmentally the royal will, so today all ministers are appointed to exercise the powers of the Crown, together with such other powers as have been statutorily conferred upon them directly.

My Lords, it will, I hope, be apparent from the foregoing that "the Crown" and "Her Majesty" are terms of art in constitutional law. They correspond, though not exactly, with terms of political science like "the Executive" or "the Administration" or "the Government," barely known to the law, which has retained the historical terminology.

·   ·   ·   ·   ·

If such terms as "aspects of the Crown" or "emanations of (or 'from') the Crown" or "participants of royal authority" are considered to be too cloudy for legal usage, the legal concept which seems to me to fit best the contemporary situation is to consider the Crown as a corporation aggregate headed by the Queen. The departments of state including the ministers at their head (whether or not either the department or the minister has been incorporated) are then themselves members of the corporation aggregate of the Crown. But on this approach two riders must be added. First, the legal concept still does not correspond to the political reality. The legal substratum is overlaid by constitutional convention. The Queen does not now command those legally her servants who are heads or subordinate members or subject to the control of the departments of state. On the contrary she acts on the formally tendered collective advice of those ministers who constitute the Cabinet. Secondly, when the Queen is referred to by the symbolic title of "Her Majesty," it is the whole corporation aggregate, the Crown, which is generally indicated. This distinction between "The Queen" and "Her Majesty" reflects the ancient distinction between "the King's two bodies," "natural" and "politic": see *The Case of the Dutchy of Lancaster* (1567) 1 Plowden 212, 213.

It follows that prima facie in public law a minister or a Secretary of State is an aspect or member of the Crown. Except in application of the doctrine of precedent analogies are to be regarded warily in legal reasoning. But in view of all the foregoing the analogy of the human body and its members is, I think, an apt one in relation to the problem facing your Lordships. It is true to say: "My hand is holding this pen." But it is equally true to say—it is another way of saying: "*I* am holding this pen." What is nonsensical is to say: "My hand is holding this pen as my agent, or as trustee for me."

Appeal allowed.

Notes

1. For a lengthy discussion of the Crown's position as trustee in public law see further *Tito* v. *Waddell (No. 2)* [1977] Ch. 106, 210 *et seq.*

2. For the meaning of the terms Crown servant and Crown agent, see *Bank voor Handel en Scheepvaart N.V.* v. *Administrator of Hungarian Property* [1954] A.C. 584; *post* p. 408 and *Tamlin* v. *Hannaford* [1950] 1 K.B. 18 *post* p. 405.

Divisibility of the Crown

R. v. Secretary of State for Foreign and Commonwealth Affairs, ex parte Indian Association of Alberta and others

[1982] 1 Q.B. 892

Court of Appeal

An application for a declaration that treaty obligations entered into by the Crown to the Indian peoples of Canada were still owed by Her Majesty in right of Her Government in the United Kingdom was dismissed by Woolf J. Leave to apply for judicial review granted by the Court of Appeal (Lord Denning M.R., Kerr and May L.JJ.

LORD DENNING M.R.: . . . [After recounting the history of relations between the Crown and the Indian peoples from the Royal Proclamation of 1763 the Master of the Rolls discussed the indivisibility of the Crown and the disappearance of that doctrine. He cited the British North America Act 1867 and continued]

The Crown of the United Kingdom was regarded at that time as still the Crown of the Dominion and of the provinces of Canada. It was all one Crown single and indivisible. As Viscount Haldane said in *Theodore* v. *Duncan* [1919] A.C. 696: "The Crown is one and indivisible throughout the Empire, and it acts in self-governing States on the initiative and advice of its own Ministers in these States."

The division of the Crown
Hitherto I have said that in constitutional law the Crown was single and indivisible. But that law was changed in the first half of this century—not by statute—but by constitutional usage and practice. The Crown became separate and divisible—according to the particular territory in which it was sovereign. This was recognised by the Imperial Conference of 1926 (1926) (Cmd. 2768). It framed the historic definition (p. 14) of the status of Great Britain and the Dominions as

"autonomonous Communities within the British Empire, equal in status, in no way subordinate one to another in any respect of their domestic or external affairs, though united by a common allegiance to the Crown, and freely associated as members of the British Commonwealth of Nations."

It was also agreed, at p. 16:

"the Governor-General of a Dominion is the representative of the Crown, holding in all essential respects the same position in relation to the administration of public affairs in a Dominion as is held by His Majesty the King in Great Britain, and that he is not the representative or agent of His Majesty's Government in Great Britain or of any Department of that Government."

Thenceforward the Crown was no longer single and indivisible. It was separate and divisible for each self-governing dominion or province or territory. Thus in 1968 it was held in this court that the Queen was the Queen of Mauritius, and the Crown in right of Mauritius could issue passports to its citizens (see *Reg.* v. *Secretary of State for the Home Department, Ex parte Bhurosah* [1948] 1 Q.B. 266); and in 1971 it was held, again in this court, that the Queen was the Queen of the Province of New Brunswick, and that province was entitled to state immunity: see *Mellenger* v. *New Brunswick Development Corporation* [1971] 1 W.L.R. 604.

As a result of this important constitutional change, I am of opinion that those obligations which were previously binding on the Crown simpliciter are now to be treated as divided. They are to be applied to the Dominion or Province or territory to which they relate: and confined to it. Thus the obligations to which the Crown bound itself in the Royal Proclamation of 1763 are now to be confined to the territories to which they related and binding only on the Crown in respect of those territories: and the treaties by which the Crown bound itself in 1875 are to be confined to those territories and binding on the Crown only in respect of those territories. None of them is any longer binding on the Crown in respect of the United Kingdom.

.   .   .   .   .

The Crown Proceedings Act 1947
In order that proceedings should be brought against the Crown in this country, it is necessary that the liability of the Crown should be a liability "in respect of His Majesty's Government in the United Kingdom": see section 40(2)(*b*) of the Crown Proceedings Act 1947.

Now at the time when the Crown entered into the obligations under the Proclamation of 1763 or the treaties of the 1870s, the Crown was in constitutional law one and indivisible. Its obligations were obligations in respect of the Government of the United Kingdom as well as in respect of Canada: see *Williams* v. *Howarth* [1905] A.C. 551. But, now that the Crown is separate and divisible, I think that the obligations under the Proclamation and the treaties are obligations of the Crown in respect of Canada. They are not obligations of the Crown in respect of the United Kingdom. It is, therefore, not permissible for the Indian peoples to bring an action in this country to enforce these obligations. Their only recourse is in the courts of Canada.

KERR L.J.: It is settled law that, although Her Majesty is the personal sovereign of the peoples inhabiting many of the territories within the Commonwealth, all rights and obligations of the Crown—other than those concerning the Queen in her personal capacity—can only arise in relation to a particular government within those territories. The reason is that such rights and obligations can only be exercised and enforced, if at all, through some governmental emanation or representation of the Crown. Thus, the Crown Proceedings Act 1947, section 40(2)(*b*) and (*c*), distinguishes between liabilities in respect of, and proceedings in right of, Her Majesty in the United Kingdom on the one hand and outside the United Kingdom on the other. In relation to the latter class, it is open to the Secretary of State under section 40(3) to issue a certificate which is conclusive for the purposes of that Act. This has not been done in the present case, though without prejudice to the respondents' contention that the legal position of the Indian peoples of Canada has no connection with the Crown in right of the United Kingdom. It is accordingly necessary to examine the constitutional principles which determine the situs of the Crown's rights and obligations in this regard, but bearing in mind that, although the relevant agreements with the Indian peoples are known as "treaties," they are not treaties in the sense of public international law. They were not treaties between sovereign states, so that no question of state succession arises.

The principles which govern the situs of rights and obligations of the Crown are conveniently summarised in *Halsbury's Laws of England*, 4th ed., vol. 6 (1974), paragraph 820, under the heading "Unity and Divisibility of the Crown in Her Majesty's Dominions." For present purposes it is sufficient to refer to two passages and to a number of authorities cited in support of these.

First, as there stated, it is clear that

"on the grant of a representative legislature, and perhaps even as from the setting up of courts, legislative council and other such structures of government, Her Majesty's Government in a colony is to be regarded as distinct from Her Majesty's Government in the United Kingdom."

Thus, in *Reg.* v. *Secretary of State for the Home Department, Ex parte Bhurosah* [1986] 1 Q.B. 266, an issue arose as to passports issued in Mauritius, which was then a dependent British colony, on behalf of the Governor. The passports were issued "in the name of Her Majesty" to persons who were British subjects and citizens of the United Kingdom and Colonies under section 1 of the British Nationality Act 1948. The issue was whether they were "United Kingdom passports" within the Commonwealth Immigrants Act 1962. It was held that they were not, because—in effect—they had been issued in the name of Her Majesty in right of the Government of Mauritius and not of the United Kingdom.

This being the position in relation to a dependent colony, the government of a Dominion is clearly in an a fortiori position, and neither of these forms of established government within the Commonwealth presents any constitutional problem for present purposes. In times long past there was such a problem, when many of the territories which are now within the Commonwealth had not yet been opened up for settlement, or even fully discovered, and there was no established government on behalf of the Crown.

·   ·   ·   ·

The second relevant principle stated in the same passage in *Halsbury* is "the liabilities of the Crown in right of, or under the laws of, one of the Crown's territories can be satisfied only out of the revenues, and by the authority of the legislature, of that territory."

In effect, the situs of obligations on the part of the Crown is to be found only in that territory within the realm of the Crown where such obligations can be enforced against a local administration. A 19th-century illustration of this principle in relation to Canada, which is interesting because the case was decided before the British North America Act 1867, was *In re Holmes* (1861) 2 Johns. & Hem. 527. This concerned disputes arising out of certain lands vested in the Crown, in the then Province of Upper Canada, in relation to which a petition of right was brought in the Court of Chancery here. It was held by Sir William Page Wood V.-C. that, whether or not the Crown was a trustee of the land, the situs of any resulting rights and obligations lay in Canada and that these were only enforceable there. He said, at p. 543: ". . . as the holder of Canadian land for the public purposes of Canada, the Queen should be considered as present in Canada, and out of the jurisdiction of this court."

In other words, any resulting rights and obligations existed only in right or respect of the Crown in what was then Upper Canada, and not in right or respect of what was then Great Britain.

MAY L.J.: . . . By the Act of 1867, therefore, the Dominion and the provinces acquired a substantial degree of self-government and their own treasuries. Between then and the Imperial Conferences of 1926 and 1930 the Dominion acquired, largely by agreement and convention, increasing independence over and above that given it by the Act of 1867 from the United Kingdom and its Parliament until, by the Statute of Westminster 1931, it and the other Dominions referred to in that statute attained complete independence subject, in the case of Canada, to section 7 which, as it was put in argument, entrenched the Constitution of Canada and its provinces in Westminster, subject to this that such Constitution can only be amended at the request and with the consent of the Dominion.

As a result of this process and on the authorities to which I have referred, I have no doubt that any treaty or other obligations which the Crown had entered into with the Indian peoples of Canada in right of the United Kingdom had become the responsibility of the Government of Canada with the attainment of independence, at the latest with the Statute of Westminster 1931. I therefore think that this application must fail.

Note
Both Kerr and May L.JJ. relied heavily on the decision of the House of Lord in *Attorney-General* v. *Great Southern and Western Railway Co. of Ireland* [1925] A.C. 754. The differing lines

of reasoning by which the Court of Appeal reached its conclusion were considered by Sir Robert Megarry V-C in *Manuel* v. *Attorney-General; Noltcho* v. *Attorney-General* [1983] Ch. 77, 89 in his consideration of the *Noltcho* claim.

Prerogative Subject to the Law

No New Prerogatives

Case of Monopolies (Darcy v. Allein)
(1602) 11 Co.Rep.84b
King's Bench

Queen Elizabeth by Letters Patent granted to Darcy, a groom of her privy chamber: (a) a sole licence for 21 years to import playing-cards and sell them within the realm, and (b) a sole licence and dispensation during the same period to make playing-cards within the realm, on rendering to the Queen 100 marks per annum. Infringement of the Patent would incur fine and imprisonment. Darcy brought an action against Allein for infringing these monopolies.

Coke, who as Attorney-General argued the case for the plaintiff, reports as follows:

... As to the first, it was ... resolved by Popham C.J. *et per totam curiam*, that the said grant to the plaintiff of the sole making of cards within the realm was utterly void, and that for two reasons: 1. That it is a monopoly, and against the common law. 2. That it is against divers Acts of Parliament.

Against the common law for four reasons: 1. All trades ... which prevent idleness ... are profitable for the commonwealth, and therefore the grant to the plaintiff to have the sole making of them is against the common law, and the benefit and liberty of the subject, and therewith agrees Fortescue in *Laudibus legum Angliae*, cap. 26.[1] ... 2. The sole trade of any mechanical artifice, or any other monopoly, is not only a damage and prejudice to those who exercise the same trade, but also to all other subjects, for the end of all these monopolies is for the private gain of the patentees. ... 3. The Queen was deceived in her grant; for the Queen, as by the preamble appears, intended it to be for the weal public, and it will be employed for the private gain of the patentee, and for the prejudice of the weal public. ... 4. This grant is *primae impression* is, for no such was ever seen to pass by Letters Patent under the Great Seal before these days, and therefore it is a dangerous innovation, as well without any precedent, or example, as without authority of law, or reason. ...

Also such charter of a monopoly, against the freedom of trade and traffic, is against divers Acts of Parliament, *sc.* 9 Edw. 3, cc. 1 and 2. ...

As to the second question, it was resolved that the dispensation or licence to have the sole importation and merchandising of cards (without any limitation or stint) notwithstanding the said Act of 3 Edw. 4, is utterly against law. ... But when the wisdom of the Parliament has made an Act to restrain *pro bono publico* the importation of many foreign manufactures, to the intent that the subjects of the realm might apply themselves to the making of the said manufactures, etc. ... now for a private gain to grant the sole importation of them to one, or divers (without any limitation) notwithstanding the said Act, is a monopoly against the common law, and against the end and scope of the Act itself. ... And King Edward 3, by his Letters Patent, granted to one John Peche the sole importation of sweet wine into London, and at a Parliament held 50 Edw. 3, this grant was adjudged void. ...

And our Lord the King that now is, in a book which he in zeal to the law and justice commanded to be printed *anno* 1610, intituled, "A Declaration of His Majesty's Pleasure, etc.," p. 13, has published, that monopolies are things against the laws of this realm; and therefore expressly commands, that no suitor presume to move him to grant any of them.

---

[1] The reference should apparently be to cap. 36.

Legislation

Case of Proclamations
(1610) 12 Co.Rep. 74; 2 St.Tr. 723

Resolution of the Judges

This arose out of the Petition of Grievances. On September 20, 1610, Coke C.J. was called before the Privy Council; and it was referred to him whether the King, by Proclamation, might prohibit new buildings in London, or the making of starch of wheat, these having been preferred to the King by the House of Commons as grievances and against law. Coke asked leave to consider with his colleagues, since the questions were of great importance, and they concerned the answer of the King to the Commons.

Coke reports the following resolution:

In the same term it was resolved by the two Chief Justices, Chief Baron, and Baron Altham, upon conference betwixt the Lords of the Privy Council and them, that the King by his proclamation cannot create any offence which was not an offence before, for then he may alter the law of the land by his proclamation in a high point; for if he may create an offence where none is, upon that ensues fine and imprisonment: also the law of England is divided into three parts, common law, statute law, and custom; but the King's proclamation is none of them: also *malum aut est malum in se, aut prohibitum,* that which is against common law is *malum in se, malum prohibitum* is such an offence as is prohibited by Act of Parliament, and not by proclamation.

Also it was resolved, that the King hath no prerogative but that which the law of the land allows him.

But the King for prevention of offences may by proclamation admonish his subjects that they keep the laws, and do not offend them: upon punishment to be inflicted by the law.

Lastly, if the offence be not punishable in the Star Chamber, the prohibition of it by proclamation cannot make it punishable there: and after this resolution, no proclamation imposing fine and imprisonment was afterwards made.

Administration of Justice

Prohibitions Del Roy (Case of Prohibitions)
(1607) 12 Co.Rep. 63
Resolution of the Judges

Coke reports as follows:

Note, upon Sunday the 10th of November in this same term, the King, upon complaint made to him by Bancroft, Archbishop of Canterbury, concerning prohibitions [from the King's Bench to the Ecclesiastical Courts], the King was informed that when the question was made of what matters the Ecclesiastical Judges have cognisance, either upon the exposition of the statutes concerning tithes or any other thing ecclesiastical, or upon the statute 1 Eliz., concerning the high commission or in any other case in which there is not express authority in law, the King himself may decide it in his royal person: and that the Judges are but the delegates of the King, and that the King may take what cause he shall please to determine, from the determination of the Judges, and may determine them himself. And the Archbishop said that this was clear in divinity, that such authority belongs to the King by the word of God in the Scripture.

To which it was answered by me, in the presence, and with the clear consent of all the Judges of England, and Barons of the Exchequer, that the King in his own person cannot adjudge any case, either criminal, as treason, felony, etc., or betwixt party and party, concerning his inheritance, chattels, or goods etc., but this ought to be determined and adjudged in some Court of Justice, according to the law and custom of England; and always judgments are given, *ideo consideratum est per curiam*, so that the Court gives the judgment: . . . in the King's Bench he may sit, but the Court gives the judgment: and it is commonly said in our books, that the King is always present in Court in the judgment of law; and upon this he cannot be nonsuit: but the judgments are always given *per curiam*; and the Judges are sworn to execute justice according to the law and custom of England. . . .

A controversy of land between parties was heard by the King, and sentence given, which was repealed for this, that it did belong to the common law: then the King said that he thought the law was founded upon reason, and that he and others had reason, as well as the judges: to which it was answered by me, that true it was, that God had endowed His Majesty with excellent science, and great endowments of nature: but His Majesty was not learned in the laws of his realm of England, and causes which concern the life, or inheritance, or goods, or fortunes of his subjects, are not to be decided by natural reason but by the artificial reason and judgment of the law, which law is an art which requires long study and experience, before that a man can attain to the cognizance of it: that the law was the golden metwand and measure to try the causes of the subjects; and which protected His Majesty in safety and peace: with which the King was greatly offended, and said, that then he should be under the law, which was treason to affirm, as he said; to which I said, that Bracton saith, *quod Rex non debet esse sub homine, sed sub Deo et lege.*

No Suspending Power

Fitzgerald v. Muldoon

[1976] N.Z.L.R. 615

Supreme Court

Shortly after taking office the Prime Minister of New Zealand announced his intention to introduce legislation to abolish the existing State Superannuation Scheme. He also indicated that no further payments to the fund needed to be made by employers and employees in the period before the passing of the necessary legislation. In the light of the announcement the Superannuation Board decided to take no steps to enforce the payment of contributions under the existing law. The plaintiff challenged the legality of the Prime Minister's statement.

WILD C.J.: (After stating the facts): I come now to consider the basic allegation of the plaintiff on which this action is founded. It asserts a breach of s.1 of the Bill of Rights (1688) (Eng) the material part of which, as printed in 6 *Halsbury's Statutes of England* (3rd ed.) 490, is in these words: "That the pretended power of suspending of laws or the execution of laws by regall authority without consent of Parlyament is illegall."

It is a graphic illustration of the depth of our legal heritage and the strength of our constitutional law that a statute passed by the English Parliament nearly three centuries ago to extirpate the abuses of the Stuart Kings should be available on the other side of the earth to a citizen of this country which was then virtually unkown in Europe and on which . . . no Englishman was to set foot for almost another hundred years. And yet it is not disputed that the Bill of Rights is part of our law. The fact that no modern instance of its application was cited in argument may be due to the fact that it is rarely that a litigant takes up such a cause as the present, or it may be because governments usually follow established constitutional procedures. But it is not a reason for declining to apply the Bill of Rights where it is invoked and a litigant makes out his case.

. . . . . .

[The Chief Justice examined the terms of the Prime Minister's statement and continued]

The Act of Parliament in force required that those deductions and contributions must be made, yet here was the Prime Minister announcing that they need not be made. I am bound to hold that in so doing he was purporting to suspend the law without consent of Parliament. Parliament had made the law. Therefore the law could be amended or suspended only by Parliament or with the authority of Parliament.

"The principle of Parliamentary sovereignty means neither more nor less than this, namely, that Parliament thus defined has, under the English constitution, the right to make or unmake any law whatever; and, further, that no person or body is recognised by the law of England as having a right to override or set aside the legislation of Parliament" (*Dicey's Law of the Constitution* (10th ed) 39).

The question whether "the pretended power of suspending" was "by regall authority" within the meaning of s.1 of the Bill of Rights is, I think, to be determined by reference to the powers of the Prime Minister and the position occupied by him, which are of fundamental importance in our system of government. He is the Prime Minister, the leader of the government elected to office, the chief of the executive government. He had lately received his commission by royal authority, taken the oaths of office, and entered on his duties. In my opinion his public announcement of 15 December, made as it was in the course of his official duties as Prime Minister, must therefore be regarded as made "by regall authority" within the meaning of s.1. The authority accorded it by the officials concerned is abundantly evident from the resolution of the Superannuation Board, and the decision of the State Services Co-ordinating Committee and the various branches of the state services. While I reject the allegation that the Prime Minister gave instructions to these officials I think it is perfectly clear that they acted because of his public announcement of 15 December. Had it not been made they would have continued as before.

I am unable to accept the Solicitor-General's submission that there was no breach of s.1 because there was no assertion in the press statement that the operation of the New Zealand Superannuation Act 1974 was being lawfully suspended. In my view it was implicit in the statement, coming as it did from the Prime Minister, that what was being done was lawful and had legal effect.

. . . . .

For the reasons given I must conclude that the Prime Minister's public announcement of 15 December was illegal as being in breach of s.1 of the Bill of Rights, and that the plaintiff is entitled to a declaration to the effect.

The other claims for injunctions against the Prime Minister, for declarations and mandamus against the members of the Superannuation Board for declarations against the Attorney-General and the Controller and Auditor-General, are all matters within the discretion of the court. There can be no doubt as to the government's intention to introduce the legislation indicated in the Prime Minister's public announcement. There can be little doubt that that legislation will be enacted. The evidence is that Parliament is summoned to assemble on 22 June. In that situation, and in the light of the facts earlier mentioned, it would be an altogether unwarranted step to require the machinery of the New Zealand Superannuation Act 1974 now to be set in motion again, when the high probabilities are that all would have to be undone again within a few months.

In my opinion, the law and the authority of Parliament will be vindicated by the making of the declaration I have indicated, and the appropriate course is to adjourn all other matters in issue for six months from this date.

Judicial Review of Prerogative Powers

Council of Civil Service Unions v. Minister for the Civil Service

[1985] A.C. 374

House of Lords

By the Civil Service Order in Council 1982 power to regulate the terms of employment of the Civil Service was given to the Minister for the Civil Service—at the time of the litigation, the Prime Minister. Acting under the Order in Council the Minister gave an instruction that the terms of employment of civil servants working at the Government Communications Headquarters (GCHQ) should be revised so as to exclude membership of any trade union other than a departmental staff association approved by the director of GCHQ. An affidavit made by Sir Robert Armstrong, Secretary of the Cabinet and Head of the Home Civil Service, set out the history of industrial action at GCHQ which was believed to justify the instruction given by the Minister. Before Glidewell J. in the High Court argument centered on the right of the Unions to be consulted before the instruction was made (the legitimate expectation point : see *post*, p. 287 and the jurisdiction of the Court to review the exercise of prerogative powers; [1984] I.R.L.R. 309. In the Court of Appeal (Lord Lane, L.C.J., Watkins and May LJJ: [1984] I.R.L.R. 354) and subsequently in the House of Lords national security emerged as an important issue.

LORD FRASER OF TULLYBELTON: . . . The appeal raises a number of questions. I shall consider first the question which I regard as the most important and also the most difficult. It concerns the royal prerogative.

The royal prerogative
The mechanism on which the Minister for the Civil Service relied to alter the terms and conditions of service at GCHQ was an "instruction" issued by her under the Order in Council of 1982, article 4. That article so far as relevant provides as follows:

"As regards Her Majesty's Home Civil Service—(a) the Minister for the Civil Service may from time to time make regulations or give instructions— . . . (ii) for controlling the conduct of the service, and providing for the classification of all persons employed therein and . . . the conditions of service of all such persons; . . ."

The Order in Council was not issued under powers conferred by any Act of Parliament. Like the previous Orders in Council on the same subject it was issued by the sovereign by virtue of her prerogative, but of course on the advice of the government of the day. In these circumstances (Counsel for the Minister) submitted that the instruction was not open to review by the courts because it was an emanation of the prerogative. This submission involves two propositions: (1) that prerogative powers are discretionary, that is to say they may be exercised at the discretion of the sovereign (acting on advice in accordance with modern constitutional practice) and the way in which they are exercised is not open to review by the courts; (2) that an instruction given in the exercise of a delegated power conferred by the sovereign under the prerogative enjoys the same immunity from review as if it were itself a direct exercise of prerogative power. . . .
The first of these propositions is vouched by an impressive array of authority, which I do not propose to cite at all fully. Starting with *Blackstone's Commentaries*, 15th ed. (1809), p. 251 and *Chitty's Prerogatives of the Crown* (1820), pp. 6–7 they are at one in stating that, within the sphere of its prerogative powers, the Crown has an absolute discretion. In more recent times the best known definition of the

prerogative is that given in Dicey, *Law of the Constitution*, 8th ed. (1915), p. 421 which is as follows:

> "The prerogative is the name for the remaining portion of the Crown's original authority, and is therefore, as already pointed out, the name for the residue of discretionary power left at any moment in the hands of the Crown, whether such power be in fact exercised by the King himself or by his ministers."

Dicey's definition was quoted with approval in this House in *Attorney-General* v. *De Keyser's Royal Hotel Ltd.* [1920] A.C. 508, 526 by Lord Dunedin and was impliedly accepted by the other Law Lords in that case. In *Burmah Oil Co. Ltd.* v. *Lord Advocate*, 1964 S.C. (H.L.) 117 Lord Reid, at p. 120, referred to Dicey's definition as being "always quoted with approval" although he said it did not take him very far in that case. It was also referred to with apparent approval by Roskill L.J. (as my noble and learned friend then was) in *Laker Airways Ltd.* v. *Department of Trade* [1977] Q.B. 643, 719. As *De Keyser's* case shows, the courts will inquire into whether a particular prerogative power exists or not, and, if it does exist, into its extent. But once the existence and the extent of a power are established to the satisfaction of the court, the court cannot inquire into the proprietary of its exercise. That is undoubtedly the position as laid down in the authorities to which I have briefly referred and it is plainly reasonable in relation to many of the most important prerogative powers which are concerned with control of the armed forces and with foreign policy and with other matters which are unsuitable for discussion or review in the law courts. In the present case the prerogative power involved is power to regulate the Home Civil Service, and I recognise there is no obvious reason why the mode of exercise of that power should be immune from review by the courts. Nevertheless to permit such review would run counter to the great weight of authority to which I have briefly referred. Having regard to the opinion I have reached on [Counsel's] second proposition, it is unnecessary to decide whether his first proposition is sound or not and I prefer to leave that question open until it arises in a case where a decision upon it is necessary. I therefore assume, without deciding, that his first proposition is correct and that all powers exercised directly under the prerogative are immune from challenge in the courts. I pass to consider his second proposition.

The second proposition depends for its soundness upon whether the power conferred by article 4 of the Order in Council of 1982 on the Minister for the Civil Service of "providing for ... the conditions of service" of the Civil Service is subject to an implied obligation to act fairly. (Such an obligation is sometimes referred to as an obligation to obey the rules of natural justice, but that is a less appropriate description, at least when applied, as in the present case, to a power which is executive and not judicial.) There is no doubt that, if the Order in Council of 1982 had been made under the authority of a statute, the power delegated to the Minister by article 4 would have been construed as being subject to an obligation to act fairly.I am unable to see why the words conferring the same powers should be construed differently merely because their source was an Order in Council made under the prerogative. It is all the more difficult in the face of article 6(4) of the Order in Council of 1982 which provides that the Interpretation Act 1978 shall apply to the Order; it would of course apply to a statutory order. There seems no sensible reason why the words should not bear the same meaning whatever the source of authority for the legislation in which they are contained. The Order in Council of 1982 was described by Sir Robert Armstrong in his first affidavit as primary legislation; that is, in my opinion, a correct description, subject to the qualification that the Order in Council, being made under the prerogative, drives its authority from the sovereign alone and not, as is more commonly the case with legislation, from the sovereign in Parliament. Legislation frequently delegates power from the legislating authority—the sovereign alone in one case, the sovereign in Parliament in the other—to some other person or body and, when that is done, the delegated powers are defined more or less closely by the legislation, in this case by article 4. But whatever their source, powers which are defined, either by reference to their object or by reference to procedure for their exercise, or in some other way, and whether the definition is expressed or implied, are in my opinion normally subject to judicial control to ensure that they are not exceeded. By "normally" I mean provided that considerations of national security do not require otherwise.

The duty to consult

. . . . .

It is clear that the employees did not have a legal right to prior consultation. The Order in Council confers no such right, and article 4 makes no reference at all to consultation. The Civil Service handbook (*Handbook for the new civil servant*, 1973 ed. as amended 1983) which explains the normal method of consultation through the departmental Whitley Council, does not suggest that there is any legal right to consultation; indeed it is careful to recognise that, in the operational field, considerations of urgency may make prior consultation impracticable. ....

But even where a person claiming some benefit or privilege has no legal right to it, as a matter of private law, he may have a legitimate expectation of receiving the benefit or privilege, and, if so, the courts will protect his expectation by judicial review as a matter of public law. This subject has been fully explained by my noble and learned friend, Lord Diplock, in *O'Reilly* v. *Mackman* [1983] 2 A.C. 237[1] and I need not repeat what he has so recently said. Legitimate, or reasonable, expectation may arise either from an express promise given on behalf of a public authority or from the existence of a regular practice which the claimant can reasonably expect to continue.[2] In the present case the evidence shows that, ever since GCHQ began in 1947, prior consultation has been the invariable rule when conditions of service were to be significantly altered. Accordingly in my opinion if there had been no question of national security involved, the appellants would have had a legitimate expectation that the minister would cost them before issuing the instruction of 22 December 1983. The next question, therefore, is whether it has been shown that consideration of national security supersedes the expectation.

National security
The issue here is not whether the minister's instruction was proper or fair or justifiable on its merits. These matters are not for the courts to determine. The sole issue is whether the decision on which the instruction was based was reached by a process that was fair to the staff at GCHQ. As my noble and earned friend Lord Brightman said in *Chief Constable of the North Wales Police* v. *Evans* [1982] 1 W.L.R. 1155, 1173: "Judicial review is concerned, not with the decision, but with the decision-making process."

I have already explained my reasons for holding that, if no question of national security arose, the decision-making process in this case would have been unfair. The respondent's case is that she deliberately made the decision without prior consultation because prior consultation "would involve a real risk that it would occasion the very kind of disruption [at GCHQ] which was a threat to national security and which it was intended to avoid."

[Counsel for the Unions] conceded that a reasonable minister could reasonably have taken that view, but he argued strongly that the respondent had failed to

---

[1] *Post* p. 97.
[2] Cf. *Reg* v. *Liverpool Corporation Ex parte Liverpool Taxi Fleet Operators' Association* [1972] 2 Q.B; *Attorney General of Hong Kong* v. *Ng Yuen Shiu* [1983] 2 A.C. 629; *post* p. 333.

show that that was in fact the reason for her decision.

·   ·   ·   ·   ·

The question is one of evidence. The decision on whether the requirements of national security outweigh the duty of fairness in any particular case is for the Government and not for the courts; the Government alone has access to the necessary information, and in any event the judicial process is unsuitable for reaching decisions on national security. But if the decision is successfully challenged, on the ground that it has been reached by a process which is unfair, then the Government is under an obligation to produce evidence that the decision was in fact based on grounds of national security. Authority for both these points is found in *The Zamora* [1916] 2 A.C. 77.[3] The former point is dealt with in the well known passage from the advice of the Judicial Committee delivered by Lord Parker of Waddington, at p. 107:

> "Those who are responsible for the national security must be the sole judges of what the national security requires. It would be obviously undesirable that such matters should be made the subject of evidence in a court of law or otherwise discussed in public."

The second point, less often referred to, appears at p. 106 and more particularly at p. 108 where this passage occurs:

> "In their Lordships' opinion the order appealed from was wrong, not because, as contended by the appellants, there is by international law no right at all to requisition ships or goods in the custody of the court, but because the judge had before him *no satisfactory evidence* that such a right was exercisable." (Emphasis added.)

What was required was evidence that a cargo of copper in the custody of the Prize Court was urgently required for national purposes, but no evidence had been directed to that point. The claim on behalf of the Crown that it was entitled to requisition the copper therefore failed; considering that the decision was made in 1916 at a critical stage of the 1914–1918 war, it was a strong one. In *Chandler* v. *Director of Public Prosecutions* [1964] A.C. 763, which was an appeal by persons who had been convicted of a breach of the peace under section 1 of the Official Secrets Act 1911 by arranging a demonstration by the Campaign for Nuclear Disarmament on an operational airfield at Wethersfield, Lord Reid said, at p. 790:

> "The question more frequently arises as to what is or is not in the public interest. I do not subscribe to the view that the Government or a minister must always or even as a general rule have the last word about that. But here we are dealing with a very special matter—interfering with a prohibited place which Wethersfield was."

But the court had had before it evidence from an Air Commodore that the airfield was of importance for national security. Both Lord Reid and Viscount Radcliffe, at p. 796, referred to the evidence as being relevant to their refusal of the appeal.

The evidence in support of this part of the respondent's case came from Sir Robert Armstrong in his first affidavit.

·   ·   ·   ·   ·

The affidavit, read as a whole, does in my opinion undoubtedly constitute evidence that the Minister did indeed consider that prior consultation would have involved a risk of precipitating disruption at GCHQ. I am accordingly of opinion that the respondent has shown that her decision was one which not only could

---

[3] "Surely one of the more courageous of judicial decisions even in our long history"; *per* Lord Scarman at p. 404.

reasonably have been based, but was in fact based, on considerations of national security, which outweighed what would otherwise have been the reasonable expectation on the part of the appellants for prior consultation. For these reasons I would dismiss the appeal.

LORD SCARMAN: . . . My Lords, I would wish to add a few, very few, words on the reviewability of the exercise of the royal prerogative. Like my noble and learned friend Lord Diplock, I believe that the law relating to judicial review has now reached the stage where it can be said with confidence that, if the subject matter in respect of which prerogative power is exercised is justiciable, that is to say if it is a matter upon which the court can adjudicate, the exercise of the power is subject to review in accordance with the principles developed in respect of the review of the exercise of statutory power. Without usurping the role of legal historian, for which I claim no special qualification, I would observe that the royal prerogative has always been regarded as part of the common law, and that Sir Edward Coke had no doubt that it was subject to the common law: *Prohibitions del Roy* (1608) 12 Co. Rep. 63 and the *Proclamations Case* (1611) 12 Co. Rep. 74. In the latter case he declared, at p. 76, that "the King hath no prerogative, but that which the law of the land allows him.' It is, of course, beyond doubt that in Coke's time and thereafter judicial review of the exercise of prerogative power was limited to inquiring into whether a particular power existed and, if it did, into its extent: *Attorney-General* v. *De Keyser's Royal Hotel Ltd.* [1920] A.C. 508. But this limitation has now gone, overwhelmed by the developing modern law of judicial review: *Reg.* v. *Criminal Injuries Compensation Board, Ex parte Lain* [1967] 2 Q.B. 864 (a landmark case comparable in its generation with the *Proclamations Case*, 12 Co.Rep. 74) and *Reg.* v. *Secretary of State for Home Affairs, Ex parte Hosenball* [1977] 1 W.L.R. 766. Just as ancient restrictions in the law relating to the prerogative writs and orders have not prevented the courts from extending the requirement of natural justice, namely the duty to act fairly, so that it is required of a purely administrative act, so also has the modern law, a vivid sketch of which my noble and learned friend Lord Diplock has included in his speech, extended the range of judicial review in respect of the exericise of prerogative power. Today, therefore, the controlling factor in determining whether the exercise of prerogative power is subject to judicial review is not its source but its subject matter.

Subject to these few comments, I agree with the speeches delivered by my noble and learned friends Lord Diplock and Lord Roskill. I am in favour of dismissing the appeal only because the respondent has established by evidence that the interest of national security required in her judgment that she should refuse to consult the unions before issuing her instruction. But for this I would have allowed the appeal on the procedural ground that the respondent had acted unfairly in failing to consult unions or staff before making her decision.

LORD DIPLOCK: . . . The reason why the Minister for the Civil Service decided on 22 December 1983 to withdraw this benefit was in the interests of national security. National security is the responsibility of the executive government; what action is needed to protect its interests is, as the cases cited by my learned friend, Lord Roskill, establish and common sense itself dictates, a matter upon which those upon whom the responsibility rests, and not the courts of justice, must have the last word. It is par excellence a non-justiciable question. The judicial process is totally inept to deal with the sort of problems which it involves.

The executive government likewise decided, and this would appear to be a collective decision of cabinet ministers involved, that the interests of national security required that no notice should be given of the decision before administrative action had been taken to give effect to it. The reason for this was the risk that advance notice to the national unions of the executive government's intention would attract the very disruptive action prejudicial to the national security the recurrence of which the decision barring membership of national trade unions to civil servants employed at GCHQ was designed to prevent.

There was ample evidence to which reference is made by others of your Lordships that this was indeed a real risk; so the crucial point of law in this case is whether procedural propriety must give way to national security when there is conflict between (1) on the one hand, the prima facie rule of "procedural propriety" in public law, applicable to a case of legitimate expectations that a benefit ought not to be withdrawn until the reason for its proposed withdrawal has been communicated to the person who has theretofore enjoyed that benefit and that person has been given an opportunity to comment on the reason, and (2) on the other hand, action that is needed to be taken in the interests of national security, for which the executive government bears the responsibility and alone has access to sources of information that qualify it to judge what the necessary action is. To that there can, in my opinion, be only one sensible answer. That answer is 'Yes.'

I agree with your Lordships that this appeal must be dismissed.

LORD ROSKILL: ... My Lords, before considering this issue it is necessary to consider a further important question which arises by reason of the fact that the instructions given under article 4 of the Order in Council of 1982 were by means of the exercise of a prerogative power. The appellants in their printed case invited the House to consider and if necessary to reconsider the reviewability of executive acts done under the prerogative. Mr. Alexander for the respondent understandably did not press the argument that no action taken under the prerogative could ever be the subject of judicial review. But, helpfully, he thought it right to make available to your Lordships a selection from the classic pronouncements of many famous writers in this field from Locke through Blackstone and Chitty to Dicey and from the writings of distinguished modern authorities including de Smith, Wade, Hood Phillips and Heuston designed to show first the historic view that acts done under the prerogative were never reviewable and secondly the extent to which that classic doctrine may at least in this century be said to have been diluted.

Dicey's classic statement in *Law of the Constitution*, 10th ed. (1959), p. 424, that the prerogative is "the residue of discretionary or arbitrary authority, which at any given time is legally left in the hands of the Crown" has the weight behind it not only of the author's own authority but also of the majority of this House in *Burmah Oil Co. Ltd.* v. *Lord Advocate* [1965] A.C. 75: see *per* Lord Reid, at p. 99. But as Lord Reid himself pointed out this definition "does not take us very far." On the other hand the attempt by Lord Denning M.R. in *Laker Airways Ltd.* v. *Department of Trade* [1977] Q.B. 643, 705 (obiter since the other members of the Court of Appeal did not take so broad a view) to assert that the prerogative "if ... exercised improperly or mistakenly" was reviewable is, with great respect, far too wide. The Master of the Rolls sought to support his view by a quotation from *Blackstone's Commentaries*, 15th ed., vol. 1, p. 252. But unfortunately and no doubt inadvertently he omitted the opening words of the paragraph.

> "In the exercise therefore of those prerogatives, which the law has given him, the King is irresistible and absolute, according to the forms of the constitution. And yet, if the consequence of that exertion be manifestly to the grievance or dishonour of the kingdom, the parliament will call his advisers to a just and severe account."

In short the orthodox view was at that time that the remedy for abuse of the prerogative lay in the political and not in the judicial field.

But fascinating as it is to explore this mainstream of our legal history, to do so in connection with the present appeal has an air of unreality. To speak today of the acts of the sovereign as "irresistible and absolute" when modern constitutional convention requires that all such acts are done by the sovereign on the advice of and will be carried out by the sovereign's ministers currently in power is surely to hamper the continual development of our administrative law by harking back to what Lord Atkin once called, albeit in a different context, the clanking of mediaeval chains of the ghosts of the past: see *United Australia Ltd.* v. *Barclays Bank Ltd.* [1941] A.C. 1, 29. It is, I hope, not out of place in this connection to quote a letter written in 1896 by the great legal historian F. W. Maitland to Dicey himself: "The only direct utility of legal history (I say nothing of its thrilling interest) lies in the lesson that each generation has an enormous power of shaping its own law": see *Richard A. Cosgrove, The Rule of Law: Albert Venn Dicey, Victorian Jurist* (1980), p. 177. Maitland was in so stating a greater prophet than even he could have foreseen for it is our legal history which has enabled the present generation to shape the development of our administrative law by building upon but unhampered by our legal history.

My Lords, the right of the executive to do a lawful act affecting the rights of the citizen, whether adversely or beneficially, is founded upon the giving to the executive of a power enabling it to do that act. The giving of such a power usually carries with it legal sanctions to enable that power if necessary to be enforced by the courts. In most cases that power is derived from statute through in some cases, as indeed in the present case, it may still be derived from the prerogative. In yet other cases, as the decisions show, the two powers may coexist or the statutory power may by necessary implication have replaced the former prerogative power. If the executive in pursuance of the statutory power does an act affecting the rights of the citizen, it is beyond question that in principle the manner of the exercise of that power may today be challenged on one or more of the three grounds which I have mentioned earlier in this speech. If the executive instead of acting under a statutory power acts under a prerogative power and in particular a prerogative power delegated to the respondent under article 4 of the Order in Council of 1982, so as to affect the rights of the citizen, I am unable to see, subject to what I shall say later, that there is any logical reason why the fact that the source of the power is the prerogative and not statute should today deprive the citizen of that right of challenge to the manner of its exercise which he would possess were the source of the power statutory. In either case the act in question is the act of the executive. To talk of that act as the act of the sovereign savours of the archaism of past century. In reaching this conclusion I find myself in agreement with my noble and learned friends Lord Scarman and Lord Diplock whose speeches I have had the advantage of reading in draft since completing the preparation of this speech.

But I do not think that that right of challenge can be unqualified. It must, I think, depend upon the subject matter of the prerogative power which is exercised. Many examples were given during the argument of prerogative powers which as at present advised I do not think could properly be made the subject of judicial review. Prerogative powers such as those relating to the making of treaties, the defence of the realm, the prerogative of mercy, the grant of honours, the dissolution of Parliament and the appointment of ministers as well as others are not, I think, susceptible to judicial review because their nature and subject matter are such as not to be amenable to the judicial process. The courts are not the place where to determine whether a treaty should be concluded or the armed forces disposed in a particular manner or Parliament dissolved on one date rather than another.

In my view the exercise of the prerogative which enabled the oral instructions of 22 December 1983 to be given does not by reason of its subject matter fall within what for want of a better phrase I would call the "excluded categories" some of which I have just mentioned. It follows that in principle I can see no reason why those instructions should not be the subject of judicial review.

[After reviewing the earlier case law and the facts set out in Sir Robert Armstrong's affidavit Lord Roskill concluded]

My Lords, I have therefore reached the clear conclusions, first, that the respondent has established that the work at GCHQ was a matter of grave national security, second, that that security would have been seriously compromised had industrial action akin to that previously encountered between 1979 and 1981 taken place, third, that consultation with the appellants prior to the oral instructions would have served only further to reveal the vulnerability of GCHQ to such industrial action, fourth, that it was in the interest of nation security that that should not be allowed to take place, and fifth, that accordingly the respondent was justified in the interests of national security in issuing the instructions without prior consultation with the appellants.

LORD BRIGHTMAN: My Lords, I also would dismiss this appeal for one reason only, namely, on the ground of national security. . . . There is nothing which I can usefully add to the comprehensive survey which your Lordships have already made of the authorities on the reviewability of decisions taken under the royal prerogative. There is no difference between the conclusions reached by your Lordships except on one isolated point: whether the reviewability of an exercise of a prerogative power is limited to the case where the power has been delegated to the decision-maker by Order in Council, so that the decision-making process which is sought to be reviewed arises under and must be exercised in accordance with the terms of that order; or whether reviewability may also extend, in an appropriate case, to a direct exercise of a prerogative power. Like my noble and learned friend, Lord Fraser of Tullybelton, I would prefer to leave the resolution of that question to a case where it must necessarily be determinded.

For the reason indicated, I would dismiss this appeal.

Appeal dismissed.

Note

The prerogative power to issue or refuse a passport has been held to be subject to judicial review in *R. v. Secretary of State for Foreign and Commonwealth Affairs Ex parte Everett, The Times,* December 10, 1987.

The treaty making power and foreign relations have been held not to be subject to judicial review: *Ex parte Molyneux, post; R. v. Secretary of State for Foreign and Commonwealth Affairs Ex parte Trawnik, The Times,* February 21, 1986 (C.A.); post; p. 403.

On national security as a ground for excluding judicial review see *R. v. Secretary of State for Home Affairs Ex parte Hosenball* [1977] 1 W.L.R. 766; *R. v. Secretary of State for the Home Department Ex parte Ruddock* [1987] 2 All E. R. 518, 524.

In *R. v. Secretary of State for the Home Office, Ex parte Chubb* [1986] Crim.L.R. 809, The Divisional Court (Stephen Brown L.J. and Otton J.) held that there was no jurisdiction to review the refusal of the Home Secretary to make an *ex gratia* payment to a person imprisoned on the basis of a conviction which was subsequently set aside as having been wrongfully imposed.

Ex parte Molyneaux
[1986] 1 W.L.R. 331
Queen's Bench Division

TAYLOR J: This application concerns an agreement which was signed on 15 November 1985 by the Prime Minister, on behalf of Her Majesty's Government, and by Dr. Garret Fitzgerald, for the Government of the Republic of Ireland. The agreement provides for the establishment of an Intergovernmental Conference concerned with Northern Ireland and its relations with the Irish Republic.

The four applicants are all members and officers of the Ulster Unionist Council. They make application for leave to apply for judicial review of the agreement. . . . I am prepared to assume, in the applicants' favour, without deciding, that they have in law a sufficient interest in the matters they raise to entitle them to apply for leave. What they seek is a declaration that it would be contrary to law for Her Majesty's Government to implement the agreement without the authority of the Queen in Parliament in the form of new legislation.

[The learned judge rejected various arguments based on the alleged conflict between the terms of the agreement and the Union with Ireland Act 1800 and The Northern Ireland Constitution Act 1973. He concluded]

As its name indicates, the Intergovernmental Conference between the Government of the United Kingdom and that of another sovereign state would be of an international nature. The agreement itself is in the field of international relations. It is akin to a treaty. It concerns relations between the United Kingdom and another sovereign state and it is not the function of this court to inquire into the exercise of the prerogative in entering into such an agreement or by way of anticipation to decide whether the method proposed of implementing the agreement is appropriate.

Application dismissed.

Mutasa v. Attorney General
[1980] Q.B. 114
Queen's Bench Division

The plaintiff, a British subject and a citizen of Southern Rhodesia was resident in that territory at the time of its unilateral declaration of independence. He was arrested and detained without trial before being released on condition that he left Southern Rhodesia for the United Kingdom. Subsequently, he brought an action against the Attorney General of the United Kingdom seeking a declaration that his detention had been unlawful and that Her Majesty's Government had failed in its duty to protect him. He also claimed damages.

BOREHAM J: On behalf of the Crown, it is conceded that the plaintiff being resident in one of Her Majesty's territories, and being a British subject, the Crown did owe him a duty to protect from unlawful arrest and detention, and that that duty has not been carried out. It is argued, however, first, that what is called by the plaintiff "a legal duty" is not more than a political or moral duty or obligation; it is not a legal duty. Secondly, that even if it is to be regarded as a legal duty it is not enforceable, nor would its breach be actionable, in this court. Next, it is argued that, even if the defendant is wrong in those contentions, the plaintiff is precluded from bringing these particular proceedings by the provisions of section 40(2)(*b*) of the Crown Proceedings Act 1947.

.   .   .   .   .

In support of his contention for a legal duty, [Counsel for the plaintiff] relies upon a number of citations from well known text books on constitutional and administrative law. It is sufficient if I quote from one, for the others are to the like effect, and I quote from O. Hood Phillips' *Constitutional and Adminstrative Law*, 6th ed. (1978), p. 272:

> " 'The principal duty of the King is, to govern his people according to law,' says Blackstone, quoting Bracton and Fortescue to like effect. Blackstone cites the Coronation Oath, but adds that 'doubtless the duty of protection is impliedly as such incumbent on the Sovereign before coronation as after.' "[1]

To like effect is a quotation from S. A. de Smith, *Constitutional and Administrative Law*, 3rd ed. (1977), p. 121[2]. Before leaving those text books, it is to be observed that in each case the writer asserts, by way of preface to the words already quoted, that the sovereign in theory has duties but these are not legally enforceable.

On behalf of the plaintiff it is argued that that latter assertion as to the non-enforceability of those duties is unsupported by authority, and he says is ill founded in law. It is true that there is no authority directly in point, but there are authorities which relate to similar duties, and which in my judgment are helpful in this particular context. The first to which I make reference is *Attorney-General* v. *Tomline* (1880) 14 Ch.D. 58. That was a case where the duty was somewhat different from that which is asserted here, though it falls, in my view, into the same category. There the duty was the duty of the Crown to protect the realm from the inroads of the sea. Brett L.J. had no doubt that the duty existed, nor did his brethren, and he said, at p. 66:

> "Now, I confess to my mind that is a duty of what is called imperfect obligation. Supposing that the King were to neglect that duty, I know no legal means—that is, no process of law—common law or statute law—by which the Crown could be forced to perform that duty, but there is that duty of

---

[1]   (7th ed., 1987) p. 270.
[2]   (5th ed., 1985) p. 148.

imperfect obligation on the part of the royal authority, and that duty on the part of the King gives a corresponding right to the subject, but inasmuch as the duty of the King seems to me to be a duty of imperfect obligation, the right of the subject is also an imperfect right. It is a right which as against the Crown the subject has no means to enforce: nevertheless the right exists. The right of the subject exists and the duty of the King."

There followed, in 1931, *China Navigation Co. Ltd.* v. *Attorney-General* (1931) 40 Ll.L.R. 110. There again the duty is somewhat different. The duty alleged in that case, in the court of first instance, was a duty cast upon the Crown to protect His Majesty's subjects in British ships upon the high seas. In the course of his judgment, Rowlatt J. came to the point where he was comparing the duty of officers of the Crown with the duty of the Crown itself. He said, at pp.112-113:

"It seems to me, as was said in another case, that the analogy fails because the word 'duty' in the two cases is made to describe two totally different things. In the case of the officers they have the duty to perform the duties confided to them by the statutes in question, *i.e.*, a duty in the eye of the courts of law. But in the case of the Crown and the use of its forces, what is called the duty is not that sort of thing at all. It has not any obligation, as I understand it, which comes within the purview of the courts of law. It is a different sort of thing in a different region altogether. It is merely what I venture to call a political duty, using the word 'political' in its proper and original sense. It is what any government would be expected to do for its people, but the court cannot examine it. Nobody could come to the court and say whether the government of any country did or did not perform its duty in that respect. That confusion with the double use of the word 'duty' lies at the bottom of the whole argument in this case. The case for the plaintiffs is on a complete fallacy."

That decision was tested in the Court of Appeal: see *China Navigation Co. Ltd.* v. *Attorney-General* [1932] 2 K.B. 197. There the argument shifted somewhat. Whereas in the court below it has rested upon the assertion of an unqualified duty to protect, in the Court of Appeal the shift of emphasis was towards an assertion that the Crown had no right to charge for affording protection. It is sufficient to say that in the judgments, in particular that of Lawrence L.J., the dictum of Brett L.J. in the *Tomline* case, and the decision of Rowlatt J. on the question of duty and its non-enforceability were completely confirmed.

It seems to me that the principles which are to be gleaned from those authorities apply to the duty here alleged by the plaintiff and conceded by the Attorney-General. In my judgment, therefore, the duty here relied upon is not in the proper sense a legal duty, namely one which can be enforced in a court of law or the breach of which would give rise to a cause of action in a court of law. The duty here is to protect from arrest and imprisonment, and whatever the extent of that duty may be it is one, as Brett L.J. said, of imperfect obligation and is not enforceable in this court.

That, in my view, is sufficient to dispose of the plaintiff's claim, but other questions, as I have indicated, have been extensively canvassed and I turn to them now. First, as to the effect of section 40 of the Crown Proceedings Act 1947. As I have indicated, it is Mr. Blom-Cooper's contention that section 40, and in particularly subsection (2)(*b*), precludes the plaintiff from bringing these proceedings in the present circumstances. The relevant part of the subsection reads:

"(2) Except as therein otherwise expressly provided, nothing in this Act shall:— . . . (*b*) authorise proceedings to be taken against the Crown under or in accordance with this Act in respect of any alleged liability, of the Crown arising otherwise than in respect of Her Majesty's Government in the United Kingdom . . ."

Mr. Blom-Cooper's contention is short; it is this. That the liability alleged in this case is a liability of the Crown which does arise otherwise than in respect of Her Majesty's Government of the United Kingdom.

[His Lordship accepted the argument that the liability, if any, arose otherwise than in respect of Her Majesty's Government of the United Kingdom despite the terms of the Southern Rhodesia Act 1965.]

Plaintiff's claim dismissed.

PREROGATIVE IN RELATION TO ACT OF PARLIAMENT

Prerogative Subject to Act of Parliament

Attorney-General v. De Keyser's Royal Hotel Ltd.
[1920] A.C. 508
House of Lords

The respondents were the lessees of the De Keyser's Royal Hotel, the business of which was being carried on by Mr. Whinney as receiver for the debenture-holders. The premises being required by the War Office and negotiations having broken down over the amount of rent, possession was taken by the Army Council under the Defence of the Realm Regulations and upon the terms that compensation would be *ex gratia*, the amount to be determined by the Defence of the Realm Losses Commission. Whinney gave possession but rejected the reference to arbitration and claimed full compensation as of right. The premises were at first used by members of the Air Service, but when the Air Board was formed, the Air Service moved elsewhere and De Keyser's Royal Hotel was subsequently used by the Government for other sections of the War Office. It was throughout used for administrative purposes.

Peterson J. dismissed the petition, Holding that he was bound by the decision of the Court of Appeal in *Re X's Petition of Right*.[1] The Court of Appeal reversed his decision. The House of Lords (Lord Dunedin, Lord Atkinson, Lord Moulton, Lord Sumner and Lord Parmoor), on an appeal by the Crown, unanimously confirmed the decision of the Court of Appeal, *i.e.* decided against the Crown.

LORD DUNEDIN [after stating the facts, and holding that there was no implied contract that the Crown should pay a reasonable sum for use and occupation of the premises, said]: Now, that the act of taking by the Crown was in itself legal is necessarily admitted by both sides. It is the basis of the case for the Crown, who said at the time that they took under the Defence of the Realm Act, and now add in argument that whether that was so or not they took *de facto* and can justify that taking under the powers of the prerogative. It must necessarily be admitted by the respondents, for if taking in itself was purely illegal, then it would be a tort not committed by the Crown, who cannot commit a tort,[2] but by the officers of the Crown, and the petition of right would not lie. The question in the case is therefore narrowed to one point and one point only: the Crown having legally taken, is it bound to pay compensation *ex lege*, or is the offer to pay compensation *ex gratia*, as that compensation may be fixed by the Losses Commission, a sufficient offer and an answer to all demands? I have already quoted the letter of May 1, which shows that the War Office proposed to take possession of the hotel under the Defence of the Realm Regulations, but in the argument in the court below and before your Lordships the taking has been justified by the power of the prerogative alone, and there has been a very exhaustive citation of authority on the powers of the Crown in virtue of the prerogative.

I do not think it necessary to examine and comment on the various cases cited. The foundations of the contention are to be found in the concessions made in the speech of Mr. St. John in *Hampden's* case,[3] and in the opinion of the consulted judges in *The Saltpetre Case*.[4] . . . The most that could be taken from them is that the King, as *suprema potestas* endowed with the right and duty of protecting the realm, is for the purpose of the defence of the realm in times of danger entitled to take any

---

[1] [1915] 3 K.B. 649.
[2] [See now the Crown Proceedings Act 1947].
[3] (1637) 3 St.Tr. 82.
[4] (1606) 12 Co.Rep. 12.

man's property, and that the texts give no certain sound as to whether this right to take is accompanied by an obligation to make compensation to him whose property is taken. In view of this silence it is but natural to inquire what has been the practice in the past. An inquiry as to this was instituted in this case, and there has been placed before your Lordships a volume of extracts from the various records. . . . I shall refer to the statutes presently, but, speaking generally, what can be gathered from the records as a matter of practice seems to resolve itself into this. There is a universal practice of payment resting on bargain before 1708, and on statutory power and provision after 1708. On the other hand, there is no mention of a claim made in respect of land taken under the prerogative, for the acquisition of which there was neither bargain nor statutory sanction. Nor is there any proof that any such acquisition had taken place. I do not think that from this usage of payment there can be imposed on the Crown a customary obligation to pay, for once the taking itself is admitted to be as of right the usage of payment so far as not resting on statutory provision is equally consistent with a payment *ex lege*, and a payment *ex gratia*. On the other hand, I think it admissible to consider the statutes in the light of the admitted custom to pay, for in the face of a custom of payment it is not surprising that there should be consent on the part of the Crown that this branch of the prerogative should be regulated by statute. It is just here that the full investigation into the statutory history which has been made in this case, and of which the Court of Appeal and your Lordships have had the advantage, serve to dislodge a view which I cannot help thinking was very influential in determining the judgment of the Court of Appeal in the case of *Re X's Petition of Right*. . . .

Now the view which I think prevailed in *Re X's Petition of Right* was that the prerogative gives a right to take for use of the moment in a time of emergency, that when you come to the Defence Acts of 1803 and 1842 you find a code for the taking of land permanently in times of peace as well as of war, and that consequently the two systems could well stand side by side: and then, as there was no direct mention of the prerogative in the statutes, you were assisted by the general doctrine that the Crown is not bound by a statute unless specially mentioned. That in cases where a burden or tax is imposed the Crown must be specifically mentioned no one doubts. Instances are given by the Master of the Rolls in the cases of *Wheaton* v. *Maple & Co.*[5] and *Coomber* v. *Berks Justices*,[6] and there are many others. Nonetheless, it is equally certain that if the whole ground of something which could be done by the prerogative is covered by the statute it is the statute which rules. On this point I think that the observation of the learned Master of the Rolls is unanswerable. He says: "what use would there be in imposing limitations, if the Crown could at its pleasure disregard them and fall back on prerogative?" The prerogative is defined by a learned constitutional writer as "the residue of discretionary or arbitrary authority which at any given time is legally left in the hands of the Crown."[7] Inasmuch as the Crown is a party to every Act of Parliament it is logical enough to consider that when the Act deals with something which before the Act could be effected by the prerogative and specially empowers the Crown to do the same thing, but subject to conditions, the Crown assents to it, and, by the Act, to the prerogative being curtailed.

[After discussing the legislation preceding the Defence Act 1842 his Lordship continued]: It thus appears that the inception of the legislation was during that very period and connected with that very requirement which, if the argument in *Re X's Petition of Right* was sound, was satisfied by the powers of the prerogative alone, that is to say, it dealt with temporary acquisition during a period of war, and the Act of 1842 only continued that legislation. It is therefore impossible, in

---

[5] [1893] 3 Ch.48.
[6] (1883) 9 App.Cas. 61.
[7] Lord Dunedin was citing Dicey, *Law of the Constitution:* see now 10th ed., p. 424.

my opinion, to say that the whole field of the prerogative in the matter of the acquisition of land or rights therein was not covered by the Act of 1842. It follows from what I have said above that there is no room for asserting an unrestricted prerogative right as existing alongside with the statutory powers authorising the Crown to acquire on certain terms. The conclusion is that the Crown could not take the petitioners' property by the powers of the prerogative alone.

I now come to the Defence of the Realm Consolidation Act 1914, the Act under the powers of which the Crown professes to take. Now just as the statutes must be interpreted in view of what the rights and practices antecedent to them had been, so we must look at the Act of 1914 in view of the law as it stood previous to its passing. The Defence of the Realm Consolidation Act 1914, passed on November 27, 1914, declares, by section 1(1), that His Majesty has power during the continuance of the war to issue regulations for securing the public safety and the defence of the realm. Subsection (2) says that any such regulations may provide for the suspension of any restrictions on the acquisition or user of land under the Defence Acts 1842 to 1875. Pursuant to this Act a regulation was issued, on November 28, 1914, which empowered the competent naval or military authority, or any person authorised by him, "where for the purpose of securing the public safety or the defence of the realm it is necessary so to do, (a) to take possession of any land," and "(b) to take possession of any buildings." It is clear that under these subsections the taking possession of De Keyser's Hotel was warranted, but there was no necessity for the public safety or the defence of the realm that payment should not be made, such payment being, on the hypothesis that the views above expressed as to the Act of 1842 were sound, a necessary concomitant to taking. The very structure of the Act points the same way. Why provide by subsection (2) of section 1 for the suspension of restrictions under the existing Act which allowed of taking land if a mere taking *simpliciter* was all that was wanted? The thing may be tested in another way. Suppose the regulation as to taking land had had added to it the words "without making any payment therefor." That would have left no doubt as to the regulation. The question would have been: Was it *ultra vires*? It could only be *intra vires* if it were necessary for the safety of the realm, and that is the same question over again, and again the existence of the powers of subsection (2) of section 1 of the Act can be appealed to. The argument is practically analogous to the argument which prevailed, and I think rightly prevailed, in the judgment of Salter J. in the case of *Newcastle Breweries Ltd.* v. *R.*,[8] where the taking of the goods was held a necessity, but the extrusion of the subject, whose goods were taken, from the King's Courts in the event of non-agreement as to value was not. It will have been noticed that the regulation which authorises the taking of land says nothing about doing away with restrictions, or, in other words, does not specifically purport to be made in virtue of subsection (2) of section 1 of the Act. Nonetheless, it may well be held to be virtually so. There are various restrictions as to the initiation of proceedings, notices, etc., which I have not thought it necessary to quote. These may be taken as swept away by the simple authority to take. There remains the question whether the obligation to pay can be considered as a restriction and also swept away. I think that it cannot. The word "restriction" seems to me appropriate to the various provisions as to notice, but not at all appropriate to the obligation to make compensation. . . .

On the whole matter I am therefore of opinion that the judgment of the Court of Appeal was right and ought to be affirmed, and the appeal dismissed with costs.

LORD ATKINSON: . . . It is quite obvious that it would be useless and meaningless for the Legislature to impose restrictions and limitations upon, and to attach conditions to the exercise by the Crown of the powers conferred by a statute, if the

---

[8] [1920] 1 K.B. 854.

Crown were free, as its pleasure, to disregard all these provisions, and by virtue of its prerogative do the very thing which the statute empowered it to do. One cannot in the construction of a statute attribute to the Legislature, in the absence of compelling works, an intention so absurd. It was suggested that when a statute is passed empowering the Crown to do a certain thing which it might theretofore have done by virtue of its prerogative, the prerogative is merged in the statute. I confess that I do not think the word "merged" is happily chosen. I should prefer to say that when such a statute expressing the will and intention of the King and of the three estates of the realm is passed, it abridges the Royal prerogative while it is in force to the extent: that the Crown can only do the particular thing under and in accordance with the statutory provisions, and that its prerogative power to do that thing is in abeyance. Whichever mode of expression be used, the result intended to be indicated is, I think, the same—namely, that after the statute has been passed and while it is in force the thing which it empowers the Crown to do can thenceforth only be done by and under the statute, and subject to all the limitations, restrictions and conditions thereby imposed, however unrestricted the Royal prerogative may theretofore have been. ...

LORD MOULTON: ... What effect has this course of legislation upon the Royal prerogative? I do not think that it can be said to have abrogated that prerogative in any way, but it has given to the Crown statutory powers, which render the exercise of that prerogative unnecessary, because the statutory powers which have been conferred upon it are wider and more comprehensive than those of the prerogative itself. But it has done more than this. It has indicated unmistakably that it is the intention of the nation that the powers of the Crown in these respects should be exercised in the equitable manner set forth in the statute, so that the burden shall not fall on the individual, but shall be borne by the community. This being so, when powers covered by this statute are exercised by the Crown, it must be presumed that they are so exercised under the statute and therefore subject to the equitable provision for compensation, which is to be found in it. There can be no excuse for reverting to prerogative powers—*simpliciter*—if indeed they ever did exist in such a form as would cover the proposed acquisition, a matter which is far from clear in such a case as the present—when the Legislature has given to the Crown statutory powers which are wider than anyone ever were those that it possessed under the prerogative, and which cover all that can be necessary for the defence of the nation, and are moreover accompanied by safeguards to the individual, which are in agreement with the demands of justice. Accordingly if the commandeering of the buildings in this case had not been expressly done under statutory powers, I should have held that the Crown must be presumed to have acted under these statutory powers, and thus given the subject the statutory right to compensation. ...

LORD SUMNER: ... The regulation has the force of statute, and under its amelioration of the Defence Acts everything could be done for this purpose that could be done under the prerogative, equally efficiently and with equal speed. One difference, and one only, can be found. According to the argument, under the prerogative the subject could claim no compensation for losing the use of his property; under the statute he could. Is it to be supposed that the Legislature intended merely to give the Executive, as advisers of the Crown, the power of discriminating between subject and subject, enriching one by electing to proceed under the statute, and impoverishing another when it requisitions under the alleged prerogative? To presume such an intention seems to me contrary to the whole trend of our constitutional history for over 200 years. Nor is it a reasonable interpretation to say that the object of the Defence Acts was merely to supplement the prerogative by enabling the Crown to pay compensation out of public funds to a subject damnified by the exercise of the prerogative, which otherwise it would not be able to do. A prerogative right to take without paying must have been a right to take without paying out of the Royal funds; but, in truth, prerogative can at most extend to taking, and stands quite apart from payment. There is no prerogative right to elect not to pay. Conversely, if there is adequate power to do all that is required by proceeding under the statute, where is the emergency and public necessity which is the foundation for resort to the prerogative? . . .

LORD PARMOOR: . . . I am further of opinion that the plea of the appellant that the prerogative right of the Crown, whatever it may have been, has not been abated, abridged, or curtailed by any of the Defence Acts 1842 to 1873, or by any other statute, cannot be maintained . . . . The constitutional principle is that, when the power of Executive to interfere with the property or liberty of subjects has been placed under Parliamentary control and directly regulated by statute, the Executive no longer derives its authority from the Royal prerogative of the Crown, but from Parliament, and that, in exercising such authority, the Executive is bound to observe the restrictions which Parliament has imposed in favour of the subject. I think that the statutory provisions applicable to the interference by the Executive with the land and buildings of the respondents bring the case within the above principle. It would be an untenable proposition to suggest that courts of law could disregard the protective restrictions imposed by statute law where they are applicable. In this respect the sovereignty of Parliament is supreme. The principles of construction to be applied in deciding whether the Royal prerogative has been taken away or abridged are well ascertained. They may be taken away or abridged by express words, by necessary implication, or, as stated in Bacon's *Abridgement*, where an Act of Parliament is made for the public good, the advancement of religion and justice and to prevent injury and wrong. Statutes which provide rent or compensation as a condition to the right of the Executive to take over the temporary possession of land or buildings on the occasion of public exigency come, in my opinion, within the category of statutes made for the advancement of justice and to prevent injury and wrong. This is in accord with the well-established principle that, unless no other interpretation is possible, justice requires that statutes should not be construed to enable the land of a particular individual to be confiscated without payment. I am further of opinion that, where a matter has been directly regulated by statute, there is a necessary implication that the Regulation must be obeyed, and that, as far as such Regulation is inconsistent with the claim of a Royal prerogative right, such right can no longer be enforced. . . .
Appeal dismissed.

Treaties and Legislation

Blackburn v. Attorney–General
[1971] 1 W.L.R. 1037
Court of Appeal

Blackburn brought two actions against the Attorney-General claiming declarations to the effect that, by signing the Treaty of Rome, Her Majesty's Government would irreversibly surrender in part the sovereignty of the Crown in Parliament, and in so doing would be acting in breach of the law.

The Master struck out the statement of claim as disclosing no reasonable cause of action, and Eveleigh J. upheld the Master's order.

The Court of Appeal (Lord Denning M.R. Salmon and Stamp L.JJ.) dismissed the plaintiff's appeal.

LORD DENNING M.R.: In this case Mr. Blackburn—as he has done before—has shown eternal vigilance in support of the law. This time he is concerned about the applications of Her Majesty's Government to join the Common Market and to sign the Treaty of Rome. He brings two actions against the Attorney-General in which he seeks declarations to the effect that, by signing the treaty of Rome. Her Majesty's Government will surrender in part the sovereignty of the Crown in Parliament and will surrender it for ever. He says that in so doing the government will be acting in breach of the law. The Attorney-General has applied to strike out the statements of claim on the ground that they disclose no reasonable cause of action. Master Jacob and Eveleigh J. have struck them out. Mr. Blackburn, with our leave, appeals to this court. He thinks it is important to clear the air.

Much of what Mr. Blackburn says it quite correct. It does appear that if this country should go into the Common Market and sign the Treaty of Rome, it means that we will have taken a step which is irreversible. The sovereignty of these islands will thenceforward be limited. It will not be ours alone but will be shared with others. Mr. Blackburn referred us to a decision by the Court of Justice of the European Communities, *Costa* v. *Ente Nazionale Per L'Energia Elettrica* (*ENEL*)[1] in February 1964, in which the European court in its judgment said: ". . . the member-states, albeit within limited spheres, have restricted their sovereign rights and created a body of law applicable both to their nationals and to themselves."

Mr. Blackburn points out that many regulations made by the European Economic Community will become automatically binding on the people of this country: and that all the courts of this country, including the House of Lords, will have to follow the decisions of the European court in certain defined respects, such as the construction of the treaty.

I will assume that Mr. Blackburn is right in what he says on those matters. Nevertheless, I do not think these courts can entertain these actions. Negotiations are still in progress for us to join the Common Market. No agreement has been reached. No treaty has been signed. Even if a treaty is signed, it is elementary that these courts take no notice of treaties as such. We take no notice of treaties until they are embodied in laws enacted by Parliament, and then only to the extent that Parliament tells us. That was settled in a case about a treaty between the Queen of England and the Emperor of China. It is *Rustomjee* v. *The Queen.*[2] Lord Coleridge C.J. said: "She"—that is, the Queen—

> "acted throughout the making of the treaty and in relation to each and every of its stipulations in her sovereign character, and by her own inherent

[1] [1964] C.M.L.R. 425, 455.
[2] (1876) 2 Q.B.D. 69, 74.

authority; and, as in making the treaty, so in performing the treaty, she is beyond the control of municipal law, and her acts are not to be examined in her own courts."[3]

Mr. Blackburn acknowledged the general principle, but he urged that this proposed treaty is in a category by itself, in that it diminishes the sovereignty of Parliament over the people of this country. I cannot accept the distinction. The general principle applies to this treaty as to any other. The treaty-making power of this country rests not in the courts, but in the Crown; that is, Her Majesty acting upon the advice of her Ministers. When her Ministers negotiate and sign a treaty, even a treaty of such paramount importance as this proposed one, they act on behalf of the country as a whole. They exercise the prerogative of the Crown. Their action in so doing cannot be challenged or questioned in these courts.

Mr. Blackburn takes a second point. He says that, if Parliament should implement the treaty by passing an Act of Parliament for this purpose, it will seek to do the impossible. It will seek to bind its successors. According to the treaty, once it is signed, we are committed to it irrevocably. Once in the Common Market, we cannot withdraw from it. No Parliament can commit us, says Mr. Blackburn, to that extent. He prays in aid the principle that no Parliament can bind its successors, and that any Parliament can reverse any previous enactment. He refers to what Professor Maitland said about the Act of Union between England and Scotland. Professor Maitland in his *Constitutional History of England* (1908) said, at p. 322: "We have no irrepealable laws; all laws may be repealed by the ordinary legislature, even the conditions under which the English and Scottish Parliaments agreed to merge themselves in the Parliament of Great Britain."

We have all been brought up to believe that, in legal theory, one Parliament cannot bind another and that no Act is irreversible. But legal theory does not always march alongside political reality. Take the Statute of Westminster 1931, which takes away the power of Parliament to legislate for the Dominions. Can any one imagine that Parliament could or would reverse that Statute? Take the Acts which have granted independence to the Dominions and territories overseas. Can anyone imagine that Parliament could or would reverse those laws and take away their independence? Most clearly not. Freedom once given cannot be taken away. Legal theory must give way to practical politics. It is as well to remember the remark of Viscount Sankey L.C. in *British Coal Corporation* v. *The King*[4]: "... the Imperial Parliament could, as matter of abstract law, repeal or disregard section 4 of theStatute of Westminster. But that is theory and has no relation to realities."

What are the realities here? If Her Majesty's Ministers sign this treaty and Parliament enacts provisions to implement it, I do not envisage that Parliament would afterwards go back on it and try to withdraw from it. But, if Parliament should do so, then I say we will consider that event when it happens. We will then say whether Parliament can lawfully do it or not.

Both sides referred us to the valuable article by Professor H. W. R. Wade ("The Basis of Legal Sovereignty") in the *Cambridge Law Journal*, 1955, at p. 196, in which he said that "sovereignty is a political fact for which no purely legal authority can be constituted ... ." That is true. We must wait to see what happens before we pronounce on sovereignty in the Common Market.

So, whilst in theory Mr. Blackburn is quite right in saying that no Parliament can bind another, and that any Parliament can reverse what a previous Parliament has done, nevertheless so far as this court is concerned, I think we will wait till that day comes. We will not pronounce upon it today.

A point was raised as to whether Mr. Blackburn has any standing to come before the court. That is not a matter which we need rule upon today. He says that he feels very strongly and that it is a matter in which many persons in this country

[3] See *Winfat Enterprises (HK) Co Ltd* v. *Att-Gen of Hong Kong* [1985] 1 A.C. 733; *post* p. 117.
[4] [1935] A.C. 500, 520.

are concerned. I would not myself rule him out on the ground that he has no standing. But I do rule him out on the ground that these courts will not impugn the treaty-making power of Her Majesty, and on the ground that in so far as Parliament enacts legislation, we will deal with that legislation as and when it arises.

I think the statements of claim disclose no cause of action, and I would dismiss the appeal.

SALMON L.J.: Whilst I recognise the undoubted sincerity of Mr. Blackburn's views, I deprecate litigation the purpose of which is to influence political decisions. Such decisions have nothing to do with these courts. These courts are concerned only with the effect of such decisions if and when they have been implemented by legislation. Nor have the courts any power to interfere with the treaty-making power of the Sovereign. As to Parliament, in the present state of the law, it can enact, amend and repeal any legislation it pleases. The sole power of the courts is to decide and enforce what is the law and not what it should be—now, or in the future.

I agree that this appeal should be dismissed.

STAMP L.J.: I agree that the appeal should be dismissed; but I would express no view whatsoever upon the legal implications of this country becoming a party to the Treaty of Rome. In the way Mr. Blackburn put it I think he confused the division of the powers of the Crown, Parliament and the courts. The Crown enters into treaties; Parliament enacts laws; and it is the duty of this court in proper cases to interpret those laws when made; but it is no part of this court's function or duty to make declarations in general terms regarding the powers of Parliament, more particularly where the circumstances in which the court is asked to intervene are purely hypothetical. Nor ought this court at the suit of one of Her Majesty's subjects to make declarations regarding the undoubted prerogative power of the Crown to enter into treaties.

Appeals dismissed with costs.

Note

See also *Ex parte Molyneux* [1986] 1 W.L.R. 331; *ante* p. 105.

Winfat Enterprises (HK) Co. Ltd. v. Attorney-General of Hong Kong
[1985] 1 A.C. 733
Privy Council

In 1898 the Emperor of China leased land (the New Territories) to the Crown for a period of 99 years to be administered as part of the colony of Hong Kong. The convention effecting the lease stated that there would be "no expropriation or expulsion of the inhabitants of the district included [within the lease] and that if land is required for public purposes it shall be bought at a fair price." Subsequently a system of leaseholding, subject to restrictive covenants, was introduced by the Crown in the place of the pre-existing customary Chinese tenure. The appellants owned land in the New Territories. They had been refused permission to build on part of the land. They claimed the restrictions on the use to which they could put their land and the limited period for which they could hold it constituted expropriation of their customary rights. Another part of their land had been resumed (*i.e.* compulsorily acquired) by the Crown. The compensation payable under Hong Kong law did not, the owners claimed, amount to a fair price. In the High Court (Kempster, J.) and the Court of Appeal (Roberts C.J., Cons and Fuad JJ.A.) the land owners' actions failed. They appealed to the Privy Council (Lord Fraser of Tullybelton, Lord Wilberforce, Lord Diplock, Lord Brightman and Lord Templeman).

LORD DIPLOCK: . . . The land developers' claim does not lack boldness. At the time of the cession of the New Territories the greater part of the land was occupied by Chinese peasants and used for agricultural purposes: the growing of rice, of vegetables, of fruit and other foodstuffs. Although nominally the property of the Emperor of China, to whom land tax was payable, the land was held by its occupiers upon common or customary Chinese tenure by individuals or families or clans. It suffices for present purposes to note that it was a perpetual interest, heritable and assignable and subject to no restrictions upon building on the land.

· · · · ·

Put in an nutshell the land developers' claim was that, notwithstanding the 99–year cession under the Peking Convention, they held the retained land, of which they were successors in title to the Chinese inhabitants of the New Territories at the time of the cession, upon the same common or customary Chinese tenure as those Chinese inhabitants had themselves held it, that is to say a perpetual interest, heritable and assignable and free from any restriction upon building on the land. As respects the resumed land they claimed that its purported compulsory acquisition by the government was void because the above-cited provisions for compensation did not amount to a "fair price' and so resulted in the Crown Lands Resumption Ordinance being *ultra vires*.

· · · · ·

The elementary fallacy of British constitutional law which vitiates the land developers' claim is the contention that this vaguely expressed understanding, stated in the Peking Convention, that there shall not be expropriation or expulsion, is capable of giving rise to rights enforceable in the municipal courts of Hong Kong or by this Board acting in its judicial capacity. Although there are certain *obiter dicta* to be found in cases which suggest the propriety of the British Government giving effect as *an act of state* to promises of continued recognition of existing private titles of inhabitants of territory obtained by cession, there is clear long-standing authority by decision of this Board that no municipal court has authority to enforce such an obligation. This was laid down by Lord Halsbury L.C. in *Cook v. Sprigg* [1899] A.C. 572, 578–579, and by Lord Dunedin in *Vajesingji Joravarsingji v. Secretary of State for India in Council* (1924) L.R. 51 Ind.App. 357, 360–361.

What the High Court and Court of Appeal of Hong Kong are bound to enforce in the New Territories is the municipal law of Hong Kong made in the manner authorised by the Constitution as a British colony that has been granted to Hong Kong by the British Crown as sovereign of those territories for the duration of the cession.

Appeal dismissed.

EXECUTIVE POWERS OF THE CROWN

The Queen's Peace

R. v. Secretary of State for the Home Department Ex Parte Northumbria Police Authority [1988] 1 All E.R. 556

Court Of Appeal

The Northumbria Police Authority sought judicial review of a decision by the Home Secretary to issue a circular relating to the use by police forces of plastic baton rounds (plastic bullets) and CS gas. The circular stated:

"1. In July 1981 the Home Secretary announced that plastic baton rounds and CS would be made available to chief officers of police for use in the last resort, and under strict conditions, in situations of serious public disorder. It is now proposed that all police requirements for this equipment should be met from a central store. These arrangements will also extend to the provision of equipment in cases where a chief officer has been unable to obtain his police authority's agreement to purchase, and the chief officer's assessment of need is endorsed by HM Inspector of Constabulary. . . .
4. Where a chief officer decides that he needs plastic baton round or CS equipment and anticipates that he will have difficulty in obtaining the approval of his police authority, he should consult HM Inspector of Constabulary. The chief officer should report the views of the HMI to the police authority. If the HMI endorses the chief officer's assessment of need but nonetheless the police authority withholds approval for such equipment, the HMI will make arrangements with the Home Office for equipment to be supplied from the central store. The chief officer should inform the police authority that this is being done. The HMI will also make arrangements, through the Home Office, for further supplies to be provided, as required. The police authority should also be notified by the chief officer whenever this is done. Where baton rounds are supplied to a police force under the arrangements set out in this paragraph, the stock of baton rounds held by the force at any one time will normally be limited to 1,000 rounds. This will include rounds used for training purposes . . . '

The Divisional Court (Watkins L.J. and Mann J.) refused to grant a declaration that the Home Secretary had no power to issue plastic bullets or CS gas to a chief constable, without the consent of the local police authority, save in a grave emergency. The police authority appealed to the Court of Appeal (Purchas, Croom-Johnson and Nourse L.JJ.)

CROOM-JOHNSON L.J. (giving the first judgment at the invitation of Purchas L.J.).

The legal background is the Police Act 1964, which replaced a large number of Acts of Parliament which until then had governed the police forces in England and Wales. Section 1 provides that a police force shall be maintained in each police area in these countries. The Northumbria police area in its present form was delimited by the Local Government Act 1985, s.25 and Schedule 11. Section 2 of the 1964 Act established a police authority for each police area, and also its composition. Section 4 deals with the general functions of police authorities. Section 4(1) reads:

"It shall be the duty of the police authority for every police area for which a police force is required to be maintained by section 1 of this Act to secure the maintenance of an adequate and efficient police force for the area, and to exercise for that purpose the powers conferred on a police authority by this Act."

Section 4(2) places on the police authority the duty of appointing the chief constable, subject to the approval of the Secretary of State Section 4(3) reads:

"The police authority for any such police area may, subject to the consent of the Secretary of State, provide and maintain such buildings, structures and premises . . . as may be required . . ."

Section 4(4) reads:

"The police authority for any such police area may, subject to any regulations under Part II of this Act, provide and maintain such vehicles, apparatus, clothing and other equipment as may be required for police purposes of the area."

It will be noticed that s.4(1) imposes a duty, while s.4(3) and (4) gives power which may or may not be used.

Section 5 lays down the duties of the chief constable. The only part relevant for present purposes is sub–s.(1), which provides:

"The police force maintained for a police area under section 1 of this Act shall be under the direction and control of the chief constable appointed under section 4(2) of this Act."

It is common ground that the chief constable has complete operational control of his force. Neither the police authority nor the Home Secretary may give him any directions about that. The relationship between police forces and their appropriate local authorities was exhaustively examined by McCardie J in *Fisher* v *Oldham Corp* [1930] 2 KB 364, [1930] All ER Rep 96.

In that case it was held that the police were not the servants of the watch committee of a borough corporation so as to make the corporation civilly liable for wrongs committed by the police. The police perform their duties as constables wholly independently of the watch committee (or police authority). McCardie J gave this illustration ([1930] 2 KB 364 at 372–373, [1930] All ER Rep 96 at 102):

"Suppose that a police officer arrested a man for a serious felony? Suppose, too, that the watch committee of the borough at once passed a resolution directing that the felon should be released? Of what value would such a resolution be? Not only would it be the plain duty of the police officer to disregard the resolution, but it would also be the duty of the chief constable to consider whether an information should not at once be laid against the members of the watch committee for a conspiracy to obstruct the course of justice."

The independence of a constable, and a fortiori a chief constable, from outside control whether by a local authority or the executive, has been repeatedly upheld (see, A-G *for News South Wales* v *Perpetual Trustee Co Ltd* [1955] 1 All ER 846, [1955] AC 457 and *R.* v. *Metropolitan Police Comr, ex p. Blackburn* [1968] 1 All ER 763, [1968] 2 QB 118). In the latter case Lord Denning MR said of the commissioner, and so of every chief constable ([1968] 1 All ER 763 at 769, [1968] 2 QB 118 at 136):

"No Minister of the Crown can tell him that he must, or must not, keep observation on this place or that; or that he must, or must not, prosecute this man or that one. Nor can any police authority tell him so. The responsibility for law enforcement lies on him. He is answerable to the law and to the law alone."

This independence of the police goes back a long way. It is not the creation of the Police Act 1964.

The financial provisions of the 1964 Act are contained in section 8, as amended by Local Government Act 1985, s.25 and Schedule II. The effect is that all receipts of the police authority shall be paid into the police fund and all expenditure of any such police authority shall be paid out of that fund. That fund is in the exclusive control of the police authority.

Part II of the Act is headed "Central Supervision, Direction and Facilities." Section 28 sets out the general duty of the Home Secretary. It reads:

"The Secretary of State shall exercise his powers under this Act in such manner and to such extent as appears to him to be best calculated to promote the efficiency of the police."

It indicates the object to be achieved by the exercise of powers conferred on him elsewhere.

By Section 31 he may make grants to the police authority in respect of expenses incurred for police purposes. By section 33 he has a power to make regulations, none of which are relevant for present purposes. Section 38 provides for the appointment and functions of inspectors of constabulary, who are to inspect and report to the Home Secretary on the efficiency of all police forces. They shall also carry out such other duties for the purpose of furthering police efficiency as the Secretary of State may from time to time direct.

Section 41 is important. It begins a part of the Act sub-headed "Central services." It was under this section that the circular letter was sent. Section 41 says:

"The Secretary of State may provide and maintain, or may contribute towards the provision or maintenance of, a police college, district police training centres, forensic science laboratories, wireless depots and such other organisations and services as he considers necessary and expedient for promoting the efficiency of the police."

Before the Divisional Court the police authority contended that Section 41 does not give the Secretary of State power to supply equipment to the police force without the consent of the police authority. On that point the Divisional Court found in favour of the police authority. In this court the Secretary of State has argued that the Divisional Court was wrong, and that he does have the power. The Divisional Court however accepted an argument advanced for the Home Secretary that, alternatively, he may supply equipment, without the permission of the police authority, under the royal prerogative. Against that finding the police authority now appeals.

It is convenient to take the section 41 point first. It is a straight matter of construction of the section, when placed in the context of the statute as a whole.

It is not now contended by the Home Secretary that he can (as is stated in the circular) propose that all police requirement for plastic baton rounds and CS gas must be met from his central store. The police authority agree that section 41 gives the Home Secretary power to maintain a central store (which it is conceded would be an "organisation" within the meaning of that section) but it is argued that section 4(4) reserves to the authority the exclusive right to obtain equipment in discharge of its duty to secure the maintenance of an efficient police force. That the authority has financial control over the police fund is prayed in aid. This interpretation is said to be consistent with the general scheme of the statute, which divides the respective functions for providing an efficient force into three: an authority to maintain, provide and equip; a chief constable to control and operate; and a Home Secretary to supervise and regulate. The authority's case is that the 1964 Act sets out a complete and comprehensive code which defines and limits the functions of each of those three entities. It is correct that there is a general scheme as described by the authority. The question is whether the functions are as closely limited and exclusive as is suggested.

Section 4 places a duty on the authority; and gives it a discretion how the duty is to be discharged. Section 8 provides it with the funds with which to do so. But section 28 places a duty on the Home Secretary to use his powers so as to promote the efficiency of the police. Those powers include the provision of central services.

It is too narrow a construction of section 41 to say, as the authority contends, that the establishments mentioned in the section are only organisations and no more, and that the central store would be another. It ignores the word "services" in the section. If the Home Secretary gives instruction at a police college, or if a forensic science laboratory examines material sent to it by a force, he is providing service. Similarly, the supply of baton rounds or CS gas from the store is another service. It is not permissible to read into section 41 words which are not there, such as "with the consent of the police authority." There is no need to do so. Such services may be asked for by a chief constable in the ordinary course of carrying out his duty of efficient policing. If some payment for the service used is required, it would have to come from the police fund concerned, but if the Home Secretary is willing to make no charge there is no reason why the chief constable may not avail himself of what is available without asking the authority.

To read into section 41 the words which are suggested would involve an interference by the authority in the operational discretion of the chief constable. The provisions in section 43 relating to the payment of policemen who are seconded for service under the Crown in providing the central services have no bearing on the point now at issue.

Counsel for the police authority recognised that a distinction between organisations and services was artificial.

He also recognised that an operational requirement for baton rounds and CS gas may arise suddenly and with no prior warning. There would be no time in which to obtain the consent of the Northumbria police authority. Therefore another argument was advanced. This was that, if supply is permitted under section 41, yet that supply could only be given "without consent" in an emergency. There was some discussion as to what would constitute an emergency. Riots and civil disturbances such as Broadwater Farm, or those at Brixton, erupted very suddenly and without any prior warning having been given to the police, and if such riots took place in Northumbria it would be pointless to require the chief constable to draw the equipment from the Home Secretary's central store in order to deal with them. Moreover, the Northumbria police would not have been trained in the use of the baton rounds.

This argument by the police authority would require even more words to be read into the section. Not only would it be necessary to write into it a requirement for the consent of the authority before any service could be used by the force, but then to add an exception to it saying "save in an emergency."

I do not consider that the general scheme of powers under the 1964 Act justifies any such reading of section 41. The judgment of what is an emergency must be within the operational powers of the chief constable, unsubjected to any control on the part of the police authority. It was submitted to us in argument that not even the Broadwater Farm or Brixton riots could be regarded as "emergency," but in my view that decision would be for the chief constable and not for the authority.

Accordingly, the Divisional Court was mistaken in construing section 41 as not authorising the Home Secretary to supply the equipment from the central store in the way described in paragraph 4 of the circular. All he is proposing to do is to hold the equipment and make it available for supply on request and without charge to such extent as appears to him to be best calculated to promote the efficiency of the police.

The second question is, on the assumption that section 41 gives no statutory power to the Home Secretary to supply this equipment to chief constables, then does the royal prerogative supply it?

Although there has always been what is called the war prerogative, which is the Crown's right to make war and peace, counsel for the police authority has submitted that there is no corresponding prerogative to enforce the keeping of what is popularly called the Queen's peace within the realm. He based his submission by reference to Chitty, *A Treatise on the Law of the Prerogatives of the*

Crown (1820) and pointed out that there is no power referred to in it for keeping the peace. It does, however, contain an extensive section on "the King as the Fountain of Justice" and courts and gaols (see chap. 7, p. 75 ff). The argument is that if there was no prerogative power to keep the peace in 1820, at which date no organised police force existed, then all police forces exist and are controlled only by the later statutes by which they were created, and there is no residual prerogative power to draw on in cases of necessity.

In contrast to this submission, Professor. O Hood Phillips in *Constitutional and Administrative Law* (6th ed. 1978) ch. 21, p. 399 states unequivocally:

> "Although the preservation of the peace, which is a royal prerogative, is one of the primary functions of any state, the administration of the police has always been on a local basis in this country."[1]

It may be that the King's power to establish courts and gaols and to administer justice was no more than the larger power to see that the peace was kept. There were constables long before the establishment of Peel's metropolitan police in 1829.

At all events, the assumption was early made that keeping the peace was part of the prerogative. The position of the Home Secretary is that he is one of a number of Secretaries of State through whom the prerogative power is exercised. In *Harrison* v. *Bush* (1855) 5E. & B. 344 at 353, 119 E.R. 509 at 513 Lord Campbell C.J. stated:

> "In practice, to the Secretary of State for the Home Department . . . belongs peculiarly the maintenance of the peace within the Kingdom, with the superintendance of the administration of justice as far as the Royal prerogative is involved in it."

That case does not establish the existence of the power with regard to the police, but only that status of the Home Secretary.

In *Coomber (Surveyor of Taxes)* v. *Berks Justices* (1883) 9 App. Cas. 61 the question for decision was whether a block of buildings comprising county assize courts and a police station were liable to income tax under Schedule A. If they were erected as part of the function of government in the administration of justice, then, notwithstanding the fact that they were built by the country and paid for out of the country rates, the Crown's exemption from payment of taxes would apply. The House of Lords held that they both were exempt, the police being ultimately a Crown responsibility. Lord Blackburn said (at 67):

> "I do not think it can be disputed that the administration of justice, both criminal and civil, and the preservation of order and prevention of crime by means of what is now called police, are among the most important functions of Government, nor that by the constitution of this country these functions do, of common right, belong to the Crown. In England a subject may have a franchise, giving him the right to administer justice in a particular locality in Courts held by him; and he may also have a right to name the constables. In early times, such local franchises were of value for the revenue derived from the fees, and, no doubt, as increasing the local influence of the grantee. But it was always held that on a proceeding in quo warranto the Crown could call on the person in possession of such a franchise to shew his title, on the ground that they were among the matters *quae mere spectant ad regem*, and that unless he shewed a title by grant from the Crown, or by prescription, the franchises were seized and he was ousted. (See Comyn's Digest, Quo Warranto A, and the authorities there collected). In the present case there is no question raised as to any franchise in the hands of a subject. From very early times, judges acting under the King's commission went down to administer

[1] (7th ed., 1987) p. 407.

justice in countries. The sheriff, the head officer of the county, but appointed by the Crown, was always called upon to attend them, and to provide lodging and accommodation for them. He did this at the cost of the county. I do not stop to inquire by what machinery the cost was in early times defrayed. It is now provided for by the statutes referred to, and comes out of the county rate. The sheriff also was bound to raise the hue and cry, and call out the *posse comitatus* of the county whenever it was necessary for any police purposes; in so doing he was acting for the Crown, but the burthen fell on the inhabitants of the county. By modern legislation, the county police are arrayed at the expense of the county, defrayed by a police rate on the county, supplemented, in some cases, by grants from the imperial revenues."

A recent instance of exercise of the royal prerogative in the context of preserving law and order was the creation of the Criminal Injuries Compensation Board in 1964 (see *R.* v. *Criminal Injuries Compensation Board, ex p. Lain* [1967] 2 All E.R. 770 at 777, 780–781, 783–784, [1967] 2 Q.B. 864 at 881, 886, 891 *per* Lord Parker C.J., Diplock L.J. and Ashworth J.). By its very nature, the subject of maintaining the Queen's peace and keeping law and order has over the years inevitably been dealt with by statute much more than the war prerogative has been. Instances of the way in which such a prerogative may be used are more readily provided by example than by being placed in categories, but I have no doubt that the Crown does have a prerogative power to keep the peace, which is bound up with its undoubted right to see that crime is prevented and justice administered. This is subject to the next submission of counsel for the police authority, which was that any prerogative power may be lost by being overtaken by statute law.

Counsel for the police authority adopted the dictum of Dicey in *Introduction to the Study of the Law of the Constitution* (10th ed., 1959) p. 424 that the prerogative is "the residue of discretionary or arbitrary authority, which at any given time is legally left in the hands of the Crown." *A-G* v. *De Keyser's Royal Hotel Ltd.* [1920] A.C. 508 [1920] All E.R. Rep. 80 was the decision which establishes that in the exercise of the war prerogative the Crown's power to requisition property had been limited by Defence Act 1842 so as to require compensation to be paid to the subject. Lord Dunedin said ([1920] A.C. 508 at 546, [1920] All E.R. Rep 80 at 86):

"Inasmuch as the Crown is a party to every Act of Parliament it is logical enough to consider that when the Act deals with something which before the Act could be effected by the prerogative, and specially empowers the Crown to do the same thing, but subject to conditions, the Crown assents to that, and by the Act, to the prerogative being curtailed."

Lord Parmoor stated ([1920] A.C. 508 at 575, [1920] All E.R. Rep.80 at 109):

"The constitutional principle is that when the power of the Executive to interfere with the property or liberty of subjects has been placed under Parliamentary control, and directly regulated by statute, the Executive no longer derives its authority from the Royal Prerogative of the Crown but from Parliament, and that in exercising such authority the Executive is bound to observe the restrictions which Parliament has imposed in favour of the subject."

Counsel for the police authority also placed reliance on the speech of Lord Atkinson (see [1920] A.C. 508 at 539, [1920] All E.R. Rep. 80 at 92).

It is clear that the Crown cannot act under the prerogative if to do so would be incompatible with statute. What is said here is that the Home Secretary's proposal under the circular would be inconsistent with the powers expressly or impliedly conferred on the police authority by section 4 of the 1964 Act. The Divisional Court rejected that submission for reasons with which I wholly agree, namely that section 4 does not expressly grant a monopoly, and that granted the possibility of an authority which declines to provide equipment required by the chief constable there is every reason not to imply a parliamentary intent to create one.

The last submission of counsel for the police authority was that if there is a prerogative power it can only be used in emergency and that this does not allow its use beforehand in circumstances of peace and quiet.

One need only quote, and adapt, two passages from the speeches in *Burmah Oil Co. (Burma Trading) Ltd.* v. *Lord Advocate* [1964] 2 All E.R. 348 at 353, 382, [1965] A.C. 75 at 100, 144. That was a case concerning the war prerogative, but the same point was taken. Lord Reid said: ". . . it would be very strange if the law prevented or discouraged necessary preparations until a time when it would probably be too late for them to be effective." Lord Pearce said:

> "The prerogative power in the emergency of war must be one power, whether the peril is merely threatening or has reached the ultimate stage of crisis. Bulwarks are as necessary for the public safety when they are constructed in good time against a foreseen invasion as when they are hastily improvised after the enemy has landed. The Crown must have power to act before the ultimate crisis arises . . ."

The same reasoning must apply to the provision of equipment to the police, and to their being trained in its use, in times when there is reason to apprehend outbreaks of riot and serious civil disturbance. The steps contemplated by the circular are within prerogative powers, and in my view the declaration now asked for should not be granted.

I would dismiss this appeal and allow the appeal on the Home Secretary's cross-notice.

NOURSE L.J. . . . References in reported cases and authorities texts to a prerogative of keeping the peace within the realm are admittedly scarce. The police authority relies especially on Chitty's silence as to that matter in his *Treatise on the Law of the Prerogatives of the Crown* (1820). I do not think that the scarcity is of any real significance. It has not at any stage in our history been practicable to identify all the prerogative powers of the Crown. It is only by a process of piecemeal decision over a period of centuries that particular powers are seen to exist or not to exist, as the case may be. From time to time a need for more exact definition arises. The present need arises from a difference of view between the Secretary of State and a police authority over what is necessary to maintain public order, a phenomenon which has been observed only in recent times. There has probably never been a comparable occasion for investigating a prerogative of keeping the peace within the realm.

The Crown's prerogative of making war and peace, the war prerogative, has never been doubted. Its origins may not have been fully explored. Here it is important to remember that the royal prerogative was never regarded as a collection of mere powers, to be exercised or not at the will of the Sovereign. The King owed certain duties to his subjects, albeit duties of imperfect obligation whose performance could not be enforced by legal process. Nowadays these duties are taken to be expressed in the coronation oath, whose modern form derives from the Coronation Oath Act 1688. They included a duty to protect the lives and property of the King's subjects. Thus, *Chitty* p. 7:

> "The *duties* arising from the relation of sovereign and subject are reciprocal. Protection, that is, the security and governance of his dominions according to law, is the duty of the sovereign; and allegiance and subjection, with reference to the same criterion, the constitution and laws of the country, form, in return, the duty of the governed, as will be more fully noticed hereafter. We have already partially mentioned this duty of the sovereign, and have

observed that the prerogatives are vested in him for the benefit of his subjects, and that his Majesty is under, and not above, the laws. This doctrine is laid down by several writers; and is expressly ratified by the coronation oath, wherein the King swears to govern according to law, to execute judgment in mercy, and to maintain the established religion . . ."

A duty of protection seems to have been recognised from earliest times. In *Calvin's Case* (1608) 7 Co. Rep. 1a at 4b, 77 E.R. 377 at 382 we find this statement based on some observations of Glanville on the connection which there ought to be between a lord and his tenant by homage: "But between the Sovereign and the subject there is without comparison a higher and greater connexion: for as the subject oweth to the King his true and faithful ligeance and obedience, so the Sovereign is to govern and protect his subjects . . ." A later passage is to the same effect (7 Co. Rep. 1a at 5a. 77 E.R. 377 at 382): ". . . ligeance is the mutual bond and obligation between the King and his subjects, whereby subjects are called his liege subjects, because they are bound to obey and serve him; and he is called their liege lord, because he should maintain and defend them."

These passages express the essential theory (and originally the practice) of feudalism, a system developed to remedy the chaos and perils to human life and property which succeeded the decline of the Roman empire in Europe. Although we should be careful not to propound too romanticised a view of the feudal system in England, I feel sure that the great Plantagenet kings, notably Edward I, would never have questioned the existence of a duty or prerogative of protection. In *China Navigation Co Ltd*. v. *A-G* [1932] 2 K.B. 197, [1932] All E.R. Rep. 626, the only modern decision on the point, it was held that the Crown is under no legal duty to afford military protection to British subjects abroad. But the question whether there is a duty at home was left open: see, in particular, the judgment of Lawrence L.J. ([1932] 2 K.B. 197 at 221–223, [1932] All E.R. Rep. 626 at 634–635).

Reverting to the war prerogative, it is natural to suppose that it was founded, at least in part, on the wider prerogative of protection. That seems to have been the view of Lord Erskine, speaking in the House of Lords in 1808: 'What is termed the war prerogative of the King is created by the perils and exigencies of war for the public safety, and by its perils and exigencies it is therefore limited."
(See *Chitty*, p. 50.) The wider prerogative must have extended as much to unlawful acts within the realm as to the menaces of a foreign power. There is no historical or other basis for denying to the war prerogative a sister prerogative of keeping the peace within the realm.

I have already expressed the view that the scarcity of references in the books to the prerogative of keeping the peace within the realm does not disprove that it exists. Rather it may point to an unspoken assumption that it does. That assumption is, I think, made in the judgment of Lord Campbell C.J. in *Harrison* v. *Bush* (1855) 5 E. & B. 344 at 353, 119 E.R. 509 at 513. Professor Hood Phillips has taken it for granted, and so may other learned authors whose works do not specifically refer to it. Of especial importance for their demonstration of the Crown's part in keeping the peace are these words of Lord Blackburn, which may have been based on Blackstone (I Bl Com. (14th edn) 343): "The sheriff also was bound to raise the hue and cry, and call out the posse comitatus of the country whenever it was necessary for any police purposes; in so doing he was acting for the Crown, but the burthen fell on the inhabitants of the country."
(See *Coomber (Surveyor of Taxes)* v. *Berks Justices* (1883) 9 App.Cas. 61 at 67.)

The posse comitatus was a civilian body, consisting in theory of all the able-bodied male inhabitants of the country, other than those in holy orders. In *R.* v. *Pinney* (1832) 3 B & Ad 947 at 962, 110 E.R. 349 at 355 (the case of the Bristol riots) Littledale J; another judge of great learning, said that, although the posse comitatus might be called out by a justice of the peace, it was generally done by the sheriff. This duty was given statutory recognition by the Sheriffs Act 1887, s.8(1) of which imposed liability to a fine on any who failed to respond to the sheriff's call. Although that particular provision has now been repealed (see s.10(2) of and Schedule 3, Part. III to the Criminal Law Act 1967), the sheriff's duties in keeping the peace, along with his other common law powers and duties, were preserved by section. 39(1)(d) of the 1887 Act. Their continued existence is attested by the warning which the Privy Council gave the sheriffs in 1939 that, in the event of invasion, they might have to exercise their powers to call on the civilian population to assist them in the defence of their counties: see 42 Halsbury's Laws (4th ed.) para. 1132, note I. True it is that for many years now it has been the invariable practice to leave the maintenance of public order to the police, who are for all relevant purposes independent of the executive. But the powers and duties of the sheriff show that the Crown retains, at the least, a general supportive power, which, if exercisable by one of its officers, is as well exercisable by the Secretary of State. At all events, there being no decision to the contrary, I decline to hold that a power so valuable to the common good no longer exists.

For these reasons I am of the opinion that a prerogative of keeping the peace within the realm existed in medieval times, probably since the Conquest and, particular statutory provision apart, that is has not been surrendered by the Crown in the process of giving its express or implied assent to the modern system of keeping the peace through the agency of independent police forces. I therefore conclude that, if the necessary power had not been available under section 41 of the 1964 Act, the terms and implementation of para. 4 of the Home Office circular would have been within the prerogative powers of the Crown.

Prerogative and Emergencies

Burmah Oil Co. Ltd. v. Lord Advocate
[1965] A.C. 75
House of Lords

The Company's oil installations in Burma (then a British colony) had been destroyed by order of the commander of the British forces in 1942, to prevent them from falling into the hands of the invading Japanese forces who would have found them of great strategic value. The Company (which was registered in Scotland) some years later brought an action in Scotland against the Lord Advocate under the Crown Suits Acts 1857 claiming compensation.

On an appeal to the House of Lords on the preliminary issue their Lordships (Lord Reid, Lord Pearce and Lord Upjohn, Viscount Radcliffe and Lord Hodson dissenting) held that the circumstances of the destruction gave the appellants a right to claim compensation.

LORD REID [after stating the facts said]: The appellants' case is that the demolitions were carried out by an exercise of the royal prerogative. At one time this was denied. It was said that this was an operation which any subject was entitled to carry out in the defence of the country and that neither the Crown nor a subject can have any obligation to pay compensation for such an operation. No doubt there are occasions when a subject is entitled to act on his own initiative in the defence of the realm, particularly if there is no one in authority there to direct him. But I find it impossible to suppose that any subject could have been entitled to carry out these demolitions on his own initiative. As this point was not argued before your Lordships it is unnecessary to deal with it further. So we must now take it that these demolitions were carried out by an exercise of the royal prerogative, and the question for decision is whether such an exercise of the royal prerogative gives any legal right to compensation to the persons who have suffered loss thereby.

It is not easy to discover and decide the law regarding the royal prerogative and the consequences of its exercise. Apart from *In re a Petition of Right*[1] and *Attorney-General* v. *De Keyser's Royal Hotel Ltd.*[2] there have been no cases directly raising the matter for some centuries, and obiter dicta and the views of institutional writers and text writers are not always very helpful. The definition of Dicey (*Law of the Constitution*, (10th ed.) p. 424)), always quoted with approval: "The residue of discretionary or arbitrary authority, which at any given time is legally left in the hands of the Crown," does not take us very far. It is extremely difficult to be precise because in former times there was seldom a clear-cut view of the constitutional position. I think we should beware of looking at older authorities through modern spectacles. We ought not to ignore the many changes in constitutional law and theory which culminated in the Revolution Settlement of 1688–89, and there is practically no authority between that date and 1915. . . . So it appears to me that we must try to see what the position was after it had become clear that sovereignty resided in the King in Parliament. Any rights thereafter exercised by the King (or the executive) alone must be regarded as a part of sovereignty which Parliament chose to leave in his hands. There is no doubt that control of the armed forces has been left to the prerogative (see *Chandler* v. *Director of Public Prosecutions*[3]) subject to the power of Parliament to withhold supply and to refuse to continue legislation essential for the maintenance of a standing army: and so also has the waging of war. . . .

[1] [1915] 3 K.B. 649.
[2] [1920] A.C. 508.
[3] [1964] A.C. 763.

The reason for leaving the waging of war to the King (or now the executive) is obvious. A schoolboy's knowledge of history is ample to disclose some of the disasters which have been due to parliamentary or other outside attempts at control. So the prerogative certainly covers doing all those things in an emergency which are necessary for the conduct of war. It has been suggested that some greater right arises in an extreme emergency, but it would be very strange if the law prevented or discouraged necessary preparations until a time when it would probably be too late for them to be effective. But, as I shall try to show later, there are some kinds of action for which the need only arises in an extreme emergency in face of the enemy, and there the position is different.

There is difficulty in relating the prerogative to modern conditions. In fact no war which has put this country in real peril has been waged in modern times without statutory powers of an emergency character. The taking of property for defence purposes was authorised by statute, not only in the last war and in the 1914 war, but also in the Napoleonic wars, and it could only be taken subject to payment of compensation.

What we have to determine in this case is whether or when, in a case not covered by any statute, property can be taken by virtue for the prerogative without compensation. That could only be an exceptional case, because it would be impracticable to conduct a modern war by use of the prerogative alone, whether or nor compensation was paid. The mobilisation of the industrial and financial resources of the country could not be done without statutory emergency powers. The prerogative is really a relic of a past age, not lost by disuse, but only available for a case not covered by statute. So I would think the proper approach is a historical one: how was it used in former times and how has it been used in modern times?

As regards modern times, extensive investigation in connection with the *De Keyser* case[4] failed to disclose a single instance of taking or interfering with land without payment. And if moveables had been taken without compensation at any time after 1660 I feel sure that historians would have found evidence of that. People in influential positions may have been very willing to give their services but they were very sensitive about property. It would certainly have been a grievance if property had been taken without payment, yet there is no mention of such a grievance either in 1688–89, or at any other time. Negative evidence may not amount to proof, but it is so strong that I would hold it established that prerogative was never used or attempted to be used in that way in modern times before 1914.

As regards earlier times I think that the Ship Money case (*Rex* v. *Hampden*[5]) deserves rather more consideration than it received in the *De Keyser* case[6] or than it has received in this case. In the course of very long and elaborate arguments and opinions, extending to 425 columns in the report, every aspect of the royal prerogative connected with defence was examined and every known precedent was set out and discussed. I have not attempted to study the whole report but I find many instances given where the King paid for goods taken to supply and equip his troops on active service. Some are given by Mr. St. John[7] immediately before the passage in his argument on which the Crown rely. And I have not noticed any reference to any instance in which the King took the property of a subject without payment, except in conditions where both parties were agreed that it was the right and duty of every man to take and use anything he could lay hands on in order to fight the approaching enemy. Looking at some similar passages scattered among the arguments and judgments, I thing that Mr. St. John

---

4 [1920] A.C. 508.
5 (1637) 3 St.Tr. 825.
6 [1920] A.C. 508.
7 3 St.Tr. 826, 890 *et seq.*

must have had that sort of thing in mind in the passage quoted from his argument. And I feel sure that if there were any passage in the report showing any wider use of the prerogative or any argument supporting any wider right we would have been referred to it. What the King was contending for was a right to require his subjects to contribute to defence expenditure. The argument seems to have been that it was the duty of the King to defend his subjects, and that if imminent danger required extraordinary expenditure his subjects must be bound to contribute, because all ought to pay their share of expenditure made for the benefit of all. There is no suggestion that I can find that the King could have avoided at least part of this expenditure even in time of war by taking for nothing supplies or other property required for the conduct of the war. Without further investigation I would not rely too much on this case, but it does seem to indicate that, even at the zenith of the royal prerogative, no one thought that there was any general rule that the prerogative could be exercised, even in times of war or imminent danger, by taking property required for defence without making any payment for it.

Before turning to the cases which arose out of the 1914 war I would make these observations. First, there is nothing novel in the idea that a prerogative right to take property carries with it an obligation to pay compensation: that has apparently always been recognised with regard to the prerogative rights of purveyance and angary. And, secondly, it was well established that taking or destroying property in the course of fighting the enemy did not give rise to any claim for compensation, whether that was done by the armed forces of the Crown or by individuals taking arms to defend their country or by the enemy. What had never been clarified was the question whether compensation was payable when property was taken deliberately for defence purposes, and in modern times such purposes would at least include training of troops, manufacture of munitions, obtaining the wide variety of supplies necessary to maintain the forces on active service, and economic warfare and various purposes essential to the conduct of the war but not immediately concerned with the maintenance of the fighting services. I may say at this point that it was rightly not argued that the fact that property is taken for destruction and not for use can make any difference.

I must now turn to examine the authorities which arose out of the 1914 war. . . .

[His Lordship referred to *In re a Petition of Right*[8] and *De Keyser's* case[9] and continued]: Taking the series of cases which arose out of the 1914 war, the present question never had to be decided and diverse opinions about it were expressed. But my conclusion is that, on balance, the weight of opinion was against there being any general rule that no compensation can be due for loss caused by an exercise of this prerogative . . .

[His Lordship then referred to Scots law,[10] Grotius, *De Jure Belli ac Pacis*, Vattel, *Droit des Gens* the exception of "battle damage" and *United States* v. *Caltex (Phillipines) Inc.*,[11] and continued]: it follows that, in my judgment, the appeals must succeed and I must not seek to anticipate questions which may arise if the facts proved should differ from those averred by the appellants. But there is one matter on which I must say a word to avoid any misunderstanding. I am deciding nothing about the proper measure of compensation. The appellants appear to be claiming the full value of these installations in time of peace. I am holding that they are entitled to compensation, and it will be necessary to consider whether compensation must not be related to their loss in the sense of what difference it

---

[8] [1915] 3 K.B. 649.
[9] [1920] A.C. 508.
[10] The litigation had been conducted on the basis that Scots law was applicable. While Lord Reid did not think that it followed that, because the company was Scottish the relevant law was Scots, nothing turned on the question since there was no material difference between the law of England, the law of Scotland and the law applicable in Burma in 1942: [1965] A.C. 75 at pp. 98–99.
[11] 344 U.S. 149 (1952).

would have made to them if their installations had been allowed to fall into the hands of the enemy instead of being destroyed. . . .

VISCOUNT RADCLIFFE [in the course of his *dissenting* judgment said]: To begin with one must clear the ground with one or two short propositions. There is not in our history any known case in which a court of law has declared such compensation to be due as of right. There is not any known instance in which a subject, having suffered from such a taking, has instituted legal proceedings for the recovery of such compensation in a court of law. No payment has been identified as having been made by the Crown in recognition of a legal right to such compensation irrespective of the institution of legal proceedings for its recovery. Lastly, no text writer of authority has stated that there is this legal right under our law.

If, then, such a legal right is to be declared for the first time, its existence has to be deduced from some general current of lawyers' thinking so strong as to make the denial of it unacceptable in principle. Certainly, the war prerogative itself has been acknowledged for many centuries: has there been a similar tradition of a right to compensation, not as something that ought to be provided by Parliament or Crown on a fair understanding of their public duty, but as something to which the subject is absolutely entitled by the judgment of a court of law?

We must get what help we can from the English authorities. I should say that they fall into two groups for this purpose, first, those decided prior to the end of the seventeenth century and, secondly, those of later date, which second group means in practice cases decided in relation to the war of 1914–18. I agree that there is a great gulf fixed between these two, if only because so much that could be said about the war prerogative as an active power before the days of the Civil War has been rendered out of date by the encroachment of statutory provision upon the field of the prerogative and its consequent erosion. I do not think, therefore, that the first group calls for anything but brief notice.

What we get from them down to *The Saltpetre Case* in 1607, is merely a general recognition that in times of sudden peril to general safety, such as the outbreak of fire or the arrival of enemy forces or a storm threatening a ship, the common law authorised private property rights to be ignored, as by destroying houses, entering or occupying land, damaging crops and trees, or jettisoning cargo. The law provided no remedy for this, given the emergency; a man must suffer for the sake of the common weal. The actions envisaged are not specifically those of the Crown, nor are they spoken of as prerogative acts: on the contrary, they seem to be acts of one's "neighbours" acting in the public interest. The background is one of a rather rudimentary social organisation, poor communications and local self-help.

The Saltpetre Case[12] is on a different footing, though I do not regard it as having any direct bearing on the present case. There the judges recognised in the Crown a prerogative right to enter upon the land of subjects in order to dig for and acquire saltpetre. The justification for this was said to be that saltpetre was a muniment required for the defence of the realm, but the right was not treated as an emergency or war-time prerogative, nor was it limited to the occasion of war. The court prescribed an elaborate set of conditions subject to which this right was to be exercisable, including an obligation to restore and make good the land dug up. It is odd that among all these conditions they did not mention an obligation to pay the owner for the value of his saltpetre (which was no royal mineral), but, since they described and, I think, intended to justify the taking of it as a "purveyance," they may well have meant to imply the necessity of payment, since purveyance as a royal prerogative was historically a pre-emptive right of purchase or hire for the

[12] 12 Co.Rep. 12.

use of the King's household or his castles and garrisons. . . . What is interesting in this decision and at any rate of some importance is that the prerogative of the Crown to override property rights in cases of public extremity is, in effect, deduced from the old common law rule that "every man may come upon my land for the defence of the realm" and that "for the commonwealth a man shall suffer damage"; and the familiar instances appear, destined to be resorted to so often in this context, of gravel dug for the making of bulwarks, houses plucked down against the spread of fire and suburbs destroyed to secure a city's defence. These are not put forward as compensable (to use the ancient word) actions, nor would they have been compensable by the old common law right of necessity: but is is said that, "after the danger is over, the trenches and bulwarks ought to be removed so that the owner shall not have prejudice by his inheritance." This last qualification, which may conceivably be a reflection of Magna Carta's pledge against disseisin, calls for restoration of land to its former state, but the judges do not seem to have had in mind anything amounting to indemnity against loss by occupation and disturbance.

Once we leave the times of the Spanish Armada and the seventeenth century there is nothing to say about the war prerogative until the period of the French Revolutionary or Napoleonic Wars. History gives us nothing firm to go upon with regard to the Jacobite landings of 1715 and 1745. What we do know is that, so far as concerned the taking of land for defence purposes in time of peace or war, Parliament from the beginning of the eighteenth century onwards had begun to step in and to confer and regulate by statute the necessary power. It was invariable practice to require the payment of full compensation. . . .

To treat the matter this way seems to me equivalent to saying that in the crisis of the war emergency the sovereign power, when in the face of the enemy, has authority to commit acts of war upon the property of its own subjects without incurring any legal liability for the consequences. It is a harsh doctrine, but the emergencies of war are harsh too. . . .

My second conclusion is that, where war damage is concerned, the long-standing absence of any recognition that there is jurisdiction in the courts to award compensation is based on sound considerations of public policy. Such damage is a matter, being unpredictable in extent and range, that must be controlled by that department of the sovereign power that is responsible for the raising and expenditure of public money. There is not a legal line between those divisions of that damage that carry a legal right to compensation and those that do not. Damage inflicted by the enemy may be terrible individual loss, and it is certainly suffered in the common cause. Moreover, it is likely to fall with disproportionate weight on some citizens who suffer in that cause, a fact familiar in the last war to those whose homes or places of business were close to an object of strategic importance and so peculiarly exposed to air or missile attack. Damage inflicted by one's own side, accidentally or to prevent its capture and the enrichment of the enemy, does not seem to me different in kind. . . . And no one can find an equation between the personal loss that war inflicts and its inroads upon property.

None of this is an argument against the propriety or, indeed, urgent desirability of the state providing compensation schemes to take care, so far as possible, of all war damage, of person or property. But it is for those who fill and empty the public purse to decide when, by whom, on what conditions and within what limitations such compensation is to be made available. After all, states lose wars as well as win them: and at the conclusion of a war that has seen massive destruction, whether self-inflicted through the medium of a "scorched earth" policy or inflicted by the enemy, there may well be urgent claims for reconstruction priorities that make it impossible in advance to mortgage the public treasury to legal claims for full individual compensation for such destruction as we have now to consider. Indeed, what in legal terms does "compensation" mean in this case?

The act of destruction was lawful, that is conceded (though I should myself prefer to say that it was not unlawful), so we are not to think of damages and the legal rules for their assessment. Has the law any principle for measuring compensation as a legal right when an act has been done in circumstances so special that the ordinary conceptions of property do not apply to it? Can the state be asked to pay a requisition price for something for which there was at the time no conceivable purchaser? I do not think so, but, if this action is to proceed on its way, it is better that I should not trench further on this point.

For the reasons that I have given I think that this appeal ought to be dismissed. . . .

Appeals allowed.

Note

The War Damage Act 1965 nullified this decision retrospectively so far as *war* damage by the Crown is concerned. The Act does not cover *unlawful* acts by officers or servants of the Crown or the mere taking possession of property by requisition or angary.

Act of State
Salaman v. Secretary of State for India
[1906] 1 K.B. 613
Court of Appeal

Salaman, the trustee in bankruptcy of the Prince Victor Albert Jay Duleep Singh, brought an action against the Secretary of State for India, as successor to the East India Company under the Government of India Act 1858. Shortly before the passing of that Act, the East India Company entered into various agreements with the regents of the infant Maharajah of the Punjab, by which the Maharajah resigned the sovereignty of the Punjab all the property of the State was confiscated to the East India Company and the Company was to pay a pension to the Maharajah. The Maharajah died in 1893 and was succeeded by his son, the Prince, who went bankrupt in 1902.

The plaintiff allegedthat the Company, and subsequently the Secretary of State for India, became trustee of the amount of the pension; that as such trustee the defendant was liable to pay the arrears of the pension accrued during the Maharajah's lifetime: and that the Company and afterwards the defendant, became possessed of certain *private* property of the Maharajah as guardians, and afterwards as trustees, and that the defendant was liable to account therefore to the plaintiff.

Bucknill J., at chambers, dismissed the action on the ground that it was frivolous and vexatious and an abuse of the process of the court.

The plaintiff appealed to the Court of Appeal. The Court (Vaughan Williams, Stirling and Fletcher Moulton L.JJ.) held that inasmuch as the facts stated in the claim disclosed that the various acts done were "acts of State" done by the East India Company as trustees for the Crown, the action ought to be dismissed as frivolous and vexatious, but that an opportunity should be given to amend the claim and adduce evidence in support. Fletcher Moulton L.J. thought that the claim relating to the *private* property of the Maharajah might be capable of substantiation, though the evidence might show that even here what was done was in the circumstances an act of State.

The plaintiff then applied for leave to amend the claim, and filed an affidavit in support. The Court of Appeal (Fletcher Moulton L.J. dissenting) refused the application and dismissed the appeal, being of opinion that the further facts brought forward only tended to show that the taking possession of the Maharajah's private property was an act of State, and that there was no intention of holding the property as trustee.

The following extract is taken from the judgment read by Fletcher Moulton L.J. at the original hearing in the Court of Appeal.

FLETCHER MOULTON L.J. . . . An act of State is essentially an exercise of sovereign power, and hence cannot be challenged, controlled, or interfered with by municipal courts. Its sanction is not that of law, but that of sovereign power, and, whatever it be, municipal courts must accept it as it is without question. But it may and often must be part of their duty to take cognisance of it. For instance, if an act is relied upon as being an act of State, and as thus affording an answer to claims made by a subject, the courts must decide whether it was in truth an act of State, and what was its nature and extent, an example of this is to be found in the case of *Forester* v. *Secretary of State for India in Council*.[1] But in such an inquiry the court must confine itself to ascertaining what the act of State in fact was, and not what in their opinion it ought to have been. In like manner, municipal courts may have to consider the results of acts of State—that is, their effects on the rights of individuals, and even of the Government itself.

[1] (1872) L.R. Ind.App Supp. Vol. at p. 10.

Acts of State are not all of one kind; their nature and consequences may differ in an infinite variety of ways, and thus may profoundly affect the position of municipal courts with regard to them. For instance, an act of State may fix the relations between two States, each of which continues to possess an independent existence. The consequences of such an act of State are entirely beyond the cognisance of municipal courts, because they do not administer treaty obligations between independent States. An example of such an act of State may be found in the case of *Carnatic (Nabob)* v. *East India Co.*[2] But the object and effect of an act of State are not necessarily of this kind. Its intention and effect may be to modify and create rights as between the Government and individuals, who are, or who are about to become, subjects of the Government. In such cases the rights accruing therefrom may have to be adjudicated upon by municipal courts. Let me take a simple example. Let us suppose that a Government by an act of State annexes a neighbouring country, and formally takes over all the property and liabilities of the former ruler, and that part of such property consists of debts due to him. The Government is not compelled to collect such debts *vi et armis*; it may avail itself of the assistance of its courts of law for the purpose, in the same way as though the debts had accrued due to it otherwise than by an act of State. But in deciding on such a claim the courts must loyally accept the act of State as effective. Evidence that the debt was due to the former ruler would thereby become evidence of its being due to the existing Government; and I see no reason why in such a case a claim of a converse character might not equally be entertained by municipal courts, and a subject recover from the existing Government by the processes of law applicable to such a case any debts due from the former ruler. The judgments in the case of *Frith* v. *R.*[3] seem to me to give support to this view.

The true view of an act of State appears to me to be that it is a catastrophic change, constituting a new departure. Municipal law has nothing to do with the act of change by which this new departure is effected. Its duty is simply to accept the new departure; and its power and its duty to adjudicate upon, and enforce, rights of individuals, or of the Government, in the future, appear to me to be precisely the same whether the origin of such rights be an act of State or not. But, although this be so, it must not be supposed that the principles of interpretation applicable to an act of State are the same as those which apply to other acts. For instance, if an act of State be expressed in a document purporting to confer benefits on an individual, it by no means necessarily follows that there is any intention to create a contract, or that the document should be construed by the same canons of interpretation as would be adopted in the case of a contract between two individuals. A Government in the exercise of its sovereign power may well desire to reserve to itself discretionary powers quite inconsistent with contractual relations. There is no presumption in the case of an act of State that this is not the case, and, if the language of the document, and the circumstances of the case, point to such a conclusion, the court is bound to accept it, however vague and indefinite it may make the effect of the act of State. An example of this is to be found, in my opinion, in the present case, though for other reasons it may not be necessary to decide the point.

Starting, therefore, from the premiss that the claims are not necessarily beyond the cognisance of municipal courts, merely because their origin is connected more or less directly with an act of State, I proceed to examine specifically the several heads of claim, to ascertain their nature, and to determine what it is the court is asked to do. ...

[His Lordship, after finding that the first two heads of claim disclosed acts of State, proceeded to consider the claim relating to the taking and sale of the private property of the Maharajah and continued]: The plaintiff asserts that, so far as the

---

[2] (1793) 2 Ves. 56.
[3] (1872) L.R. 7 Ex. 365.

Company thus dealt with the private property of the Maharajah it was on his behalf and for his benefit, and was done not by virtue of the "Terms of Lahore" but under the ample powers which they possessed as having the infant under their care and his property in their absolute control. The plaintiff does not set up a claim in tort on the ground that this was a wrongful conversion. On the contrary, he treats the action of the Company as perfectly lawful, considering the position of the parties, but claims that such action on the part of the Company did not change the beneficial interest in the property, and that the Company held the proceeds in trust for the Maharajah during his lifetime and that therefore the defendant now holds them in trust for the plaintiff as trustee in bankruptcy of his residuary legatee.

Now, if the "Terms of Lahore" fully define the act of State so far as it concerns the property of the late Maharajah, I think that the above constitutes a claim of a nature such that the court ought not to prevent the plaintiff raising it, and obtaining a decision upon it, by the ordinary process of an action. But I do not shut my eyes to the possibility that the defendant may meet this claim by an allegation that apart from the question whether this property passed to the Company in accordance with Clause II of the "Terms of Lahore," the seizure and sale of this property was in itself an act of State—an intentional exercise of soverign power independent of the rights taken by the Company at the time of the granting of the "Terms of Lahore"—and that such act of State, like all acts of State, cannot be reviewed or criticised by a municipal court. If this allegation can be substantiated it would bean answer to the plaintiff's claim.

An act of State need not rest upon or be expressed in documents. It may be evidenced by the nature of the acts done and the circumstances under which they were done; and, if an act is in this way shown to have been actually done in such a way as to constitute it an act of State, it is no answer to say that it was in excess of previous or contemporary acts of State to which it might be expected to conform.

An excellent instance of such an independent act of State so evidenced is given by the case to which I have just referred [*Secretary of State in Council of India* v. *Kamachee Boye Sahaba*[4] where the seizure of the private property of the deceased Rajah of Tanjore by the Company and their disregard of the claims thereon (except so far as they chose in their own absolute discretion to recognise them) was held by the court to be in itself an act of State, though probably not coming within the act of State which annexed the territory and took possession of the State property. But in that case the court heard and decided this as a fact and upon evidence. In the present case no such subsequent and independent act of State is as yet alleged. It will be for the defendant to allege it, and probably it will be for him to prove it, if he is in a position to do so. . . .

Note

See *Blackburn* v. *Att.-Gen.* [1971] 1 W.L.R. 1037 (C.A.), *ante* for the treaty-making power of the Crown in relation to Parliament and the courts.

See also *McWhirter* v. *Att.-Gen.* [1972] C.M.L.R. 882 (C.A.), where application was made for a declaration that the executive acts leading to and culminating in the signing of the Treaty of Accession to the Treaty of Rome were unlawful as being contrary to the Bill of Rights, which declares that the full power of government is vested in the Crown. The originating summons was struck out as disclosing no reasonable cause of action, vexatious and an abuse of the process of the court. The courts, said Lord Denning M.R., do not let treaties signed by the Crown impinge on the rights or liberties of any men unless and until they are incorporated into our law by Act of Parliament.

[4] (1859) 7 Moo.Ind.App. 476; 13 Moo.P.C.C. 22.

Johnstone v. Pedlar
[1921] 2 A.C. 262
House of Lords

Pedlar, a naturalised citizen of the United States, was arrested in Dublin (which was at that time within the United Kingdom), convicted of illegal drilling and sentenced to six months' imprisonment. He brought an action in the Irish courts against Johnstone, Chief Commissioner of the Dublin Metropolitan Police, for the return of a cheque and certain money which were found on him at the time of his arrest and had since been detained by the police. Johnstone contended (paragraph 3 of defence) that the money and cheque were the property of an illegal association and were in Pedlar's possession for the illegal purpose of the said association. He contended, further (paragraph 4 of defence), that the plaintiff was an alien and that the money and cheque were taken and detained by an officer of the Crown by the direction of the Crown as an act of State for the defence of the realm and for the prevention of crime. On the latter point, he produced a certificate signed by the Chief Secretary for Ireland, formally ratifying the seizure and detention. Johnstone was successful before Pim J. and the Irish Divisional Court but the Irish Court of Appeal found for Pedlar.

Johnstone now appealed to the House of Lords. The Court (Viscount Finlay, Viscount Cave, Lord Atkinson, Lord Sumner and Lord Phillimore) dismissed his appeal.

VISCOUNT FINLAY: . . . The case turns upon the question whether the defence of "Act of State" is available as against the present plaintiff. Paragraph 3 of the defence was not proved.

It is the settled law of this country, applicable as much to Ireland as to England, that if a wrongful act has been committed against the person or the property of any person, the wrongdoer cannot set up as a defence that the act was done by the command of the Crown. The Crown can do no wrong, and the Sovereign cannot be sued *in tort*,[1] but the person who did the act is liable in damages, as any private person would be. This rule of law has, however, been held subject to qualification in the case of acts committed abroad against a foreigner. If an action be brought in the British courts in such a case, it is open to the defendant to plead that the act was done by the orders of the British Government, or that after it had been committed it was adopted by the British Government. In any such case the act is regarded as an act of State of which a municipal court cannot take cognisance. The foreigner who has sustained injury must seek redress against the British Government through his own Government by diplomatic or other means. This was established in 1848 in the well-known case of *Buron* v. *Denman*.[2] The defendant in that case, Captain Denman, was a British naval officer engaged on the coast of Africa in measures for the suppression of the slave trade. The plaintiff was a Spaniard engaged in that trade. The acts in respect of which the action was brought were the destruction by the defendant of the barracoons in which plaintiff kept slaves for shipment, and the release of the slaves. The case was tried at Bar, and the summing up was delivered by Parke B. He laid down the law with regard to acts of State, as I have above stated it, and the jury found for the defendant.

This doctrine has no application to any case in which the plaintiff is a British subject. If authority be wanted for the proposition that a British subject's right of action for any wrong to his person or property is not subject to this qualification with regard to acts of State, it is enough to refer to the case of *Walker* v. *Baird*.[3] In

[1] [But see now Crown Proceedings Act 1947, s. 2.]
[2] (1848) 2 Ex. 167.
[3] [1892] A.C. 491.

that case the officers of the Crown had, with the authority of the Government, seized a lobster factory in Newfoundland belonging to British subjects. An action was brought in the courts of Newfoundland against the officers engaged. The Superior Court of Newfoundland held that, in an action of this description, in which the plaintiffs are British subjects, for a trespass within British territory in time of peace, it was no answer to say in exclusion of the jurisdiction of the municipal courts that the trespass was an act of state. An appeal to His Majesty in Council was dismissed. Lord Herschell said[4] that the suggestion that these acts could be justified as acts of State was wholly untenable.

The cases in which the defence of "Act of State" has hitherto been recognised have been cases in which the acts complained of were committed out of British territory. The plaintiffs have been foreigners, and no question arose as to their being in any sense subjects of the British Crown, as it might have arisen if the wrongs complained of had been done in British territory. An alien in British territory is normally regarded as a British subject for the time being in virtue of local allegiance, and it is for this reason that, in dealing with the defence of "Act of State," it is often said that the act must have been abroad as well as against a foreigner in order that the defence should succeed.

The plaintiff is not a subject of the British Crown, but he was, at the time of his arrest, within British territory. It was contended for him that he must be treated for the purposes of the present case as a British subject, inasmuch as he was at the time resident in Ireland. Lord Hale, in his *Pleas of the Crown* (Vol. 1, p. 542), after discussing a statute of Henry VIII (21 Hen. 8, c.11) giving to any of the King's subjects whose goods have been taken away the right to a writ of restitution on conviction of the thief, says: "Tho the statute speak of the King's subjects, it extends to aliens robbed: for tho they are not the King's natural-born subjects, they are the King's subjects, when in England, by local allegiance." The subject of a State at peace with His Majesty, while permitted to reside in this country, is under the King's protection and allegiance, and may be convicted of high treason in respect of acts committed here.

The proposition put forward on behalf of the appellant was that residence in this country does not put an alien in the same position as a British subject in respect of acts of State of the Government, and does not entitle him to bring an action against a *tortfeasor*, whose act has been ordered or adopted by the Government. I am quite unable to accept this proposition as a correct statement of our law. On such a view of the law, aliens in this country, instead of having the protection of British law, would be at the mercy of any department entitled to use the name of the Crown for an "Act of State." It would have effects upon aliens in the country of a far-reaching nature as to person and property. If an alien be wrongfully arrested, even by order of the Crown, it cannot be doubted that a writ of habeas corpus is open to him, and it would be surprising if he has not the right to recover damages from the person who has wrongfully imprisoned him. He has corresponding rights as regards his property. I am unable to find any ground either of principle or of authority for a proposition so sweeping, which would profoundly modify the position in this country of many aliens whose conduct, while resident here, has been quite without reproach. . . .

It follows that this appeal must be dismissed with costs.

Appeal dismissed.

---

[4] [1892] A.C. 491 at p. 497.

Nissan v. Attorney-General
[1970] A.C. 179
House of Lords

Nissan, a citizen of the United Kingdom and Colonies, was lessee of a hotel in Cyprus, an independent republic in the Commonwealth. The hotel was occupied by British forces for several months as part of a truce force under an agreement between the governments of the United Kingdom and Cyprus for the purpose of restoring peace in the civil strife between the Greek and Turkish communities. The British forces then continued to occupy the hotel for a period as part of a United Nations Peace-keeping Force, on the recommendation of the Security Council of the United Nations and with the consent of the Cyprus Government. Nissan brought an action against the Crown in England, claiming declarations that he was entitled to compensation for damage to the contents of the hotel and the destruction of stores, on the ground that this was a lawful exercise of the prerogative; and that the Crown was liable in damages for trespass to chattels by the British troops.

This case was fought on four preliminary issues, *viz.* whether the British troops in the first period were agents of the Cyprus Government, whether in the second period they were agents of the United Nations, whether there was a contract (express or implied) that Nissan would be compensated, and whether the acts of the British forces were acts of State. It being decided that the troops were not the agents of either the Cyprus Government or the United Nations, and the question of contract being left to the trial court, the question remained whether the Crown was liable to pay compensation for the loss and damage.

John Stephenson J. thought the matter was non-justiciable as an act of State. The Court of Appeal (Lord Denning M.R., Winn and Danckwerts L.JJ.) held that the Crown was liable to compensate on various grounds. The House of Lords (Lord Reid, Lord Morris of Borth-y-Gest, Lord Pearce, Lord Wilberforce and Lord Pearson) dismissed the appeal by the Attorney-General. Their Lordships (other than Lord Reid) held that the acts concerned were not themselves acts of State, although they were incidental to an act of State, *viz.* the agreement with the Cyprus Government; Lord Pearce, like Lord Denning M.R. in the Court of Appeal, thought there was an exercise of the prerogative (involving an obligation to pay compensation, as it was not covered by the War Damage Act 1965).

LORD REID [in the course of his judgment said]: The next question is whether taking possession of the hotel was an act of state with the consequence that this act of state and its consequence are not within the jurisdiction of a British court, and no action can lie for relief against them. "Act of State" is a phrase which has often been used, but by no means always with the same meaning. It seems to me to be useless to attempt to define it until one has determined in what circumstances a person, injured by an act ordered or ratified by the British Government, can, and in what circumstances he cannot, obtain redress from the English courts. The question may arise in several ways. A servant of the Crown may by his act infringe the rights of an individual so as to cause him damage. Then, if that servant of the Crown is sued, the question is whether it is a defence to him to prove that his act was ordered or ratified by the Government. Or, secondly, the action of the Government or of its servants may cause consequential loss to an individual although it does not infringe any of his ordinary rights. Or, again, the action of the Government or its servants may be in exercise of the royal prerogative in which case the action is not unlawful but the question is whether the individual is entitled to compensation.

Where an act of a servant of the Crown in this country infringes the rights of a British subject it has been settled law for centuries that it is no defence to plead that the act was ordered or ratified by the Crown or the Government. And since the decision of this House in *Johnstone* v. *Pedlar*[1] it has, I think, been equally clear that an alien in this country—other than an enemy alien—is in the same position. And not that it is possible to sue the Crown directly by virtue of the Crown Proceedings Act 1947, the position must be the same as it would have been if the action had been brought against the individual wrongdoer.

The other case which is, I think, clear is where the act complained of was done against an alien outside Her Majesty's dominion. Since *Buron* v. *Denman*,[2] it has been accepted that if the act was ordered or has been ratified by the British Government the English courts cannot give redress to that alien. He may enlist the support of his own government who may make diplomatic representations, but he has no legal remedy in England.

There is as yet no decision as to rights of a British subject who complains of an infringement of his ordinary rights of property by an act of a servant of the Crown done outside Her Majesty's dominions. The respondent contends that he is as much entitled to legal redress against arbitrary actions of servants of the Crown as is a British subject within the realm. The appellant on the other hand contends that he has no legal protection or redress against such acts if they have been ordered or ratified by the Government: all he can do is to try to get some Member of Parliament to take up his case in Parliament.

There are dicta favouring the respondent's contention, generally in cases where the plaintiff's property was within British territory. And there are dicta favouring the appellants' contention, generally in cases where the plaintiff was an alien outside British territory. I do not think that they can all be reconciled. But it would, in my view, be a strange result if it were found that those who have struggled and fought through the centuries to establish the rights of the subject to be protected from arbitrary acts of the King's servants have been completely successful with regard to acts done within the realm, but completely unsuccessful in gaining any legal protection from British subjects who have gone beyond the territorial waters of the King's dominions. ...

In the present case the Crown claims that the taking and retention of possession of this hotel was an act of state. For all we know—and we cannot inquire—it may have been a matter of ministerial policy to take this hotel. One possibility might be that it was thought better as a matter of policy to take the property of British subjects, so as to avoid any question with the Cyprus Government, if the property of citizens of Cyprus was taken. Or the Crown may simply have decided to ratify as an act of state the action of its officers in taking the hotel.

If I thought that any act done against the person or property of a British subject wherever situated could be an act of state in the sense that he was deprived of all right to apply to an English court for redress, then I would think that the taking of this hotel was an act of state. But for the reasons which I have already given I am of opinion that a British subject—at least if he is also a citizen of the United Kingdom and Colonies—can never be deprived of his legal right to redress by any assertion by the Crown or decision of the court that the acts of which he complains were acts of state. It seems to me that no useful purpose is served by inquiring whether an act in respect of which a British subject claims legal redress is or is not an act of state, because a decision of that question can make no difference to the result.

In my judgment, both on principle and on the balance of authority this act was not of such a character that the courts have no jurisdiction to entertain the present action. This is sufficient to dispose of the preliminary issue. ...

LORD MORRIS OF BORTH-Y-GEST [in the course of his judgment said]: The

---

[1] [1921] 2 A.C. 262.
[2] (1848) 2 ex. 167.

question has been raised whether the defence of act of state can be pleaded against a British subject. I can imagine circumstances in which an event abroad, which could be described as an act of state because deliberately (and as a matter of policy) commanded by the executive, caused damage to a large number of people whose nationality was unknown: if it subsequently transpired that one out of the large number was a British subject would the result be that act of state could be successfully pleaded against all the others but not against him? In this connection, having in mind the provisions of the British Nationality Act 1948[3] it would be necessary to have clear definition as to the range of those covered by the description of British subject. Would the description have to be limited to those owing allegiance to the Crown? But quite apart from this point I do not find it necessary in this preliminary issue to express any opinion on this wider question. . . .

LORD PEARCE [in the course of his judgment said]: There is some force in the argument that the interference by the Crown with a subject's liberties of person or property abroad cannot be barred from consideration in the courts by the plea of an act of state. But this is a difficult subject with wide implications. In the present case it is not necessary to decide it. For the taking of the Cornaro Hotel does not come within the category of an act of state. Whatever might be the situation if a clause in the treaty said expressly that British troops must be stationed in the Cornaro Hotel, in the present case there was no such necessity. No doubt it was a sensible place for them to be stationed. But had it not existed, they would have been stationed elsewhere. There is nothing in the facts pleaded to suggest that the occupation of the hotel was a *sine qua non* of the performance of the treaty. It was quite a subsidiary matter. In my opinion it did not have the character of an act of state. . . .

LORD WILBERFORCE [after considering the question whether the British forces were agents of the Cyprus Government, continued]: The second point of law referred by the master's order is raised in paragraph 4 (third sentence) of the defence in the following words: "Alternatively the actions of the British elements were acts of state of Her Majesty on the territory of an independent sovereign power performed in pursuance of an agreement between Her Majesty and the said power which equally are not so cognisable." It will be seen that this plea seeks to withdraw the matter from cognisance by the courts on the two grounds that the acts complained of were (i) performed abroad and (ii) performed in pursuance of a treaty. It was made clear by counsel for the Crown that it was the combination of these characteristics upon which he relied. This necessitates at least some consideration of the doctrine of act of state as it affects British subjects and I shall have to deal, if only provisionally, with some arguments of general scope.

Naturally, to start with one looks for a definition. One which is well known is as follows: ". . . an act of the executive as a matter of policy performed in the course of its relations with another state, including its relations with the subjects of that state, unless they are temporarily within the allegiance of the Crown."[4] This is less a definition than a construction put together from what has been decided in various cases; it covers as much ground as they do, no less, no more. It carries with it the warning that the doctrine cannot be stated in terms of a principle but develops from case to case: it has perhaps the disadvantage that it includes within itself two different conceptions or rules. The first rule is one which provides a defendant, normally a servant of the Crown, with a defence to an act otherwise tortious or criminal, committed abroad, provided that the act was authorised or subsequently ratified by the Crown. It is established that this defence may be

---

[3] Now the British Nationality Act 1981. See C & A.L. 283.

[4] Professor E.C.S. Wade in *British Yearbook of International Law* (1934). Vol. XV. p. 103, adopted by *Halsbury's Laws of England* (3rd ed., 1954) Vol. VII, p. 279, n. (i). See now (4th ed., 1977): Vol. 18, para. 1413.

pleaded against an alien, if done abroad, but not against a friendly alien if the act
was done in Her Majesty's Dominions. It is supported in its positive aspect by the
well-known case of *Buron* v. *Denman*[5] and in its negative aspect by *Johnstone* v.
Pedlar.[6]

The second rule is one of justiciability: it prevents British municipal courts from
taking cognisance of certain acts. The class of acts so protected has not been
accurately defined ... From the terms of the pleading it appears that it is this
aspect of the rule upon which the Crown seeks to rely.

Most of the decided cases are concerned with acts of annexation, or transfer of
territory, and although in our present situation these have become of historical
interest they may still give us some guidance on principle. The respondent sought
to discount their relevance by saying that they decide nothing more than that a
claim cannot be entertained by the courts if the person making it has to rely, as
part of his case, upon an act of this character. I have no doubt that this principle
does underlie some of the decisions, but I do not think that it is sufficient to
dispose of them. The principle is wider than this and must in my opinion, extend
equally to cases where the "act of state" is complained of, as where it is relied
upon. In either case, the courts are not bound to accept the *ipse dixit* of the
executive but have the right to decide for themselves whether the act is, in this
sense, an "act of state" (see *Forester* v. *Secretary of State for India in Council;*[7] *Secretary
of State in Council of India* v. *Kamachee Boye Sahaba*.[8] "The next question is, what is
the real character of the act done in this case" *per* Lord Kingsdown: *Salaman* v.
Secretary of State for India.[9] But once the character of the act is decided, whether it is
raised by way of defence to a claim (*Salaman's* case, *Cook* v. *Sprigg*,[10] a case of
doubtful authority) or is the basis of complaint (*Secretary of State in Council of India*
v. *Kamachee Boye Sahaba* where the act complained of was of a tortious character—
see *Secretary of State for India* v. *Bai Rajbai*[11]) or is sought to be relied on by the
claimant (*West Rand Central Gold Mining Co. Ltd.* v. *The King*[12]) cognisance cannot
be taken of it by a municipal court. Whether, in this type of case, any distinction is
to be drawn between claims by British subjects and claims by others is not brought
out by the decisions. One may in fact wonder why, if the character of the act is
what makes it non-cognisable, the quality of nationality of the plaintiff should
enter into the matter. Certainly in some cases, and probably in others, the plaintiff
was a British subject but generally no reference to this either way appears, nor is
this circumstance, or its absence, a ground of decision. If any guidance on this
point is to be obtained from authority, it must rather be found in *Walker* v. *Baird*[13]
and *Johnstone* v. *Pedlar*.[14]

Walker v. *Baird* was an appeal to the Privy Council from Newfoundland where
the acts complained of took place. These were the seizure of the lobster factory of
the respondents, who were British subjects, by the appellant commanding
H.M.S. Emerald acting, under instruction, to enforce an agreement as to lobster
fishing between Her Majesty and the French Government. The defendant submitted that the acts complained of "were acts and matters of state arising out of the
political relations between Her Majesty the Queen and the Government of the
Republic of France, that they involved the construction of treaties ..."[15] and the

[5] (1848) 2 Exch. 167.
[6] [1921] 2 A.C. 262.
[7] (1872) L.R.Ind.App.Supp. 10.
[8] (1859) 13 Moo.P.C.C. 22, 77.
[9] [1906] 1 K.B. 613, 639.
[10] [1899] A.C. 572.
[11] (1915) L.R. 42 Ind. App. 229, 238.
[12] [1905] 2 K.B. 391.
[13] [1892] A.C. 491.
[14] [1921] 2 A.C. 262.
[15] [1892] A.C. 491, 496.

validity of this defence was submitted (as here) to the court by way of a preliminary point of law. The Judicial Committee held that the defence disclosed no answer and the limited scope of the decision is worth observing:

> "... this judgment [of the Supreme Court of Newfoundland] was clearly right, unless the defendant's acts can be justified on the ground that they were done by the authority of the Crown for the purpose of enforcing obedience to a treaty or agreement entered into between Her Majesty and a foreign power. The suggestion that they can be justified as acts of state ... is wholly untenable."[16]

Lord Herschell went on to refer to the Attorney-General's argument. The latter had not, he said, argued generally for a right to invade the rights of private individuals whenever it was necessary in order to compel obedience to the provisions of a treaty. He contended (it seems under judicial pressure) for a more limited proposition: that the Crown had this power in relation to a treaty arrived at to put an end to a state of war. If this be so, the power, he contended, must extend to the provisions of a treaty for the preservation of peace. As to this, Lord Herschell concludes, at p. 497:

> "Whether the power contended for does exist in the case of treaties of peace, and whether if so it exists equally in the case of treaties akin to a treaty of peace, or whether in both or either of these cases interference with private rights can be authorised otherwise than by the legislature, are grave questions upon which their Lordships do not find it necessary to express an opinion."[17]

When so eminent a Board expresses itself with such caution as this in relation to acts done within Her Majesty's dominions, we may be entitled to feel some hesitation in attempting any general proposition of law in the much more difficult case where the action takes place outside them.

These hesitations are hardly dispelled by *Johnstone* v. *Pedlar*.[18] This was a straightforward case of a tort committed within Her Majesty's dominions (Ireland, then part of the United Kingdom). The questions debated were whether the defence of act of state could be raised against the plaintiff who was regarded as an alien and whether he had forfeited his rights by violation of his allegiance. It was unanimously held in this House that he was entitled to recover. There are certain passages in the speeches which, in words, suggest that in no circumstances, wherever the act complained of took place, can a defence of act of state be set up against a British subject. These have been quoted and I shall not repeat them. They are open to the familiar counterpart arguments that, read literally they support the proposition, read in their context and *secundum materiam* they do not. I shall not extend the discussion since I do not believe that anything said at this stage of the present case can elevate the status of these dicta in the former decisions. But it is perhaps fair to remark that two of their Lordships, whose speeches contain, in words, perhaps the strongest dicta as regards the nonapplicability of "act of state" to British subjects, firmly rest their observations on *Walker* v. *Baird*[19] which is undoubtedly a case where the act took place within the dominions of the Crown[20] and those of another are founded upon a deduction from some remarks of Lord Halsbury in *Cook* v. *Sprigg*[21] which, with respect, seems not to follow from what Lord Halsbury said.[22] Finally, the type of act with

[16] [1892] A.C. 496–497.
[17] [1892] A.C. 496, 497.
[18] [1921] 2 A.C. 262.
[19] [1892] A.C. 491.
[20] [1921] 2 A.C. 262, 272, *per* Viscount Finlay and [1921] 2 A.C. 262, 295, *per* Lord Phillimore.
[21] [1899] A.C. 572.
[22] [1921] 2 A.C. 262, 280–281 *per* Lord Atkin.

which *Johnstone* v. *Pedlar* was concerned (the seizure of money found on the plaintiff's person) is vastly different in character from the type of act which the plea (if it exists) seems adapted to protect, namely acts in the conduct of foreign relations, or acts in the execution of a treaty. So I cannot regard *Johnstone* v. *Pedlar* as laying down any rule as to the matter with which we are concerned, or, if it does, as defining its limits.

Textbook writers, on this subject, are no more conclusive than the cases. ....

Finally, an attempt was made to derive a rule from constitutional principle: but this in my opinion, is precarious. The settlement of 1688 may be said to have produced the result that, as regards the United Kingdom and its colonies, the rights of British subjects, and of resident friendly aliens, cannot be affected by the conclusion of treaties, or other acts in the field of foreign relations, without legislation making them locally binding: but I can find no logical compulsion to apply this doctrine abroad. The subject has, unquestionably, left the Crown or the executive, a free hand in the conduct of foreign relations, and I do not know where, in our constitutional principles, or otherwise than in a general feeling of benevolence to anyone having a claim against the government, to find an answer to the question whether, and how far, he is to be taken to assent to consequent executive action. The converse doctrine that legislation is always required to cover any action affecting British subjects wherever taken is not one that commands automatic assent, nor is the proposition that, in such situations as the present justice, as between the claimant and the British tax-payer who will have to pay if the claim succeeds, is dependent upon recourse to the courts rather than upon appraisal by the executive.

In this state of authority and doctrine it appears to me to be impossible to accept the broad proposition that in no case can the plea of act of state, in the sense that a particular act by the Crown is not cognisable by a British court, be raised against a British subject. On the contrary, as regards acts committed abroad in the conduct of foreign relations with other states, the preponderance of authority and of practice seems to me to be the other way. No doubt the scope of the Crown's prerogative, and the consequent non-justiciability of its acts, is uncertain—as uncertain as such expressions as "the conduct of foreign relations" or "in the performance of treaties." This is why I am with the Privy Council in *Walker* v. *Baird* in thinking that caution in the stating of general propositions is required. What fortunately is possible, on consideration of the cases, is to decide whether the defence as pleaded is a good defence. As to this, I am of opinion that the acts here alleged are as clearly outside the non-cognisance principle as were the acts complained of in *Walker* v. *Baird*—and for very similar reasons. The plea is directed not to the "taking" of the respondent's hotel, but generally and universally to the "actions of the British elements," expressions which might include or seem intended to include, the selection of this hotel for occupation, the manner in which it was used or damaged, the consumption of stores therein and the interference with the respondent's business. Between these acts and the pleaded agreement with the Government of Cyprus the link is altogether too tenuous, indeed it is not even sketched out: if accepted as sufficient to attract the description of act of state it would cover with immunity an endless and indefinite series of acts, judged by the officers in command of the troops to be necessary, or desirable, in their interest. That I find entirely unacceptable.

Before stating a conclusion on the appeal it is necessary to say something as to other pleaded matters which were debated. First there is the claim that what was done was done under the prerogative. I think it is unfortunate that we have been called upon at this stage in the action to consider this elusive concept. As the matter stood in the Queen's Bench Division, it did not arise: John Stephenson J. said that he was not hearing an application to strike out this head of claim; he assumed that it might be made good and he then proceeded on this assumption, to examine the validity of the defence of act of state. This was strictly in accordance with the master's order. In the Court of Appeal the discussion took a wider range. By agreement, so it appears, an additional question was added to the master's order, wide enough to let in arguments as to the validity in law of any claim or cause of action pleaded in the statement of claim. Accordingly, the judgments in the Court of Appeal, though not their formal order contain observations as to the plaintiff's right to compensation by virtue of the prerogative or otherwise: thus Lord Denning M.R. held[23] that the prerogative extends to the taking or destruction of the property of a British subject ("one of Her Majesty's subjects") in a foreign land, by way of extension of the *Burmah Oil* case[24] and went on to express the opinion that in any event an obligation arose at common law. With all respect I am of opinion that these matters cannot be decided without a knowledge certainly of the circumstances in which the plaintiff's hotel was taken or occupied and I would also think of the local law. What rule of English law ought thereafter to be applied is a matter which, in my view, ought to be left entirely open: for as at present advised I find great difficulty in seeing how the exercise of the prerogative in the independent territory of Cyprus, where, by statute (Cyprus Act 1960) the Crown enjoys no sovereignty, can be justified, or why the prerogative or the English common law should apply as regards an immovable situated in Cyprus, or why the legality of the act in Cyprus, if it was legal, should not be a defence (vide *Carr* v. *Fracis Times & Co.*[25]. If these, to me, remarkable consequences are to follow and if the *Burmah Oil* case is to be applied by analogy or by extension, that must be by virute of a very special set of facts yet to be established. I think it unwise to anticipate their establishment. . . .

LORD PEARSON [in the course of his judgment said]: But it does not follow that everything which the Truce Force, or elements of it, did in the foreign territory constituted an act of state. It is not alleged that the Truce Force had to engage in any fighting or that there was any urgent military necessity to occupy the hotel. The mere stationing of the Truce Force in the territory may have been sufficient to keep the peace. The Truce Force would nevertheless need supplies and accommodation. Conceivably they might have seized the supplies and accommodation in a high-handed, extra-legal manner as an act of state with the intention of denying to those affected any right of redress in any municipal court. But it is unlikely that they would so act in a friendly country, being present there with the consent and for the assistance of the government of the country. It is not reasonable to infer an intention that the occupation of the hotel should be an act of state. The probable intention was to take the hotel for the needs of the army and to leave those affected to pursue whatever legal remedies they might have. In my opinion, the assumed facts do not show that there was an act of state.

I wish to reserve the question whether an act done outside the realm could ever be an act of state in relation to a British subject. The dicta in decided cases are important, but not decisive, and there are problems involved. Should the same rule apply to acts on the high seas and to acts in independent sovereign countries? What is the positon, if, in a foreign country, a British army or truce force seizes in one operation a row of ten houses of which one belongs to a British subject and the other nine to foreigners? What is the position if, in a foreign country, a British army or truce force seizes a building and goods both belonging to a partnership, of which some partners are British subjects and others are foreigners? Then there is the case of the person of British nationality who has settled in a foreign country and there acquired a business and made a home for himself and his family: he belongs to the community of that country: any damage to his property there is a blow to the economy of that country and any compensation paid to him is a benefit to the economy of that country: the government of that country has an

---

[23] [1968] 1 Q.B. 286, 340.
[24] [1965] A.C. 75.
[25] [1902] A.C. 176.

interest in his welfare: he owes local allegiance to that government and is entitled to its protection, if the law of that country is the same as English law. How does the rule in regard to acts of state apply in his case?

Another problem is this: If the plea of act of state is not available in any circumstances against a British subject, what is the meaning of the expression "British subject" for this purpose? Does it mean only a citizen of the United Kingdom and Colonies? Or does it include anyone who is a "British subject" within the wide definition contained in section 1 of the British Nationality and Status of Aliens Act 1948?[26] Or does it have some other meaning? . . .
Appeal dismissed.

[26] See n. 3 *ante.*

4. ADMINISTRATION OF JUSTICE

Attorney-General v. B.B.C.
[1981] A.C. 303
House of Lords

The Attorney-General brought proceedings for an injunction to restrain the defendants from broadcasting a programme dealing with matters which related to an appeal pending before a local valuation court on the ground that it would constitute contempt of court. The Divisional Court (Lord Widgery, L.C.J., Wien and Kenneth Jones JJ.) concluded that the valuation court was a court for the purposes of the law of contempt and the B.B.C. gave an undertaking not to broadcast the programme. The Court of Appeal (Eveleigh L.J. and Sir Stanley Rees, Lord Denning M.R. dissenting) dismissed the appeal. Counsel for the Attorney-General suggested 14 identifying characteristics of a court which the local valuation court satisfied:

1. The members are selected from a panel approved by the Minister.
2. Witnesses can be compelled to attend by subpoena.
3. It sits in public.
4. It has power to administer oaths.
5. Its decisions are final, subject to appeal.
6. An appeal is to the Lands Tribunal, which hears the case de novo: and the Lands Tribunal is undoubtedly a "court."
7. It has rules of procedure like any court.
8. It deals with matters of public interest.
9. It is judicial, not executive or administrative.
10. The proceedings taken there form a lis.
11. It is named in its title as a "court."
12. Although its decisions are not directly enforceable, they amount to a declaration which is binding on those concerned.
13. They administer the law.
14. They have exclusive jurisdiction within their allotted sphere.

Eveleigh L.J. suggested six characteristics of a court:

"the first is that it should have been created by the State. At one time courts were created or recognised by the Monarch. Now they are created by Parliament. Thus, while an arbitration tribunal may contain many of the attributes of a court, it will lack this first essential one. Secondly, it must conduct its procedure in accordance with the rules of natural justice. Thirdly, that procedure will involve a public hearing with the power at least to receive evidence orally, to permit the oral examination and cross-examination of witnesses and to hear argument upon the issue before it. Fourthly, it arrives at a decision which is final and binding as long as it stands. Fifthly, there will be two parties at least before it, one of whom may be the Crown, who are interested in the decision. Sixthly, the decision will be concerned with legal rights."

He specifically dissented from the view of Lord Denning M.R. that a court should include or have connected with it someone who is legally qualified or experienced.

"It is not necessary that there should be a lawyer presiding, in my opinion, or indeed that there should be a legally trained clerk. A coroner's court is a court. It lacks or may lack these attributes when a doctor presides as he so frequently does. In practice the clerk actually present in the magistrates' court is not always legally qualified. So too at quarter sessions the chairman used not to have to be a person with legal training and it was not essential for there to be present a legally trained clerk."

The B.B.C. appealed to the House of Lords (Viscount Dilhorne, Lord Salmon, Lord Edmund-Davies, Lord Fraser of Tullybelton and Lord Scarman).

VICOUNT DILHORNE: My Lords, on February 9, 1978, the B.B.C. advertised in the "Radio Times" their intention to broadcast a television programme about a sect called the Exclusive Brethren. It was a repeat of a television programme broadcast by the B.B.C. on September 26, 1976. Your Lordships have not seen the text of the proposed broadcast and have not seen any evidence as to the activities of the sect. Lord Denning M.R. at the commencement of his judgment, . . . gave a short account of their tenets and activities which he said "must be taken with reserve" as their activities had not been proved by evidence. Among other things he said that their doctrine had caused such distress that "it is said that in Andover it led to two deaths which the coroner described as murder and suicide."

It is not necessary for the purposes of this appeal to express any opinion about the Exclusive Brethren. It suffices to say that Lord Denning M.R. who had seen a transcript of the broadcast, which your Lordships have not, described it as "extremely hostile to, and critical of" the Exclusive Brethren.

Among other things, he said that it stated that they were not entitled to exemption from liability for rates on their meeting rooms by virtue of section 39 of the General Rate Act 1967 as it was said that their meeting rooms were not open to the public and so were not "places of public religious worship" coming within that section.

The Exclusive Brethren had applied for the exemption from rates of their meeting room at Andover. To this both the local authority and the valuation officer objected and the question whether they were entitled to exemption was to come before the local valuation court at Andover on March 10, 1978.

The Exclusive Brethren demanded that the broadcast should not be made on the ground that its content would prejudice the hearing of their case before the local valuation court and interfere with the administration of justice. When the B.B.C. refused to accede to this demand, the matter was brought to the attention of the Attorney-General who on February 17, 1978, two days before the proposed broadcast, issued a writ claiming an injunction restraining the B.B.C. from making it. The same day an application was made to the Divisional Court for an interlocutory injunction. Unknown to the parties to the action, the Attorney-General and the B.B.C., though presumably not unknown to other Exclusive Brethren, there was then no prospect of the claim to rate relief being heard by the local valuation court on March 10, the local authority and the valuation officer having withdrawn their objection to the claim on February 16.[1]

Before the Divisional Court, where naturally the matter had to be dealt with in a great hurry, it not being known to that court that there would be no hearing before the local valuation court, it appears to have been assumed that the broadcast would be prejudicial to the hearing and the only question considered was whether the local valuation court was a court coming within R.S.C., Ord. 52, r.1 which so far as material reads as follows:

"(2) Where contempt of court—(a) is committed in connection with—(i) any proceedings before a Divisional Court of the Queen's Bench Division, or (ii) criminal proceedings, except where the contempt is committed in the face of the court or consists of disobedience to an order of the court or a breach of an undertaking to the court, or (iii) proceedings in an inferior court, . . . then . . . an order of committal may be made only by a Divisional Court of the Queen's Bench Division."

On the Divisional Court holding that it did, the B.B.C. undertook not to broadcast the programme until after March 10. . . .

It is most unusual for this House to pronounce on hypothetical questions. Ordinarily we refuse to do so and it is with some reluctance that in this case I am prepared to depart from our usual practice. I do so for the following reasons. Both parties want us to do so. The B.B.C. naturally do not wish to commit contempt of court. They want to know where they stand. If they repeat the broadcast, they want to know if they are liable to be proceeded against for contempt should there happen to be an application pending before one of the many local valuation courts in the country by the Exclusive Brethren for rate relief. For the Attorney-General it was suggested that if a local valuation court is a court coming within the rule, the following tribunals must also be courts coming within the rule: agricultural land tribunals, the commons commissioners, immigration adjudicators, the Immigration Appeal Tribunal, the Lands Tribunal, the Mines and Quarries Tribunal, pension appeal tribunals, the Performing Right Tribunal, the Plant Varieties and Seeds Tribunal, the Transport Tribunal and value added tax tribunals, of which according to the Annual Report of the Council of Tribunals for 1978/79 (H.C. 359) there are well over 500 in this country. If this suggestion is well founded, it means that the media are at risk of being proceeded against for contempt should anything be published which is likely to affect a hearing before any of these tribunals.

If the reasoning of the Court of Appeal is accepted, and unless your Lordships deal with this case it will be, then it means that until the question has been litigated in respect of each of these tribunals, there will be great and undesirable uncertainty as to the extent of the Divisional Court's jurisdiction to punish for contempt.

I think the desirability of your Lordships, if possible, removing or diminishing this uncertainty, justifies the taking of the exceptional course of considering this now hypothetical question.

Local valuation courts are a comparatively modern innovation. They were created in 1948 by section 44 (1) of the Local Government Act of that year (now replaced by the General Rate Act 1967, section 88) which stated:

"Local valuation courts constituted as hereinafter provided shall be convened . . . for the purpose of hearing and determining appeals . . . against draft valuation lists and against objections to proposals for the alteration of valuation lists."

Before 1948 it was the task of assessment committees to deal with these matters. The Act of 1948 provided, and the Act of 1967 now provides, that a local valuation court is to consist of three persons, a chairman or deputy chairman and two others all drawn from a local valuation panel in accordance with a scheme submitted by each county and county borough council and approved by the minister; that each scheme was to state by whom the members of the panel were to be appointed; that the court should normally sit it public; that it could take evidence on oath and for that purpose administer the oath; that the parties to an appeal should be entitled to examine witnesses and to call witnesses; that after hearing an appeal the court was to give such directions as to the manner in which the hereditament in question was to be dealt with in the valuation list as appeared necessary and that it was the duty of the valuation officer to give effect to those directions.

Under the Act of 1948 an appeal lay from a local valuation court to the county court. Under the General Rate Act 1967 it now lies to the Lands Tribunal.

Under the scheme shown to us all members of the local valuation panel were to be appointed by the county council. The Acts do not provide, nor did this scheme, that any member of the panel or the clerk to the local valuation court should have any legal qualification. But for his view that to be a court a member or the clerk must have legal qualifications, it would seem that Lord Denning M.R. would have agreed with the other members of the court that a local valuation court was a court.

That in my view is the first question to be decided in this appeal. Despite these statutory provisions the appellants submit that the local valuation court is not a court but this is not only question to be considered. If it is a court, it clearly is an inferior court but is it a court contempt of which the Divisional Court has jurisdiction to punish?

In my opinion it is a court but my conclusion is based on a different ground from those put forward on behalf on the Attorney-General and those accepted by the Court of Appeal. Mr. Kidwell for the Attorney-General submitted that a court must be established by Parliament and must administer public justice in public. Eveleigh L.J. in his judgment in the Court of Appeal listed six characteristics which he said a court must have and found those present in a valuation court.

In my view when an Act of Parliament provides that a court shall be constituted, no other conclusion is possible that that it is a court. And here the Act of 1948 provided that the court to be constituted should have all the features that one associated with a court.

I know of no authority for the view that a tribunal is not a court unless a member or the clerk to the court has legal qualifications. A coroner's court is just one example of a court without any requirement of legal qualifications.

There is a wide variety of courts; so there is of tribunals as the long list in the Appendix to the Annual Report of the Council on Tribunals for 1978/79 shows. While every court is a tribunal, the converse is not true. There are many tribunals which are not courts despite the fact that they are charged with dealing with certain matters and have features in common with courts. A distinction is drawn in this country between tribunals which are courts and those which are not. Sometimes that which is called a tribunal is declared by the Act creating it to be a court. Instances of this are the Iron and Steel Arbitration Tribunal which by section 44 (1) of the Iron and Steel Act 1949 was declared to be a court of record and the Transport Tribunal which also by Schedule 10 to the Transport Act 1962 is declared to be a court of record. There are other instances. Generally I would say that just because a tribunal has features resembling those of a court, it should not he held to be a court. Tribunals created by or under Acts of Parliament are not as a general rule courts unless constituted as such by the Act creating them. The only exception to this that I can find is the Lands Tribunal which has a status which singles it out from the rest. Apart from the Lands Tribunal and the Transport Tribunal, I do not regard any of these tribunals which it was suggested were courts if a local valuation court is a court, as courts despite their similarity to that court.

In 1958 the Council on Tribunals was created by the Tribunals and Inquiries Act of that year. One of the tasks of the council was to keep under review the tribunals listed in Schedule 1 to that Act. That Schedule did not include local valuation courts. That Act has now been replaced by the Tribunals and Inquiries Act 1971 which states that the council is to keep under review the tribunals listed in Schedule 1 to that Act and that Schedule includes local valuation courts. I do not know why this change was made. Local valuation courts are the only courts named in the list. It may be that in 1971 Parliament thought that though called a court, a local valuation court was not a court but this, in view of the terms of the Local Government Act and of the General Rate Act, is, I think, most unlikely. I think that the more likely explanation is that Parliament thought them to be courts of such a character—and as I have said, all courts are tribunals—as to make it desirable that they should be subject to the supervision of the council.

However this may be, the inclusion of local valuation courts in the list does not in my opinion suffice to establish that an Act stating that courts are to be constituted can properly be interpreted as creating something which is not a court.

I now turn to the question whether it is a court, contempt of which the Divisional Court has power to punish. This involves consideration of the jurisdiction of that court. It may be limited to protecting inferior courts which are courts of law. It may extend to all courts which have been established as courts by the state or it may extend beyond that to all tribunals which have the same features as courts. I have come to the conclusion that it does not extend as far as that. It can be argued that it should but to hold that it does, would, in my view, be to trespass on the field of the legislature. As I have pointed out, Parliament has on occasions enacted that a tribunal shall be a court. When it has refrained from doing so, save in the case of the Lands Tribunal I am not prepared to hold that a tribunal it has created, no matter how much it resembles a court, is a court. And the jurisdiction of the Divisional Court in relation to contempt only extends to courts.

I need not dilate on the uncertainty that would result from the contrary view or upon its effect on freedom of speech. This case, when so much argument has been directed to detailed examination of the functions of valuation courts, illustrates the complexities involved in determining whether the similarities are such that a particular tribunal, not declared to be a court, is nevertheless one.

I do not think that the Divisional Court's jurisdiction extends to all courts created by the state for I think that a distinction has to be drawn between courts which discharge judicial functions and those which discharge administrative ones, between courts of law which form part of the judicial system of the country on the one hand and courts which are constituted to resolve problems which arise in the course of administration of the government of this country. In my opinion a local valuation court comes within the latter category. It discharges functions formerly performed by assessment committees. It has to resolve disputes as to the valuation of hereditaments, while its decisions will affect an occupier's liability for rates, it does not determine his liability. It is just part of the process of rating. It has to act judicially but that does not make it a court of law. The fact that it has to act judicially means as Fry L.J. said in (*Royal Aquarium and Summer and Winter Garden Society Ltd.* v. *Parkinson*) [1892] 1 Q.B. 431 that its proceedings must be "conducted with the fairness and impartiality which characterise proceedings in courts of justice, and are proper to the function of a judge" and not, though established by law, that it is a court of law and part of the judicial system of the country. In *Reg.* v. *Assessment Committee of St. Mary Abbotts, Kensington* [1891] 1 Q.B. 378 Lord Esher M.R. said that an assessment committee was not a court or tribunal exercising judicial functions in the legal acceptation of the term. A local valuation court, as I have said, discharges the same functions as an assessment committee did and they have not changed their character. I hold that such a court's functions are administrative not judicial. No case was cited to us of the law of contempt being applied to tribunals or courts discharging, albeit judicially, administrative functions and I for my part am not prepared to extend the law by applying it to such tribunals or courts.

I recognise that this conclusion still leaves an area of uncertainty. If your Lordships agree with me about this, it will still leave it open to argument whether a court established by Parliament discharges administrative or judicial functions, about whether or not it is a court of law but the area of uncertainty will be much diminished.

To sum up, my conclusions are as follows: (1) a local valuation court is a court; (2) it is a court which discharges administrative functions and is not a court of law;

(3) consequently, the jurisdiction in relation to contempt of the Divisional Court does not extend to it; and (4) that court's jurisdiction only extends to courts of law and R.S.C., Ord. 52, r. 1 when it refers to "inferior courts" must be taken to mean inferior courts of law.

For these reasons I would allow the appeal.

LORD SALMON: I agree that a local valuation court has some of the attributes of the long-established "inferior courts." There is today a plethora of such tribunals which may well resemble the old "inferior courts." In my view, it does not by any means follow that the modern inferior courts need the umbrella of contempt of court nor that they come under it. Indeed, in my opinion, public policy requires that most of the principles relating to contempt of court which have for ages necessarily applied to the long-established inferior courts such as county courts, magistrates courts, courts-martial, coroners' courts and consistory courts shall not apply to valuation courts and the host of other modern tribunals which may be regarded as inferior courts; otherwise the scope of contempt of court would be unnecessarily extended and accordingly freedom of speech and freedom of the press would be unnecessarily contracted.

These two freedoms are two of the pillars of liberty. They should never be diminished unless justice so requires, e.g. if a man is charged with a criminal offence it would be a gross contempt of court for the press to publish any of his past wrongdoings or indeed to write prejudicial articles about him. There would be a grave danger that such conduct might prevent him from having a fair trial; juries are sometimes seriously prejudiced by what they hear or read. The media however are very careful to avoid these pitfalls whether in criminal trials or civil trials by jury.

LORD EDMUND-DAVIES: . . . At the end of the day it has unfortunately to be said that there emerges no sure guide, no unmistakable hall-mark by which a "court" or "inferior court" may unerringly be identified. It is largely a matter of impression. My own firm view is that a local valuation court is not such a body. I would add that, if Parliament had it in mind to bring local valuation courts within the contempt procedure by which the Divisional Court is empowered to protect "inferior courts," it is regrettable that they did not make this clear by legislation, as they have already done in several other Acts of Parliament cited to your Lordships and ranging from the Tribunals of Inquiry (Evidence) Act 1921, section 1(2) to the Parliamentary Commissioner Act 1967, s.9. Yet nothing of the sort has been done, and this despite the recurring opportunities of conveniently doing so which have arisen since the Local Government Act 1948 first created local valuation courts.

LORD FRASER OF TULLYBELTON: . . . The contention on behalf of the Attorney-General was that the class of inferior courts to which Order 52 applied consisted of all bodies which possess certain characteristics, including having been created by the Crown or by Parliament, and administering justice in public, even though they were not courts of justice in the full sense. But that definition is open to two grave objections; it is too uncertain and it is probably too wide. Uncertainty is a serious objection because of the large number of tribunals set up by modern legislation, may of which might be on the borderline. It is undesirable that anyone intending to publish information in the newspapers or on radio or television relating to proceedings pending before a tribunal should have to examine in detail the functions and constitution of the tribunal in order to ascertain whether it is protected by the law against contempt. The second objection is even more serious, because, if protection is extended widely, the right to freedom of expression would be correspondingly reduced. The objection would have great weight with a English court without reference to the Convention,[2] and it is reinforced by the Convention. The contention of the Attorney-General cannot therefore be

---

[2] *i.e.* the European Convention for the Protection of Human Rights, (1953) Cmd. 8969.

accepted, and in my opinion, the class of inferior courts protected by the law against contempt should be limited to those which are truly courts of law, exercising the judicial power of the state. Not all bodies which are called courts will be included; for example, a court of referees under the Unemployment Insurance Act 1920 would not qualify—see (*Collins* v. *Henry Whiteway & Co. Ltd.*) [1927] 2 K.B. 378—nor, I think, would a court of inquiry under Part II of the Industrial Courts Act 1919. Both these courts perform administrative acts and are not courts of justice.

I recognise that limiting the protection against contempt in this way is difficult to justify in strict logic. It may well be that the need for protection against interference from newspaper articles or television programmes relating to pending proceedings before a tribunal is greater when the tribunal is not a court of law than when it is, because members of a tribunal which is not a court of law are often laymen who may find more difficulty in excluding irrelevant matter from their minds that the professional lawyers who constitute or preside over most courts of law. Nevertheless, strict logic must give way to the practical convenience of having a test which can be applied with reasonable certainty and of avoiding too great a curtailment of the right of freedom of expression.

For the reasons explained by others of your Lordships I agree that the local valuation court is not a court of law, but a body whose functions are of an administrative character. It is therefore not within the class of inferior courts to which the law of contempt applies.

I would allow the appeal.

LORD SCARMAN: The appeal raises two questions: (1) whether a local valuation court is truly a court; and, if it is, (2) does it "come within the contempt jurisdiction of the High Court, whereby in a proper case its proceeding may be protected by contempt proceedings before the High Court." (I borrow these words from paragraph 2 of the respondent's written case). The way in which the case was conducted before the Divisional Court and in the Court of Appeal has left the impression that the decisive question is the first. But it is not. The second is the critical question. And for the reasons which I shall endeavour to explain I have reached the conclusion that, though a local valuation court is a court, it is not one to which the law of contempt of court applies. . . .

Much of the statutory law relating to rating and valuation in England and Wales was consolidated in the General Rate Act 1967. The consolidation included the provisions constituting the local valuation courts. The language and style of these provisions (sections 76 to 93) are consistent only with an intention by Parliament to create a court, albeit with a jurisdiction strictly limited by the statute.

But, in my judgment, not every court is a court of judicature, *i.e.* a court in law. Nor am I prepared to assume that Parliament intends to establish a court as part of the country's judicial system whenever it constitutes a court. The word "court" does, in modern English usage, emphasise that the body so described has judicial functions to exercise: but it is frequently used to describe bodies which, though they exercise judicial functions, are not part of the judicial system of the Kingdom. Fry L.J. made the point in the passage I have quoted, and there is an abundance of modern instances of this usage of the word. When, therefore, Parliament entrusts a body with a judicial function, it is necessary to examine the legislation to discover its purpose. The mere application of the "court" label does not determine the question; nor, I would add, does the absence of the label conclude the question the other way. In *Collins* v. *Henry Whiteway & Co. Ltd* [1927] 2 K.B. 378, Horridge J. held that the court of referees constituted under the Unemployment Insurance Act 1920 had an administrative purpose and that, though it exercised a judicial function, it was not a court of law. He did not consider himself bound by Parliament's label. In the constitutionally complex case of *Shell Co. of Australia Ltd.* v. *Federal Commissioner of Taxation* [1931] A.C. 275, the Privy Council held that the board of review, created by federal statute to review the decisions of the Commissioner of Taxation, was not a court exercising the judicial power of the Commonwealth but was an administrative tribunal. . . .

Though the United Kingdom has no written constitution comparable with that of Australia, both are common law countries: and in both judicial power is an exercise of sovereign power. I would identify a court in (or "of") law, *i.e.* a court of judicature, as a body established by law to exercise, either generally or subject to defined limits, the judicial power of the state. In this context judicial power is to be contrasted with legislative and executive (*i.e.* administrative) power. If the body under review is established for a purely legislative or administrative purpose, it is part of the legislative or administrative system to the state, even though it has to perform duties which are judicial in character. Though the ubiquitous presence of the state makes itself felt in all sorts of situations never envisaged when our law was in its formative stage, the judicial power of the state exercised through judges appointed by the state remains an independent, and recogisably separate, function of government. Unless a body exercising judicial functions can be demonstrated to be part of this judicial system, it is not, in my judgment, a court in law. I would add that the judicial system is not limited to the courts of the civil power. Court-martial and consistory courts (the latter since 1540) are as truly entrusted with the exercise of the judicial power of the state as are civil courts: *Rex* v. *Daily Mail, Ex parte Farnsworth* [1921] 2 K.B. 773 and *Rex* v. *Daily Herald, Ex parte Bishop of Norwich* [1932] 2 K.B. 402.

My Lords, a local valuation court fails this test. Its function is essentially administrative, though it must act judicially in discharging it. Its purpose is, upon objection being made, to give directions as to the manner in which a hereditament is to be treated in the valuation list: General Rate Act 1967, s.76 (5). The fact, which is plain upon the face of the statute that it must act judicially in hearing and determining objections, do not alter its administrative purpose: compare *Ranaweera* v. *Wickramasinghe* [1970] A.C. 951. The fact that it is a court (Parliament's description) with an administrative purpose does not make it part of the judicial system of the Kingdom. The limits of its jurisdiction, as explored by Lord Radcliffe in *Hope's* case, [1960] A.C. 551, reinforce the administrative nature of the purpose it serves. At the end of the day its one power is to correct a valuation list. It imposes no tax, no liability upon the citizen to pay any money or do any act. It has an important role in the machinery for determining a rate, and must act judicially: but it does not determine the amount of the rate or impose a liability to pay it. Its work is strictly comparable with the judicial responsibility of its predecessor, the assessment committee. I conclude, therefore, that a local valuation court is an administrative court, but not a court in law. Though I rest no part of my argument on the law relating to income tax, I would think it is wholly consistent with the view taken by the courts of the character of the Income Tax Commissioners: see *Inland Revenue Commissioners* v. *Sneath* [1932] 2 K.B. 362.

The second question may now be re-phrased. Does a body established for an administrative purpose but required to act judicially in the achievement of that purpose attract to itself the protection of the doctrine of contempt of court?

The High Court has power to punish summarily, i.e. without trial by jury upon indictment, for contempt of its own proceedings. The Court of King's Bench, now a constituent part of the High Court of Justice, has power to punish summarily for contempt of inferior courts: *Rex* v. *Parke* [1903] 2 K.B. 432 and *Rex* v. *Davies* [1906] 1 K.B. 32. This jurisdiction is today regulated by R.S.C., Ord. 52, r. 1. The question for your Lordships is whether this power, which admittedly extends to inferior courts which are part of the judicial system of the Kingdom, extends to administrative courts, or to bodies not so described but required in pursuit of their administrative purpose to act judicially.

.   .   .   .

Neither the meagre authorities available in the books nor the historical origins of contempt of court require the House to extend the doctrine to administrative courts and tribunals. Legal policy in today's world would be better served, in my judgment, if we refused so to extend it. If Parliament wishes to extend the doctrine to a specific institution which it establishes, it must say so explicitly in its enactment; as it has done on occasion, *e.g.*, Tribunals of Inquiry (Evidence) Act 1921. I would not think it desirable to extend the doctrine, which is unknown, and not apparently needed, in most civilised legal systems, beyond its historical scope, namely the proceeding of courts of judicature. If we are to make the extension, we have to ask ourselves, if the United Kingdom is to comply with its international obligations, whether the extension is necessary in our democratic society. Is there "a pressing social need" for the extension? For that, according to the European Court of Human Rights, 2 E.H.R.R. 245, 275, is what the phrase means. It has not been demonstrated to me that there is.

For these reasons I would allow the appeal.
Appeal allowed.

JUDICIAL IMMUNITY

In Re McC (A Minor)
[1985] A.C. 528
House of Lords

A boy of 14 was sentenced by magistrates in Belfast to a period of detention at a training school. The magistrates had failed to comply with statutory requirements that such a sentence should not be imposed on a person who was not legally represented in that court and had not been previously sentenced to that punishment by a court in any part of the United Kingdom, unless either—(a) he applied for legal aid and the application was refused on the grounds that it did not appear his means were such that he required assistance: or (b) having been informed of his right to apply for legal aid and had the opportunity to do so, he refused or failed to apply.

(Treatment of Offenders (Northern Ireland) Order 1976, article 15 (1)).

The young delinquent had never before been sentenced to detention. In the proceedings before the Belfast Juvenile Court he was not legally represented and he had never applied for legal aid. The Divisional Court (Lord Lowry L.C.J. and Jones L.J.) quashed the training school order and the minor issued a writ for damages for false imprisonment against the magistrates.

Section 15 of the Northern Ireland Act of 1964 provided as follows:

> "No action shall succeed against any person by reason of any matter arising in the execution or purported execution of his office of resident magistrate or justice of the peace, unless the court before which the action is brought is satisfied that he acted without jurisdiction or in excess of jurisdiction."

Hutton J. decided a preliminary point of law, whether the magistrates had, on the facts as pleaded, acted "without jurisdiction or in excess of jurisdiction," in favour of the magistrates. The Court of Appeal (Lord Lowry L.C.J., Jones and O'Donnell L.JJ.) reversed the order of Hutton J. and the magistrates appealed to the House of Lords (Lord Keith of Kinkel, Lord Elwyn-Jones, Lord Bridge of Harwich, Lord Brandon of Oakbrook and Lord Templeman.)

LORD BRIDGE OF HARWICH. . . . This is, so far as I know, the first case ever to come before this House related specifically to the civil liability of justices arising from the performance or purported performance of their duties as such. It is obviously desirable, so far as it may be possible, that the House, beyond deciding the appeal on its particular facts, should make some attempt, however daunting the prospect may seem, to discover and pronounce any principles of general application in relation to justices' civil liability and, if essentially the same principles apply both in Northern Ireland on the one hand and in England and Wales on the other, to say so.

[Lord Bridge then referred to the provisions of the Justices Protection Act 1848, which related to England, and the Justices Protection (Ireland) Act 1849. Section 1 of each Act envisaged actions for acts done within the justice's jurisdiction, if done maliciously. Section 2 related to acts in excess of jurisdiction, in which case no allegation of malice was required. The 1849 Act was re-enacted in the Northern Ireland Act 1964.[1] The provisions of section 1 disappeared; Section 2 became Section 15, the terms of which are set out, *supra*. A new provision, Section 20, provided that any damages awarded against a magistrate should be defrayed by the Ministry of Home Affairs.[2] The English Act of 1848 remained in force until repealed by the Justices of the Peace Act 1979. Section 2 became section 45. Section

---

[1] See now the Magistrates' Courts (Northern Ireland) Order 1981.
[2] The Lord Chancellor under current legislation.

1 was not repealed but replaced by section 44 which begins

"If apart from this section any action lies against a justice of the peace for an act done by him in the execution of his duty as such a justice, with respect to any matter within his jurisdiction as such a justice, the action . . ."

Section 53 provides for the indemnification of justices out of local funds.]

The language of section 15 of the Northern Ireland Act of 1964 plainly abolishes the old common law "action on the case as for a tort" against a justice in respect of anything done by him maliciously and without reasonable and probable cause *within* his jurisdiction.

It was not open to the draftsman of the Act of 1979 to take the same course in England. In the process of consolidation (there being no relevant Law Commission recommendation: see Justices of the Peace Bill (1979) (Law Commission No. 94, Cmnd. 7583) he was constrained to reproduce the previous statutory provisions, which are purely procedural in character, but was entitled by using the opening words: "If apart from this section any action lies etc . . ." to manifest his doubt as to the survival of the old common law cause of action.

My Lords, I am fully conscious that anything I say on this topic is obiter, since no question of malice, either within or without jurisdiction, arises in this appeal. But when the whole subject of justices' liability arising out of the execution or purported execution of their office is under consideration by this house for the first time, even though this aspect of the subject was not argued, I should be sorry to pass it by without comment. It is, of course, clear that the holder of any judicial office who acts in bad faith, doing what he knows he has no power to do, is liable in damages. If the Lord Chief Justice himself, on the acquittal of a defendant charged before him with a criminal offence, were to say: "That is a perverse verdict," and thereupon proceed to pass a sentence of imprisonment, he could be sued for trespass. But, as Lord Esher M.R. said in *Anderson* v. *Gorrie* [1895] 1 Q.B. 668, 670:

"the question arises whether there can be an action against a judge of a court of record for doing something within his jurisdiction, but doing it maliciously and contrary to good faith. By the common law of England it is the law that no such action will lie."

The principle underlying this rule is clear. If one judge in a thousand acts dishonestly within his jurisdiction to the detriment of a party before him, it is less harmful to the health of society to leave that party without a remedy than that nine hundred and ninety nine honest judges should be harassed by vexatious litigation alleging malice in the exercise of their proper jurisdiction.

If the old common law rule was different in relation to justices of the peace, I suspect the different rule had its origins in society's view of the justice, reflected in Shakespeare's plays, as an ignorant buffoon. How long this view persisted and how long there was any justification for it, I am not a good enough legal or social historian to say. But it clearly has no application whatever in today's world either to stipendiary magistrates or to lay benches. The former are competent professional judges, the latter citizens from all walks of life, chosen for their intelligence and integrity, required to undergo some training before they sit, and advised by legally qualified clerks. They give unstinting voluntary service to the community and conduct the major part of the criminal business of the courts. Without them the system of criminal justice in this country would grind to a halt. In these circumstances, it would seem to me a ludicrous anachronism that, whilst a judge sued for an act within his jurisdiction alleged to have been done maliciously is entitled to have the proceedings dismissed in limine, a magistrate, in the like case, should have to go to trial to defend himself against the accusation of malice. It follows that, in my opinion, the old common law "action on the case as for a tort" against justices acting within their jurisdiction maliciously and without reasonable and probable cause no longer lies.

By contrast with section 1, the position is entirely different in relation to the re-enacted provisions of section 2 of the English Act of 1848 and the Irish Act of 1849. Whether or not the language used was, as Hutton J. in my opinion rightly held it was, declaratory of the common law, the words "may maintain an action against such justice in the same form and in the same case as he might have done before the passing of this Act" gave statutory force, which survives in section 15 of the Northern Ireland Act of 1964 and section 45 of the Act of 1979, to the old common law rule that justices were civilly liable for actionable wrongs suffered by citizens pursuant to orders made without jurisdiction. It follows that it is now a statutory rule expressed in positive terms in section 45(2) of the Act of 1979. I have already indicated my opinion that the negative form in which the rule is expressed in section 15 of the Northern Ireland Act of 1964 has a similar positive effect. It must follow from this that both courts below were right to reject the argument based on the judgment of Lord Denning M.R. in *Sirros* v. *Moore* [1975] Q.B. 118, which sought to equate the immunity from suit of those purporting to exercise the limited jurisdiction of inferior courts, including justices, with that of judges of the superior courts. Whatever the juridical basis for the distinction between superior and inferior courts in this regard, and however anomalous it may seem to some, the distinction unquestionably remains part of the law affecting justices and will continue to do so as long as the language of either section 15 of the Northern Ireland Act of 1964 or section 45 of the Act of 1979 remains in legislative force in the two jurisdictions.

The provisions introduced in 1964, which have the effect of indemnifying justices against personal liability in appropriate circumstances, have two significant consequences. First, they must contemplate that a justice may be liable for having acted "without jurisdiction or in excess of jurisdiction" even though he was in no way blameworthy, and the statutory phrase must be so construed as to cover this possibility. Secondly, they go far to meet Lord Denning M.R.'s concern expressed in the passage from his judgment in *Sirros* v. *Moore* [1975] Q.B. 118, 136 where he had said:

> "Each should be protected from liability to damages when he is acting judicially. Each should be able to do his work in complete independance and free from fear. He should not have to turn the pages of his books with trembling fingers, asking himself: 'If I do this, shall I be liable in damages?' "

Finally, I can find nothing in the language of section 15 of the Northern Ireland Act of 1964 which suggests that it set out to amend, as opposed to consolidate, the previous law or, in particular, that the phrase "he acted without jurisdiction or in excess of jurisdiction" should convey any different meaning than the words in section 2 of the Irish Act of 1849 "for any act done by a justice in the peace in a matter of which by law he has not jurisdiction, or in which he shall have exceeded his jurisdiction." This is an a fortiori conclusion in relation to section 45 of the Act of 1979, which reproduces verbatim in subsection (1)(*a*) the language of section 2 of the English Act of 1848.

[Lord Bridge then distinguished "excess of jurisdiction" sufficient to justify quashing a conviction by *certiorari* and the "excess of jurisdiction" required to ground liability in damages.]

But once justices have duly entered upon the summary trial of a matter within their jurisdiction, only something quite exceptional occurring in the course of their proceeding to a determination can oust their jurisdiction so as to deprive them of protection from civil liability for a subsequent trespass. As *Johnston* v. *Meldon*, 30 L.R.Ir. 15 shows, an error (whether of law or fact) in deciding a collateral issue on which the jurisdiction depends will not do so. Nor will the absence of any evidence to support a conviction: *Rex (Martin)* v. *Mahony* [1910] 2 I.R. 695; *Rex* v. *Nat Bell Liquors Ltd.* [1922] 2 A.C. 128. It is clear, in my opinion, that no error of law committed in reaching a finding of guilt would suffice, even if it arose from a misconstruction of the particular legislative provision to be applied, so that it could be said that the justices had asked themselves the wrong question. I take this view because, as I have intimated earlier, I do not believe that the novel test of excess of jurisdiction which emerges from the *Anisminic* case [1969] 2 A.C. 147,[3] however valuable it may be in ensuring that the supervisory jurisdiction of the superior courts over inferior tribunals is effective to secure compliance with the law and is not lightly to be ousted by statute, has any application whatever to the construction of section 15 of the Northern Ireland Act of 1964 or section 45 of the Act of 1979.

Justices would, of course, be acting "without jurisdiction or in excess of jurisdiction" within the meaning of section 15 if, in the course of hearing a case within their jurisdiction they were guilty of some gross and obvious irregularity of procedure, as for example if one justice absented himself for part of the hearing and relied on another to tell him what had happened during his absence, or of the rules of natural justice, as for example if the justices refused to allow the defendant to give evidence. But I would leave for determination if and when they arise other more subtle cases one might imagine in which it could successfully be contended in judicial review proceedings that a conviction was vitiated on some narrow technical ground involving a procedural irregularity or even a breach of the rules of natural justice. Such convictions, if followed by a potential trespass to person or goods would not, in my opinion, necessarily expose the justices to liability in damages.

[The error in the instant case gave rise to an excess of jurisdiction which involved liability in damages.]

These three cases[4] establish the clear principle that justices, though they have "jurisdiction of the cause" and conduct the trial impeccably, may nevertheless be liable in damages on the ground of acting in excess of jurisdiction if their conviction of the defendant before them or other determination of the complaint against him does not provide a proper foundation in law for the sentence imposed on him or order made against him and in pursuance of the sentence or order he is imprisoned or his goods are seized.

I turn, at long last, to consideration of the decision in *Sirros* v. *Moore* [1975] Q.B. 118, upon which Hutton J. relied for his decision in favour of the appellants. It was a very unusual case. The plaintiff, a Turkish citizen, had been convicted by a stipendiary magistrate for breach of the Aliens Order 1953 (S.I. 1953 No. 1671). He was fined and recommended for deportation. Pending a decision by the Home Secretary whether or not to implement that recommendation, he would have been liable to be detained unless the magistrate made a direction to the contrary, which in fact he did. The plaintiff appealed to the Crown Court. That court, although a superior court of record when trying cases on indictment, is a court of limited jurisdiction when exercising its appellate jurisdiction from magistrates' courts, which it inherited from the previous courts of quarter sessions, at least in this sense, that its proceedings are subject to judicial review by the High Court as were the proceedings of quarter sessions.

In the course of the appeal to the Crown Court, the plaintiff, unrepresented, made clear that he was only challenging the recommendation for deportation, not the fine. The judge of the Crown Court, erroneously thinking that he had no jurisdiction to entertain an appeal against the recommendation for deportation,

---

[3] *Post* p. 389

[4] *Groome* v. *Forrester* (1816) 5 M&S.314; *M'Creadie* v. *Thomson* 1907 S.C. 1176; *O'Connor* v. *Isaacs* [1956] 2 Q.B. 288.

dismissed the appeal. As the plaintiff was leaving the court, or just after, the judge ordered that he should be detained. Later the same day the judge refused an application made on the plaintiff's behalf by counsel for bail. On the following day the plaintiff was released pursuant to an order of habeas corpus made by the Divisional Court.

The plaintiff sued the judge and the police officers who had detained him pursuant to the judge's order for damages for false imprisonment. The issue came before the Court of Appeal on appeal from an order to strike out the plaintiff's writ and statement of claim, which the Court of Appeal affirmed. I have already indicated my view that, in the light of the statutory provisions relating to the liability of justices acting without jurisdiction in excess of jurisdiction, the sweeping judgment of Lord Denning M.R. in favour of abolishing the distinction between superior and inferior courts in this respect cannot possibly be supported in relation to justices. The narrower question whether other courts of limited jurisdiction can and should be given the same immunity from suit as the superior courts, in which Lord Denning M.R. was supported in his view by Ormrod L.J., is one on which I express no concluded opinion, though my inclination is to think that this distinction is so deeply rooted in our law that it certainly cannot be eradicated by the Court of Appeal and probably not by your Lordship's House, even in exercise of the power declared in the *Practice Statement (Judicial Precedent)* [1966] 1 W.L.R. 1234 made by the House. So fundamental a change would, in my present view, require appropriate legislation.

The decision to strike out the writ and statement of claim in *Sirros* v. *Moore* [1975] Q.B. 118 was, however, supported on a much narrower ground by Buckley L.J., and as an alternative to his main grounds, by Ormrod L.J. It was their reasoning which was applied in the instant case by Hutton J. The essence of this approach is expressed in the judgment of Buckley L.J., which Hutton J. cited and on which he relied, in the following terms, at pp. 143–144:

"If it was within the powers of the judge to determine whether Mr. Sirros should or should not be detained in custody consequent on hearing the appeal, the fact that he may have followed an irregular course in doing so would not render the judge personally liable to a claim such as Mr. Sirros seeks to prosecute in this action. If the judge had jurisdiction to procure Mr. Sirros's detention, any irregularity of procedure may afford good grounds for appeal but cannot deprive the judge's act of its judicial character, so as to render it coram non judice. It is suggested that when the judge gave his direction to 'stop him' he was already functus officio, as the hearing of the appeal had then been concluded, with the consequence that the direction was not a judicial act at all. I feel unable to accept this argument. The judge, in my opinion, clearly thought and intended that the order which he had made would result without more in the detention of Mr. Sirros in custody. The direction to 'stop him' was not a new and distinct decision. It was an implementation of the consequence which the judge believed and intended to follow from the order which he had made. This would, in my opinion, hold good, whether the judge gave the direction at the moment when he saw Mr. Sirros disappearing through the door of the court or some minutes later. I would, however, accept the judge's evidence that the former was the truth. If the judge was mistaken, as I think he was, in thinking that it would follow from his order without more that Mr. Sirros should be detained in custody, but he could have produced that result by an order in some other form, his error was one of form or procedure, not of jurisdiction."

In my opinion, the decision in *Sirros* v. *Moore* [1975] Q.B. 118 can be supported on this very narrow ground. The Crown Court judge was seized of the appeal. He had jurisdiction to determine the case de novo. If he thought it appropriate to affirm the recommendation for deportation but to overrule the magistrate's direction that, pending the Home Secretary's decision, the plaintiff should not be detained, he was authorised to do so. By refusing bail after the plaintiff's detention, he demonstrated that this was indeed his intention. He implemented this intention by a hopelessly irregular procedure, which properly resulted in the plaintiff's release by order of habeas corpus the next day. But the irregularity of procedure was not shown to deprive him, for the purpose of his immunity from civil liability, of the protection attaching to acts done within his jurisdiction, when the order he had made irregularly had produced exactly the same result as the order which he could and, by inference, would have made if the procedure adopted had followed its regular course.

Can it be said that the appellants' omission to inform the respondent of his right to apply for legal aid was a mere procedural irregularity? I have reached the conclusion that it cannot. The language of article 15(1) of the Order of 1976, in any case in which it applies, prohibits in the clearest terms the imposition of any of the custodial sentences mentioned unless one or other of the conditions referred to in paragraphs (a) and (b) of the subsection has been satisfied. As already mentioned, section 21(1) of the Powers of Criminal Courts Act 1973 has the same effect. Parliament plainly attached importance to ensuring that none of these custodial sentences should be imposed for the first time on a defendant not legally represented unless the defendant's lack of representation was of his own choice. The philosophy underlying the provision must be that no one should be liable to a first sentence of imprisonment, borstal training or detention, unless he has had the opportunity of having his case in mitigation presented to the court in the best possible light. For an inarticulate defendant, as so many are, such presentation may be crucial to his liberty. It is impossible to say in this or any other case that, if the requirements of article 15(1) had been satisfied, it would have made no difference to the result. For these reasons I am of opinion that the fulfilment of this statutory condition precedent to the imposition of such a sentence as the appellants here passed on the respondent is no less essential to support the justices' jurisdiction to pass such a sentence than, for example, in the case of a sentence of immediate imprisonment, a prior conviction of an offence for which a sentence of imprisonment can lawfully be passed. There is an analogy here between fulfilment of this statutory condition precedent, necessary to give justices jurisdiction to pass an otherwise appropriate sentence and the fulfilment, at an earlier stage, of the statutory condition precedent, where applicable, requiring the defendant to be informed of his right to elect trial by jury which is necessary to give the justices "jurisdiction of the cause," i.e. to try the case summarily. In neither case can the omission to fulfil the condition precedent be considered a mere procedural irregularity.

It follows that the appellants acted "without jurisdiction or in excess of jurisdiction" within the meaning of the Northern Ireland Act of 1964 and I would accordingly dismiss the appeal with costs.

LORD TEMPLEMAN: . . . In my opinion the authorities disclose that a magistrate is not liable in damages for the consequences of an unlawful sentence passed by him in his judicial capacity in a properly constituted and convened court if he has power to try the offence and the offender, duly convicts the offender of the offence and imposes a sentence which he has power to impose for the offence and on the offender. If the magistrate fails to convict the offender of the offence or if he imposes a sentence which he has no power to impose on the offender for the offence he acts without jurisdiction and if the sentence results in imprisonment, is liable to the accused in a civil action for damages for false imprisonment.

If in the course of a trial which a magistrate is empowered to undertake, the magistrate misbehaves or does not accord the accused a fair trial, or is guilty of some other breach of the principles of natural justice or reaches a result which is vitiated by any error of fact or law, the decision may be quashed but the magistrate acting as such acts within jurisdiction. Similarly if the magistrate after a lawful trial imposes a sentence which he is authorised to impose on the defendant for the offence, but follows a procedure which is irregular, the sentence may be quashed but the magistrate acts within jurisdiction.

In the present case the magistrates were given power to try and to convict the respondent for the offence of which he has in fact convicted. The magistrates were given power to impose a sentence of detention for the offence. But the magistrates were not given power to impose a sentence of detention on the respondent because article 15(1) of the Treatment of Offenders (Northern Ireland) Order 1976 expressly prohibited the imposition of such a sentence on the respondent. The magistrates accordingly acted without jurisdiction.

For these reasons and for reasons advanced by my noble and learned friend, Lord Bridge of Harwich, I would dismiss the appeal.

This appeal demonstrates that the time is ripe for the legislature to reconsider the liability of a magistrate and the rights of a defendant if an unlawful sentence results in imprisonment. There is no liability on a judge of the High Court acting as such and no right for a defendant to damages for an unlawful sentence imposed by a High Court judge; harm may be prevented or cut short by bail and an appeal procedure which results in the sentence being quashed.

> "The High Court constitutes the sole arbiter (though subject to correction on appeal) as to what matters fall between its own jurisdiction. In my judgment, it should now be taken as settled both on authority and on principle that a judge of the High Court is absolutely immune from personal civil liability in respect of any judicial act which he does in his capacity as a judge of that court. He enjoys no such immunity, however, in respect of any act not done in his capacity as a judge."

Per Buckley L.J. in *Sirros* v. *Moore* [1975] Q.B. 118, 139–140, in which case the principles and the authorities are fully discussed.

On the other hand a magistrate is personally liable where an innocent error of law or fact results in an unlawful sentence of imprisonment imposed without jurisdiction. A magistrate is not personally liable for an innocent error of law or fact which results in an unlawful sentence of imprisonment within jurisdiction. So far as the defendant is concerned imprisonment produces the same suffering whether the unlawful sentence is defective but within jurisdiction or defective and made without jurisdiction. I agree with my noble and learned friend, Lord Bridge of Harwich, that the former cause of action against a magistrate for acting within jurisdiction but maliciously and without reasonable and probable cause is obselete or obsolescent. The principles which protect High Court judges from harassment by civil suits alleging malice apply equally to magistrates. Magistrates are better selected, better trained and better advised than they were in the days when Palmerston tried poachers. A possible solution is to extend to magistrates the immunity which protects the High Court judge acting as such. An appellate court or an independent tribunal could be accorded a discretionary power to award compensation to a defendant who suffers an unlawful sentence of imprisonment whether the court acted within or without jurisdiction in imposing the sentence.

Appeal dismissed with costs.

Notes

1. Lord Keith of Kinkel expressed

> "some reservations upon the question, which does not require to be decided in the present appeal, whether the liability of justices for acts done within their jurisdiction but with malice and without probable cause should be treated as having fallen into

desuetude. I should prefer to leave this question to be decided after full argument in an appropriate case."

Lord Brandon of Oakbrook agreed with Lord Bridge of Harwich that liability for malicious acts within the jurisdiction was absolute in Northern Ireland. So far as England was concerned, he thought the question was not wholly free from doubt and preferred to reserve his opinion.

2. Liability for acts done in excess of jurisdiction is limited to one penny if the circumstances fall within section 52 of the Justices of the Peace Act 1979.

(1) The provisions of this section shall have effect where, in any action brought against a justice of the peace for anything done by him in the execution of his office as such a justice, the plaintiff is (apart from this section) entitled to recover damages in respect of a conviction or order, and proves the levying or payment of a penalty or sum of money under the conviction or order as part of the damages which he seeks to recover, or proves that he was imprisoned under the conviction or order and seeks to recover damages for the imprisonment, but it is also proved—

(a) that the plaintiff was actually guilty of the offence of which he was so convicted, or that he was liable by law to pay the sum he was so ordered to pay, and
(b) where he was imprisoned, that he had undergone no greater punishment than that assigned by law for the offence of which he was so convicted for non-payment of the sum he was so ordered to pay.

(2) In the circumstances specified in subsection (1) above, the plaintiff shall not be entitled to recover the amount of the penalty or sum levied or paid as mentioned in that subsection or (as the case may be) to recover any sum beyond the sum of one penny as damages for the imprisonment, and shall not be entitled to any costs.

In R. v. Waltham Forest Justices Ex parte Solanke [1986] Q.B. 479 the Court of Appeal upheld the judgment of Woolf J. in the course of which he said

"Having regard to the framework of the section to which I have referred, I am satisfied that counsel for the justices is correct in his submission that as long as the justice in question is purporting to act in his capacity as a justice sitting in court dealing with the cases before him, he is acting in the execution of his office. The consequence is that notwithstanding that the justices on 12 September 1977 were acting without jurisdiction, they were still acting in the execution of their respective offices."

[The justices had sentenced S. to imprisonment for failure to pay money due to his wife under a High Court order. They had overlooked the fact that the order had not been registered in the magistrates' court so that they had no jurisdiction to commit.]

See further R. v. Manchester City Magistrates' Court ex parte Davies [1988] 1 W.L.R. 667.

PRIVILEGE

Hasselblad (G.B.) Ltd. v. Orbinson
[1985] 1 Q.B. 475
Court of Appeal

As a result of a complaint made to it, the Commission of the European Communities began proceedings to investigate whether the plaintiff company was carrying on business in breach of Article 85 of the E.E.C. Treaty. The complainant forwarded to the Commission a letter from a dissatisfied purchaser of one of the plaintiff's products and the Commission sent a copy to the plaintiff for comment. The plaintiff replied that the allegations in the letter were untrue and brought an action for defamation against the defendant, its author. Comyn J. ruled that the letter was absolutely privileged: Hasselblad appealed.

SIR JOHN DONALDSON M.R.: This is a completely novel issue and one which is of very considerable importance in the light of our increasing involvement with the Commission.

Absolute privilege
The last occasion upon which the House of Lords considered this defence was in *Trapp* v. *Mackie* [1979] 1 W.L.R. 377. Dr Trapp had been dismissed from his post as headmaster of a Scottish school and a local inquiry was held before a commissioner appointed by the Secretary of State for Scotland pursuant to statutory powers. In the course of the inquiry Mr. Mackie gave evidence which Dr. Trapp alleged to be both false and malicious. The House of Lords held that the evidence was protected by absolute privilege, but the importance of the decision lies in the guidance given by Lords Diplock and Fraser of Tullybelton on the approach which should be adopted by courts charged with the duty of deciding whether this defence is available. Lord Diplock said, at pp. 378-380:

"That absolute privilege attaches to words spoken or written in the course of giving evidence in proceedings in a court of justice is a rule of law, based on public policy, that has been established since earliest times. That the like privilege extends to evidence given before tribunals which, although not courts of justice, nevertheless act in a manner similar to that in which courts of justice act, was established more than a hundred years ago by the decision of this House in *Dawkins* v. *Lord Rokeby* (1875) L.R. 7 H.L. 744, where the unanimous answer of the judges to the question asked them by the House was adopted and the ratio decidendi of the judgment of the Court of Exchequer Chamber (1873) L.R. 8 Q.B. 255 was approved.

"The kind of tribunal in which the evidence of witnesses is entitled to absolute privilege was described by Lord Atkin in *O'Connor* v. *Waldron* [1935] A.C. 76, 81, as a tribunal which 'has similar attributes to a court of justice or acts in a manner similar to that in which such courts act.' That the 'or' in this phrase is not intended to be disjunctive is apparent from the fact that Lord Atkin was confirming the accuracy of the law as it had been stated by Lord Esher M.R. in *Royal Aquarium and Summer and Winter Garden Society Ltd.* v. *Parkinson* [1892] 1 Q.B. 431, 442. Lord Esher, having spoken of 'an authorised inquiry which, though not before a court of justice, is before a tribunal which has similar attributes,' went on to explain that what he meant by similar attributes was 'acting . . . in a manner as nearly as possible similar to that in which a court of justice acts in respect of an inquiry before it.'

"In the course of the hearing which, as in both courts below, has been conducted by Dr. Trapp in person with skill and erudition, your Lordships' attention has been drawn to what must be nearly every reported case upon this topic in Scotland, and in England where most of the authorities are to be found. I do not find it necessary to refer to them. They provide examples of inquiries and tribunals which have been held to fall upon one or other side of a line which as Lord Atkin said in *O'Connor* v. *Waldron* [1935] A.C. 76, 81 'is not capable of very precise limitation.'

"No single touchstone emerges from the cases; but this is not surprising for the rule of law is one which involves the balancing of conflicting public policies, one general: that the law should provide a remedy to the citizen whose good name and reputation is traduced by malicious falsehoods uttered by another; the other particular: that witnesses before tribunals recognised by law should, in the words of the answer of the judges in *Dawkins* v. *Lord Rokeby*, L.R. 7 H.L. 744, 753 'give their testimony free from any fear of being harassed by an action on an allegation, *whether true or false*, that they acted from malice.'

"So, to decide whether a tribunal acts in a manner similar to courts of justice and thus is of such a kind as will attract absolute, as distinct from qualified, privilege for witnesses when they give testimony before it, one must consider first, under what authority the tribunal acts, secondly the nature of the question into which it is its duty to inquire; thirdly the procedure adopted by it in carrying out the inquiry; and fourthly the legal consequences of the conclusion reached by the tribunal as a result of the inquiry.

"To attract absolute privilege for the testimony of witnesses the tribunal, by whatever name it is described, must be 'recognised by law,' a phrase first used by the Court of Exchequer in *Dawkins* v. *Lord Rokeby*, L.R. 8 Q.B. 255, 263. This is a sine qua non; the absolute privilege does not attach to purely domestic tribunals. Although the description 'recognised by law' is not necessarily confined to tribunals constituted or recognised by Act of Parliament (see *Lincoln* v. *Daniels* [1962] 1 Q.B. 237) it embraces all that are, and so includes the local inquiry in the instant case. . . ."

Lord Fraser of Tullybelton said, at pp. 385-386:

"It will be convenient first to consider the legal principles to be applied. It is, and has long been, well settled that no action will lie against a witness for words spoken in giving evidence in a court even if the evidence is falsely and maliciously given. In *Watson* v. *M'Ewan* [1905] A.C. 480, 486, Lord Halsbury L.C. said that was 'settled law and cannot be doubted.' He went on: 'The remedy against a witness who has given evidence which is false and injurious to another is to indict him for perjury; but for very obvious reasons, the conduct of legal procedure by courts of justice, *with the necessity of compelling witnesses to attend*, involves as one of the necessities of the administration of justice the immunity of witnesses from actions being brought against them in respect of evidence they have given.' (My italics) That case decided that the same immunity attached to statements made on precognition with a view to giving evidence. The rule was reaffirmed recently in *Roy* v. *Prior* [1971] A.C. 470 and its justification was explained by Lord Wilberforce, at p. 480: 'The reasons why immunity is traditionally (and for this purpose I accept the tradition) conferred upon witnesses in respect of evidence given in court, are in order that they may give their evidence fearlessly and to avoid a multiplicity of actions in which the value or truth of their evidence would be tried over again. Moreover, the trial process contains in itself, in the subjection to cross-examination and confrontation with other evidence, some safeguard against careless, malicious or untruthful evidence.'

"The rule has been extended beyond courts of justice and has been held to apply to authorised inquiries before tribunals which, though not courts of justice, have similar attributes: see *Royal Aquarium and Summer and Winter Garden Society Ltd.* v. *Parkinson* [1892] 1 Q.B. 431, 442 *per* Lord Esher M.R. In

O'Connor v. *Waldron* [1935] A.C. 76, 81 Lord Atkin giving the advice of the Judicial Committee said: 'In their Lordships' opinion the law on the subject was accurately stated by Lord Esher in *Royal Aquarium etc., Ltd.* v. *Parkinson* where he says that the privilege "applies wherever there is an authorized inquiry which, though not before a court of justice, is before a tribunal which has similar attributes. . . . This doctrine has never been extended further than to courts of justice and tribunals acting in a manner similar to that in which such courts act." The question therefore in every case is whether the tribunal in question has similar attributes to a court of justice or acts in a manner similar to that in which such courts act. This is of necessity a differentia which is not capable of very precise limitation.' "

Lord Fraser of Tullybelton continued, at p. 388:

"Consideration of the cases shows that, provided the tribunal is one recognised by law, there is no single element the presence or absence of which will be conclusive in showing whether it has attributes sufficiently similar to those of a court of law to create absolute privilege. It is not essential that the tribunal itself should have power to determine the issue before it, and a statement by Lord Sankey L.C. in *Shell Co. of Australia Ltd.* v. *Federal Commissioner of Taxation* [1931] A.C. 275, 295, which at first sight appears to indicate the contrary is not truly in pari materia. It was directed to the different question of the meaning of 'judicial power' in section 71 of the Australian Constitution. Cases such as *Dawkins*, L.R. 7 H.L. 744 and *Barratt* [1905] 1 K.B. 504, show that absolute privilege may apply if the inquiry is a step leading directly towards determination of an issue by the authority who appointed it. In each case the object of the tribunal, its constitution and its manner of proceeding must all be considered before the question can be answered."

In *Watson* v. *M'Ewan* [1905] A.C. 480 absolute privilege was accorded to a precognition, or witness's proof, on the grounds expressed in the speech of the Earl of Halsbury L.C. when he said, at p. 487:

"If it were otherwise, I think what one of the learned counsel has with great cogency pointed out would apply—that from time to time in these various efforts which have been made to make actual witnesses responsible in the shape of an action against them for the evidence they have given, the difficulty in the way of those who were bringing the action would have been removed at once by saying, 'I do not bring the action against you for what you said in the witness-box, but I bring the action against you for what you told the solicitor you were about to say in the witness-box.' If that could be done the object for which the privilege exists is gone, because then no witness could be called; no one would know whether what he was going to say was relevant to the question in debate between the parties. A witness would only have to say, 'I shall not tell you anything; I may have an action brought against me tomorrow if I do; therefore I shall not give you any information at all.' It is very obvious that the public policy which renders the protection of witnesses necessary for the administration of justice must as a necessary consequence involve that which is a step towards and is part of the administration of justice—namely, the preliminary examination of witnesses to find out what they can prove. It may be that to some extent it seems to impose a hardship, but after all the hardship is not to be compared with that which would arise if it were impossible to administer justice, because people would be afraid to give their testimony."

The first question which arises is whether this letter is to be regarded as sufficiently closely connected to the process of giving evidence, for it to be necessary to extend absolute privilege to it, assuming always that absolute privilege would attach to evidence to the like effect given to the Commission.

[The Master of the Rolls, after considering the facts, concluded that the letter was sufficiently closely connected.]

I therefore turn to the criteria identified by Lord Diplock in *Trapp* v. *Mackie* [1979] 1 W.L.R. 377, 379, as aids to deciding whether a body which is not a court of justice is a tribunal which acts in a manner similar to courts of justice.

(a) *The authority under which the Commission acts*
It is conceded, as it must be, that the Commission is recognised by the law of this country. Its general duties are laid down by article 155 of the E.E.C. Treaty. More specifically in relation to competition and articles 85 [matters "incompatible with the common market"] and 86 [abuse by undertakings of "dominant position within the common market"], article 89 requires it to investigate suspected infringements of the principles enshrined in those articles and to take appropriate measures to bring them to an end. Article 87 arms the Commission with the power to impose fines and periodic penalty payments. In addition to these provisions, the Council has legislated (Council Regulation (E.E.C.) No. 17/62 [Official Journal of the European Communities, 204/62, p. 87]) giving the Commission special powers and the Commission itself has made regulations governing its hearings (Regulation No. 99/63 E.E.C. of the Commission). Finally the decisions of the Commission are subject to review by the Court of Justice under article 173.

(b) *The nature of the question into which it is the duty of the Commission to inquire*
The Commission is charged with the duty of inquiring whether there have been infringements of article 85 or 86 of the Treaty, not with a view to reporting the facts to others, but with a view to reaching a definitive decision, subject to any review by the Court of Justice, and imposing penalties, again subject to any such review.

(c) *The legal consequences of its conclusion*
Decisions of the Commission enforceable under article 192 of the E.E.C. Treaty are known as "Community judgments" and are enforceable by the High Court under R.S.C., Ord. 71, rr. 15–24, without further proof, other than of authenticity.

Thus far I can detect nothing which indicates that the Commission in its role in relation to alleged breaches of articles 85 and 86 is other than a tribunal which could be said to be one which, though not a court of justice, had similar attributes: see Lord Fraser of Tullybelton's speech [1979] 1 W.L.R. 377, 385–386. However, the picture changes when one comes to look at the remaining criterion listed by Lord Diplock.

(d) *The procedure adopted by the Commission*
The starting point is either a complaint from outside the Commission or the Commission being put on inquiry by published materials, but it is simpler to consider an investigation which begins with a complaint, this being the more usual situation and the one which obtained in the present instance.

The complaint is considered within the Commission by an examiner and a case team. They can and do make further inquiries including, in an appropriate case, making use of the Commission's right to enter and search the premises of the alleged infringer on the lines of the *Anton Piller* jurisdiction: see article 14(3) of Regulation No. 17/62. Once the Commission's own preliminary investigations are complete, a decision is made whether to take no further action or to serve a statement of objections on the alleged infringer. If the decision is that no further action be taken, the complaint is informed and can, if he wishes, seek judicial review from the Court of Justice. If a statement of objections is served, it is accompanied by a letter setting out the alleged infringer's time for reply, rights of defence and rights of access to the Commission's file. The letter ends by inviting the alleged infringer to a hearing, if he requires it.

The next stage consists of the hearing. The chairman is now an officer of the Commission who is to some extent independent, but, at the time with which we are concerned, the chairman or hearing officer was Mr. Ferry, who had been involved in evaluating the complaint at an earlier stage. The parties present at the hearing are the alleged infringer , the complainant, third parties with a sufficient interest and representatives of the Commission. All these can have legal advisers. Member states of the E.E.C. also send representatives.

The hearing begins with a brief outline of the matter by the hearing officer of the Commission. The alleged infringer then presents his case and is free to call witnesses. The hearing officer can ask questions and he can and does permit questions by representatives of the competition department of the Commission and on occasion by those of other directorates, *e.g.* agriculture, industrial policy, etc. Unlike the position of the Commission, the other parties are not allowed to ask questions. The complainant and third parties then present their case by calling evidence and making submissions. Finally the hearing officer closes the proceedings and, in an appropriate case, can invite the parties, but not the Commission, to submit any further evidence in writing within a time limit. The fact that the Commission is not invited to submit further evidence is both significant and easily explicable. The hearing is a hearing by or on behalf of the Commission and it is open to it to take account of such new evidence as it may acquire at any time before a decision is reaches. No formal procedures are necessary.

After the hearing has been concluded, the hearing officer presents his conclusions to the Director General. If his recommendation is that the case proceed no further, the matter is considered by the Director General.The hearing officer has direct access to the Commissioners. If a decision is taken to drop the case, the complainants are informed and given the opportunity to comment and may seek judicial review of the decision in some circumstances. If, on the other hand, the decision is that the case should proceed, then a preliminary draft decision is prepared for approval and forwarded to an advisory committee consisting of representatives of the ten member states. This advisory committee considers the draft and issues a confidential opinion for consideration by the Commission itself. That draft is scrutinised by the legal service. Thereafter it is submitted to the Commission with the opinion of the Advisory committee and any opinion of the hearing officer. The Commissioner to whom the draft is submitted places it before his fellow Commissioners for adoption. The decision, once adopted, is promulgated and there upon becomes fully enforceable throughout the European Community.

This procedure is wholly dissimilar to that of any court or judicial tribunal operating under the common law system, but I do not think that that is the test. When in *Trapp* v. *Mackie* [1979] 1 W.L.R. 377, 379, Lord Diplock referred to a tribunal acting "in a manner similar to courts of justice" and Lord Fraser of Tullybelton at p. 385G to tribunals having "similar attributes" to courts of justice, I think that they must have had a wider concept in mind which would embrace courts of justice operating both under common law and under civil law procedures. The fact that the Commission quite clearly has regard to the rules of natural justice, as shown inter alia by the procedure which gives the alleged infringer a right to an oral hearing, does not advance the matter, because those who take purely administrative decisions are often required to have regard to those rules. However, the fact that the decision is reached by Commissioners, who have not attended the hearing, on the basis of advice from representatives of the European Community nations, who are not directly concerned, seems to me to show that the Commission is acting in a manner which is dissimilar to that of either civil or common law courts of justice and that its attributes are dissimilar to such courts. This is not a criticism of the Commission and its procedures. It is merely an acceptance that the Commission and its procedures fall into a different category, better labelled as administrative rather than judicial or quasi judicial.

O'Connor L.J. concurred. The appeal, however, was dismissed on the ground of public interest: see *post* p.455 May L.J. dissented.

CONTEMPT OF COURT

Attorney-General v. Newspaper Publishing PLC
[1987] 3 W.L.R. 942
Court of Appeal.

Interlocutory injunctions had been granted at the instance of the Attorney-General restraining the *Observer* and *The Guardian* newspapers from publishing material taken from the memoirs of Peter Wright, formerly a member of the British Security Service. Subsequently *The Independent* and two other newspapers published extracts from the same memoirs. The Attorney-General moved to commit the three papers for contempt of court. Sir Nicolas Browne-Wilkinson V-C held that the injunctions against the *Observer* and *The Guardian* could only act *in personam* and therefore the disregard of those orders by third parties did not constitute contempt of court. The Attorney-General appealed to the Court of Appeal (Sir John Donaldson M.R., Lloyd and Balcombe L.JJ.).

SIR JOHN DONALDSON M.R.: . . . If the parties are arguing about the ownership of a horse or a car, it may not matter who keeps the horse or car pending the trial. If, as things turn out, the court has given it to the wrong party, it can get it back and give it to the right party after the trial, together with damages to compensate for having been deprived of the horse or car for the time being. Not so with confidential information where, as here, one party says that it is his private property and the other says that he is entitled to publish it to the world. If, pending the trial, the court prohibits publication, the information can still be published after the trial if the defendant succeeds. But if, pending the trial, the court allows publication, there is no point in having a trial since the cloak of confidentiality can never be restored. Confidential information is like an ice cube. Give it to the party who undertakes to keep it in his refrigerator and you still have an ice cube by the time the matter comes to trial. Either party may then succeed in obtaining possession of the cube. Give it to the party who has no refrigerator or will not agree to keep it in one, and by the time of the trial you just have a pool of water which neither party wants. It is the inherently perishable nature of confidential information which gives rise to unique problems.

The situation with which we are faced is novel in the sense that there is no reported decision which provides any direct guidance. It is therefore appropriate to start with the first principles of the law of contempt of court and indeed by distancing myself from that phrase itself. As Lord President Clyde pointed out in *Johnson* v. *Grant*, 1923 S.C. 789, 790:

> "The phrase 'contempt of court' does not in the least describe the true nature of the class offence with which we are here concerned . . . The offence consists in interfering with the administration of the law; in impeding and perverting the course of justice. . . . It is not the dignity of the court which is offended—a petty and misleading view of the issues involved—it is the fundamental supremacy of the law which is challenged."

Despite its protean nature, contempt has been classified under two heads, namely, "civil contempt" and "criminal contempt." Whatever the value of this classification in earlier times, I venture to think that it now tends to mislead rather than assist, because the standard of proof is the same, namely, the criminal standard, and there are now common rights of appeal. Of greater assistance is a re-classification as (a) conduct which involves a breach, or assisting in the breach, of a court order and (b) any other conduct which involves an interference with the due administration of justice, either in a particular case or, more generally, as a continuing process, the first category being a special form of the latter, such interference being a characteristic common to all contempts: *per* Lord Diplock in *Attorney-General* v. *Leveller Magazine Ltd.* [1979] A.C. 440, 449. What distinguishes the two categories is that in general conduct which involves a breach, or assisting in the breach, of a court order is treated as a matter for the parties to raise by complaint to the court, whereas other forms of contempt are in general considered to be a matter for the Attorney-General to raise. In doing so he acts not as a government minister or legal adviser, but as the guardian of the public interest in the due administration of justice. There is a further, but less important, distinction in that in the case of a failure to comply with some court orders, for example those relating to procedural timetables, the appropriate reaction of the court is not punishment in the form of committal, attachment or a fine, but an order striking out all or part of a claim, or refusing to entertain the whole or part of a defence.

The Attorney-General's complaint is not that the respondent newspapers and their editors have breached or assisted in the breach of the orders which he obtained in the Guardian and Observer actions, but that the conduct complained of "was intended or calculated to impede, obstruct or prejudice the administration of justice."

This raises two issues. What is the conduct complained of? Can it be said to have been intended or calculated to impede, obstruct or prejudice the administration of justice? The latter is clearly a question which cannot be answered in the abstract, but depends upon the course which the administration of justice has taken and is intended by the court to take. It is for this reason, and this reason alone, that it is necessary to take account of the course which the Guardian and Observer actions had pursued, including the orders made restraining "The Guardian" and the "Observer," but no other newspapers, from publishing what I may describe as "Wright material," *i.e.* information obtained by Mr. Wright in his capacity as a member of the British Security Service and which was known or reasonably believed to have come or been obtained, whether directly or indirectly, from Mr. Wright or any information concerning the British Security Service which was attributed to Mr. Wright.

[After surveying the history of the earlier litigation Sir John Donaldson M.R. continued]

It is against this background that I ask myself whether at the end of July 1986, when the interim injunctive order was made against "The Guardian" and the "Observer," a publication by "The Independent" of new, and apparently more authentic, Wright material, allegedly based upon possession of a copy of Mr. Wright's manuscript, which neither "The Guardian" nor the "Observer" ever claimed or admitted having had, would "be calculated to impede obstruct or prejudice the administration of justice," to quote the words of the Attorney-General's application or "involve an interference with the due administration of justice," to quote the words of Lord Diplock in *Attorney-General* v. *Leveller Magazine Ltd.* [1979] A.C. 440, 449. To that question I think that there can be only one answer, namely that it would. The issue in the Guardian and the Observer actions was not whether the information had been confidential to the Crown, but whether for one reason or another that confidentiality had evaporated or was overridden by a countervailing public interest. Millett J., and this court on appeal, had not only prohibited publication, including republication, by "The Guardian" and the "Observer," but had held that, to quote Millett J., indirect publication of Mr. Wright's memoirs, the direct publication of which was prohibited by the Australian courts, would "permanently deprive the Attorney-General of his rights in advance of the trial." It could not have been made clearer. The court was making an order for the preservation of the confidentiality of the Wright material pending the trial. Publication meanwhile, whether by those defendants or others, would deprive the Attorney-General of his rights in advance of the trial, because information once published, at least on the scale achieved by publication in national newspapers, can never be truly confidential again.

I then ask myself whether this situation had changed in April 1987 when "The Independent," "The London Evening Standard" and "The London Daily News" in fact published further Wright material. It is true that the Australian trial had concluded by then, and the judge had ruled that Mr. Wright was entitled to publish, but the decision was under appeal and the Guardian and the Observer actions still awaited a full trial. The answer is plain. The publication of Mr. Wright's memoirs in full at that time would have prevented any effective adjudication upon the Attorney-General's claim in the Guardian and the Observer actions and the publications complained of, whilst not going to this length, were very far from being of minimal effect. To the extent that they placed Wright material into the public domain, which had not previously been there, they deprived the Attorney-General of a part of the rights which he was asserting in these actions and to this extent made it impossible for the court to do justice between the parties.

Summary
Although it has been necessary to explore this matter in considerable detail and depth, I can summarise the position very shortly. (1) Confidential information, whatever its nature—personal, financial, technical or security—has one essential common characteristic. It is *irremediably* damaged in its confidential character by every publication and the more widespread the publication, the greater the damage. (2) If a prima facie claim to confidentiality can be established, but this is opposed by a claim of a right to publish, whether on grounds of the public interest or otherwise, these opposing and wholly inconsistent claims must be evaluated and balanced the one against the other. (3) The public interest in ensuring that disputes are resolved justly and by due process of law may require a different balance to be struck at different stages. Thus, pending the trial of the action, the balance will normally come down in favour of preserving confidentiality, for the very obvious reason that, if this is not done and publication is permitted, there will be nothing left to have a trial about. (4) It is for the courts, and not for either of the opposing parties, to decide where, in the public interest, that balance lies. (5) Third parties—strangers to the action—who know that the court has made orders or accepted undertakings designed to protect the confidentiality of the information pending the trial, commit a serious offence against justice itself if they take action which will damage or destroy the confidentiality which the court is seeking to protect and so render the due process of law ineffectual. (6) If such third parties, having a legitimate interest in so doing, wish to contest the court's decision to protect the confidentiality of the information on any grounds, including in particular that they have special rights or interests of which account has not been taken, they should apply to the court which will hear them and make any modification of its orders which may be appropriate. This is a well-established procedure which works speedily and well in the context of ex parte orders, such as those made in the exercise of the *Mareva* and *Anton Piller* jurisdictions. Similarly they should apply to the court if they have doubts whether the action which they contemplate taking is lawful. (7) It is for the courts, and not for third parties, to decide whether, balancing competing public and private interests including those of the third parties, confidentiality should continue to be preserved at any particular time.
I would answer the question raised on this appeal by holding that the conduct of the respondents could constitute a criminal contempt of court, but that it is impossible to say whether it did or did not do so until they have been given an opportunity of being further heard and the court has determined whether, in so conducting themselves, the respondents intended to impede or prejudice the administration of justice. I would allow the appeal and remit the matter to the High Court.
Appeal allowed.

Note

This was not a case of strict liability contempt. For the requisite mental element in intentional contempts, see *post* p. 178.

In *Attorney-General* v. *Observer Ltd.* [1988] 1 All E.R. 385 Knox J. had to exercise the "novel" jurisdiction recognised in the sixth point of Sir John Donaldson M.R.'s summary and consider at the request of the Derbyshire County Council whether supplying *Spycatcher* in libraries under its control might constitute contempt of the interlocutory injunctions granted by the House of Lords in *Attorney-General* v. *Guardian Newspapers Ltd.* [1987] 1 W.L.R. 1248. The learned judge held that making the book available would constitute the actus reus of contempt and that it would be "in the highest degree improbable" that a council could in the circumstances fail to have the necessary mens rea. The learned judge also held that failing to examine magazines and newspapers available in the library to see if they contained material from *Spycatcher* would not constitute contempt;

> "Beyond that I am not prepared to go. In particular I am not prepared to make a finding that making newspapers, magazines and periodicals available to the public could not in any circumstances amount to a contempt of court because a great deal would depend on those circumstances, and it is no part of this court's function to give general advice as to future courses of conduct."

The Strict Liability Rule

Attorney-General v. English
[1983] 1 A.C. 116
House of Lords

In October 1981 the editor and owners of a newspaper published an article in support of a candidate at a forthcoming parliamentary by-election who was seeking election as an independent "pro-life" candidate. The article supported the candidate's view that every person, however severely handicapped, had the right to life and stated that the chances of such a baby surviving today would be very small, since someone would be likely to recommend letting the child die of starvation or otherwise disposing of him. It asked whether human beings were to be culled like livestock so that there would be no more hereditary idiots or mongoloid children and then contrasted that approach with the Christian view of the sanctity of life. The article was published on the third day of the trial of a consultant paediatrician, for the murder of a mongol baby. The trial received wide publicity, the prosecution case being that the doctor in accordance with the wishes of the parents, had caused or intended to cause the child's death by starvation. The doctor was subsequently acquitted.

On the Attorney-General's application for an order against the respondents for contempt of court, pursuant to the Contempt of Court Act 1981, the Divisional Court (Watkins L.J., Boreham and Glidewell J.J.) held that the "strict liability rule" defined in section 1 of the Act applied by virtue of section 2(2), since the article had created a substantial risk of serious prejudice to the course of justice in the doctor's trial, and that appellants were not entitled to the protection of section 5 because the words complained of were not "merely incidental" to a discussion of general public interest.

The House of Lords (Lord Diplock, Lord Elwyn-Jones, Lord Keith of Kinkel, Lord Scarman and Lord Brandon of Oakbrook) allowed an appeal by the editor and the owners of the newspaper.

LORD DIPLOCK. . . . My Lords, that part of the Contempt of Court Act 1981 which is relevant to this appeal is to be found in the first seven sections. These appear under the crossheading "Strict liability." They deal with the publication to the public or a section of the public of matter which tends to interfere with the course of justice in particular legal proceedings, and they seek to hold the balance between the competing public interest of what American lawyers pithily described as "fair trial and free press." Apart from the provisions of sections 11 and 12 of the Administration of Justice Act 1960, of which the former is now repealed and replaced by section 3 of the Contempt of Court Act 1981, the law as to contempt of court before the passing of the Act of 1981 was entirely "judge-made" law, and the remedies for it lay within a virtually unfettered discretion of the individual judge or Divisional Court which remained unappealable until by the Administration of Justice Act 1960 a right of appeal to the Court of Appeal, and ultimately to this House, was granted in matters of contempt of court. The distinction was blurred between publications that did *not* amount to a contempt of court and those which, although "technically" they did, were regarded by the court before which the matter came as being so venial as not to merit any punishment or even an order to pay the costs; and the criteria for determining where in a particular case the balance lay between fair trial and free press can hardly be said to have been rendered clear-cut by obiter dicta to be found in the five separate speeches in this House in *Attorney-General v. Times Newspapers Ltd.* [1974] A.C. 273. These were two-fold mischiefs which, as it seems to me, the first seven sections of the Act of 1981 were intended to remedy.

In the instant appeal your Lordships will be primarily concerned with the construction of section 2(2) and section 5 of the Act; but for this purpose it is helpful to read them in the context of the remaining sections appearing under the cross-heading "Strictliability".

It is convenient to reproduce all seven sections here.

"Strict liability

"1. In this Act 'the strict liability rule' means the rule of law whereby conduct may be treated as a contempt of court as tending to interfere with the course of justice in particular legal proceedings regardless of intent to do so.

"2. (1) The strict liability rule applies only in relation to publications, and for this purpose 'publication' includes any speech, writing, broadcast or other communication in whatever form, which is addressed to the public at large or any section of the public. (2) The strict liability rule applies only to a publication which creates a substantial risk that the course of justice in the proceedings in question will be seriously impeded or prejudiced. (3) The strict liability rule applies to a publication only if the proceedings in question are active within the meaning of this section at the time of the publication. (4) Schedule 1 applies for determining the times at which proceedings are to be treated as active within the meaning of this section.

"3. (1) A person is not guilty of contempt of court under the strict liability rule as the publisher of any matter to which that rule applies if at the time of publication (having taken all reasonable care) he does not know and has no reason to suspect that relevant proceedings are active. (2) A person is not guilty of contempt of court under the strict liability rule as the distributor of a publication containing any such matter if at the time of distribution (having taken all reasonable care) he does not know that it contains such matter and has no reason to suspect that it is likely to do so. (3) The burden of proof of any fact tending to establish a defence afforded by this section to any person lies upon that person. (4) Section 11 of the Administration of Justice Act 1960 is repealed.

"4. (1) Subject to this section a person is not guilty of contempt of court under the strict liability rule in respect of a fair and accurate report of legal proceedings held in public, published contemporaneously and in good faith. (2) In any such proceedings the court may, where it appears to be necessary for avoiding a substantial risk of prejudice to the administration of justice in those proceedings, or in any other proceedings pending or imminent, order that the publication of any report of the proceedings, or any part of the proceedings, be postponed for such period as the court thinks necessary for that purpose. (3) For the purposes of subsection (1) of this section and of section 3 of the Law of Libel Amendment Act 1888 (privilege) a report of proceedings shall be treated as published contemporaneously—(a) in the case of a report of which publication is postponed pursuant to an order under subsection (2) of this section, if published as soon as practicable after that order expires; (b) in the case of a report of committal proceedings of which publication is permitted by virtue only of subsection (3) of section 8 of the Magistrates' Courts Act 1980, if published as soon as practicable after publication is so permitted. (4) Subsection (9) of the said section 8 is repealed.

"5. A publication made as or as part of a discussion in good faith of public affairs or other matters of general public interest is not to be treated as a contempt of court under the strict liability rule if the risk of impediment or prejudice to particular legal proceedings is merely incidental to the discussion.

"6. Nothing in the foregoing provisions of this Act—(a) prejudices any defence available at common law to a charge of contempt of court under the strict liability rule; (b) implies that any publication is punishable as contempt of court under that rule which would not be so punishable apart from those provisions; (c) restricts liability for contempt of court in respect of conduct intended to impede or prejudice the administration of justice.[1]

"7. Proceedings for a contempt of court under the strict liability rule (other than Scottish proceedings) shall not be instituted except by or with the consent of the Attorney-General or on the motion of a court having jurisdiction to deal with it."

The long title of the Act is "An Act to amend the law relating to contempt of court and related matters" and it is apparent from 6(*a*) and (*b*) that such changes as sections 1 to 5 make in the existing law are intended to effect some reduction in its severity in its application to those responsible for publications which may have a tendency to interfere with the course of justice in particular legal proceedings. So far as the reported cases go, the "strict liability rule," as defined in section 1, had only been applied to conduct which involved some publication of offending material; and it can reasonably be inferred from the provision in section 2 (1) which confines the ambit of the fasciculus of sections to publications addressed to the public at large or a section of the public, that the principal intended beneficiaries of any reduction in severity were the media, *viz*, the press, television and radio. It is true that public speakers also are included—but unless their speeches are reported by the media these are likely to be exonerated by section 2(2).

There is, of course, no question that the article in the "Daily Mail" of which complaint is made by the Attorney-General was a "publication" within the meaning of section 2(1). That being so, it appears to have been accepted in the Divisional Court by both parties that the onus of proving that the article satisfied the conditions stated in section 2(2) lay upon the Attorney-General and that, if he satisfied that onus, the onus lay upon the appellants to prove that it satisfied the conditions stated in section 5. For my part, I am unable to accept that this represents the effect of the relationship of section 5 to section 2(2). Section 5 does not take the form of a proviso or an exception to section 2(2). It stands on an equal footing with it. It does not set out exculpatory matter. Like section 2(2) it states what publications shall *not* amount to contempt of court despite their tendency to interfere with the course of justice in particular legal proceedings.

For the publication to constitute a contempt of court under the strict liability rule, it must be shown that the publication satisfies the criterion for which section 2(2) provides, *viz*, that it "creates a substantial risk that the course of justice in the proceedings in question will be seriously impeded or prejudiced." It is only if it falls within section 5 that anything more need be shown. So logically the first question always is: has the publication satisfied the criterion laid down by section 2(2).

My Lords, the first thing to be observed about this criterion is that the risk that has to be assessed is that which was created by the publication of the allegedly offending matter at the time when it was published. The public policy that underlies the strict liability rule in contempt of court is deterrence. Trial by newspaper or, as it should be more compendiously expressed today, trial by the media, is not to be permitted in this country. That the risk that was created by the publication when it was actually published does not ultimately affect the outcome of the proceedings is, as Lord Goddard C.J. said in *Reg.* v. *Evening Standard Co. Ltd.* [1954] 1 Q.B. 578, 582 "neither here nor there." If there was a reasonable possibility that it might have done so if in the period subsequent to the publication the proceedings had not taken the course that in fact they did and Dr. Arthur was acquitted, the offence was complete. The true course of justice must not at any stage be put at risk.

Next for consideration is the concatenation in the subsection of the adjective "substantial" and the adverb "seriously," the former to describe the degree of risk, the latter to describe the degree of impediment or prejudice to the course of justice. "Substantial" is hardly the most apt word to apply to "risk" which is a

[1] *Post*, page 181.

noumenon. In combination I take the two words to be intended to exclude a risk that is only remote. With regard to the adverb "seriously" a perusal of the cases cited in *Attorney-General* v. *Times Newspapers Ltd.* [1974] A.C. 273 discloses that the adjective "serious" has from time to time been used as an alternative to "real" to describe the degree of risk of interfering with the course of justice, but not the degree of interference itself. It is, however, an ordinary English word that is not intrinsically inapt when used to describe the extent of an impediment or prejudice to the cause of justice in particular legal proceedings, and I do not think that for the purposes of the instant appeal any attempt to paraphrase it is necessary or would be helpful. The subsection applies to all kinds of legal proceedings, not only criminal prosecutions before a jury. If, as in the instant case and probably in most other criminal trials upon indictment, it is the outcome of the trial or the need to discharge the jury without proceeding to a verdict that is put at risk, there can be no question that that which in the course of justice is put at risk is as serious as anything could be.

Mr Lords, that Mr. Malcolm Muggeridge's article was capable of prejudicing the jury against Dr. Arthur at the early stage of his trial when it was published, seems to me to be clear. It suggested that it was a common practice among paediatricians to do that which Dr. Arthur was charged with having done, because they thought that it was justifiable in the interest of humanity even though it was against the law. At this stage of the trial the jury did not know what Dr. Arthur's defence was going to be; and whether at that time the risk of the jury's being influenced by their recollection of the article when they came even-tually to consider their verdict appeared to be more than a remote one, was a matter which the judge before whom the trial was being conducted was in the best position to evaluate, even though his evaluation, although it should carry weight, would not be binding on the Divisional Court or on your Lordships. The judge thought at that stage of the trial that the risk was substantial, not remote. So, too, looking at the matter in retrospect, did the Divisional Court despite the fact that the risk had not turned into an actuality since Dr. Arthur had by then been acquitted. For my part I am not prepared to dissent from this evaluation. I consider that the publication of the article on the third day of what was to prove a lengthy trial satisfied the criterion for which section 2(2) of the Act provides.

The article, however, fell also within the category dealt with in section 5. It was made, in undisputed good faith, as a discussion in itself of public affairs, viz., Mrs. Carr's candidature as an independent pro-life candidate in the North West Croydon by-election for which the polling day was in one week's time. It was also part of a wider discussion on a matter of general public interest that had been proceeding intermittently over the last three months, upon the moral justification of mercy killing and in particular of allowing newly born hopelessly handicapped babies to die. So it was for the Attorney-General to show that the risk of prejudice to the fair trial of Dr. Arthur which I agree was created by the publication of the article at the stage the trial had reached when it was published was not "merely incidental" to the discussion of the matter with which the article dealt.

My Lords, any article published at the time when Dr. Arthur was being tried which asserted that it was a common practice among paediatricians to let severely physically or mentally handicapped new born babies die of starvation or other-wise dispose of them would (as, in common with the trial judge and the Divisional Court, I have already accepted) involve a substantial risk of prejudicing his fair trial. But an article supporting Mrs. Carr's candidature in the by-election as a pro-life candidate that contained no such assertion would depict her as tilting at imaginary windmills. One of the main planks of the policy for which she sought the suffrage of the electors was that these things did happen and ought to be stopped.

I have drawn attention to the passages principally relied upon by the Divisional Court as causing a risk of prejudice that was not "merely incidental to the discussion." The court described them as "unnecessary" to the discussion and as "accusations." The test, however, is not whether an article could have been written as effectively without these passages or whether some other phraseology might have been substituted for them that could have reduced the risk of prejudicing Dr. Arthur's fair trial; it is whether the risk created by the words actually chosen by the author was "merely incidental to the discussion," which I take to mean: no more than an incidental consequence of expounding its main theme. The Divisional Court also apparently regarded the passages complained of as disqualified from the immunity conferred by section 5 because they consisted of "accusations" whereas the court considered that "discussion" was confined to "the airing of views and the propounding and debating of principles and arguments." I cannot accept this limited meaning of "discussion" in the section. As already pointed out, in the absence of any accusation, believed to be true by Mrs. Carr and Mr. Muggeridge, that it was a common practice among some doctors to do what they are accused of doing in the passages complained of, the article would lose all its point whether as support for Mrs. Carr's parliamentary candidature or as a contribution to the wider controversy as to the justifiability of mercy killing. The article would be emasculated into a mere contribution to a purely hypothetical problem appropriate, it may be, for debate between academic successors of the mediaeval schoolmen, but remote from all public affairs and devoid of any general public interest to readers of the "Daily Mail."

My Lords, the article that is the subject of the instant case appears to me to be in nearly all respects the antithesis of the article which this House (pace a majority of the judges of the European Court of Human Rights) held to be a contempt of court in *Attorney-General* v. *Times Newspapers Ltd.* [1974] A.C. 273. There the whole subject of the article was the pending civil actions against Distillers Co. (Biochemicals) Ltd. arising out of their having placed upon the market the new drug thalidomide, and the whole purpose of it was to put pressure upon that company in the lawful conduct of their defence in those actions. In the instant case, in contrast, there is in the article no mention at all of Dr. Arthur's trial. It may well be that many readers of the "Daily Mail" who saw the article and had read also the previous day's report of Dr. Arthur's trial, and certainly if they were members of the jury at that trial, would think, "that is the sort of thing that Dr. Arthur is being tried for; it appears to be something that quite a lot of doctors do." But the risk of their thinking that and allowing it to prejudice their minds in favour of finding him guilty on evidence that did not justify such a finding seems to me to be properly described in ordinary English language as "merely incidental" to any meaningful discussion of Mrs. Carr's election policy as a pro-life candidate in the by-election due to be held before Dr. Arthur's trial was likely to be concluded, or to any meaningful discussion of the wider matters of general public interest involved in the current controversy as to the justification of mercy killing. To hold otherwise would have prevented Mrs. Carr from putting forward and obtaining publicity for what was a main plank in her election programme and would have stifled all discussion in the press upon the wider controversy about mercy killing from the time that Dr. Arthur was charged in the magistrates' court in February 1981 until the date of his acquittal at the beginning of November of that year; for those are the dates between which, under section 2(3) and Schedule 1, the legal proceedings against Dr. Arthur would be "active" and so attract the strict liability rule.

Such gagging of bona fide public discussion in the press of controversial matters of general public interest, merely because there are in existence contemporaneous legal proceedings in which some particular instance of those controversial matters may be in issue, is what section 5 of the Contempt of Court Act 1981 was in my view intended to prevent. I would allow this appeal.

Appeal allowed.

Section 6(c) and Intentional Contempt

Attorney-General v. Newspaper Publishing PLC.
[1987] 3 W.L.R. 942
Court of Appeal

See *supra*. p. 169 for the facts.

Sir John Donaldson M.R. ... Here the newspapers without doubt have interfered with the administration of justice by rendering the trial of the government's claims against the Guardian and the Observer less effective. They have therefore committed the actus reus. The real question is whether they had the necessary mens rea or criminal intent. It is to that question that I now turn.

Mens rea in the law of contempt is something of a minefield. The reason is that it is wholly the creature of the common law and has developed on a case by case basis, as no doubt it will continue to do. The Act of 1981 did not seek to systematise the approach of the courts. It simply defined by section 1 a term of art, namely, "the strict liability rule," as meaning:

> "the rule of law whereby conduct may be treated as a contempt of court as tending to interfere with the course of justice in particular legal proceedings, regardless of intent to do so."

There may well be instances of conduct which would be treated as contempt of court regardless of intent to do so, but which do not fall within this defined term. One example may be *Attorney-General* v. *Butterworth* [1963] 1 Q.B. 696, because the act complained of—punishing a witness for having given evidence in proceedings after those proceedings had been concluded—was calculated to interfere with future proceedings in general and not "particular legal proceedings." Another would be the offence of marrying a ward of court or taking the ward out of the jurisdiction without in each case first obtaining the court's permission, because the gravamen of the charge is not interfering with the course of justice in proceedings.

The contempt alleged against the three newspapers quite clearly falls within the category of contempt to which the Act applies and accordingly the limitations and defences set out is sections 2 to 5 apply. The most important of these is section 2(3) which provides:

> "The strict liability rule applies to a publication only if the proceedings in question are active within the meaning of this section at the time of the publication."

The proceedings between the Government and "The Guardian" and the "Observer" newspapers were not active in this sense when the three newspapers published the Wright material and accordingly they cannot be charged with contempt of court on a strict liability basis. This, Mr. Laws, for the Attorney-General, fully accepts. But this does not mean that they cannot be charged on a basis which involves having regard to intent and indeed section 6(c) expressly contemplates and saves such a possibility when it provides:

> "Nothing in the foregoing provisions of this Act— ... (c) restricts liability for contempt of court in respect of conduct intended to impede or prejudice the administration of justice."

This at once raises the question, "What kind of intent?" Mr. Laws contending for a general or basic intent and the newspapers for a specific intent. In the light of the policy of Parliament as evidenced by section 8 of the Criminal Justice Act 1967, and the likelihood that in passing the Act of 1981 Parliament intended to accept the recommendations of the Phillimore Committee (Report of the Committee on Contempt of Court (1974) (Cmnd. 5794)), I am quite satisfied that what is contemplated, and what is "saved," is the power of the court to commit for contempt where the conduct complained of is specifically intended to impede or prejudice the administration of justice. Such an intent need not be expressly avowed or admitted, but can be inferred from all the circumstances, including the foreseeability of the consequences of the conduct. Nor need it be the sole intention of the contemnor. An intent is to be distinguished from motive or desire: see *per* Lord Bridge of Harwich in *Reg.* v. *Moloney* [1985] A.C. 905, 926.

LLOYD L.J.: . . . The purpose of section 2 of that Act was to confine strict liability as defined within narrow limits. Thus it was common ground that strict liability does not apply to the facts of the present case, because the proceedings against "The Guardian" were not active, within the statutory definition, at the time of publication. But the fact that "The Independent" could not be liable here under the strict liability rule does not mean that "The Independent" cannot be liable at all. Section 6 (c) specifically provides that nothing in section 2 shall restrict liability in respect of conduct intended to impede or prejudice the administration of justice. The question is what is the nature of that intent?

There are three possibilities. The first is that the contemnor is liable if he intends to do the act in question, in this case publish the article, even though he does not intend to impede or prejudice the administration of justice. It is sufficient if the article in fact impedes or prejudices the administration of justice. The second possibility is that the contemnor is liable if he intends to interfere with the course of justice—I use that phrase for brevity—or is reckless whether or not he interferes with the course of justice. The third possibility is that the contemnor is only liable if he intends to interfere with the course of justice.

Mr. Laws did not seek to support the first possibility. But he argued strongly in favour of the second. There was, he says, nothing in the pre-existing law to suggest that contempt of court was ever a crime of specific intent. If therefore it was necessary to show a guilty mind on the part of the contemnor, in other words when the strict liability rule did not apply, it was sufficient to show either that he intended to interfere with the course of justice, *or* that he was reckless whether he did so or not. This would be in accordance with the ordinary principle of criminal law. Moreover, if it were necessary to show in every case that the contemnor intended to interfere with the course of justice, the protection afforded by the law of contempt to the administration of justice would be undermined. Mr. Laws relied on the following passage from *Arlidge and Eady, The Law of Contempt,* p. 82, para. 2–80:

> "The best view is that contempt of court is a crime of general intent. There is insufficient authority to indicate that it is a crime of specific intent and the purpose of the jurisdiction might be too easily defeated if it were."

He also relied on a later passage, at p. 177, para. 4–46, where the authors sound less certain note:

> "Since this type of offence has hitherto been absolute, there are no authorities which indicate the precise nature of the mens rea required in the case of prejudicial publications which fall outside the Act but which are nevertheless prima facie contempts. On principle the contemnor must know the publication contains matter capable of prejudicing particular proceedings; he must know the proceedings are pending or imminent; and he must intend to prejudice these proceedings. It may be that if he is reckless as to any or all of these requirements he will also be guilty."

If reckless interference with the course of justice was a ground of liability before the Act, as Mr. Laws submits it was, then there is nothing in the Act itself which restricts that ground of liability. It is true that section 6(c) refers to conduct intended to impede or prejudice the administration of justice, and there is nothing about recklessness. But section 6(c) was enacted for the avoidance of doubt. Since there is nothing in section 1 or 2 to restrict liability based on recklessness, there was no need to refer to recklessness in section 6(c). Alternatively, "intent" in section 1 and "intended to impede etc.," in section 6(c) must refer to *general* intent, *i.e.* basic mens rea, which would include recklessness.

Such was Mr. Laws's argument. I cannot accept it. Mr Clarke is surely right when he submits that the statutory purpose behind the Contempt of Court Act 1981 was to effect a permanent shift in the balance of public interest away from the protection of the administration of justice and in favour of freedom of speech. Such a shift was forced upon the United Kingdom by the decision of the European Court in *The Sunday Times* v. *United Kingdom* [1979] 2 E.H.R.R. 245, and was in any event foreshadowed by the recommendations of the Phillimore Committee, Report of the Committee on Contempt of Court (1974) (Cmnd. 5794). If we were to hold that, where the strict liability rule does not apply (because, for example, the publication does not create a *substantial* risk that the course of justice would be *seriously* impeded, but only some lesser risk, or some minor impediment), the publisher might nevertheless be liable if he is reckless, we would certainly not be furthering the statutory purpose.

But Mr. Clarke has a narrower, and even more compelling, point based on the language of section 1. The strict liability rule is expressed to be a rule whereby a person may be liable "regardless of intent." Now, whatever else recklessness may or may not mean (and the cases show that the concept is not without its difficulties) it is clear that it is independent of, and frequently contrasted with, intent. Liability based on recklessness is thus a liability regardless of intent. If that is so, then liability based on recklessness is included within the statutory description of the strict liability rule, and is therefore subject to the restrictions imposed by section 2. It must follow that recklesssness does not provide the Attorney-General with an avenue of escape from section 2, which is the essence of Mr. Laws's submission.

Putting the matter another way, section 6(c) of the Act saves from the operation of sections 1 and 2 conduct which is intended to impede or prejudice the administration of justice. If it was the object of Parliament to save also conduct which is reckless, then Parliament would surely have said so. Sections 1, 2 and 6(c) cover the whole ground. In cases covered by the Act to which the strict liability rule does not apply, there is no room for a state of mind which falls short of intention. There is no middle way.

I would therefore hold that the mens rea required in the present case is an intent to interfere with the course of justice. As in other branches of the criminal law, that intent may exist, even though there is no desire to interfere with the course of justice. Nor need it be the sole intent. It may be inferred, even though there is no overt proof. The more obvious the interference with the course of justice, the more readily will the requisite intent be inferred.

Balcombe L.J. agreed with the views expressed by Sir John Donaldson M.R. and Lloyd L.J.

Attorney-General v. News Group Newspapers Ltd.
The Times, February 20, 1988
Divisional Court

The Attorney-General brought proceedings against the proprietors of *The Sun* newspaper for contempt of court arising out of the publication of a number of articles relating to allegations that a doctor had raped a girl of eight. Counsel had advised that there was insufficient evidence to justify a prosecution of the doctor. *The Sun* provided financial help for a private prosecution which ended in the doctor being acquitted in December 1986. The articles complained of appeared in March 1986 under headlines such as "Rape case doc: Sun acts"; "He's a real swine"; "Beast must be named, says MP" and "Rape case doc groped."

WATKINS L.J. said that the 1981 Act had made extensive provision for what might be called statutory contempt, but section 6(c) provided that nothing in the Act " . . . restricts liability for contempt of court in respect of conduct intended to impede or prejudice the administration of justice." In his Lordship's view the content of the articles and the financial support offered to the mother justified the inference that the editor intended to interfere with the administration of justice.

His Lordship could not accept that an experienced editor could have failed to have foreseen that the material which he published and the steps he announced he was taking to assist the mother to prosecute would incur a real risk of prejudicing the fairness of the doctor's trial.

It was an inescapable inference that he became so convinced of the doctor's guilt and incensed by that and the failure to prosecute him that he endeavoured to persuade the readers of *The Sun* to take similar view, some of whom could possibly have formed part of a jury to try the doctor.

That was trial by newspaper, a form of activity which struck directly at a jury's impartiality. Furthermore, what conceivable reason could there be for publishing the article headed "Doc groped" unless it was intended to prejuduce a fair trial by bringing to readers' attention extremely damaging matter affecting the doctor which would be inadmissible as evidence in his trial.

But a further vital issue had to be resolved before it could be established that contempt at common law had been committed . . .

No such contempt was committed unless the conduct complained of was carried out at a time when proceedings were either pending or imminent. . . .

"Imminent proceedings" was a vague and uncertain phrase which could not be confined to any particular length of time as a matter of principle; its application depended on all the circumstances.

There were cases where although proceedings were not yet active they were likley to be commenced in the near future; some proceedings were imminent when there was a likelihood or a real risk that they would be instituted in the near future, and when there was a real risk that the kind of publication would interfere with the course of justice;

In the instant case proceedings were imminent; the newspaper intended they should be commenced at their expense as soon as possible and actively pursued that goal because they were determined to see the doctor charged, tried and convicted.

Alternatively, if the proceedings could not be said to be imminent, common law contempt applied nonetheless in the whole circumstances of the case. That was because the purpose of the contempt jurisdiction was to prevent interference with the course of justice. The contents of the articles created a real risk that a fair trial would be impeded.

The authorities were not concerned with the scope of common law contempt where such an intent existed in relation to proceedings in the contemplation of an alleged contemnor who deliberately assisted a private prosecutor to prosecute as soon as possible.

His Lordship said that the circumstances in which a criminal contempt at common law could be committed were not necessarily confined to those in which proceedings were either pending or imminent.

The common law was not a worn-out jurisprudence rendered incapable of further development by the ever-increasing incursion of parliamentary legislation. It was a lively body of law capable of adaption and expansion to meet fresh needs calling for the exertion of the discipline of law.

The need for a free Press was axiomatic but the Press could not be allowed to charge about like a wild unbridled horse. It had to a necessary degree in the public interest to be curbed.

The curb was in no circumstances more necessary than when the principle that every man accused of crime should have a fair trial was at stake. It was a principle which, in his Lordship's experience, newspaper proprietors and editors were usually as alert as anyone to avoid violating.

In the present case the kind of threat which the articles complained of posed to the proper administration of justice was by no means novel. The newspaper had very much in mind particular proceedings which they were determined, as far as lay within their power and influence, to ensure took place.

If it was necessary for the Attorney-General to establish that the proposed proceedings were imminent he had done so in the present case.

Lord Justice Mann agreed.

The court imposed a fine of £75,000.

Section 10 and Disclosure of Sources

Secretary of State for Defence v. Guardian Newspapers Ltd.

[1985] A.C. 339

In interlocutory proceedings before Scott J. the Crown successfully relied on section 10 of the Contempt of Court Act 1981 to secure the delivery up of a document alleged to be Crown property that had been "handed in" anonymously to *The Guardian* newspaper on October 22, 1983 and published verbatim in that newspaper on October 31. The only reason why the Crown wanted delivery up of the document was to assist it in identifying the civil servant by whom it had been "leaked" to the press. The interlocutory order was affirmed by the Court of Appeal (Sir John Donaldson, M.R., Griffiths and Slade L.JJ.) on the following day. It was complied with on the same day. *The Guardian* appealed to the House of Lords (Lord Diplock, Lord Fraser of Tullybelton, Lord Scarman, Lord Roskill and Lord Bridge of Harwich) which heard the appeal because of the importance of the issue involved—the meaning of section 10—even though the civil servant involved had, before the appeal could be heard, been identified and convicted of an offence under section 2 of the Official Secrets Act 1911.

LORD DIPLOCK: . . . Section 10 of the Contempt of Court Act 1981 is in the following terms:

> "No court may require a person to disclose, nor is any person guilty of contempt of court for refusing to disclose, the source of information contained in a publication for which he is responsible, unless it be established to the satisfaction of the court that disclosure is necessary in the interests of justice or national security or for the prevention of disorder or crime."

It is to be observed that the statutory protection created by the section from being compelled by order of a court which is enforceable by legal sanctions to disclose sources of information contained in a publication in what for convenience I may call the "media" does not differentiate between disclosure in interlocutory proceedings for discovery prior to the trial and disclosure at the actual trial itself.

In this respect and also in the respect that it eliminates any discretion on the part of the judge at the trial as to whether or not the non-disclosure rule should be applied, the section alters what had been the previous practice of the courts under the so-called newspaper rule of which detailed discussion and analysis can be found in the speeches in this House in *British Steel Corporation* v. *Granada Television Ltd.* [1981] A.C. 1096, and in particular that of my noble and learned friend, Lord Fraser of Tullybelton (pp. 1197–1199). The section is so drafted as to make it a question of fact not of discretion as to whether in the particular case a requirement for disclosure of sources of information falls within one of the express exception introduced by the word "unless." If it does not, the statutory right to refuse disclosure of sources of information in the media is absolute. With all respect to Mr. Kentridge I do not think that the process of ascertaining the true construction of the section is advanced by dubbing this a "constitutional right." For my part I would repudiate this evocative phrase if it is intended to mean anything more than that in ascertaining the extent of the rights which it confers the section should be given a purposive construction and, that being done, the right, like other rights conferred on persons by statute, effect must be given to it in the courts.

. . . . .

My Lords, I have said that I think it is unfortunate that this question of the true construction of section 10 of the Contempt of Court Act of 1981 which is of great general importance primarily to the "media" (but having regard to the wide definition of "publication" in section 2(1) of the Act of 1981, not exclusively to them) should have come before your Lordships in the form of an interlocutory appeal. As I have pointed out section 10 applies to interlocutory proceedings and to actual trial alike. I understand that all your Lordships are agreed not only upon the true construction of the section but also that if the action had proceeded to a speedy trial and the facts as they were known to the Government at the date of the application for the interlocutory order had been the subject of explicit oral evidence the Crown would have succeeded in establishing that disclosure of the source of the document was necessary in the interests of national security and thus that it was entitled to final judgment for delivery up of the document as a means of discovering that source. So all that divides us is whether the facts stated in the affidavit evidence of Mr. Hastie-Smith, the principal establishment officer of the Ministry of Defence, to establish that identification of the civil servant who had been resonsible for the leak was necessary in the interests of national security, were sufficiently explicit to justify the inference that such necessity had been sufficiently shown. In common with all three members of the Court of Appeal, (Sir John Donaldson M.R., Griffiths and Slade L.JJ.) two of your Lordships with whom I align myself, are of opinion that those facts, when read in conjunction with those stated in the affidavit evidence of the editor of *The Guardian* and in the light of matters of public notoriety of which judicial notice might legitimately be taken were just enough, although there was material available to him at the date of his affidavit, November 23, 1983, which if Mr. Hastie-Smith had included it, as he would certainly have been wise to do, could have put beyond all doubt, without requiring any resort to the doctrine of judicial notice, that it was necessary in the interest of national security to identify the "leaker" as soon as possible.

.   .   .   .   .   .

The construction of section 10

My Lords, save that the subject matter of the Act 1981 is limited to contempt of court, as its long title shows, there is no consistent theme that can be identified as being common to all its sections. It consists of a number of miscellaneous amendments to the previous law of contempt of court both criminal and civil; and all that can be predicated as an aid in giving a purposive construction to a particular section is that it presupposes the existence of what in section 1(1) are referred to as "particular legal proceedings." (For present purposes the species of contempt of court which consists of "scandalising the judges" and is virtually obsolescent in England may be ignored; it is not dealt with by the Act.)

Section 10 is concerned solely with the power of a court of justice (or by virtue of the extended definition in section 19, any other tribunal or body exercising the judicial power of the State) to order a person to disclose the source of information contained in a publication for which he is responsible; a power which is exercisable only where the identity or nature of such sources is relevant to some issue that falls to be determined by the court in the particular proceedings. The section confers no powers upon a court additional to those powers, whether discretionary or not, which already existed at common law or under rules of court, to order disclosure of sources of information; its effect is restrictive only. As I have pointed out, the disclosure of sources of information with which the section deals is not, like the old "newspaper rule" at common law, limited to disclosure upon discovery where disobedience to the order for discovery would fall into the category of a civil contempt; it applies also to disclosure in response to a question put to a witness at the trial, where a refusal to answer the question if ordered to by the judge to do so would constitute a contempt committed in the face of the court and thus a criminal.

Under the common law as it had developed by the time of the passing of the Act of 1981, the judge already had a discretion to decline to order disclosure of sources of information whether by means of discovery or by oral questions at the trial, despite their relevance to an issue in the particular proceedings where to require such disclosure would be contrary to some public interest. The classical example of the exercise of this discretion was where disclosure of the identity of police informers was sought; but the discretion was not confined to refusing to require disclosure of sources of information on which criminal prosecutions were based. It was extended by this House to sources of information supplied to the Gaming Board for the purpose of their exercise of their statutory functions (*Reg.* v. *Lewes Justices, Ex parte Secretary of State for the Home Department* [1973] A.C. 388) and to sources of information supplied to the N.S.P.C.C. for the purpose of exercising their statutory powers in relation to the care and custody of children: *D.* v. *National Society for the Prevention of Cruelty to Children* [1978] A.C. 171. The rationale of the existence of this discretion was that unless informants could be confident that their identity would not be disclosed there was a serious risk that sources of information would dry up. So the exercise of the discretion involved weighing the public interest in eliminating this risk against the conflicting public interest that information which might assist a judicial tribunal to ascertain facts relevant to an issue on which it is required to adjudicate should not be withheld from that tribunal. Unless the balance of competing public interest tilted *against* disclosure, the right to disclosure of sources of information in cases where this was relevant prevailed.

In the exercise of this common law discretion, the protection of some general right, albeit of imperfect obligation, which members of the public had to be informed of reprehensible conduct by persons in responsible positions or of future action intended to be taken by government and other bodies entitled to exercise executive powers, does not appear to have been treated as a factor to be put into the balance when weighing the competing public interests in favour of and against disclosure of sources of information. There is no mention of it in the judgments and the discretion to refuse to require disclosure where this would otherwise be relevant to the determination of an issue in the particular legal proceedings was not limited to sources of information that was contained in publications to which members of the public had access.

Such then is the setting of existing law in which section 10 falls to be construed. The first thing to be noted is that it is limited to information contained in a publication. This expression by virtue of section 19 (the interpretation section) bears the meaning assigned to it in section 2(1) which deals with the strict liability rule. It is there defined as including "any speech, writing, broadcast or other communication in whatever form, which is addressed to the public at large or any section of the public." Although in section 2(1) this definition is introduced by the words "includes" rather than "means," the context in which it appears in that subsection which speaks of "publications" in the plural makes it clear that it is intended as a complete and comprehensive definition of the term.

Section 10 thus recognises the existence of a prima facie right of ordinary members of the public to be informed of any matter that anyone thinks it appropriate to communicate to them as such, though this does not extent to that information's source. The right so recognised is, so far as members of the public are directly concerned, of imperfect obligation. It encourages purveyors of information to the public, but a member of the public as such has no right conferred on him by this section to compel purveyance to him of any information. The choice of what information shall be communicated to members of the public lies with the publisher alone; it is not confined to what, in an action for defamation would be regarded as matters of public interest, or even, going down the scale, information published in order to pander to idle curiosity and thus promote sales of the publication; nor is the section confined to publications by "the media" although no doubt the media will in practice be the chief beneficiaries of it. Provided that it is addressed to the public at large or to any section of it every publication of information falls within the section and is entitled to the protection granted by it unless the publication falls within one of the express exceptions introduced by the word "unless."

The nature of the protection is the removal of compulsion to disclose in judicial proceedings the identity or nature of the source of any information contained in the publication, even though the disclosure would be relevant to the determination by the court of an issue in those particular proceedings; and the only reasonable inference is that the purpose of the protection is the same as that which underlay the discretion vested in the judge at common law to *refuse* to compel disclosure of sources of information; videlicet—unless informers could be confident that their identity would not be revealed sources of information would dry up.

The words with which the section starts, before it comes to specifying any exceptions, impose a prohibition on the court itself that is perfectly general in its terms: "No court may require a person to disclose . . . the source of information contained in a publication for which he is responsible . . ." This prohibition is in no way qualified by the nature of the judicial proceedings, or of the claim or cause of action in respect of which such judicial proceedings, if they are civil, are brought. So I am unable to accept Scott J.'s construction of the section as being inapplicable to a claim for detention of goods in which an order for the delivery of the goods, without the option to the defendant to pay damages by reference to their value instead, is sought under section 3(2)(a) of the Torts (Interference with Goods) Act 1977. I defer for later reference the relevance of section 10 of the Contempt of Court Act 1981 to the exercise of the discretion, conferred upon the judge by section 3(3)(b) of the Act of 1977, whether or not to order delivery of the goods under section 3(2)(a).

Again, what the court is prohibited from requiring is not described by reference to the form the requirement takes, but by reference to its consequences, *viz.* disclosure of the source of information. If compliance with the requirement, whatever form it takes, will, or is sought in order to enable, another party to the proceedings to identify the source by adding to the pieces already in possession of that party the last piece to a jigsaw puzzle in which the identity of the source of information would remain concealed unless that last piece became available to put into position, the requirement will fall foul of the ban imposed by the general words with which the section starts. I therefore, with respect, do not share the doubts expressed by Slade L.J. as to whether section 10 of the Act of 1981 applies to anything other than an order of a court which *in terms* (his italics) directs disclosure of the identity of the source by oral evidence or affidavit; nor do I accept his alternative, though tentative, suggestion that in order to rely upon section 10 of the Act of 1981 to resist delivery up of a document the person responsible for its publication must establish by affirmative evidence that compliance will (not just may) compel him to reveal a source of information. If he can show that there is a reasonable chance that it will do so, then (subject always to the exceptions provided for later in the section) this will suffice to bring the prohibition into effect.

I find myself in full agreement with the judgment of Griffiths L.J., where he says that he sees no harm in giving a wide construction to the opening words because in the latter part of the section the court is given ample powers to order the source to be revealed where in the circumstances of a particular case the wider public interest makes it necessary to do so.

So I turn next to the exceptions that the latter part of section 10 provides to the general ban upon the court requiring disclosure of sources of information that is imposed by the opening words. There are only four interests, and each of these is specific, that are singled out for protection, viz.: (a) justice, (b) national security, (c) the prevention of disorder, and (d) the prevention of crime.

The exceptions include no reference to "the public interest" generally and I would add that in my view the expression "justice," the interests of which are entitled to protection, is not used in a general sense as the antonym of "injustice" but in the technical sense of the administration of justice in the course of legal proceedings in a court of law, or, by reason of the extended definition of "court" in section 19 of the Act of 1981 before a tribunal or body exercising the judicial power of the State.

The onus of proving that an order of the court has or may have the consequence of disclosing the source of information falls within any of the exceptions lies upon the party by whom the order is sought. The words "unless it be established to the satisfaction of the court" make it explicit and so serve to emphasise what otherwise might have been left to be inferred from the application of the general rule of statutory construction: the onus of establishing that he falls within an exception lies upon the party who is seeking to rely upon it. Again, the section uses the words "necessary" by itself, instead of using the common statutory phrase "necessary or expedient," to describe what must be established to the satisfaction of the court—which latter phrase gives to the judge a margin of discretion; expediency, however great, is not enough; section 10 requires actual necessity to be established; and whether it has or not is a question of fact that the judge has to find in favour of necessity as a condition precedent to his having any jurisdiction to order disclosure of sources of information.

In the instant case the Crown relied upon the interests of national security and not upon any of the other three exceptions. It was to national security alone that Mr. Hastie-Smith's affidavit was directed, and with the contents of this affidavit I shall be dealing later. In view of the course that the case took before Scott J., however, it is necessary to say something about another exception: the interests of justice. This, as I have already pointed out, refers to the administration of justice in particular legal proceedings already in existence or, in the type of "bill of discovery" case revived after long disuse and exemplified by *Norwich Pharmacal Co.* v. *Customs and Excise Commissioners* [1974] A.C. 133 (to which incidentally section 10 of the Act of 1981 would not have applied) a particular civil action which it is proposed to bring against a wrongdoer whose identity has not yet been ascertained.

I find it difficult to envisage a civil action in which section 10 of the Contempt of Court Act 1981 would be relevant other than one for defamation or for detention of goods where the goods, as in the instant case and in *British Steel Corporation* v. *Granada Television Ltd.* [1981] A.C. 1096, consist of or include documents that have been supplied to the media in breach of confidence. The instant case does not provide a convenient occasion for saying anything about the effect of section 10 on actions for defamation. As respects actions for the detention of documents section 10 does not destroy the cause of action or affect its nature; what it does is to affect what interlocutory orders may be made by the court in the action, what questions witnesses may be compelled to answer and what documents (or other things) they may be required to produce at the actual trial, and what relief under the Torts

(Interference with Goods) Act 1977 may be granted by the judgment given in it.

Where the only, or the predominant, purpose of the action is to obtain posses-sion of a document in order to find out from examining it the identity of the source of information that had been contained in a publication, it is in my view plain that the provisions of section 10 would be a matter that the judge would be required to take into consideration in deciding how to exercise the discretion conferred upon him by section 3(3)(b) of the Torts (Interference with Goods) Act 1977. Unless he had found as a fact that the case fell within one of the four exceptions specified in section 10 of the Contempt of Court Act 1981, he should not give judgment in a form that granted relief under section 3(2)(a) of the Act of 1977 which compelled delivery up of the document itself. In any such case the intrinsic value of the document as a physical object is likely to be small, not to say tiny, as it was in the instant case. Having regard to the emphatic terms in which section 10 of the Contempt of Court Act 1981 is cast, I have not found it possible to envisage any case that might occur in real life, in which, since the passing of that Act, it would be necessary in the interests of justice to order delivery up of the document and thus constitute a permissible exercise of the discretion under section 3(3)(b) of the Act of 1977 to make such an order. Since this would be so in the case of an order in the final judgment in the action for delivery of goods a fortiori it would be so in an interlocutory order.

However, in the instant appeal what are relied upon as bringing the case within the exceptions to the general rule laid down in the first part of section 10 are not the interests of justice but those of national security. To these interests quite different considerations apply. To their application to the facts of the instant case at the interlocutory stage that it has reached, which is the only matter on which your Lordships are divided, I will now turn.

LORD ROSKILL: My Lords, with all respect to those who have either taken a different view from that of Griffiths L.J. or have felt doubts about the correctness of the construction which he preferred, I am of the clear opinion that his view was correct. The opening words of section 10 are plain, "No court may require a person to disclose . . . the source of information contained in a publication . . . unless . . ." There then follow four specific exceptions. I can see no reason for adding to those four specific exceptions by cutting down the natural and unqualified meaning of the section's opening words. The view which appealed to Scott J. involves doing precisely that. If it is to be said that the section has no application where the case is (say) one of unchallenged proprietory rights, that involves writing or implying into the opening words of the section words which are not there and that I must decline to do. Accordingly I find myself on this, the all important issue in this appeal, in complete agreement with Griffiths L.J. [1984] Ch. 156, 167. The appel-lants must therefore be entitled to the protection of section 10 unless the case is proved to fall within one or more of the four specific exceptions.

But before I turn to that question I must note in order to reject one part of the able arguments of Mr. Kentridge for the appellants. He urged that section 10 was akin to an "entrenched" provision in a written constitution; indeed he went so far as to describe it as such. I understood Mr. Kentridge to be using the word "entrenched" in its accurate sense in constitutional law, that is to say as a provision in a written constitution which cannot be altered save by some special legislative process beyond the ordinary parliamentary process. I can only say that with all respect to the persuasiveness of the argument, I cannot accept it and for two reasons. First in a country such as our own without a written constitution, to speak of an "entrenched" provision in a statute or of a provision in a statute as "akin to an entrenched provision" is constitutionally incorrect. Secondly the fact that a section affects specific freedoms or confers specific privileges or immunities whether on individuals or on the media does not give it a special constitutional status in our law. The language of the relevant statute is subject to the ordinary rules of statutory construction, always remembering first that neither additions nor subtractions should be made to the natural meaning of the words used unless they are essential in order to give an intelligible meaning to the statutory language and second that courts should always be slow to cut down as a matter of construction plain words designed to create a privilege or immunity accorded by statute, especially in a case where to put the matter no higher, doubts had long existed as to the extent of any comparable privilege or immunity which was or may have been previously accorded at common law.

Lord Fraser of Tullybelton, Lord Scarman and Lord Bridge of Harwich reached similar conclusions on the construction of section 10.

Lord Diplock, Lord Roskill and Lord Bridge concluded on the evidence before the trial judge that the Crown had proved that delivery of the documents was necessary in the interests of national security; Lord Fraser and Lords Scarman dissented.

Appeal dismissed.

In re An Inquiry Under the Company
Securities (Insider Dealing) Act 1985
[1988] 2 W.L.R. 33
House of Lords

Inspectors, appointed under section 177 of the Financial Services Act 1986, questioned a journalist responsible for two newspaper articles which appeared to have been based on unpublished price-sensitive information. He refused to answer questions which he considered might lead to the identification of his sources. The Inspectors sought the assistance of the High Court under section 178 of the Act which provides:

"(1) If any person—(a) refuses to comply with any request under section 177(3) above; or (b) refuses to answer any question put to him by the inspectors appointed under that section with respect to any matter relevant for establishing whether or not any suspected contravention has occurred, the inspectors may certify that fact in writing to the court and the court may inquire into the case.
(2) 'If, after hearing any witness who may be produced against or on behalf of the alleged offender and any statement which may be offered in defence, the court is satisfied that he did without reasonable excuse refuse to comply with such a request or answer any such question, the court may—(a) punish him in like manner as if he had been guilty of contempt of the court; . . ."

Hoffman J. dismissed the Inspectors' application. The Court of Appeal (Slade and Lloyd L.JJ. and Sir George Waller) allowed an appeal by the inspectors. The journalist appealed to the House of Lords (Lord Keith of Kinkel, Lord Roskill, Lord Griffiths, Lord Oliver of Aylmerton and Lord Goff of Chieveley.)

LORD GRIFFITHS: [The Contempt of Court Act 1981] has not been specifically applied to any inquiry under section 178. I therefore conclude that section 10 of the Act of 1981 has no direct application to a reference under section 178 of the Act of 1986. However, this is, as I have said, an academic point. Parliament has recognised the privilege of a journalist to protect his source and spelled out the limitations on that privilege in section 10. When deciding upon the limits of the privilege in whatever circumstances it is claimed a court should follow the guidance of Parliament and apply the test provided in section 10.

The judge in deciding whether or not a journalist has a "reasonable excuse" for refusing to reveal his sources is not carrying out a balancing exercise between two competing areas of public interest. The judge starts the inquiry with the presumption that the journalist's refusal to reveal his sources does provide a reasonable excuse for refusing to answer the inspectors' questions and the burden is upon the inspectors to satisfy the judge as a question of fact that the identification of his sources is necessary for the prevention of crime: see per Lord Diplock and Lord Bridge of Harwich in Secretary of State for Defence v. Guardian Newspapers Ltd. [1985] A.C. 339, 350 and 372. If the inspectors are able to discharge this burden, then, as a general rule, the judge should hold that there was no reasonable excuse for refusing to answer the inspectors' questions as to the source of the journalist's information. I say as a general rule because section 10 is not framed in language that compels a judge to order a journalist to reveal his sources and I can conceive of extreme cases in which the judge might properly refuse to do so if, for instance, the crime was of a trivial nature or, at the other end of the scale, the journalist's life might be imperilled if he revealed his source. However, it is not suggested that this is such an extreme case and Mr. Warner accepts that if it has been established that the identification of his sources is necessary for the prevention of crime he has no "reasonable excuse" for refusing to do so. I should add that even if the decision goes against him, Mr. Warner says he will accept punishment rather than reveal his source, but that is not a matter which can be taken into account in deciding this appeal.

What then is meant by the words "necessary" ... for the prevention of ... crime" in section 10? I do not think that much light is thrown upon this question by an elaborate discussion of the meaning of the word "necessary." "Necessary" is a word in common usage in everyday speech with which everyone is familiar. Like all words, it will take colour from its context; for example, most people would regard it as "necessary" to do everything possible to prevent a catastrophe but would not regard it as "necessary" to do everything possible to prevent some minor inconvenience. Furthermore, whether a particular measure is necessary, although described as a question of fact for the purpose of section 10, involves the exercise of a judgment upon the established facts. In the exercise of that judgment different people may come to different conclusions on the same facts; for an example of this one has to look no further than *Secretary of State for Defence* v. *Guardian Newspapers Ltd*. But this cannot be avoided and the task of the judge will not be lightened by substituting for the familiar word "necessary" some other set of words with a similar meaning. I do not myself think that it helps to consider the meaning of "necessary" when used in the narrow context of discovery of documents and then apply it to the very broad considerations that will arise when considering the four heads of public interest identified in Section 10. I therefore derive no assistance from the discussion of the word "necessary" in *Air Canada* v. *Secretary of State for Trade* [1983] 2 A.C. 394.

I doubt if it is possible to go further than to say that "necessary" has a meaning that lies somewhere between "indispensable" on the one hand, and "useful" or "expedient" on the other, and to leave it to the judge to decide towards which end of the scale of meaning he will place it on the facts of any particular case. The nearest paraphrase I can suggest is "really needed."

The words "prevention of ... crime" do, however, admit of more than one construction. Hoffmann J. adopted a narrow construction for which Mr. Warner contends. He held that: "it must appear probable that in the absence of disclosure by the journalist further crimes are likely to be committed." And later he said: "The facts to which the inspectors deposed do not therefore in my judgment show a probability that only the disclosure of his sources by Mr. Warner can prevent further insider dealing."

No one can be so optimistic as to believe that any measure will ever prevent crime, including "insider dealing," being committed in the future. Mr Kentridge submits that this narrow construction means that "prevention of ... crime" is limited to a situation in which the identification of the source will allow steps to be taken to prevent the commission of a particular identifiable future crime or crimes: for example, the source knows the plans for the hijack of a wages van and the police urgently need to question him so that they may take steps to ambush the robbers and thus prevent the crime from being committed. In an inquiry such as this it is highly unlikely that the inspectors will be able to discharge such a burden. It is not the job of the inspectors to take immediate action to frustrate a particular crime. Their task is to probe into and lay bare the whole dishonest web of this suspected insider dealing so that measures can be taken to deter and contain, so far as possible, this type of financial dishonesty. Mr. Kentridge freely acknowledges that on the narrow construction a journalist could rarely, if ever, be called upon to identify his sources in aid of this type of inquiry, and submits that section 10 is designed to ensure that inspectors will get little or no help from the press. If Parliament had wished to confer a complete protection on journalists from revealing their sources in this type of inquiry, they could have specifically provided such protection, as they have for legal professional privilege: see section 177(7) of the Act of 1986. But Parliament has not done so and I am reluctant to believe that it was the intention that, by a side wind, the same effect should be achieved by giving a very narrow construction to the meaning of the words "prevention of ... crime" in Section 10 of the Act of 1981.

The phrase "prevention of ... crime" carries, to my mind, very different overtones from "prevention of a crime" or even "prevention of crimes." There are frequent articles and programmes in the media on the prevention of crime. The subject on these occasions is discussed from many points of view including the social background in which crime breeds, detection, deterrence, retribution, punishment, rehabilitation and so forth. The prevention of crime in this broad sense is a matter of public and vital interest to any civilised society. Crime is endemic in society and will probably never be eradicated but its containment is essential. If crime gets the upper hand and becomes the rule rather than the exception, the collapse of society will swiftly follow. By identifying "prevention of ... crime" as one of the four heads of public interest to which the journalist's privilege may occasionally have to yield, I am satisfied that Parliament was using the phrase in its wider and, I think, natural meaning, rather than in the restricted sense for which the appellant contends.

Mr. Kentridge relied upon article 10 of the Convention for the Protection of Human Rights and Fundamental Freedoms (1953) (Cmd. 8969) and the judgment of the European Court of Human Rights in *The Sunday Times* v. *United Kingdom* [1979] 2 E.H.R.R. 245 to support a narrow construction of "prevention of ... crime."

Article 10 provides:

"1. Everyone has the right to freedom of expression. This right shall include freedom to hold opinions and to receive and impart information and ideas without interference by public authority regardless of frontiers. ... 2. The exercise of these freedoms, since it carries with it duties and responsibilities, may be subject to such formalities, conditions, restrictions or penalties as are prescribed by law and are necessary in a democratic society, in the interests of national security, territorial integrity or public safety, for the prevention of disorder or crime, for the protection of health or morals, for the protection of the reputation or rights of others, for preventing the disclosure of information received in confidence, or for maintaining the authority and impartiality of the judiciary."

When considering the breadth of such expression as "public safety," "the protection of health or morals" and "maintaining the authority and impartiality of the judiciary," which are used in association with "prevention of ... crime," it is clear I think that "prevention of ... crime" is being used in its broad general sense in article 10. The passage from the judgment of the European Court relied upon is that quoted in the speech of Lord Templeman in *Attorney-General* v. *Guardian Newspapers Ltd*. [1987] 1 W.L.R. 1248, 1297:

"[The court] is faced not with a choice between two conflicting principles, but with a principle of freedom of expression that is subject to a number of exceptions which must be narrowly interpreted. ... It is not sufficient that the interference involved belongs to that class of exceptions listed in article 10(2) which has been invoked; neither is it sufficient that the interference was imposed because its subject matter fell within a particular category or was caught by a legal rule formulated in general or absolute terms: the court has to be satisfied that the interference was necessary having regard to the facts and circumstances prevailing in the specific case before it"(p. 281, para. 65).

In this passage the European Court is not giving a restricted meaning to any of the exceptions but stressing that before interference with freedom of expression can be justified it must be shown to be necessary on the facts of the particular case. In so far as any assistance is to be gained from the Convention and this decision it supports the wider construction of "prevention of ... crime."

Appeal dismissed.

ENFORCEMENT OF THE LAW

Functions of the Attorney-General

Gouriet v. Union of Post Office Workers
[1978] A.C. 435
House of Lords

It was publicly announced that the Union of Post Office Workers (UPW) and the Post Office Engineering Union (POEU) proposed to call on their members not to handle mail to South Africa for a week, in protest against the South African Government's policy of *apartheid*. Gouriet, Secretary of the National Association for Freedom, applied to the Attorney-General for his consent to act as plaintiff in relator proceedings for an injunction to restrain the UPW from procuring persons wilfully to detain or delay postal packets between England and South Africa, which would constitute an offence under the Telegraph Act 1863 and the Post Office Act 1953, as amended. The Attorney-General, "having considered all the circumstances including the public interest," declined to give his consent.

Gouriet then issued a writ in his own name and applied to the judge in chambers (Stocker J.) for a final injunction, which the judge refused. Gouriet appealed to the Court of Appeal (Lord Denning M.R., Lawton and Ormrod L.JJ.) which granted him an interim injunction against the UPW, and also gave him leave to join the POEU as defendants and to join the Attorney-General as a defendant. In face of that order the proposed boycott by Post Office employees did not take place. At the resumed hearing Gouriet claimed permanent injunctions against both trade unions, and a declaration that the Attorney-General by refusing his consent had acted improperly and had wrongfully exercised his discretion. At the end of the hearing, the declaration sought against the Attorney-General was provisionally amended to claim that notwithstanding his refusal to consent to relator proceedings, the plaintiff was entitled to proceed with his claim for final injunctions against the two unions.

The Court of Appeal, allowing Gouriet's appeal, held: (i) (by a majority) that the court had no power to review the decision of the Attorney-General in refusing consent to relator proceedings; (ii) (by a majority) the plaintiff was not entitled to a permanent injunction in the terms sought; but that (iii) the plaintiff could claim declarations, and that pending a decision on this claim the court could grant interim injunctions. (The injunctions were in fact discharged as being no longer necessary.)

All parties appealed to the House of Lords, Gouriet no longer claiming that the Attorney-General's refusal of consent to relator proceedings was improper or that it could be reviewed by the court. The House of Lords (Lord Wilberforce, Viscount Dilhorne, Lord Diplock, Lord Edmund Davies and Lord Fraser of Tullybelton) allowed the appeals by the trade unions and dismissed Gouriet's appeal.

Viscount Dilhorne [after reciting the facts and arguments, continued]: On the Saturday the statement of claim was also amended to include a claim for a declaration that the Attorney-General had acted improperly in refusing his consent to relator proceedings and had wrongly exercised his discretion. At the hearing the following Tuesday the Attorney-General's refusal to give his reasons for withholding his consent was regarded by Lord Denning M.R. as a direct challenge to the rule of law, a statement with which I feel I must express my complete dissent.

In the course of his judgment on January 27 Lord Denning M.R. said that he accepted that the court could not inquire into the giving of consent by the Attorney-General to the institution of a relator action but in his opinion his refusal of consent could be reviewed by the courts. Lawton L.J. and Ormrod L.J. did not agree. On the last day of the hearing Mr. Gouriet abandoned his contention that the courts had power to review the Attorney-General's exercise of his powers, but in view of Lord Denning's observations and those of Lawton L.J. on the Saturday to which I have referred and the importance of the question, I feel I should say something with regard thereto.

The Attorney-General has many powers and duties. He may stop any prosecution on indictment by entering a nolle prosequi. He merely has to sign a piece of paper saying that he does not wish the prosecution to continue. He need not give any reasons. He can direct the institution of a prosecution and direct the Director of Public Prosecutions to take over the conduct of any criminal proceedings and he may tell him to offer no evidence. In the exercise of these powers he is not subject to direction by his ministerial colleagues or to control and supervision by the courts. If the court can review his refusal of consent to a relator action, it is an exception to the general rule. No authority was cited which supports the conclusion that the courts can do so. Indeed such authority as there is points strongly in the opposite direction.

[His Lordship referred to the judgments of Lord Halsbury L.C. and Lord Macnaghten in *London County Council* v. *Attorney-General* [1902] A.C. 165, 168–169, 170 and continued]: Mr. Gouriet's contention now is that the Attorney-General can only refuse his consent to the institution of a relator action if it is frivolous, vexatious or oppressive and that as the action for which he sought the Attorney-General's consent did not fall under any of these heads, the Attorney-General had acted improperly. The ancient cases to which we were referred show that there was a time when Attorneys-General freely gave their consent to such actions but since the days of Lord Eldon, Attorneys-General have exercised considerable control. The figures with which we were supplied show that over the last 25 years or so the number of applications for the Attorney-General's consent has increased, and while a good percentage of them are refused, the number of such actions has also increased. A relator action is not something to be regarded as archaic and obsolete. The courts have power to dismiss an action which is frivolous, vexatious or oppressive. If indeed the only purpose of requiring an application for the Attorney-General's consent was to give him the opportunity of saying in advance of the courts that an action was frivolous, vexatious or oppressive, this function of his would serve little useful purpose. Again in my opinion this contention for which no authority was cited must be rejected. The Attorney-General did not in my opinion act improperly as now suggested on behalf of Mr. Gouriet. "There is no greater nonsense talked about the Attorney-General's duty," said Sir John Simon in 1925, "than the suggestion that in all cases the Attorney-General ought to decide to prosecute merely because he thinks there is what the lawyers call 'a case.' It is not true, and no one who has held that office supposes it is." (See *Edwards, The Law Officers of the Crown*, p. 222.)

However clear it appears to be that an offence has been committed, it is, as Sir Hartley Shawcross then Attorney-General said in 1951, the Attorney-General's duty "in deciding whether or not to authorise the prosecution, to acquaint himself with all the relevant facts, including, for instance, the effect which the prosecution, successful or unsuccessful as the case may be, would have upon public morale and order." (See *Edwards*, p. 223.)

This approach which the Attorney-General should make when considering whether a prosecution should be started, is in my opinion the kind of approach he should have made to the question of giving his consent to Mr. Gouriet's application.

In deciding whether or not to prosecute "there is only one consideration which is altogether excluded," Sir Hartley Shawcross said, "and that is the repercussion of a given decision upon my personal or my party's or the Government's political fortunes." (See *Edwards*, pp.222–223.) In the discharge of any of the duties to which I have referred, it is, of course, always possible that an Attorney-General may act for reasons of this kind and may abuse his powers. One does not know the reasons for the Attorney-General's refusal in this case but it should not be inferred from his refusal to disclose them that he acted wrongly. For all one knows he may have attached considerable importance to the fact that the injunction sought did no more than repeat the language of the sections of the Post Office Act 1953. On the Friday he may indeed have thought that to start proceedings so speedily for an injunction which did no more than that was not likely to serve any useful purpose and might indeed exacerbate the situation. Instances of applications by Attorneys-General to the civil courts for aid in enforcing the criminal law are few in number and exceptional in character. In the Court of Appeal a number of observations were made as to the inability of the courts to "enforce the law" if the Attorney-General refused his consent to an application for such an injunction. A breach of the law was impending according to Lord Denning M.R. "Are the courts to stand idly by?" was the question he posed on the Saturday. On January 27 he said [1977] Q.B. 729, 761: "If he" (the Attorney-General) "does not act himself—or refuses to give his consent to his name being used—then the law will not be enforced. If one Attorney-General after another does this, if each in his turn declines to take action against those who break the law—then the law becomes a dead letter."

With great respect the criminal law does not become a dead letter if proceedings for injunctions to restrain the commission of offences or for declarations that certain conduct is unlawful are not brought. The criminal law is enforced in the criminal courts by the conviction and punishment of offenders, not in the civil courts. The jurisdiction of the civil courts is mainly as to the determination of disputes and claims. They are not charged with responsibility for the administration of the criminal courts. The question "Are the courts to stand idly by?" might be supposed by some to suggest that the civil courts have some executive authority in relation to the criminal law. The line between the functions of the executive and the judiciary should not be blurred.

There are a number of statutory offences for the prosecution of which the consent of the Attorney-General or of the Director of Public Prosecutions is required but apart from these offences, anyone can if he wishes start a prosecution without obtaining anyone's consent. The enforcement of the criminal law does not rest with the civil courts or depend on the Attorney-General alone.

An enactment by Parliament defining and creating a criminal offence amounts to an injunction by Parliament restraining the commission of the acts made criminal. If the injunction in the Act is not obeyed—and in these days it frequently is not—the statute normally states the maximum punishment that can be awarded on conviction. If, in addition to the enactment, an injunction is granted in the civil courts to restrain persons from doing the acts already made criminal by Parliament, an injunction which does no more than embody the language of the statute, has that any greater potency than the injunction by Parliament contained in the Act? An injunction in the terms sought when the application in this case was made to the Attorney-General does not appear to me to be one that can with any accuracy of language be regarded as "enforcing the law." Repetition is not enforcement. The granting of such an injunction merely imposes a liability to fine or imprisonment for contempt additional to the maximum Parliament has thought fit to prescribe on conviction for the same conduct.

Great difficulties may arise if "enforcement" of the criminal law by injunction became a regular practice. A person charged, for instance, with an offence under section 58 or 68 of the Post Office Act 1953 has the right of trial by jury. If, before he commits the offence, an injunction is granted restraining him from committing an offence under those sections and he is brought before the civil courts for contempt, his guilt will be decided not by a jury but by a judge or judges. If he is subsequently tried for the criminal offence, might not the finding of guilt by a judge or judges prejudice his trial? This question is not to my mind satisfactorily answered by saying that juries can be told to ignore certain matters. It was suggested that this difficulty might be overcome by adjourning the proceedings for contempt until after the conclusion of the criminal trial. If that was done, the question might arise then as to the propriety of imposing a punishment in the contempt proceedings additional to that imposed on conviction for the same conduct in the criminal court.

Such considerations may have been present to the mind of the Attorney-General when he considered Mr. Gouriet's application on the Friday and may have provided valid grounds for his refusal of consent. Whether they did so or not, one does not know but I have mentioned them as they seem to me suffice to show that even if good legal reasons for his decision were not immediately apparent, the inference that he abused or misused his powers is not one that should be drawn.

An Attorney-General is not subject to restrictions as for the applications he makes, either ex officio or in relator actions, to the courts. In every case it will be for the court to decide whether it has jurisdiction to grant the application and whether in the exercise of its discretion it should do so. It has been and in my opinion should continue to be exceptional for the aid of the civil courts to be invoked in support of the criminal law and no wise Attorney-General will make such an application or agree to one being made in his name unless it appears to him that the case is exceptional.

One category of cases in which the Attorney-General has successfully sought an injunction to restrain the commission of criminal acts is where the penalties imposed for the offence have proved wholly inadequate to deter its commission: see *Attorney-General* v. *Sharp* [1931] 1 Ch. 121; *Attorney-General* v. *Premier Line Ltd.* [1932] 1 Ch. 303; *Attorney-General* v. *Bastow* [1957] 1 Q.B. 514 and *Attorney-General* v. *Harris* [1961] 1 Q.B. 74 where the defendant had been convicted on no less than 142 occasions of breaches of the Manchester Police Regulation Act 1844.

In *Attorney-General* v. *Chaundry* [1971] 1 W.L.R. 1614 an injunction was granted at the instance of the Attorney-General in a relator action to restrain the defendant from using a building as a hotel without a certificate under the London Building Acts. There was a serious fire risk and it was not possible to secure the early hearing of a summons charging the defendant with a criminal offence in so using the building without a certificate. In those circumstances an interlocutory injunction was granted prohibiting the use of the building as a hotel until the necessary certificate was granted.

I do not wish to suggest that the cases to which I have referred are the only types of cases in which the civil courts can and should come to the aid of the criminal law by granting injunctions at the instance of the Attorney-General but they, I think, serve to show that the exercise of that jurisdiction at the instance of the Attorney-General is exceptional.

As after the hearing on the Saturday the proposed action by members of the unions was called off, there was no occasion when the hearing was resumed for the grant of injunctions. The Court of Appeal allowed the statement of claim to be amended to add claims for declarations. I do not propose to spend time considering the terms of the declarations sought against the unions. It suffices to say that they were that it would be unlawful for the unions their servants and agents to do the acts made criminal by sections 58 and 68 of the Post Office Act 1953 and section 45 of the Telegraph Act 1863. The question for decision is not whether in the exercise of their discretion the Court of Appeal should have declared that what Parliament had made criminal was unlawful but whether the court had any jurisdiction to entertain Mr. Gouriet's application.

That is the main question to be decided in this appeal and the main thrust of Mr. Gouriet's contention, which was, it appears to me, accepted by the Court of Appeal, was that it was wrong in principle that the Attorney-General should, by the refusal of his consent to a relator action, be able to block recourse to the civil courts when a widespread breach of the criminal law was threatened. There were frequent references in the course of the argument to the courts being "immunized" by his refusal. It has been asserted that the Attorney-General stands between members of the public and the courts and by his refusal can deny access thereto. This would appear to be the basis for Lord Denning M.R.'s observation that his refusal of consent in this case was a direct challenge to the rule of law.

It was also urged that if, as is undoubtedly the case, any person can start a prosecution for a criminal offence without, save in those cases where the consent of the Attorney-General or the Director of Public Prosecutions is required by statute, the consent of anyone, why should not any member of the public be entitled to apply to the civil courts for an injunction in an endeavour to prevent the commission of an offence? Why, when the Attorney-General is not the only person who can start a prosecution, should he be the only person who can apply for such an injunction?

The reply to this made on behalf of the Attorney-General and the unions was that Mr. Gouriet was not qualified to act on behalf of the public to prevent injury to public rights and the courts had not jurisdiction to entertain his claim.

Mr. Gouriet does not as I have said assert a private right of any kind. He does not claim that he would have suffered any loss or damage by reason of the interruption of postal services to and from South Africa. If he had suffered any such loss or damage, he would have no cause of action against the Post Office or in tort against the unions and their members: see the Post Office Act 1969, sections 9(4) and 29(1).

It is not necessary therefore to consider the long line of cases dealing with the rights of individuals to secure injunctions and declarations when their private rights are threatened though it is not without interest to note that in *Springhead Spinning Co.* v. *Riley* (1868) L.R. 6 Eq. 551 it was held that an injunction could be granted at the instance of a person to prevent the commission of a crime if, but only if, that person would be damaged thereby . . . .

In *Cutler* v. *Wandsworth Stadium Ltd.* [1949] A.C. 398 Lord Simonds, referring to the Betting and Lotteries Act 1934, observed, at p. 408: "the sanction of criminal proceedings emphasises that this statutory obligation, like many others which the Act contains, is imposed for the public benefit and that the breach of it is a public not a private wrong."

So here in my opinion the sanction of criminal proceedings in sections 58 and 68 of the Post Office Act 1953 and in section 45 of the Telegraph Act 1863 was imposed for the public benefit and breach of them is a public and not a private wrong.

That the Attorney-General can, if he thinks it in the public interest to do so, take proceedings to prevent the commission of a public wrong is not disputed. As Professor Edwards said at p. 286 in his book *The Law Officers of the Crown* this aspect "of the Attorney-General's role as protector of public rights [is] of great antiquity."

An instance of its exercise is to be found in *Attorney-General* v. *Bastow* [1957] 1 Q.B. 514 where Devlin J. said that a relator action was one over which the Attorney-General retains complete control. I venture to think that no one who has held the office of Attorney-General would agree with the view expressed by Ormrod L.J. in the present case that there is a fictional element in relator actions. While it is true that the conduct of the proceedings in such an action is left in the hands of the relator, it is in his hands as agent for the Attorney-General and its conduct is always under his control and direction.

In that case Devlin J. cited the following observation of Jessel M.R. in *Attorney-General* v. *Cockermouth Local Board*, L.R. 18 Eq. 172, 176: "Except for the purposes of costs, there is no difference between an ex officio information at an information at the relation of a private individual. In both cases the Sovereign, as parens patriae, sues by the Attorney-General."

No useful purposes would I think be served by my referring to all the cases cited in argument. While the contention that if a private individual can start a prosecution, he should be able to take steps directed to preventing the commission of a crime appears at first sight attractive and logical, I do not find anything to support it in the decided cases. *Dyson* v. *Attorney-General* [1911] 1 K.B. 410 is not a case where the plaintiff was asserting a public right or the existence of a public wrong. He was seeking to protect himself. . . .

The conclusion to which I have come in the light of the many authorities to which we were referred is that it is the law, and long established law, that save and in so far as the Local Government Act 1972, section 222, gives local authorities a limited power so to do, only the Attorney-General can sue on behalf of the public for the purpose of preventing public wrongs and that a private individual cannot do so on behalf of the public though he may be able to do so if he will sustain injury as a result of a public wrong. In my opinion the cases establish that the courts have no jurisdiction to entertain such claims by a private individual who has not suffered and will not suffer damage.

If these conclusions are right, then when the Attorney-General gives his consent to a relator action, he is enabling an action to be brought which an individual alone could not bring. When he refuses his consent, he is not denying the right of any individual and barring his access to the courts for the courts have no jurisdiction to entertain a claim by an individual whose only interest is as a member of the public in relation to a public right. Consequently, any suggestions that his refusal constitutes a challenge to the rule of law appears to me to be entirely misconceived, and though views may differ as to where the balance of public interest lies, it should not be lightly assumed that his refusal of consent in a particular case was unjustified and not grounded on considerations of public interest.

There are a few other matters with which I desire to deal. I do not think that there is any true analogy between the giving of consent to relator actions and the issue of prerogative writs and we are not therefore in my opinion called upon to express views upon the correctness of the observations made as to the issue of mandamus in *Reg.* v. *Commissioner of Police of the Metropolis, Ex parte Blackburn* [1968] 2 Q.B. 118.

In *Attorney-General ex rel. McWhirter* v. *Independent Broadcasting Authority* [1973] Q.B. 629 Lord Denning M.R. made some obiter observations to the effect that a member of the public can apply to the court when the Attorney-General refuses leave in a proper case for the institution of relator proceedings. It follows from what I have said that these obiter observations do not in my opinion correctly state the law. The courts cannot review the Attorney-General's decision and they have no jurisdiction to entertain an application by a member of the public which he alone can make, either ex officio or in a relator action . . . .

In my opinion the Attorney-General was right in his contention that the court had no jurisdiction to grant the interim injunctions. It had no jurisdiction to grant declarations or a final injunction in this suit by Mr. Gouriet.

In conclusion, as I see it, we were asked not just to extend the existing law but to override a mass of authority and to say that long established law should no longer prevail. That is a question for the legislature to consider and in the light of what I have said about the exceptional character of requests by the Attorney-General to the civil courts to come to the aid of the criminal law and of the occasions when that has been given, I must confess to considerable doubt whether it would be in the public interest that private individuals such as Mr. Gouriet should be enabled to make such applications in cases where such interest as they have is in common with all other members of the public and when the object is the enforcement of public rights.

For these reasons in my opinion the appeals of the Attorney-General and the unions should be allowed and that of Mr. Gouriet dismissed. His claim should be struck out and, the Attorney-General not seeking costs in this House, Mr. Gouriet should pay the unions' costs here in addition to the costs in the courts below which were ordered to be costs in cause.

LORD EDMUND-DAVIES [in the course of his speech said]: Although the majority of the Court of Appeal in the instant case accepted that they had no right to review the Attorney-General's refusal of consent to a relator action, they inconsistently held that where the proposed civil action aims at upholding the *criminal* law they can review such refusal and are free to express the view, for example, that "there is no discernible reason why threatened breaches of the criminal law should not be declared illegal and possibly restrained" (*per* Lawton L.J. [1977] Q.B. 729 at p. 771F), and, having done so, to allow the private citizen to proceed. Such a conclusion strikes at the roots of the Attorney-General's unique role, and it is backed by no more authority than that available to support the view expressed obiter in *McWhirter's* case [1973] Q.B. 629 that a private citizen may act if the Attorney-General unreasonably delays in giving his consent or refuses it in what was there described as "a proper case." It should be added that none of the circumstances there predicated have been shown to exist in the present case. And the trouble about opening that particular door is that it involves proceeding upon the basis that the Attorney-General is in no better position than any other citizen to decide what is best in the public interest. That is a mistake, as Pearce L.J. demonstrated in *Attorney-General* v. *Harris* [1961] 1 Q.B. 74, 92, for he frequently has sources of information not generally available and must bear in mind considerations which may be undervalued when one considers injury to the public merely in terms of immediate injury: see also *Edwards, The Law Officers of the Crown*, pp. 222–223.

The law being perfectly clear, does the public interest require that it be changed? All three members of the Court of Appeal sternly condemned the Attorney-General's conduct. He had acted "contrary to the whole spirit of the law of England," and, by refusing to explain his refusal, he had made "a direct challenge to the rule of law." So said Lord Denning M.R., [1977] Q.B. 729, at pp. 753A and 758G, quoting Baggallay L.J., who had said in *Attorney-General* v. *Great Eastern Railway Co.* (1879) 11 Ch.D. 449, 500, that: "It is the interest of the public that the law should in all respects be respected and observed, and if the law is transgressed or threatened to be transgressed . . . it is the duty of the Attorney-General to take the necessary steps to enforce it, nor does it make any difference whether he sues ex officio, or at the instance of relators."

But it is *not* the law that every criminal act must lead to a prosecution (*Buckoke* v. *Greater London Council* [1971] Ch. 655, *per* Lord Denning M.R., at p. 668D-H), and, even if it were, the Attorney-General is unquestionably entitled to halt prosecutions in the manner already indicated. In other words, it is ultimately a matter for his unfettered discretion. The Court of Appeal regarded the manner of its exercise in the present case as so inexplicable that, in the words of Lawton L.J., at p. 739: ". . . until such times as there is some explanation as to why the Attorney-General did not intervene, then on the face of it his failure to do so must have been for some reason which was not a good reason in law." And yet lip-service was paid to the proposition that the Attorney-General's exercise of his discretion cannot be reviewed by the courts. For my part, I venture to reiterate by way of a contrast the striking fact that my noble and learned friend, Viscount Dilhorne, has expressed the affirmative view that the Attorney-General may well have acted in the public interest in withholding his consent. This highlights the undesirability of making the matter one of disputation in the courts, instead of in Parliament.

Accepting as I do that the Attorney-General's discretion is absolute and non-reviewable, there was accordingly, in my judgment, no basis upon which the plaintiff should have been granted the final injunction he sought. It remains to be considered whether he should have been granted *any* relief or whether, as the

three defendants submit, the proceedings should have been dismissed as showing no reasonable cause of action. . . .

In considering it [Gouriet's claim for a declaration], one may usefully begin with
Dyson v. *Attorney-General* [1911] 1 K.B. 410; [1912] 1 Ch. 158, the case most strongly
relied upon for Mr. Gouriet. Professor de Smith regarded the decision as the
turning point in the development of declaratory relief (see p. 428)[1] a remedy which
Atkin L.J. once described as "one of the most valuable contributions that the
courts have made to the commercial life of this country": see *Spettabile Consorzio
Veneznaio di Armamento e Navigazione* v. *Northumberland Shipbuilding Co. Ltd.* (1919)
121 L.T. 628, 635. Mr. Vinelott Q.C. for the Attorney-General, on the other hand,
stigmatised *Dyson* as a "red herring" introduced into these proceedings. Shortly
stated, the facts were that the Inland Revenue Commissioners issued to Dyson (a
taxpayer) a form and a notice requiring him under penalty to submit certain
particulars. Relying on R.S.C., Ord. 25, r. 5, he sued the Attorney-General for
declarations that the requisition was unauthorised and that he was under no
obligation to comply with it inasmuch as it was ultra vires the Finance Act. The
Court of Appeal granted the declarations sought, and Professor de Smith commented (*Judicial Review of Administrative Action,* (3rd ed.), p. 429)[2] ". . . this was a
case in which the plaintiff had no 'cause of action' that would have entitled him to
any other form of judicial relief: the threat to his interests created by the unlawful
demand that had been made upon him could be directly averted only by the
award of a binding declaration." But it is noteworthy that the defendant against
whom a declaration was sought was none other than the Attorney-General
himself, concerning whom Cozens-Hardy M.R. said [1911] 1 K.B. 410, 415: "I start
with this proposition, that the penalty which is threatened to be enforced against
the plaintiff is one which the Attorney-General must sue for in this court: Inland
Revenue Regulations Act 1890, sections 21 and 22. This suggests that the Attorney-General ought to be liable to an action in so far as he threatens to enforce a
penalty based upon non-compliance with an unauthorised notice."

The fact is that, as Mr. Vinelott rightly submitted, Mr. Dyson (though only one
among a very large number) had been threatened with penalties if he refused to
comply with an invalid demand. He therefore had a special interest and thus a
locus standi to institute what were, in effect, quia timet proceedings to protect his
private rights, and this nonetheless because the different private rights of many
others were similarly threatened. *Dyson* v. *Attorney-General*, in my judgment,
does not justify the declaration granted on the Court of Appeal's initiative to Mr.
Gouriet. . . .

Conclusion

The plaintiff is confronted by insurmountable difficulties. For *either* (*a*) he is
asserting a public right, which (since no private right, were invaded and he
neither feared nor suffered any special damage in consequence) he cannot do
without the concurrence of the Attorney-General in a relator action: or (*b*) he is
asserting a private right by means of an action in tort, and that is barred against the
defendant trade unions by section 14 of the Trade Union and Labour Relations Act
1974 and section 29 of the Post Office Act 1969.

So clear and well-established is the law that those who regard it as ill serving the
public interest must seek the aid of Parliament to remedy the position, for the
massive and fundamental revision involved before such plaintiffs as Mr. Gouriet
can be granted relief is beyond the proper capacity of your Lordships' House. We
accordingly cannot accede to Mr. French's supplication to break the "mould."

For these reasons, I hold that the appeals of the Attorney-General and the two
trade unions should be allowed and that of Mr. Gouriet dismissed.

Appeals of H.M. Attorney-General and of the Post Office unions allowed.

[1] *Judicial Review of Administrative Action* (4th ed., 1980) 479.
[2] (4th ed.) p.480.

Appeal of the plaintiff dismissed.

Notes

1. See *Dyson* v. *Attorney-General, post,* p. 424.

2. The use of the injunction to enforce the criminal law is further discussed by the House of Lords in *Stoke-on-Trent City Council* v. *B. & Q. (Retail) Ltd.* [1984] A.C. 754 (Section 222, Local Government Act 1972: deliberate and flagrant flouting of the law.) See also *City of London Corporation* v. *Bovis Construction, The Times,* April 21, 1988 (C.A.).

The effect of a Royal Pardon

R. v. Foster
[1985] 1 Q.B. 115
Court of Appeal

The appellant, following a plea of guilty, was convicted of various sexual offences. Some years later it was proved that these offences had been committed by another man. The appellant was granted a royal pardon and then sought to leave to appeal against conviction. Leave was granted by the Court of Appeal (Watkins and May L.JJ and Butler Sloss J.).

WATKINS L.J.: [delivering the judgment of the Court] It seems so we were told, generally to be thought that the effect of a free pardon is to wipe away the stain of conviction—put in a more legalistic way, to quash it. Mr. Arlidge informed us that there had been many pardons given over the decade between 1973 and 1983. There have been 12 persons at the time in prison pardoned in respect of offences of which they were convicted and 2,284 persons pardoned who were not in prison, the vast majority of whom had been convicted of some kind of road traffic offence . . .
The words of the pardon are instructive in themselves:

> "Now know ye that We in consideration of some circumstances humbly represented unto Us, are Graciously pleased to extend Our Grace and Mercy unto the said Barry Arthur Foster and to grant him Our Free Pardon in respect of the said conviction, thereby pardoning, remitting and releasing unto him all pains penalties and punishments whatsoever that from the said conviction may ensue."

It would seem from those words that the beneficiary of the pardon is pardoned in respect of all pains, penalties and punishments ensuing from the conviction, but not pardoned in respect of the conviction itself.

·   ·   ·   ·   ·

Many of the extracts we have been shown from textbooks and articles, some of them written centuries ago, tend to support the proposition that a pardon leaves the existence of a conviction untouched. These extracts include the works of Bracton on the Laws and Customs of England (1968) Vol. 2, pp.362–363, 369–370, 372, 378, Blackstone's Commentaries (1830) Vol 4, pp. 396–402, Hawkins' Pleas of the Crown (8th ed., 1824) Vol. 2, pp. 543, 548, 549 and Holdsworth, *A History of English Law*, (2nd ed., 1937) Vol. 6 p. 630.

·   ·   ·   ·   ·

Although the courts in this country have not, in recent times anyway, considered the position of pardon vis-á-vis conviction, Commonwealth countries have not been idle in the matter. Not for the first time this court is grateful for the research of counsel and judges of the Commonwealth and for the decisions appearing in reported cases. We refer above all in this context to *Rex* v. *Cosgrove* [1948] Tas.S.R. 99, in which judgment was given by the Supreme Court of Tasmania. In that case a pardon had been granted. It was a case which involved corruption. It was held that the pardon granted was not the equivalent of an acquittal.
Finally, so far as quotation from authority is concerned, we refer to *In re Royal Commission on Thomas Case* [1980] 1 N.Z.L.R. 602. In 1979 Thomas was granted a free pardon in respect of his conviction for the murders of David and Jeanette

Crewe ... It is quite obvious from the judgment in the case that much of the argument presented to the court by counsel was devoted to the question of the impact of a free pardon upon conviction. The High Court (Full Court) at Auckland held, among other things at pp. 602–603:

> "The effect of the pardon was to remove the criminal element of the offence named in the pardon, but not to create any factual fiction, or to raise the inference that the person pardoned had not in fact committed the crime for which the pardon was granted. Thomas, by reason of the pardon, was deemed to have been wrongly convicted, and he could not again be charged with the murders of the Crewes."

We respectfully agree that the effect of a free pardon is as stated in the judgments in the Tasmanian and New Zealand cases. In other words, the effect of a free pardon is such as, in the words of the pardon itself, to remove from the subject of the pardon, "all pains penalties and punishments whatsoever that from the said conviction may ensue," but not to eliminate the conviction itself.
Appeal allowed.

5. RIGHTS AND DUTIES OF THE INDIVIDUAL

"UBI JUS IBI REMEDIUM"

Ashby v. White and others
(1703) 2 Ld.Raym. 938; (1704) 3 L.Raym. 320; 14 St.Tr. 695;
1 Smith L.C. (13th ed.) 253.
Queen's Bench

ASHBY, a poor Whig cobbler recently come to settle in Aylesbury, had been warned out of the parish by the overseers of the poor, and application had been made to the justices to remove him. While this matter was still unsettled, he tendered his vote in an election of burgesses to represent the borough in Parliament; but his vote was refused by White (the Tory Mayor) and the constables (the returning officers), because in their opinion he was not a settled inhabitant there, neither had he contributed to the Church or the poor. The candidates for whom Ashby would have voted were duly elected. Nevertheless, he brought an action on the case at the Assizes against White and the other returning officers, alleging that they knew that his vote ought to be admitted, but that they, fraudulently and maliciously intending to damnify him, absolutely refused to permit him to give his vote. He obtained judgment for £5 damages and costs.

On motion in the Queen's Bench in arrest of judgment, on the ground that the action did not lie as the Commons had exclusive jurisdiction to determine claims to the franchise, the court (Powell, Powys and Gould JJ., Holt C.J. dissenting) gave judgment for the defendants. Upon writ of error in the House of Lords this was reversed on the grounds set forth by Holt C.J. in the court below that where there is a right there is a remedy.

This was a question of the (property) right of the individual. Holt C.J. prepared a revised version of his judgment, probably for the House of Lords, in which he emphasised the point that fraud and malice were alleged and proved.

HOLT C.J.: The single question in this case is, whether, if a free burgess of a corporation, who has an undoubted right to give his vote in the election of a burgess to serve in Parliament, be refused and hindered to give it by the officer, an action on the case will lie against such officer?

I am of opinion that judgment ought to be given in this case for the plaintiff. My brothers differ from me in opinion; and they all differ from one another in the reasons of their opinion; but notwithstanding their opinion, I think the plaintiff ought to recover, and that this action is well maintainable, and ought to lie. I will consider their reasons. My brother Gould thinks no action will lie against the defendant, because, as he says, he is a judge[1]; my brother Powys indeed says he is no judge, but *quasi* judge; but my brother Powell is of opinion, that the defendant neither is a judge, nor anything like a judge, and that is true; for the defendant is only an officer to execute the precept, *i.e.* only to give notice to the electors of the time and place of election, and to assemble them together in order to elect, and upon the conclusion to cast up the poll, and declare which candidate has the majority.

But to proceed, I will do these two things: First, I will maintain that the plaintiff has a right and a privilege to give his vote: Secondly, in consequence thereof, that if he be hindered in the enjoyment or exercise of the right, the law gives him an action against the disturber, and that this is the proper action given by the law.

---

[1] *i.e.* the returning officer was acting in a judicial capacity.

205

I did not at first think it would be any difficulty to prove that the plaintiff has a right to vote, nor necessary to maintain it, but from what my brothers have said in their arguments I find it will be necessary to prove it. It is not to be doubted, but that the Commons of England have a great and considerable right in the government, and a share in the legislative, without whom no law passes; but because of their vast numbers this right is not exercisable by them in their proper persons, and therefore, by the Constitution of England, it has been directed that it should be exercised by representatives, chosen by and out of themselves, who have the whole right of all the Commons of England vested in them. . . .

[Holt C.J. then went on to show that parliamentary electors had a right to vote, founded on the common law, but recognised by many statutes, and that the franchise was at that time of a proprietary nature, being incident to various kinds of land tenure which were made necessary qualifications by statute.] The right of voting at the election of burgesses is a thing of the highest importance, and so great a privilege, that it is a great injury to deprive the plaintiff of it. These reasons have satisfied me as to the first point.

2. If the plaintiff has a right, he must of necessity have a means to vindicate and maintain it, and a remedy if he is injured in the exercise or enjoyment of it; and indeed it is a vain thing to imagine a right without a remedy[2]; for want of right and want of remedy are reciprocal. . . . Where a man has but one remedy to come at his right, if he loses that, he loses his right. It would look very strange, when the Commons of England are so proud of their right of sending representatives to Parliament, that it should be in the power of a sheriff or other officer to deprive them of that right, and yet that they should have no remedy; it is a thing to be admired at[3] by all mankind. Supposing then that the plaintiff had a right of voting, and so it appears on the record, and the defendant has excluded him from it, nobody can say that the defendant has done well; then he must have done ill, for he has deprived the plaintiff of his right, so that the plaintiff having a right to vote, and the defendant having hindered him of it, it is an injury to the plaintiff. Where a new Act of Parliament is made for the benefit of the subject, if a man be hindered from the enjoyment of it, he shall have an action against such person who so obstructed him. . . . If then, where a statute gives a right, the party shall have an action for the infringement of it, is it not as forceable when a man has his right by the common law? This right of voting is a right in the plaintiff by the common law, and consequently he shall maintain an action for the obstruction of it. But there wants not a statute, too, in his case, for by West. I, 3 Edw. 1, c. 5, it was enacted "that for as much as electing ought to be free, the King forbids upon grievous forfeiture, that any great man, or other, by power of arms, or by malice, or menaces, shall disturb to make free election": 2 Inst. 168, 169. And this statute, as my Lord Coke observes, is only an enforcement of the common law; and if the Parliament thought the freedom of elections to be a matter of that consequence, as to give their sanction to it, and to enact that they should be free, it is a violation of that statute to disturb the plaintiff in this case in giving his vote at an election, and consequently actionable.

And I am of opinion that this action on the case is a proper action. My brother Powell indeed thinks that an action upon the case is not maintainable because there is no hurt or damage to the plaintiff; but surely every injury imports a damage, though it does not cost the party one farthing, and it is impossible to prove the contrary; for a damage is not merely pecuniary, but an injury imports a damage, when a man is thereby hindered of his right . . . . So if a man gives another a cuff on the ear, though it cost him nothing, no not so much as a little *diachylon*, yet he shall have his action, for it is a personal injury. So a man shall have an action against another for riding over his ground, though it do him no damage: for it is an invasion of his property, and the other has no right to come there; and in these cases the action is brought *vi et armis*. But for invasion of another's franchise trespass *vi et armis* does not lie, but an action of trespass on the case .... So here in the principal case, the plaintiff is obstructed of his right, and shall therefore have his action.

And it is no objection to say that it will occasion multiplicity of actions: for if men will multiply injuries, actions must be multiplied too, for every man that is injured ought to have his recompense. Suppose the defendant had beat forty or fifty men, the damage done to each one is peculiar to himself and he shall have his action. So if many persons receive a private injury by a public nuisance, every man shall have his action as is agreed in *William's Case*,[4] and *Westbury* and *Powell*.[5] Indeed, where many men are offended by one particular act, there they must proceed by way of indictment, and not of action; for in that case the law will not multiply actions. But it is otherwise when one man only is offended by that act; he shall have his action; as if a man dig a pit in a common, every commoner shall have an action on the case . . .; for every commoner has a several right. But it would be otherwise if a man dig a pit in a highway; every passenger shall not bring his action, but the[6] party shall be punished by indictment, because the injury is general, and common to all that pass. But when the injury is particular and peculiar to every man, each man shall have his action. In the case of *Turner* v. *Sterling*,[7] the plaintiff was not elected; he could not give in evidence the loss of his place as a damage, for he was never in it; but the *gist* of the action is, that the plaintiff having a right to stand for the place, and it being difficult to determine who had the majority, he had therefore a right to demand a poll, and the defendant, by denying it, was liable to an action. If public officers will infringe men's rights, they ought to pay greater damages than other men, to deter and hinder other officers from the like offences. ...

But in the principal case, my brother [Powell J.] says we cannot judge of this matter, because it is a parliamentary thing. O! by all means be very tender of that. Besides it is intricate, that there may be contrariety of opinions. But this matter can never come in question in Parliament, for it is agreed that the persons for whom the plaintiff voted were elected, so that the action is brought for being deprived of his vote; and if it were carried for the other candidates against whom he voted, his damage would be less. To allow this action will be to make public officers more careful to observe the constitutions of cities and boroughs, and not to be so partial as they commonly are in all elections, which is indeed a great and growing mischief, and tends to the prejudice of the peace of the nation. But they say that this is a matter out of our jurisdiction, and we ought not to enlarge it. I agree that we ought not to encroach or enlarge our jurisdiction; by doing so we usurp both on the right of the Queen and the people; but sure we may determine on a charter granted by the King, or on a matter of custom or prescription, when it comes before us, without encroaching on the Parliament. And if it be a matter within our jurisdiction, we are bound by our oaths to judge of it. This is a matter of property determinable before us. Was ever such a petition heard of in Parliament, as that a man was hindered of giving his vote, and praying them to give him a remedy? The Parliament undoubtedly would say, take your remedy at law. It is not like the case of determining the right of election between the candidates. ...

Let us consider where in the law consists, and we shall find it to be, not in particular instances and precedents, but in the reason of the law, and *ubi eadem ratio, idem jus*. This privilege of voting does not differ from any other franchise

---

[4] (1592) 5 Co. 73a.
[5] Co.Litt. 56a.
[6] See (1699) 1 Ld.Raym. 486.
[7] (1672) 2 Lev. 50; 2 Vent. 25. Gould J., in *Ashby* v. *White*, said that *Turner* v. *Sterling* was a case of *loss* of a profitable place, *viz.*, Bridgemaster of London.

whatsoever . . .; but we must not be frightened, when a matter of property comes before us, by saying it belongs to the Parliament; we must exert the Queen's jurisdiction. My opinion is founded on the law of England. The case of *Morse* and *Slue*[8] was the first action of that nature; but the novelty of it was no objection to it. So the case of *Smith* and *Crawshaw*[9] that an action of the case lay for falsely and maliciously indicating the plaintiff for treason; though the objections were strong against it, yet it was adjudge, that if the prosecution were without probable cause, there was as much reason the action should be maintained as in other cases. . . . So in the case of *Herring* and *Finch*[10] nobody scrupled but that the action well lay, for the plaintiff was thereby deprived of his right. And if an action is maintainable against an officer for hindering the plaintiff from voting for a mayor of a corporation, who cannot bind him in his liberty nor estate, to say that yet this action will not lie in our case, for hindering the plaintiff to vote at an election of his representative in Parliament, is inconsistent. Therefore my opinion is, that the plaintiff ought to have judgment.

Note

This case was followed by *Paty's Case* or the *Case of the Aylesbury Men* (R. v.*Paty* (1704) 2 Ld.Raym. 1105; 14 St.Tr. 849) in which Holt C.J. delivered another important dissenting judgment which has subsequently been approved by the legal profession.

The classification of the Parliamentary franchise as a proprietary right is now obsolete. The Representation of the People Act 1983, s.63, provides that returning officers, etc., who commit breaches of official duty in connection with Parliamentary elections are liable to a fine but not to an action for damages.

[8] (1672) 1 Vent. 190, 238.
[9] (1625) Cro.Car. 15; W. Jones 93.
[10] (1679) 2 Lev. 250.

Malone v. Metropolitan Police Commissioner
1979 1 Ch. 344
Chancery Division

Malone sought declarations that the tapping of his telephone by police on the authority of the Secretary of State was illegal. Although the law has been changed since this case was decided—by the Interception of Communications Act 1985— much of Sir Robert Megarry V.-C.'s judgment remains of importance.

SIR ROBERT MEGARRY V.-C.: [The Vice Chancellor first considered whether he had jurisdiction to make a declaration that telephone tapping was contrary to Article 8 of the European Convention for the Protection of Human Rights]

It was common ground that the status of the Convention was that of a treaty, and that it did not have the force of law in England. R.S.C., Ord. 15, r. 16, runs as follows:

> "No action or other proceeding shall be open to objection on the ground that a merely declaratory judgment or order is sought thereby, and the court may make binding declarations of right whether or not any consequential relief is or could be claimed."

Mr. Ross-Munro's contention was that this wording was very wide, and enabled the court to make declarations not only as to legal rights, but also as to moral or international obligations. Further, the Convention was unlike an ordinary treaty, since it gave individuals the right to petition the Commission established under the Convention in respect of alleged breaches of the terms of the Convention. He relied on certain passages in *Guaranty Trust Co. of New York* v. *Hannay & Co.* [1915] 2 K.B. 536, and especially the judgment of Bankes L.J. at p. 571. This emphasised that rule 16 had two limbs, the first stating that the proceedings should not be open to objection on the ground that "a merely declaratory judgment or order is sought thereby," and the second providing that the court may make "binding declarations of right," whether or not any consequential relief is or could be claimed. Even though the second limb might be confined to cases of legally enforceable rights (as opposed to moral obligations and so on), said Mr. Ross-Munro, the first limb, which did not contain the word "right," was not thus circumscribed. Bankes L.J. had held at p. 571 that the rule contemplated making "declaratory judgments and orders which may not be declarations of right"; and although he held that the plaintiff must be claiming some "relief," he also held that the relief was not confined to relief in respect of a cause of action. Provided it would not be unlawful, unconstitutional or inequitable for the court to grant the relief claimed, or contrary to the accepted principles on which the court exercises its jurisdiction, the jurisdiction was unfettered and "the rule should receive as liberal a construction as possible": see at p. 572.

This, I think, is the high water mark of the authority relied on by Mr. Ross-Munro in support of his contention. . . .

The language of Bankes L.J. in the *Guaranty* case is indeed wide, and in some respects a little puzzling; but I do not think that it supports Mr. Ross-Munro's contention. That case was concerned with a claim to a declaration that the plaintiffs were not subject to certain obligations. What Bankes L.J. was pointing out (and I put it in my own words) was that in addition to making declarations of the right the court can make declarations of non-liability. True, a plaintiff who seeks such a declaration may have no cause of action; but it suffices if he is claiming "relief." This, I think, means relief from "[some] real liability or disadvantage or difficulty" which affects him (see *Thorne Rural District Council* v. *Bunting* [1972] Ch. 470, 477, 478), and not mere matters of interest or curiosity or the like. The illustrations which Bankes L.J. gives ([1915] 2 K.B. 536, 573) make it plain, I think, that he is throughout referring to rights and liabilities that are enforceable in the courts, and not merely moral, social or political rights or liabilities that are not. It would indeed be remarkable if by seeking a declaration instead of other relief a litigant could require the court to adjudicate on matters that otherwise would be outside its jurisdiction. It would be even more remarkable if it were to be held that although the second limb of the rule is confined to legal rights, the first limb extends to all liabilities, whether legal, moral, social or otherwise. (I use the word "legal" to include "equitable," of course.)

In my judgment, the power to make declarations is confined to making declarations on matters that are justiciable in the courts. This is emphasised by the contrast in drafting in the rule. The second limb is cast in the form of conferring a positive power of making declarations of right. The first limb, on the other hand, is expressed in terms not of conferring any positive power but only of removing one possible objection to proceedings, namely, that a merely declaratory judgment is sought. Every other objection remains open, and so if the proceedings are brought in respect of moral, social or political matters in which no legal or equitable rights arise, the objection to the court deciding such matters remains.

This view seems to me to be supported by ample authority.[1]

·   ·   ·   ·   ·

As I have indicated, I can see nothing in Ord. 15, r. 16, to open the doors to the making of declarations on a wide range of extra-legal issues. I shall not discuss the engaging examples which emerged in argument, ranging from moral obligations to the decisions of referees in football matches. I shall only say that I cannot believe that the court could, or should, grant a declaration that, for instance, a referee was right (or wrong) in awarding a penalty kick. The short answer to Mr. Ross-Munro on the present point is that declarations will be made only in respect of matters justiciable in the courts; treaties are not justiciable in this way, the Convention is a treaty with nothing in it that takes it out of that category for this purpose; and I therefore have no power to make the declaration claimed under paragraph 4 of the prayer for relief in the statement of claim. Even if I had jurisdiction, I think that in my discretion I would refuse to make the declaration, and would leave it to the bodies set up under the Convention to decide the matter. Accordingly I refuse to make that declaration, and dismiss the claim to it.[2]

[The Vice Chancellor then summarised the three main submissions put forward by Counsel for the Plaintiff]

Although the royal prerogative was mentioned from time to time, no claim was made that there was any prerogative power to tap telephones, and so I need say nothing of that. As they finally emerged, I think Mr. Ross-Munro's three main submissions maybe summarised as follows. First, he said that it was unlawful for anyone to intercept or monitor the telephone conversations of another without the consent of that other. He rested this contention on the right of property, on the right of privacy, and on the right of confidentiality. Second, he relied on article 8 of the Convention, as construed by the European Court of Human Rights, especially in *Klass and Others*, July 4, 1978. He relied on this in two respects. First, he said that it conferred a direct right on all citizens of the United Kingdom. Second, he said that it aided the courts of this country. It guided those courts in interpreting and applying English law so as to make it accord as far as possible with the Convention; and it provided a guide in cases of ambiguity or a lack of clarity in English

---

[1] The learned Vice-Chancellor cited *Republic of Italy* v. *Hambros Bank Ltd.* [1950] Ch.134, 329 *per* Vaisey J; his own unreported decision, *Uppal* v. *Home Office*, October 20, 1978; *Gouriet* v. *Union of Post Office Workers* [1978] A.C. 435, 483, 495, 501, 508, 522; *Nixon* v. *Attorney-General* [1930] 1 Ch.566, 574 *per* Clauson J.; affirmed [1930] 1 Ch.581; [1931] A.C. 184; *Kynaston* v. *Attorney-General* (1932) 49 T.L.R. 114.

[2] See also *Dyson* v. *Attorney-General* [1911] 1 K.B. 410; *post* p.424.

law. Mr. Ross-Munro's third main contention was based on the absence of any grant of powers to the executive to tap telephones, either by statute or by the common law.

[Counsel's] first proposition rested in the first place on a right of property. To tap a person's telephone conversation without his consent, he said, was unlawful because that person had rights of property in his words as transmitted by the electrical impulses of the telephone system, and so the tapping constituted an interference with his property rights. An analogy that he suggested was that the important part of a letter was the words that it contained rather than the paper that it was written on. I regret to say that Mr. Ross-Munro found it difficult to persuade me that there was any reality in this contention, and he did not struggle long. I do not see how words being transmitted by electrical impulses could themselves (as distinct from any copyright in them) fairly be said to be the subject matter of property. At all events, no argument which even began to support such a proposition was put before me.

The second ground on which [Counsel] sought to support his first proposition was that of the right of privacy. He accepted that the books assert that in English law there is no general right to privacy, and he referred me to a passage in *Halsbury's Laws of England*, Vol. 8 (4th ed., 1974), p. 557 to this effect. But he contended that there was a particular right of privacy which the books did not mention, namely, the right to hold a telephone conversation in the privacy of one's home without molestation.

I now turn to the third ground on which Mr. Ross-Munro supports his first proposition, the right of confidentiality. This is an equitable right which is still in course of development. . . . It may be, however, that a new tort is emerging (see *Goff and Jones, The Law of Restitution*, (2nd ed., 1978), pp. 518, 519, and Gareth Jones (1970) 86 L.Q.R. 463, 491), though this has been doubted: see *Street, The Law of Torts*, (6th ed. 1976) p. 377. Certainly the subject raises many questions that are so far unresolved, some of which are discussed in the Younger Report[3] at pp. 296–299.

The application of the doctrine of confidentiality to the tapping of private telephone lines is that in using a telephone a person is likely to do it in the belief that it is probable (though by no means certain) that his words will be heard only by the person he is speaking to. I do not think that it can be put higher than that. As the Younger Report[3] points out at p. 168, those who use the telephone are

> "aware that there are several well understood possibilities of being over-heard. A realistic person would not therefore rely on the telephone system to protect the confidence of what he says because, by using the telephone, he would have discarded a large measure of security for his private speech."

Extension lines, private switchboards and so-called "crossed lines," for example, all offer possibilities of being overheard. The report then pointed out that what would not be taken into account would be an unauthorised tap by induction coil or infinity transmitter. The report, which was dealing only with incursions into privacy by individuals and companies, and not the public sector, said nothing about tapping authorised by the Home Secretary. However, the substantial publicity attending the Birkett Report, and the general interest in films, television and affairs of notoriety in other countries, must mean that few telephone users can be ignorant of the real possibility that telephones are subject to the risk (which most people will probably regard as being very small in their own cases) of being tapped by some governmental body with access to the telephone system.

· · · · · ·

With that, I turn to [Counsel's] second main contention, based on the Convention. As I have mentioned, there were two limbs: first, that the Convention

[3] (1972) Cmnd. 5012.

conferred direct rights on citizens of the United Kingdom, and, second, that the Convention should be applied as a guide in interpreting and applying English law in so far as it is ambiguous or lacking in clarity. . . . The main trust of his argument, which had a number of facets to it, was that although a treaty forms no part of the law of this country, it might nevertheless have some effect in English law. In this case, he said, the Convention . . . could and should have a significant effect in determining what the law was on a point which, like this, was devoid of any direct authority. On this, he put before me a number of recent authorities in the Court of Appeal. In these, the high water mark for his purpose was, I think, the judgment of Scarman L.J. in *Pan-American World Airways Inc.* v. *Department of Trade* [1976] 1 Lloyd's Rep. 257, 261. After stating that the treaty there in question was "no part of the law of England," Scarman L.J. referred to a situation where it would be proper for the courts to take note of an international convention. That arose when two courses were reasonably open to the court, but

> "one would lead to a decision inconsistent with Her Majesty's international obligations under the convention while the other would lead to a result consistent with those obligations. If statutory words have to be construed or a legal principle formulated in an area of the law where Her Majesty has accepted international obligations, our courts—who, of course, take notice of the acts of Her Majesty done in the exercise of her sovereign power—will have regard to the convention as part of the full content or background of the law. Such a convention, especially a multilateral one, should then be considered by courts even though no statute expressly or impliedly incorporates it into our law."

There was then a reference of two of the cases which were cited to me, both of which concerned the Convention now before me. See also the subsequent case of *Reg.* v. *Chief Immigration Officer, Heathrow Airport, Ex parte Salamat Bibi* [1976] 1 W.L.R. 979, especially at p. 984, *per* Lord Denning M.R., and contrast p. 986, *per* Roskill L.J., questioning the dictum of Scarman L.J.

It is not for me, sitting at first instance, to resolve the variant shades of meaning in the dicta, and I do not attempt to do so. For the present, all that I say is that I take note of the Convention . . . and I shall give it due consideration in discussing English law on the point. As for the direct right which the Convention confers, it seems to me to be plain that this is a direct right in relation to the European Commission of Human Rights and the European Court of Human Rights, the bodies established by the Convention, but not in relation to the courts of this country. The Convention is plainly not of itself law in this country, however much it may fall to be considered as indicating what the law of this country should be, or should be construed as being.

Finally, there is the contention that as no power to tap telephones has been given by either statute or common law, the tapping is necessarily unlawful. The underlying assumption of this contention, of course, is that nothing is lawful that is not positively authorised by law. As I have indicated, England is not a country where everything is forbidden except what is expressly permitted. One possible illustration is smoking. I inquired what positive authority was given by the law to permit people to smoke. [Counsel] accepted that there was none; but tapping, he said, was different. It was in general disfavour, and it offended against usual and proper standards of behaviour, in that it was an invasion of privacy and an interference with the liberty of the individual and his right to be let alone when lawfully engaged on his own affairs.

I did not find this argument convincing. A stalward non-smoker, whether life-long or redeemed, might consider that most or all of what Mr. Ross-Munro said applied with equal force to the not inconsiderable numbers of non-smokers. . . . The notion that some express authorisation of law is required for acts which meet with "general disfavour," and "offend against proper standards of behaviour," and so on, would make the state of the law dependent on subjective views on indefinite concepts, and would be likely to produce some remarkable and contentious results.

[Counsel's] first main contention was that by reason of the right of privacy and the right of confidentiality it was unlawful to tap a telephone, even under the authority of a warrant of the Home Secretary. I need not mention the argument based on property as I have already rejected it.

First, I do not think that any assistance is obtained from the general warrant cases, or other authorities dealing with warrants. At common law, the only power to search premises under a search warrant issued by a justice of the peace is to search for stolen goods: see *Entick* v. *Carrington,* 19 St.Tr. 1029, 1067. However, many statutes authorise searches under search warrants for many different purposes; and there is admittedly no statute which in terms authorises the tapping of telephones, with or without a warrant. Nevertheless, any conclusion that the tapping of telephones is therefore illegal would plainly be superficial in the extreme. The reason why a search of premises which is not authorised by law is illegal is that it involves the tort of trespass to those premises: and any trespass, whether to land or goods or the person, that is made without legal authority is prima facie illegal. Telephone tapping by the Post Office, on the other hand, involves no act of trespass. The subscriber speaks into his telephone, and the process of tapping appears to be carried out by Post Office officials making recordings, with Post Office apparatus on Post Office premises, of the electrical impulses on Post Office wires provided by Post Office electricity. There is no question of there being any trespass on the plaintiff's premises for the purpose of attaching anything either to the premises themselves or to anything on then: all that is done is done within the Post Office's own domain. As Lord Camden C.J. said in *Entick* v. *Carrington,* 19 St.Tr. 1029, 1066, "the eye cannot by the laws of England be guilty of a trespass"; and, I would add, nor can the ear.

[The Vice-Chancellor then considered the status in law of a warrant issued by the Home Secretary under the statutes then in force and concluded that by the Post Office Act 1969 Parliament has provided a clear recognition of the warrant of the Home Secretary as having an effective function in law, both as providing a defence to certain criminal charges, and also as amounting to an effective requirement for the Post Office to do certain acts.]

.   .   .   .   .   .

Third, there is the right of privacy. Here the contention is that although at present no general right of privacy has been recognised by English law, there is a particular right of privacy, namely, the right to hold a telephone conversation in the privacy of one's home without molestation. That, it was said, ought to be recognised and declared to be part of English law, despite the absence of any English authority to this effect. As I have indicated, I am not unduly troubled by the absence of English authority: there has to be a first time for everything, and if the principles of English law, and not least analogies from the existing rules, together with the requirements of justice and common sense, pointed firmly to such a right existing, then I think the court should not be deterred from recognising the right.

On the other hand, it is no function of the courts to legislate in a new field. The extension of the existing laws and principles is one thing, the creation of an altogether new right is another. At times judges must, and do, legislate; but as Holmes J. once said, they do so only interstitially, and with molecular rather than molar motions: see *Southern Pacific Co.* v. *Jensen* (1917) 244 U.S. 205, 221, in a dissenting judgment. Anything beyond that must be left for legislation. No new right in the law, fully-fledged with all the appropriate safeguards, can spring from the head of a judge deciding a particular case: only Parliament can create such a right. [The Vice-Chancellor concluded that the plaintiff's claim based on the right on privacy must fail.]

Fourth, there is the right of confidentiality. Let me at the outset dispose of one point. If telephone services were provided under a contract between the telephone subscriber and the Post Office, then it might be contended that there was some implied term in that contract that telephone conversations should remain confidential and be free from tapping. To meet such a possible contention, the Solicitor-General took me through a series of statutes and cases on the point, ending with certain sections of the Post Office Act 1969. The combined effect of sections 9 and 28 is that the Post Office is under a duty to provide certain services, including telephone services (thought this duty is not enforceable by proceedings in court), and that the Post Office has power to make a scheme of charges and other terms and conditions for those services, the charges being recoverable "as if" they were simple contract debts. Under section 28, the Post Office Telecommunication Scheme 1976 was duly made, bearing the name Scheme T1/1976: this was published as a supplement to the "London Gazette" of May 25, 1976. By paragraph 6 of the scheme, neither the scheme, nor anything done under it, nor any request for any service for which the scheme fixes or determines any charges, terms or conditions, it to "constitute or lead to the formation of a contract between the Post Office and any other person; . . ." At the end of the Solicitor-General's submissions on the point Mr. Ross-Munro conceded that there was no contract as such between the plaintiff and the Post Office; and that, I think is the end of any contention based on implied terms.

The right of confidentiality accordingly falls to be considered apart from any contractual right. In such a case, it has been said that three elements are normally required if a case of breach of confidence is to succeed. First, the information itself, in the words of Lord Greene M.R. in *Saltman Engineering Co. Ltd.* v. *Campbell Engineering Co. Ltd.* (1948) 65 R.P.C. 203, 215, "must 'have the necessary quality of confidence about it.' Secondly, that information must have been imparted in circumstances importing an obligation of confidence. Thirdly, there must be an unauthorised use of that information to the detriment of the party communicating it": see *Coco* v. *A. N. Clark (Engineers) Ltd.* [1969] R.P.C. 41, 47, cited by Lord Widgery C.J. in *Attorney-General* v. *Jonathan Cape Ltd.* [1976] Q.B. 752, 769, Of the second requirement, it was said in the *Coco* case, at pp. 47–48:

> "However secret and confidential the information, there can be no binding obligation of confidence if that information is blurted out in public or is communicated in other circumstances which negative any duty of holding it confidential."

What was in issue in the *Coco* case was a communication by an inventor or designer to a manufacturer, and the alleged misuse of that information by the manufacturer. In the present case, the alleged misuse is not by the person to whom the information was intended to be communicated, but by someone to whom the plaintiff had no intention of communicating anything: and that, of course, introduces a somewhat different element, that of the unknown overhearer.

It seems to me that a person who utters confidential information must accept the risk of any unknown overhearing that is inherent in the circumstances of communication. Those who exchange confidences on a bus or a train run the risk of a nearby passenger with acute hearing or a more distant passenger who is adept at lip-reading. Those who speak over garden walls run the risk of the unseen neighbour in a tool-shed nearby. Office cleaners who discuss secrets in the office when they think everyone else has gone run the risk of speaking within earshot of an unseen member of the staff who is working late. Those who give confidential information over an office intercommunication system run the risk of some third party being connected to the conversation. I do not see why someone who has overheard some secret in such a way should be exposed to legal proceedings if he uses or divulges what he has heard. No doubt an honourable man would give some warning when he realises that what he is hearing is not intended for his ears; but I have to concern myself with the law, and not with moral standards. There are, of course, many moral precepts which are not legal enforceable.

When this is applied to telephone conversations, it appears to me that the speaker is taking such risks of being overheard as are inherent in the system. . . . So much publicity in recent years has been given to instances (real or fictional) of the deliberate tapping of telephones that it is difficult to envisage telephone users who are genuinely unaware of this possibility. No doubt a person who uses a telephone to give confidential information to another may do so in such a way to impose an obligation of confidence on that other: but I do not see how it could be said that any such obligation is imposed on those who overhear the conversation, whether by means of tapping or otherwise.

Fifth, there is [Counsel's] second main head, based on the European Convention for the Protection of Human Rights and Fundamental Freedoms. The first limb of this relates to the direct rights conferred by the Convention. Any such right is, as I have said, a direct right in relation to the European Commission of Human Rights and the European Court of Human Rights, and not in relation to the courts of this country; for the Convention is not law here. Article 1 of the Convention provides that the High Contracting Parties "shall secure to everyone within their jurisdiction the rights and freedoms defined in Section I of this Convention"; and those rights and freedoms are those which are set out in articles 1 to 18 inclusive. The United Kingdom, as a High Contracting Party which ratified the Convention of March 8, 1951, has thus long been under an obligation to secure these rights and freedoms to everyone. That obligation, however, is an obligation under a treaty which is not justiciable in the courts of this country. Whether that obligation has been carried out is not for me to say. It is, I suppose, possible to contend that the de facto practice in this country sufficiently secures these rights and freedoms, without legislation for the purpose being needed. It is also plainly possible to contend that, among other things, the existing safeguards against unbridled telephone tapping, being merely administrative in nature and not imposed by law, fall far short of making any rights and freedoms "secure" to anyone. However, as I have said, that is not for me to decide. All that I do is to hold that the Convention does not as a matter of English law, confer any direct rights on the plaintiff that he can enforce in the English courts.

Sixth, there is the second limb of [the] contention based on the Convention. . . . as assisting the court to determine what English law is on a point on which authority is lacking or uncertain. Can it be said that in this case two courses are reasonably open to the court, one of which is inconsistent with the Convention and the other consonant with it? I refer, of course, to the words of Scarman L.J. in the Pan-American case [1976] 1 Lloyd's Rep. 257 that I have already quoted. I readily accept that if the question before me were one on construing a statute enacted with the purpose of giving effect to obligations imposed by the Convention, the court would readily seek to construe the legislation in a way that would effectuate the Convention rather that frustrate it. However, no relevant legislation of that sort is in existence. It seems to me that where Parliament has abstained from legislation on a point that is plainly suitable for legislation, it is indeed difficult for the court to lay down new rules of common law or equity that will carry out the Crown's treaty obligations, or to discover for the first time that such rules have always existed.

It appears to me that to decide this case in the way that [Counsel] seeks would carry me far beyond any possible function of the Convention as influencing English law that has ever been suggested; and it would be most undesirable. Any regulation of so complex a matter as telephone tapping is essentially a matter for

Parliament, not the courts; and neither the Convention nor the *Klass* can, I think, play any proper part in deciding the issue before me. Accordingly, the second limb of counsel's second main contention also fails.

I would only add that, even if it was not clear before, this case seems to me to make it plain that telephone tapping is a subject which cries out for legislation. Privacy and confidentiality are, of course, subjects of considerable complexity. Yet however desirable it may be that they should at least to some extent be defined and regulated by statute, rather than being left for slow and expensive evolution in individual cases brought at the expense of litigants and the legal aid fund, the difficulty of the subject matter is liable to discourage legislative zeal. Telephone tapping lies in a much narrower compass; the difficulties in legislation on the subject ought not to prove insuperable; and the requirements of the Convention should provide a spur to action, even if belated. This, however, is not for me to decide. I can do no more than express a hope, and offer a proleptic welcome to any statute on the subject.

Seventh, there is counsel's third main contention, based on the absence of any grant of powers to the executive to tap telephones. I have already held that if such tapping can be carried out without committing any breach of the law, it requires no authorisation by statute or common law; it can lawfully be done simply because there is nothing to make it unlawful. Now that I have held that such tapping can indeed be carried out without committing any breach of the law, the contention necessarily fails. I may also say that the statutory recognition given to the Home Secretary's warrant seems to me to point clearly to the same conclusion.

.   .   .   .   .

Plaintiff's claim dismissed.

Note

For another unsuccessful attempt to challenge the legality of telephone tapping, before the enactment of the Interception of Communications Act 1985, see *R.* v. *Secretary of State for the Home Department Ex parte Ruddock* [1987] 2 All E.R. 518.

DISCRIMINATION

Gill v. El Vino Co. Ltd.
[1983] 1 Q.B. 425
Court of Appeal

The plaintiffs, both women, entered a wine bar in Fleet St. and attempted to buy a drink at the bar. The barman refused to serve them: the management required women customers to sit at one of the tables on the premises if they wishs to be served. They sought a declaration at the Mayor's and City of London Court that the defendants, the owners of the bar, had acted in breach of the Sex Discrimination Act 1975, s. 29. On judgment being given for the defendants, they appealed to the Court of Appeal.

Section 1(1) of the Sex Discrimination Act 1975 provides:

A person discriminates against a woman in any circumstances relevant for the purposes of any provision of this Act if—(a) on the ground of her sex he treats her less favourably than he treats or would treat a man . . .

Section 29 (1) of the Act provides:–

It is unlawful for any person concerned with the provision (for payment or not) of goods, facilities or services to the public or a section of the public to discriminate against a woman who seeks to obtain or use those goods, facilities or services—(a) by refusing or deliberately omitting to provide her with any of them, or (b) by refusing or deliberately omitting to provide her with good, facilities or services of the like quality, in the like manner and on the like terms as are normal in his case in relation to male members of the public or (where she belongs to a section of the public) to male members of that section.

Subsection (2) provides:–

The following are examples of the facilities and services mentioned in subsection (1)—(a) access to and use of any place which members of the public or a section of the public are permitted to enter . . . (e) facilities for entertainment, recreation or refreshment.

EVELEIGH L.J.: The judge came to the conclusion, on the facts of this case, that there was no discrimination in that he found that the ladies were not treated less favourably by the defendants than they treated a man or men. In coming to that conclusion the judge was, in my opinion, influenced by reference to other cases, and in particular by reference to *Ministry of Defence* v. *Jeremiah* [1980] Q.B. 87 and he quoted the words of Brightman L.J. at p. 103, where he said:

"I do not say that the mere deprivation of choice for one sex, or some other differentiation in their treatment, is necessarily unlawful discrimination. The deprivation of choice, or differentiation, in the sort of case we are considering, must be associated with a detriment."

It seems to me that the judge in this case took the view that he could not call it a detriment for women to be refused the facilities afforded in the particular area in El Vino's which we have to consider and therefore there was no discrimination.

In my judgment, the correct way to approach this case is to take the simple words of the statute and try to apply them. It sometimes is helpful in judgments to substitute some other phraseology which the judge thinks is more apposite in the particular case under consideration, but that is by no means always necessary and if it can be avoided it is desirable to do so. It is also, in my view, desirable to avoid looking at cases where substituted phraseology has been evoked, because the next step is that one goes on to rephrase the substituted phraseology, and on and on one goes and departs further and further from the approach which the statute indicates. Now this is not a technical statute and, therefore, is not of a kind where one should or need go for the meaning of words to other decided cases. It is a simple statute seeking to deal with ordinary everyday behaviour and the relative positions of men and women.

The reference to "detriment" in Brightman L.J.'s passage was necessary because that was a case under section 6 (2) of the Act of 1975, and that read: "It is unlawful for a person, in the case of a woman employed by him at an establishment in Great Britain, to discriminate against her . . . (b) by dismissing her, or subjecting her to any other detriment."

So that the words "subjecting her to any other detriment" refer to the manner or the means used in discriminating. Compare in the present case the words of section 29 (1) "by refusing or deliberately omitting to provide her with" goods, facilities or services or the corresponding words in section 29 (1) (b). One has to ask in the present case: was she refused, or was there deliberate omission to provide her with, goods, facilities or services? In *Ministry of Defence* v. *Jeremiah* [1980] Q.B. 87 there had to be asked: was she subjected to a detriment? But once those questions have been answered, it is then necessary to go simply to section 1 (1) (a) and ask the question: when that happened, was she treated less favourably than a man would have been treated? In other words, to apply section 1 of the Act, one has to make a comparison between the treatment of a man and a woman.

What is the comparison in this case? A woman is denied certain things that a man can have. As a matter of fact in this case what are they? She was denied the opportunity to drink where others drank, to mix with other people who were drinking in El Vino's. . . .

It is said here that this is de minimis. In coming to the conclusion that it was de minimis the judge again was influenced by the emphasis upon "detriment." In the present case, as I have said, we are not enjoined to ask if there was detriment—although, in passing, I myself, on the usual understanding of that word, would say there was, but we are not enjoined to ask that. We are enjoined to ask: was there a refusal of a facility? There clearly was. Can it be said that the refusal of that facility was a matter that could be classified as de minimis? In other words, it seems to me that involves saying: "Well, she was less favourably treated but only very slightly." I find it very difficult to evoke the maxim de minimis non curat lex in a situation where that which has been denied to the plaintiff is the very thing that Parliament seeks to provide, namely facilities and services on an equal basis. But on the facts of this particular case the whole rather special attractiveness of the particular area of the premises in question is denied to the woman. Its popularity is undoubted. It affords a unique atmosphere which is clearly greatly appreciated and is in great demand by men, and I cannot, therefore, assume that there is no true demand for it by women. . . .

I would allow the appeal.

GRIFFITHS L.J.: I agree. El Vino's is no ordinary wine bar, it has become a unique institution in Fleet Street. Every day it is thronged with journalists, solicitors, barristers exchanging the gossip of the day. No doubt it is the source of many false rumours which have dashed the hopes of many an aspirant to a High Court appointment. Now if a man wishes to take a drink in El Vino's he can drink, if he wishes, by joining the throng which crowds round the bar and there he can join his friends and pick up, no doubt, many an interesting piece of gossip, particularly if he is a journalist. Or, if he wishes, he can go and sit down at one of the two tables that are on the right immediately behind the main door of the premises. Thirdly, if he wishes, he can pass through the partition and enter the little smoking room at the back, which is equipped with a number of tables and chairs.

But there is no doubt that very many men choose to stand among the throng drinking at the bar.

But if a woman wishes to go to El Vino's she is not allowed to join the throng before the bar. She must drink either at one of the two tables on the right of the entrance, or she must pass through the throng and drink in the smoking room at the back. There is no doubt whatever that she is refused facilities that are accorded to men, and the only question that remains is: is she being treated less favourably than men? I think that permits of only one answer: of course she is . . .

This appeal must be allowed.

Sir Roger Ormrod delivered judgment to the same effect.

Appeal allowed.

Mandla v. Dowell Lee
[1983] 2 A.C. 548
House of Lords

The appellants were Sikhs, father and son. The father had wished to enter his son at a school owned by a company in which the respondent (the headmaster of the school) and his wife were principal shareholders. The respondent refused to admit the son if he insisted on wearing his turban. The father accordingly found another school for his son and then complained to the Commission for Racial Equality which took up the case.

Section 1 of the Race Relations Act 1976 provides:

> A person discriminates against another in any circumstances relevant for the purposes of any provision of this Act if—(a) on racial grounds he treats that other less favourably than he treats or would treat other persons; or (b) he applies to that other a requirement or condition which he applies or would apply equally to persons not of the same racial group as that other but—(i) which is such that the proportion of persons of the same racial group as that other who can comply with it is considerably smaller than the proportion of persons not of that racial group who can comply with it; and (ii) which he cannot show to be justifiable irrespective of the colour, race, nationality or ethnic or national origins of the person to whom it applied; and (iii) which is to the detriment of that other because he cannot comply with it.

Section 3 (1) provides:

> " 'racial group' means a group of persons defined by reference to colour, race, nationality or ethnic or national origins, and references to a person's racial group refer to any racial group into which he falls."

In the County Court the judge held that Sikhs were not a racial group and therefore there had been no discrimination contrary to the Act of 1976. The Court of Appeal (Lord Denning M.R., Oliver and Kerr L.JJ.) agreed. The House of Lords (Lord Fraser of Tullybelton, Lord Edmund-Davies, Lord Roskill, Lord Brandon of Oakbrook and Lord Templeman) allowed an appeal from that decision.

LORD FRASER OF TULLYBELTON: The case against the respondent under section 1 (1) (b) is that he discriminated against the second appellant because he applied to him a requirement or condition (namely, the "No turban" rule) which he applied equally to pupils not of the same racial group as the second respondent (i.e. to pupils who were not Sikhs) but (i) which is such that the proportion of Sikhs who can comply with it is considerably smaller than the proportion of non-Sikhs who can comply with it and (ii) which the respondent cannot show to be justifiable irrespective of the colour, etc. of the second appellant, and (iii) which is to the detriment of the second appellant because he cannot comply with it. As I have already said, the first main question is whether the Sikhs are a racial group. If they are, then two further questions arise. Question two is what is the meaning of "can" in paragraph (i) of section 1 (1) (b), and question three is, what is the meaning of "justifiable" in paragraph (ii) of that subsection?

.   .   .   .   .

It is not suggested that Sikhs are a group defined by reference to colour, race, nationality or *national* origins. In none of these respects are they distinguishable from many other groups, especially those living, like most Sikhs, in the Punjab. The argument turns entirely upon whether they are a group defined by "*ethnic* origins." It is therefore necessary to ascertain the sense in which the word "ethnic" is used in the Act of 1976.

. . . . .

My Lords, I recognise that "ethnic" conveys a flavour of race but it cannot, in my opinion, have been used in the Act of 1976 in a strictly racial or biological sense. For one thing, it would be absurd to suppose that Parliament can have intended that membership of a particular racial group should depend upon scientific proof that a person possessed the relevant distinctive biological characteristics (assuming that such characteristics exist). The practical difficulties of such proof would be prohibitive, and it is clear that Parliament must have used the word in some more popular sense. For another thing, the briefest glance at the evidence in this case is enough to show that, within the human race, there are very few, if any, distinctions which are scientifically recognised as racial. I respectfully agree with the view of Lord Simon of Glaisdale in *Ealing London Borough Council* v. *Race Relations Board* [1972] A.C. 342, 362, referring to the long title of the Race Relations Act 1968 (which was in terms identical with part of the long title of the Act of 1976) when he said:

> "Moreover, 'racial' is not a term of art, either legal or, I surmise, scientific. I apprehend that anthropologists would dispute how far the word 'race' is biologically at all relevant to the species amusingly called homo sapiens."

A few lines lower down, after quoting part of section 1 (1) of the Act, the noble and learned Lord said:

> "This is rubbery and elusive language—understandably when the draftsman is dealing with so unprecise a concept as 'race' in its popular sense and endeavouring to leave no loophole for evasion."

. . . . .

In my opinion, the word "ethnic" still retains a racial flavour but it is used nowadays in an extended sense to include other characteristics which may be commonly thought of as being associated with common racial origin.

For a group to constitute an ethnic group in the sense of the Act of 1976, it must, in my opinion, regard itself, and be regarded by others, as a distinct community by virtue of certain characteristics. Some of these characteristics are essential; others are not essential but one or more of them will commonly be found and will help to distinguish the group from the surrounding community. The conditions which appear to me to be essential are these: (1) a long shared history, of which the group is conscious as distinguishing it from other groups, and the memory of which it keeps alive; (2) a cultural tradition of its own, including family and social customs and manners, often but not necessarily associated with religious observance. In addition to those two essential characteristics the following characteristics are, in my opinion, relevant; (3) either a common geographical origin, or descent from a small number of common ancestors; (4) a common language, not necessarily peculiar to the group; (5) a common literature peculiar to the group; (6) a common religion different from that of neighbouring groups or from the general community surrounding it; (7) being a minority or being an oppressed or a dominant group within a larger community, for example a conquered people (say, the inhabitants of England shortly after the Norman conquest) and their conquerors might both be ethnic groups.

A group defined by reference to enough of these characteristics would be capable of including converts, for example, persons who marry into the group, and of excluding apostates. Provided a person who joins the group feels himself or herself to be a member of it, and is accepted by other members, then he is, for the purposes of the Act, a member. That appears to be consistent with the words at the end of section 3 (1): "references to a person's racial group refer to any racial group into which he falls." In my opinion, it is possible for a person to fall into a particular racial group either by birth or by adherence, and it makes no difference, so far as the Act of 1976 is concerned, by which route he finds his way into the group. This view does not involve creating any inconsistency between direct discrimination under paragraph (*a*) and indirect discrimination under paragraph (*b*). A person may treat another relatively unfavourably "on racial grounds" because he regards that other as being of a particular race, or belonging to a particular racial group, even if his belief is, from a scientific point of view, completely erroneous.

The respondent admitted rightly in my opinion, that, if the proper construction of the word "ethnic" in section 3 of the Act of 1976 is a wide one, on lines such as I have suggested, the Sikhs would qualify as a group defined by ethnic origins for the purposes of the Act. It is, therefore, unnecessary to consider in any detail the relevant characteristics of the Sikhs. They were originally a religious community founded about the end of the 15th century in the Punjab by Guru Nanak, who was born in 1469. But the community is no longer purely religious in character. Their present position is summarised sufficiently for present purposes in the opinion of the learned judge in the county court in the following passage:

> "The evidence in my judgment shows that Sikhs are a distinctive and self-conscious community. They have a history going back to the 15th century. They have a written language which a small proportion of Sikhs can read but which can be read by a much higher proportion of Sikhs than of Hindus. They were at one time politically supreme in the Punjab."

The result is, in my opinion, that Sikhs are a group defined by a reference to ethnic origins for the purpose of the Act of 1976, although they are not biologically distinguishable from the other peoples living in the Punjab. That is true whether one is considering the position before the partition of 1947, when the Sikhs lived mainly in that part of the Punjab which is now Pakistan, or after 1947, since when most of them have moved into India. It is, therefore, necessary to consider whether the respondent has indirectly discriminated against the appellants in the sense of section 1 (1) (*b*) of the Act. That raises the two subsidiary questions I have already mentioned.

"Can comply"
It is obvious that Sikhs, like anyone else, "can" refrain from wearing a turban, if "can" is construed literally. But if the broad cultural/historic meaning of ethnic is the appropriate meaning of the word in the Act of 1976, then a literal reading of the word "can" would deprive Sikhs and members of other groups defined by reference to their ethnic origins of much of the protection when Parliament evidently intended the Act to afford to them. They "can" comply with almost any requirement or condition if they are willing to give up their distinctive customs and cultural rules. On the other hand, if ethnic means inherited or unalterable, as the Court of Appeal thought it did, then "can" ought logically to be read literally. The word "can" is used with many shades of meaning. In the context of section 1 (1) (*b*) (i) of the Act of 1976 it must, in my opinion, have been intended by Parliament to be read not as meaning "can physically," so as to indicate a theoretical possibility, but as meaning "can in practice" or "can consistently with the customs and cultural conditions of the racial group." The latter meaning was attributed to the word by the Employment Appeal Tribunal in *Price* v. *Civil Service Commission* [1978] I.C.R. 27, on a construction of the parallel provision in the Sex Discrimination Act 1975. I agree with their construction of the word in that context. Accordingly I am of opinion that the "No turban" rule was not one with

which the second appellant could, in the relevant sense, comply.

"Justifiable"
The word "justifiable" occurs in section 1 (1) (*b*) (ii). It raises a problem which is, in my opinion, more difficult than the problem of the word "can." But in the end I have reached a firm opinion that the respondent has not been able to show that the "No turban" rule was justifiable in the relevant sense. Regarded purely from the point of view of the respondent, it was no doubt perfectly justifiable. He explained that he had no intention of discriminating against Sikhs. In 1978 the school had about 300 pupils (about 75 per cent. boys and 25 per cent. girls) of whom over 200 were English, five were Sikhs, 34 Hindus, 16 Persians, six negroes, seven Chinese and 15 from European countries. The reasons for having a school uniform were largely reasons of practical convenience—to minimise external differences between races and social classes, to discourage the "competitive fashions" which he said tend to exist in a teenage community, and to present a Christian image of the school to outsiders, including prospective parents. The respondent explained the difficulty for a headmaster of explaining to a non-Sikh pupil why the rules about wearing correct school uniform were enforced against him if they were relaxed in favour of a Sikh. In my view these reasons could not, either individually or collectively, provide a sufficient justification for the respondent to apply a condition that is prima facie discriminatory under the Act.

An attempted justification of the "No turban" rule, which requires more serious consideration, was that the respondent sought to run a Christian school, accepting pupils of all religions and races, and that he objected to the turban on the ground that is was an outward manifestation of a non-Christian faith. Indeed he regarded it as amounting to a challenge to that faith. I have much sympathy with the respondent on this part of the case and I would have been glad to find that the rule was justifiable within the meaning of the statute, if I could have done so. But in my opinion that is impossible. The onus under paragraph (ii) is on the respondent to show that the condition which he seeks to apply is not indeed a necessary condition, but that it is in all circumstances justifiable "irrespective of the colour, race, nationality or ethnic or national origins of the person to whom it is applied"; that is to say that it is justifiable without regard to the ethnic origins of that person. But in this case the principal justification on which the respondent relies is that the turban is objectionable just because it is a manifestation of the second appellant's ethnic origins. This is not, in my view, a justification which is admissible under paragraph (ii). The kind of justification that might fall within that provision would be one based on public health, as in *Panesar* v. *Nestlè Co. Ltd. (Note)* [1980] I.C.R. 144, where the Court of Appeal held that a rule forbidding the wearing of beards in the respondent's chocolate factory was justifiable within the meaning of section 1 (1) (*b*) (ii) on hygienic grounds, notwithstanding that the proportion of Sikhs who could [sc. conscientiously] comply with it was considerably smaller than the proportion of non-Sikhs who could comply with it. Again, it might be possible for the school to show that a rule insisting upon a fixed diet, which included some dish (for example, pork) which some racial groups could not conscientiously eat was justifiable if the school proved that the cost of providing special meals for the particular group would be prohibitive. Questions of that sort would be questions of the fact for the tribunal of fact, and if there was evidence on which it could find the condition to be justifiable its finding would not be liable to be disturbed on appeal.

But in the present case I am of opinion that the respondents have not been able to show that the "No turban" rule was justifiable.

LORD TEMPLEMAN: . . . In the course of the argument attention was directed to the dictionary definitions of the adjective "ethnic." But it is common ground that some definitions constitute the Sikhs a relevant group of ethnic origin whereas other definitions would exclude them. The true construction of the expression "ethnic origins" must be deduced from the Act. A racial group means a group of persons defined by reference to colour, race, nationality or ethnic or national origins. I agree with the Court of Appeal that in this context ethnic origins have a good deal in common with the concept of race just as national origins have a good deal in common with the concept of nationality. But the statutory definition of a racial group envisages that a group defined by reference to ethnic origin may be different from a group defined by reference to race, just as a group defined by reference to national origins may be different from a group defined by reference to nationality. In my opinion, for the purposes of the Race Relations Act a group of persons defined by reference to ethnic origins must possess some of the characteristics of a race, namely group descent, a group of geographical origin and a group history. The evidence shows that the Sikhs satisfy these tests. They are more than a religious sect, they are almost a race and almost a nation. As a race, the Sikhs share a common colour, and a common physique based on common ancestors from that part of the Punjab which is centred on Amritsar. They fail to qualify as a separate race because in racial origin prior the the inception of Sikhism they cannot be distinguished from other inhabitants of the Punjab. As a nation the Sikhs defeated the Moghuls, and established a kingdom in the Punjab which they lost as a result of the first and second Sikh wars; they fail to qualify as a separate nation or as a separate nationality because their kingdom never achieved a sufficient degree of recognition or permanence. The Sikhs qualify as a group defined by ethnic origins because they constitute a separate and distinct community derived from the racial characteristics I have mentioned. They also justify the conditions enumerated by my noble and learned friend, Lord Fraser of Tullybelton. The Sikh community has accepted converts who do not comply with those conditions. Some persons who have the same ethnic origins as the Sikh have ceased to be members of the Sikh community. But the Sikhs remain a group of persons forming a community recognisable by ethnic origins within the meaning of the Act.

Appeal allowed.

ACCESS TO THE COURTS

Chester v. Bateson
[1920] 1 K.B. 829
King's Bench Division

Chester appealed by way of case stated by the magistrates of Ulveston, Lancashire, who had dismissed a complaint preferred by him under the Small Tenements Act 1838 for recovery of possession of his house and the ejectment of Bateson (the tenant). The magistrates dismissed the complaint on the ground that he was precluded from taking proceedings by regulation 2A (2) of the Defence of the Realm Regulations 1914. By this Regulation the Minister of Munitions was empowered, with respect to any area in which war production was being carried on, to declare such area to be a special area if he was of opinion that the ejectment of workmen employed in such work was calculated to impede that work. The regulation continued: "Whilst the order remains in force no person shall without the consent of the Minister of Munitions, take, or cause to be taken, any proceedings for the purpose of obtaining an order or decree for the recovery of possession of, or for the ejectment of a tenant of, any dwelling-house or other premises situate in the special area, being a house or premises in which any workman so employed is living, so long as the tenant continues duly to pay his rent and to observe the other conditions of the tenancy, other than any condition for the delivery up of possession. If any person acts in contravention of this regulation he shall be guilty of a summary offence against these regulations."

The court (Darling, Avory and Sankey JJ.) allowed his appeal.

DARLING J.: read the following judgment: This case came before this court on a case stated by the justices sitting for the petty sessional division of Lonsdale North, Lancashire, and during the argument for the appellant (the respondent not being represented) we reserved judgment. The case raises the question whether regulation 2A (2) of the Defence of the Realm Regulations 1914 goes beyond the authority by the statute 5 Geo. 5, c. 8, confided to His Majesty in Council, to be exercised during the continuance of the war, for the defence of the realm. [His Lordship read the regulation.] The authority to make this regulation is to be found, if anywhere, in 5 Geo. 5, c. 8, s.1 (1) (e): "Otherwise to prevent assistance being given to the enemy, or the successful prosecution of the war being endangered." It is objected that the regulation is bad, because it forbids any person, without the consent of the Minister of Munitions, to take, or cause to be taken, any proceedings to recover possession of his own house, or to eject a tenant from it, where the tenant is employed in certain work connected with war material.

Counsel for the appellant has contended that this regulation violates Magna Carta, where the King declares: "To no one will we sell, to none will we deny, to none will we delay, right or justice." I could not hold the regulation to be bad on that ground were there sufficient authority given by a statute of the realm to those by whom the regulation was made. Magna Carta has not remained untouched; and, like every other law of England, it is not condemned to that immunity from development or improvement which was attributed to the laws of the Medes and Persians. I found my judgment rather on the passage in R. v. Halliday[1] where Lord Finlay says that Parliament may entrust great powers to His Majesty in Council, feeling certain that such powers will be reasonably exercised and further on these words of Lord Atkinson in the same case[2]: "It by no means follows, however, that if on the face of a regulation it enjoined or required something to be

[1] [1917] A.C. 260 at pp. 268, 269.
[2] [1917] A.C. 260 at pp. 272–273.

done which could not in any reasonable way aid in securing the public safety and the defence of the realm it would not be *ultra vires* and void. It is not necessary to decide this precise point on the present occasion, but I desire to hold myself free to deal with it when it arises."

Here, I think it does at last arise; and I ask myself whether it is a necessary, or even reasonable, way to aid in securing the public safety and the defence of the realm to give power to a minister to forbid any person to institute any proceedings to recover possession of a house so long as a war-worker is living in it.

The main question to be decided is whether the occupant is a workman so employed; and the regulation might have been so framed as to make this a good answer to the application for possession, still leaving that question to be decided by a court of law. But the regulation, as framed, forbids the owner of the property access to all legal tribunals in regard to this matter. This might, of course, legally be done by Act of Parliament; but I think this extreme disability can be inflicted only by direct enactment of the legislature itself, and that so grave an invasion of the rights of all subjects was not intended by the legislature to be accomplished by a departmental order, such as this one of the Minister of Munitions.

There are some instances in which Parliament has deliberately deprived certain persons of the ordinary right of citizens to resort to the King's courts for the righting of alleged wrongs. The most notorious of these is the Vexatious Actions Act 1896[3] which by section 1 provides:

"It shall be lawful for the Attorney-General to apply to the High Court for an Order under this Act, and if he satisfies the High Court that any person has habitually and persistently instituted vexatious legal proceedings without any reasonable ground for instituting such proceedings, whether in the High Court or in any inferior court, and whether against the same person or against different persons, the court may, after hearing such persons or giving him an opportunity of being heard, after assigning counsel in case such person is unable on account of poverty to retain counsel, order that no legal proceedings shall be instituted by that person in the High Court or any other court, unless he obtains the leave of the High Court or some judge thereof, and satisfies the court or judge that such legal proceedings is not an abuse of the process of the court, and that there is prima facie ground for such proceeding. A copy of such order shall be published in the *London Gazette*."

Let it be observed how carefully, even when so high an official as the King's Attorney-General intervenes, resort to the courts of justice is preserved, and contrast this with the power of veto uncontrolled which is claimed for the Minister of Munitions.

This exceptional statute has been already enforced, as may be seen by reference to *Re Boaler*. In giving judgment in that case Scrutton L.J. uses these words[4]:

"One of the valuable rights of every subject of the King is to appeal to the King in his courts if he alleges that a civil wrong has been done to him, or if he alleges that a wrong punishable criminally has been done to him, or has been committed by another subject of the King. This right is sometimes abused and it is, of course, quite competent to Parliament to deprive any subject of the King of it either absolutely or in part. But the language of any such statute should be jealously watched by the courts, and should not be extended beyond its least onerous meaning unless clear words are used to justify such extension."

It is to be observed that this regulation not only deprives the subject of his ordinary right to seek justice in the courts of law, but provides that merely to

---

[3] 59 & 60 Vict. c. 51. [See now Supreme Court Act, 1981, s. 42; *Re Fletcher, The Times*, June 12, 1984 (C.A.)]

[4] [1915] 1 K.B. 21 at p. 36.

resort there without the permission of the Minister of Munitions first had and obtained shall, of itself, be a summary offence, and so render the seeker after justice liable to imprisonment and fine. I allow that in stress of war we may rightly be obliged, as we should be ready, to forgo much of our liberty, but I hold that this elemental right of the subject of the British Crown cannot be thus easily taken from him. Should we hold that the permit of a departmental official is a necessary condition precedent for a subject of the realm who would demand justice at the seat of judgment, the people would be in that unhappy condition indicated, but not anticipated, by Montesquieu, where he writes in his treatise, *De l'Esprit des Loix*: "Les Anglois, pour favoriser la libertè, ont ôté toutes les puissances intermediaries qui formoient leur monarchie. Ils ont bien raison de conserver cette liberte; s'ils venoient a la perdre, ils seroient un des peuples les plus esclaves de la terre" (Livre II, Chap. 4).

AVORY J.: [in the course of his judgment, said]: . . . The purpose in view when the regulation was made—namely, to prevent the disturbance of munition workers in their dwellings—may, without doubt, be said to be reasonable; and a regulation designed to prevent such disturbance, providing that no order for ejectment should be made except under conditions prescribed, would probably be held to be *intra vires* the statute. But the objection which is made to the regulation as it stands is that it deprives the King's subjects of their right of access to the courts of justice, and renders them liable punishment if they have the temerity to ask for justice in any of the King's courts. It is not difficult to conceive a case in which a landlord might honestly believe that the rent had not been paid, or some other condition of the tenancy had been violated by the tenant which would justify him in applying to a court of justice for an order of ejectment without the consent of the Ministry of Munitions; but if it should be determined that he was mistaken either in law or fact, he would be liable to punishment for having instituted the proceedings. . . .

SANKEY J.: [in the course of his judgment, said]: . . . It might have been competent, under the words of the statute, although I express no opinion on the point, to make regulations, constituting the consent of the Minister of Munitions, in a proper case, a condition of the making of an order for the recovery of possession of, or for the ejectment of a tenant of, any dwelling-house or other premises of the character referred to. It was not, however, competent for his Majesty in Council to make a regulation enacting that a man who seeks the assistance or the protection of the King's courts should be exposed to fine and imprisonment for having done so.

It would have been astonishing if Parliament had conferred such a power. See what would have happened in a doubtful case. A man, believing in all good faith that he was entitled to bring proceedings, finds he is wrong on the evidence; but the mere fact of his having brought them is to make him guilty of an offence, and liable to fine and imprisonment.

I am of opinion that the regulation so made is beyond the powers conferred by the Act of Parliament. I should be slow to hold that Parliament ever conferred such a power, unless it expressed it in the clearest possible language, and should never hold that it was given indirectly by ambiguous regulations made in pursuance of any Act. . . .

Appeal allowed.

Notes

1. See also *Commissioners of Customs and Excise* v. *Cure & Deeley Ltd.* [1962] 1 Q.B. 340, *post* p. 294.

2. Only four of the original thirty seven clauses of Magna Carta, as confirmed by Henry III, remain in force. For the story of the repeal of the other clauses see Ann Pallister, *Magna Carta, The Heritage of Liberty*, (Oxford, 1971) Chap. 7.

Raymond v. Honey

[1983] A.C. 1

House of Lords

R, while serving a term of imprisonment, wrote a letter to his solicitors which H, the Governor refused to be allowed to be sent because it contained not only matter relating to pending legal proceedings, but also allegations against an assistant governor. R there upon prepared an application to commit H for contempt of court. The Governor prevented this application from being forwarded. The Divisional Court held that stopping the letter did not constitute contempt of court but the stopping of the application did constitute contempt. The Governor appealed and the prisoner cross-appealed.

Control over prisoner's correspondence is exercised through Rules and Standing Orders made under the Prison Act 1952, s. 47.

"(1) The Secretary of State may make rules for the regulation and management of prisons, remand centres, detention centres and Borstal institutions respectively, and for the classification, treatment, employment, discipline and control of persons required to be detained therein. (2) Rules made under this section shall make provision for ensuring that a person who is charged with any offence under the rules shall be given a proper opportunity of presenting his case."

Rule 33 allows for restrictions on communications between prisoners and other persons with a view to securing discipline and the prevention of crime.It also authorises the governor to read and stop any letter on the ground that its contents are objectionable.

Rule 34 (8) provides that a prisoner shall not be entitled to communicate with any person in connection with any legal or other business, or with any person other than a relative or friend, except with the leave of the Secretary of State. Rule 37A provides for correspondence between a prisoner who is a party to any legal proceedings and his solicitor. Under Standing Orders letters from prisoners may not make allegations against officers. Standing Order 29 (1) provides that

When a prisoner makes an allegation against an officer in a letter, the letter will be stopped and the governor informed. The governor will then explain to the prisoner the correct procedure to follow in making a complaint against an officer.

The correct procedure is for the prisoner to make a formal complaint with a view to an internal investigation. A prisoner may pursue his complaint through the courts only after there has been an investigation of this kind.

LORD WILBERFORCE: I deal first with the appeal. In considering whether any contempt has been committed by the appellant, there are two basic principles from which to start.

First, any act done which is calculated to obstruct or interfere with the due course of justice, or the lawful process of the courts, is a contempt of court. These are the well known words of Lord Russell of Killowen C.J. in *Reg.* v. *Gray* [1900] 2 Q.B. 36, 40.

Since 1900, the force of this principle has in no way been diminished. In *Attorney-General* v. *Times Newspapers Ltd.* [1974] A.C. 273, Lord Diplock, with whom Lord Simon of Glaisdale agreed, clearly stated that to inhibit suitors from availing themselves of their constitutional right to have their legal rights and obligations ascertained and enforced by courts of law, could amount to contempt of court (p. 310): whether the particular action there involved had that effect is immaterial to the present case. The principle has been strongly affirmed by the European Court of Human Rights in the case of *Golder* v.*United Kingdom* (1975) 1 E.H.R.R. 524. The court there decided that access to a court was a right protected by article 6 of the European Convention for the Protection of Human Rights and Fundamental Freedoms, and, while not expressly ruling upon the compatibility with the Convention of rules 33, 34 and 37 of the Prison Rules 1964 (as to which see below), and while accepting that the right might be subject to limitations, applied this ruling to a convicted United Kingdom prisoner, who (inter alia) wished to direct proceedings against a member of the prison staff, and to a hindrance of a temporary character.

Secondly, under English law, a convicted prisoner, in spite of his imprisonment, retains all civil rights which are not taken away expressly or by necessary implication: see *Reg.* v. *Board of Visitors of Hull Prison, Ex parte St. Germain* [1979] Q.B. 425, 455 and *Solosky* v. *The Queen* (1979) 105 D.L.R. (3d) 745, 760, Canadian Supreme Court, *Per* Dickson J.

These two principles are not disputed by the appellant. The question is to what extent (if any) the respondent's rights were taken away, or affected by, the Prison Rules 1964 or by Standing Orders made by the Secretary of State.

.   .   .   .   .

In my opinion, there is nothing in the Prison Act 1952 that confers power to make regulations which would deny, or interfere with, the right of the respondent, as a prisoner, to have unimpeded access to a court. Section 47, which has already been quoted, is a section concerned with the regulation and management of prisons and, in my opinion, is quite insufficient to authorise hindrance or interference with so basic a right. The regulations themselves must be interpreted accordingly, otherwise they would be ultra vires. So interpreted, I am unable to conclude that either rule 34 (8)—which is expressed in very general terms—or rule 37A (4), whether taken by themselves or in conjunction with Standing Orders, is in any way sufficiently clear to justify the hindrance which took place. The standing orders, if they have any legislative force at all, cannot confer any greater powers than the regulations, which, as stated, must themselves be construed in accordance with the statutory power to make them.

The action of the appellant was clearly such as to deny, albeit temporarily, the respondent's right of access to the court and, on the principle above stated, constituted a contempt.

(Lord Bridge of Harwich delivered a speech to the same effect. Lord Elwyn-Jones, Lord Russell of Killowen and Lord Lowry concurred).
Appeal dismissed.
[The House also dismissed the cross-appeal].

Note
In addition to the cases cited in C. & A.L. pp.512–516 the House of Lords has recently held that prisoners have no right to legal representation at disciplinary hearings before boards of

visitors: whether they were allowed legal representation or the assistance of a friend or adviser depended on the facts of each case: *R.* v. *Board of Visitors of H.M. Prison, The Maze, Ex parte Hone* [1988] 2 W.L.R. 177.

Contrary to earlier decisions, the House of Lords has now held that decisions of prisoner governors in the exercise of their disciplinary powers are subject to judicial review: *Leech* v. *Deputy Governor of Parkhurst Prison* [1988] 2 W.L.R. 290.

R. v. Secretary of State for the Home Department
Ex parte Ruddock
[1987] 2 All E.R.518
Queen's Bench Division

Counsel for the Secretary of State argued that the Court ought not in its discretion agree to hear applications relating to alleged illegal telephone tapping because of considerations relating to national security. In rejecting the argument and deciding to exercise his discretion in favour of the applicants Taylor J. said: I bear in mind that every citizen has a right to come to the courts for relief, and it is well established that even where statute is relied on, only the most clear and unequivocal words would entitle the courts to deny him access (see *R. & W. Paul Ltd.* v. *Wheat Commission* [1936] 2 All E.R. 1243 at 1247, [1937] A.C. 139 at 153 *per* Lord Macmillan, *Pyx Granite Co. Ltd.* v. *Ministry of Housing and Local Government* [1959] 3 All E.R. 1 at 6, [1960] A.C. 260 at 286 *per* Viscount Simonds, *Raymond* v. *Honey* [1982] 1 All E.R. 756 at 762, [1983] 1 A.C. 1 at 14 *per* Lord Bridge). Such clear and unequivocal words are now enacted in the Interception of Communications Act 1985. However, it did not come into force until 10 April 1986 and does not therefore apply to these proceedings.

FREEDOM OF THE PERSON

Habeas Corpus

Quigley v. Chief Constable, Royal Ulster Constabulary
[1983] N.I. 238
Court of Appeal

Mrs. Quigley's sisters applied for habeas corpus on the ground that she was being detained by the R.U.C. against her will. The R.U.C. maintained that Mrs. Quigley and her children were being protected by the police until after her husband had given evidence in a trial involving charges of terrorist offences.

LORD LOWRY L.C.J.: This appeal is from the refusal by Gibson L.J. on 20 April 1983 of the application on behalf of the appellant for an order that a writ of habeas corpus should issue directed to the Chief Constable of the Royal Ulster Constabulary to have the body of Linda Quigley before the Queen's Bench Division of the High Court.

· · · · ·

The prerogative writ of habeas corpus ad subjiciendum is an extraordinary remedy, issued upon cause shown where ordinary legal remedies are inapplicable or inadequate. Both at common law and by statute the writ may be granted only upon reasonable cause for its issue being shown. It is not a writ of course, but it is a writ of right and may not in general be refused merely because there exists an alternative remedy by which the validity of an alleged detention can be questioned: *Halsbury's Laws of England* (4th ed.), Vol. 11, para. 1455 and cases there cited.

The wrong for which habeas corpus is the remedy is the tort of false imprisonment.[1]

· · · · ·

Mr. Ferguson who appeared with Mr. Morgan for the applicant, submits that the evidence supports a prima facie case that Mrs. Quigley has been falsely imprisoned by or on behalf of the Chief Constable and that the affidavits raise questions of fact proper to be decided on the return to a writ of habeas corpus. In particular he submits that the uncontradicted evidence of Kathleen Taylor and Mr. Kearney tends to show that Mrs. Quigley was prevented by the R.U.C. from fulfilling her wish to meet with the members of her family who were in the courthouse. In support of his interference he points to the two requests she is said to have made to her solicitor and (something which could have been contradicted if it had not happened) her wish expressed in open court and the Learned Recorder's comment thereon. Clearly enough (to judge from Mr. Kearney's affidavit and from Chief Inspector Johnston's statements that he was responsible for the safety of Mrs. Quigley and that, in the interests of her safety, he did not consider it possible to arrange a meeting with relatives at the courthouse) the police were keeping a careful eye on Mrs. Quigley.

It has not been suggested that, in so acting, the police were inspired by any wrongful intent towards Mrs. Quigley, and nothing had so far emerged which would justify the fears of her safety expressed in paragraph 7 of Kathleen Taylor's affadavit, but this court is asked to infer that by preventing the desired meeting with relatives the police must have been putting a restraint on Mrs. Quigley's liberty against her will.

[1] Lord Lowry referred to *Halsbury's Law of England* (3rd Ed.), Vol. 38, pages 764–6, *Clerk & Lindsell on Torts* (15th Ed.), para. 14–13 et seq., *Bullen & Leake & Jacob on Pleadings (12th Ed.), pages 426–31, Winfield & Jolowicz on Tort* (9th Ed.), pages 35–43, *Salmond & Heuston on Torts* (18th Ed.), pages 116–7 and *Roscoe's Nisi Prius Evidence* (18th Ed.), Vol. II, pages 917–21.

Most of the authorities deal with the situation where the fact of restraint is not contested, and therefore the only issue was whether the restraint was justified. Therefore care must be used when applying the principles to a case like the present, where the only issue is whether Mrs. Quigley was or is restrained or, to use the technical word, imprisoned by or on behalf of the respondent. If she was or is so restrained, this would amount to *false* imprisonment because the *alleged* imprisonment is not sought to be justified, if indeed it exists. The onus to prove imprisonment is on the applicant and only when that is proved does the respondent incur an onus to justify.

It is, however, subject to this caution, useful to look at the cases, Mr. Ferguson relied on R. v. *Governor of Brixton Prison (ex parte Ahsan)* [1969] 2 Q.B. 222 *per* Lord Parker C.J. at pages 230E and 231D to illustrate the appropriate procedure on the return to the writ pursuant to the Habeas Corpus Act 1816. He referred also to R. v. *Reynolds* 6 T.R.; 101 E.R. 667 for the statement of Kenyon C.J.:

"If the writ of habeas corpus had been properly issued, and a question had arisen on the merits of the case, we would not have gone into it on affidavits, but would have required the party to make a return."

Counsel further relied on *Barnardo* v. *Ford* [1892] A.C. 326 for two propositions illustrated in the speech of Lord Herschell at page 339:

(1) "(This indicates that) the very basis of the writ is the allegation and the prima facie evidence in support of it that the person to whom the writ is directed is unlawfully detaining another in custody."
(2) "(But) where the Court entertains a doubt whether this be the fact," (i.e., whether the party challenged had ceased to have control over the party alleged to be detained) "it is unquestionably entitled to use the pressure of the writ to test the truth of the allegation and to require a return to be made to it."

Reference was also made to the judgment of Scrutton L.J. in R. v. *Secretary of State (ex parte O'Brien)* [1923] 2 Q.B. 361, 382, 392.

In order to emphasise the need to prove a prima facie case Mr. Carswell, who appeared with Mr. Coghlin for the respondent, brought to our notice *Greene* v. *Secretary of State for Home Affairs* [1942] A.C. 284 *per* Lord Wright at page 302 and *Azam* v. *Secretary of State for the Home Department* [1974] A.C. 18 *per* Lord Denning M.R. in the Court of Appeal at page 32C. He also rightly pointed out the danger of applying uncritically cases in which detention is admitted and lawfulness is the sole issue.

As to the facts, Mr. Carswell, taking issue on the burden of proof, submitted that, the question being whether Mrs. Quigley was at any material time in the detention or custody of the R.U.C., the evidence in *all* the affidavits had to be taken as a whole and that when this was done, the applicant did not discharge the onus of showing a sufficient case or, as the authorities have it, a prima facie case. While conceding that a return could be ordered to resolve a case of conflict or doubt, he maintained that the evidence here did not pose a conflict which required that kind of investigation.

Mr. Carswell further stressed that the evidence of the R.U.C. officers had not been controverted and that they had not been required to be cross-examined on their affidavits. Their evidence, he argued, clearly showed that Mrs. Quigley was not and never had been in the custody of, or constrained or confined by the R.U.C.

I find myself, however, unable to accept the respondent's arguments, nor do I consider that the absence of a request to cross-examine endows the respondent's affidavits with the power, at this stage of the proceedings, to nullify the case made by the applicant. It may well be—and certainly I have seen no evidence to the contrary—that in general Mrs. Quigley is more than content that she and her children should be with her husband. It is equally possible that she is not generally subject to a restraint which could be recognised as imprisonment. On the other hand, relying on the discussion of imprisonment with which I began this judgment and applying to the facts the principles to be extracted from the textbooks (and the cases on which they are based), I consider that the inevitable prima facie inference is that Mrs. Quigley was prevented and restrained from meeting her relatives on 14 April and that she would have been physically restrained (it may be, entirely with her welfare and safety in mind) if she had tried to do so. And, as Lord Wright put it in *Greene's case supra* at page 302, the question is "whether (Mrs. Quigley's) freedom was unlawfully interfered with". For this purpose the motive is irrelevant. There is also a presumption of continuance which the respondent has to contend with. This interference does not necessarily contradict the spirit of the police officers' affidavits but it seems to me prima facie to contradict their averments in point of law, and therefore also in point of fact.

Accordingly, in my opinion, this is a proper case for the issue of a writ of habeas corpus ad subjiciendum directed to the Chief Constable in respect of Mrs. Linda Quigley. I further consider that the writ should be directed also to Detective Superintendent Nesbitt who appears to be in charge of operations relating to the case in which Mr. Quigley is a witness.

I conclude by adapting to this case a comment made by Lord Herschell in *Barnardo's case supra*, where he said (at page 340):

> "I must not be understood as indicating that I think the story told by the appellant" (in this case, the respondent) "is untrue. But, as the matter is to undergo further investigation, it would obviously be improper to enter upon any discussion of the statements contained in the affidavits, or to express any opinion upon them."

In Re Quigley
[1983] N.I. 245
Queen's Bench Division

Following the decision of the Court of Appeal, *supra*, a writ of habeas corpus was issued in the following terms:

"ELIZABETH THE SECOND, by the Grace of God, of the United Kingdom of Great Britain and Northern Ireland and of Our other realms and territories Queen, Head of the Commonwealth, Defender of the Faith; To; Chief Constable of the Royal Ulster Constabulary and Detective Superintendent Thomas James Nesbitt, Royal Ulster Constabulary, greeting;

We command you that you have in the Queen's Bench Division of Our High Court of Justice, in Northern Ireland, at the Royal Courts of Justice, Chichester Street, Belfast, on the day and at the time specified in this Notice served with this Writ the body of Linda Quigley being taken and detained under your custody as is said, together with the day and cause of her being taken and detained, by whatsoever name she may be called therein, that Our Court may then and there examine and determine whether such cause is legal, and have you there then this writ."

In the return to the writ it was denied that Mrs. Quigley was being detained against her will by the Chief Constable or anyone on his behalf or any member of the R.U.C. and therefore it was impossible to produce the body of Mrs. Quigley to the Court.

Counsel for the applicants argued that the failure to produce the body on the day specified in the Notice served with the writ was a contempt of court.

HUTTON J.: . . . It is relevant that the writ does not refer to the body of the person "taken and detained under your custody"—it refers to the body of the person "taken and detained under your custody, *as is said.*" In my judgment the writ does not require the respondent to have in the court the body of the person named therein whom the respondent claims, in a return good and valid on its face, never to have been at any time detained, confined or restrained by him or in his custody, and which return on examination by the court under section 3 of the 1816 Act may be shown to be truthful.

[Section 3 of Habeas Corpus Act 1816 provides:

In all cases provided for by this Act, although the return to any writ of habeas corpus shall be good and sufficient in law, it shall be lawful for the justice or baron, before whom such writ may be returnable, to proceed to examine into the truth of the facts set forth in such return by affidavit or by affirmation (in cases where an affirmation is allowed by law); and to do therein as to justice shall appertain.]

.   .   .   .   .

The proper procedure in this case is to examine into the truth of the facts set forth in the return before ordering Mrs. Quigley to be produced in court or ordering her release.

[On a subsequent date Hutton J. dealt with the procedure to be followed to ascertain the truth of the facts set forth in the return.]

It is relevant to note that section 3 of the Habeas Corpus Act 1816 provides that "it shall be lawful for the justice . . . to examine into the truth of the facts set forth in such return . . ." The procedure under section 3 was described as follows by Drake J. in *In re Shahid Iqbal* [1979] 1 Q.B. 264 at page 274H:

"Long ago the return to the writ of habeas corpus was all important. It was the beginning and the ending of the matter, and the court acted solely on the reasons for detention stated on the face of the return. If the reason shown was bad the person detained was entitled to be released; if the reason was good he was not entitled to habeas corpus, although it may have been open to him to pursue some other remedy, such as certiorari, under which the court would go behind the return and inquire into the evidence on which the detention was said to be justified.

But since the Habeas Corpus Act 1816 the court is empowered to inquire into the truth of the facts stated in the return. Indeed that is precisely the procedure relied on by applicants in the majority of applications which come before this court . . . In my judgment the overriding function of the court is to see that no injustice is done to the person detained; and in order to see that justice is done the court should inquire into the true facts and not be hampered by the wording of the return."

The authorities make it clear that the inquiry by the court should be a searching one. In *Barnardo* v. *Ford* [1892] A.C. 326 at page 340 Lord Macnaghten stated:

"I cannot say that this is a case in which there ought not to be an opportunity of further inquiry into the circumstances under which Dr. Barnardo parted with the child, and ascertaining beyond all doubt whether the child is or is not still under Dr. Barnardo's control or within his reach."

And in *R.* v. *Secretary of State for Home Affairs, ex parte O'Brien* [1923] 2 K.B. 361 at page 375 Bankes L.J. stated:

"The duty of the court is clear. The liberty of a subject is in question. The court must inquire, and inquire closely, into the question whether the order of internment complained of was or was not lawfully made."

Where a writ of habeas corpus issues the concern of the court is to protect the liberty of the subject.

In *Cox* v. *Hakes* [1890] 15 A.C. 506 at page 527 Lord Herschell stated:

"My Lords, the preliminary question argued upon the hearing of this appeal is one of the great importance. It touches closely the liberty of the subject, and the protection afforded by discharge from custody under a writ of habeas corpus. The law of this country has been very jealous of any infringement of personal liberty, and a great safeguard against it has been provided by the manner in which the Courts have exercised their jurisdiction to discharge under a writ of habeas corpus those detained unlawfully in custody."

And in *Secretary of State for Home Affairs* v. *O'Brien* [1923] A.C. 603 at page 609 Lord Birkenhead stated:

"To-day the substitution of more modern remedies has left the writ ad subjiciendum, more shortly known as the writ of habeas corpus, in almost exclusive possession of the field. It is perhaps the most important writ known to the constitutional law of England, affording as it does a swift and imperative remedy in all cases of illegal restraint or confinement. It is of immemorial antiquity, an instance of its use occurring in the thirty-third year of Edward I. It has through the ages been jealously maintained by courts of law as a check upon the illegal usurpation of power by the executive at the cost of the liege."

But the circumstances of the present case are most unusual and, whilst the court must ever have present to its mind the overriding importance of preserving the effectiveness of the procedure under the writ of habeas corpus in order to protect the liberty of the subject, the court must also have regard to the background to this case and to certain dangers which exist.

[After hearing argument from Counsel as to whether he should call Mrs. Quigley to give evidence the learned judge concluded.]

Having regard to the duty of the court to make a searching inquiry into the question which arises subsequent to the issue of the writ of habeas corpus and to the importance of arriving at the truth in this matter, I consider that I should require Mrs. Quigley to attend to give evidence in chambers.

I therefore order that a writ of subpoena ad testificandum do issue directing Mrs. Quigley to attend as a witness before me in chambers.

[Subsequently Hutton J. announced that having seen Mrs. Quigley in his chambers he was satisfied that the facts stated in the return were true.]

Note

See further the speech of Lord Scarman in *R.* v. *Home Secretary Ex Parte Khawaja* [1984] A.C. 74: *infra*.

Judicial Review

R. v. Home Secretary Ex Parte Khawaja

[1984] A.C. 74

House of Lords

The two appellants had been granted permission to enter the United Kingdom but subsequently had been declared to be illegal entrants and ordered to leave the United Kingdom. Khera applied unsuccessfully to the Divisional Court (Donaldson L.J. and Hodgson J.) for a declaration that he was lawfully in the United Kingdom and *certiorari* to quosh the Secretary of State's decision to have him removed as an illegal entrant. The Court of Appeal (Ormrod and Dunn L.JJ., and Sir Sebag Shaw) dismissed his appeal. Khawaja had similarly failed in an application for judicial review before Forbes J. and on appeal to the Court of Appeal (Lord Denning M.R., Eveleigh and Donaldson L.JJ.). Both appealed to the House of Lords (Lord Fraser of Tullybelton, Lord Wilberforce, Lord Scarman, Lord Bridge of Harwich and Lord Templeman).

LORD SCARMAN: ... Two questions of law fall to be considered in the two appeals. Both arise under the Immigration Act 1971 (the Act). One is as to the construction to be put upon the definition of "illegal entrant" which is contained in section 33 (1) of the Act. The other is as to the proper scope of judicial review where the immigration authority has decided to exercise its statutory power to remove an illegal entrant from the United Kingdom and detains him, or permits his temporary admission into the country subject to restrictions pending removal.

Both questions were considered and answered by the House in the recent case of *Reg.* v. *Secretary of State for the Home Department, Ex parte Zamir* [1980] A.C. 930. The House in these two appeals is being invited to reconsider that decision and to depart from it using the power to depart from precedent which the House declared by its Practice Statement of 1966 it was prepared to use in certain circumstances: *Practice Statement (Judicial Precedent)* [1966] 1 W.L.R. 1234.

.   .   .   .   .

Three propositions of law were enunciated in *Reg.* v. *Secretary of State for the Home Department, Ex parte Zamir* [1980] A.C. 930 by a unanimous House: (1) that a person who has succeeded in entering the United Kingdom by committing an offence under the Immigration Act is an illegal entrant as defined by section 33 (1) ofthe Act: he has entered "in breach of the immigration laws": (2) that a person who has to seek leave to enter the United Kingdom owes to the immigration authority a positive duty of candour, *i.e.* a duty to disclose material facts even though he be asked no questions and has neither expressly nor by his conduct implicitly made any false representation as to them: (3) that, if the immigration authority has reasonable grounds for believing that a person is an illegal entrant, the decision to remove him and to detain him until he is removed is for the authority. It is not subject to review by the courts, save to the limited extent recognised by what has come to be called "the *Wednesbury* principle."

.   .   .   .   .

I entertain no doubt that in *Zamir's* case the House correctly construed the definition of "illegal entrant" in section 33 (1) of the Immigration Act 1971 as covering one who has obtained leave to enter by deception. It is an offence for a person who is being examined by an immigration officer to make a statement or representation which he knows to be false or does not believe to be true: section 26 (1) (c) of the Act. Silence can, of course, constitute a representation of fact; it depends upon conduct and circumstances. If the offence is committed, it is a breach of the immigration laws. The definition therefore covers a person who by committing the offence obtains leave to enter the United Kingdom.

It was strenuously argued that the definition must be limited to persons who enter the country by evading immigration control, *e.g.* clandestinely over the beach. Even if I were disposed to accept this submission, I would not do so in the face of the unanimous decision in *Zamir's* case. I see nothing unjust in the construction the House then put upon the statutory definition, nor any threat to the proper development of the law.

In *Zamir's* case deception was proved. . . . It was not necessary, therefore, for the House to consider whether even where there is no deliberate deception a person seeking leave to enter the United Kingdom owes a positive duty of candour to the immigration authority. The House's expression of opinion that he does was obiter. It is certainly an entrant's duty to answer truthfully the questions put to him and to provide such information as is required of him: paragraph 4 of Schedule 2. But the Act goes no further. . . . The Immigration Act does impose a duty not to deceive the immigration officer. It makes no express provision for any higher or more comprehensive duty: nor is it possible, in my view, to imply any such duty. Accordingly I reject the view that there is a duty of positive candour imposed by the immigration laws and that mere non-disclosure by an entrant of material facts in the absence of fraud is a breach of the immigration laws.

Real difficulties, however, arise in respect of the third proposition of law in *Reg. v. Secretary of State for the Home Department, Ex parte Zamir* [1980] A.C. 930. This was part of the ratio decidendi. The House approved a line of authority (beginning with *Reg. v. Secretary of State for the Home Department, Ex parte Hussain* [1978] 1 W.L.R. 700) which put a gloss upon the words of the critical provision in the Immigration Act, *i.e.* paragraph 9 of Schedule 2 to the Act. The paragraph declares an illegal entrant to be liable to removal. It provides that where an illegal entrant is not given leave to enter or remain in the United Kingdom an immigration officer may give directions for his removal. Unless he (or the Secretary of State, paragraph 10) may give such directions, no power to detain him arises: for paragraph 16 (2) provides a power to detain only in respect of a person who may be so removed. Similarly, paragraph 21 of the Schedule empowers the release of a person from detention and his temporary admission into the United Kingdom subject to restrictions as to residence and reporting to the police only if that person may be lawfully removed from the country. The gloss which the House in *Zamir's* case put upon the words of paragraph 9 was to read them as meaning not "where a person is an illegal entrant" but "where the immigration officer *has reasonable grounds for believing a person to be an illegal entrant*" he may be removed if not given leave to enter. If it be sought to justify the gloss as a proper construction of the statutory language, there is a difficulty. The gloss requires the introduction into the paragraph of words that are not there. Must they, then, be implied? This question lies at the heart of the problem.

In *Zamir's* case the House was impressed with the difficulties arising if the implication were not to be made. The House attached importance to three considerations: (1) the line of cases beginning with *Reg v. Secretary of State for the Home Department, Ex parte Hussain* [1978] 1 W.L.R. 700 in which the Court of Appeal had held it necessary to make the implication: (2) the scheme of the Immigration Act and especially, (3) the nature and process of the power of decision conferred by the Act upon immigration officers.

These considerations, in the view of the House, made it necessary to reject the appellant's argument based upon the well-establishes principle that, where the exercise of an executive power depends upon the precedent establishment of an objective fact, it is for the court, if there be a challenge by way of judicial review, to decide whether the precedent requirement had been satisfied.

My Lords, in most cases I would defer to a recent decision of your Lordships' House on a question of construction, even if I thought it wrong. I do not do so in this context because for reasons which I shall develop I am convinced that the *Zamir* reasoning gave insufficient weight to the important—I would say fundamental—consideration that we are here concerned with, the scope of judicial review of a power which inevitably infringes the liberty of those subjected to it. This consideration, if it be good, outweighs, in my judgment, any difficulties in the administration of immigration control to which the application of the principle might give rise. The *Zamir* construction of paragraph 9 deprives those subjected to the power of that degree of judicial protection which I think can be shown to have been the policy of our law to afford to persons with whose liberty the executive is seeking to interfere. It does therefore, in my view, tend to obstruct the proper development and application of the safeguards our law provides for the liberty of those within its jurisdiction. If I can make good this view of the law, it must be right to depart from the precedent of *Zamir's* case. I, therefore, now turn to the reasons why I conclude that it is correct.

The *Zamir* decision would limit judicial review, where the executive has decided to remove someone from the country as being an illegal entrant, to "the *Wednesbury* principle." This principle is undoubtedly correct in cases where it is appropriate. But, as I understand the law, it cannot extend to interference with liberty unless Parliament has unequivocally enacted that it should. The principle was formulated by Lord Greene M.R. in *Associated Provincial Picture Houses Ltd.* v. *Wednesbury Corporation* [1948] 1 K.B. 223. The case concerned the conditions imposed upon the issue of a licence. The principle formulated was that the courts will not intervene to quosh the decision of a statutory authority unless it can be shown that the authority erred in law, was guilty of a breach of natural justice or acted "unreasonably." If the authority has considered the matters which it is it's duty to consider and has excluded irrelevant matters, its decision is not reviewable unless so absurd that no reasonable authority could have reached it. The principle excludes the court from substituting its own view of the facts for that of the authority.

Such exclusion of the power and duty of the courts runs counter to the development of the safeguards which our law provides for the liberty of the subject. The law has largely developed through the process of habeas corpus. But in the common law habeas corpus was itself of limited scope, though a rapid and effective remedy where it applied. It brought the gaoler and his prisoner into court; but, if the respondent's return to the writ was valid on its face, that was the end of the matter. The court could not take the case further. The great statute of 1816, Habeas Corpus Act 1816 (56 Geo. 3, c. 100), "An Act for more effectually securing the liberty of the subject" substantially extended the scope of the process. It conferred upon the judges the power in non-criminal cases to inquire into the truth of the facts contained in the return. Section 3 is the beginning of the modern jurisprudence the effect of which is to displace, unless Parliament by plain words otherwise provides, the *Wednesbury* principle in cases where liberty is infringed by an act of the executive. The section deserves quotation:

> "3 . . . in all cases provided for by this Act, although the return to any writ of habeas corpus shall be good and sufficient in law, it shall be lawful for the justice or baron before whom such writ may be returnable, to proceed to examine into the truth of the facts set forth in such return . . . and to do therein as to justice shall appertain: . . ."

The court's duty is to examine into the truth of the facts set forth in the return: the section thereby contemplates the possibility of an investigation by the court so that it may satisfy itself where the truth lies. There is here a principle which the judges, faced with decisions by statutory authorities which restrict or take away liberty, have accepted as being justly met by the rule, the existence of which was recognised in *Zamir's* case though not applied, that where the exercise of executive power depends upon the precedent establishment of an objective fact, the courts will decide whether the requirement has been satisfied.

The classic dissent of Lord Atkin in *Liversidge* v. *Anderson* [1942] A.C. 206 is now accepted (*Reg.* v. *Inland Revenue Commissioners, Ex parte Rossminster Ltd.* [1980] A.C. 952, 1011, 1025) as correct not only on the point of construction of regulation 18 (b) of the then emergency Regulations but in its declaration of English legal principle. Lord Atkin put it thus, at p. 245: "that in English law every imprisonment is prima facie unlawful and that it is for a person directing imprisonment to justify his act."

In an earlier Privy Council decision Lord Atkin had made the same point in the specific case of an executive decision. In *Eshugbayi Eleko* v. *Government of Nigeria* [1931] A.C. 662, 670, Lord Atkin said:

> "In accordance with British jurisprudence no member of the executive can interfere with the liberty or property of a British subject except on the condition that he can support the legality of his action before a court of justice. And it is the tradition of British justice that judges should not shrink from deciding such issues in the face of the executive."

For, as Blackstone said of habeas corpus, describing it as a high prerogative writ: "the king is at all times entitled to have an account why the liberty of any of his subjects is restrained, wherever that restraint may be inflicted": *Commentaries*, Bk. III, p. 131, 12th ed. (Christian) 1794.

There are, of course, procedural differences between habeas corpus and the modern statutory judicial review. *Reg.* v. *Secretary of State for the Home Department, Ex parte Zamir* [1980] A.C. 930 was a case of habeas corpus: in the instant cases the effective relief sought is certiorari to quash the immigration officers' decision. But the nature of the remedy sought cannot affect the principle of the law. In both cases liberty is in issue. "Judicial review" under R.S.C., Ord. 53 and the Supreme Court Act 1981 is available only by leave of the court. The writ of habeas corpus issues as of right. But the difference arises not in the law's substance but from the nature of the remedy appropriate to the case. The writ issues as of right summoning into court the person in whose custody the subject is. It gets the custodian into court: but discharge from custody is not possible unless "the party hath a probable cause to be delivered," as Vaughan C.J. put it (in *Bushell's Case* (1670) T.J. 13, p. 132) in words quoted by Blackstone, Bk. III. This remains the law today and effectually puts habeas corpus in like case with the other form of judicial review. Whatever the process, the party seeking relief carries the initial burden of showing he has a case fit to be considered by the court. Accordingly, faced with the jealous care our law traditionally devotes to the protection of the liberty of those who are subject to its jurisdiction. I find it impossible to imply into the statute words the effect of which would be to take the provision, paragraph 9 of Schedule 2 to the Act, "out of the 'precedent fact' category" (Lord Wilberforce, *Zamir's* case at p. 948). If Parliament intends to exclude effective judicial review of the exercise of a power of restraint of liberty, it must make its meaning crystal clear.

Two points remain. First, does our law's protection extend to aliens and non-patrials? There is a suggestion that because an alien is liable to expulsion under the royal prerogative and a non-patrial has no right of abode, it is less difficult to infer a Parliamentary intention to deprive them of effective judicial review of a decision to infringe their liberty. And, secondly, the problem of proof.

Habeas corpus protection is often expressed as limited to "British subjects." Is it really limited to British nationals? Suffice it to say that the case law has given an emphatic "no" to the question. Every person within the jurisdiction enjoys the equal protection of our laws. There is no distinction between British nationals and others. He who is subject to English law is entitled to its protection. This principle has been in the law at least since Lord Mansfield freed "the black" in *Sommerset's Case* (1772) 20 St.Tr. 1. There is nothing here to encourage in the case of aliens or non-patrials the implication of words excluding the judicial review our law normally accords to those whose liberty is infringed.

Secondly, there is the problem of proof. The initial burden is upon the applicant. At what stage, if at all, is it transferred to the respondent? And, if it is transferred, what is the standard of proof he has to meet? It is clear from the passages cited from Lord Atkin's opinions in *Liversidge* v. *Anderson* [1942] A.C. 206 and *Eshugbayi Eleko* v. *Government of Nigeria* [1931] A.C. 662 that in case where the exercise of executive discretion interferes with liberty or property rights he saw the burden of justifying the legality of the decision as being upon the executive. Once the applicant has shown a prima facie case, this is the law. It was so recognised by Lord Parker C.J. in *Reg.* v. *Governor of Brixton Prison, Ex parte Ahsan* [1969] 2 Q.B. 222, and by Lord Denning M.R. in the Court of Appealin *Reg.* v. *Governor of Pentonville Prison, Ex parte Azam* [1974] A.C. 18, 32. And, I would add, it is not possible to construe section 3 of the Habeas Corpus Act 1816, as meaning anything different.

The law is less certain as to the standard of proof. The choice is commonly thought to be between proof beyond reasonable doubt, as in criminal cases, and the civil standard of the balance of probabilities: and there is distinguished authority for the view that in habeas corpus proceedings the standard is beyond reasonable doubt, since liberty is at stake. This appears to have been the view of Lord Atkin (*Eshugbayi Eleko* v. *Government of Nigeria* [1931] A.C. 662, 670), and certainly was the view of Lord Parker C.J. (*Reg.* v. *Governor of Brixton Prison, Ex parte Ahsan* [1969] Q.B. 222). But there is a line of authority which casts doubt upon their view. The Court of Appeal was held that the standard of proof of criminal offences is that of the balance of probabilities: *Hornal* v. *Neuberger Products Ltd.* [1957] 1 Q.B. 247. As judicial review whether under the modern statutory procedure or section 3 of the Habeas Corpus Act 1816 is a civil proceeding, it would appear to be right, if *Hornal's* case was correctly decided, to apply the civil standard of proof. My Lords, I have come to the conclusion that the choice between the two standards is not one of any great moment. It is largely a matter of words. There is no need to import into this branch of the civil law the formula used for the guidance of juries in criminal cases. The civil standard as interpreted and applied by the civil courts will meet the ends of justice. . . .

Accordingly, it is enough to say that, where the burden lies on the executive to justify the exercise of a power of detention, the facts relied on as justification must be proved to the satisfaction of the court. A preponderance of probability suffices: but the degree of probability must be such that the court is satisfied. The strictness of the criminal formula is unnecessary to enable justice to be done: and its lack of flexibility in a jurisdiction where the technicalities of the law of evidence must not be allowed to become the master of the court could be a positive disadvantage inhibiting the efficacy of the developing safeguard of judicial review in the field of public law.

For these reasons I conclude that in these two appeals, once the applicant had shown, as each did, that he had entered the United Kingdom with the leave of the immigration officer, the burden of proving that he had obtained leave by deception was upon the executive and the standard of proof was the balance of probabilities. In Khera's case, the executive failed to prove that he was guilty of deception. In Khawaja's case the evidence that he decieved the immigration authority was overwhelming. Accordingly, I would allow the appeal of Khera and dismiss that of Khawaja.

Appeal by Khewa allowed.
Appeal by Khawaja dismissed.

Note

Contrast *R.* v. *Secretary of State for the Home Department, Ex parte Bugdaycay* [1987] A.C. 514 where the House of Lords refused to examine whether in fact an immigrant was a refugee.

Lord Bridge of Harwich distinguished *Khawaja*:
"[It was argued that] the court, on an application for judicial review, is not confined to considering whether there was evidence to support the decision of the Secretary of State, but must examine the evidence and make its own decision. Only if the court is satisfied on a balance of probabilities that the person claiming asylum is *not* a refugee can the decision to remove him to his country of origin be affirmed.

This line of reasoning is said to be supported by analogy by the decision in *Khawaja* v *Secretary of State for the Home Dept*. [1983] 1 All E.R. 765, [1984] A.C. 74 that, when directions given pursuant to para. 9 of Sched. 2 to the 1971 Act for the removal of an illegal entrant are challenged on an application for judicial review, it is for the immigration officer or the Secretary of State, as the case may be, to establish the fact of illegal entry.

The reason why this argument cannot be sustained is that all questions of fact on which the discretionary decision whether to grant or withhold leave to enter or remain depends must necessarily be determined by the immigration officer or the Secretary of State in the exercise of the discretion which is exclusively conferred on them by s.4 (1) of the 1971 Act. The question whether an applicant for leave to enter or remain is or is not a refugee is only one, even if a particularly important one required by para. 73 of H.C. Paper (1982–83) no. 169 to be returned to the House Office, of a multiplicity of questions which immigration officers and officials of the Home Office acting for the Secretary of State must daily determine in dealing with applications for leave to enter or remain in accordance with the rules, as, for example, whether an applicant is a bona fide visitor, student, businessman, dependant, etc. Determination of such questions is only open to challenge in the courts on well-known *Wednesbury* principles (see *Associated Provincial Picture Houses Ltd.* v. *Wednesbury Corp.* [1947] 2 All E.R. 680, [1948] 1 K.B. 223). There is no ground for treating the question raised by a claim to refugee status as an exception to this rule. For the reasons explained at length in the speeches in *Khawaja's* case the court's fundamentally different approach to an order for removal on the ground of illegal entry is dictated by the terms of the statute itself, since the power to direct removal under para. 9 of Sched. 2 is only available in the case of a person who is in fact an "illegal entrant."

See also *R.* v. *Secretary of State for the Home Department, Ex parte Sivakumaran* [1988] 2 W.L.R. 92.

On the *Wednesbury* principles, referred to by Lord Scarman in *Khawaja* and by Lord Bridge in *Bugdaycay* see *post* p.300 *et seq*.

244 RIGHTS AND DUTIES OF THE INDIVIDUAL

General Warrant for Arrest

Leach v. Money and Others
(1765) 3 Burr. 1692, 1742; 19 St.Tr. 1001
King's Bench

An action was brought in the Court of Common Pleas by John Wilkes's printer against three King's Messengers for trespass and false imprisonment. The defendants justified their conduct under a warrant of Lord Halifax, a principal Secretary of State, which required the defendants to search for the authors, printers, and publishers of an alleged seditious libel entitled *The North Briton*, and to apprehend them together with their papers. The plaintiff was apprehended and released after four days as he turned out not to be the printer.

The jury found for the plaintiff—£400 damages. Pratt C.J.[1] was required to seal a bill of exceptions.

On the hearing of the Bill in the King's Bench, sitting as a Court of Error, it was argued that such warrants had been sanctioned by long custom; and that a Secretary of State as a sentinel of the public peace, must have the power to issue them. As a conservator of the peace, he was protected by a statute of 1609 and the Constables Protection Act 1750.

The court (Lord Mansfield C.J., Wilmot, Yates and Aston JJ.) held that a general warrant to seize a person or persons unnamed was illegal and void, and affirmed the judgment of Pratt C.J.

LORD MANSFIELD C.J.: [after discussing the question whether a Secretary of State acting as a conservator of the peace fell within the statutes mentioned, said]: "The last point is, Whether this general warrant be good."

One part of it may be laid out of the case: for, as to what relates to the seizing of his papers, that part of it was never executed, and therefore it is out of the case. . . .

At present—as to the validity of the warrant, upon the single objection of the uncertainty of the person, being neither named nor described—the common law, in many cases, gives authority to arrest without warrant; more especially, where taken in the very act: and there are many cases where particular Acts of Parliament have given authority to apprehend, under general warrants; as in the case of writs of assistance, or warrants to take up loose, idle, and disorderly people. But here, it is not contended that the common law gave the officer authority to apprehend; nor that there is any Act of Parliament which warrants this case.

Therefore it must stand upon principles of common law.

It is not fit, that the receiving or judging of the information should be left to the discretion of the officer. The magistrate ought to judge; and should give certain directions to the officer. This is so, upon reason and convenience.

Then as to authorities—Hale and all others hold such an uncertain warrant void: and there is no case or book to the contrary.

It is said, "that the usage has been so; and that many such have been issued, since the Revolution, down to this time." But a usage, to grow into law, ought to be a general usage, *communiter usitata et approbata*; and which, after a long continuance, it would be mischievous to overturn. This is only the usage of a particular office, and contrary to the usage of all other justices and conservators of the peace. There is the less reason for regarding this usage; because the form of the warrant probably took its rise from a positive statute; and the former precedents were inadvertently followed after that law was expired.

WILMOT J.: declared that he had no doubt, nor ever had, upon these warrants: he thought them illegal and void.

[1] [Afterwards Lord Camden].

Neither had the other two judges, Yates and Aston JJ., any doubt (upon this first argument) of the illegality of them: for no degree of antiquity can give sanction to a usage bad in itself. And they esteemed this usage to be so. They were clear and unanimous in opinion, that this warrant was illegal and bad.

FREEDOM OF PROPERTY

General Warrant to Search and Seize

Wilkes v. Wood

(1763) 19 St. Tr. 1153; Lofft, Michaelmas Term, 1763, p. 1

Court of Common Pleas

Wood, who was Under-Secretary of State, with a constable and several King's Messengers, entered into John Wilkes's house, broke open his locks, and seized his papers. The warrant, issued by the Secretary of State, Lord Halifax, directed the messengers "to make strict and diligent search for the authors, printers and publishers of a seditious and treasonable paper, entitled *The North Briton*, No. 45, and these or any of them being found, to apprehend and seize, together with their papers." Wilkes brought an action of trespass against Wood. The action was tried before Pratt C.J. and a special jury.

PRATT C.J.: [in his charge to the jury, after dealing with the questions of fact] then went upon the warrant, which he declared was a point of the greatest consequence he had ever met with in his whole practice. The defendants claimed a right, under precedents, to force person's houses, break open escrutores [escritoires], seize their papers, etc., upon a general warrant, where no inventory is made of the things thus taken away, and where no offender's names are specified in the warrant, and therefore a discretionary power given to messengers to search wherever their suspicions may chance to fall. If such a power is truly invested in a Secretary of State, and he can delegate this power, it certainly may affect the person and property of every man in this kingdom, and is totally subversive of the liberty of the subject.

And as for the precedents, will that be esteemed law in a Secretary of State which is not law in any other magistrate of this kingdom? If they should be found to be legal, they are certainly of the most dangerous consequences; if not legal, must aggravate damages. Notwithstanding what Mr. Solicitor-General [Norton] has said, I have formerly delivered it as my opinion on another occasion, and I still continue of the same mind, that a jury have it in their power to give damages for more than the injury received. Damages are designed not only as a satisfaction to the injured person, but likewise as a punishment to the guilty to deter from any such proceeding in the future, and as a proof of the detestation of the jury to the action itself.

... It is my opinion the office precedents, which had been produced since the Revolution, are no justification for a practice in itself illegal, and contrary to the fundamental principles of the constitution; though its having been the constant practice of the office, might fairly be pleaded in mitigation of damages. ...

The jury found a general *verdict for the plaintiff*, with £1,000 damages.

The court sat at nine o'clock in the morning, and the verdict was brought in at twenty minutes past eleven o'clock at night.

Entick v. Carrvariousington
(1765) 19 St.Tr. 1029; 2 Wils. 275
Court of Common Pleas

Carrington, with three other persons, King's Messengers, acting under a warrant from a Secretary of State, forcibly entered Entick's house, he being alleged to be the author of a seditious libel (the *Monitor, or British Freeholder*), and carried away his books and papers. Entick brought an action of trespass against Carrington and the other messengers.

The jury returned a special verdict, stating that the defendants had acted upon a warrant from a Secretary of State (Lord Halifax), authorising the arrest of the plaintiff by name and the seizure of his papers, and that it had been the custom for Secretaries of State since the Revolution to issue such warrant; they assessed the damages at £300 of the defendants were liable.

This special verdict was twice argued, and the judgment of the court was delivered by Lord Camden C.J. for the plaintiff.

LORD CAMDEN C.J.:[1] . . . The messenger, under this warrant, is commanded to seize the person described, and to bring him with his papers to be examined before the Secretary of State. In consequence of this, the house must be searched; the lock and doors of every room, box, or trunk must be broken open; all the papers and books without exception, if the warrant be executed according to its tenor, must be seized and carried away; for it is observable, that nothing is left either to the discretion or to the humanity of the officer.

This power so assumed by the Secretary of State is an execution upon all the party's papers, in the first instance. His house is rifled; his most valuable secrets are taken out of his possession, before the paper for which he is charged is found to be criminal by any competent jurisdiction, and before he is convicted either of writing, publishing, or being concerned in the paper.

This power, so claimed by the Secretary of State, is not supported by one single citation from any law book extant. It is claimed by no other magistrate in this kingdom but himself: the great executive head of criminal justice, the Lord Chief Justice of the Court of King's Bench, Scroggs C.J. excepted, never having assumed this authority.

The arguments, which the defendants' counsel have thought fit to urge in support of this practice, are of this kind:

That such warrants have been issued frequently since the Revolution, which practice has been found by the special verdict. . . .

That the case of the warrants bears a resemblance to the case of search for stolen goods.

They say, too, that they have been executed without resistance upon many printers, booksellers, and authors, who have quietly submitted to the authority; that no action hath hitherto been brought to try the right. . . .

And it is further insisted, that this power is essential to government, and the only means of quieting clamours and sedition.

These arguments, if they can be called arguments, shall all be taken notice of; because upon this question I am desirous of removing every colour or plausibility. . . .

If it is law, it will be found in our books. If it is not to be found there, it is not law.

The great end, for which men entered into society, was to secure their property. That right is preserved sacred and incommunicable in all instances, where it has not been taken away or abridged by some public law for the good of the whole. The cases where this right of property is set aside by positive law are various.

---

[1] [As to the authenticity of this report of Lord Camden's judgment, see note in 19 St. Tr. 1029–1030].

Distresses, executions, forfeitures, taxes, etc., are all of this description; wherein every man by common consent gives up that right, for the sake of justice and the general good. By the laws of England, every invasion of private property, be it ever so minute, is a trespass. No man can set his foot upon my ground without my licence, but he is liable to an action, though the damages be nothing. . . . If he admits the fact he is bound to show by way of justification that some positive law has empowered or excused him. . . .

According to this reasoning, it is now incumbent upon the defendants to show the law by which this seizure is warranted. If that cannot be done, it is a trespass.
. . . Where is the written law that gives any magistrate such a power? I can safely answer, there is none; and therefore it is too much for us without such authority to pronounce a practice legal, which would be subversive of all the comforts of society.

But though it cannot be maintained by any direct law, yet it bears a resemblance, as was urged, to the known case of search and seizure for stolen goods. I answer, that the difference is apparent. . . . The case of searching for stolen goods crept into the law by imperceptible practice. It is the only case of the kind that is to be met with. No less a person than my Lord Coke (4 Inst. 176) denied its legality; and therefore, if the two cases resembled each other more than they do, we have no right, without an Act of Parliament, to adopt a new practice in the criminal law, which was never yet allowed from all antiquity.

Observe, too, the caution with which the law proceeds in this singular case [of stolen goods]. . . . On the contrary, in the case before us nothing is described, nor distinguished: no charge us requisite to prove that the party has any criminal papers in his custody: no person present to separate or select: no person to prove in the owner's behalf the officer's misbehaviour. To say the truth, he cannot easily misbehave, unless he pilfers; for he cannot take more than all. . . .

I come now to the practice since the Revolution, which has been strongly urged.
. . . If the practice began then, it began too late to be law now. If it was more ancient, the Revolution is not to answer for it. . . . With respect to the practice itself, if it goes no higher, every lawyer will tell you it is much too modern to be evidence of the common law. . . .

This is the first instance I have met with, where the ancient immemorable law of the land, in a public matter, was attempted to be proved by the practice of a private office. . . .

The defendants upon this occasion have stopped short at the Revolution. But I think it would be material to go further back, in order to see how far the search and seizure of papers have been countenanced in the antecedent reigns. . . . I find no trace of such a warrant before that period, except a very few that were produced the other day in the reign of King Charles II. . . .

It is then said that it is necessary for the ends of government to lodge such a power with a State officer, and that it is better to prevent the publication before than to punish the offender afterwards. I answer, if the legislature be of that opinion, they will remove the Licensing Act. But if they have not done that, I conceive they are not of that opinion. And with respect to the argument of State necessity, of a distinction that has been arrived at between State offences and others, the common law does not understand that kind of reasoning, nor do our books take notice of any such distinctions.

Serjeant Ashley was committed to the Tower in the third [year] of Charles I by the House of Lords, only for asserting in argument that there was a "law of State" different from the common law; and the Ship-Money Judges were impeached for holding, first, that State-necessity would justify the raising money without consent of Parliament; and secondly, that the King was judge of that necessity.

If the King himself has no power to declare when the law ought to be violated for reasons of State, I am sure we his Judges have no such prerogative. . . .

I have not taken notice of everything that has been urged upon the present point; and upon the whole we are all of opinion, that the warrant to seize and carry away the party's papers in the case of a seditious libel, is illegal and void.

Statutory Powers

R. v. Inland Revenue Commissioners, Ex parte Rossminster
[1980] A.C. 952
House of Lords

Section 20C of the Taxes Management Act 1970, as amended, provides:

"(1) If the appropriate judicial authority is satisfied on information on oath given by an officer of the board that—(a) there is reasonable ground for suspecting that an offence involving any form of fraud in connection with, or in relation to, tax has been committed and that evidence of it is to be found on premises specified in the information; ... the authority may issue a warrant in writing authorising an officer ... to enter the premises, if necessary by force, at any time within 14 days from the time of issue of the warrant, and search them. ...

(3) On entering the premises with a warrant under this section, the officer may seize and remove any things whatsoever found there which he has reasonable cause to believe may be required as evidence for the purposes of proceedings in respect of such an offence as is mentioned in subsection (1) above. ..."

Suspecting that some tax fraud had been committed, a senior revenue officer placed information before a circuit judge on July 12, 1979, and obtained search warrants for named revenue officers to search specified premises and seize anything which they had reasonable cause to believe might be required as evidence in proceedings in respect of a tax fraud, in accordance with section 20C of the Taxes Management Act 1970 as amended. At 7 a.m. on Friday, July 13, 1979, teams of revenue officers accompanied by police officers arrived at the premises, including those of the applicants, and having gained entry, searched those premises. They seized anything which they claimed that they had reasonable cause to believe might be require as evidence of a tax fraud, but they did not inform the applicants of the offences suspected or of the persons suspected of having committed them. In addition, the warrant contained no such particulars. The applicants applied to the Divisional Court (Eveleigh L.J., Park and Woolf JJ.) for certiorari; to quash the warrants and a declaration that the revenue officers were not entitled to remove the documents seized. The Divisional Court refused the application. The Court of Appeal (Lord Denning M.R., Browne and Goff L.JJ.) reversed that decision and granted a declaration. The Inland Revenue appealed to the House of Lords (Lord Wilberforce, Viscount Dilhorne, Lord Diplock, Lord Salmon and Lord Scarman). The following extracts relate to the validity of the warrants. The availability of declaratory relief is discussed *post* p.426.

LORD WILBERFORCE: My Lords, the organised searches by officers of the Inland Revenue on Friday, July 13, 1979, on the respondents' offices and private premises were carried out under powers claimed to be conferred by Act of Parliament—the Finance Act 1976, section 57, and Schedule 6, section 20C amending the Taxes Management Act 1970, section 20.

The integrity and privacy of a man's home and of his place of business, an important human right has, since the second world war, been eroded by a number of statutes passed by Parliament in the belief, presumably, that this right of privacy ought in some cases to be over-ridden by the interest which the public has in preventing evasions of the law. Some of these powers of search are reflections of dirigisme and of heavy taxation, others of changes in mores. Examples of them are to be found in the Exchange Control Act 1947, the Finance Act 1972 (in relation to VAT) and in statutes about gaming or the use of drugs. A formidable number of officials now have powers to enter people's premises, and to take property away, and these powers are frequently exercised, sometimes on a large scale. Many people, as well as the respondents, think that this process has gone too far; that is an issue to be debated in Parliament and in the press.

The courts have the duty to supervise, I would say critically, even jealously, the legality of any purported exercise of these powers. They are the guardians of the citizens' right to privacy. But they must do this in the context of the times, i.e. of increasing Parliamentary intervention, and of the modern power of judicial review. In my respectful opinion appeals to 18th century precedents of arbitrary action by Secretaries of State and references to general warrants do nothing to throw light on the issue. Furthermore, while the courts may look critically at legislation which impairs the rights of citizens and should resolve any doubt in interpretation in their favour, it is no part of their duty, or power, to restrict or impede the working of legislation, even of unpopular legislation; to do so would be to weaken rather than to advance the democratic process.

It is necessary to be clear at once that Parliament, in conferring these wide powers, has introduced substantial safeguards. Those relevant to this case are three:

(1) No action can be taken under section 20C without the approval of the Board of Inland Revenue—viz., two members, at least, acting personally. This board consists of senior and responsible officials expert in the subject matter, who must be expected to weigh carefully the issues of public interest involved.

(2) No warrant to enter can be issued except by a circuit judge, not, as is usually the case, by a magistrate. There has to be laid before him information on oath, and on this he must be satisfied that there is reasonable ground for suspecting the commission of a "tax fraud" and that evidence of it is to be found in the premises sought to be searched. If the judge does his duty (and we must assume that the learned Common Serjeant did in the present case) he must carefully consider for himself the grounds put forward by the revenue officer and judicially satisfy himself, in relation to each of the premises concerned, that these amount to reasonable grounds for suspecting, etc. It would be quite wrong to suppose that he acts simply as a rubber stamp on the revenue's application.

(3) The courts retain their full powers of supervision of judicial and executive action. There is nothing in section 20C which cuts these down: on the contrary, Parliament, by using such phrases as "is satisfied," "has reasonable cause to believe" must be taken to accept the restraints which courts in many cases have held to be inherent in them. The courts are concerned, in this case, only with two matters bearing upon legality.

First, were the warrants valid? Secondly, can the actual action taken under subsection (3) be challenged on the ground that the officers did not have, or could not have had, reasonable cause to believe that the documents they seized might be required as evidence for the purposes of proceedings in respect of a "tax fraud"? A third possible issue, namely, that there was not before the judge sufficient material on which to be satisfied as the section requires was not pursued, nor thought sustainable by the Court of Appeal. It is not an issue now.

The two first mentioned are the only issues in the case. Three judges have decided them in favour of each side. For myself I have no doubt that the view taken by the Divisional Court on each was correct and I am willing to adopt their judgment. I add a few observations of my own.

1. I can understand very well the perplexity, and indeed indignation, of those present on the premises, when they were searched. Beyond knowing, as appears in the warrant, that the search is in connection with a "tax fraud," they were not told what the precise nature of the fraud was, when it was committed, or by whom it was committed. In the case of a concern with numerous clients, for example, a bank, without this knowledge the occupier of the premises is totally unable to protect his customers' confidential information from investigation and seizure. I cannot believe that this does not call for a fresh look by Parliament. But,

on the plain words of the enactment, the officers are entitled if they can persuade the board and the judge, to enter and search *premises* regardless of whom they belong to: a warrant which confers this power is strictly and exactly within the parliamentary authority, and the occupier has no answer to it. I accept that some information as regards the person(s) who are alleged to have committed an offence and possibly as to the approximate dates of the offences must almost certainly have been laid before the board and the judge. But the occupier has no right to be told of this at this stage, nor has he the right to be informed of the "reasonable grounds" of which the judge was satisfied. Both courts agree as to this: all this information is clearly protected by the public interest immunity which covers investigations into possible criminal offences. With reference to the police, Lord Reid stated this in these words:

> "The police are carrying on an unending war with criminals many of whom are today highly intelligent. So it is essential that there should be no disclosure of anything which might give any useful information to those who organise criminal activities. And it would generally be wrong to require disclosure in a civil case of anything which might be material in a pending prosecution: but after a verdict has been given or it has been decided to take no proceedings there is not the same need for secrecy." (*Conway* v. *Rimmer* [1968] A.C. 910, 953–954).

The Court of Appeal took the view that the warrants were invalid because they did not sufficiently particularise the alleged offence(s). The court did not make clear exactly what particulars should have been given—and indeed I think that this cannot be done. The warrant followed the wording of the statute "fraud in connection with or in relation to tax": a portmanteau description which covers a number of common law (cheating) and statutory offences (under the Theft Act 1968 et al.). To require specification at this investigatory stage would be impracticable given the complexity of "tax frauds" and the different persons who may be involved (companies, officers of companies, accountants, tax consultants, tax-payers, wives of taxpayers etc.). Moreover, particularisation, if required, would no doubt take the form of a listing of one offence and/or another or others and so would be of little help to those concerned. Finally, there would clearly be power, on principles well accepted in the common law, after entry had been made in connection with one particular offence, to seize material bearing upon other offences within the portmanteau. So, particularisation, even if practicable, would not help the occupier.

I am unable, therefore, to escape the conclusion, that adherence to the statutory formula is sufficient.

The warrants, being valid, confer an authority to enter and search: see section 20C (1). This being in terms stated in the Act, I do not appreciate the relevance of an inquiry into the form of search warrants at common law (which in any case admitted of some flexibility in operation) still less into that of warrants of arrest. There is no mystery about the word "warrant": it simply means a document issued by a person in authority under power conferred in that behalf authorising the doing of an act which would otherwise be illegal. The person affected, of course, has the right to be satisfied that the power to issue it exists: therefore the warrant should (and did) contain a reference to that power. It would be wise to add to it a statement of satisfaction on the part of the judicial authority as to the matters on which he must be satisfied but this is not a requirement and its absence does not go to validity. To complain of its absence in the present case when, as is admitted, no challenge can be made as to the satisfaction, in fact, of the judge, would be technical and indeed irrational. I can find no ground for holding these warrants invalid.

The validity of the warrant
LORD DIPLOCK: ...What has to be disclosed upon the face of the search warrant

depends upon the true construction of the statute. The construing court ought, no doubt, to remind itself, if reminder should be necessary, that entering a man's house or office, searching it and seizing his goods against his will are tortious acts against which he is entitled to the protection of the court unless the acts can be justified either at common law or under some statutory authority. So if the statutory words relied upon as authorising the acts are ambiguous or obscure, a construction should be placed upon them that is least restrictive of individual rights which would otherwise enjoy the protection of the common law. But judges in performing their constitutional function of expounding what words used by Parliament in legislation mean, must not be over-zealous to search for ambiguities or obscurities in words which on the face of them are plain, simply because the members of the court are out of sympathy with the policy to which the Act appears to give effect.

My Lords, it does not seem to me that in construing section 20C of the Taxes Management Act 1970 any assistance is to be gained from a consideration of those mid-18th century cases centring on John Wilkes and culminating in *Entick* v. *Carrington* (1765) 2 Wils. 275, which established the illegality of "general warrants" and were cited by Lord Denning M.R. in his judgment in the instant case. *Rex* v. *Wilkes* (1763) 2 Wils. 151 was not concerned with a warrant for arrest and seizure of documents but with a warrant of commitment to the Tower of London of John Wilkes by name and was decided on a point of parliamentary privilege from arrest alone. *Huckle* v. *Money* (1763) 2 Wils. 205 was a case reported on the question of the right of the Court of Common Pleas to order a new trial on the ground that excessive damages had been awarded by a jury. It was an action for false imprisonment brought by a journeyman printer who apparently had played no part in printing the famous issue No.45 of "The North Briton" but had been arrested under a warrant issued by a Secretary of State authorising a King's messenger to arrest the authors, printers and publishers of that issue (without naming or identifying any of them), to seize all their papers and to bring them before the Secretary of State to be examined by him. Pratt C.J. referred to the fact that in this particular case the warrant did not name the persons to be arrested under it as a matter which might be taken into account in aggravation of damages; but as was ultimately held in *Entick* v. *Carrington* 2 Wils. 275 the invalidity of warrants of this kind did not depend on the absence of the name of the person to be arrested, for Entick was so named. Their invalidity was more fundamental; a Secretary of State, it was held, did not have any power at common law or under the prerogative to order the arrest of any citizen or the seizure of any of his property for the purpose of discovering whether he was guilty of publishing a seditious libel.

In the instant case the search warrant did not purport to be issued by the circuit judge under any common law or prerogative power but pursuant to section 20C (1) of the Taxes Management Act 1970, alone. That subsection makes it a condition precedent to the issue of the warrant that the circuit judge should himself be satisfied by information upon oath that facts exist which constitute reasonable ground for suspecting that an offence involving some form of fraud in connection with or in relation to tax has been committed, and also for suspecting that evidence of the offence is to be found on the premises in respect of which the warrant to search is sought. It is not, in my view, open to your Lordships to approach the instant case on the assumption that the Common Serjeant did not satisfy himself on both these matters, or to imagine circumstances which might have led him to commit so grave a dereliction of his judicial duties. The presumption is that he acted lawfully and properly; and it is only fair to him to say that, in my view, there is nothing in the evidence before your Lordships to suggest the contrary; nor, indeed, have the respondents themselves so contended.

All that the subsection expressly requires shall be specified in the warrant are the address of the premises to be searched and the name of the officer or officers of the board who are authorised to search them. The premises need not be in the occupation of the person suspected of the offence; they may be premises of some wholly innocent custodian or third party. The matter is still at the investigatory stage; good grounds must exist for suspecting that a tax fraud has been committed, but as yet there is not sufficient evidence in a form admissible at a criminal trial to prove it. The sole purpose of the search is to obtain such evidence.

Even though the statute may not strictly so require (a matter on which I express no concluded opinion) the warrant in my view ought to state upon its face the statutory authority under which it has been issued. This the form of warrant issued in the instant case does, though I agree with my noble and learned friend, Viscount Dilhorne, that the wording of the recital of the fulfilment of the two statutory conditions precedent to its issue might be improved. But for the reference to section 20C in accordance with whose provisions the information is stated to have been laid, the wording of the warrant would be consistent with its meaning that the information had not specified for consideration by the judge the grounds of suspicion on which the informant relied; but the express reference to the section, in my view, resolves any ambiguity and makes untenable the suggestion that the preamble to the warrant constitutes an admission by the judge that he had adopted blindly a statement of the informant that there existed some reasonable grounds for suspicion the nature of which however, was not disclosed. This was not a contention that the respondents were willing to advance. The warrant, in my view, ought also to state what are things found on the premises that the searching officers are entitled to seize and to remove, i.e. potential evidence of a particular category of offences. This form of warrant in the instant case also does by reproducing the terms of section 20C (3).

Ought it to disclose more in order to be a valid warrant under the section? It was submitted on behalf of the respondents that it was defective in three respects. First, it was said, it ought to identify the suspected offender, secondly, it ought to specify which one or more of the six or more species of offences which fall within the genus "an offence involving any form of fraud in connection with, or in relation to, tax," the suspect is suspected of having committed, and thirdly it ought to state the date of any offences of which he is suspected.

My Lords, if the subsection does indeed require that any of this additional information should be disclosed upon the face of the warrant, this must be by necessary implication only. There is no express requirement; and for my part I cannot see that any such implication is justified. The information would not protect the innocent; it might well assist the guilty to destroy or to remove beyond the jurisdiction of the court of trial the documentary evidence of their tax frauds. Tax frauds generally involve the use of confederates, whether ignorant of or parties to the fraud. To identify a suspect where the search extends to premises that are not in his personal occupation is to alert him to the suspicions of the revenue and if they are well founded, it may give him an opportunity of covering his tracks; while if the suspicions ultimately turn out to be groundless, his reputation with those whose premises have been searched will be unnecessarily besmirched. It is to be observed that the form of warrant at common law to search premises for stolen goods does not state who is alleged to have been the thief. As regards more detailed specification in the warrant of the offence of which the circuit judge was satisfied that there were reasonable grounds for suspecting had been committed this would not help the person whose premises were searched to know what documents were liable to be seized, since the right of seizure under subsection (3) is not limited to documents that may be required as evidence in proceedings for that offence alone but, on the true construction of the subsection, extends to documents that may be required as evidence in proceedings for any other offence that falls within the genus of offences "involving any kind of fraud in connection with, or in relation to, tax." This, as it seems to me, is the plain meaning of the words "such an offence as is mentioned in subsection (1) above." Nor do I find it surprising that Parliament should grant a power of search under the warrant wider in its scope than those things which it was already suspected would be found on the premises when the warrant was issued. Even at common law as it had developed by the time the Act was passed a warrant to search premises for stolen goods particularised in the warrant justified seizure of other goods found upon the premises at the time the warrant was executed if there were reasonable grounds for believing that those other goods were stolen: *Chic Fashions (West Wales) Ltd.* v. *Jones* [1968] 2 Q.B. 299.[1]

In agreement with the Divisional Court I would accordingly uphold the sufficiency and validity of the search warrant.

[Viscount Dilhorne and Lord Scarman similarly upheld the validity of the warrants; Lord Salmon dissented.]

Appeal allowed.

---

[1] See now the Police and Criminal Evidence Act 1984, S. 19.

FREEDOM OF SPEECH

Verrall v. Great Yarmouth Borough Council
[1981] 1 Q.B. 202
Court of Appeal

The defendant local authority granted a licence to the National Front to use a hall for two days for the organisation's annual conference. Following a change in political control the local authority repudiated its agreement. Watkins J. and the Court of Appeal (Lord Denning M.R., Roskill and Cumming-Bruce L.JJ.) concluded that the court had jurisdiction as a matter of substantive law to enforce by specific performance a contract to grant a licence over land.

LORD DENNING M.R.: . . . All technical objections being on one side, we come to the real point in the case: whether or not, as a matter of discretion, we should order specific performance of this contract.

Watkins J. ordered the new council to perform the contract. He did so because of the importance of freedom of speech and freedom of assembly. These are among our most precious freedoms. Freedom of speech means freedom not only for the views of which you approve, but also freedom for the views you most heartily disapprove. This is a land, in the words of the poet:

"where a man may speak the things he will. A land of settled government. A land of just and old renown where freedom broadens slowly down from precedent to precedent."

But, mark you, freedom of speech can be abused. It can be used so as to promote violence; to propagate racial hatred and class warfare; and to undermine the structure of society itself. History provides examples. Such as when Hitler led the Germans to believe that they were the master race, and inflamed them so that they expelled and massacred the Jews. Or when the communists have used their freedom to destroy the freedom of others. If there were any evidence that the National Front were abusing this freedom, it might turn the scale. But there is no evidence of it here.

Freedom of assembly is another of our precious freedoms. Everyone is entitled to meet and assemble with his fellows to discuss their affairs and to promote their views: so long as it is not done to propagate violence or do anything unlawful. On this point I would stress—and it is very important that it should be stressed—that this is a private meeting of this political party. I will read what the plaintiff said in his affidavit:

"The conference which is to be held in Great Yarmouth is a private meeting. It is open to members and to invited members of the press only. Each person attending the meeting will be required to produce a current membership card validated by a regional officer of the National Front. A panel of senior members of the National Front will scrutinise the credentials of every person seeking entry to the meeting.

"There have been 12 such conferences in the past. There has never been any trouble inside such a meeting."

That is the meeting which is contemplated. It is essential under the constitution of this party that it should hold the meeting; that it should elect its officers and members for the ensuing year and the like; and that it should do all such things as are done at an annual conference of this kind.

The evidence is that if there is any trouble it will not be at the meeting at all. If it does occur, it will be outside caused by opponents of the National Front. There are societies such as the Anti-Nazi League who object to all the goings on of the

National Front. Their members may threaten or assault the members of the National Front: or try to stop their meeting. It would then be those interrupters who would be the destroyers of freedom of speech. They cannot be allowed to disrupt the meeting by mass pickets, or by violent demonstrations, and the like. The police will, I hope, be present in force to prevent such disruptions.

In this case, in April the Great Yarmouth Borough Council made a deliberate decision. They took everything into account. They had all information before them. They must have decided that the dangers were not such as to lead them to withhold the use of their halls for the conference. The dangers are just the same now. The newly constituted council is bound by what the old constituted council did. The newly constituted council must honour the contract. I see no sufficient reason for not holding the council to their contract. In the interests of our fundamental freedoms—freedom of speech, freedom of assembly, and the importance of holding people to their contracts—we ought to grant specific performance in this case, as the judge did.

I would therefore dismiss the appeal.

ROSKILL L.J:. . . . It is said that if we insist on this contract being fulfilled there is a risk of public disorder, and evidence has been sought to be given that there have been other disorders on other occasions. I venture to echo what Lord Denning M.R. and Watkins J. have said about the right of speech. It would be a sorry day if this court, fearful because an attempt might be made to prevent those who wish to air their views, however unpopular, prevented the performance of due contractual rights for which they have paid merely because others might seek to disrupt a private meeting by the use of unlawful force. If, as has happened in the past in times of national emergency such as the last war, the government of the day has found it necessary to stop free expressions of opinion because they are thought contrary to the national good, there are and have been in the past ways and means of stopping them. But unless and until some political organisations are proscribed as unlawful or legislation such as the Public Order Act is extended to make their activities unlawful, it is the duty of the court to treat all political parties as equal before the law and (irrespective of whether particular views may be distasteful to the courts or to some members of the public) allow those views to find expression particularly at a meeting which it is said is going to be private.

CUMMING-BRUCE L.J:. . . . On the matter of discretion, I would only say this. Anyone who has been at the scene of mob violence is likely to regard with deep horror and distaste the risks of personal injury and to personal property which the antics of infuriated political enthusiasts are likely to cause. Having been in some such situations in other countries myself, I am very much alive to the apprehensions that the threats of mobs must arouse in the minds of responsible people in Great Yarmouth. But, when that is said, one has to consider, as did the judge whose discretion it was in the first instance to exercise, that it was his duty to consider, as he did, the implications of the course that the council invite this court to take. A solemn contractual obligation for valuable consideration has been entered into. The council are under a legal duty, which they no longer dispute, to comply with that obligation. They deliberately repudiate it. The reason that they deliberately repudiate it is because, after a change of political party in the local government elections, they take a different view of the pros and cons of the bargain from the view taken by their predecessors on the council who made the contract. In that situation, although there is a solemn legal obligation whereby the National Front are entitled to hold their annual general meeting in the hall that has been licensed to them, because of the threats of mobs and the fear of unlawful violence on the part of groups who, I suppose, if they are not already in Yarmouth are intending to go to Yarmouth in order to prevent this political party from exercising its constitutional right, they invite the court to step in and say, "Free speech should be silenced. The constitutional rights enjoyed in this country, at any rate since the Bill of Rights, should come to an end." If that proposition is right, then, if you look at the other side of the penny, those political enthusiasts described as "left-wing bodies" who wish to hold meetings, who wish to organise politically, would find themselves faced with the same difficulty because the ferocious mobs who take the opposite view will claim the assistance of the court to prevent them speaking or holding meetings.

Such implications appear to me to be profoundly dangerous. If there is a case for silencing a group which wishes to organise as a political party, it is for the Crown in Parliament by statute to restrict the right of free speech or free association. It is not appropriate to come to this court and invite the court to begin a slide down such a slippery slope.

For those reasons I too would dismiss the appeal.

Appeal dismissed.

Criminal Libel

R. v. Wells Street Stipendiary Magistrate, Ex Parte Deakin
[1980] A.C. 477
House of Lords

A private prosecution had been brought against the authors and publishers of a book, charging them with criminal libel. At the committal proceedings the accused sought leave to call evidence of the general bad reputation of the prosecutor. The magistrates held that they had no jurisdiction to hear such evidence at the committal stage. After committal orders were made the accused unsuccessfully applied for *certiorari* and *mandamus* to the Divisional Court (Lord Widgery L.C.J., Boreham and Drake JJ.). On appeal to the House of Lords (Lord Diplock, Viscount Dilhorne, Lord Edmund-Davies, Lord Keith of Kinkel and Lord Scarman).

LORD DIPLOCK: My Lords, the speeches of my noble and learned friends Viscount Dilhorne and Lord Scarman, which I have had the opportunity of reading in advance, contain references to all the earlier authorities, which it is necessary to cite for the purposes of this appeal. I agree with the conclusions that they draw from those authorities and for the reasons that they give I too would dismiss the appeal.

The examination of the legal characteristics of the criminal offence of the defamatory libel as it survives today, which has been rendered necessary in order to dispose of this appeal, has left me with the conviction that this particular offence has retained anomalies which involve serious departures from accepted principles upon which the modern criminal law of England is based and are difficult to reconcile with international obligations which this country has undertaken by becoming a party to the European Convention for the Protection of Human Rights and Fundamental Freedoms (1953) (Cmd. 8969).

The original justification for the emergence of the common law offence of defamatory libel in a more primitive age was the prevention of disorder—to use the words of article 10.2 of the European Convention which describes the various grounds on which public authority may interfere to restrict or penalise freedom of expression. The reason for creating the offence was to provide the victim with the means of securing the punishment of his defamer by peaceful process of the law instead of resorting to personal vioence to obtain revenge. But risk of provoking breaches of the peace has ceased to be an essential element inthe criminal offence of defamatory libel; and the civil action for damages for libel and an injunction provides protection for the reputation of the private citizen without necessity for any interference by public authority with the alleged defamer's right to freedom of expression.

My Lords, under article 10.2 of the European Convention, the exercise of the right of freedom of expression may be subjected to restrictions or penalties by a contracting state, only to the extent that those restrictions or penalties are necessary in a democratic society for the protection of what (apart from the reputation of individuals and the protection of information received in confidence) may generically be described as the public interest. In contrast to this the truth of the defamatory statement is not in itself a defence to a charge of defamatory libel under our criminal law; so here is a restriction on the freedom to impart information which states that are parties to the Convention have expressly undertaken to secure to everyone within their jurisdiction. No onus lies upon the prosecution to show that the defamatory matter was of a kind that it is necessary in a democratic society to suppress or penalise in order to protect the public interest. On the contrary, even though no public interest can be shown to be injuriously affected by imparting to others accurate information about seriously discreditable conduct of an individual, the publisher of the information must be convicted unless he himself can prove to the satisfaction of a jury that the publication of it was for the public benefit.

This is to turn article 10 of the Convention on its head. Under our criminal law a person's freedom of expression, wherever it involves exposing seriously discreditable conduct of others, is to be repressed by public authority unless he can convince a jury ex post facto that the particular exercise of the freedom was for the public benefit; whereas article 10 requires that freedom of expression shall be untrammelled by public authority except where its interference to repress a particular exercise of the freedom is necessary for the protection of the public interest.

My Lords, public authority, represented in criminal matters by the Director of Public Prosecutions and the police, has had minimal recourse in recent years to prosecutions for the offence of defamatory libel; and I have no reason to doubt that in each of the prosecutions which its representatives have brought it could be shown not only that the defamatory matter was false but also that by reason of its nature or the circumstances in which it was published, repression of the publication by penal sanctions was necessary in the public interest. But private prosecutions for this offence are still available and in the last two years there are two instances in which private prosecutions (of which this is the second) have been instituted by individuals who have been defamed. As private prosecutors they are not under any duty to consider whether the prosecution is necessary in the public interest as distinct from serving their own private interests. It is this that has brought into the light of day the present sorry state of the law of criminal libel in this country.

My Lords, the law of defamation, civil as well as criminal, has proved an intractable subject for radical reform. There is, however, one relatively simple step that could be taken which would at least avoid the risk of our failing to comply with our international obligations under the European Convention for the Protection of Human Rights and Fundamental Freedoms. That step is to require the consent of the Attorney-General to be obtained for the institution of any prosecution for criminal libel. In deciding whether to grant his consent in the particular case, the Attorney-General could then consider whether the prosecution was necessary on any of the grounds specified in article 10.2 of the Convention and unless satisfied that it was, he should refuse his consent. For this additional reason I support the recommendation of my noble and learned friends Viscount Dilhorne and Lord Scarman which is to the same effect.

VISCOUNT DILHORNE: In argument it was contended for the appellants that there was no prima facie case of publishing a criminal libel unless the public interest was involved to such an extent as to require a prosecution, the suggestion being that Mr. Gleaves' general bad character, if established, meant that there was no such public interest requiring a prosecution.

When an application is made for leave to institute the prosecution of a newspaper for criminal libel, a judge has to consider whether the public interest requires a prosecution (see Goldsmith v. Pressdram Ltd. [1977] Q.B. 83, per Wien J. and Law of Libel Amendment Act 1888, section 8) but examining justices are not charged with the responsibility of deciding whether or not a prosecution should be instituted. When a case comes before them, the prosecution has been instituted and in my opinion it is not their task to decide whether the public interest is involved to such an extent as to require a prosecution before deciding whether or not to commit for trial. "Public interest" has no precise meaning and views as to what it comprehends may differ widely: Some may think that public interest requires regard to be had to matters which others would think were wholly irrelevant. In my opinion examining magistrates do not have to and should not enter into this uncharted field. All they have to decide is whether there is sufficient evidence to put the accused on trial for the alleged offence.

. . . . .

In *Rex* v. *Wicks* [1936] 1 All E.R. 384, du Parcq J. delivering the judgment of the Court of Criminal Appeal said, at p. 386:

"... a criminal prosecution for libel ought not to be instituted and, if instituted, will probably be regarded with disfavour by judge and jury, when the libel complained of is of so trivial a character as to be unlikely either to disturb the peace of the community or seriously affect the reputation of the person defamed."

He went on to cite, at p. 387, the following passage from the judgment of Mansfield C.J. in *Thorley* v. *Lord Kerry* (1812) 4 Taunt. 355, 364:

"There is no doubt that this was a libel, for which the plaintiff in error might have been indicted and punished; because, though the words impute no punishable crimes, they contain that sort of imputation which is calculated to vilify a man, and bring him, as the books say, into hatred, contempt, and ridicule; for all words of that description an indictment lies. ..."

This, du Parcq J. said, remained the law.

A criminal libel must be serious libel, If the libel is of such a character as to be likely to disturb the peace of the community or to provoke a breach of the peace, then it is not to be regarded as trivial. But to hold as du Parcq J. did, in my view rightly, that the existence of such a tendency suffices to show that the libel is a serious one, is a very different thing from saying that proof of its existence is necessary to establish guilt of the offence. Evidence of the bad character of the person libelled is irrelevant to the question whether the libel has any such tendency.

An examining magistrate may regard the libel as a serious one even if the person libelled has the bad character alleged. The fact that a man has a bad character does not mean that anyone can publish what he likes about him with impunity. If the magistrate thinks the libel a serious one even if the person libelled has the bad character alleged, proof that the allegations of bad character are well founded will serve no useful purpose and consequently they are irrelevant.

In the present case I see no ground for holding that the examining magistrate should, even if the prosecutor has the bad character alleged, have regarded any of the libels as of a trivial character.

It would, I think, be an improvement in our law if no prosecution for criminal libel could be instituted without leave. There are many precedents for the leave of the Attorney-General or the Director of Public Prosecutions being required for the institution of prosecutions. In considering whether or not to give his consent, the Attorney-General and the Director must have regard to the public interest. The leave of a judge must be obtained for the institution of a prosecution for criminal libel against a newspaper (Law of Libel Amendment Act 1888, section 8), and where such leave is sought, the judge must consider whether a prosecution is required in the public interest: see *Goldsmith* v. *Pressdram Ltd.* [1977] Q.B. 83. As I do not myself regard it as very desirable that judges have any responsibility for the institution of prosecutions, I would like to see it made the law that no prosecution for criminal libel could be brought without the leave of the Attorney-General or of the Director of Public Prosecutions.

LORD EDMUND-DAVIES: I abstain from ventilating at length such views as I entertain regarding the desirability of law reform in the matter of criminal libel. For this may well be regarded as not a wholly suitable occasion to do so, and, even if it be, the most zealous law reformer must feel discouraged by the well-nigh total apathy that has reigned since the publication in 1975 of the stimulating Report of the Committee on Defamation (Cmnd. 5909) presided over by Faulks J. It has, indeed, been strongly urged in some quarters that proceedings for criminal libel, rarely resorted to, should be abolished altogether. But I share the view of the Faulks Committee and of Mr. Spencer in [1977] Crim.L.R. 465, 473, that such proceedings do serve some useful purpose and should not be abolished unless and until adequate substitute provisions have been made. If, however, they are to be retained, either in their present form or another, the two following pieces of reform are badly needed:

(A) No such proceedings should be capable of being instituted at the unrestricted whim of anyone. Under the Newspaper Libel and Registration Act 1881, section 3, no criminal proceedings could be instituted against a newspaper proprietor, publisher or editor "without the written fiat or allowance of the Director of Public Prosecutions in England or Her Majesty's Attorney-General in Ireland being first had and obtained." The Law of Libel Amendment Act 1888, section 8, substituted therefor the order of "a judge at chambers," the person sought to be accused being given notice of the intended application for the order and having an opportunity to be heard in opposition. Such provisions should be extended to *all* criminal proceedings for defamatory libel, and I, in common with your Lordships, favour the fiat of the Attorney-General being rendered necessary.

(B) A provision similar to section 5 of the Defamation Act 1952 should be made applicable. The position at present is that if an alleged criminal libel contains several distinct allegations and the defendant fails to prove the truth of any one of them, the jury should in duty convict (*Reg.* v. *Newman* (1853) 1 El. & Bl. 558), whereas if the allegation complained of is general in its nature it is sufficient to prove as much of the plea of truth as would justify the libel. (*Reg.* v. *Labouchere,* 12 Q.B.D. 320). Section 5 of the Act of 1952 provides that: ". . . a defence of justification shall not fail by reason only that the truth of every charge is not proved if the words not proved to be true do not materially injure the plaintiff's reputation having regard to the truth of the remaining charges."

But by reason of section 17 (2) this has no application to criminal libel. It is high time it did, for no-one should be liable to be convicted in the circumstances envisaged.

[Lord Keith of Kinkel and Lord Scarman expressed similar views]

Appeal dismissed.

Blasphemy: the Origins of the Criminal Libels: Mens Rea

R. v. Lemon
[1979] A.C. 617
House of Lords

The appellants were the editor and publisher of a magazine called Gay News. In one issue a poem was published "The Love that Dares to Speak its Name." It was accompanied by a drawing illustrating its subject matter. A private prosecution for blasphemy was brought against the editor and publisher on the ground that the poem and drawing "[vilified] Christ in His life and in His crucifixion." After a trial before Judge King-Hamilton Q.C. the jury found the accused guilty. An appeal to the Court of Appeal (Roskill and Eveleigh L.JJ. and Stocker J.) was dismissed.

On appeal to the House of Lords (Lord Diplock, Viscount Dilhorne, Lord Edmund-Davies, Lord Russell of Killowen and Lord Scarman):

LORD DIPLOCK: . . . The issue in this appeal is not whether the words and drawing are blasphemous. The jury, though only by a majority of ten to two, have found them to be so. As expressed in the charge against the appellants they "vilify Christ in His life and in His crucifixion."

.   .   .   .   .

The only question in this appeal is whether in 1976 the mental element or mens rea in the common law offence of blasphemy is satisfied by proof only of an intention to publish material which in the opinion of the jury is likely to shock and arouse resentment among believing Christians or whether the prosecution must go further and prove that the accused in publishing the material in fact intended to produce that effect upon believers, or (what comes to the same thing in criminal law), although aware of the likelihood that such effect might be produced, did not care whether it was or not, so long as the publication achieved someother purpose that constituted his motive for publishing it. Wherever I speak hereafter of "intention" I use the expression as a term of art in that extended sense.

My Lords, the offence of publishing a blasphemous libel has a long and at times inglorious history in the common law. For more than 50 years before the prosecution in the instant case was launched the offence seemed to have become obsolete, the last previous trial for it having taken place in 1922. . . . I feel bound to concede that by the beginning of the present century the law as to the mental elements in the offence of blasphemous libel was still uncertain. The task of this House in the instant appeal is to give to it certainty now, and to do so in a form that will not be inconsistent with the way in which the general law as to the mental element in criminal offences has developed since then.

Two things emerge clearly from the earlier history, first, that between the 17th century and the last quarter of the 19th, when Sir James Fitzjames Stephen published his *History of the Criminal Law of England* (1883), the characteristics of the substantive offence of blasphemous libel had undergone progressive changes; and secondly that, as Stephen reluctantly acknowledges in his chapter on "Seditious Offences" (Vol.II, p. 298), those changes (which he personally regretted) were largely shaped by the procedural changes in the trial of prosecutions for all forms of criminal libel resulting from Fox's Libel Act of 1792 and by the passing of Lord Campbell's Libel Act of 1843.

In the post-Restoration politics of 17th and 18th century England, Church and State were thought to stand or fall together. To cast doubt on the doctrines of the established church or to deny the truth of the Christian faith upon which it was founded was to attack the fabric of society itself; so blasphemous and seditious libel were criminal offences that went hand in hand. Both were originally what would now be described as offences of strict liability. To constitute the offence of blasphemous libel it was enough for the prosecution to prove that the accused, or someone for whose acts the law of libel held him to be criminally responsible, had published matter which (in trials held before Fox's Libel Act) the judge ruled, or (in trials held after that) the jury found, to be blasphemous, whether the accused knew it to be so or not. Furthermore, criminal libel in its four manifestations—seditious, blasphemous, obscene and defamatory—was unique among common law offences in imputing to any person who carried on the business of publisher or bookseller vicarious criminal liability for acts of publications done by persons in his employment even though these were done without his authority, consent or knowledge. Since in practice prosecutions were brought against publishers and booksellers rather than against authors, so long as this remained the law, as it did until the passing of section 7 of Lord Campbell's Libel Act in 1843, it could not logically be reconciled with the notion that the accused's own actual intention was a relevant element in the offence.

The severity of the law of blasphemous libel had, however, been somewhat mitigated before 1843 by judicial rulings not as to the mens rea but as to the actus reus of the offence. To publish opinions denying the truth of doctrines of the established Church or even of Christianity itself was no longer held to amount to the offence of blasphemous libel so long as such opinions were expressed in temperate language and not in terms of offence, insult or ridicule. *Reg.* v. *Hetherington* (1841) 4 St.Tr.N.S. 563. This introduces into the concept of the actus reus, in addition to the act of publication itself, the effect that the material published is likely to have upon the minds of those to whom it is published.

At a period when an accused could not give evidence in his own defence and his intention to produce a particular result by his acts, where this was an ingredient of the offence, was ascertained by applying the presumption that a man intends the natural consequences of his acts, the distinction was often blurred between the *tendency* of the published words to produce a particular effect upon those to whom they were published and the *intention* of the publisher to produce that effect. So that one finds Holt in his textbook on *The Law of Libel* published in (2nd ed., 1816) defining blasphemous libel as requiring the publication to be made ". . . with an *intent* to subvert man's faith in God, or to impair his reverence of him" (p. 64) and during the 20 years before Lord Campbell's Libel Act in 1843 one also finds in reported summings up of various judges occasional references to the *intention* of the accused.

The abolition in 1843 of vicarious criminal liability for blasphemous libel and the growing influence of Starkie's text book on the law of the criminal libel (*Starkie's Slander and Libel,* (1st ed., 1813); (2nd ed., 1830); (3rd ed., 1869); (4th ed., 1876), opened the way for a further development in the definition of the crime of blasphemous libel; but this time in its mental element or mens rea which was brought into closer harmony with the changed concept of the actus reus. Starkie was one of the Criminal Law Commissioners during the 1840s and became Downing Professor of Law at Cambridge. He adopted Holt's definition and elaborated it in a paragraph (4th ed., p. 599) later to be adopted as an accurate statement of the law by Lord Coleridge C.J. in *Reg.* v. *Ramsay and Foote* (1883) 15 Cox C.C. 231, 236:

"The law visits not the honest errors, but the malice of mankind. A wilful intention to pervert, insult, and mislead others, by means of licentious and contumelious abuse applied to sacred subjects, or by wilful misrepresentations or artful sophistry, calculated to mislead the ignorant and unwary, is the criterion and test of guilt. A malicious and mischievous intention, or what is the equivalent to such an intention, in law, as well as moral,—a state of apathy and indifference to the interests of society,—is the broad boundary between right and wrong."

The language in which this statement is expressed is perhaps more that of the advocate of law reform than of the draftsman of a criminal code. The reference to misleading others is probably outdated in this more sceptical and agnostic age unless what misleads is couched in terms that are likely to shock and arouse resentment among believing Christians. Nevertheless, the statement clearly requires intent on the part of the accused himself to produce the described effect on those to whom the blasphemous matter is published and so removes blasphemous libel from the special category of offences in which mens rea as to one of the elements of the actus reus is *not* a necessary constituent of the offence.

.   .   .   .   .

My own feeling of outrage at the blasphemous material with which the instant appeal is concerned makes it seem to me improbable that, if Mr. Lemon had been permitted to give evidence of his intentions, the jury would have been left in any doubt that, whatever his motives in publishing them may have been, he knew full well that the poem and accompanying drawing were likely to shock and arouse resentment among believing Christians and indeed many unbelievers. Nevertheless, Mr. Lemon was entitled to his opportunity of sowing the seeds of doubt in the jury's mind. By the judge's ruling he was denied this opportunity. For this reason, if the decision had lain with me, I would have allowed the appeal.

VISCOUNT DILHORNE: I now come to the first of the two cases which I regard as the leading cases in this field. Prior to *Reg.* v. *Bradlaugh* (1883) 15 Cox C.C. 217 there had been very considerable controversy about what constituted blasphemy. In the 18th century and before, it appears to have been thought that any attack or criticism, no matter how reasonably expressed, on the fundamental principles of the Christian religion and any discussion hostile to the inspiration and perfect purity of the Scriptures was against the law. That was Stephen's view (*History of the Criminal Law of England*, Vol. II, pp. 473 et seq.) but in this case it was rejected by Lord Coleridge C.J., who told the jury that he thought the law had been accurately stated in *Starkie's Slander and Libel*, (4t ed.) p. 599, in the following terms, at p. 226:

" 'The wilful intention to insult and mislead others by means of licentious and contumelious abuse offered to sacred subjects, or by wilful misrepresentations or wilful sophistry, calculated to mislead the ignorant and unwary, is the criterion and test of guilt. A malicious and mischievous intention, or what is equivalent to such an intention, in law, as well as morals—a state of apathy and indifference to the interests of society—is the broad boundary between right and wrong.' "

At first sight the citation this passage by Lord Coleridge C.J. might appear to give support to the view that such an intenton the part of the accused had to be proved but it is to be noted that Lord Coleridge C.J. began his summing up by telling the jury that there were two questions to be considered, first, whether the publications in question were blasphemous libels, and, secondly, whether, assuming them to be so, Mr. Bradlaugh was guilty of publishing them. He did not at any time tell the jury that they had to consider Mr. Bradlaugh's intent, an astonishing omission if he regarded it necessary to prove that he had a blasphemous intent, and the passage he cited from *Starkie's Slander and Libel*, (4th ed.), p. 599 was cited by him as providing the test for determining whether or not the publication itself was blasphemous.

This, to my mind, is shown beyond doubt by the fact that, after citing *Starkie*, he said, at p. 226:

"That I apprehend to be a correct statement of the law, and if you think the broad boundary between right and wrong that is laid down in the passage, has been overpast in the articles which are the subject matter of this indictment, then it will be your duty to answer the first question . . . against the defendant"

and by his saying at the end of his summing up, at pp. 230–231:

"It is a question, first of all, whether these things are not in any point of view blasphemous libels, whether they are not calculated and intended to insult the feelings and the deepest religious convictions of the great majority of the persons amongstwhom we live; and if so they are not to be tolerated any more than any other nuisance is tolerated. We must not do things that are outrages to the general feeling of propriety among the persons amongst whom we live. That is the first thing. Then the second thing is: Is Mr. Bradlaugh made out to have joined in the publication of these?"

"To say that crime lies in the manner and not in the matter appears to me an attempt to evade and explain away a law which has no doubt ceased to be in harmony with the temper of the times" was Stephen's view (*History of the Criminal Law of England*, Vol. II, p. 475) but since 1883 it has been accepted that it is the manner in which they are expressed that may constitute views expressed in a publication a blasphemous libel and this passage from *Starkie's Slander and Libel*, (4th ed.), p. 599, has been relied on as providing the test for determining whether the publication exceeds that which is permissible. It is the intention revealed by the publication that may lead to its being held to be blasphemous. There was nothing in Lord Coleridge C.J.'s summing up to support the view that there was a third question for the jury to consider, namely the intent of the accused.

This case was followed by *Reg.* v. *Ramsay and Foote*, 48 L.T. 773, a case greatly relied on by the appellants, a case of great importance and also tried by Lord Coleridge C.J. Again he told the jury that there were two questions for them to consider:

"First, are these publications in themselves blasphemous libels? Secondly, if they are so, is the publication of them traced home to the defendants so that you can find them guilty?" (p. 734.)

He went on to say, at p. 734: "The great point still remains, are these articles within the meaning of the law blasphemous libels?" Again he cited the passage from *Starkie's Slander and Libel*, (4th ed.), p. 599, not as indicating that it must be shown that the accused had an intention to blaspheme but as providing the test for determining whether the articles exeeded the permissible bounds. Again Lord Coleridge C.J. gave no direction to the jury as to the intent of the accused, an omission which I regard as of great significance.

In the light of the authorities to which I have referred and for the reasons I have stated, I am unable to reach the conclusion that the ingredients of the offence of publishing a blasphemous libel have changed since 1792. Indeed, it would, I think, be surprising if they had. If it be accepted, as I think it must, that that which it is sought to prevent is the publication of blasphemous libels, the harm is done by their intentional publication, whether or not the publisher intended to blaspheme.

I would dismiss these appeals.

LORD EDMUND-DAVIES: [The question relating to mens rea] cannot be answered without regard being had to the actus reus of blasphemous libel. Nor should one overlook the fact that seditious libel, blasphemous libel, obscene libel and defamatory libel all had their common origin in the Star Chamber, which (in the words of J. R. Spencer [1977] Crim.L.R. 383):

> ". . . regarded with the deepest suspicion the printed word in general, and anything which looked like criticism of the established institutions of Church or State in particular."

It was on the abolition of the Star Chamber in 1641 that the Court of King's Bench inherited its criminal jurisdiction, and shortly after the Restoration it tried the dramatist Sir Charles Sedley for indecency and blasphemy (*Rex* v. *Sedley* (1663) 17 St.Tr. 155; *Pepys' Diary*, July 1, 1663). For centuries thereafter

> ". . . a published attack on a high state official . . . might be prosecuted as either a seditious or a defamatory libel, and an attack on the Church or its doctrine might be prosecuted as either a blasphemous or a seditious libel. What the attack in question was called seems to have depended largely on the taste in vituperative epithet of the man who drafted the indictment or information. Thus in one case a man was prosecuted for seditious rather than blasphemous libel when he published a book contrary to the teaching of the Church of England: *Rex* v. *Keach* (1665) 6 St.Tr. 701."

As to the actus reus, as late as 1841 the Commissioners on Criminal Law reported that "The law distinctly forbids *all* denial of the Christian religion," but nevertheless added that in actual practice ". . . the course has been to withhold the application of the penal law unless insulting language is used." [*Sixth Report of Her Majesty's Commissioners on Criminal Law* (1841) (Parliamentary Reports (1841) x).] These last words mark the second stage in the development of the actus reus of blasphemy, and echo the ruling of Lord Denman C.J. a year earlier in *Reg.* v. *Hetherington*, 4 St.Tr.N.S. 563, 590 that criminality lies " . . . not altogether [on] a matter of opinion, but that it must be, in a great degree, a question as to the tone, and style, and spirit, . . ."

My Lords, during the long years when the actus reus of blasphemy was constituted by the mere denial (however decently expressed) of the basic tenets of Christianity or, later, the couching of that denial in scurrilous language, there was no necessity to explore the intention of the accused, for his words were regarded as revealing in themselves what that intention was. And that was so notwithstanding the fact that indictments for blasphemy habitually contained assertions regarding the defendant's intention.

.   .   .   .   .

[Lord Edmund-Davies then examined *R.* v. *Bradlaugh* and *R.* v. *Ramsay and Foote* (*supra*) and concluded, contrary to the view of Viscount Dilhorne, that Lord Coleridge L.C.J. had regarded intent as an essential element in blasphemy]

My Lords, we have seen that sedition and blasphemy were in origin twin types of criminal libel, the latter consisting in its earliest stage as *any* attack upon the Christian Church, as part of the State, and Lord Hale C.J. declaring in *Taylor's case* (1676) 1 Vent. 293 that "Christianity is parcel of the laws of England." I understood the respondents to this appeal to accept that, in relation to *sedition*, the intention of the defendant is an essential ingredient, and such cases as *Reg.* v. *Burns* (1886) 16 Cox C.C. 355, 360 and *Rex* v. *Caunt* (unreported)[1] proceeded upon that basis. It would be inexplicable were intention relevant in the one case but not in the other. *Reg.* v. *Burns* is also important as illustrating the lessening respect paid, as the 19th century progressed, to the presumption as to intention, Cave J. saying, at p. 364:

[1] See *The Times*, November 18, 1947; E. C. S. Wade, (1948) 64.

"In order to make out the offence of speaking seditious words there must be a criminal intent upon the part of the accused, they must be words spoken with a seditious intent; and, although it is a good working rule, to say that a man must be taken to intend the natural consequences of his acts, and it is very proper to ask a jury to infer, if there is nothing to show the contrary, that he did intend the natural consequences of his acts, yet, if it is shown from other circumstances that he did not actually intend them, I do not see how you can ask a jury to act upon what has then become a legal fiction."

My Lords, allow me to summarise. This appeal raises the questions whether it is sufficient for conviction that the defendants intended to *publish* the blasphemous words for which they were indicted, as the learned trial judge held. Or was it necessary that they should have also known of their offensive character and have intended to offend, alternatively that they published with reckless indifference to the consequences of publication? Different answers to these questions were called for at different stages in the evolution of the law of blasphemy. In the earliest stage it was clearly a crime of strict liability and consisted merely of any attack upon the Christian Church and its tenets. In the second stage the original harshness of the law was ameliorated, and the attack was not punishable unless expressed in intemperate or scurrilous language. In the third stage, opinions were mixed. Some judges held that the subjective intention of author or publisher was irrelevant, others that it was of the greatest materiality.

The preponderance of authority was nevertheless increasingly and markedly in favour of the view that intention to blaspheme must be established if conviction was to ensue. In my judgment, such is now indeed the law, and any 20th century cases in conflict with it—such as *Rex* v. *Aldred*, 22 Cox C.C. 1—should be regarded as wrongly decided.

[To adopt such a view of the law would be in accord with] the increasing tendency in our law to move away from strict liability in relation both to statutory offences (see *Sweet* v. *Parsley* [1970] A.C. 132, especially at pp. 149c and 163c) and to common law crimes (see *Lim Chin Aik* v. *The Queen* [1963] A.C. 160, 172 and *Reg.* v. *Morgan* [1976] A.C. 182, 210G-H). For in truth it is with strict liability that we are concerned in this appeal, for ". . . an offence is regarded—and properly regarded—as one of strict liability if no mens rea need be proved as to a single element in the actus reus" (Smith and Hogan, *Criminal Law*, (4th ed., 1978), p. 79).

There are those who dislike this tendency. But to treat as irrelevant the state of mind of a person charged with blasphemy would be to take a backward step in the evolution of a humane code. Unfortunately, despite the exemplary care taken by the learned trial judge, lacking as he did the prolonged and patient probing into the law of which this House has had the benefit, I am afraid that that is what has happened in this case. Accordingly, despite my strong feelings of revulsion over this deplorable publication, I find myself most reluctantly compelled to answer the certified question in the negative and to hold that these appeals against convicton should be allowed.

LORD RUSSELL OF KILLOWEN: My Lords, it must be made at the outset absolutely clear that it is accepted by the appellants that the publication of a blasphemous libel is still a criminal offence: it is no part of your Lordships' function in this case to hold the contrary.

Moreover, if the only ingredient of the offence is the knowing publication of matter which will in fact shock and outrage the feelings of ordinary Christians it must equally be made clear that, as the jury found, this publication was a blasphemous libel. It is not for your Lordships to agree or disagree with that finding: though speaking for myself as an ordinary Christian, I found the publication quite appallingly shocking and outrageous.

So I return to the question of intent. The authorities embrace an abundance of apparently contradictory or ambivalent comments. There is no authority in your Lordships' House on the point. The question is open for decision. I do not, with all respect to the speech of my noble and learned friend Lord Diplock, consider that the question is whether this is an offence of strict liability. It is necessary that the editor or publisher should be aware of that which he publishes.

.   .   .   .   .

Why then should this House, faced with a deliberate publication of that which a jury with every justification has held to be a blasphemous libel, consider that it should be for the prosecution to prove, presumably beyond reasonable doubt, that the accused recognised and intended it to be such or regarded it as immaterial whether it was? I see no ground for that. It does not to my mind make sense: and I consider that sense should retain a function in our criminal law. The reason why the law considers that the publication of a blasphemous libel is an offence is that the law considers that such publication should not take place. And if it takes place, and the publicationis deliberate, I see no justification for holding that there is no offence when the publisher is incapable for some reason particular to himself of agreeing with a jury on the true nature of the publication.

Accordingly I would answer the certified question of law in the affirmative and dismiss the appeal.

LORD SCARMAN: My Lords, I do not subscribe to the view that the common law offence of blasphemous libel serves no useful purpose in the modern law. On the contrary, I think that there is a case for legislation extending it to protect the religious beliefs and feelings of non-Christians. The offence belongs to a group of criminal offences designed to safeguard the internal tranquillity of the kingdom. In an increasingly plural society such as that of modern Britain it is necessary not only to respect the differing religious beliefs, feelings and practices of all but also to protect them from scurrility, vilification, ridiculeand contempt.

I have permitted myself these general observations at the outset of my opinion because, my Lords, they determine my approach to this appeal. I will not lend my voice to a view of the law relating to blasphemous libel which would render it a dead letter, or diminish its efficacy to protect religious feeling from outrage and insult. My criticism of the common law offence of blaspphemy is not that it exists but that it is not sufficiently comprehensive. It is shackled by the chains of history.

While in my judgmeent it is not open to your Lordships' House, even under the Lord Chancellor's policy announcement of July 26, 1966 (H.L. Debates, July 26, 1966, col. 677) [*Practice Statement (Judicial Precedent)* [1966] 1 W.L.R. 1234], to extend the law beyond the limits recognised by the House in *Bowman* v. *Secular Society Ltd.* [1917] A.C. 406, or to make by judicial decision the comprehensive reform of the law which I believe to be beneficial, this appeal does offer your Lordships the opportunity of stating the existing law in a form conducive to the social conditions of the late 20th century rather than to those of the 17th, the 18th, or even the 19th century.

.   .   .   .   .

What, then, is the "mens rea" required by law to constitute the crime? No one has suggested that blasphemy is a crime of strict liability. The issue is as to the nature of the intention which has to be proved. As Eveleigh L.J. is reported to have put it in argument in this case [1979] Q.B. 10, 16:

"must the defendants have had an intention of offend in the manner complained of, or is it enough that he or they intended to publish that which offends?"

Bowman v. *Secular Society Ltd.* [1917] A.C. 406 throws no light upon the point.

The history of the law is obscure and confused. The point is, therefore, open for your Lordships' decision as a matter of principle. And in deciding the point your Lordships are not saying what the law was in the past or ought to be in the future but what is required of it in the conditions of today's society.

. . . . .

I am of the opinion that historically the law has required no more than an intention to publish words found by the jury to be blasphemous. Yet I recognise that another view, such as that developed by my noble and learned friend Lord Edmund-Davies, has great persuasive force. Indeed, it has the formidable support of my noble and learned friend Lord Diplock.

The issue is, therefore, one of legal policy in the society of today. There is some force in the lawyer's conceptual argument that in the matter of "mens rea" all four species of criminal libel (seditious, blasphemous, obscene and defamatory) should be the same. It is said that an intention to stir up sedition is necessary to constitute the crime of seditious libel. I am not sure that it is or ought to be: contrast *Rex* v. *Aldred*, 22 Cox C.C. 1 with Birkett J.'s direction in *Rex* v. *Caunt* (unreported). Prior to the enactment of the Obscene Publications Act 1959 it was not necessary to establish an intention to deprave and corrupt in order to prove an obscene libel: *Reg.* v. *Hicklin* 1868 L.R. 3 Q.B. 360. At worst, the common law may be said to have become fragmented in this area of public order offences: at best, it may be said (as I believe to be true) to be moving towards a position in which people who know what they are doing will be criminally liable if the words they choose to publish are such as to cause grave offence to the religious feelings of some of their fellow citizens or are such as to tend to deprave and corrupt persons who are likely to read them.

The movement of the law is illustrated by recent statutes. The Obscene Publications Act 1959 focuses attention upon the words or article published, not the intention of the author or publisher. The test of obscenity depends on the article itself. Section 5 of the Public Order Act 1936 has been significantly amended by the addition of a new section, 5A. The Race Relations Act 1976, s.70 (2), by providing that section 5A be added, has made it unnecessary to prove an intention to provoke a breach of the peace in order to secure a conviction for incitement to racial hatred. All this makes legal sense in a plural society which recognises the human rights and fundamental freedoms of the European Convention [Convention for the Protection of Human Rights and Fundamental Freedoms (1950) (Cmd. 8969)]. Article 9 provides that every one has the right to freedom of religion, and the right to manifest his religion in worship, teaching, practice and observance. By necessary implication the article imposes a duty on all of us to refrain from insulting or outraging the religious feelings of others. Article 10 provides that every one shall have the right to freedom of expression. The exercise of this freedom "carries with it duties and responsibilities" and may be subject to such restrictions as are prescribed by law and are necessary "for the prevention of disorder or crime, for the protection of health or morals, for the protection of the reputation or rights of others . . ." It would be intolerable if by allowing an author or publisher to plead the excellence of his motives and the right of free speech he could evade the penalties of the law even though his words were blasphemous in the sense of constituting an outrage upon the religious feelings of his fellow citizens. This is no way forward for a successful plural society. Accordingly, the test of obscenity by concentrating attention on the words complained of is, in my judgment, equally valuable as a test of blasphemy. The character of the words published matter; but not the motive of the author or publisher.

For these reasons as well as for those developed in the speeches of my noble and learned friends, Viscount Dilhorne and Lord Russell of Killowen, with both of which I agree, I would dismiss these appeals.

Appeal dismissed.

Notes

1. The law relating to incitement to racial hatred is now to be found in the Public Order Act 1986, Part VII.

2. Contrast with the views of Lord Scarman those of the Law Commission expressed in *Offences against Religion and Public Worship* (1985) Law Com. No. 145.

3. Is Lord Scarman's view of the meaning of Article 10 of the European Convention of Human Rights the only possible view? Would the enactment of the Convention as part of domestic law remove the divergency of judicial views as to what the law should be on any particular issue?

The obligation of confidentiality

Attorney-General v. Jonathan Cape Ltd.
[1976] 1 Q.B. 752
Queen's Bench Division

From 1964 to 1970, Mr. R.H.S. Crossman, while a Cabinet Minister, with the knowledge of his Cabinet colleagues, kept a diary in which he recorded Cabinet discussions and political events. In 1975, after his death, extracts from the diary appeared in the *Sunday Times* and the Attorney-General applied for injunctions to restrain further publication.

Lord Widgery L.C.J.: It has always been assumed by lawyers and, I suspect, by politicians, and the Civil Service, that Cabinet proceedings and Cabinet papers are secret, and cannot be publicly disclosed until they have passed into history. It is quite clear that no court will compel the production of Cabinet papers in the course of discovery in an action,[1] and the Attorney-General contends that not only will the court refuse to compel the production of such matters, but it will go further and positively forbid the disclosure of such papers and proceedings if publication will be contrary to the public interest.

The basis of this contention is the confidential character of these papers and proceedings, derived from the convention of joint Cabinet responsibility whereby any policy decision reached by the Cabinet has to be supported thereafter by all members of the Cabinet whether they approve of it or not, unless they feel compelled to resign. It is contended that Cabinet decisions and papers are confidential for a period to the extent at least that they must not be referred to outside the Cabinet in such a way as to disclose the attitude of individual Ministers in the argument which preceded the decision. Thus, there may be no objection to a Minister disclosing (or leaking, as it was called) the fact that a Cabinet meeting has taken place, or, indeed, the decision taken, so long as the individual views of Ministers are not identified.

There is no doubt that Mr. Crossman's manuscripts contain frequent references to individual opinions of Cabinet Ministers, and this is not suprising because it was his avowed object to obtain a relaxation of the convention regarding memoirs of ex-Ministers to which Sir John Hunt referred. There have, as far as I know, been no previous attempts in any court to define the extent to which Cabinet proceedings should be treated as secret or confidential, and it is not surprising that different views on this subject are contained in the evidence before me. The Attorney-General does not attempt a final definition but his contention is that such proceedings are confidential and their publication is capable of control by the courts at least as far as they include (a) disclosure of Cabinet documents or proceedings in such a way as to reveal the individual views or attitudes of Ministers; (b) disclosure of confidential advice from civil servants, whether contained in Cabinet papers or not; (c) disclosure of confidential discussions affecting the appointment or transfer of such senior civil servants.

The Attorney-General contends that all Cabinet papers and discussions are prima facie confidential, and that the court should restrain any disclosure thereof if the public interest in concealment outweighs the public interest in a right to free publication. The Attorney-General further contends that, if it is shown that the public interest is involved, he has the right and duty to bring the matter before the court. In this contention he is well supported by Lord Salmon in *Reg.* v. *Lewes Justices, Ex parte Secretary of State for the Home Department* [1973] A.C. 388, 412, where Lord Salmon said:

"when it is in the public interest that confidentiality shall be safeguarded,

---

[1] *Post*, p. 436 *et seq.*

then the party from whom the confidential document or the confidential information is being sought may lawfully refuse it. In such a case the Crown may also intervene to prevent production or disclosure of that which in the public interest ought to be protected."

. . . . .

The defendants' main contention is that whatever the limits of the convention of joint Cabinet responsibility may be, there is no obligation enforceable at law to prevent the publication of Cabinet papers and proceedings, except in extreme cases where national security is involved. In other words, the defendants submit that the confidential character of Cabinet papers and discussions is based on a true convention as defined in the evidence of Professor Henry Wade, namely, an obligation founded in conscience only. Accordingly, the defendants contend that publication of these Diaries is not capable of control by any order of this court.

If the Attorney-General were restricted in his argument to the general proposition that Cabinet papers and discussion are all under the seal of secrecy at all times, he would be in difficulty. It is true that he has called evidence from eminent former holders of office to the effect that the public interest requires a continuing secrecy, and he cites a powerful passage from the late Viscount Hailsham to this effect. The extract comes from a copy of the Official Report (House of Lords) for December 21, 1932, [at col. 527] in the course of a debate on Cabinet secrecy.

The defendants, however, in the present action, have also called distinguished former Cabinet Ministers who do not support this view of Lord Hailsham, and it seems to me that the degree of protection afforded to Cabinet papers and discussion cannot be determined by a single rule of thumb. Some secrets require a high standard of protection for a short time. Others require protection until a new political generation has taken over. In the present action against the literary executors, the Attorney-General asks for a perpetual injunction to restrain further publication of the Diaries in whole or in part. I am far from convinced that he has made out a case that the public interest requires such a Draconian remedy when due regard is had to other public interests, such as the freedom of speech: see Lord Denning M.R. in *In re X (A Minor) (Wardship: Jurisdiction)* [1975] Fam. 47.

Some attempt has been made to say that the publication of these Diaries by Mr. Crossman would have been a breach of his oath as a Privy Councillor, and an echo of this argument is, of course, to be found in Lord Hailsham's words recently quoted. This is, however, not seriously relied upon in the two actions now before me, and the Attorney-General concedes that the present defendants are not in breach of the Official Secrets Acts. It seems to me, therefore, that the Attorney-General must first show that whatever obligation of secrecy or discretion attaches to former Cabinet Ministers, that obligation is binding in law and not merely in morals.

I have read affidavits from a large number of leading politicians, and the facts, so far as relevant, appear to be these. In 1964, 1966 and 1969 the Prime Minister (who was in each case Mr. Harold Wilson) issued a confidential document to Cabinet Ministers containing guidance on certain questions of procedure. Paragraph 72 of the 1969 edition provides:

"The principle of collective responsibility and the obligation not to disclose information acquired whilst holding Ministerial office apply to former Ministers who are contemplating the publication of material based upon their recollections of the conduct of Cabinet and Cabinet committee business in which they took part."

The general understanding of Ministers while in office was that information obtained from Cabinet sources was secret and not to be disclosed to outsiders.

There is not much evidence of the understanding of Ministers as to the protection of such information after the Minister retires. It seems probable to me that those not desirous of publishing memoirs assumed that the protection went on until the incident was 30 years old, whereas those interested in memoirs would discover on inquiry at the Cabinet Office that draft memoirs were normally submitted to the Secretary of the Cabinet for his advice on their contents before publication. Manuscripts were almost always submitted to the Secretary of the Cabinet in accordance with the last-mentioned procedure. ... In recent years, successive Secretaries of the Cabinet, when giving advice on the publication of a Minister's memoirs, were much concerned about (a) disclosure of individual views of Members of the Cabinet in defiance of the principle of joint responsibility; (b) disclosure of advice given by civil servants still in office; (c) disclosure of discussions relating to the promotion or transfer of senior civil servants.

Mr. Crossman, as appears from the introduction to volume one of his Diaries, disapproved of the submission of manuscripts to the Secretary of the Cabinet. He made no attempt to admit the three categories of information just referred to, and expressed the intention to obtain publication whilst memories were green.

Mr. Crossman made no secret of the fact that he kept a diary which he intended to use for the writing of his memoirs. It was contended on behalf of the literary executors that any bond of confidence or secrecy normally attending upon Cabinet material had been lifted in Mr. Crossman's case by consent of his colleagues. Even if, as a matter of law, a Minister can release himself from a bond of secrecy in this way, I do not find that Mr. Crossman effectively did so. It is not enough to show that his colleagues accepted the keeping of the diary. It was vital to show that they accepted Mr. Crossman's intention to use the diary whether it passed the scrutiny of the Secretary of the Cabinet or not.

· · · · ·

I have already indicated some of the difficulties which face the Attorney-General when he relied simply on the public interest as a ground for his actions. That such ground is enough in extreme cases is shown by the universal agreement that publication affecting national security can be restrained in this way. It may be that in the short run (for example, over a period of weeks or months) the public interest is equally compelling to maintain joint Cabinet responsibility and the protection of advice given by civil servants, but I would not accept without close investigation that such matters must, as a matter of course, retain protection after a period of years.

However, the Attorney-General has a powerful reinforcement for his argument in the developing equitable doctrine that a man shall not profit from the wrongful publication of information received by him in confidence. This doctrine, said to have its origin in *Prince Albert* v. *Strange* (1849) 1 H. & T. 1, has been frequently recognised as a ground for restraining the unfair use of commercial secrets transmitted in confidence. Sometimes in these cases there is a contract which may be said to have been breached by the breach of confidence, but it is clear that the doctrine applies independently of contract: see *Saltman Engineering Co. Ltd.* v. *Campbell Engineering Co. Ltd.* (1948) 65 R.P.C. 203.

Even so, these defendants argue that an extension of the principle of the *Argyll*[2] case to the present dispute involves another large and unjustified leap forward, because in the present case the Attorney-General is seeking to apply the principle to public secrets made confidential in the interests of good government. I cannot see why the courts should be powerless to restrain the publication of public secrets, while enjoying the *Argyll* powers in regard to domestic secrets. Indeed, as already pointed out, the court must have power to deal with publication which threatens national security, and the difference between such a case and the present case is one of degree rather than kind. I conclude, therefore, that when a Cabinet Minister receives information in confidence the improper publication of

[2] *Argyll (Margaret, Duchess of)* v. *Argyll (Duke of)* [1967] Ch. 302.

such information can be restrained by the court, and his obligation is not merely to observe a gentleman's agreement to refrain from publication.

It is convenient next to deal with the submission that the evidence does not prove the existence of a convention as to collective responsibility, or adequately define a sphere of secrecy. I find overwhelming evidence that the doctrine of joint responsibility is generally understood and practised and equally strong evidence that it is on occasion ignored. The general effect of the evidence is that the doctrine is an established feature of the English form of government, and it follows that some matters leading up to a Cabinet decision may be regarded as confidential. Futhermore, I am persuaded that the nature of the confidence is that spoken for by the Attorney-General, namely, that since the confidence is imposed to enable the efficient conduct of the Queen's business, the confidence is owed to the Queen and cannot be released by the members of Cabinet themselves. I have been told that a resigning Minister who wishes to make a personal statement in the House, and to disclose matters which are confidential under the doctrine obtains the consent of the Queen for this purpose. Such consent is obtained through the Prime Minister. I have not been told what happened when the Cabinet disclosed divided opinions during the European Economic Community referendum. But even if there was here a breach of confidence (which I doubt) this is no ground for denying the existence of the general rule. I cannot accept the suggestion that a Minister owes no duty of confidence in respect of his own views expressed in Cabinet. It would only need one or two Ministers to describe their own view to enable experienced observers to identify the views of the others.

. . . . .

The Cabinet is at the very centre of national affairs, and must be in possession at all times of information which is secret or confidential. Secrets relating to national security may require to be preserved indefinitely. Secrets relating to new taxation proposals may be of the highest importance until Budget day, but public knowledge thereafter. To leak a Cabinet decision a day or so before it is officially announced is an accepted exercise in public relations, but to identify the Ministers who voted one way or another is objectionable because it undermines the doctrine of joint responsibility.

It is evident that there cannot be a single rule governing the publication of such a variety of matters. In these actions we are concerned with the publication of diaries at a time when 11 years have expired since the first recorded events. The Attorney-General must show (a) that such publication would be a breach of confidence; (b) that the public interest requires that the publication be restrained, and (c) that there are no other facts of the public interest contradictory of and more compelling than that relied upon. Moreover, the court, when asked to restrain such a publication, must closely examine the extent to which relief is necessary to ensure that restrictions are not imposed beyond the strict requirement of public need.

Applying those principles to the present case, what do we find? In my judgment, the Attorney-General has made out his claim that the expression of individual opinions by Cabinet Ministers in the course of Cabinet discussion are matters of confidence, the publication of which can be restrained by the court when this is clearly necessary in the public interest.

The maintenance of the doctrine of joint responsibility within the Cabinet is in the public interest, and the application of that doctrine might be prejudiced by premature disclosure of the views of individual Ministers.

There must, however, be a limit in time after which the confidential character of the information, and the duty of the court to restrain publication, will lapse. Since the conclusion of the hearing in this case I have had the opportunity to read the whole of volume one of the Diaries, and my considered view is that I cannot believe that the publication at this interval of anything in volume one would inhibit free discussion in the Cabinet of today, even though the individuals involved are the same, and the national problems have a distressing similarity with those of a decade ago. It is unnecessary to elaborate the evils which might flow if at the close of a Cabinet meeting a Minister proceeded to give the press an analysis of the voting, but we are dealing in this case with a disclosure of information nearly 10 years later.

It may, of course, be intensely difficult in a particular case, to say at what point the material loses its confidential character, on the ground that publication will no longer undermine the doctrine of joint Cabinet responsibility. It is this difficulty which prompts some to argue that Cabinet discussions should retain their confidential character for a longer and arbitrary period such as 30 years, or even for all time, but this seems to me to be excessively restrictive. The court should intervene only in the clearest of cases where the continuing confidentiality of the material can be demonstrated. In less clear cases—and this, in my view, is certainly one—reliance must be placed on the good sense and good taste of the Minister or ex-Minister concerned.

In the present case there is nothing in Mr. Crossman's work to suggest that he did not support the doctrine of joint Cabinet responsibility. The question for the court is whether it is shown that publication now might damage the doctrine notwithstanding that much of the action is up to 10 years old and three general elections have been held meanwhile. So far as the Attorney-General relies in his argument on the disclosure of individual ministerial opinions, he has not satisfied me that publication would in any way inhibit free and open discussion in Cabinet hereafter.

It remains to deal with the Attorney-General's two further argument's, namely, (a) that the Diaries disclose advice given by senior civil servants who cannot be expected to advise frankly if their advice is not treated as confidential; (b) the Diaries disclose observations made by Ministers on the capacity of individual senior civil servants and their suitability for specific appointments. I can see no ground in law which entitle the court to restrain publication of these matters. A Minister is, no doubt, responsible for his department and accountable for its errors even though the individual fault is to be found in his subordinates. In these circumstances, to disclose the fault of the subordinate may amount to cowardice or bad taste, but I can find no ground for saying that either the Crown or the individual civil servant has an enforceable right to have the advice which he gives treated as confidential for all time.

For these reasons I do not think that the court should interfere with the publication of volume one of the Diaries, and I propose, therefore, to refuse the injunction sought but to grant liberty to apply in regard to material other than volume one if it is alleged that different considerations may there have to be applied.

Confidentiality and Public Interest

Francome v. Mirror Group Newspapers Ltd.
[1984] 1 W.L.R. 892
Court of Appeal

Unidentified persons tapped telephone conversations made to and from the plaintiffs' home. The eavesdroppers offered for sale to a national newspaper tapes of the telephone conversations which it was alleged revealed breaches of the rules of racing by the first plaintiff, a well-known jockey. The plaintiffs became aware of the existence of the tapes when two journalists employed by the newspaper approached the first plaintiff to confirm the authenticity of tapes. Thereupon the plaintiffs issued a writ against the newspaper, its editor and the two journalists claiming, inter alia, damages for breach of confidence. On the plaintiffs' application for interlocutory relief, Bingham J. ordered, inter alia, that the defendants be restrained until trial from publishing any article based on the contents of the tapes. The defendants appealed to The Court of Appeal (Sir John Donaldson M.R., Fox and Stephen Brown L.JJ.) which allowed the appeal in relation to issues not here relevant but upheld the granting of an interlocutory injunction.

SIR JOHN DONALDSON M.R.: ... The plaintiffs say that the defendants cannot be allowed to make any use of the tapes or of the conversations which they record. There is a two-fold basis for this contention. The first is that both the eavesdroppers and the defendants know full well that the conversations were confidential. Although users of the telephone take the risk of crossed lines and of official telephone tapping, they are entitled to regard their conversations as confidential and anyone overhearing those conversations knows that that is the position. It is therefore idle for an eavesdropper, and particularly a deliberate eavesdropper, to contend that he did not know that the conversations were confidential. The plaintiffs say that in the circumstances revealed by the evidence, the defendants were in the same position as the eavesdroppers. Both were under a duty to preserve the confidentiality of the plaintiff's private conversations.

The second basis for this contention is that, as the defendants well knew, tapes and transcripts came into existence by means of acts which constituted criminal offences under the Wireless Telegraphy Act 1949 and, as the plaintiffs say, disclosure of, inter alia, the contents of the messages contained in those conversations would also constitute such an offence. ... The defendants accept that the plaintiffs may have various causes of action against the eavesdroppers, but rightly say that this is not directly relevant. They go on to say that the plaintiffs have no right of action against them. So far as trespass is concerned, they were not parties to it. This may well be right. They go on to say that there is no cause of action against them or the eavesdroppers for breach of an obligation of confidentiality. The authority for this rather surprising proposition is said to be *Malone* v. *Metropolitan Police Commissioner* [1979] Ch. 344. Suffice it to say that Sir Robert Megarry V.-C. expressly stated, at p. 384, that he was deciding nothing on the position when tapping was effected for purposes other than the prevention, detection and discovery of crime and criminals or by persons other than the police. This is thus a live issue.

The defendants then go on to submit that whatever their obligations towards the plaintiffs upon grounds of confidentiality, they can rely upon the classic, but ill-defined, exception of what is quaintly called "iniquity." The basis of this exception is that whilst there is a public interest in maintaining confidentiality, there is a countervailing public interest in exposing conduct which involves a breach of the law or which is "anti-social." I use the term "anti-social," without defining it, to describe activities which, whilst not in breach of the law, are seriously contrary to the public interest. In the defendants' submission the tapes revealed breaches by Mr. Francome of the rules of racing and, bearing in mind the large sums of money which are staked on the results of the races, this conduct they say is "anti-social" within the meaning of the inquity rule and may also involve criminal offences. Let me say at once that it is not for me to say whether the tapes bear this interpretation and I express no view on that point. That will also be an issue. . . .

The Wireless Telegraphy Act 1949
    Section 5 is in the following terms:

> "Any person who— . . . (b) otherwise than under the authority of the Post-master General or in the course of his duty as a servant of the Crown, either—(i) uses any wireless telegraphy apparatus with intent to obtain information as to the contents, sender or addressee of any message (whether sent by means of wireless telegraphy or not) which neither the person using the apparatus nor any person on whose behalf he is acting is authorised by the Postmaster General to receive; or (ii) except in the course of legal proceedings or for the purpose of any report thereof, discloses any information as to the contents, sender or addressee of any such message, being information which would not have come to his knowledge but for the use of wireless telegraphy apparatus by him or by another person, shall be guilty of an offence under this Act."

Section 14 is headed "Penalties and legal proceedings." It prescribes penalties for offences, including offences under section 5, and continues in subsection (7):

> "Nothing in the preceding provisions of this section shall limit any right of any person to bring civil proceedings in respect of the doing or apprehended doing of anything rendered unlawful by any provision of this Act . . ."

For the defendants it is submitted that this subsection shows that section 5 gives rise to no right enforceable by a private individual: see the judgment of Lord Denning M.R. in *McCall* v. *Abelesz* [1976] 1 Q.B. 585. It would follow, so it is submitted, that the plaintiffs have no right to rely upon section 5 of the Act of 1949.
    Suffice it to say that I am far from sure that the plaintiffs do not have rights under the Act of 1949, if they have suffered damage by breach of the Act which is special to them: see *Gouriet* v. *Union of Post Office Workers* [1978] A.C. 435. This again will be an issue.
    Mr. Molloy, the editor of the *Daily Mirror*, adverted to the Act of 1949 in his affidavit. He said in paragraph 3:

> "I have not yet finally decided whether to publish this story and its exact wording will depend upon further inquiries . . . Any story will be carefully vetted by a barrister in the first defendant's legal department and I shall also have to give careful consideration to the probability that publication would be an offence under section 5(*b*) of the Wireless and Telegraphy Act, although I would not regard this fact as an absolute bar to publication if I considered that publication was justifiable in the public interest."

I draw attention to the use of the word "probability" which I regard as wholly accurate. Mr Molloy thus claims the right in what he judges to be the public interest to comply or not comply with the law of the land made by Parliament by the constitutional processes. Furthermore, his counsel submits that it is not for any civil court to restrain him or to make any order which might incidentally have this effect, although not couched in the terms of the statute.
    I hope that Mr. Molloy will acquit me of discourtesy if I say with all the emphasis at my command that I regard his assertion as arrogant and wholly unacceptable. Parliamentary democracy as we know it is based upon the rule of law. That

requires all citizens to obey the law, unless and until it can be changed by due process. There are no privileged classes to whom it does not apply. If Mr. Molloy and the *Daily Mirror* can assert this right to act on the basis that the public interest, as he sees it, justifies breaches of the criminal law, so can any other citizen. This has only to be stated for it to be obvious that the result would be anarchy.

It is sometimes said, although to be fair to Mr. Molloy he has not said it, that all are free to break the law if they are prepared to pay the penalty. This is pernicious nonsense. The right to disobey the law is not obtainable by the payment of a penalty or licence fee. It is not obtainable at all in a parliamentary democracy, although different considerations arise under a totalitarian regime.

In saying this I nevertheless recognise that, in very rare circumstances, a situation can arise in which the citizen is faced with a conflict between what is, in effect, two inconsistent laws. The first law is the law of the land. The second is a moral imperative, usually, but not always, religious in origin. An obvious example is the priest's obligation of silence in relation to the confessional, but others can be given. In conducting the business of the courts, judges seek to avoid any such conflict, but occasionally it is unavoidable. Yielding to the moral imperative does not excuse a breach of the law of the land, but it is understandable and in some circumstances may even be praiseworthy. However, I cannot over-emphasise the rarity of the moral imperative. Furthermore, it is almost unheard of for compliance with the moral imperative to be in the financial or other best interests of the person concerned. Anyone who conceives himself to be morally obliged to break the law, should also ask himself whether such a course furthers his own interests. If it does, he would be well advised to re-examine his conscience.

The "media," to use a term which comprises not only the newspapers, but also television and radio, are an essential foundation of any democracy. In exposing crime, anti-social behaviour and hypocrisy and in campaigning for reform and propagating the views of minorities, they perform an invaluable function. However, they are peculiarly vulnerable to the error of confusing the public interest with their own interest. Usually these interest march hand in hand, but not always. In the instant case, pending a trial, it is impossible to see what public interest would be served by publishing the contents of the tapes which would not equally be served by giving them to the police or to the Jockey Club. Any wider publication could only serve the interests of the *Daily Mirror*. . . . I stress, once again, that we are not at this stage concerned to determine the final rights of the parties. Our duty is to make such orders, if any, as are appropriate pending the trial of the action. It is sometimes said that this involves a weighing of the balance of convenience. This is an unfortunate expression. Our business is justice, not convenience. We can and must disregard fanciful claims by either party. Subject to that, we must contemplate the possibility that either party may succeed and must do our best to ensure that nothing occurs pending the trial which will prejudice his rights. Since the parties are usually asserting wholly inconsistent claims, this is difficult, but we have to do our best. In so doing, we are seeking a balance of justice, not of convenience. . . . Such disclosure as has taken place in affidavits is authorised by the exception in section 5 of the Wireless Telegraphy Act 1949 as being a disclosure "in the course of legal proceedings." For the injunction granted by the judge, I would substitute an injunction restraining "the defendants by themselves, their servants or agents from disclosing, otherwise than under the authority of the appropriate minister of the Crown as the successor of the Postmaster General or in the course of legal proceedings, any information as to the contents, sender or addressee of any telephone messages passing to or from telephones at the home of the plaintiffs, being information which would not have come to the knowledge of the defendants, but for the use or wireless telegraphy apparatus "by the defendants or any of them or by another person."".

The defendants have submitted that such an injunction can only be granted at the suit of the Attorney-General. I disagree. We have a complete discretion as to what order to make in order best to preserve the rights of the parties. In my judgment an order forbidding the defendants to commit what would probably constitute a criminal offence, but otherwise leaving them free to pursue such course as they deem proper, will best achieve this object.

Assuming that the tapes reveal evidence of the commission of a criminal offence or a breach of the rules of racing—and I stress that this is an assumption—it may well be in the public interest that the tapes and all the information to be gleaned therefrom be made available to the police and to the Jockey Club. Accepting the defendants' expressed desire to promote the public interest, it will be open for them to apply to the appropriate minister of the Crown for authority to disclose all the information to one or other or both of these authorities. Furthermore, if the defendants wish to publish statements which are prima facie defamatory of Mr. Francome—and they have disavowed any intention of making such statements about Mrs. Francome—the exception contained in the injunction which I propose and in the section of the Act of 1949 will leave them free to use the tapes as evidence in support of a plea of justification.

I would allow the appeal accordingly.

Appeal allowed in part.

Lion Laboratories v. Evans
[1985] 1 Q.B. 526
Court of Appeal

The plaintiffs manufactured a device (the Lion Intoximeter 3000) used by police to test the breath of drivers suspected of driving having more than the permitted statutory quantity of alcohol in their blood. Two employees of the plaintiffs offered to newspapers for publication confidential memoranda which cast doubt on the accuracy of the device. The newspapers maintained that, as the proper functioning of the instrument was of the utmost importance for drivers who were tested by the instrument and, on the basis of its readings, were charged, and possibly convicted, for drunken driving with consequences which followed, it was important for the public to be informed of the instrument's doubtful functioning. The plaintiffs claimed an injunction and damages for breach of confidentiality and copyright. Pending the trial Leonard J. issued an interlocutory injunction restraining publication by the newspapers. The Court of Appeal (Stephenson, O'Connor and Griffiths L.JJ.) discharged the interlocutory injunction.

STEPHENSON L.J.: . . . The problem before the judge and before this court is how best to resolve, before trial, a conflict of two competing public interests. The first public interest is the preservation of the right of organisations, as of individuals, to keep secret confidential information. The courts will restrain breaches of confidence, and breaches of copyright, unless there is just cause or excuse for breaking confidence or infringing copyright. The just cause or excuse with which this case is concerned is the public interest in admittedly confidential information. There is confidential information which the public may have a right to receive and others, in particular the press, now extended to the media, may have a right and even a duty to publish, even if the information has been unlawfully obtained in flagrant breach of confidence and irrespective of the motive of the informer. The duty of confidence, the public interest in maintaining it, is a restriction on the freedom of the press which is recognised by our law, as well as by article 10(2) of the Convention for the Protection of Human Rights and Fundamental Freedoms (1953)(Cmd. 8969); the duty to publish, the countervailing interest of the public in being kept informed of matters which are of real public concern, is an inroad on the privacy of confidential matters.[1] . . . .

There are four further considerations. First, "there is a wide difference between what is interesting to the public and what it is in the public interest to make known" said Lord Wilberforce in *British Steel Corporation* v. *Granada Television Ltd.*, at p. 1168. The public are interested in many private matters which are no real concern of theirs and which the public have no pressing need to know. Secondly, the media have a private interest of their own in publishing what appeals to the public and may increase their circulation or the numbers of their viewers or listeners; and (I quote from Sir John Donaldson M.R. in *Francome* v. *Mirror Group Newspapers Ltd.* [1984] 1 W.L.R. 892, 898B), "they are peculiarly vulnerable to the error of confusing the public interest with their own interest." Thirdly, there are cases in which the public interest is best served by an informer giving the confidential information, not to the press but to the police or some other responsible body, as was suggested by Lord Denning M.R. in *Initial Services Ltd.* v. *Putterill* [1968] 1 Q.B. 396, 405–406 and by Sir John Donaldson M.R. in

---

[1] Stephenson L.J. then referred to "the illuminating judgments of Lord Denning M.R. in *Initial Services Ltd.* v. *Putterill* [1968] 1 Q.B. 396; *Fraser* v. *Evans* [1969] 1 Q.B. 349; *Hubbard* v. *Vosper* [1972] 2 Q.B. 84; *Woodward* v. *Hutchins* [1977] 1 W.L.R. 760. He also cited Lord Denning M.R.'s dissenting judgment in *Schering Chemicals Ltd.* v. *Falkman Ltd.* [1982] Q.B. 1 and the speeches of Lord Wilberforce, Lord Salmon and Lord Fraser of Tulleybelton in *British Steel Corporation* v. *Granada Television Ltd.* [1981] A.C. 1096.

Francome v. *Mirror Group Newspapers Ltd.* [1984] 1 W.L.R. 892, 898. Fourthly, it was said by Wood V.-C.in 1856, in *Gartside* v. *Outram* (1856) 26. L.J.Ch. 113, 114, "there is no confidence as to the disclosure of iniquity"; and though Mr. Hoolahan concedes on the plaintiffs' behalf that, as Salmon L.J. said in *Initial Services Ltd.* v. *Putterill* [1968] 1 Q.B. 396, 410, "what was iniquity in 1856 may be too narrow or . . . too wide for 1967," and in 1984 extends to serious misdeeds or grave misconduct, he submits that misconduct of that kind is necessary to destroy the duty of confidence or excuse the breach of it, and nothing of that sort is alleged against the plaintiffs in the evidence now before the court.

I agree with the judge in rejecting the "no iniquity, no public interest" rule; and in respectfully adopting what Lord Denning M.R. said in *Fraser* v. *Evans* [1969] 1 Q.B. 349, 362, that some things are required to be disclosed in the public interest, in which case no confidence can be prayed in aid to keep them secret, and "[iniquity] is merely an instance of just cause or excuse for breaking confidence."

GRIFFITHS L.J.: . . . The first question to be determined is whether there exists a defence of public interest to actions for breach of confidentiality and copyright, and if so, whether it is limited to situations in which there has been serious wrongdoing by the plaintiffs—the so-called "iniquity" rule.

I am quite satisfied that the defence of public interest is now well established in actions for breach of confidence and, although there is less authority on the point, that it also extends to breach of copyright: see by way of example *Fraser* v. *Evans* [1969] 1 Q.B. 349; *Hubbard* v. *Vosper* [1972] 2 Q.B. 84; *Woodward* v. *Hutchins* [1977] 1 W.L.R. 760 and *British Steel Corporation* v. *Granada Television Ltd.* [1981] A.C. 1096.

I can see no sensible reason why this defence should be limited to cases in which there has been wrongdoing on the part of the plaintiffs. I believe that the so-called iniquity rule envolved because in most cases where the facts justified a publication in breach of confidence, it was because the plaintiff had behaved so disgracefully or criminally that it was judged in the public interest that his behaviour should be exposed. No doubt it is in such circumstances that the defence will usually arise, but it is not difficult to think of instances where, although there has been no wrongdoing on the part of the plaintiff, it may be vital in the public interest to publish a part of his confidential information.

. . . .

When there is an admitted breach of confidence and breach of copyright, there will usually be a powerful case for maintaining the status quo by the grant of an interlocutory injunction to restrain publication until trial of the action. It will, I judge, be an exceptional case in which a defence of public interest which does not involve iniquity on the part of the plaintiff will justify refusing the injunction. But I am bound to say that I think this is such a case.

Attorney-General v. The Observer Ltd.
The Times, February 11, 1988
Court of Appeal

After a number of earlier reported decisions relating to claims for interlocutory injunctions (*Attorney-General* v. *Guardian Newspapers Ltd*. [1987] 1 W.L.R. 1248) and contempt of court (see *Attorney-General* v. *Newspaper Publishing Plc*. [1987] 3 W.L.R. 942, *ante* p. 169 the substantive question whether the Crown was entitled to permanent injunctions to restrain newspapers from publishing information contained in *Spycatcher*, the memoirs of Mr. Peter Wright, a former member of MI5 was litigated before Scott J. His Lordship concluded that the Crown was not entitled to permanent injunctions *inter alia* on the grounds that there was a public interest in knowing of some of the allegations contained in the book (*e.g.* a plot to assassinate President Nasser) and that the information contained in the book had been so widely disseminated that it was no longer confidential. Publication of extracts from the book in *The Sunday Times* did constitute a breach of confidentiality and the Crown was entitled to an account of profits. The Attorney General appealed to the Court of Appeal (Sir John Donaldson M.R., Dillon and Bingham L.JJ.) *The Sunday Times* cross-appealed.

Lord Justice Dillon said that the main English authority relied on as showing what the court's approach should be to the balancing exercise when the Crown sought to restrain publication of confidential material on grounds of protecting the public interest was the decision of Lord Widgery C.J. in *Attorney General* v. *Jonathan Cape Ltd*.

The issue there was that the Crown has sought to restrain, on public interest and confidentiality grounds, the publishing of the diaries which a Cabinet Minister had kept while in office and which included his accounts of the proceedings of Cabinet committees whose meetings he had attended.

Lord Widgery's judgment had been accepted as a correct statement of the law and applied by Mr. Justice Mason in the High Court of Australia in *Commonwealth of Australia* v. *John Fairfax & Son Ltd*. ((1980) 147 C.L.R. 39).

Those cases contained the tests which the court had to apply to the issues in the present case. They recognized that there was an important public interest in freedom of speech which had in any balancing exercise to be weighed against the other interests involved.

His Lordship turned to consider the issue whether the judge has been right to refuse to continue the injunctions because of the publication of *Spycatcher* in the United States and elsewhere. That involved considering the publication of the book as a whole.

Accordingly, questions which had been discussed in argument, such as how far publication was franked by the iniquity defence, how far particular allegations of iniquity had already been inquired into and whether there was any genuine basis for regarding previous inquiries as unsatisfactory and whether the subject matter of particular allegations could no longer be regarded as secret because they had been published before in this country, were merely aspects of the general test, and not separate questions the court had to answer.

Obviously the fact that *Spycatcher* had been so widely published in the United States and other countries had had the effect that all the contents were well-known to every hostile, or potentially hostile, power which was at all interested in the activities of the British security services.

Any adverse effect which publication would be likely to have on the readiness of the intelligence services of friendly powers to impart confidential information to the British services had by now largely been suffered.

His Lordship doubted whether that effect could have been all that great, since the intelligence services of friendly powers must already have been too well aware of the cases of Maclean, Burgess, Philby, Blunt, Blake and others and of the publication of Mr. Chapman Pincher's books.

The Crown relied on other aspects of inquiry to the public interest which, it was submitted, would be likely to be suffered if the injunctions were not continued permanently.

Among the more important were the risk that Mr. Wright might be moved to make further disclosures and the risk that other present or past members of the security services might be harassed or cajoled by the media into disclosing further secrets either for gain or from a more honourable, if misplaced, desire to set the record straight and refute statements made in *Spycatcher* which they believed to be calumnies.

As against those matters it was urged that any former member of the security services who was minded to make any disclosure of secret information would have to emigrate and leave the country for good in order to avoid prosecution.

More fundamentally, there was the point that (whether or not anything in the book was technically still confidential) for the courts to continue the injunctions further would be futile and just plain silly, now that *Spycatcher* had been so widely circulated.

The arguments for or against the continuation of the injunctions were set out as persuasively as possible each way in the speeches of Lord Templeman and Lord Ackner on the one hand and Lord Bridge of Harwich and Lord Oliver of Aylmerton on the other hand in the recent interlocutory hearing ([1988] 1 W.L.R. 1248).

Nothing said there bound the court, since the actual decision was merely to continue the injunctions until trial. His Lordship preferred, without hesitation, the views of Lord Bridge and Lord Oliver.

Accordingly, the injunctions should not be continued against any of the three newspapers. No injunction should be granted to restrain any public library from stocking copies of *Spycatcher* or lending them out, or to restrain booksellers from stocking copies of the book bought from abroad.

That conclusion was reached by the balancing exercise indicated by Lord Widgery, on which the appropriateness of the remedy had often to be one of the factors.

The court was not constrained to follow beyond the point of absurdity the logic of Mr. Alexander's argument that any person who came into possession of information contained in *Spycatcher*, knowing as he must that that information had been published by Mr. Wright in breach of his duty of secrecy, necessarily came under the same duty of secrecy and was precluded in conscience from disseminating that information any further.

The continuation of the injunctions was not necessary to protect the public interest in national security and would go beyond any strict requirement of public need, when due regard was had to the public interest in freedom of speech.

It was generally accepted that matters stated or read out in open court might be taken down and then published as part of a fair report of the proceedings unless the court had ordered otherwise.

That general principle had nothing to do with *The Observer* and *The Guardian* articles of June 22 and 23, since they had been published before any hearing in open court of the Australian proceedings had begun.

The newspapers had been fully entitled to report, as a matter of public interest to their readers, that proceedings were due to be heard in court in Sydney. The question was whether they were entitled to go further and include the brief descriptions of some of the matters mentioned in Mr. Wright's memoirs.

That involved a balancing act in the light of all the circumstances. The court had been fully entitled to infer that the journalists must have received the information on which they had based the articles either from someone in the offices of the

Australian publishers or from someone in the offices of the Australian solicitors for Mr. Wright and the publishers.

The court should also infer that *The Observer* and *The Guardian* were aware of the undertakings against disclosure then subsisting in the Australian proceedings.

His Lordship could not see how the injunctions in the Australian proceedings could operate extra-territorially. The question was whether on a proper balancing exercise *The Observer* and *The Guardian* was entitled by English law to publish such details as they had done in the two articles.

They were only seeking in June 1986 to report the nature of the Australian proceedings, which was a matter of public interest. There was nothing at that stage to suggest that they then intended to go beyond reporting the nature of the proceedings and then reporting the proceedings as they came on.

The articles had been brief and had given little detail of the allegations. In so far as the detail given went beyond what had been previously published, his Lordship could see no detriment to national security or the public interest, to outweigh the benefit of free speech and the advantage in the public interest of restrained and responsible but adequately detailed reports of the Australian proceedings.

Applying Lord Widgery's test again, *The Observer* and *The Guardian* were entitled to publish those June 1986 articles.

The judge had distinguished between those articles and the serialization in *The Sunday Times* on the ground that the extract in *The Sunday Times* had been "indiscriminate."

The important question in the context of the case was not whether the editor had published indiscriminately but whether he had been saved by having by instinct, intuition or otherwise got the right answer.

Since the whole object of *The Sunday Times* in publishing the instalment when it had was to get in ahead of the consequences of the United States publication of the books, his Lordships did not accept it was a justification that hostile eyes would shortly get a full sight of the book from the United States publication.

The pending publication would not have justified Heinemann in publishing *Spycatcher* on the date of the first instalment, and *The Sunday Times*, serializing by licence from Heinemann, were not then in any better position.

. . . *The Sunday Times* had not been entitled to punish the instalment. The order for an account followed, and for what it was worth it should be upheld. The cross appeal should also be dismissed.

In the present circumstances, and as there was no claim in copyright, there should not be an injunction to restrain *The Sunday Times* from further serialization. To grant such an injunction would be futile.

The judge had also been asked to grant injunctions which would prevent the publication of a supposed second volume of Mr. Wright's memoirs. He had declined to do so.

In the Court of Appeal the argument had ranged more widely. Mrs. Alexander had produced in the course of argument a draft of the wide form of the injunction sought, not limited to future disclosures by Mr. Wright alone.

His Lordship would not be prepared to grant the wide form of the injunction proposed, nor a form of *quia timet* injunction limited to further disclosures by Mr. Wright alone.

His Lordship would affirm the decision of Mr. Justice Scott on all points and dismiss the Crown's appeal.

Sir John Donaldson M.R. dissented from the majority view that *The Observer* and *The Guardian* had not been in breach of the duty of confidentiality in reporting the Australian proceedings relating to *Spycatcher* and that no injunction should be granted to restrain publication of future instalments by *The Sunday Times*.

Bingham L.J. dissented on the liability of *The Sunday Times* to account. His

Lordship said the judge held *The Sunday Times* in breach of a duty of a confidentiality in publishing a serialized extract of *Spycatcher*. He had found against the newspaper on two grounds.

The first had been that publication had been indiscriminate. The second had been that the extract had included a good deal of material which could not be said to raise a public interest in disclosure capable of outweighing the interest of national security in non-disclosure. Neither of those conclusions was justified.

Those were not, however, the crucial considerations, because even if disclosure of Mr. Wright's major allegations had been in principle justified on the iniquity ground, that would not of itself justify publication of that long and detailed extract.

The question turned on the correct view of the impending publication of the book in the United States.

On July 12 it had been a virtual certainty that widespread publication of the book in the United States would imminently take place. Whether on the assumption of limited circulation in this country but widespread circulation in the United States an injunction should have been granted was a difficult question.

It was made no easier by the editor's devious and surreptitious behaviour. But disapproval of the means employed to publish should not pre-empt the substantial question whether there was a pressing social need to restrain *The Sunday Time's* freedom to publish.

His Lordship concluded that there was not. On that one point he disagreed with Mr. Justice Scott.

Appeal dismissed; cross appeal dismissed.

6. JUDICIAL CONTROL OF PUBLIC AUTHORITIES

I. JUDICIAL REVIEW
Council of Civil Service Unions v. Minister
for Civil Service
[1985] A.C. 374
House of Lords

[For the facts, see *ante*, p. 97].

LORD DIPLOCK: My Lords, the English law relating to judicial control of administrative action has been developed upon a case to case basis which has virtually transformed it over the last three decades. The principles of public law that are applicable to the instant case are in my view well established by authorities that are sufficiently cited in the speech that will be delivered by my noble and learned friend, Lord Roskill. This obviates the necessity of my duplicating his citations: though I should put on record that after reading and rereading Lord Devlin's speech in *Chandler* v. *Director of Public Prosecutions* [1964] A.C. 763, I have gained no help from it, for I find some of his observations that are peripheral to what I understand to be the ratio decidendi difficult to reconcile with the actual decision that he felt able to reach and also with one another.

. . . . .

Judicial review, now regulated by R.S.C., Ord. 53, provides the means by which judicial control of administrative action is exercised. The subject matter of every judicial review is a decision made by some person (or body of persons) whom I will call the "decision-maker" or else a refusal by him to make a decision.

To qualify as a subject for judicial review the decision must have consequences which affect some person (or body of persons) other than the decision-maker, although it may affect him too. It must affect such other person either:

(a) by altering rights or obligations of that person which are enforceable by or against him in private law; or

(b) by depriving him of some benefit or advantage which either (i) he had in the past been permitted by the decision-maker to enjoy and which he can legitimately expect to be permitted to continue to do until there has been communicated to him some rational grounds for withdrawing it on which he has been given an opportunity to comment; or (ii) he has received assurance from the decision-maker will not be withdrawn without giving him first an opportunity of advancing reasons for contending that they should not be withdrawn. (I prefer to continue to call the kind of expectation that qualifies a decision for inclusion in class (b) a "legitimate expectation" rather than a "reasonable expectation," in order thereby to indicate that it has consequences to which effect will be given in public law, whereas an expectation or hope that some benefit or advantage would continue to be enjoyed, although it might well be entertained by a "reasonable" man, would not necessarily have such consequences. The recent decision of this House in *In re Findlay* [1985] A.C. 318 presents an example of the latter kind of expectation. "Reasonable" furthermore bears different meanings according to whether the context in which it is being used is that of private law or of public law. To eliminate confusion it is best avoided in the latter.)

For a decision to be susceptible to judicial review the decision-maker must be empowered by public law (and not merely, as in arbitration, by agreement between private parties) to make decisions that, if validly made, will lead to administrative action or abstention from action by an authority endowed by law with executive powers, which have one or other of the consequences mentioned in the preceding paragraph. The ultimate source of the decision-making power is nearly always nowadays a statute or subordinate legislation made under the statute; but in the absence of any statute regulating the subject matter of the decision the source of the decision-making power may still be the common law itself, *i.e.*, that part of the common law that is given by lawyers the label of "the prerogative." Where this is the source of decision-making power, the power is confined to executive officers of central as distinct from local government and in constitutional practice is generally exercised by those holding ministerial rank.

It was the prerogative that was relied on as the source of the power of the Minister for the Civil Service in reaching her decision of December 22, 1983 that membership of national trade unions should in future be barred to all members of the home civil service employed at GCHQ.

My Lords, I intend no discourtesy to counsel when I say that, intellectual interest apart, in answering the question of law raised in this appeal, I have derived little practical assistance from learned and esoteric analyses of the precise legal nature, boundaries and historical origin of "the prerogative," or of what powers exercisable by executive officers acting on behalf of central government that are not shared by private citizens qualify for inclusion under this particular label. It does not, for instance, seem to me to matter whether today the right of the executive government that happens to be in power to dismiss without notice any member of the home civil service upon which perforce it must rely for the administration of its policies, and the correlative disability of the executive government that is in power to agree with a civil servant that his service should be on terms that didnot make him subject to instant dismissal, should be ascribed to "the prerogative" or merely to a consequence of the survival, for entirely different reasons, of a rule of constitutional law whose origin is to be found in the theory that those by whom the administration of the realm is carried on do so as personal servants of the monarch who can dismiss them at will, because the King can do no wrong.

Nevertheless, whatever label may be attached to them there have unquestionably survived into the present day a residue of miscellaneous fields of law in which the executive government retains decision-making powers that are not dependent upon any statutory authority but nevertheless have consequences on the private rights or legitimate expectations of other persons which would render the decision subject to judicial review if the power of the decision-maker to make them were statutory in origin. From matters so relatively minor as the grant of pardons to condemned criminals, of honours to the good and great, of corporate personality to deserving bodies of persons, and of bounty from moneys made available to the executive government by Parliament, they extend to matters so vital to the survival and welfare of the nation as the conduct of relations with foreign states and—what lies at the heart of the present case—the defence of the realm against potential enemies. Adopting the phraseology used in the European Convention on Human Rights 1953 (Convention for the Protection of Human Rights and Fundamental Freedoms (1953) (Cmd. 8969)) to which the United Kingdom is a party it has now become usual in statutes to refer to the latter as "national security."

My Lords, I see no reason why simply because a decision-making power is derived from a common law and not a statutory source, it should *for that reason only* be immune from judicial review. Judicial review has I think developed to a stage today when without reiterating any analysis of the steps by which the development has come about, one can conveniently classify under three heads the grounds upon which administrative action is subject to control by judicial review. The first grounds I would call "illegality," the second "irrationality" and the third "procedural impropriety." That is not to say that further development on a case by case basis may not in course of time add further grounds. I have in mind particularly the possible adoption in the future of the principle of "proportionality"[1] which is recognised in the administrative law of several of our fellow members of the European Economic Community; but to dispose of the instant case the three already well-established heads that I have mentioned will suffice.

By "illegality" as a ground for judicial review I mean that the decision-maker must understand correctly the law that regulates his decision-making power and must give effect to it. Whether he has or not is par excellence a justiciable question to be decided, in the event of dispute, by those persons, the judges, by whom the judicial power of the state is exercisable.

By "irrationality" I mean what can by now be succinctly referred to as "*Wednesbury* unreasonableness" (*Associated Provincial Picture Houses Ltd.* v. *Wednesbury Corporation* [1948] 1 K.B. 223). It applies to a decision which is so outrageous in its defiance of logic or of accepted moral standards that no sensible person who had applied his mind to the question to be decided could have arrived at it. Whether a decision falls within this category is a question that judges by their training and experience should be well equipped to answer, or else there would be something badly wrong with our judicial system. To justify the court's exercise of this role, resort I think is today no longer needed to Viscount Radcliffe's ingenious explanation in *Edwards* v. *Bairstow* [1956] A.C. 14 of irrationality as a ground for a court's reversal of a decision by ascribing it to an inferred though unidentifiable mistake of law by the decision-maker. "Irrationality" by now can stand upon its own feet as an accepted ground on which a decision may be attacked by judicial review.

I have described the third head as "procedural impropriety" rather than failure to observe basic rules of natural justice or failure to act with procedural fairness towards the person who will be affected by the decision. This is because susceptibility to judicial review under this head covers also failure by an administrative tribunal to observe procedural rules that are expressly laid down in the legislative instrument by which its jurisdiction is conferred, even where such failure does not involve any denial of natural justice. But the instant case is not concerned with the proceedings of an administrative tribunal at all.

My Lords, that a decision of which the ultimate source of power to make it is not a statute but the common law (whether or not the common law is for this purpose given the label of "the prerogative") may be the subject of judicial review on the ground of illegality is, I think, established by the cases cited by my noble and learned friend, Lord Roskill, and this extends to cases where the field of law to which the decision relates is national security, as the decision of this House itself in *Burmah Oil Co. Ltd.* v. *Lord Advocate*, 1964 S.C. (H.L.) 117 shows. While I see no a priori reason to rule out "irrationality" as a ground for judicial review of a ministerial decision taken in the exercise of "prerogative" powers, I find it difficult to envisage in any of the various fields in which the prerogative remains the only source of the relevant decision-making power a decision of a kind that would be open to attack through the judicial process upon this ground. Such decisions will generally involve the application of government policy. The reasons for the decision-maker taking one course rather than another do not normally involve questions to which, if disputed, the judicial process is adapted to provide the right answer, by which I mean that the kind of evidence that is admissible under judicial procedures and the way in which it has to be adduced tend to exclude from the attention of the court competing policy considerations which, if the executive discretion is to be wisely exercised, need to be weighed against one another—a balancing exercise which judges by their upbringing and experience are ill-qualified to perform. So I leave this as an open question to be dealt with on a case to case basis if, indeed, the case should ever arise.

---

[1]   In addition to the cases cited in C. & A.L., p.662, n.6, see also *R.* v. *Crown Court Ex parte Smalley* [1987] 1 W.L.R. 237; *R.* v. *Brent L.B.C. Ex parte Assegai, The Times,* June 18, 1987; *R.* v. *Secretary of State for the Home Department Ex parte Yeboah* [1987] 1 W.L.R. 1586.

As respects "procedural propriety" I see no reason why it should not be a ground for judicial review of a decision made under powers of which the ultimate source is the prerogative. Such indeed was one of the grounds that formed the subject matter of judicial review in *Reg.* v. *Criminal Injuries Compensation Board, Ex parte Lain* [1967] 2 Q.B. 864. Indeed, where the decision is one which does not alter rights or obligations enforceable in private law but only deprives a person of legitimate expectations, "procedural impropriety" will normally provide the only ground on which the decision is open to judicial review. But in any event what procedure will satisfy the public law requirement of procedural propriety depends upon the subject matter of the decision, the executive functions of the decision-maker (if the decision is not that of an administrative tribunal) and the particular circumstances in which the decision came to be made.

LORD ROSKILL: This appeal is concerned with and only with judicial review. Judicial review, as my noble and learned friend Lord Brightman stated in *Chief Constable of the North Wales Police* v. *Evans* [1982] 1 W.L.R. 1155, 1174, "is not an appeal from a decision, but a review of the manner in which the decision was made." It is the appellants' case, stated in a sentence, that the oral instruction of December 22, 1983 should be judicially reviewed and declared invalid because of the manner in which the decision which led to those instructions being given was taken, that is to say without prior consultation of any kind with the appellants or indeed others. Initially the respondents also sought judicial review of the two certificates to which I have referred but that claim has been abandoned.

Before considering the rival submissions in more detail, it will be convenient to make some general observations about the process now known as judicial review. Today it is perhaps commonplace to observe that as a result of a series of judicial decisions since about 1950 both in this House and in the Court of Appeal there has been a dramatic and indeed a radical change in the scope of judicial review. That change has been described—by no means critically—as an upsurge of judicial activism. Historically the use of the old prerogative writs of certiorari, prohibition and mandamus was designed to establish control by the Court of King's Bench over inferior courts or tribunals. But the use of those writs, and of their successors the corresponding prerogative orders, has become far more extensive. They have come to be used for the purpose of controlling what would otherwise be unfettered executive action whether of central or local government. Your Lordships are not concerned in this case with that branch of judicial review which is concerned with the control of inferior courts or tribunals. But your Lordships are vitally concerned with that branch of judicial review which is concerned with the control of executive action. This branch of public or administrative law has evolved, as with much of our law, on a case by case basis and no doubt hereafter that process will continue. Thus far this evolution has established that executive action will be the subject of judicial review on three separate grounds. The first is where the authority concerned has been guilty of an error of law in its action as for example purporting to exercise a power which in law it does not possess. The second is where it exercises a power in so unreasonable a manner that the exercise becomes open to review upon what are called, in lawyers' shorthand, *Wednesbury* principles (*Associated Provincial Picture Houses Ltd.* v. *Wednesbury Corporation* [1948] 1 K.B. 223). The third is where it has acted contrary to what are often called "principles of natural justice." As to this last, the use of this phrase is no doubt hallowed by time and much judicial repetition, but it is a phrase often widely misunderstood and therefore as often misused. That phrase perhaps might now be allowed to find a permanent resting-place and be better replaced by speaking of a duty to act fairly. But that latter phrase must not in its turn be misunderstood or misused. It is not for the courts to determine whether a particular policy or particular decisions taken in fulfilment of that policy are fair. They are only concerned with the manner in which those decisions have been taken and the extent of the duty to act fairly will vary greatly from case to case as indeed the decided cases since 1950 consistently show. Many features will come into play including the nature of the decision and the relationship of those involved on either side before the decision was taken.

My noble and learned friend, Lord Diplock, in his speech has devised a new nomenclature for each of these three grounds, calling them respectively "illegality," "irrationality" and "procedural impropriety"—words which, if I may respectfully say so, have the great advantage of making clear the differences between each ground.

In the present appeal your Lordships are not concerned with the first two matters already mentioned, with the exercise of a power which does not exist or with *Wednesbury* principles. But this appeal is vitally concerned with the third, the duty to act fairly.

The particular manifestation of the duty to act fairly which is presently involved is that part of the recent evolution of our administrative law which may enable an aggrieved party to evoke judicial review if he can show that he had "a reasonable expectation" of some occurrence or action preceding the decision complained of and that that "reasonable expectation" was not in the event fulfilled.

The introduction of the phrase "reasonable expectation" into this branch of our administrative law appears to owe its origin to Lord Denning M.R. in *Schmidt* v. *Secretary of State for Home Affairs* [1969] 2 Ch. 149, 170 (when he used the phrase "legitimate expectation"). Its judicial evolution is traced in the opinion of the Judicial Committee delivered by my noble and learned friend, Lord Fraser of Tullybelton, in *Attorney-General of Hong Kong* v. *Ng Yuen Shiu* [1983] 2 A.C. 629, 636–638. Though the two phrases can, I think, now safely be treated as synonymous for the reasons there given by my noble and learned friend, I prefer the use of the adjective "legitimate" in this context and use it in this speech even though in argument it was the adjective "reasonable" which was generally used. The principle may now be said to be firmly entrenched in this branch of the law. As the cases show, the principle is closely connected with "a right to be heard." Such an expectation may take many forms. One may be an expectation of prior consultation. Another may be an expectation of being allowed time to make representations especially where the aggrieved party is seeking to persuade an authority to depart from a lawfully established policy adopted in connection with the exercise of a particular power because of some suggested exceptional reasons justifying such a departure.

ILLEGALITY: ULTRA VIRES

Administrative Powers

R. v. Liverpool City Council Ex parte Ferguson
The Times, November 20, 1985. Lexis
Divisional Court

In the financial year 1985–1986 Liverpool Council delayed making a rate until June of that year. The rate which it made was admittedly too low to cover the Council's budgeted expenditure. The City Solicitor warned the Council that in setting such a rate it was acting contrary to the law.[1] (The General Rates Act 1967, s.2 required the making of "such rate as would be sufficient to provide for the total expenditure to be incurred by the authority during the period in respect of which the rate is made.") As a consequence of the level at which the rate was made the Council in due course became unable to pay its employees. In September it sent notices to teachers employed in local authority schools terminating their employment. Under section 8 of the Education Act 1944 "(1) It shall be the duty of every local education authority to secure that there shall be available for their area sufficient schools—(a) for providing primary education, that is to say, full-time education suitable to the requirements of junior pupils; and (b) for providing secondary education, that is to say, full-time education suitable to the requirements of senior pupils, other than such full-time education as may be provided for senior pupils in pursuance of a scheme made under the provisions of this Act relating to further education; and the schools available for an area shall not be deemed to be sufficient unless they are sufficient in number character, and equipment to afford for all pupils opportunities for education offering such variety of instruction and training as may be desirable in view of their different ages, abilities, and aptitudes, and of the different periods for which they may be expected to remain in school, including practical instruction and training appropriate to their respective needs."

Teachers employed by the Council applied to the Divisional Court (Watkins L.J., Woolf and Tucker JJ.) for a declaration that the decision of the Council to dismiss all teachers employed by it was *ultra vires* and void.

WATKINS L.J.: (reading the judgment of the Court) ... The decision to dismiss the teachers was a direct consequence of the decision of the Council to make an illegal rate contrary to the provisions of the General Rate Act 1967. Making of the illegal rate was followed by a failure to consider or implement the options which could have been taken to balance the budget. The decision to dismiss the teachers was the result of this failure and if the teachers remain dismissed education in Liverpool will stop, with the closing of the schools, for at least a month and possible three months. Steps which are taken with this result were not taken legitimately in furtherance of the Council's duties as the local education authority. The steps were not taken for educational reasons, but because the Council was not prepared to depart from the unlawful course it had embarked upon when it made its decision to make an unlawful rate. The resolution of the Council to dismiss the teachers and the purported dismissal of the teachers is therefore unlawful on the grounds of illegality. It is illegal ... because it is the direct consequence of an illegal act, because it was not taken for proper education purposes and because its consequences are a breach of the Council's statutory duties as the local education authority.

[Counsel for the authority] argues that until the rate which was made on June 14, 1985, is set aside, it is the rate and therefore it cannot be regarded as illegal. It is

[1] See further, *Lloyd* v. *McMahon* [1987] A.C. 625; *post* p.339.

true that until the rate is set aside it is binding. However, this does not mean that when considering the consequences of that rate the court has to ignore the fact that with full knowledge of the position it was deliberately made in contravention of the law. Counsel for the applicants accepts that there is no previous authority justifying this approach but, as he submits, the explanation for this could be that there is no precendent in the long history of local government litigation of the court having to consider the sort of behaviour by democratically elected members of the Council which is revealed by the facts of this case. As the rate could undoubtedly be quashed on the grounds of illegality if an application for this was made, the court is perfectly entitled to look at the true nature of the decision which was made by the Council on June 14, 1985.

As an alternative to their argument based on illegality, the applicants advanced an argument based on irrationality. Having regard to the conclusion which has just been reached on illegality, it is not necessary to do more than to say that, in our judgment, it is undoubtedly irrational to take a decision which is so flawed by illegality.

Declaration granted.

Delegated Legislation

Commissioners of Customs and Excise v.
Cure & Deeley Ltd.
[1962] 1 Q.B. 340
Queen's Bench Division

The Commissioners of Customs and Excise were empowered by the Finance (No. 2) Act 1940, s.33(1), to make regulations providing for any matter for which provision appeared to them to be necessary for the purpose of giving effect to the provisions of the Act and of enabling them to discharge their functions thereunder. Regulation 12 of the Purchase Tax Regulations 1945 provided that: "If any person fails to furnish a return as required by these Regulations or furnishes an incomplete return the commissioners may ... determine the amount of tax appearing to them to be due from such person, and demand payment thereof, which amount shall be deemed to be the proper tax due from such person and shall be paid within seven days of such demand unless within that time it is shown to the satisfaction of the commissioners that some other amount is the proper tax due. . . ." The commissioners sued the defendants for a sum demanded more than seven days previously under a determination made by them under regulation 12 of the Purchase Tax Regulations.

Sachs J. held on a preliminary issue that regulation 12 was *ultra vires* the Finance (No. 2) Act 1940, s.33.

SACHS J. [after summarising the arguments, continued]: To my mind a court is bound before reaching a decision on the question whether a regulation is *intra vires* to examine the nature, objects, and scheme of the piece of legislation as a whole, and in the light of that examination to consider exactly what is the area over which powers are given by the section under which the competent authority is purporting to act. In taking that view I respectfully apply the line of approach adopted by Lord Greene in the above cited cases,[1] where he referred to the need for the acts of the competent authority to fall within the four corners of the powers given by the legislature. ...

Having reached the above conclusion, I now turn to the legislation under consideration in the present case. Of its nature it concerns the taxation of the subject and is thus widely different from both emergency legislation and legislation calling for administrative decisions in relation to planning. Its scheme I have already discussed and at this stage merely repeat that until one reaches regulation 12 one finds a quite normal set of provisions which define the good and transactions which attract tax and leave it to the courts to decide disputes between the executive and the subject in a normal way.

As already mentioned, section 31(2) in particular provides that the tax shall be recoverable as a debt and enables the subject thus to obtain decisions on points in dispute.

It is in relation to this general scheme that the functions of the commissioners are by section 30 provided to be as follows: "(1) The tax shall be under the care and management of the commissioners. (2) The commissioners may do all such acts as may be deemed necessary and expedient for raising, collecting, receiving, and accounting for the tax in the like and as full and ample a manner as they are authorised to do with relation to any duties under their care and management."

It is next to be observed that it is fully practicable to draft a regulation which enables the commissioners to assess tax where there has been no return or an incomplete return without in that regulation providing that the assessment can-

---

[1] *Carltona Ltd.* v. *Commissioners of Works* [1943] 2 All E.R. 560 at p. 564; *Point of Ayr Collieries Ltd.* v. *Lloyd George* [1943] 2 All E.R. 546 at p. 547.

not be made the subject of an appeal. Indeed, no parallel provision of any Act was cited to me which excluded all right of appeal to an independent tribunal. Whilst the present case relates to an incomplete return, it is pertinent that regulation 12 equally applies whenever any person fails to furnish a return "as required by these regulations." ...

It is against the background of the above examination of the relevant legislation that the court has to interpret the words "for the purpose of giving effect to the provisions of this Part of the Act and of enabling them to discharge their functions thereunder" to see what is the area over which the power of the commissioners to make regulations extends. The word "and," as was rightly conceded by Mr. Cumming-Bruce, is one which, if the court can (contrary to his main submission) consider the ambit of the powers given by section 33, necessitates the regulations being such as are required for the discharge of the commissioners' functions as well as their being related to the provisions of the Act.

On the above footing it is, to my mind, clear that regulation 12 is *ultra vires* on at any rate three grounds, which, to my mind, are distinct in law though they overlap in so far as they may be different ways of expressing the result of certain facts. First, it is no part of the functions assigned to the commissioners to take upon themselves the powers of a High Court judge and decide issues of fact and law as between the Crown and the subject. Secondly, it renders the subject liable to pay such tax as the commissioners believe to be due, whereas the charging sections impose a liability to pay such tax as in law is due. Thirdly, it is capable of excluding the subject from access to the courts and of defeating pending proceedings. This last is a distinct ground that needs to be stated separately, not least because there is nothing in the regulation to preclude the commissioners from making a determination on a transaction whilst proceedings are pending in the High Court either for a declaration or for the determination of a case stated on a section 21 arbitration. The regulation thus enables the commissioners to oust the subject's right to have issues determined in the courts not only before relevant proceedings are commenced but whilst they are pending.

The first ground derives from the proper construction of the word "functions" in section 33; the second from the fundamental repugnance of regulation 12 to the charging provisions of the relevant legislation; and the third from a general examination of the nature, objects and scheme of the legislation.

There also exists, parallel to the third ground, a subsidiary repugnance between the regulation and that part of section 21 which makes obligatory the reference of certain disputes to arbitration.

In the result this attempt to substitute in one segment of the taxpayer's affairs the rule of tax collectors for the rule of law fails.

The defendants, accordingly, here succeed at the first stage of the two-tier approach, *i.e.* upon an examination as to what is the area within which the commissioners can exercise powers. It is thus not necessary to consider whether at the second stage the courts are invariably as powerless as Mr Cumming-Bruce suggested to examine whether a particular regulation is one which can be said to be proper and "necessary" in the exercise of those powers. In particular, nothing that I have said must be taken as encouraging the view that in the particular and perhaps peculiar sphere of tax legislation the subject can merely by regulation validly be ousted from access to the courts: still less that a court would, upon the *ipse dixit* of the competent authority, inevitably be bound to hold that denial of justice to the subject was something that could properly be termed "necessary." ...

Judgment for the defendants: action dismissed with costs.

Notes

1. This decision was followed by the Purchase Tax Act 1963, which gave the Commissioners power, where proper records were not produced, to estimate the amount of tax due, unless

in an action the person liable proved the amount properly due and that amount was less than the estimate. But the principle of Sachs J.'s judgment remains of great importance.

Similarly, the decision in *R.* v. *Customs and Excise Commissioners Ex parte Hedges & Butler Ltd.* [1986] 1 All E.R. 164 that regulations made by the Commissioners were *ultra vires* was swiftly nullified by the Finance Act 1986, s.5 and Sched. 3.

2. Unreasonableness *per se* is probably not a ground for holding delegated legislation made by a minister *ultra vires*, in contrast to by-laws: *Kruse* v. *Johnson, infra*: C. & A.L. p. 60, n. 59.

Local By-laws and Unreasonableness

Kruse v. Johnson
[1898] 2 Q.B. 91
Divisional Court

Kruse, who was conducting an open-air religious service, congregated with others within fifty yards of a dwelling-house in a village in Kent, and continued singing a hymn after he had been requested by a police constable to desist. Johnson, a superintendent of police, preferred an information against him for contravention of a by-law made by the Kent County Council, as follows: "No person shall sound or play upon any musical or noisy instrument or sing in any public place or highway within fifty yards of any dwelling-house after being required by any constable or by an inmate of such house personally or by his or her servant, to desist." The magistrates convicted Kruse, who appealed by way of case stated to the High Court. He contended that the by-law was unreasonable and therefore invalid, as it ought to show on its face that it prohibited acts which caused a nuisance or annoyance.

The judges of a Divisional Court having differed in opinion, the present court (Lord Russell of Killowen C.J., Sir F. H. Jeune, Chitty L.J. and Mathew, Wright, Darling and Channell JJ.) was specially constituted to re-hear the case. They affirmed the conviction, Mathew J. dissenting.

LORD RUSSELL OF KILLOWEN C.J.: The question reserved for this court is whether the by-law is valid. If valid, the conviction is to stand. It is objected that the by-law is *ultra vires*, on the ground that it is unreasonable, and therefore bad. It is necessary, therefore, to see what is the authority under which the by-law in question has been made, and what are the relations between its framers and those affected by it. But first it seems necessary to consider what is a by-law. A by-law of the class we are here considering I take to be an ordinance affecting the public or some portion of the public, imposed by some authority clothed with statutory powers, ordering something to be done or not to be done, and accompanied by some sanction or penalty for its non-observance. It necessarily involves restriction of liberty of action by persons who come under its operation as to acts which, but for the by-law, they would be free to do or not to do as they pleased. Further, it involves this consequence—that, if validly made, it has the force of law within the sphere of its legitimate operation—see *Edmonds v. Watermen's Co.*[1] In the present case we are dealing with a by-law made by a local representative body—namely, the County Council of Kent—which is created under the Local Government Act 1888 and is endowed with the powers of making by-laws given to municipal corporate bodies under the Municipal Corporations Act 1882. ... We thus find that Parliament has thought fit to delegate to representative public bodies in towns and cities, and also in counties, the power of exercising their own judgment as to what are the by-laws which to them seem proper to be made for good rule and government in their own localities. But that power is accompanied by certain safeguards; there must be antecedent publication of the by-law, with a view, I presume, of eliciting the public opinion of the locality upon it, and such by-laws shall have no force until after they have been forwarded to the Secretary of State. ... I agree that the presence of these safeguards in no way relieves the court of the responsibility of inquiring into the validity of by-laws where they are brought in question, or in any way affects the authority of the court in the determination of their validity or invalidity. It is to be observed, moreover, that the by-laws having come into force they are not like the laws, or what were said to be the laws, of the Medes and Persians—they are not unchangeable. The power is to make by-laws

[1] (1855) 24 L.J.M.C. 124.

from time to time as to the authority shall seem meet, and if experience shows that in any respect existing by-laws work hardly or inconveniently the local authority, acted upon by the public opinion, as it must necessarily be, of those concerned, has full power to repeal or alter them. It need hardly be added that should experience warrant that course, the legislature, which has given, may modify or take away the powers it has delegated. I have thought it well to deal with these point in some detail, and for this reason—that the great majority of the cases in which the question of by-laws has been discussed are not cases of by-laws of bodies of a public representative character entrusted by Parliament with delegated authority, but are for the most part cases of railway companies, dock companies, or other like companies which carry on their business for their own profit, although incidentally for the advantage of the public. In this class of case it is right that the courts should jealously watch the exercise of these powers and guard against their unnecessary or unreasonable exercise to the public disadvantage. But when the court is called upon to consider the by-laws of public representative bodies clothed with the ample authority which I have described, and exercising that authority accompanied by the checks and safeguards which have been mentioned, I think the consideration of such by-laws ought to be approached from a different standpoint. They ought to be supported if possible. They ought to be, as has been said, "benevolently" interpreted, and credit ought to be given to those who have to administer them that they will be reasonably administered. This involves the introduction of no new canon of construction. But, further, looking to the character of the body legislating under the delegated authority of Parliament, to the subject-matter of such legislation, and to the nature and extent of the authority given to deal with matters which concern them and in the manner which to them shall seem meet, I think courts of justice ought to be slow to condemn as invalid any by-laws so made under such conditions on the ground of supposed unreasonableness. Notwithstanding what Cockburn C.J. said in *Bailey* v. *Williamson*[2]—an analogous case—I do not mean to say that there may not be cases in which it would be the duty of the court to condemn by-laws made under such authority as these were made as invalid because unreasonable. But unreasonable in what sense? If, for instance, they were found to be partial and unequal in their operation as between different classes, if they were manifestly unjust, if they disclosed bad faith, if they involved such oppressive or gratuitous interference with the rights of those subject to them as could find no justification in the minds of reasonable men, the court might well say Parliament never intended to give authority to make such rules; they are unreasonable and *ultra vires*. But it is in this sense, and in this sense only as I conceive, that the question of unreasonableness can properly be regarded. A by-law is not unreasonable merely because particular judges may think that it goes further than is prudent or necessary or convenient, or because it is not accompanied by a qualification or an exception which some judges may think ought to be there. Surely it is not too much to say that, in matters which directly and mainly concern the people of the county who have the right to choose those whom they think best fitted to represent them in their local government bodies, such representatives may be trusted to understand their own requirements better than judges. . . .

I now come to the by-law in question. It is admitted that the County Council of Kent were within their authority in making a by-law in relation to the subject-matter which is dealt with by the impeached by-law. In other words, it is conceded—and properly so—that the local authority might make a by-law imposing conditions under which musical instruments and singing might be permitted or prevented in public in places. But it is objected that they had no authority to make a by-law on that subject in the terms of this by-law. Further, it is not contended that the by-law should, in order to be valid, be confined to cases where the playing

---

[2] (1873) L.R. 8 Q.B. 118.

or singing amounted to a nuisance; but the objections are, as I understand them, that the by-law is bad—first, because it is not confined to cases where the playing or singing is in fact causing annoyance, and the next because it enables a police-constable to bring it into operation by a request on his part to the player or singer to desist. As to the first of these objections, if the general principles upon which these by-laws ought to be dealt with are those which I have already stated, it is clear that the absense of this qualification cannot make the by-law invalid. But further, such a qualification, in my judgment, would render the by-law ineffective. What is to be the standard of annoyance? What may be a cause of annoyance to one person may be of no annoyance, and may even be pleasurable, to another person. Again, who is to be the judge in such a case of whether there is or is not an annoyance? Is it to be the resident of the house within fifty yards of the playing or singing, or is it to be the magistrate who hears the charge? It is enough to say that, in my judgment, the absence of the suggested qualification cannot make they by-law invalid, even if it be admitted that its presence would be an improvement. As to the second objection—namely, that the policeman has the power of putting the by-law into operation by requiring the player or singer to desist—I again say that, even if the absence of this power would be an improvement and would make the by-law in the apprehension of some more reasonable, it is not on the principles I have already stated any ground for declaring the by-law to be invalid. In support of this objection pictures have in argument been drawn (more or less highly coloured) of policemen who, without rhyme or reason, would or might gratuitously interfere with what might be a source of enjoyment to many. In answer, I say a policeman is not an irresponsible person without check or control; if he acts capriciously or vexatiously he can be checked by his immediate superiors, or he can be taught a lesson by the magistrates should he prefer vexatious charges. If the policeman persisted in saying that the musician should desist when the people in the neighbourhood desire his music, his gratuitous interference would promptly come to an end. Nor is it correct to say (as has been erroneously stated in some of the cases cited) that the magistrate would be bound in every case to convict where the musician did not desist when called upon. It is clear that, under section 16 of the Summary Jurisdiction Act 1879, the magistrate, if he thinks the case of so trifling a nature that it is inexpedient to inflict any punishment, may without proceeding to conviction dismiss the information. The facts of this case are certainly no illustration of the by-law having been gratuitously or vexatiously put in force. The case states that although it was not proved that the occupier of the house within fifty yards had on the day in question requested the constable to require the appellant to desist, yet it was proved that the singing was an annoyance to the occupier, and that he had on previous occasions complained to the police of such singing. . . .

. . . In my opinion, judged by the test of reasonableness, even in its narrower sense, this is a reasonable by-law; but, whether I am right or wrong in this view, I am clearly of opinion that no court of law can properly say that it is invalid. In the result the conviction appealed from must, in my opinion, be affirmed. . . .
Conviction affirmed.

Notes
1. A by-law is also open to challenge on the ground that it is repugnant to the general law of the land: *Powell* v.*May* [1946] K.B. 330.

2. The validity of by-laws may be inquired into by justices in the course of a prosecution for breach of a by-law. The defendant in such proceeding is not required to challenge a by-law by way of judicial review under R.S.C. Ord. 53: *R.* v. *Reading Crown Court Ex parte Hutchinson* [1987] 3 W.L.R. 1062 (D.C.); distinguishing *Quietlynn Ltd.* v. *Plymouth City Council* [1987] 3 W.L.R. 189 (D.C.) A petition for leave to appeal in *Hutchinson's* case was refused by the Appeal Committee: [1988] 1 W.L.R. 308.

IRRATIONALITY

Misuse of Discretion

Padfield v. Minister of Agriculture, Fisheries and Food
[1968] A.C. 997
House of Lords

The Agricultural Marketing Act 1958, s.19(3), provided: "A committee of investigation shall . . . (*b*) be charged with the duty, if the Minister in any case so directs, of considering, and reporting to the Minister . . . any complaint made to the Minister as to the operation of any scheme which, in the opinion of the Minister, could not be considered by a consumers' committee . . . ." The South-Eastern dairy farmers complained to the Minister about the operation of a milk marketing scheme involving the fixing of price differentials by the Milk Marketing Board, but the Minister refused to refer the complaint to a committee of investigation. They accordingly applied for an order of mandamus.

A Divisional Court (Lord Parker C.J., and Sachs and Nield L.JJ.) made an order against the Minister, which was set aside by the Court of Appeal (Diplock and Russell L.JJ., Lord Denning M.R. dissenting). The House of Lords (Lord Reid, Lord Hodson, Lord Pearce and Lord Upjohn, Lord Morris of Borth-y-Gest dissenting) allowed the plaintiffs' appeal and granted mandamus.

LORD REID [after stating the facts, said]: The question at issue in this appeal is the nature and extent of the Minister's duty under section 19(3)(*b*) of the Act of 1958 in deciding whether to refer to the committee of investigation a complaint as to the operation of any scheme made by persons adversely affected by the scheme. The respondent contends that his only duty is to consider a complaint fairly and that he is given an unfettered discretion with regard to every complaint either to refer it or not to refer it to the committee as he may think fit. The appellants contend that it is his duty to refer every genuine and substantial complaint, or alternatively that his descretion is not unfettered and that in this case he failed to exercise his discretion according to law because his refusal was caused or influenced by his having misdirected himself in law or by his having taken into account extraneous or irrelevant considerations.

In my view, the appellants' first contention goes too far. There are a number of reasons which would justify the Minister in refusing to refer a complaint. For example, he might consider it more suitable for arbitration, or he might consider that in an earlier case the committee of investigation had already rejected a substantially similar complaint, or he might think the complaint to be frivolous or vexatious. So he must have at least some measure of discretion. But is it unfettered?

It is implicit in the argument for the Minister that there are only two possible interpretations of this provision—either he must refer every complaint or he has an unfettered discretion to refuse to refer in any case. I do not think that is right. Parliament must have conferred the discretion with the intention that it should be used to promote the policy and objects of the Act; the policy and objects of the Act must be determined by construing the Act as a whole and construction is always a matter of law for the court. In a matter of this kind it is not possible to draw a hard and fast line, but if the Minister, by reason of his having misconstrued the Act or for any other reason, so uses his discretion as to thwart or run counter to the policy and objects of the Act, then our law would be very defective if persons aggrieved were not entitled to the protection of the court. So it is necessary first to construe the Act.

The approval of Parliament shows that this scheme was thought to be in the public interest, and in so far as it necessarily involved detriment to some persons, it must have been thought to be in the public interest that they should suffer it. But in sections 19 and 20 Parliament drew a line. They provide machinery for investigating and determining whether the scheme is operating or the board is acting in a manner contrary to the public interest.

The effect of these sections is that if, but only if, the Minister and the committee of investigation concur in the view that something is being done contrary to the public interest the Minister can step in. Section 20 enables the Minister to take the initiative. Section 19 deals with complaints by individuals who are aggrieved. I need not deal with the provisions which apply to consumers. We are concerned with other persons who may be distributors or producers. If the Minister directs that a complaint by any of them shall be referred to the committee of investigation, that committee will make a report which must be published. If they report that any provision of this scheme or any act or omission of the board is contrary to the interests of the complainers *and* is not in the public interest, then the Minister is empowered to take action, but not otherwise. He may disagree with the view of the committee as to public interest, and, if he thinks that there are other public interests which outweigh the public interest that justice should be done to the complainers, he would be not only entitled but bound to refuse to take action. Whether he takes action or not, he may be criticised and held accountable in Parliament but the court cannot interfere.

I must now examine the Minister's reasons for refusing to refer the appellants' complaint to the committee. I have already set out the letters of March 23 and May 3, 1965. I think it is right also to refer to a letter sent from the Ministry on May 1, 1964, because in his affidavit the Minister says he has read this letter and there is no indication that he disagrees with any part of it. It is as follows: [His Lordship read the letter and continued]:

The first reason which the Minister gave in his letter of March 23, 1965, was that this complaint was unsuitable for investigation because it raised wide issues. Here it appears to me that the Minister has clearly misdirected himself. Section 19(6) contemplates the raising of issues so wide that it may be necessary for the Minister to amend a scheme or even to revoke it. Narrower issues may be suitable for arbitration but section 19 affords the only method of investigating wide issues. In my view it is plainly the intention of the Act that even the widest issues should be investigated if the complaint is genuine and substantial, as this complaint certainly is.

Then it is said that this issue should be "resolved through the arrangements available to producers and the board within the framework of the scheme itself." This re-states in a condensed form the reasons given in paragraph 4 of the letter of May 1, 1964, where it is said "the Minister owes no duty to producers in any particular region," and reference is made to the "status of the Milk Marketing Scheme as an instrument for the self-government of the industry," and to the Minister "assuming an inappropriate degree of responsibility." But, as I have already pointed out, the Act imposes on the Minister a responsibility whenever there is a relevant and substantial complaint that the board are acting in a manner inconsistent with the public interest, and that has been relevantly alleged in this case. I can find nothing in the Act to limit this responsibility or to justify the statement that the Minister owes no duty to producers in a particular region. The Minister is, I think, correct in saying that the board is an instrument for the self-government of the industry. So long as it does not act contrary to the public interest the Minister cannot interfere. But if it does act contrary to what both the committee of investigation and the Minister hold to be the public interest the Minister has a duty to act. And if a complaint relevantly alleges that the board has so acted, as this complaint does, then it appears to me that the Act does impose a duty on the Minister to have it investigated. If he does not do that he is rendering nugatory a safeguard provided by the Act and depriving complainers of a remedy which I am satisfied that Parliament intended them to have.

Paragraph 3 of the letter of May 1, 1964, refers to the possibility that, if the complaint were referred and the committee were to uphold it, the Minister "would be expected to make a statutory Order to give effect to the committee's recommendations." If this means that he is entitled to refuse to refer a complaint because, if he did so, he might later find himself in an embarrassing situation, that would plainly be a bad reason. . . . In the first place it appears that the Minister has come to no decision as to the merits of the appellant's case and, secondly, the Minister has carefully avoided saying what he would do if the committee were to uphold the complaint.

It was argued that the Minister is not bound to give any reasons for refusing to refer a complaint to the committee, that if he gives no reasons his decision cannot be questioned, and that it would be very unfortunate if giving reasons were to put him in a worse position. But I do not agree that a decision cannot be questioned if no reasons are given. If it is the Minister's duty not to act so as to frustrate the policy and objects of the Act, and if it were to appear from all the circumstances of the case that that has been the effect of the Minister's refusal, then it appears to me that the court must be entitled to act.

A number of authorities were cited in the course of the argument but none appears to me to be at all close to the present case. . . .

. . . I have found no authority to support the unreasonable proposition that it must be all or nothing—either no discretion at all or an unfettered discretion. Here the words "if the Minister in any case so directs" are sufficient to show that he has some discretion but they give no guide as to its nature or extent. That must be inferred from a construction of the Act read as a whole, and for the reasons I have given I would infer that the discretion is not unlimited, and that it has been used by the Minister in a manner which is not in accord with the intention of the statute which conferred it.

As the Minister's discretion has never been properly exercised according to law, I would allow this appeal. It appears to me that the case should now be remitted to the Queen's Bench Division with a direction to require the Minister to consider the complaint of the appellants according to law. . . .

Appeal allowed.

Note

After this decision the Minister referred the complaint to the Committee of Investigation, which reported that the milk marketing scheme was contrary to the reasonable interests of the complainants and was not in the public interest; but the Minister told the House of Commons that, after considering all the issues and implications involved—including wider questions of policy that were beyond the scope of the Committee's inquiry—he had concluded that it would not be in the public interest for the Committee's conclusions to be implemented.

Congreve v. Home Office
[1976] Q.B. 629
Court of Appeal

At a time when the annual licence fee for a colour television set cost £12, the Home Secretary announced that from April 1st—a date some time in the future—the fee would be increased to £18. A number of licence holders renewed their licences before their old ones expired in order to be able to do so at the pre-April fee. The Home Office initially threatened to revoke licences so renewed unless the "overlappers" paid a further £6. Subsequently the Home Office announced that it would, if the extra sum were not paid, revoke "overlapping" licences eight months from the date of issue. Congreve, a television licence holder, sought a declaration that the threatened revocation was unlawful. Phillips J. refused a declaration. Congreve appealed to the Court of Appeal (Lord Denning M.R., Roskill and Geoffrey Lane L.JJ.)

LORD DENNING M.R.: (After stating the facts).

The statutory provisions
The granting of television licences is governed by the Wireless Telegraphy Act 1949 and the regulations made under it. The Act of 1949 says (so far as material):
"1 (1) No person shall . . . instal or use any apparatus for wireless telegraphy except under the authority of a licence in that behalf granted by the Postmaster General . . . (2) A licence . . . may be issued subject to such terms, provisions and limitations as the Postmaster General may think fit . . . (3) A wireless telegraphy licence shall, unless previously revoked by the Postmaster General, continue in force for such period as may be specified in the licence. (4) A wireless telegraphy licence may be revoked, or the terms, provisions or limitations thereof varied, by a notice in writing of the Postmaster General . . .
"2 (1) On the issue or renewal of a . . . licence, and . . . at such times thereafter as may be prescribed by the regulations, there shall be paid to the Postmaster General by the person to whom the licence is issued such sums as may be prescribed by regulations . . . "
The Wireless Telegraphy (Broadcast Licence Charges & Exemption) Regulations 1970 and the Wireless Telegraphy (Broadcast Licence Charges & Exemption) Amendment (No. 2) Regulations 1971 provided (by regulation 4 (3)): "On and after [July 1, 1971], on the issue of a broadcast receiving licence . . . the licensee shall pay an issue fee of the amount specified . . . in Schedule 3, whatever may be the duration of the licence." The amount specified in Schedule 3 for colour television was £12.
The Wireless Telegraphy (Broadcast Licence Charges & Exemption) (Amendment) Regulations 1975 came into operation on April 1, 1975, and said: "1. These regulations . . . shall come into operation on April 1, 1975. . . . 3. The principal regulations shall be amended by substituting . . . for £12 . . . £18."

The carrying out of the statutory provisions
Undoubtedly those statutory provisions give the Minister a discretion as to the issue and revocation of licences. But it is a discretion which must be exercised in accordance with the law, taking all relevant considerations into account, omitting irrelevant ones, and not being influenced by any ulterior motives. One thing which the Minister must bear in mind is that the owner of a television set has a right of property in it; and, as incident to it, has a right to use it for viewing pictures in his own home, save in so far as that right is prohibited or limited by law. Her Majesty's subjects are not to be delayed or hindered in the exercise of that right except under the authority of Parliament. The statute has conferred a

licensing power on the Minister: but it is a very special kind of power. It invades a man in the privacy of his home, and it does so solely for financial reasons so as to enable the Minister to collect money for the revenue. It is a ministerial power which is exercised automatically by clerks in the post office. They cannot be expected to exercise a discretion. They must go by the rules. The simple rule—as known to the public—is that if a man fills in the form honestly and correctly and pays his money, he is to be issued with a licence.

A first licence

Test it by taking a first licence. Suppose a man buys on March 26, 1975, a television set for the first time for use in his own home. He goes to the post office and asks for a licence and tenders the £12 fee. He would be entitled to have the licence issued to him at once; and it would be a licence to run from March 26, 1975, until February 29, 1976. I say "entitled," and I mean it. The Home Secretary could not possibly refuse him. Nor could he deliberately delay the issue for a few days—until after April 1, 1975—so as to get a fee of £18 instead of £12. That would not be a legitimate ground on which he could exercise his discretion to refuse. The Minister recognises this. He allows newcomers who apply for a licence before April 1, 1975, to get their licence for the next 12 months for the £12 fee.

A second licence

But the Minister says that it is different with a man who already has a licence for a television set expiring on March 31, 1975. The Minister says that he is entitled to refuse to issue such a man with a new licence until after the old licence has expired. .... To my mind any man is entitled, if he pleases, to take out an overlapping licence: and the Minister has no discretion to stop him. It would be a misuse of his power for him to do so. In the present case, however, there is no difficulty. On March 26, 1975, Mr. Congreve went to the post office. The Minister did not refuse to issue him with a licence. The lady clerk did not even ask him whether he had an existing licence. Mr. Congreve filled in the form. He paid his money—£12. She issued him with a licence from March 26, 1975, to last until February 29, 1976. That licence was obtained perfectly lawfully. The Minister cannot dispute it. Nor does he now—though he did before the judge.

The power of revocation

But now the question comes: can the Minister revoke the overlapping licence which was issued so lawfully? He claims that he can revoke it by virtue of the discretion given him by section 1(4) of the Act. But I think not, the licensee has paid £12 for the 12 months. If the licence is to be revoked—and his money forfeited—the Minister would have to give good reasons to justify it. Of course, if the licensee had done anything wrong—if he had given a cheque for £12 which was dishonoured, or if he had broken the conditions of the licence—the Minister could revoke it. But when the licensee has done nothing wrong at all, I do not think the Minister can lawfully revoke the licence, at any rate, not without offering him his money back, and not even then except for good cause. If he should revoke it without giving reasons, or for no good reason, the courts can set aside his revocation and restore the licence. It would be a misuse of the power conferred on him by Parliament: and these courts have the authority—and, I would add, the duty—to correct a misuse of power by a Minister or his department, no matter how much he may resent it or warn us of the consequences if we do. *Padfield* v. *Minister of Agriculture, Fisheries and Food*[1] is proof of what I say. It shows that when a Minister is given a discretion—and exercises it for reasons which are bad in law—the courts can interfere so as to get him back on to the right road. Lord Upjohn put it well when he said, at pp. 1061–1062: "[A Minister] is a public officer charged by Parliament with the discharge of a public discretion

---

[1]   [1968] A.C. 997.

affecting Her Majesty's subjects; if he does not give any reason for his decision it may be, if circumstances warrant it, that a court may be at liberty to come to the conclusion that he had no good reason for reaching that conclusion and order a prerogative writ to issue accordingly."

The reasons here

What then are the reasons put forward by the Minister in this case? He says that the increased fee of £18 was fixed so as to produce enough revenue for future requirements. It was calculated on previous experience that no one would take out an overlapping licence before April 1, 1975—or, at any rate, that no appreciable number of people would do so. When he found out that many more were doing so, he tried to prevent it so far as he could. He gave instructions to the clerks that anyone who applied towards the end of March 1975 for an overlapping £12 licence should be told to come back on or after April 1, 1975, and thus made to pay the increased fee of £18. His policy would be thwarted, he says, and the revenue rendered insufficient, if large numbers of people were allowed to take out overlapping licences. He says, too, that other licence holders (being the vast majority) would have a legitimate grievance. So he considered it proper to revoke the overlapping licences of those who had acted contrary to his policy.

Are those good reasons?

I cannot accept those reasons for one moment. The Minister relies on the intention of Parliament. But it was not the policy of Parliament that he was seeking to enforce. It was his own policy. And he did it in a way which was unfair and unjust. The story is told in the *Seventh Report of the Parliamentary Commissioner for Administration*. Session 1974–75 (680). Ever since February 1, 1975, the newspapers had given prominence to the bright idea. They had suggested to readers that money could be saved by taking out a new colour licence in March 1975 instead of waiting till after April 1, 1975. The Minister did nothing to contradict it. His officials read the articles and drew them to his attention. They raised the query: Should a letter be written to *The Times*, or should an inspired question be put in Parliament, so as to put a stop to the bright idea? But the Minister decided to do nothing. He allowed the bright idea to circulate without doing anything to contradict it. And all the time he kept up his sleeve his trump card—to revoke all overlapping licences. Thousands of people acted on the bright idea: only to be met afterwards by the demand: "Pay another £6."

The conduct of the Minister, or the conduct of his department, has been found by the Parliamentary Commissioner to be maladministration. I go further. I say it was unlawful. His trump card was a snare and a delusion. He had no right whatever to refuse to issue an overlapping licence, or, if issued, to revoke it. His original demand, "Pay £6 or your licence will be revoked," was clearly unlawful—in the sense that it was a misuse of power—especially as there was no offer to refund the £12, or any part of it. His later demand, "Pay £6 or your licence will be revoked after eight months," was also unlawful. Suppose that, owing to mistaken calculation, the original £12 had been found inadequate. Would it be legitimate for the Minister to say after eight months: "I am going to revoke your licence now and you must take out a new licence"? I should think not. The licence is granted for 12 months and cannot be revoked simply to enable the Minister to raise more money. Want of money is no reason for revoking a licence. The real reason, of course, in this case was that the department did not like people taking out overlapping licences so as to save money. But there was nothing in the Regulations to stop it. It was perfectly lawful: and the department's dislike of it cannot afford a good reason for revoking them. So far as other people (who did not have the foresight to take out overlapping licences) are concerned I doubt whether they would feel aggrieved if these licences remain valid. They might only say: "Good luck to them. We wish we had done the same."

There is yet another reason for holding that the demands for £6 to be unlawful. They were made contrary to the Bill of Rights. They were an attempt to levy money for the use of the Crown without the authority of Parliament: and that is quite enough to damn them: see *Attorney-General* v. *Wilts United Dairies Ltd.*[2]

My conclusion is that the demands made by the Minister were unlawful. So were the attempted revocations. The licences which were issued lawfully before April 1, 1975, for £12 cannot be revoked except for good cause: and no good cause has been shown to exist. They are, therefore, still in force and the licensees can rely on them until they expire at the date stated on them. . . .

ROSKILL L.J. [in the course of his judgment, said]: I confess I have been greatly troubled by the Home Office claim that the Secretary of State has an unfettered discretion to grant or withhold a licence unless, as Mr. Parker conceded, the refusal was wholly arbitrary. I am well aware of what has been said in *Associated Provincial Picture Houses Ltd.* v. *Wednesbury Corporation*[3] and *Padfield* v. *Minister of Agriculture, Fisheries and Food*[4] regarding judicial control over the exercise of executive powers. Nothing I am about to say goes in any way outside or beyond what was authoritatively laid down in those cases. But the law does not stand still, and those cases, while stating the relevant principles, leave open their application to the particular facts of particular cases which from time to time come before the courts.

I ventured to put to Mr. Parker in argument what the position would have been on his argument on the facts of this case if the counter clerk on instructions had in fact refused the plaintiff a licence on March 26 and April 1 had been a Sunday or Bank Holiday on which no licence could have been obtained. Was it not inevitable that on April 1 the plaintiff, if he used his set, would have committed a criminal offence? If it was, was it a proper exercise of discretion to refuse a licence if it must or even in all probability would, if the plaintiff, being a busy man, was unable to find time to buy a licence on an April 1 which was not a Sunday or Bank Holiday, lead to the commission of a criminal offence? On those assumed facts might not the plaintiff, if he were swift to move as he has been in this case, have obtained an order of mandamus on some day between March 27 and 31 directed to the Secretary of State to issue such a licence so as to avoid the plaintiff committing a criminal offence on April 1?

I was surprised by Mr. Parker's reply that this was legal fantasy, because these were not the facts of the present case. It was, he suggested, fanciful to suppose that there could or would be a prosecution on those facts which I have posed. With great respect, the commission of a criminal offence depends upon whether one is committed and not upon whether there is an executive decision not to prosecute for fear of some outraged judicial comment that would, as Mr. Parker conceded, be likely to follow a prosecution based on facts such as I have posed. So to exercise an executive discretion as inevitably to cause or to be likely to cause a breach of the criminal law seems to me hardly likely to encourage respect for the law or indeed for those who would then in those circumstances be directly responsible for its breach. I do not find it necessary to decide this point, since a licence, as I think a valid licence, was issued to the plaintiff on March 26. But I wish to make it clear that for my part I am not without further argument accepting that the Secretary of State in such a case has such an unfettered discretion or that the courts could not in such a case interfere with that discretion without going one centimetre outside the principles laid down in the *Wednesbury Corporation* and *Padfield* cases. If the Secretary of State wishes to put his position in this respect beyond all argument, he should seek the necessary Parliamentary powers—if he can obtain them.

[2] (1921) 37 T.L.R. 884; (1922) 38 T.L.R. 781.
[3] [1948] 1 K.B. 223.
[4] [1968] A.C. 997.

I have already said that I think the licence issued on March 26 was a valid licence. . . .

Is it then a lawful exercise of the undoubted power of revocation possessed by the Secretary of State for him subsequently to seek to revoke that licence in order to exact from the plaintiff in relation to a part of the licence period arising on and after April 1, 1975, a sum of money which could not lawfully have been exacted from him in relation to that same or indeed any other period of time when the licence was first issued?

That, I think, is the real question which has to be answered on this appeal. I hope I do no injustice to Mr. Parker's argument if I say that it really rested upon the submission that only in this way could effect be given to what he claimed to have been the plain intention of Parliament that on and after April 1 the licence fee should be £18 and that that plain intention could not and should not be allowed to be thwarted by persons such as the plaintiff who before April 1, 1975, had successfully procured the issue of television licences extending beyond that date when there was no needfor them to do so since they possessed a licence which was valid at least up to that date.

It was noticeable how much Mr. Parker relied upon the Report of the Parliamentary Commissioner in order to support this argument. That the intention of the Home Office emerges from that Report is clear. But that intention and the intention of Parliament are two different things. The latter, at any rate in the majority of cases, is to be ascertained only from the relevant legislation, be it statute or delegated legislation. How the Home Office interpreted or sought to administer that legislation is irrelevant. I therefore turn back to the relevant legislation. Reading the 1975 Order with the 1970 and 1971 Orders which it amends, I read these as enacting no more and no less than that on and after April 1, 1975, every licensee shall on the issue of the relevant type and description of broadcast receiving licence pay an issue fee of (so far as relevant) £18. I am quite unable to read this legislation as having any application at all to anyone who has lawfully taken out a licence before April 1, 1975, whether or not in law he required such a licence before that date. I can see nothing in these Orders which would justify me in imputing to Parliament an intention to prevent the early issue of television licences. Assuming—as already stated, it is only an assumption—that the Secretary of State could lawfully have refused to issue the plaintiff with a licence before April 1, he did not so refuse. Can he then properly exercise his power of revocation so as to force the plaintiff for all practical purposes into the same position as if there had been such an initial refusal before April 1, 1975? As I have already said, it would not have been difficult to frame the 1975 Order so as to achieve the result for which the Home Office now contends, though it would probably have involved altering the structure of the various Orders issued between 1970 and 1975: a simple amendment such as the 1975 Order made would not have sufficed. But that is neither here nor there. If the Home Office want to attain the result they have sought to attain, they must obtain the necessary legislative powers. In my view they have not got them and did not possess them at the material time and they cannot be allowed to act as if they had possessed them through what I regard as a misuse of the power of revocation. . . .

GEOFFREY LANE L.J. concluded his judgment as follows: Mr. Parker contends that the matter should be viewed in the following way. The Minister undoubtedly has powers to revoke. If he had done so, he would have refunded the £12 paid for the licence. The plaintiff would have had to buy another licence. The fee would then have been £18. By requesting the payment of £6, therefore, all that the Minister was doing was to condense the sequence of events and to produce the same result as if each step had been duly and separately taken. Unhappily this was not the way it was put in any of the letters to the plaintiff. Nor was the plaintiff ever told by the Minister that his £12 would be refunded upon revocation. It is interesting to note that regulation 8 of the Regulations of 1970 provides as follows: "On the revocation ... of a licence no part of any fee already paid ... shall be refunded ... unless the Minister ... with the consent of the Treasury so determines."

Mr. Parker concedes and the Parliamentary Commissioner has found that there was maladministration by the Home Office and their agents; that distress and confusion were caused because insufficient attention had been paid to make policy officially and openly clear to the public.

No court would declare the actions of a government department void and illegal merely because it had acted ineptly or without tact. But is that the limit of the proper criticism which can be made here, or did the Home Office exceed the powers which were conferred upon them by statute and regulation? In my judgment they did.

Viewed objectively, the effect of the various letters written to the plaintiff was to demand the sum of £6 as the price of not exercising the powers to revoke the licence. The licence was a valid one at the time of its issue. At that time the new regulation increasing the fee to £18 had not come into operation and therefore did not in law exist. There was no power to demand the extra £6 nor to receive it. The fact that the demand came after April 1 did not make it any more lawful.

It is, however, the legality of the proposed revocation which is the crucial question. In my judgment it is illegal for two reasons. First, it is coupled with an illegal demand which taints the revocation and makes that illegal too. Secondly, or possibly putting the same matter in a different way, it is an improper exercise of a discretionary power to use a threat to exercise that power as a means of extracting money which Parliament has given the executive no mandate to demand: see *Attorney-General* v. *Wilts United Dairies Ltd.*[5]

The plaintiff is entitled to his declaration, and I would allow the appeal accordingly.

Appeal allowed with costs.

Declaration that purported revocation of plaintiff's licence issued on March 26, 1975, was unlawful, invalid and of no effect.

Leave to appeal refused.

Note

A later increase in the television licence fee was announced by the Home Secretary at midnight immediately before the appointed day so as to prevent forestalling.

[5] (1921) 37 T.L.R. 884.

Unreasonable Exercise of Discretion
Secretary of State for Education and Science v. Tameside Metropolitan Borough Council
[1977] A.C. 104
House of Lords

A Labour–controlled local education authority proposed to bring all the schools in its area under the comprehensive principle. Its scheme was approved by the Secretary of State in 1975 and implementation of the scheme was envisaged for the beginning ofthe school year in September 1976. Meanwhile, in May 1976, local government elections were held and, in the authority's area, the survival of grammar schools was a strongly fought issue. The Conservative party gained control of the authority and, considering that it had a mandate to review its predecessor's education policy, it proposed (*inter alia*) to postpone plans for converting three grammar schools into comprehensive schools or sixth form colleges. Two of the grammar schools would retain that status and a number of places would be available for pupils selected by a combination of reports, records and interviews. In June 1976 the Secretary of State, acting under section 68 of the Education Act 1944 ("if the Secretary of State is satisfied . . . that any local educa-tion authority . . . have acted or are proposing to act unreasonably. . . . "), directed the authority to give effect to the proposals approved by him in 1975 and to implement the arrangements previously made for allocation of pupils to second-ary schools for the coming year on a non-selective basis.

A week later the Secretary of State applied for an order of mandamus ordering the authority to comply with the direction. The Divisional Court (Lord Widgery L.C.J., Cusack and May JJ.) made the order, largely on the ground that, since it appeared that the teachers would not be willing to co-operate in putting the proposed selection procedure into effect, the Secretary of State was justified in saying that there was no time to carry out the proposed selection procedure by September, and accordingly there had been material on which he had been entitled to express himself as satisfied that the authority was going to act unreasonably.

The Court of Appeal (Lord Denning M.R., Scarman and Geoffrey Lane L.JJ.), which received evidence to the effect that the selection procedure proposed by the authority was well known and tried and workable and that sufficient teachers were available to form a selection panel, allowed the authority's appeal and quashed the order of mandamus. The House of Lords (Lord Wilberforce, Vis-count Dilhorne, Lord Diplock, Lord Salmon and Lord Russell of Killowen) unani-mously dismissed the appeal by the Secretary of State.

Lord Wilberforce [after stating the facts, continued]: I must now set the legal scene. The direction of June 11, 1976, was given under section 68 of the Education Act 1944. . . .

Under the Act responsibility for secondary education rests upon a fourfold foundation: the Minister (as he was then called); local authorities; parental wishes; and school managers and governors. All have their part to play. The primary responsibility rests on the Minister. He has to promote the education of the people of England and " . . . to secure the effective execution by local authori-ties, under his control and direction, of the national policy for providing a varied and comprehensive" (old meaning) "educational service in every area" (s.1). But local education authorities, which are elected, have their place defined. It is they who are responsible for "providing secondary education" in schools " . . . suffi-cient in number, character, and equipment to afford for all pupils opportunities for education offering such variety of instruction and training as may be desirable in view of their different ages, abilities, and aptitudes, . . . " (s.8).

Section 13 is an important section—it is that which was acted on in 1975. It enables local education authorities to make "significant changes" in the character of any school but requires them to make proposals to that effect to the Secretary of State. So the initiative is theirs; ultimate control is with the Secretary of State: there is no obligation, before or after his approval, on the authority to carry its proposals out. Section 68 must be quoted in full: "If the Secretary of State is satisfied, either on complaint by any person or otherwise, that any local education authority or the managers or governors of any county or voluntary school have acted or are proposing to act unreasonably with respect to the exercise of any power conferred or the performance of any duty imposed by or under this Act, he may, notwith-standing any enactment rendering the exercise of the power or the performance of the duty contingent upon the opinion of the authority or of the managers or governors, give such directions as to the exercise of the power or the performance of the duty as appear to him to be expedient. . . . " This section does not say what the consequences of the giving of directions are to be, but I accept, for the purposes of the appeal, that the consequences are to impose on the authority a statutory duty to comply with them which can be enforced by an order of mandamus.

Analysis of the section brings out three cardinal points.

(1) The matters with which the section is concerned are primarily matters of educational administration. The action which the Secretary of State is entitled to stop is unreasonable action with respect to the exercise of a power or the perform-ance of a duty—the power and the duty of the authority are presupposed and cannot be interfered with. Local education authorities are entitled under the Act to have a policy, and this section does not enable the Secretary of State to require them to abandon or reverse a policy just because the Secretary of State disagrees with it. Specifically, the Secretary of State cannot use power under this section to impose a general policy of comprehensive education upon a local education authority which does not agree with the policy. He cannot direct them to bring in a scheme for total comprehensive education in their area, and if they have done so he cannot direct them to implement it. If he tries to use a direction under section 68 for this purpose, his direction would be clearly invalid. A direction under section 68 must be justified on the ground of unreasonable action in doing what under the Act the local authority is entitled to do, and under the Act it has a freedom of choice. I do not think that there is any controversy upon these propositions.

The critical question in this case, and it is not an easy one, is whether, on a matter which appears to be one of educational administration, namely whether the change of course proposed by the council in May 1976 would lead to educa-tional chaos or undue disruption, the Secretary of State's judgment can be challenged.

(2) The section is framed in a "subjective" form—if the Secretary of State "is satisfied." This form of section is quite well known, and at first sight might seem to exclude judicial review. Sections in this form may, no doubt, exclude judicial review on what is or has become a matter of pure judgment. But I do not think that they go further than that. If a judgment requires, before it can be made, the existence of some facts, then, although the evaluation of those facts is for the Secretary of State alone, the court must inquire whether those facts exist, and have been taken into account, whether the judgment has been made upon a proper self-direction as to those facts, whether the judgment has not been made upon other facts which ought not to have been taken into account. If these requirements are not met, then the exercise of judgment, however bona fide it may be, becomes capable of challenge: see *Secretary of State for Employment* v. *ASLEF (No. 2),*[1] *per* Lord Denning M.R., at p. 493.

(3) The section has to be considered within the structure of the Act. In many

[1] [1972] 2 Q.B. 455.

statutes a minister or other authority is given a discretionary power and in these cases the court's power to review any exercise of the discretion, though still real, is limited. In these cases it is said that the courts cannot substitute their opinion for that of the minister: they can interfere on such grounds as that the minister has acted right outside his powers or outside the purpose of the Act, or unfairly, or upon an incorrect basis of fact. But there is no universal rule as to the principles on which the exercise of a discretion may be reviewed: each statute or type of statute must be individually looked at. This Act, of 1944, is quite different from those which simply create a ministerial discretion. The Secretary of State, under section 68, is not merely exercising a discretion: he is reviewing the action of another public body which itself has discretionary powers and duties. He, by contrast with the courts in the normal case, may substitute his opinion for that of the authority: this is what the section allows, but he must take account of what the authority, under the statute, is entitled to do. The authority—this is vital—is itself elected, and is given specific powers as to the kind of schools it wants in its area. Therefore two situations may arise. One is that there may be a difference of policy between the Secretary of State (under Parliament) and the local authority: the section gives no power to the Secretary of State to make his policy prevail. The other is that, owing to the democratic process involving periodic elections, abrupt reversals of policy may take place, particularly where there are only two parties and the winner takes all. Any reversal of policy if at all substantial must cause some administrative disruption—this was as true of the 1975 proposals as of those of the respondents. So the mere possibility, or probability, of disruption cannot be a ground for issuing a direction to abandon the policy. What the Secretary of State is entitled, by a direction if necessary, to ensure is that such disruptions are not "unreasonable," *i.e.* greater than a body, elected to carry out a new programme, with which the Secretary of State may disagree, ought to impose upon those for whom it is responsible. After all, those who voted for a new programme, involving a change of course, must also be taken to have accepted some degree of disruption in implementing it.

The ultimate question in this case, in my opinion, is whether the Secretary of State has given sufficient, or any, weight to this particular factor in the exercise of his judgment. . . .

What the Secretary of State was entitled to do, under his residual powers, was to say something to the effect: "the election has taken place; the new authority may be entitled to postpone the comprehensive scheme: this may involve some degree of selection and apparently the parents desire it. Nevertheless from an educational point of view, whatever some parents may think, I am satisfied that in the time available this, or some part of it, cannot be carried out, and that no reasonable authority would attempt to carry it out." Let us judge him by this test—though I do not think that this was the test he himself applied. Was the procedure to be followed for choosing which of the applicants were to be allotted the 240 selective places such that no reasonable authority could adopt it? The authority's letter of June 7 said that selection would be by "a combination of reports, records and interviews." They had about three months in which to carry it out. The plan was lacking in specification, but it must have conveyed sufficient to the experts at the department to enable them to understand what was proposed. Selection by 11-plus examination was not the only selection procedure available. Lancashire, part of which was taken over by Tameside, had evolved and operated a method of selection by head teacher recommendation, ranking of pupils, reports and records and standardised verbal reasoning tests. The Tameside authority had set up in May a panel of selection to operate a procedure of this kind, the chairman of which was experienced in the Lancashire method. He, as he deposed in an affidavit before the Court of Appeal, was of opinion that even though a verbal reasoning test might not be practicable in the time there would be no difficulty in selecting the number of pupils required. There were other

opinions, expressed with varying degrees of confidence by experts, and no doubt
the procedure could not be said to be perfect, but I do not think that such defects
as there were could possibly, in the circumstances, having regard to the comparatively small number of places involved, enable it to be said that the whole of the
authority's programme of which this was a part was such that no reasonable
authority would carry it out.

But there is a further complication. The authority's selection plans were
opposed by a number of the teachers' unions, and there was the likelihood of
non-co-operation by some of the head teachers in the primary schools in production of records and reports. The department letters and affidavits do not rely upon
this matter, for understandable reasons, but they must be assumed to have had it
in mind. Is this a fact upon which the Secretary of State might legitimately form
the judgment that the authority was acting unreasonably?

To rephrase the question: on June 11, 1976 (this is the date of the direction, and
we are not entitled to see what happened thereafter), could it be said that the
authority was acting unreasonably in proceeding with a selection procedure
which was otherwise workable in face of the possibility of persistent opposition
by teachers' unions and individual teachers, or would *the only* (not "the more")
reasonable course have been for the authority to abandon its plans? This is, I
think, the ultimate factual question in the case. And I think that it must be
answered in the negative—*i.e.*, that it could not be unreasonable, in June 1976,
and assuming that the Secretary of State did not interfere, for the authority to put
forward a plan to act on its approved procedure. The teachers, after all, are public
servants, with responsibility for their pupils. They were under a duty to produce
reports. These reports and the records in the primary schools are public property.
I do not think that it could be unreasonable (not "was unreasonable") for the
authority to take the view that if the Secretary of State did not intervene under his
statutory powers the teachers would co-operate in working the authority's procedure—a procedure which had, in similar form, been operated in part of this very
area.

On the whole case, I come to the conclusion that the Secretary of State, real
though his difficulties were, fundamentally misconceived and misdirected himself as to the proper manner in which to regard the proposed action of the
Tameside authority after the local election of May 1976: that if he had exercised his
judgment on the basis of the factual situation in which this newly elected
authority was placed—with a policy approved by its electorate, and massively
supported by the parents—there was no ground—however much he might
disagree with the new policy, and regret such administrative dislocation as was
brought about by the change—upon which he could find that the authority was
acting or proposing to act unreasonably. In my opinion the judgments in the
Court of Appeal were right and the appeal must be dismissed.

LORD DIPLOCK [in the course of his speech, said]: The Secretary of State's
power to overrule their choice by giving them a direction under section 68 to act in
some other way that he himself preferred and they did not, was exercisable only if
he had satisfied himself that the council were proposing to act "unreasonably."

My Lords, in public law "unreasonable" as descriptive of the way in which a
public authority has purported to exercise a discretion vested in it by statute has
become a term of legal art. To fall within this expression it must be conduct which
no sensible authority acting with due appreciation of its responsibilities would
have decided to adopt.

The very concept of administrative discretion involves a right to choose between more than one possible course of action upon which there is room for
reasonable people to hold differing opinions as to which is to be preferred. It has
from beginning to end of these proceedings been properly conceded by counsel
for the Secretary of State that his own strong preference and that of the govern-

ment of which he is a member for non-selective entry to all secondary schools is not of itself a ground upon which he could be satisfied that the Tameside council would be acting unreasonably if they gave effect to their contrary preference for the retention of selective entry to the five grammar schools in their area. What he had to consider was whether the way in which they proposed to give effect to that preference would, in the light of the circumstances as they existed on June 11, 1976, involve such interference with the provision of efficient instruction and training in secondary schools in their area that no sensible authority acting with due appreciation of its responsibilities under the Act could have decided to adopt the course which the Tameside council were then proposing.

It was for the Secretary of State to decide that. It is not for any court of law to substitute its own opinion for his; but it is for a court of law to determine whether it has been established that in reaching his decision unfavourable to the council he had directed himself properly in law and had in consequence taken into consideration the matters which upon the true construction of the Act he ought to have considered and excluded from his consideration matters that were irrelevant to what he had to consider: see *Associated Provincial Picture Houses Ltd*. v. *Wednesbury Corporation*,[2] *per* Lord Greene M.R., at p. 229. Or, put more compendiously, the question for the court is, did the Secretary of State ask himself the right question and take reasonable steps to acquaint himself with the relevant information to enable him to answer it correctly?

Appeal dismissed.

Notes

1. Lord Wilberforce in the final paragraph of his speech quoted above (at p. 312) refers to the fact that the Council's policy had the support of the electorate. Viscount Dilhorne referred to the Council having a mandate for its policy. Lord Salmon said the authority "rightly considered" that they had a mandate for the policy. The House had to deal more explicitly with the weight to be given to a mandate by the majority party in local authorities in *Bromley L.B.C.* v. *G.L.C.* [1983] 1 A.C. 768 where a plan to increase the grant from the G.L.C. to the London Transport Executive was held invalid, either as being *ultra vires* or unreasonable (in the *Wednesbury* sense). Lord Wilberforce said, in response to the argument that the majority party had a mandate for its course of action:

> The G.L.C., though a powerful body, with an electorate larger and a budget more considerable than those of many national states, is the creation of statute and only has powers given to it by statute. The courts will give full recognition to the wide discretion conferred upon the council by Parliament and will not lightly interfere with its exercise. But its actions, unlike those of Parliament, are examinable by the courts, whether on grounds of vires, or on principles of administrative law (those two may overlap). It makes no difference on the question of legality (as opposed to reasonableness—see *Secretary of State for Education and Science* v. *Tameside Metropolitan Borough Council* [1977] A.C. 1014), whether the impugned action was or was not submitted to or approved by the relevant electorate: that cannot confer validity upon ultra vires action.
>
> Lord Diplock said: A council member once elected is not the delegate of those who voted in his favour only; he is the representative of all the electors (*i.e.* adult residents) in his ward. If he fought the election on the basis of policies for the future put forward in the election manifesto of a particular political party, he presumably himself considered that in the circumstances contemplated in the manifesto those policies were in the best interest of the electors in his ward, and, if the democratic system as at present practised in local government is to survive, the fact that he received a majority of votes of those electors who took enough interest in the future policies to be adopted by the G.L.C. to cause them to cast their votes, is a factor to which considerable weight ought to be given by him when participating in the collective duty of the G.L.C. to decide whether to implement those policies in the circumstances that exist at the time that the decision falls to be made. That this may properly be regarded as a weighty factor is implicit in the speeches in this House in *Secretary of State for Education and Science* v. *Tameside Metropolitan Borough Council* [1977] A.C. 1014; although the issues dealt with in that case were

[2] [1948] 1 K.B. 223.

very different from those arising in the present appeals. In this respect, I see no difference between those members of the G.L.C. who are members of what as a result of the election becomes the majority party and those who are members of a minority party. In neither case when the time comes to play their part in performing the collective duty of the G.L.C. to make choices of policy or action on particular matters, must members treat themselves as irrevocably bound to carry out pre-announced policies contained in election manifestos even though, by that time, changes of circumstances have occurred that were unforeseen when those policies were announced and would add significantly to the disadvantages that would result from carrying them out.

2. Compare with the *Tameside* Case the wider power of ministerial control in *R. v. Secretary of State for the Environment, Ex parte Norwich City Council* [1982] 1 Q.B. 808, *infra*.

R. v. Secretary of State for the Environment
Ex parte Norwich City Council
[1982] 1 Q.B. 808
Court of Appeal

The Housing Act 1980 gave the right to council tenants to buy their homes from their council landlords. Section 23(1) of the Act provided

"Where it appears to the Secretary of State that tenants generally, or a tenant or tenants of a particular landlord, or tenants of a description of landlords have or may have difficulty in exercising the right to buy effectively and expeditiously, he may, after giving the landlord or landlords notice in writing of his intention to do so and while the notice is in force, use his powers under the following provisions of this section; and any such notice shall be deemed to be given 72 hours after it has been sent."

Section 23(3) authorised the Secretary of State to "do all such things as appear to him necessary or expedient" to enable tenants to exercise the right to buy.
[The current legislation is to be found in the Housing Act 1985, s.164].
Tenants in Norwich complained to the Secretary of State about delays in exercising their right to buy. The process of valuation was slow. Tenants who wished to buy were required to go to council staff for "counselling advice." In 7 months not one sale had been completed. After negotiations with the authority the Secretary of State concluded that it was not prepared to move more quickly. He then wrote to warn the council of his intention to invoke his powers under section 23. In the light of the council's unsatisfactory response to his letter the Secretary of State made an order under section 23. The council sought to have the order quashed by *certiorari* on the ground that no reasonable Secretary of State could have made the order. The Division Court (Donaldson L.J. and Robert Goff J.) dismissed the application. The council appealed to the Court of Appeal (Lord Denning M.R. Kerr and May L.JJ.)

KERR L.J.: . . . [The section] may well be without precedent in legislation of this nature. Section 23 applies when it appears to the minister that a certain state of fact exists, viz. that tenants "have or may have difficulty in exercising the right to buy effectively and expeditiously." These words are not qualified by any reference to the consideration whether that state of fact was due to any unreasonable conduct on the part of the local authority. I cannot see any basis for reading any words to this effect into the section without re-writing it, which would not be permissible. . . .

It follows that in my judgment all the submissions put forward on behalf of the council, to the effect that its approach to its obligations under the Act was reasonable or not unreasonable are of no direct relevance. The question of reasonableness only enters into the construction of section 23 in relation to the minister's decision to invoke his powers under the section on the basis of the facts which, upon a proper self direction, appear to him they exist by reference to the words of the section.

MAY L.J.: . . . In my opinion the wording of section 23(1) of the Act is clear and the question which the Secretary of State has to consider is just what the section says, namely whether the tenants have or may have difficulty in exercising their right to buy effectively and expeditiously. If the answer to that question is in the affirmative, then he has the powers under the section which Parliament has given him therein. . . .

Nevertheless, as I have said, I have no doubt that the Secretary of State must act fairly and reasonably in exercising the powers given him by section 23 of the Act in accordance with the principles set out in the passages from the judgments and speeches in *Secretary of State for Employment* v. *ASLEF (No. 2)* [1972] 2 Q.B. 455 and *Secretary of State for Education and Science* v. *Tameside Metropolitan Borough Council* [1977] A.C. 1014 which have already been quoted. ...

It follows not only from this, but also from my view that in construing section 23 there is no need to insert any word that is not already there, that I cannot agree that the Secretary of State is only empowered by the section to issue a notice under it in circumstances where it can be said that the relevant local authority has acted unreasonably. This clearly would involve reading words to that effect into section 23. I respectfully think that in the passage from Lord Brandon of Oakwood's speech in the recent case of *Bromley London Borough Council* v. *Greater London Council* [1982] 2 W.L.R. 62, 130, to which Lord Denning M.R. referred, Lord Brandon was referring to a different question from the one which we are presently considering. Just as in that case, Lord Brandon took the view that the courts could interfere where it could be shown that a local authority was acting in a way in which no reasonable local authority would act, so also would the courts interfere in a case such as the present if the Secretary of State took a decision to intervene under section 23 in circumstances in which no reasonable Secretary of State would do so. It in no way follows from this proposition, nor indeed from the wording and scope of section 23 of the Act of 1980, that a Secretary of State is only entitled to intervene when the relevant local authority, in its turn, is acting unreasonably, that is to say is acting in a way in which no other reasonable local authority would act.

Appeal dismissed.

Unreasonableness (or unfairness?)

Wheeler v. Leicester City Council
[1985] 1 A.C. 1054
House of Lords

The Leicester Football Club, a rugby club, had for many years used a recreation ground owned by the Leicester City Council. In 1984 the English Rugby Football Union announced that it had agreed to tour South Africa; the touring party was to include three members of the Leicester Club. The City Council was concerned that maintaining sporting links with South Africa might be seen as supporting apartheid. It was particularly anxious that its objection to apartheid should be clear because about one quarter of Leicester's population had Asian or Afro-Caribbean origins. A meeting was arranged between the Club and representatives of the Council at which four questions were put to the Club:

"1. Does the Leicester Football Club support the government opposition to the tour?
"2. Does the Leicester Football Club agree that the tour is an insult to the large proportion of the Leicester population?
"3. Will the Leicester Football Club press the Rugby Football Union to call off the tour?
"4. Will the Leicester Football Club press the players to pull out of the tour?"

Subsequently the Club wrote to the Council. It affirmed its opposition to apartheid and indicated that it had supplied to the three players a memorandum prepared by the anti-apartheid movement and had asked them to seriously consider its contents. The Club also pointed out that the players, as amateurs, were free to choose where to play and that the government had not made sporting contacts illegal. The reply concluded, "The club are and always have been multi-racial and will continue that principle for the benefit of Leicester and rugby football." The Council decided that the Club's answer was unsatisfactory and withdrew its permission to use the Council's recreation ground. Members of the club unsuccessfully sought judicial review of the Council's decision. An appeal to the Court of Appeal was unsuccessful (Ackner L.J. and Sir George Waller; Browne-Wilkinson L.J. dissenting). The House of Lords (Lord Roskill, Lord Bridge of Harwick, Lord Brightman, Lord Templeman and Lord Griffiths) upheld a further appeal and reversed the decision of the Court of Appeal.

LORD ROSKILL: . . . The reasons for the imposition of the ban are clearly set out in paragraph 13 of Mr. Soulsby's affidavit. I quote that paragraph in full:

"I refute any suggestion that the purported sanction against the club was imposed in response to the actions of their players. I wish to make it clear that the action taken by the council was in response to the attitude taken by the club in failing to condemn the tour and to discourage its members from playing. The council has taken its steps therefore because of what the club did or did not do. It was always recognised that the club were not in the position of employers and could not instruct their players. However, the club is, as the applicants' evidence shows, a premier rugby football club and an influential member of the Rugby Football Union. At no time was the club asked to do anything by the city council which was beyond their powers to do. The steps taken by the city council have not been taken in order to penalise the club for having members who went to South Africa, still less, to penalise the club in order to penalise the players."

It is important to emphasise that there was nothing illegal in the action of the three members in joining the tour. The government policy recorded in the well-known Gleneagles agreement has never been given the force of law at the instance of any government, whatever its political complexion, and a person who acts otherwise than in accordance with the principles of that agreement, commits no offence even though he may by his action earn the moral disapprobation of large numbers of his fellow citizens. That the club condemns apartheid, as does the council, admits of no doubt. But the council's actions against the club were not taken, as already pointed out, because the club took no action against its three members. They were taken, according to Mr. Soulsby, because the club failed to condemn the tour and to discourage its members from playing. The same point was put more succinctly by Mr. Sullivan Q.C., who appeared for the council— "The club failed to align themselves whole-heartedly with the council on a controversial issue." The club did not condemn the tour. They did not give specific affirmative answers to the first two questions. Thus, so the argument ran, the council, legitimately bitterly hostile to the policy of apartheid, were justified in exercising their statutory discretion to determine by whom the recreation ground should be used so as to exclude those, such as the club, who would not support the council's policy on the council's terms. The club had, however, circulated to those involved the powerfully reasoned and impressive memorandum which had been sent to the R.F.U. on March 12, 1984 by the anti-apartheid movement. Of the club's own opposition to apartheid as expressed in its memorandum which was given to Mr. Soulsby, there is no doubt. But the club recognised that those views, like those of the council, however passionately held by some, were by no means universally held, especially by those who sincerely believed that the evils of apartheid were enhanced rather than diminished by a total prohibition of all sporting links with South Africa.

The council's main defence rested in section 71 of the Race Relations Act 1976. That section appears as the first section in Part X of the Act under the cross-heading "Supplemental." For ease of reference I will set out the section in full:

"Without prejudice to their obligation to comply with any other provision of this Act, it shall be the duty of every local authority to make appropriate arrangements with a view to securing that their various functions are carried out with due regard to the need,—(a) to eliminate unlawful racial discrimination; and (b) to promote equality of opportunity, and good relations, between persons of different racial groups."

My Lords, it was strenuously argued on behalf of the club that this section should be given what was called a "narrow" construction. It was suggested that the section was only concerned with the actions of the council as regards its own internal behaviour and was what was described as "inward looking." The section had no relevance to the general exercise by the council or indeed of any local authority of their statutory functions, as for example in relation to the control of open spaces or in determining who should be entitled to use a recreation ground and on what terms. It was said that the section was expressed in terms of a "duty." But it did not impose any duty so as to compel the exercise by a local authority of other statutory functions in order to achieve the objectives of the Act of 1976.

My Lords, in respectful agreement with both courts below, I unhesitatingly reject this argument. I think the whole purpose of this section is to see that in relation to matters other than those specifically dealt with, for example, in Part II, employment, and in Part III, education, local authorities must in relation to "their various functions" make "appropriate arrangements" to secure that those functions are carried out "with due regard to the need" mentioned in the section.

It follows that I do not doubt that the council were fully entitled in exercising their statutory discretion under, for example, the Open Spaces Act 1906 and the various Public Health Acts, which are all referred to in the judgments below, to pay regard to what they thought was in the best interests of race relations.

The only question is, therefore, whether the action of the council of which the club complains is susceptible of attack by way of judicial review. It was forcibly argued by Mr. Sullivan Q.C. for the council, that once it was accepted, as I do accept, that section 71 bears the construction for which the council contended, the matter became one of the political judgment only, and that by interfering the courts would be trespassing across that line which divides a proper exercise of a statutory discretion based on a political judgment, in relation to which the courts must not and will not interfere, from an improper exercise of such a discretion in relation to which the courts will interfere.

My Lords, the House recently had to consider problems of this nature in *Council of Civil Service Unions* v. *Minister for the Civil Service* [1985] A.C. 374. In his speech at pp. 410–411, my noble and learned friend Lord Diplock classified three already well established heads or sets of circumstances in which the court will interfere. First, illegality, second, irrationality and third, procedural impropriety. If I may be forgiven for referring to my own speech in the case, a similar analysis appears on p. 415. Those three heads are not exhaustive, and as Lord Diplock pointed out, further grounds may hereafter require to be added. Nor are they necessarily mutually exclusive.

To my mind the crucial question is whether the conduct of the council in trying by their four questions, whether taken individually or collectively, to force acceptance by the club of their own policy (however proper that policy may be) on their own terms, as for example, by forcing them to lend their considerable prestige to a public condemnation of the tour, can be said either to be so "unreasonable" as to give rise to "*Wednesbury* unreasonableness" (*Associated Provincial Picture Houses Ltd.* v. *Wednesbury Corporation* [1948] 1 K.B. 223) or to be so fundamental a breach of the duty to act fairly which rests upon every local authority in matters of this kind and thus justify interference by the courts.

I do not for one moment doubt the great important which the council attach to the presence in this midst of a 25 per cent. population of persons who are either Asian or of Afro-Caribbean origin. Nor do I doubt for one moment the sincerity of the view expressed in Mr. Soulsby's affidavit regarding the need for the council to distant itself from bodies who hold important positions and who do not actively discourage sporting contacts with South Africa. Persuasion, even powerful persuasion, is always a permissible way of seeking to obtain an objective. But in a field where other views can equally legitimately be held, persuasion, however powerful, must not be allowed to cross that line where it moves into the field of illegitimate pressure coupled with the threat of sanctions. The four questions, coupled with the insistence that only affirmative answers to all four would be acceptable, are suggestive of more than powerful persuasion. The second question is to my mind open to particular criticism. What, in the context, is meant by "the club?" The committee? 90 playing members? 4,300 non-playing members? It by no means follows that the committee would all have agreed on an affirmative answer to the question and still less that a majority of their members, playing or non-playing, would have done so. Nor would any of these groups of members necessarily have know whether "the large proportion," whatever that phrase may mean in the context, of the Leicester population would have regarded the tour as "an insult" to them.

None of the learned judges in the courts below have felt able to hold that the action of the club[1] was unreasonable or perverse in the *Wednesbury* sense. They do not appear to have been invited to consider whether those actions, even if not unreasonable on *Wednesbury* principles, were assailable on the grounds of procedural impropriety or unfairness by the council in the manner in which, in the light of the facts which I have outlined, they took their decision to suspend for 12 months the use by the club of the Welford Road recreation ground.

[1] Sic. *Quaere*, Council?

I greatly hesitate to differ from four learned judges on the *Wednesbury* issue but for myself I would have been disposed respectfully to do this and to say that the actions of the council were unreasonable in the *Wednesbury* sense. But even if I am wrong in this view, I am clearly of the opinion that the manner in which the council took that decision was in all the circumstances unfair within the third of the principles stated in *Council of Civil Service Unions* v. *Minister for the Civil Service* [1985] A.C. 374. The council formulated those four questions in the manner of which I have spoken and indicated that only such affirmative answers would be acceptable. They received reasoned and reasonable answers which went a long way in support of the policy which the council had accepted and desired to be accepted. The views expressed in these reasoned and reasonable answers were lawful views and the views which, as the evidence shows, many people sincerely hold and believe to be correct. If the club had adopted a different and hostile attitude, different considerations might well have arisen. But the club did not adopt any such attitude.

In my view, therefore, this is a case in which the court should interfere because of the unfair manner in which the council set about obtaining its objective. I would not, with profound respect, rest my decision upon the somewhat wider ground which appealed to Browne-Wilkinson L.J. in his dissenting judgment.

Since preparing this speech I have had the advantage of reading in draft the speech of my noble and learned friend Lord Templeman with which I find myself in complete agreement.

I would, therefore, allow the appeal and order certiorari to issue to quash the decision of August 21, 1984, the terms of which I have already set out. I do not think that the declaration or the injunction sought is necessary at this juncture, but lest they become so, I would remit the matter to the High Court with liberty to the club to apply for such further relief as may be thought necessary to protect their rights.

LORD TEMPLEMAN: My Lords, in my opinion the Leicester City Council were not entitled to withdraw from the Leicester Football Club the facilities for training and playing enjoyed by the club for many years on the council's recreation ground for one simple and good reason. The club could not be punished because the club had done nothing wrong.

The club does not practise racial discrimination, does not support apartheid, has not been guilty of any infringement of the Race Relations Act 1976, did not support the decision of the three members to join the tour and sought to discourage them from joining the tour by sending them copies of the reasoned memorandum published by the opponents of the tour. The council does not contend that the club should have threatened or punished the three club members who participated in the tour or that the club could properly have done so. Nevertheless, the club has been punished by the council according to Mr. Soulsby for "failing to condemn the tour and to discourage its members from playing." My Lords, the laws of this country are not like the laws of Nazi Germany. A private individual or a private organisation cannot be obliged to display zeal in the pursuit of an object sought by a public authority and cannot be obliged to punish views dictated by a public authority.

The club having committed no wrong, the council could not use their statutory powers in the management of their property or any other statutory powers in order to punish the club. There is no doubt that the council intended to punish and have punished the club. When the club were presented by the council with four questions it was made clear that the club's response would only be acceptable if, in effect, all four questions were answered in the affirmative. When the club committee made their dignified and responsible response to these questions, a response which the council find unsatisfactory to the council, the council commissioned a report on possible sanctions that might be taken against the club. That report suggested that delaying tactics could be used to hold up the grant of a lease then being negotiated by the club. It suggested that land could be excluded from the new lease as it was "thought that this could embarrass the club because it had apparently granted sub-leases ... " It was suggested that the council's consent, which had already been given for advertisements by the club's sponsors, could be withdrawn although according to the report "the actual effect of this measure on the club is difficult to assess." It was suggested that "a further course is to insist upon strict observance of the tenant's covenants in the lease. However, the city estates surveyor, having inspected the premises, is of the opinion that the tenant's convenants are all being complied with." Finally, it was suggested that "the council could terminate the club's use of the recreation ground." This might cause some financial loss to the council and might "form the basis of a legal challenge to the council's decision. The club may contend that the council has taken an unreasonable action against the club in response to personal decisions of members of its team over which it had no control." Notwithstanding this warning the council accepted the last suggestion and terminated the club's use of the recreation ground. In my opinion, this use by the council of its statutory powers was a misuse of power. The council could not properly seek to use its statutory powers of management or any other statutory powers for the purposes of punishing the club when the club had done no wrong.

[His Lordship quoted from the section of Lord Denning M.R.'s judgment headed "Power of Revocation" in *Congreve* v. *Home Office* [1976] Q.B.629, *ante* p. 304, and continued.]

Similar considerations apply, in my opinion, to the present case. Of course this does not mean that the council is bound to allow its property to be used by a racist organisation or by any organisations which, by its actions or its words, infringes the letter or the spirit of the Race Relations Act 1976. But the attitude of the club and of the committee of the club was a perfectly proper attitude, caught as they were in a political controversy which was not of their making.

For these reasons and the reasons given by my noble and learned friend Lord Roskill, I would allow the appeal.

Appeal allowed.

PROCEDURAL PROPRIETY: NATURAL JUSTICE

Nemo index in re sua

Dimes v. Grand Junction Canal

(1852) 3 H.L.C. 759

House of Lords

Dimes, the lord of a manor through which the Grand Junction Canal passed, was concerned in litigation with the proprietors of the canal, and appealed to the House of Lords against a decree made by the late Lord Chancellor (Lord Cottenham). The point of this preliminary appeal, which was heard by Lords St. Leonards L.C., Brougham and Campbell, appears from the following extracts from the report.

LORD ST. LEONARDS L.C. proposed the following questions[1] for the consideration of the judges:

"A public company established for constructing a canal was incorporated, and bought some [copyhold] land for the purpose of making the canal; a person claiming adversely an interest in such land recovered the property by ejectment. The corporation then filed a bill against the claimant, and to have their title confirmed. The Lord Chancellor [Lord Cottenham] had an interest as a shareholder in the company to the amount of several thousand pounds, which was unknown to the defendant; and he (the Lord Chancellor) granted the injunction and the relief sought.

Was this a case in which the order and decree of the Lord Chancellor were void on account of his interest, and of his having decided in his own cause? . . ."

PARKE B.: In answer to the first question proposed by your Lordships, I have to state the unanimous opinion of the judges that, in the case suggested, the order or decree of the Lord Chancellor was not absolutely *void*, on account of his interest, but *voidable* only.

If this had been a proceeding in an inferior court, one to which a prohibition might go from Westminster Hall, such a prohibition would be granted, pending the proceedings, upon an allegation that the presiding judge of the court was interested in the suit. . . .

The many cases in which the Court of King's Bench has interfered (and may have gone to a great length), where interested parties have acted as magistrates, and quashed the orders made by the court of which they formed part, afford an analogy.

None of these orders is absolutely void; it would create great confusion and inconvenience if it was. The objection might be one of which the parties acting under these orders might be totally ignorant till the moment of the trial of an action for trespass for the act done; but these orders may be quashed after being removed by certiorari, and the court shall do complete justice in that respect.

We think that the order of the Chancellor is not void; but we are of opinion, that as he had such an interest which would have disqualified a witness under the old law, he was disqualified as a judge; that it was a voidable order, and might be questioned and set aside by appeal or some application to the court. . . .

LORD CAMPBELL: . . . With respect to the point upon which the learned judges

---

[1] The other question put to the judges was whether certain other orders of the late Lord Chancellor, confirming orders of the Vice-Chancellor, were void for the same reason.

were consulted, I must say that I entirely concur in the advice which they have given to your Lordships. No one can suppose that Lord Cottenham could be, in the remotest degree, influenced by the interest that he had in this concern; but my Lords, it is of the first importance that the maxim that no man is to be a judge in his own cause should be held sacred. And that is not to be confined to a cause in which he is a party, but applies to a cause in which he has an interest. Since I have had the honour to be Chief Justice of the Court of Queen's Bench, we have again and again set aside proceedings in inferior tribunals because an individual, who had an interest in a cause, took part in the decision. And it will have a most salutary influence on these tribunals when it is known that this High Court of last resort, in a case in which the Lord Chancellor of England had an interest, considered that his decree was on that account a decree not according to law, and was set aside. This will be a lesson to all inferior tribunals to take care that not only in their decrees they are not influenced by their personal interest, but to avoid the appearance of labouring under such an influence. . . .

Metropolitan Properties Co. v. Lannon
[1969] 1 Q.B. 577
Court of Appeal

Metropolitan Properties Co., one of the Freshwater Group of companies, was the landlord of flats at Oakwood Court, West Kensington, and proposed to increase the rents. The tenants of three of the flats applied to the rent officer to register a "fair rent" under the Rent Act 1965, and the landlord appealed against his assessment. The Rent Assessment Committee made drastic reductions in the rents, which gave rise to an appeal by the landlord on questions of law to a Division Court. Meanwhile, the landlord moved for an order of certiorari to quash the Rent Assessment Committee's decision on the ground that the chairman (Lannon) was disqualified from hearing the cause since there were reasonable grounds to believe that he could not give the Company an unbiased hearing. No suggestion of actual bias was made against Lannon, a solicitor residing with his parents at Regency Lodge, Swiss Cottage, in a flat of which his father was tenant. However, the landlord of Regency Lodge, which was also a company in the Freshwater Group, had recently applied to a rent officer for the future determination of a fair rent, and Lannon had advised his father about a fair rent for his flat and had been concerned also with advising other Regency Lodge tenants in dispute with their landlords. Metropolitan Properties Co. contended that the connection between the Oakwood Court flats and the Regency Lodge flats was so close that rents determined for the former would have such a powerful effect on the determination to be made for the latter that the supposition of bias would inevitably arise.

The Divisional Court (Lord Parker, C.J., Widgery and Chapman JJ.) dismissed the company's motion for certiorari: [1968] 1 W.L.R. 815, per Widgery J.; but the Court of Appeal (Lord Denning M.R., Danckwerts and Edmund Davies L.JJ.) unanimously allowed its appeal.

Cur. adv. vult.

LORD DENNING, M.R. [after stating the facts, continued]:

The Law

A man may be disqualified from sitting in a judicial capacity on one of two grounds. First, a "direct pecuniary interest" in the subject matter. Second, "bias" in favour of one side or against the other.

So far as "pecuniary interest" is concerned, I agree with the Divisional Court that there is no evidence that Mr. John Lannon had any direct pecuniary interest in the suit. He had no interest in any of the flats in Oakwood Court. The only possible interest was his father's interest in having the rent of 55 Regency Lodge reduced. It was put in this way: if the committee reduced the rents of Oakwood Court, those rents would be used as "comparable" for Regency Lodge, and might influence their being put lower than they otherwise would be. Even if we identify the son's interest with the father's. I think this is too remote. It is neither direct nor certain. It is indirect and uncertain.

So far as bias is concerned, it was acknowledged that there was no actual bias on the part of Mr. Lannon, and no want of good faith. But it was said that there was, albeit unconscious, a real likelihood of bias. This is a matter on which the law is not altogether clear: but I start with the oft–spread saying of Lord Hewart C.J. in *Rex v. Sussex Justices, ex parte McCarthy*[1]: "It is not merely of some importance, but is of fundamental importance that justice should not only be done, but should manifestly and undoubtedly be seen to be done."

In *R. v. Barnsley Licensing Justices, ex parte Barnsley and District Licensed Victuallers' Association*,[2] Devlin J. appears to have limited that principle considerably, but I

[1] [1924] 1 K.B. 256 at p. 259.
[2] [1960] 2 Q.B. 167 at p. 187, C.A.

would stand by it. It brings home this point: in considering whether there was a real likelihood of bias, the court does not look at the mind of the justice himself or at the mind of the chairman of the tribunal, or whoever it may be, who sits in a judicial capacity. It does not look to see if there was a real likelihood that he would, or did, in fact favour one side at the expense of the other. The court looks at the impression which would be given to other people. Even if he was as impartial as could be, nevertheless if right-minded persons would think that, in the circumstances, there was a real likelihood of bias on his part, then he should not sit. And if he does sit, his decision cannot stand: see *R. v. Huggins*[3]; and *R. v. Sunderland Justices*,[4] *per* Vaughan Williams L.J.[5] Nevertheless there must appear to be a real likelihood of bias. Surmise or conjecture is not enough: see *R. v. Camborne Justices, ex parte Pearce*,[6] and *R. v. Nailsworth Licensing Justices, ex parte Bird*.[7] There must be circumstances from which a reasonable man would think it likely or probably that the justice, or chairman, as the case may be, would, or did, favour one side unfairly at the expense of the other. The court will not inquire whether he did, in fact, favour one side unfairly. Suffice it that reasonable people might think he did. The reason is plain enough. Justice must be rooted in confidence: and confidence is destroyed when right-minded people go away thinking: "The judge was biased."

Applying these principles, I ask myself: Ought Mr. John Lannon to have sat? I think not. If he was himself a tenant in difference with his landlord about the rent of his flat, he clearly ought not to sit on a case against the selfsame landlord, also about the rent of a flat, albeit another flat. In this case he was not a tenant, but the son of a tenant. But that makes no difference. No reasonable man would draw any distinction between him and his father, seeing he was living with him and assisting him with his case.

Test it quite simply: if Mr. John Lannon were to have asked any of his friends: "I have been asked to preside in a case about the rents charged by the Freshwater Group of Companies at Oakwood Court. But I am already assisting my father in his case against them, about the rent of his flat in Regency Lodge, where I am living with him. Do you think I can properly sit?" The answer of any of his good friends would surely have been: "No, you should not sit. You are already acting, or as good as acting, against them. You should not, at the same time, sit in judgment on them."

No man can be an advocate for or against a party in one proceeding, and at the same time sit as a judge of that party in another proceeding. Everyone would agree that a judge, or a barrister or solicitor (when he sits ad hoc as a member of a tribunal) should not sit on a case to which a near relative or a close friend is a party. So also a barrister or solicitor should not sit on a case to which one of his clients is a party. Nor on a case where he is already acting against one of the parties. Inevitably people would think he would be biased.

I hold, therefore, that Mr. John Lannon ought not to have sat on this rent assessment committee. The decision is voidable on that account and should be avoided.

Although we are differing from the Divisional Court, I would like to say that we have had a good deal more information than the court had. In particular, we have seen the letter of January 13, 1967, and other things not before them when they gave their ruling. Otherwise I would not have thought it right to interfere.

I would allow the appeal and remit the case to another rent assessment committee. Let it be heard again as soon as may be.

Appeal allowed.

[3] [1895] 1 Q.B. 563.
[4] [1901] 2 K.B. 357 (C.A.).
[5] *Ibid.* 373.
[6] [1955] 1 Q.B. 41 at pp. 48–51; [1954] 3 W.L.R. 415; [1954] 2 All E.R. 850 (D.C.).
[7] [1953] 1 W.L.R. 1046; [1953] 2 All E.R. 652 (D.C.).

Note

Both Danckwerts and Edmund Davies L.JJ. also considered at length in their judgments the appropriate test to be satisfied before a decision is liable to be set aside on the ground of bias. The conflicting formulations were considered by Staughton J. in *Tracomin S.A.* v. *Gibbs Nathaniel(Canada)Ltd.* [1985] 1 Lloyds Rep. 586, 596:

... There is some difference of view in the cases as to the precise degree of probability needed to found a charge of imputed bias. In the *Metropolitan Properties* case Lord Denning, M.R. (at p.599) favoured real likelihood of bias, Lord Justice Danckwerts (at p. 602) reasonable doubt as to the chairman's impartiality. Lord Justice Edmund Davies (at p.606) rejected real likelihood, and adopted, as a less stringent test, reasonable suspicion of bias. In *Hannam's* case[8] Lord Justice Sachs (at pp. 941–942) preferred real danger to real likelihood. In *Ardahalian's* case[9] (at p.89) the Court of Appeal accepted real likelihood; but I do not think that there was any contest as to the standard of probability in that case. Indeed, Lord Justice Ackner referred to the case of *R.* v. *Liverpool City Justices ex parte Topping*, [1983] 1 W.I.R. 119, where he himself had adopted reasonable suspicion as a test.

In many if not most cases it will make no difference which test is applied. That is so in the present case, and I am content to adopt real likelihood, which appears to lay the heaviest burden on the person alleging bias. But I do not, with great respect, share the view of Lord Justice Cross (in *Hannam's* case) and Lord Justice Ackner (in the *Liverpool City Justices* case) that there is little if any difference between the two tests. If it had been necessary to decide the point, I would have followed what was said by Lord Justice Edmund-Davies in the *Metropolitan Properties* case [1969] 1 Q.B., at p.606:

With profound respect to those who have propounded the "real likelihood" test, I take the view that the requirement that justice must manifestly be done operates with undiminished force in cases where bias is alleged and that any development of the law which appears to emasculate that requirement should be strongly resisted. That the different tests, even when applied to the same facts, may lead to different results is illustrated by *Reg.* v. *Barnsley Licensing Justices* itself, as Devlin L.J. made clear in the passage I have quoted. But I cannot bring myself to hold that a decision may properly be allowed to stand, even though there is reasonable suspicion of bias on the part of one or more members of the adjudicating body.

---

[8] *Hannam* v. *Bradford C.C.* [1970] 1 W.L.R. 937.
[9] *Ardhalion* v. *Unifest International SA [1984] 2 Lloyd's Rep. 84.*

Audi Alteram Partem
Ridge v. Baldwin
[1964] A.C. 40
House of Lords

Ridge, Chief Constable of Brighton, was arrested in October 1957 and charged with conspiracy to obstruct the course of justice. A few days later he was suspended from duty by the watch committee. In February 1958 he was acquitted at the Old Bailey, but Donovan J., in passing sentence on two officers of the Brighton Police Force who were convicted, said that "neither of you had that professional and moral leadership which both of you should have had and were entitled to expect from the chief constable." In March 1958 on a charge of corruption against Ridge no evidence was offered, but the judge remarked on the need of the Brighton police force for a new and better leader. On his acquittal, Ridge applied to be reinstated, but the watch committee on the next day decided that he had been negligent in the discharge of his duty and dismissed him under purported exercise of their powers under the Municipal Corporations Act 1882, s. 191 (4), which provided: "The watch committee . . . may at any time suspend, and . . . dismiss any borough constable whom they think negligent in the discharge of his duty, or otherwise unfit for the same."No specific charge was notified to him, and he was not given an opportunity of being heard; but his solicitor was allowed to address a later meeting of the committee, in which he submitted that Ridge should be allowed to resign and to have his pension. The solicitor was given no further particulars of the case against Ridge, and the committee resolved to adhere to their previous decision. The Home Secretary dismissed Ridge's appeal under the then existing Police Acts and regulations.[1]

Ridge then brought an action against Baldwin and other members of the watch committee for a declaration that his dismissal was illegal, *ultra vires* and void, and for payment of salary from the date of the purported dismissal, or alternatively for payment of pension from that date and damages.

Streatfeild J. held that the watch committee's power of dismissal under the Municipal Corporations Act 1882, s. 191 (4), had to be exercised in accordance with the principles of natural justice, but that in view of the publicity of the trial and Ridge's own evidence given there, the watch committee had acted in that manner. The Court of Appeal affirmed Streatfeild J.'s judgment, but on the ground that the power of dismissal was an executive act, and that the committee were not bound to hold an inquiry of a judicial or quasi-judicial nature.

The House of Lords (Lord Reid, Lord Morris of Borth-y-Gest, Lord Hodson and Lord Devlin, Lord Evershed dissenting) allowed Ridge's appeal, holding that the dismissal was void, notwithstanding that the Home Secretary's decision was declared to be "final" by the Police Act 1927.

LORD REID summarised the facts and continued: The appellant's case is that in proceeding under the Act of 1882 the watch committee were bound to observe what are commonly called the principles of natural justice. Before attempting to reach any decision they were bound to inform him of the grounds on which they proposed to act and give him a fair opportunity of being heard in his own defence. The authorities on the applicability of the principles of natural justice are in some confusion, and so I find it necessary to examine this matter in some detail. The principle *audi alteram partem* goes back many centuries in our law and appears in a multitude of judgments of judges of the highest authority. . . . It appears to me that one reason why the authorities on natural justice have been found difficult to reconcile is that insufficient attention has been paid to the great difference between various kinds of cases in which it has been sought to apply the principle.

[1] Police Act 1919; Police (Appeals) Act 1927; Police Discipline Regulations 1952 and 1954.

What a Minister ought to do in considering objections to a scheme may be very different from what a watch committee ought to do in considering whether to dismiss a chief constable. So I shall deal first with cases of dismissal. These appear to fall into three classes: dismissal of a servant by his master, dismissal from an office held during pleasure, and dismissal from an office where there must be something against a man to warrant his dismissal.

The law regarding master and servant is not in doubt. There cannot be specific performance of a contract of service, and the master can terminate the contract with his servant at any time and for any reason or for none. But if he does so in a manner not warranted by the contract he must pay damages for breach of contract. ... The present case does not fall within this class because a chief constable is not the servant of the watch committee or indeed of anyone else.

Then there are many cases where a man holds an office at pleasure. Apart from judges and others whose tenure of office is governed by statute, all servants and officers of the Crown hold office at pleasure, and this has been held even to apply to a colonial judge (*Terrell* v. *Secretary of State for the Colonies*[2]). It has always been held, I think rightly, that such an officer has no right to be heard before he is dismissed, and the reason is clear. As the person having the power of dismissal need not have anything against the officer, he need not give any reason. That was stated as long ago as 1670 in *R.* v. *Stratford-on-Avon Corporation*,[3] where the corporation dismissed a town clerk who held office *durante bene placito*. The leading case on this matter appears to be *R.* v. *Darlington School Governors*.[4] ... But again that is not this case. In this case the Act of 1882 only permits the watch committee to take action on the grounds of negligence or unfitness. Let me illustrate the difference by supposing that a watch committee who had no complaint against their present chief constable heard of a man with quite outstanding qualifications who would like to be appointed. They might think it in the public interest to make the change, but they would have no right to do it. But there could be no legal objection to dismissal of an officer holding office at pleasure in order to put a better man in his place.

So I come to the third class, which includes the present case. There I find an unbroken line of authority to the effect that an officer cannot lawfully be dismissed without first telling him what is alleged against him and hearing his defence or explanation. An early example is *Bagg's Case*,[5] though it is more properly deprivation of the privilege of being a burgess of Plymouth. *R.* v. *Gaskin*[6] arose out of the dismissal of a parish clerk, and Lord Kenyon C.J. referred to *audi alteram partem* as one of the first principles of justice. *R.* v. *Smith*[7] was another case of dismissal of a parish clerk, and Lord Denman C.J. held that even personal knowledge of the offence was no substitute for hearing the officer: his explanation might disprove criminal motive or intent and bring forward other facts in mitigation, and in any event delaying to hear him would prevent yielding too hastily to first impressions. *Ex p. Ramshay*[8] is important. It dealt with the removal from office of a county court judge, and the form of the legislation which authorised the Lord Chancellor to act is hardly distinguishable from the form of section 191, which confers powers on the watch committee. The Lord Chancellor was empowered if he should think fit to remove on the ground of inability or misbehaviour, but Lord Campbell C.J. said[9] that this was "only on the implied condition prescribed by the principles of eternal justice." ...

---

[2] [1953] 2 Q.B. 482.
[3] (1809) 11 East 176.
[4] (1844) 6 Q.B. 682.
[5] (1615) 11 Co.Rep. 93b.
[6] (1799) 8 Term Rep. 209.
[7] (1844) 5 Q.B. 614.
[8] (1852) 18 Q.B. 173.
[9] 18 Q.B. 173 at p. 190.

That citation of authority might seem sufficient, butI had better proceed further. In *Fisher* v. *Jackson*,[10] three vicars had power to remove the master of an endowed school. But, unlike the *Darlington* case,[11] grounds on which he could be removed—briefly, inefficiency or failing to set a good example. So it was held that they could not remove him without affording him an opportunity of being heard in his own defence. Only two other cases of this class were cited in argument, *Cooper* v. *Wilson*[12] and *Hogg* v. *Scott*.[13] Both dealt with the dismissal of police officers and both were complicated by consideration of regulations made under the Police Acts. In the former, the majority at least recognised that the principles of natural justice applied, and in deciding the latter Cassels J., in deciding that a chief constable could dismiss without hearing him an officer who had been convicted of felony, appears to have proceeded on a construction of the regulations. Of course, if the regulations authorised him to do that and were *intra vires* in doing so, there would be no more to be said. . . .

Stopping there, I would think that authority was wholly in favour of the appellant, but the respondent's argument was mainly based on what has been said in a number of fairly recent cases dealing with different subject-matter. Those cases deal with decisions by Ministers, officials and bodies of various kinds which adversely affected property rights or privileges of persons who had had no opportunity or no proper opportunity of presenting their cases before the decisions were given. And it is necessary to examine those cases for another reason. The question which was or ought to have been considered by the watch committee on March 7, 1958, was not a simple question whether or not the appellant should be dismissed. There was three possible courses open to the watch committee—reinstating the appellant as chief constable, dismissing him, or requiring him to resign. The difference between the latter two is that dismissal involved forfeiture of pension rights, whereas requiring him to resign did not. Indeed, it is now clear that the appellant's real interest in this appeal is to try to save his pension rights.

It may be convenient at this point to deal with an argument that, even if as a general rule a watch committee must hear a constable in his own defence before dismissing him, this case was so clear that nothing that the appellant could have said could have made any difference. It is at least very doubtful whether that could be accepted as an excuse. But, even if it could, the respondents would, in my view, fail on the facts. It may well be that no reasonable body of men could have reinstated the appellant. But as between the other two courses open to the watch committee the case is not so clear. Certainly on the facts, as we know them, the watch committee could reasonably have decided to forfeit the appellant's pension rights, but I could not hold that they would have acted wrongly or wholly unreasonably if they had in the exercise of their discretion decided to take a more lenient course.

[His Lordship then considered authorities dealing with property rights and privileges, citing *Cooper* v. *Wandsworth Board of Works*,[14] *Hopkins* v. *Smethwick Local Board of Health*,[15] *Smith* v. *The Queen*,[16] *De Verteuil* v. *Knaggs*,[17] and *Spackman* v. *Plumstead District Board of Works*.[18]]

I shall now turn to a different class of case—deprivation of membership of a

[10] [1891] 2 Ch. 84; 7 T.L.R. 358.
[11] 6 Q.B. 682.
[12] [1937] 2 K.B. 309; 53 T.L.R. 623; [1937] 2 All E.R. 726 (C.A.).
[13] [1947] K.B. 759; 63 T.L.R. 320; [1947] 1 All E.R. 788.
[14] (1863) 14 C.B.(N.S.) 180.
[15] (1890) 24 Q.B.D. 712 at p. 714-715; 6 T.L.R. 286 (C.A.)
[16] (1878) 3 App. Cas. 614 (P.C.).
[17] [1918] A.C. 557; 54 T.L.R. 325 (P.C.).
[18] (1885) 10 App.Cas. 229; 1 T.L.R. 313 (H.L.).

professional or social body. [His Lordship discussed *Wood* v. *Woad*,[19] *Lapointe* v. *L'Association de Bienfaisance et de Retraite de la Police De Montreal*,[20] *Fisher* v. *Keane*,[21] *Dawkins* v. *Antrobus*,[22] and *Weinberger* v. *Inglis*.[23]]

I shall not at present advert to the various trade union cases because I am deliberately considering the state of the law before difficulties were introduced by statements in various fairly recent cases. It appears to me that if the present case had arisen thirty or forty years ago the courts would had no difficulty in deciding this issue in favour of the appellant on the authorities which I have cited. So far as I am aware none of these authorities has ever been disapproved or even doubted. Yet the Court of Appeal have decided this issue against the appellant on more recent authorities which apparently justify that result. How has this come about?

At least three things appears to me to have contributed. In the first place there have been many cases where it has been sought to apply the principles of natural justice to the wider duties imposed on Ministers and other organs of government by modern legislation. For reasons which I shall attempt to state in a moment, it has been held that those principles have a limited application in such cases and those limitations have tended to be reflected in other decisions on matters to which in principle they do not appear to me to apply. Secondly, again for reasons which I shall attempt to state, those principles have been held to have a limited application in cases arising out of war-time legislation; and again such limitations have tended to be reflected in other cases. And, thirdly, there has, I think, been a misunderstanding of the judgment of Atkin L.J. in *R. v. Electricity Commissioners, ex p. London Electricity Joint Committee Co.*[24]

In cases of the kind I have been dealing with the Board of Works or the Governor or the club committee was dealing with a single isolated case. It was not deciding, like a judge in a law-suit, what were the rights of the person before it. But it was deciding how he should be treated—something analogous to a judge's duty in imposing a penalty. No doubt policy would play some part in the decision—but so it might when a judge is imposing a sentence. So it was easy to say that such a body is performing a quasi-judicial task in considering and deciding such a matter, and to require to observe the essentials of all proceedings of a judicial character—the principles of natural justice.

Sometimes the functions of a Minister or department may also be of that character, and then the rules of natural justice can apply in much the same way. But more often their functions are of a very different character. If a Minister is considering whether to make a scheme for, say, an important new road, his primary concern will not be with the damage which its construction will do to the rights of individual owners of land. He will have to consider all manner of questions of public interest and, it may be, a number of alternative schemes. He cannot be prevented from attaching more importance to the fulfilment of his policy than to the fate of individual objectors, and it would be quite wrong for the courts to say that the Minister should or could act in the same kind of way as a board of works deciding whether a house should be pulled down. And there is another important difference. As explained in *Local Government Board* v. *Arlidge*[25] a Minister cannot do everything himself. His officers will have to gather and sift all the facts, including objections by individuals, and no individual can complain if the ordinary accepted methods of carrying on public business do not give him as

[19] (1874) L.R. 9 Ex. 190.
[20] [1906] A.C. 535; 22 T.L.R. 768 (P.C.).
[21] (1878) 11 Ch.D. 353.
[22] (1879) 17 Ch.D. 615 (C.A.).
[23] [1919] A.C. 606; 35 T.L.R. 399 (H.L.).
[24] [1924] 1 K.B. 171; 39 T.L.R. 715 (C.A.).
[25] [1915] A.C. 120; 30 T.L.R. 672 (H.L.).

good protection as would be given by the principles of natural justice in a different kind of case.

We do not have a developed system of administrative law—perhaps because until fairly recently we did not need it. So it is not surprising that in dealing with new types of cases the courts have had to grope for solutions, and have found that old powers, rules and procedure are largely inapplicable to cases which they were never designed or intended to deal with. But I see nothing in that to justify our thinking that our old methods are any less applicable today then ever they were to the older types of case. And if there are any dicta in modern authorities which point in that direction, then, in my judgment, they should not be followed. . . .

The matter has been further complicated by what I believe to be a misunderstanding of a much-quoted passage in the judgment of Atkin L.J. in *R. v. Electricity Commissioners, ex p. London Electricity Joint Committee Co.*[26] He said: " . . . the operation of the writs [of prohibition and certiorari] has extended to control the proceedings of bodies which do not claim to be, and would not be recognised as, courts of justice. Wherever any body of persons having legal authority to determine questions affecting the rights of subjects, and having the duty to act judicially, act in excess of their legal authority, they are subject to the controlling jurisdiction of the King's Bench Division exercised in these writs."

A gloss was put on this by Lord Hewart C.J. in *R. v. Legislative Committee of the Church Assembly, ex p. Haynes-Smith.*[27] . . . Lord Hewart said,[28] having quoted the passage from Atkin L.J.'s judgment: "The question, therefore, which we have to ask ourselves in this case is whether it is true to say in this matter, either of the Church Assembly as a whole, or of the Legislative Committee of the Church Assembly, that it is a body of persons having legal authority to determine questions affecting the rights of subjects, and having the duty to act judicially. It is to be observed that in the last sentence which I have quoted from the judgment of Atkin L.J. the word is not 'or,' but 'and.' In order that a body may satisfy the required test it is not enough that it should have legal authority to determine questions affecting the rights of subjects; there must be superadded to that characteristic the further characteristic that the body has the duty to act judicially. . . . "

I have quoted the whole of this passage because it is typical of what has been said in several subsequent cases. If Lord Hewart meant that it is never enough that a body simply has a duty to determine what the rights of an individual should be, but that there must always be something more to impose on it a duty to act judicially before it can be found to observe the principles of natural justice, then that appears to me impossible to reconcile with the earlier authorities. I could not reconcile it with what Lord Denman C.J. said in *R. v. Smith*[29] or what Lord Campbell C.J. said in *Ex p. Ramshay,*[30] or what Lord Hatherley L.C. said in *Osgood v. Nelson,*[31] or what was decided in *Cooper v. Wandsworth Board of Works*[32] or *Hopkins v. Smethwick Local Board,*[33] or what Lord Parmoor said in *De Verteuil v. Knaggs,*[34] or what Kelly C.B. said, with the subsequent approval of Lord Macnaghten, in *Wood v. Woad,*[35] or what Jessel M.R. said in *Fisher v. Keane,*[36] or what

[26] [1924] 1 K.B. 171 at p. 205; 39 T.L.R. 715.
[27] [1928] 1 K.B. 411; 44 T.L.R. 68.
[28] *Ibid.* at p.415.
[29] 5 Q.B. 615.
[30] 18 Q.B. 173.
[31] L.R. 5 H.L. 636.
[32] 14 C.B. (N.S.) 180.
[33] 24 Q.B.D. 712.
[34] [1918] A.C. 557.
[35] L.R. 9 Ex. 190.
[36] 11 Ch. D. 353.

Lord Birkenhead L.C. said in *Weinberger* v. *Inglis*,[37] the earlier authorities. And, as I shall try to show, it cannot be what Atkin L.J. meant. . . .

[Reverting to R. v. *Electricity Commissioners, supra,* Lord Reid said:] Immediately after the passage which I said has been misunderstood, he [Atkin L.J.] cited a variety of cases and in most of them I can see nothing "superadded" (to use Lord Hewart's word) to the duty itself. Certainly Atkin L.J. did not say that anything was superadded. And a later passage in his judgment convinces me that he, like Bankes L.J., inferred the judicial character of the duty from the nature of the duty itself. . . .

The authority chiefly relied on by the Court of Appeal in holding that the watch committee was not bound to observe the principles of natural justice was *Nakkuda Ali* v. *Jayaratne*.[38] . . . This House is not bound by decisions of the Privy Council, and for my own part nothing short of a decision of this House directly in point would induce me to accept the position that, although an enactment expressly requires an official to have reasonable grounds for his decision, our law is so defective that a subject cannot bring up such a decision for review however seriously he may be affected and however obvious it may be that the official acted in breach of his statutory obligation. . . .

I would sum up my opinion in this way. Between 1882 and the making of police regulations in 1920 section 191(4) has to be applied to every kind of case. The respondents' contention is that, even where there was a doubtful question whether a constable was guilty of a particular act of misconduct, the watch committee were under no obligation to hear his defence before dismissing him. In my judgment it is abundantly clear from the authorities I have quoted that at that time the courts would have rejected any such contention. In later cases dealing with different subject-matter, opinions have been expressed in wide terms so as to appear to conflict with those earlier authorities. But learned judges who expressed those opinions generally had no power to overrule those authorities, and in any event it is a salutary rule that a judge is not to be assumed to have intended to overrule or disapprove of an authority which has not been cited to him and which he does not even mention. So I would hold that the power of dismissal in the Act of 1882 could not then have been exercised and cannot now be exercised until the watch committee have informed the constable of the grounds on which they propose to proceed and have given him a proper opportunity to present his case in defence. . . .

Then there was considerable argument whether in the result the watch committee's decision is void or merely voidable. Time and again in the cases I have cited it has been stated that a decision given without regard to the principles of natural justice is void, and that was expressly decided in *Wood* v. *Woad*.[39] I see no reason to doubt these authorities. The body with the power to decide cannot lawfully proceed to make a decision until it has afforded to the person affected a proper opportunity to state his case. . . .

Accordingly, in my judgment, this appeal must be allowed. There appears to have been no discussion in the courts below as to remedies which may now be open to the appellant, and I do not think that this House should do more than declare that the dismissal of the appellant is null and void and remit the case to the Queen's Bench Division for further procedure. But it is right to put on record that the appellant does not seek to be reinstated as chief constable: his whole concern is to avoid the serious financial consequences involved in dismissal as against being required or allowed to resign.
Appeal allowed.

---

[37] [1919] A.C. 606.
[38] [1951] A.C. 66; 66 T.L.R. (Pt. 2) 214 (P.C.).
[39] (1874) L.R. 9 Ex. 190.

Attorney-General of Hong-Kong v. Ng Yuen Shiu
[1983] 2 A.C. 629
Privy Council

The respondent had entered Hong Kong illegally. He was detained after living there for some years and an order was made for his deportation. He sought to challenge the order on the ground that it had been made without granting him a hearing in accordance with the rules of natural justice. Apart from any right under the law generally he claimed that a right had arisen as a result of an assurance given publicly by the Director of Immigration that illegal immigrants of the category to which he belonged would not be deported without first being interviewed and that "Each case will be treated on its merits." Applications for habeas corpus, *certiorari* and prohibition to the High Court (Sir Denys Roberts C.J. and Rhind J.) were unsuccessful. The Court of Appeal (McMullin V-P., Li J.A. and Baber J.) allowed the appeal against refusal of an order of prohibition. The Attorney-General appealed against that decision to the Privy Council (Lord Fraser of Tullybelton, Lord Scarman, Lord Bridge of Harwich, Lord Brandon of Oakbrook and Sir John Megaw.)

LORD FRASER OF TULLYBELTON: . . . The argument for the Attorney-General raised two questions—one of wide general importance, the other of more limited scope. The general question, which both the High Court and the Court of Appeal decided in favour of the Attorney-General, is whether an alien who enters Hong Kong illegally has, as a general rule, a right to a hearing, conducted fairly and in accordance with the rules of natural justice, before a removal order is made against him. The narrower question is whether, assuming that the answer to the general question is in the negative, nevertheless the applicant has a right to such a hearing in the particular circumstances of this case. The Court of Appeal answered the latter question in favour of the applicant and therefore made the limited order of prohibition now under appeal. Having regard to the view which their Lordships have formed on the narrower question, it is unnecessary for them to decide the general question. They will therefore assume, without deciding, that the Court of Appeal rightly decided that there was no general right in an alien to have a hearing in accordance with the rules of natural justice before a removal order is made against him.

The narrower proposition for which the applicant contended was that a person is entitled to a fair hearing before a decision adversely affecting his interests is made by a public official or body, if he has "a legitimate expectation" of being accorded such a hearing. The phrase "legitimate expectation" in this context originated in the judgment of Lord Denning M.R. in *Schmidt* v. *Secretary of State for Home Affairs* [1969] 2 Ch. 1949, 170. It is many ways an apt one to express the underlying principle, though it is somewhat lacking in precision. In *Salemi* v. *MacKellar* (No. 2) (1977) 137 C.L.R. 396, 404, Barwick C.J. construed the word "legitimate" in that phrase as expressing the concept of "entitlement or recognition by law." So understood, the expression (as Barwick C.J. rightly observed) "adds little, if anything, to the concept of a right," With great respect to Barwick C.J., their Lordships consider that the word "legitimate" in that expression falls to be read as meaning "reasonable."[1] Accordingly "legitimate expectations" in this context are capable of including expectations which go beyond enforceable legal rights, provided they have some reasonable basis: see *Reg.* v. *Criminal Injuries Compensation Board, Ex parte Lain* [1967] 2 Q.B. 864. So it was held in *Reg* v. *Board of Visitors of Hull Prison, Ex parte St. Germain* (No.2) [1979] 1 W.L.R. 1041 that a prisoner is entitled to challenge, by judicial review, a decision by a prison board of

---

[1] In *Council of the Civil Service Unions* v. *Minister for the Civil Service* [1985] A.C. 374 Lord Fraser indicated that he thought "legitimate" preferable to "reasonable."

visitors, awarding him loss of remission of sentence, although he has no legal right to remission, but only a reasonable expectation of receiving it.

The decision of the Court of Appeal in the *St. Germain* case was approved by the House of Lords recently in *O'Reilly* v. *Mackman* [1983] 2 A.C. 237 where Lord Diplock, with whose speech the other Law Lords present agreed, said, at p. 275:

> "It is not, and it could not be, contended that the decision of the board awarding him forfeiture of remission had infringed or threatened to infringe any right of the appellant derived from private law, whether a common law right or one created by a statute. Under the Prison Rules remission of sentence is not a matter of right but of indulgence. So far as private law is concerned all that each appellant had was a legitimate expectation, based upon his knowledge of what is the general practice, that he would be granted the maximum remission, permitted by rule 5 (2) of the Prison Rules, of one-third of his sentence if by that time no disciplinary award of forfeiture of remission had been made against him. So the second thing to be noted is that none of the appellants had any remedy in private law.
>
> "In public law, as distinguished from private law, however, such legitimate expectation gave to each appellant a sufficient interest to challenge the legality of the adverse disciplinary award made against him by the board on the ground that in one way or another the board in reaching its decision had acted outwith the powers conferred upon it by the legislation under which it was acting; and such grounds would include the board's failure to observe the rules of natural justice: which means no more than to act fairly towards him in carrying out their decision-making process, and I prefer so to put it."

The expectations may be based upon some statement or undertaking by, or on behalf of, the public authority which has the duty of making the decision, if the authority has, through its officers, acted in a way that would make it unfair or inconsistent with good administration for him to be denied such an inquiry.

One such case was *Reg.* v. *Liverpool Corporation, Ex parte Liverpool Taxi Fleet Operators' Association* [1972] 2 Q.B. 299. Liverpool Corporation had the duty of licensing the number of taxis which they thought fit, and for some years the number had been fixed at 300. In 1971 a sub-committee of the council recommended increases in the number of licensed taxis for 1972 and again in 1973, and no limitation on numbers thereafter. The chairman of the relevant committee gave a public undertaking on August 4, 1971, that the number would not be increased beyond 300 until a private bill had been passed by Parliament and had come into effect, and his undertaking was confirmed by him orally and by the town clerk in a letter to two associations representing the holders of existing taxi licences. In November 1971 the sub-committee resolved that the number of licences should be increased in 1972, before the private bill had been passed, and the resolution was approved by the full committee and by the council in December. The association of licence holders applied to the court for an order of prohibition and certiorari. The Divisional Court refused the application, but the Court of Appeal granted an order of prohibition against the corporation from granting any increased number of licences without first hearing any representations which might be made by or on behalf of persons interested therein, including the appellant association. It is important to notice that the court order was limited to ensuring that the corporation followed a fair procedure by holding an inquiry before reaching a decision: provided such procedure was followed the decision was left with the corporation to whom it had been entrusted by Parliament. Lord Denning M.R. said, at p. 308:

> "the corporation were not at liberty to disregard their undertaking [not to increase the number without holding an inquiry]. They were bound by it so long as it was not in conflict with their statutory duty. It is said that a corporation cannot contract itself out of its statutory duties. In *Birkdale District Electric Supply Co. Ltd.* v. *Southport Corporation* [1926] A.C. 355 Lord Birken-

head said, at p. 364, that it was 'a well-established principle of law, that if a person or public body is entrusted by the legislature with certain powers and duties expressly or impliedly for public purposes, those persons or bodies cannot divest themselves of these powers and duties. They cannot enter into any contract or take any action incompatible with the due exercise of their powers or the discharge of their duties.' But that principle does not mean that a corporation can give an undertaking and break it as they please. So long as the performance of the undertaking is compatible with their public duty, they must honour it."

Roskill L.J. said, at p. 310:

"It is for the council and not for this court to determine what the future policy should be in relation to the number of taxi licences which are to be issued in the City of Liverpool. It is not for this court to consider population growths or falls or the extent of the demand for taxis within or without the city ... All those are matters for the council. This court is concerned to see that whatever policy the corporation adopts is adopted after due and fair regard to all the conflicting interests. The power of the court to intervene is not limited, as once was thought, to those cases where the function in question is judicial or quasi-judicial. The modern cases show that this court will intervene more widely than in the past."

Their Lordships see no reason why the principle should not be applicable when the person who will be affected by the decision is an alien, just as much as when he is a British subject. The justification for it is primarily that, when a public authority has promised to follow a certain procedure it is in the interest of good administration that it should act fairly and should implement its promise, so long as implementation does not interfere with its statutory duty. The principle is also justified by the further consideration that, when the promise was made, the authority must have considered that it would be assisted in discharging its duty fairly by any representations from interested parties and as a general rule that is correct.

In the opinion of their Lordships the principle that a public authority is bound by its undertakings as to the procedure it will follow, provided they do not conflict with its duty, is applicable to the undertaking given by the Government of Hong Kong to the applicant, along with other illegal immigrants from Macau, in the announcement outside the Government House on October 28, that each case would be considered on its merits. The only ground on which it was argued before the Board that the undertaking had not been implemented was that the applicant had not been given an opportunity to put his case for an exercise of discretion, which the director undoubtedly possesses, in his favour before a decision was reached. The basis of the applicant's complaint is that, when he was interviewed by an official of the Immigration Department who recommended to the director that a removal order against him should be made, he was not able to explain the humanitarian grounds for the discretion to be exercised in his favour. In particular he had no opportunity of explaining that he was not an employee but a partner in a business which employed several workers. The evidence of the applicant, contained in an affidavit to the High Court, was that at the interview he was not allowed to say anything except to answer the questions put to him by the official who was interviewing him. Sir Denys Roberts C.J., giving the judgment of the full bench, concluded that the applicant:

"should have been asked whether there were any humanitarian reasons or other special factors which he would like to be taken into account before a decision was reached. If this had been done, he would not have been able to claim that he had no opportunity of making it clear that he was a proprietor of a business and not just a technician."

When the appeal was before the Court of Appeal McMullin V.-P. pointed out that "this is the narrow factual bases upon which the appeal stands." It was emphasised by Baber J. in two striking sentences as follows:

> "It is a pity that he was not expressly asked at his interview on October 29, 1980, 'have you anything to say as to why you should be allowed to remain in Hong Kong?' and his answer recorded. This would have been an adequate opportunity to state his case and had this been done these proceedings would have been unnecessary."

Their Lordships consider that this is a very narrow case on its facts, but they are not disposed to differ from the view expressed by both the courts below, to the effect that the government's promise to the applicant has not been implemented. Accordingly the appeal ought to be dismissed. But in the circumstances their Lordships are of opinion that the order made by the Court of Appeal should be varied. The appropriate remedy is not the conditional order or prohibition made by the Court of Appeal, but an order of certiorari to quash the removal order made by the director on October 31 against the applicant. That order of certiorari is of course entirely without prejudice to the making of a fresh removal order by the Director of Immigration after a fair inquiry has been held at which the applicant has been given an opportunity to make such representations as he may see fit as to why he should not be removed.

Their Lordships will humbly advise Her Majesty that the appeal ought to be dismissed and that, in substitution for the order of prohibition made by the Court of Appeal, an order of certiorari should be made quashing the removal order dated October 31, 1980, by the Director of Immigration.

Appeal dismissed.

Note
See also O'Reilly v. Mackman [1983] 2 A.C. 237; post p. 373 and Council of the Civil Service Unions v. Minister for the Civil Service [1985] A.C. 374; ante p. 287.

Not engraved on tablets of stone

Local Government Board v. Arlidge
[1915] A.C. 120
House of Lords

Arlidge was the assignee of a lease of a dwelling-house in Hampstead. The Borough Council made a closing order under the Housing, Town Planning, etc., Act 1909 in respect of the house. After doing some repairs, Arlidge applied to the Borough Council to determine the closing order, which the Council refused to do, and he then appealed to the Local Government Board against that refusal. The Board held a public inquiry before one of its housing inspectors, at which Arlidge and his witnesses gave evidence and his solicitor argued his case. The inspector submitted to the Board his report, together with a shorthand note of the evidence and speeches. The Board then intimated its willingness to consider any further statement in writing Arlidge might desire to submit. He did not avail himself of this opportunity, but applied to the King's Bench Division for a writ of certiorari, on the ground that the appeal had not been determined in the manner required by the law. He contended that (1) the appeal had been decided neither by the Board nor by anyone lawfully authorised to act for it; (2) the procedure adopted by the Board was contrary to natural justice, in that (a) he had not been afforded an opportunity of being heard orally before the Board, and (b) the report of the inspector on the inquiry was not disclosed to him.

The Divisional Court gave judgment for the Board, but the Court of Appeal reversed this decision.

The Local Government Board now appealed to the House of Lords (Viscount Haldane L.C., Lord Shaw, Lord Moulton and Lord Parmoor), who allowed the appeal, i.e. gave judgment for the Board.

VISCOUNT HALDANE L.C.: . . . When the duty of deciding an appeal is imposed, those whose duty it is to decide it must act judicially. They must deal with the question referred to them without bias, and they must give to each of the parties the opportunity of presenting adequately the case made. The decision must be come to in the spirit and with the sense of responsibility of a tribunal whose duty is to mete out justice. But it does not follow that the procedure of every such tribunal must be the same. In the case of a court of law tradition in this country has prescribed certain principles to which in the main the procedure must conform. But what that procedure is to be in detail must depend on the nature of the tribunal. In modern times it has become increasingly common for Parliament to give an appeal in matters which really pertain to administration, rather than to the exercise of the judicial functions of an ordinary court, to authorities whose functions are administrative and not in the ordinary sense judicial. Such a body as the Local Government Board has the duty of enforcing obligations on the individual which are imposed in the interests of the community. Its character is that of an organisation with executive functions. In this it resembles other great Departments of the State. When, therefore, Parliament entrusts it with judicial duties, Parliament must be taken, in the absence of any declaration to the contrary, to have intended it to follow the procedure which is its own, and is necessary if it is to be capable of doing its work efficiently. I agree with the view expressed in an analogous case by Lord Loreburn. In *Board of Education* v. *Rice*[1] he laid down that, in disposing of a question which was the subject of an appeal to it, the Board of Education was under a duty to act in good faith and to listen fairly to both sides, inasmuch as that was a duty which lay on everyone who decided anything. But he went on to say that he did not think it was bound to treat such a question as

---

[1] [1911] A.C. 179.

though it were a trial. The Board had no power to administer an oath, and need not examine witnesses. It could, he thought, obtain information in any way which it thought best, always giving a fair opportunity to those who were parties in the controversy to correct or contradict any relevant statement prejudicial to its view. If the Board failed in this duty, its order might be the subject of certiorari, and it might itself be the subject of mandamus.

I concur in this view of the position of an administrative body to which the decision of a question in dispute between parties has been entrusted. The result of its inquiry must, as I have said, be taken, in the absence of directions in the statute to the contrary, to be intended to be reached by its ordinary procedure. In the case of the Local Government Board it is not doubtful what this procedure is. The Minister at the head of the Board is directly responsible to Parliament like other Ministers. He is responsible not only for what he himself does, but for all that is done in his department. The volume of work entrusted to him is very great, and he cannot do the great bulk of it himself. He is expected to obtain his materials vicariously through his officials, and he has discharged his duty if he sees that they obtain these materials for him properly. To try to extend his duty beyond this, and to insist that he and other members of the Board should do everything personally, would be to impair his efficiency. Unlike a judge in a court, he is not only at liberty but is compelled to rely on the assistance of his staff. When, therefore, the Board is directed to dispose of an appeal, that does not mean that any particular official of the Board is to dispose of it. . . . Provided the work is done judicially and fairly in the sense indicated by Lord Loreburn, the only authority that can review what has been done is Parliament, to which the Minister in charge is responsible. The practice of the Department in the present case was, I think, sufficiently shown by Sir Horace Monro's[2] affidavit to have been followed. In accordance with that practice the Board, in order to obtain materials with which to decide, appointed one of its health inspectors to hold a public inquiry. This was in accordance with the rules which it had made under the section of the statute which I have quoted and with its usual practice. It is said that the report of the inspector should have been disclosed. It might or might not have been useful to disclose this report, but I do not think that the Board was bound to do so, any more than it would have been bound to disclose all the minutes made on the papers in the office before a decision was come to. It is plain from Sir Horace Monro's affidavit that the order made was the order of the Board, and so long as the Board followed a procedure which was usual, and not calculated to violate the tests to which I have already referred, I think that the Board was discharging the duty imposed on it in the fashion which Parliament must be taken to have contemplated when it deliberately transferred the jurisdiction, first, from a court of summary jurisdiction to the local authority, and then, for the purposes of all appeals, from quarter sessions to an administrative Department of the State. What appears to me to have been the fallacy of the judgment of the majority in the Court of Appeal is that it begs the question at the beginning by setting up the test of the procedure of a court of justice, instead of the other standard which was laid down for such cases in *Board of Education* v. *Rice (supra)*. I do not think that the Board was bound to hear the respondent orally, provided it gave him the opportunities which he actually had. . . .

For the reasons which I have given, I have arrived at the conclusion that the judgments of the Divisional Court and of Lord Justice Hamilton, in the Court of Appeal, were right, and that this appeal should be allowed with costs here and in the Court of Appeal, and that the order of the Divisional Court should be restored. Appeal allowed.

---

[2] [Sir Horace Monro was Permanent Secretary of the Local Government Board].

Lloyd v. McMahon
[1987] A.C. 625
House of Lords

Under section 20 of the Local Government Finance Act 1982, where it appears to an auditor carrying out the audit of local government accounts under the Act that a loss or deficiency has been caused by the wilful misconduct of any person, he may certify that such sum is due from the person guilty of wilful misconduct and may take steps to recover that sum. Subsection (3) provides that any person aggrieved by such a finding may appeal to the court. The majority group on the Liverpool City Council delayed setting a rate for the City with the object of extorting the largest possible amount of financial assistance from the central government. The auditor warned of the legal consequences of failing to set a rate. When, finally, a rate for the year 1985–86 was set in June of that year, the auditor informed the members of the majority group that he proposed to consider whether to certify that the loss sustained by the city accounts from the delay was attributable to their wilful default. He invited written representations and the councillors concerned responded with a detailed, collective reply in writing. They did not, at that stage, request an oral hearing. After the auditor certified the loss as attributable to the councillors' wilful misconduct they appealed to the Divisional Court (Glidewell L.J., Caulfield and Russell JJ.) under section 20 (3) of the 1982 Act.[1] The Divisional Court held that wilful misconduct had been fully established and the failure by the auditor to offer an oral hearing did not amount to procedural unfairness. The Court itself invited the councillors to give oral evidence but they declined to do so. The Court of Appeal (Lawton, Dillon and Wolf L.JJ.) dismissed the appeal. The councillors then appealed to the House of Lords (Lord Keith of Kinkel, Lord Bridge of Harwich, Lord Brandon of Oakbrook, Lord Templeman and Lord Griffiths).

LORD KEITH OF KINKEL: . . . The argument by counsel for the appellants did not invite your Lordships to enter deeply into the merits of the question whether or not they had been guilty of wilful misconduct, nor was attention drawn to any details of the affidavits and other material placed before the Divisional Court. The substance of the argument was that the district auditor's decision had been vitiated by his failure to offer the appellants an oral hearing before reaching it, and should therefore have been quashed. The argument was supported by an examination of earlier legislation in regard to local government audits, starting with the Poor Law Amendment Act 1844 (7 & 8 Vict. c. 101), where oral hearings were the order of the day, and by reference to the Code of Local Government Audit Practice for England and Wales, made under section 14 of the Act of 1982 and approved by resolution of both Houses of Parliament. The code, by paragraphs 16 to 20, contemplates that an oral hearing will be held where the auditor is dealing with a notice of objection give under section 17(3) of the Act of 1982,[2] which itself refers to the objector attending before the auditor. The code does not deal with the procedure to be followed where the auditor takes action under section 20(1). Counsel produced a list of all instances since 1972 where a district auditor had occasion to consider an issue of wilful misconduct, indicating that in all but one of them an oral hearing had been offered. This had the effect, so it was maintained, of creating a legitimate expectation on the part of the appellants that they would be offered an oral hearing before the district auditor arrived at his decision.

My Lords, if the district auditor had reached a decision adverse to the appellants without giving them any opportunity at all of making representations to

---

[1] The Local Government Act 1986, s.1 now imposes a legal duty to make a rate for each financial year on or before April 1 of that year.

[2] The text of the relevant sections are set out in the speech of Lord Bridge of Harwich.

him, there can be no doubt that his procedure would have been contrary to the rules of natural justice and that, subject to the question whether the defect was capable of being cured on appeal to the Divisional Court, the decision would fall to be quashed. In the event, written representations alone were asked for. These were duly furnished, in very considerable detail, and an oral hearing was not requested, though that could very easily have been done, and there is no reason to suppose that the request would not have been granted. None of the appellants stated, in his or her affidavit before the Divisional Court, that they had an expectation that an oral hearing, though not asked for, would be offered. The true question is whether the district auditor acted fairly in all the circumstances. It is easy to envisage cases where an oral hearing would clearly be essential in the interests of fairness, for example where an objector states that he has personal knowledge of some facts indicative of wilful misconduct on the part of a council-lor. In that situation justice would demand that the councillor be given an opportunity to depone to his own version of the facts. In the present case the district auditor had arrived at his provisional view upon the basis of the contents of documents, minutes of meetings and reports submitted to the council from the auditor's department and their own officers. All these documents were appended to or referred to in the notice of 26 June sent by the district auditor to the appellants. Their response referred to other documents, which were duly consi-dered by the district auditor, as is shown by his statement of reasons dated 6 September 1985. No facts contradictory of or supplementary to the contents of the documents were or are relied on by either side. If the appellants had attended an oral hearing they would no doubt have reiterated the sincerity of their motives from the point of view of advancing the interests of the inhabitants of Liverpool. It seems unlikely, having regard to the position adopted by their counsel on this matter before the Divisional Court, that they would have been willing to reveal or answer questions about the proceedings of their political caucus. The sincerity of the appellants' motives is not something capable of justifying or excusing failure to carry out a statutory duty, or of making reasonable what is otherwise an unreasonable delay in carrying out such a duty. In all the circumstances I am of opinion that the district auditor did not act unfairly, and that the procedure which he followed did not involve any prejudice to the appellants.

LORD BRIDGE OF HARWICH: . . . The only challenge which must now be consi-dered is procedural. There are, I think, three facets to the challenge. First, it is said that, as a matter of law, there is an absolute obligation on a district auditor, before issuing a certificate under section 20(1) of the Act of 1982, to ask any person upon whom the certificate will impose a liability whether he wishes to make oral representations. Secondly, in the circumstances of this case, it is said that there were matters of complaint against the appellants relied on by the district auditor in his reasons for decision dated September 6, 1985 of which the appellants were not informed by, and which they could not have anticipated from, the terms of the notice given to them dated June 26, 1985. Thirdly, it is said that, apart from any general obligation to offer the appellants an oral hearing, the district auditor was under a particular obligation to do so before he could properly reject as unaccept-able any explanation of their conduct put forward by the appellants relating to their intention, motivation, or good faith. If any one of these three propositions is established, then it is submitted that there was such a want of natural justice in the proceedings leading to the decision of the district auditor as to invalidate the certificate, with the result that, on appeal, the Divisional Court, irrespective of its view on the merits, was obliged to quash it.

My Lords, the so-called rules of natural justice are not engraved on tablets of stone. To use the phrase which better expresses the underlying concept, what the requirements of fairness demand when any body, domestic, administrative or judicial, has to make a decision which will affect the rights of individuals depends on the character of the decision-making body, the kind of decision it has to make and the statutory or other framework in which it operates. In particular, it is well-established that when a statute has conferred on any body the power to make decisions affecting individuals, the courts will not only require the procedure prescribed by the statute to be followed, but will readily imply so much and no more to be introduced by way of additional procedural safeguards as will ensure the attainment of fairness. It follows that the starting-point for the examination of all the appellants' submissions on this aspect of the case is the Act of 1982. It will be convenient here to set out all the provisions which, in my opinion, throw light on the issues to be decided. They are as follows:

"17(1) At each audit by an auditor under this Part of this Act any persons interested may inspect the accounts to be audited and all books, deeds, contracts, bills, vouchers and receipts relating to them and make copies of all or any part of the accounts and those other douments. (2) At the request of a local government elector for any area to which those accounts relate, the auditor shall give the elector, or any representative of his, an opportunity to question the auditor about the accounts. (3) Subject to subsection (4) below, any local government elector for any area to which those accounts relate, or any representative of his, may attend before the auditor and make objections—(a) as to any matter in respect of which the auditor could take action under section 19 or 20 below; ... (4) No objection may be made under subsection (3) above by or on behalf of a local government elector unless the auditor has previously received written notice of the proposed objection and of the grounds on which it is to be made.

"19(1) Where it appears to the auditor carrying out the audit of any accounts under this Part of this Act that any item of account is contrary to law he may apply to the court for a declaration that the item is contrary to law except where it is sanctioned by the Secretary of State. (2) On an application under this section the court may make or refuse to make the declaration asked for, and where the court makes that declaration, then, subject to subsection (3) below, it may also—(a) order that any person responsible for incurring or authorising any expenditure declared unlawful shall repay it in whole or in part to the body in question and, where two or more persons are found to be responsible, that they shall be jointly and severally liable to repay it as aforesaid; (b) if any such expenditure exceeds £2,000 and the person responsible for incurring or authorising it is, or was at the time of his conduct in question, a member of a local authority, order him to be disqualified for being a member of a local authority for a specified period; and (c) order rectification of the accounts. (3) The court shall not make an order under subsection (2)(a) or (b) above if the court is satisfied that the person responsible for incurring or authorising any such expenditure acted reasonably or in the belief that the expenditure was authorised by law, and in any other case shall have regard to all the circumstances, including that person's means and ability to repay that expenditure or any part of it. (4) Any person who has made an objection under section 17(3)(a) above and is aggrieved by a decision of an auditor not to apply for a declaration under this section may—(a) not later than six weeks after he has been notified of the decision, require the auditor to state in writing the reasons for his decision; and (b) appeal against the decision to the court, and on any such appeal the court shall have the like powers in relation to the item of the account to which the objection relates as if the auditor had applied for the declaration. ... (6) The court having jurisdiction for the purposes of this section shall be the High Court except that, if the amount of the item of account alleged to be contrary to law does not exceed the amount over which county courts have jurisdiction in actions founded on contract, the county court shall have concurrent jurisdiction with the High Court. ...

"20(1) Where it appears to the auditor carrying out the audit of any accounts under this Part of this Act—(a) that any person has failed to bring into account any sum which should have been so included and that the failure has not been sanctioned by the Secretary of State; or (b) that a loss has been incurred or deficiency caused by the wilful misconduct of any person, he shall certify that the sum or, as the case may be, the amount of the loss or the deficiency is due from that person and, subject to subsections (3) and (5) below, both he and the body in question (or, in the case of a parish meeting, the chairman of the meeting) may recover that sum or amount for the benefit of that body; and if the auditor certifies under this section that any sum or amount is due from two or more persons, they shall be jointly and severally liable for that sum or amount. (2) Any person who—(a) has made an objection under section 17(3)(a) above and is aggrieved by a decision of an auditor not to certify under this section that a sum or amount is due from another person; or (b) is aggrieved by a decision of an auditor to certify under this section that a sum or amount is due from him, may not later than six weeks after he has been notified of the decision require the auditor to state in writing the reasons for his decision. (3) Any such person who is aggrieved by such a decision may appeal against the decision to the court and—(a) in the case of a decision to certify that any sum or amount is due from any person, the court may confirm, vary or quash the decision and give any certificate which the auditor could have given; (b) in the case of a decision not to certify that any sum or amount is due from any person, the court may confirm the decision or quash it and give any certificate which the auditor could have given; and any certificate given under this subsection shall be treated for the purposes of subsection (1) above and the following provisions of this section as if it had been given by the auditor under subsection (1) above. (4) If a certificate under this section relates to a loss or deficiency caused by the wilful misconduct of person who is, or was at the time of such misconduct, a member of a local authority and the amount certified to be due from him exceeds £2,000, that person shall be disqualified for being a member of a local authority for the period of five years beginning on the ordinary date on which the period allowed for bringing an appeal against a decision to give the certificate expires or, if such an appeal is brought, the date on which the appeal is finally disposed of or abandoned or fails for non-prosecution. (5) A sum or other amount certified under this section to be due from any person shall be payable within 14 days after the date of the issue of the certificate or, if an appeal is brought, within 14 days after the appeal is finally disposed of or abandoned or fails for non-prosecution. (6) In any proceedings for the recovery of any sum or amount due from any person under this section a certificate signed by an auditor appointed by the commission stating that that sum or amount is due from a person specified in the certificate to a body so specified shall be conclusive evidence of that fact; and any certificate purporting to be so signed shall be taken to have been so signed unless the contrary is proved. ... (9) The court having jurisdiction for the purposes of this section shall be the High Court except that, if the sum or amount alleged to be due does not exceed the amount over which county courts have jurisdiction in actions founded on contract, the county court shall have concurrent jurisdiction with the High Court."

All these provisions except section 17(1) and (2) apply to an extraordinary audit under section 22 as they apply to an ordinary audit.

I draw attention at the outset to two striking features of this statutory machinery. The first is that both the exercise of the power to declare items of account unlawful under section 19 and the ultimate power to control the issue of certificates under section 20 are entrusted to the regular courts, the county court if the amount in issue is within the county court's contractual jurisdiction, the High

Court if it is not. Under section 19 the auditor can take no effective step without invoking the jurisdiction of the court. Under section 20 the auditor's certificate will be effective unless appealed against. The second striking feature is this. The auditor may act of his own motion either in applying to the court for a declaration under section 19 or in issuing a certificate under section 20. But where, for any reason, he fails or declines to act under either section, after he has been invited to do so by a local government elector exercising his right of objection under section 17(3)(a), that elector has an unfettered right to invoke the jurisdiction of the court himself. In a case under section 19 the court will in every case be exercising its jurisdiction at first instance, but the auditor may be either seeking or opposing the declaration. In a case under section 20, the auditor may, if he has been invited to act under section 17(3)(a), be described as the tribunal of first instance, but whichever way he decides, an unfettered right of appeal to the courts lies at the instance either of the aggrieved elector or of the party from whom the relevant loss has been certified to be due. In either case if the court falls into error the error can be corrected by the Court of Appeal or, if necessary, by your Lordships' House.

So far as procedure is concerned, section 14 of the Act of 1982 provides for the issue of a code of audit practice to be approved by each House of Parliament. The code currently in force contains detailed provisions relating to objections under section 17, but none relating to the procedure to be followed when an auditor contemplates the issue of a certificate under section 20 of his own motion. The gravity of the consequences of a certificate for the person from whom the amount of a loss is certified is to be due, particularly if he is a member of a local authority and the amount exceeds £2,000, are obvious enough. No one doubts that the auditor must give to such a person adequate notice of the case against him and an adequate opportunity to present to the auditor his defence to that case. I followed with interest Mr. Blom-Cooper's carefully researched review of the history of local government audit legislaion, but I did not find that it threw any light on what, in particular, is required to provide such an opportunity in the circumstances of any particular case under the statute presently in force. Still less do I attach any significance to the fact that since 1972, when provisions substantially to the like effect as those which we find in the Act of 1982 first reached the statute book, auditors have, as a matter of practice, always invited oral representations from members of local authorities before certifying the amount of any loss or deficiency as due from them. When a single individual is thought to have failed to bring sum into account or by his wilful misconduct to have caused a loss or deficiency, it is no doubt a very appropriate practice to invite his explanation orally. But I fail to understand how that practice can constrain the courts to construe the statute as requiring an auditor proposing to act under section 20 to invite oral representations as a matter of law in every case. In this case the auditor seems to have intelligently anticipated that the Liverpool councillors who constituted the majority group would want to present a united front in their response to his notice of 26 June 1985 as they had done in their conduct of the city council's affairs during the previous year. Councillor Hamilton's letter of 19 July 1985 amply confirmed his expectation. If any councillor had wanted to put forward his own independent and individual grounds in rebuttal of the charge of wilful misconduct against himself, I have no doubt he would have done so. If any had asked to be heard orally and the auditor had refused, there would have been clear ground for a complaint of unfairness. I suppose it is conceivable that the appellants collectively might have wished to appoint a spokesman to present their case orally rather than in writing, though the case they did present, embracing as it did such a large volume of documentary material, clearly lent itself more aptly to written than oral presentation. It has never been suggested that it was unfair that the auditor did not invite the appellants to address arguments to him through solicitor or counsel. The proposition that it was, per se, in breach of the rules of natural justice not to invite oral representations in this case is quite untenable.

The second facet of the complaint of unfairness alleges that the notice of 26 June 1985 did not sufficiently particularise the case which the appellants had to meet and that new matters were relied on by the auditor in the reasons for his decision given on 6 September 1985. This is exhaustively examined in the judgments of the courts below and it would serve no good purpose to re-examine it in detail. The notice dated 26 June was sent with copies of all the previous reports to the council of the district auditor and his predecessor and identified by reference all the relevant council and committee minutes and reports made to the council by their own officers. I am fully satisfied that this gave adequate notice of the grounds on which the auditor was provisionally minded to proceed against the appellants under section 20 and indeed the character of the response shows that they were in no doubt as to the nature of the case they had to meet. The point that troubled Lawton L.J. and, to a lesser extent, Dillon L.J. was that the auditor in giving the reasons for his decision rejected the protestations of good faith in the appellants response to his notice of 26 June and did not accept that their motivation in acting as they did was as they claimed. . . . In so far as there was an issue as to whether the course on which the appellants quite deliberately embarked was one in which they acted "in good faith" or as to the motives which underlay their action or inaction, it was in essence a matter for argument rather than for evidence. When a group of 49 people act collectively they may, of course, have different subjective reasons for acting. But if they assert that their collective action was prompted by a single collective state of mind, this is inevitably to some extent a fiction. A group can have no single subjective mind. On the other hand, the objective state of mind of the group can only be inferred from what the group concurred in doing or omitting to do in given circumstances. In this case it would not have advanced the appellants' case at all if each appellant had appeared in person before the auditor and asserted his sincere belief in what had been said in the collective written response. On the other hand, if each had given his own explanation and volunteered to submit to questioning as to his own individual state of mind in relation to the council's proceedings, this would have been a departure from the collective stance which the appellants had deliberately adopted and to which they have throughout resolutely adhered. For these reasons I think the auditor was fully entitled to draw inferences from the undisputed facts which involved a rejection of the appellants' protestations of good faith and purity of motive and that his doing so without further reference to the appellants after he received their response dated 19 July 1985 involved no unfairness to them.

LORD TEMPLEMAN: . . . The auditor invited representations in writing by 19 July 1985 and intimated that he would defer making a decision until he had considered the appellants' representations.

On 19 July 1985 the appellants submitted detailed and careful representations which had been drafted with the assistance of the chief executive of Liverpool. The facts to which the auditor had drawn attention could not be and were not disputed. The appellants denied wilful misconduct on three grounds. First they said that at all times they had acted in what they sincerely believed to be the best interests of the ratepayers and citizens of Liverpool. My Lords, political leaders from Robespierre, the sea-green incorruptible, to Gandhi, the prophet of non-violence, have acted in the sincere belief that it was necessary to break the nation's laws in the interests of the nation's citizens. Only Gandhi, who broke the salt laws, acknowledged in a celebrated exchange of courtesies with the British magistrate the correctness of his conviction and the appropriate imposition of a sentence of imprisonment which, however, hastened the repeal of the salt tax and the dawn of independence for India. The sincerity of the appellants provides no defence to a charge that they deliberately delayed after they had been warned that it was wrong of them to do so. Secondly, the appellants contended that they were entitled to delay in the hope and expectation that the government would thereby be compelled or persuaded to provide more money for Liverpool. But the government in March 1985 had made it quite clear that the councillors would be responsible if they did not make a rate based on current government grants. The appellants' belief that the government did not mean that which the government stated does not justify a delay which was bound to cause loss to Liverpool whatever the government might do. Thirdly, the appellants contended that they had delayed in 1984 without dire consequences to themselves, and were entitled to believe that they would escape from the consequences of delay in 1985. But both the government and the officers of Liverpool, at an early stage, made plain to the council that 1985 circumstances were different from 1984 circumstances, and that delay in 1985 would not be tolerated or excused. An offender cannot successfully plead by way of defence that he was not prosecuted for a similar offence on a previous occasion.

The appellants did not ask the auditor for an oral hearing but it is now said that the auditor should have invited the appellants to make oral representations before he ultimately made up his mind. My Lords, a councillor might have persuaded the auditor, if he was not already persuaded, that the councillor was sincere in his belief that he could not sacrifice the policy for which he had been elected and sincere in the belief that a rigid adherence to the policy would enure for the benefit of the citizens of Liverpool even if it entailed a breach of the councillor's duty promptly to make an adequate rate to provide for the year's expenditure. But the councillor's beliefs could not alter the councillor's duty or excuse a deliberate breach of that duty. In the voluminous evidence and in the addresses of counsel I have been unable to discern any grounds for the assertion that the oral representations of a councillor could have supplied a defence which was lacking from the written representations of the appellants or could have validated or reinforced possible defences foreshadowed in those written representations. The facts disclosed by the douments were incontrovertible and damning. The auditor had no choice but to find the appellants guilty of wilful misconduct. He certified on 6 September 1985 that the loss for which the appellants were liable amounted to £106,103. . . .

If any appellant had requested an oral hearing, I think that it would have been desirable for the auditor to have granted that request, first, so that the appellant could reiterate the sincerity of his motives and, secondly, so that the appellant might satisfy himself as to the judicial and impartial quality of the auditor. But sincerity is no excuse. An oral hearing could not detract from the force of the documentary evidence or supplement the written defence of the appellants in any material respects. I do not consider that the auditor was bound to follow a procedure which the appellants, acting under competent advice, did not suggest. The judicial and impartial qualities of the auditor are not in question.

Mr. Blom-Cooper urged that although the appellants did not request an oral hearing, they were deprived of a "legitimate expectation" of being invited to an oral hearing. Mr. Blom-Cooper does not allege that the appellants in fact expected to be invited to an oral hearing and does not speculate whether they would have accepted an invitation. Mr. Blom-Cooper submits that a legitimate expectation of being invited to an oral hearing is an objective fundamental right which, if not afforded, results in a breach of law or breach of natural justice which invalidates any decision based on written material. This extravagant language does not tempt me to elevate a catch-phrase into a principle. The true principle is that the auditor, like any other decision-maker, must act fairly. It was not unfair for the auditor to reach a decision on the basis of the written material served on and submitted by the appellants. In *Council of Civil Service Unions* v. *Minister for the Civil Service* [1985] A.C. 374 it was unfair for the government to decide to deprive a civil servant of his right to belong to a trade union without first consulting the civil servant or his union; the House would have quashed the decision but for the overriding interests of national security which justified the government's decision. My noble and learned friend, Lord Roskill, pointed out, at p. 415, that "legitimate expectation" is a manifestation of the duty to act fairly. A decision may be unfair if the decision-maker deprives himself of the views of persons who will be affected by the decision. In the present case the appellants were afforded ample opportunity to express their views, and the auditor was enabled to reach a decision in the light of every defence which it was possible for the appellants to urge.

Appeal dismissed.

II. PRIVATE LAW LIABILITY

CONTRACT

Birkdale District Electric Supply Company Limited v. Corporation of Southport

[1926] A.C. 355

House of Lords

The appellant company, operating under statutory powers, entered into an agreement with the predecessors of Southport Corporation under which it agreed that the price of electricity supplied by the company in Birkdale should not exceed the price of electricity supplied in the adjoining borough of Southport. Subsequently the company began to charge higher prices than those charged in Southport. The Corporation sought an injunction to restrain the appellants from acting in breach of the agreement.

Astbury J. held that the clauses might conceivably in the future hamper the appellants in the proper performance of their statutory duties and were therefore ultra vires, and he dismissed the action. The Court of Appeal (Pollock M.R., Warrington and Sargant L.JJ.) held that the agreement was not incompatible with the exercise by the appellants of their statutory duty, and granted an injunction.

The company appealed to the House of Lords (Earl of Birkenhead, Lord Atkinson, Lord Sumner, Lord Wrenbury and Lord Carson).

EARL OF BIRKENHEAD: . . . The appellants have relied strongly on a well established principle of law, that if a person or public body is entrusted by the Legislature with certain powers and duties expressly or impliedly for public purposes, those persons or bodies cannot divest themselves of these powers and duties. They cannot enter into any contract or take any action incompatible with the due exercise of their powers or the discharge of their duties. Many authorities were referred to in support, or rather in illustration of this principle, from *Mulliner* v. *Midland Ry. Co.*[1] and *Ayr Habour Trustees* v. *Oswald*[2] down to *York Corporation* v. *Henry Leetham & Sons.*[3] A good example of the length to which the principle is carried is afforded by the case of *Paterson* v. *Provost of St. Andrews.*[4] There the magistrates of a burgh from time immemorial, for behoof of the inhabitants, held a golf links, subject to the obligation of preserving the same for the purpose of the game of golf and for the recreation and amusement of the inhabitants. The magistrates had from time to time exercised powers of management over the links. They proposed to make a macadamized road outside and along the boundary of the links where the boundary adjoined certain fens let by them in 1820, but no longer in law part of the links. An inhabitant of the burgh, and member of the golf club and others, sued for an interdict to restrain the magistrates either from making the road or permitting any road to be used in the specified place for wheeled traffic. The case was strenuously contested. Lord Selbourne L.C., Lord Blackburn and Lord Watson gave judgments. The real point in controversy reduced itself to this—whether the alteration of the surface of the site of the road, and the permission to use it for carts and carriages, would substantially interfere with the obligation of the magistrates to preserve the ground for the purpose of golf. It was held that the evidence provded that it would have no substantial interference with the practice of golfing, and that the use of the road might be

[1] (1879) 11 Ch. D. 611.
[2] 8 App. Cas. 623.
[3] [1924] 1 Ch. 557.
[4] (1881) 6 App. Cas. 833.

reconciled with its due observance; but that it was not consistent with that obligation for the magistrates to alienate any part of the ground in question, or to abdicate their existing power of administration, either by granting private easements to particular individuals or by dedicating the road when made to the public, thereby creating a public easement.

The third and fourth claims put forward by the plaintiffs were that the magistrates had no right to construct or permit or authorise the defenders, or any of them, to construct a road for carts and carriages along the northern boundary of the links, and fourth, that neither the magistrates nor the other defenders were entitled to use or to authorise or permit the use of the portion of the links adjoining the northern boundary of the parcels of ground (*i.e.*, the ground identified in the evidence) as an access for carts and carriages. Lord Blackburn said in delivering judgment[5] "Now the proposition put forward in the third and fourth [claims], that those two purposes are, under all circumstances, and in every way, beyond the power of the provost, the magistrates, and the town council, I think it is perfectly plain is too wide a proposition a great deal. Such things may be done in such a way as to interfere with the primary purposes for which the lands are held, namely, golfing and recreation, in which case I agree that they should not be done. On the other hand, such things may be done in such a way as not to interfere with this use, and though the motive may be a wish to give an advantage to a particular person who owns a house, or any other particular motive they like, yet so long as it does not injure or interfere with the rights which the inhabitants possess to have those lands preserved for the public recreation or enjoyment, more particularly for the game of golf, I do not see that the appellants have any right to complain." Lord Watson said: "My Lords, what the magistrates and town council were proposing to do at the time when this action was raised appears to me to have been this, they were acting upon the assumption that it was within their competency to confer upon the public at large a right of way over a portion of the ground which it was their duty to preserve for purposes consistent with the rights of the inhabitants; and they justified their position upon the ground that as matters stood at that date, no right of the inhabitants would be invaded thereby. I think that was a mistaken view of the law and of the extent of their power, because they would thereby have vested in others a right which might become inconsistent with the rights of the inhabitants at some future time."

In none of the authorities cited in the Court of Appeal, or, indeed, before Astbury J., was the principle I have mentioned questioned. The problem was throughout, on the facts proved, to bring the case within the principle. The *York* case[6] was somewhat severely criticised in the Court of Appeal. The facts of it are peculiar, and having regard to this peculiarity and to the acute criticism of Sargant L.J.[7] (which I adopt), I regard that case as distinguishable.

I am of opinion that the appeal fails and should be dismissed, and I so move your Lordships.

LORD SUMNER: . . . [Having concluded that the agreement was not contrary to the relevant statutory provisions he went on to ask whether it was] void at common law as being ultra vires the appellants, a trading company, incorporated to exercise statutory powers vested in them in the public interest under the authority of the Legislature? This is a doctrine, which it may be unwise to circumscribe within the limits of an inelastic definition. We have, however, a long series of decisions, extending over nearly a century, and at any rate illustrating the cases to which the rule has been understood to extend. With the exception of

[5] 6 App. Cas. 848, 851.
[6] [1924] 1 Ch. 557.
[7] (1833) 5 B. & Ad. 469.

York Corporation v. *Henry Leetham & Sons*[8] no case has been cited, in which a contract by a trading company to compound with a customer without limit of time for the price to be paid for services rendered to him, has been declared to be ultra vires, and we were told that the diligence of counsel had failed to find any other case. Certainly I have been able to go no further.

Hitherto the question has mainly arisen, where servitudes have been claimed over the property, which the alleged servient owner acquired under statutory authority and for the purposes of a public undertaking. In *Rex* v. *Inhabitants of Leake*[9] a public right of way was alleged to exist over the bank of a drain constructed by statutory Commissioners and reparable as such by the inhabitants of Leake. In *Staffordshire and Worcestershire Canal Navigation* v. *Birmingham Canal Navigations*[10] a right was claimed to have water discharged from the respondents' canal into the canal of the appellants at the bottom of a flight of locks connecting the two navigations, which the respondents had not therefore sought to recover by pumping. In *Mulliner* v. *Midland Ry. Co.*[11] land, acquired under statutory powers, had been alienated pro tanto by an express grant of a right of way through one of a series of arches, which carried the defendants' line and station over some low ground; as to this case, however, *In re Gonty and Manchester, Sheffield and Lincolnshire Ry. Co.*[12] and observations by Warrington L.J. in *South Eastern Ry. Co.* v. *Cooper*[13] should be referred to. In *Great Western Ry. Co.* v. *Solihull Rural Council*[14] a right of walking and taking recreation was claimed for the public over the banks of a reservoir, formed for the supply of the plaintiffs' canal navigation. The right in these cases (*Mulliner's* excepted) was rested on prescription and not on express grant, but the argument, which prevailed, was that the theory of dedication to the public use rests on an implied grant but none could be implied, since even an express grant would have been void as being ultra vires.

Parallel with these decisions there is line of cases, in which the servitude claimed has been upheld on the ground that a dedication would not under the circumstances have been incompatible with full observance of the terms and full attainment of the purposes for which the statutory powers had been granted. This principle is stated as early as *Rex* v. *Inhabitants of Leak*,[15] in which the dedication was upheld, and was acted on in *Grand Junction Canal Co.* v. *Petty*,[16] a case of a public right of walking on a towpath, and in *Greenwich Board of Works* v. *Maudslay*,[17] a case of a footpath along a sea wall, and was made the ground of the decision against the right in the *Solihull* case[18]; *Rochdale Canal Co.* v. *Radcliffe*[19]; *Creyke* v. *Corporation of Level of Hatfield Chase*.[20] Parke J. says, in the *Leake* case, that, if the bank was vested in the Commissioners by statute, so that they were thereby bound to use it for some special purpose, incompatible with a public right of walking along it, they must be deemed to have been incapable in law of thus dedicating their property; otherwise they were in that regard in the same position as other landowners: and see *Foster* v. *London, Chatham and Dover Ry. Co.*[21] the *Greenwich* case,[22] says "whatever is inconsistent with its doing its duty as a seawall

[8] [1924] 1 Ch. 557.
[9] (1833) 5 B. & Ad. 469.
[10] (1866) L.R. 1 H.L. 254.
[11] 11 Ch.D. 611.
[12] [1896] 2 Q.B. 439
[13] [1924] 1 Ch. 211, 229.
[14] (1902) 86 L.T. 852.
[15] 5 B. & Ad. 469.
[16] (1888) 21 Q.B.D. 273.
[17] (1870) L.R. 5 Q.B. 397.
[18] See note 14.
[19] (1852) 18 Q.B. 287.
[20] (1896) 12 Times L.R. 383.
[21] [1895] 1 Q.B. 711.
[22] See note 17.

cannot stand." Warrington L.J., in *Cooper's* case,[23] where a private level crossing was claimed, sums up the rule by saying, that statutory company has no power to grant any easement, unless expressly or impliedly authorised, but that its inability in this respect is confined to the granting of easements, the enjoyment of which is incompatible or inconsistent with the employment of the land for the statutory purposes for which it was acquired. In the *Grand Junction* case.[24] Lindley L.J. says, that such incompatibility is a matter of evidence, and, in practice, evidence has regularly been given and considered for the purpose of testing the question.

My Lords, I do not think that these cases assist the appellants in any way, but in most respects are against them, for they show that, in default of proof of incompatibility in the present case, some other consideration of a cogent kind must be found. The incompetence of the company is only an incompetence sub modo, beyond which the powers necessary to its operation may be freely exercised.

Ayr Habour Trustees v. *Oswald*[25] introduces a new matter and is nearer to the present case. Harbour trustees, whose statutory power and duty were to acquire land, to be used as need might arise for the construction of works on the coast line of the habour, sought to save money in respect of severance on the compulsory acquisition of a particular owner's land by offering him a perpetual covenant not to construct their works on the land acquired, so as to cut him off from access to the waters of the habour, or otherwise to affect him injuriously in respect of land not taken but from which the acquired land was severed. It was held that such a covenant was ultra vires. Lord Blackburn's words should be quoted. "I think," he says, "that where the legislature confer powers on any body to take land compulsorily for a particular purpose, it is on the ground that the using of that land for that purpose will be for the public good. Whether that body be one which is seeking to make a profit for shareholders, or, as in the present case, a body of trustees acting solely for the public good . . . a contract purporting to bind them and their successors not to use those powers, is void."

Founding on this case, Russell J. held in *York Corporation* v. *Henry Leetham & Sons*[26] that a contract, terminable only by the customer, to carry his traffic at a fixed annual sum was equally ultra vires. Just as the covenant in the *Ayr Habour* case[27] tied the hands of the successors to the then trustees, and prevented them from constructing works on the land acquired, however necessary they might have become for the proper management of the undertaking, so he held that the corresponding contracts with Leetham fettered the free management of the canal in perpetuity, no matter how urgent it might be to increase the revenues of the undertaking.

My Lords, I do not think that there is a true analogy between these cases. On examining the facts in the *Ayr Habour* case[27] it is plain that, in effect, the trustees did not merely propose to covenant in a manner that committed the business of the habour to restricted lines in the future; they were to forbear, once and for all, to acquire all that the statute intended them to acquire, for, though technically they acquired the whole of the land, they were to sterilise part of their acquisition, so far as the statutory purpose of their undertaking was concerned. This is some distance from a mere contract entered into with regard to trading profits. The land itself was affected in favour of the former owner in the *Ayr* case just as a towpath is affected in favour of the owner of a dominant tenement, if he is given a personal right of walking along it. If the Ayr trustees had reduced the acquisition price by covenanting with the respondent for a perpetual right to moor his barges, free of

---

[23] [1924] 1 Ch. 211, 229.
[24] (1888) 21 Q.B.D. 273.
[25] 8 App. Cas. 623, 634.
[26] [1924] 1 Ch. 557.
[27] 8 App. Cas. 623.

tolls, at any wharf, they might construct on the water front of the land acquired, the decision might, and I think would, have been different.

There is, however, another aspect of the *Ayr Harbour* case[27] whcih ought to beloyally recognised. It is certainly some ground for saying that there may be cases where the question of competence to contract does not depend on a proved incompatibility between the statutory purposes and the user, which is granted or renounced, but is established by the very nature of the grants or the contract itself. It was not proved in the *Ayr* case that there was any actual incompatibility between the general purposes of the undertaking and the arrangement by which the particular proprietor was to be spared a particular interference with the amenities or the advantages of his back land. I think the case was supposed to speak for itself and that, in effect, the trustees were held to have renounced a part of their statutory birth-right.[28] The appellants, however, contend, and Russell J. appears to have thought, that your Lordships' House extended other principles, namely, those applicable to servitudes over land acquired, to mere contracts restricting the undertakers' future freedom of action in respect to the business management of their undertaking. This point of view ought therefore to be examined.

The appellants, as I understand them, say that the doctrine is not confined to the creation of servitudes or othe derogations by grant from plenary ownership, but extends also to such covenants in perpetuity as may, in events not actually impossible, starve their undertaking and spell its ruin. Southport, they say, now standing in the shoes of the Birkdale Council as well as in its own (if I may somewhat distort their metaphor), has behind it the pockets of the ratepayers of both areas, and though these may be no more inexhaustible than their patience, at least they may prove deeper and more enduring than the paid-up or uncalled capital of the appellant company, or its shareholders' willingness to subscribe to new issues of debentures or of preference stock. The thing speaks for itself. The covenant is fraught with potential suicide for the covenantors, and so is ultra vires.

My Lords, this hypothesis is conceivable, though neither from the evidence nor the argument have I gathered why these machinations should be attributed to the respondents or be toleraged by their outraged ratepayers. Municipal finance is capable of much curious development, but I think that among ordinary ratepayers a passion to supply current below cost price to private consumers is purely academic. If it exists at Southport, I think it should be proved by testimony.

The argument must be either that it is one of the direct statutory objects of the Electric Lighting Order that the undertakers should make a profit or at least not suffer any loss, or else that this is an indirect statutory object, since, if the undertakers make no profit, they will either pursue the undertaking without zeal or will drop it, so soon as this imaginary rate-war exhausts their resources.

My Lords, I am afraid this is beyond me. It may be the policy of the Electric Lighting Acts to get trading companies to take up and work Electric Lighting Orders in hope of gain, but I cannot see that it is any part of the direct purposes of the Order, that money should be made or dividends distributed. The primary object of the Electric Lighting Order was to get a supply of electric energy for the area in question, a thing only feasible at the time by getting a trading company to undertake the business. It was not to secure that certain charges should be made or that certain results should be shown upon a profit and loss account. As for the indirect effect, which will follow if no money is made or enough money is lost, the Order itself imposes a maximum price for the current and conceivably, therefore,

---

[28] "Striking as the phrase is, it does not seem to offer much help in deciding which the principle of . . . *Oswald's* Case is to be applied;" *British Transport Commission* v. *Westmorland C.C.* [1958] A.C. 126, 155 *per* Lord Radcliffe.

might itself lead to the exhaustion of the company's funds. How, then, can it be part of the legal objects of the grant of these powers, that they should never result in financial disaster? The Order is really as little concerned with the company's ultimate ability to continue the undertaking as with its earning of a profit. The latter is the company's own affair; the former will simply lead to the revocation of the Order and the grant of a more favourable one to some one else. If this is so, there is a wide and more than sufficient difference between the contract of the Ayr Harbour Trustees not to acquire all that they were intended to acquire, and that of the appellants to obtain the transfer of the Order by covenanting among other considerations for something, which obviously is not, and may never be, incompatible with the fulfilment of all the purposes of the Order and most of the purposes of the company's trading as well.

In *York Corporation* v. *Henry Leetham & Sons*[29] there were two navigations, both vested in the Corporation of York, which appear to have differed somewhat in their incidents, the Ouse Navigation and the Foss Navigation. The original Act of 1726, which authorised the fomer, empowered trustees to levy tolls on craft using the navigation when completed, and, for the purpose of constructing the navigation, authorised them to mortgage these prospective tolls and so to raise the necessary capital. The resources of the trustees were therefore of a character wholly different from those of a limited liability company. A later Act, that of 1732, fixed a schedule of rates and provided that all commodities carried "shall" bear them, and that it should be lawful for the trustees to take the rates "by this Act directed and no others," though, if the full revenue derived from these rates proved to be more than was required to maintain the undertaking, there was power to moderate them. The Act, which authorised the latter navigation, provided for the incorporation of a company having a capital of 25,400*l.* in 100*l.* shares and borrowing powers up to 10,000*l.* No distinction appears, from the judgment of Russell J., to have been drawn in, argument between these two undertakings, but it is possible that the agreement in dispute, by which the undertakers compounded the rates with a particular customer, might be regarded as a direct breach of the mandatory charging clause of the Ouse Act of 1732, and consequently ultra vires. The same view could not arise on the Foss Act. The ratio decidendi of the judgment, however, proceeds entirely on the analogy of the *Ayr Harbour* case.[30]

My Lords, with all respect to the learned judge, I am unable to adopt this reasoning. As I have said, it is no part of the intention of the Legislature that the appellants should make a profit or avoid a loss. If, again, the agreement is to be ultra vires at all, it must be ultra vires all through. In cases like the *Ayr Harbour* case (1) the land acquired under statutory powers was fettered in the undertakers' hands from the time the agreement was made. In the present case the company's activities have not yet been and may never be impaired by the agreement at all. So far it may have been and probably has been safe and beneficial. How, then, can it have been ultra vires hitherto? There is further, in my opinion, a wide distinction between the position of the appellants and of such undertakers as the Ayr Harbour Trustees. The scheme here is that a limited liability company, not deprived of its right, as such, to go into voluntary liquidation or otherwise to terminate its enterprise, obtained the Order with the Board of Trade's consent and with the like consent may part with it. In other words, the Board of Trade is here the constituted authority, by whose discretionary intervention the supply of electricity may be secured in the interest of the locality. This is a very different scheme from a constitution of undertakers, which under the same statute establishes their existence, confers their powers, and defines their purposes.

[29] [1924] 1 Ch. 557.
[30] 8 App. Cas. 623.

It appears to me that no line can be drawn between the agreement now in question and any ordinary trading contract, if the appellants are right in testing the validity of the ontract by its ultimate and theoretic possibility of bringing upon them a crippling loss. I do not think that a speculation as to the possible effect of what they have done is a legitimate ground for relieving them from their bargain,and it seems to me that the appeal should be dismissed.
Appeal dismissed.

R. v. Hammersmith and Fulham L.B.C.
Ex parte Beddowes
[1987] 2 W.L.R. 263
Court of Appeal

The Council decided to dispose of a number of blocks of flats to private developers who would finance the modernisation of the flats and then sell them. To increase the attractiveness of the scheme to prospective purchasers the Council, in the agreement for the sale of the first block, entered into covenants under which it restricted the terms on which it could let flats in the remaining blocks in the period before they were sold. The legality of the covenants was challenged on the grounds that they constituted an unlawful fetter on the future exercise by the Council of its powers and that the decision to develop the flats for owner-occupancy was unreasonable. An application for *certiorari* was dismissed by Schiemann J. The applicants appealed to the Court of Appeal (Fox and Kerr L.JJ., and Sir Denys Buckley).

Fox L.J.: . . . The problem with which the council was faced was the modernisation of an estate laid out in blocks. The estate was 50 years old and in bad repair. It was no longer possible to limp along with day-to-day repairs which were not cost-effective, or indeed adequate. A major programme of modernisation was necessary, and the cost was high. It was estimated in November 1983 to be about £8 million, and was an amount which the council felt was too large for its own finances to sustain. The council, therefore, over a period developed a policy for dealing with the problem. The essential features of that policy in their final form were as follows.

(1) All the blocks should be sold to a developer for modernisation.

(2) The blocks, when modernised, should then be sold off as flats to the ultimate purchasers. The whole of Blocks A-G would eventually pass into the hands of owner-occupiers in this way.

(3) The preferred developers would be non-profit organisations, but the use of commercial developers was left open.

(4) The first block to be dealt with would be Block A, because it was different from the others in that it faced the Fulham Road, and it included a number of shops and it had a very ugly rear elevation which needed improvement for the benefit of the other blocks. In general, its attractive renovation was a matter of some importance in relation to the saleability of the other blocks.

(5) The council formed the view that persons buying owner-occupier flats in Block A (and in the other blocks as the development proceeded) should have a guarantee as to the user of the rest of the estate for owner-occupation. The individual purchasers of flats would be expending a substantial capital sum by way of premium, and would want binding assurances as to the user of the rest of the estate, since that would materially affect their own dwellings. The council indeed felt that if it was adopting a policy of owner-occupancy and encouraging sales of the individual flats on that basis, it was morally bound to give appropriate guarantees as to the effective implementation of what it believed to be a suitable housing policy. In the absence of certainty as to the development of the whole estate, marketing might be difficult and the whole project might flop. Although the flats were being sold at comparatively modest prices, for most purchasers the acquisition would be an important financial step.

(6) The council would not have to spend its own overstretched resources, and would indeed receive substantial capital sums which could be applied to housing purposes.

That, it seems to me, is a coherent policy which is not manifestly unreasonable. I appreciate that there may be sharp differences of opinion as to the respective merits of owner occupation and municipally rented housing, but the council's policy, as formulated, could not, I think, be struck down as "unreasonable" within the *Wednesbury* principles: *Associated ProvincialPicture Houses Ltd.* v. *Wednesbury Corporation* [1948] 1 K.B. 223:

Lord Diplock, in *Council of Civil Service Unions* v. *Minister for the Civil Service* [1985] A.C. 374, 410, said:

> "By 'irrationality' I mean what can by now be succinctly referred to as 'Wednesbury unreasonableness' (*Associated Provincial Picture Houses Ltd.* v. *Wednesbury Corporation* [1948] 1 K.B. 223). It applies to a decision which is so outrageous in its defiance of logic or of accepted moral standards that no sensible person who had applied his mind to the question to be decided could have arrived at it."

The council's policy is not open to attack on that principle.

. . . . . .

The attack as developed on the appeal is, as I have indicated, really based upon the contention that the covenants fetter the council's discretion to deal with the retained land and are bad accordingly.

The first question, I think, in relation to that contention is whether the council is entitled to impose on its retained land covenants which were restrictive of its user of that land. In my opinion it is. Fulham Court was "land acquired or appropriated by the council for the purposes of Part V of the Housing Act 1957 (as amended)." It is now held by the council for the purposes of Part II of the Housing Act 1985. Section 104 of the Act of 1957 (now incorporated in section 32 of the Act of 1985) provides:

> "(1) Without prejudice to the provisions of Chapter I of Part I of the Housing Act 1980 (right to buy public sector houses), a local authority shall have power by this section, but not otherwise, to dispose of any land which they have acquired or appropriated for the purposes of this Part of this Act. (2) A disposal under this section may be effected in any manner but is not to be made without the consent of the Minister, except in a case falling within subsection (3) below. (3) No consent is required for the letting of any land under a secure tenancy ... (5) Subject to section 104A of this Act, on any disposal under this section the local authority may impose such covenants and conditions as they think fit, but a condition of any of the kinds mentioned in subsection (6) below may only be imposed with the consent of the Minister."

A restrictive covenant does not operate merely in contract. It is an equitable interest in the burdened land. Section 104(1) of the Act of 1957 and section 32 of the Act of 1985 authorise a local authority to dispose of "land" held for housing purposes. Under Schedule 1 to the Interpretation Act 1978 " 'land' includes ... any estate, interest, easement, servitude or right in or over land." It seems to me, therefore, that a local authority could, with the consent of the Minister, create restrictive covenants over its Part V (of the Act of 1957) and Part II (of the Act of 1985) land. The nature of a restrictive covenant was referred to in argument, but no question of absence of necessary consents has been raised in this case. Subject to consent, it seems to me that the council had power to create restrictive covenants under section 104(1) and (2) of the Act of 1957.

In general, I do not understand it to be disputed that there was power in the council (as the judge held) to create restrictive covenants under the Housing Acts, or otherwise. Power to create restrictive covenants does not, however, resolve the question whether the covenants constitute an unlawful fetter. There might, possibly, be an argument that if the Minister gave consent to the covenants under section 104 of the Act of 1957 or section 32 of the Act of 1985, and a contract was made accordingly, that is a complete and lawful disposition under the Housing

Act itself, and no further question could arise as to its enforceability, but the point has not been investigated before us, and I disregard it altogether.

It is clear that a local authority cannot, in general, make declarations of policy which are binding in future on the council for the time being. A council cannot extinguish statutory powers in that way. But it may be able to do so by the valid exercise of other statutory powers. If a statutory power is lawfully exercised so as to create legal rights and obligations between the council and third parties, the result will be that the council for the time being is bound, even though that hinders or prevents the exercise of other statutory powers. Thus, in *Dowty Boulton Paul Ltd*. v. *Wolverhampton Corporation* [1971] 1 W.L.R. 204, the corporation in 1936 granted the plaintiff a right to use the municipal airport for 99 years, or for so long as the corporation should maintain it as a municipal airport (whichever should be the longer). In 1970 the corporation announced its intention to develop the site under its statutory powers as a housing authority Sir John Pennycuick V.-C. granted an interlocutory injunction to restrain the corporation from preventing the plaintiff, pending trial, from using the airport. He said, at p. 210:

> "The cases are concerned with attempts to fetter in advance the future exercise of statutory powers otherwise than by the valid exercise of a stat-utory power. The cases are not concerned with the position which arises after a statutory power has been validly exercised."

Stourcliffe Estates Co. Ltd. v. *Bournemouth Corporation* [1910] 2 Ch. 12 is an example of the same principle.

What we are concerned with in the present case are overlapping or conflicting powers. There is a power to create covenants restrictive of the use of the retained land; and there are powers in relation to the user of the retained land for housing purposes. In these circumstances, it is necessary to ascertain for what purpose the retained land is held. All other powers are subordinate to the main power to carry out the primary purpose: see *Blake (Valuation Officer)* v. *Hendon Corporation* [1962] 1 Q.B. 283, 302.

Now the purpose for which the Fulham Court estate is held by the council must be the provision of housing accommodation in the district. The council's policy in relation to the estate, as I have set it out above, seems to me to be consistent with that purpose. The estate is in bad repair, and the policy is aimed at providing accommodation in the borough of higher quality than at present by means of a scheme of maintenance and refurbishment. The policy, it is true, is designed to produce owner-occupancy and not rented accommodation. Historically, local authority housing has been rented. But a substantial inroad upon that was made by Part I of the Housing Act 1980, which gave municipal tenants the right to purchase their dwellings. In the circumstances it does not seem to me that a policy which is designed to produce good accommodation for owner-occupiers is now any less within the purposes of the Housing Acts than the provision of rented housing. We are not dealing with a policy for providing highly expensive hous-ing, but of owner accommodation at apparently reasonable prices. . . .

It seems to me that if the purpose for which the power to create restrictive covenants is being exercised can reasonably be regarded as the furtherance of the statutory object, then the creation of the covenants is not an unlawful fetter. All the powers are exercisable for the achieving of the statutory objects in relation to the land, and the honest and reasonable exercise of a power for that purpose cannot properly be regarded as a fetter upon another power given for the same purpose.

We were referred to the decision in *Ayr Harbour Trustees* v. *Oswald* (1883) 8 App. Cas. 623. But that was a case where the trustees simply "renounced part of their statutory birthright." There was an incompatibility between what they were proposing to do and the actual statutory purpose. In the present case, as it seems to me, the purpose of the contract is the same as the statutory purpose. Devlin L.J.

in *Blake (Valuation Officer)* v. *Hendon Corporation* [1962] 1 Q.B. 283, 303, said:

> "For example, a man selling a part only of his land might object to a refresh-
> ment pavilion on his boundary. Provided that the erection of a refreshment
> pavilion on that spot was not essential to the use of the land as a pleasure
> ground, the local authority could properly covenant not to erect one, not-
> withstanding that it had statutory power to do so. This illustrates the proper
> application of the principle in the *Ayr* case: see *Stourcliffe Estates Co. Ltd.* v.
> *Bournemouth Corporation* [1910] 2 Ch. 12."

I can see that there is something to be said for the view that so long as the council
retains Part V land it should retain all the powers which the statute gives in
relation to that land. That is simple and logical. But I think it is too inflexible and
takes insufficient account of the practical difficulties of administering such an
estate as Fulham Court. To bring it up to standard, money has to be found and
compromises have to be made. It is not practicable to sell the whole estate at once.
It has to be phased in order to prevent excessive voids and high loss of income. On
21 March 1986 only Block A (32 flats) was totally empty. But the scheme was quite
far advanced. Out of a total of 372 flats, 189 were empty. The policy having been
decided upon, it was necessary to press ahead with it. . . .

In general, it seems to me that we are concerned with a rational scheme which
the council could reasonably say that it was entitled to adopt as part of the housing
policy of the borough. In saying that, I do not mean that a scheme for rented
housing would have been irrational. Either could be defensible. But it is the
function of politicians to choose policies. The court is not concerned with their
merits but their legality.

SIR DENYS BUCKLEY: . . . I am clearly of the opinion that, if a statutory authority
acting in good faith in the proper and reasonable exercise of its statutory powers
undertakes some binding obligation, the fact that such obligation may thereafter
preclude the authority from exercising some other statutory power, or from
exercising its statutory powers in some other way, cannot constitute an impermissible fetter on its powers. Any other view would involve that the doctrine against
fettering would itself involve a fetter on the authority's capacity to exercise its
powers properly and reasonably as it thinks fit from time to time. So, in my view,
the decision of the present case depends primarily upon whether the council was
acting properly and reasonably in proposing to covenant with Barratts in the
terms of the second schedule covenants. For the reasons indicated by Fox L.J., I
think this was so.

KERR L.J. delivered a dissenting judgment.
Appeal dismissed.

Note
Fox L.J. referred in his judgment to "overlapping or conflicting" powers. This problem is
particularly acute in the case of local authorities which may have a wide range of duties and
discretions under various statutes, or even within the same statute. See, for example,
William Cory & Sons Ltd. v. *City of London Corporation* [1951] 2 K.B. 476 (C.A.). In *Windsor and
Maidenhead Royal Borough Council* v. *Brandrose Investments Ltd.* [1983] 1 W.L.R. 509 the Court
of Appeal considered the apparent conflict between the power of a Council to enter into a
planning agreement under section 52 of the Town and Country Planning Act 1971 and its
power under section 277(1) to designate areas as conservation areas—and so preventing
developers, in reliance on a section 52 agreement, from beginning to demolish buildings on
the land designated under 277(1). Section 52(3), in the view of Fox J. at first instance,
prohibited the council from exercising its powers under section 277(1). Section 52(3) provided that nothing in that section of the Act should be construed as restricting the exercise of
any powers under the Act so long as those powers were exercised in accordance with the
terms of the development plan. Since there was no development plan Fox J. concluded that
the exercise of powers under the Act could be restricted. The Court of Appeal, however,

differed. Lawton L.J., delivering the judgment of the Court, unencumbered by citation of authorities, said, ...

"Nor can we construe the difficult subs. (3) as restricting the exercise by a local planning authority of any of their statutory powers which they have a public duty to exercise. It is trite law that a statutory body which has public duties to perform (and a local planning authority are such a body) cannot lawfully agree not to exercise its powers ...
Whatever s.52(3) means, and we share the bemusement of counsel for the plaintiffs, it cannot in our judgment be construed as empowering a local planning authority to bind themselves not to exercise the powers given to them by s.277 of the Act which they have a public duty to exercise.
It follows that the defendants were not entitled to demolish their buildings without the plaintiffs' consent and that they have suffered no damage as a result of the plaintiffs obtaining an *ex parte* injunction on July 2, 1979. In the exercise of discretion we would not, however, grant the plaintiffs the declaration which they claimed. In our opinion this litigation should never have started. To the limited extent indicated we would allow the appeal."

Appeal allowed but in exercise of court's discretion no declaration granted.
For the extent to which the Crown may bind itself by contract see *Rederiaktiebolaget Amphitrite* v. *The King* [1921] 2 K.B. 500; *Crown Land Commissioners* v. *Page* [1960] 2 Q.B. 274.

TORT

Negligence

Mersey Docks and Harbour Board v. Gibbs

Mersey Docks and Harbour Board v. Penhallow

(1866) L.R. 1 H.L. 93

House of Lords

A ship named the *Sierra Nevada* was damaged while trying to enter one of the
Mersey docks, by reason of a mud bank negligently left at the entrance. The cargo
was also damaged. Gibbs, the owner of the cargo, and Penhallow, the owner of
the ship, brought actions for damages against the Mersey Docks and Harbour
Board Trustees.[1] It was admitted that the Harbour Board knew, or ought reasonably to have known, that the dock was in an unfit state to be navigated, and that
they did not take reasonable care to put it into a fit state for that purpose.

The findings of the Court of Exchequer Chamber, sitting in Error from the Court
of Exchequer in the case of *Gibbs*, and from the Lord Chief Baron and a special jury
in the case of *Penhallow*, were in favour of the plaintiffs.

The Harbour Board now took the matter in Error to the House of Lords. The
Lord Chancellor (Lord Cranworth) put the following questions to the judges: "In
The Mersey Docks and Harbour Board v. *Gibbs*—Does the declaration in this case state
a good cause of action? In *The Mersey Docks and Harbour Board* v. *Penhallow*—Is the
judgment of the Court of Exchequer Chamber right?" The judges, whose opinion
was delivered by Blackburn J., answered both cases in the affirmative, that is, in
favour of the plaintiffs. Their Lordships (Lord Cranworth L.C., Lord Wensleydale
and Lord Westbury) accepted this advice, and affirmed the judgment in both
cases.

BLACKBURN J.: I have the honour, in answer to your Lordships' questions in
these cases, to deliver the joint opinion of all the judges who heard the argument.
...

The Court of Exchequer Chamber, in each of the cases, based their judgment on
that of the Court of Exchequer Chamber in *The Lancaster Canal Company* v. *Parnaby*.[2] In that case the defendants were a company incorporated by Act of Parliament for the purpose of making and maintaining a canal, which was to be open to
the use of the public on the payment of rates, which the canal company were
empowered to receive for their own proper use and behoof, *i.e.* to be divided
among the shareholders. And the Court of Exchequer Chamber in that case stated
the law thus[3]:

"The facts stated in the inducement show that the company made the canal for
their profit and opened it to the public upon payment of tolls to the company; and
the common law in such a case imposes a duty upon the proprietors, not,
perhaps, to repair the canal, or absolutely to free it from obstructions, but to take
reasonable care, so long as they keep it open for the public use of all who may
choose to navigate it, that they may navigate it without danger to their lives or
property."

In the present case the Dock Board do not receive the dock rates for their own
use and behoof, *i.e.* to be divided amongst themselves or their shareholders; but
they are bound by the statutes under which they are incorporated to apply them
to the purposes of the Acts, which may in substance be stated to be to maintain the
docks and pay the very large debt contracted in making them. The Court of

[1] The action was brought in the first instance against their predecessors, the trustees of the
   Liverpool Docks.
[2] (1839) 11 Ad. & E. 223.   [3] (1839) 11 Ad. & E. 223 at p. 242.

Exchequer Chamber in both cases decided that this difference did not affect the question; that so long as the dock was left open for the public, the duty to take reasonable care that the dock and its entrance were in such a state that those who navigate it may do so without danger, was equally cast on the proprietors having the receipt of the tolls and the possession and management of the dock, whether the tolls are received for a beneficial or a fiduciary purpose. If this proposition is correct, the direction of the Lord Chief Baron excepted to was right, for a body corporate never can either take care or neglect to take care, except through their servants; and, assuming that it was the duty of the corporaton to take reasonable care that the dock was in a fit state, it seems clear that if the corporation, by their servants, had the means of knowing that the dock was in an unfit state, and were negligently ignorant of its state, they did neglect this duty, and did not take reasonable care that it was fit. And after hearing the very able arguments at your Lordships' bar, we are of opinion that the judgment of the Court of Exchequer Chamber was correct.

It is pointed out by Lord Campbell, in *The Southampton and Itchin Bridge Company v. The Southampton Local Board of Health*,[4] that in every case the liability of a body created by statute must be determined upon a true interpretation of the statutes under which it is created. It is desirable, therefore, in the first place, to state what was the effect of the legislation, so far as it applied to these docks, at the time of the accident on April 12, 1865. [His Lordship then examined the relevant statutes.]

Now, it is obvious that a shipowner who pays dock-rates for the use of the dock, or the owner of goods who pays warehouse-rates for the use of a warehouse and the services of the warehouseman, is, as far as he is concerned, exactly in the same position, however the rates may be appropriated. He pays the rates for the dock accommodation, or for warehouse accommodation and services, and he is entitled to expect that reasonable care should be taken that he shall not be exposed to danger in using the accommodation for which he has paid. It is well observed by Mellor J. in *Coe v. Wise*,[5] of corporations, like the present, formed for trading and other profitable purposes, that though such corporations may act without reward to themselves, yet in their very nature they are substitutions on a large scale for individual enterprise. And we think that, in the absence of anything in the statutes (which create such corporations) showing a contrary intention in the legislature, the true rule of construction is, that the legislature intended that the liability of corporations thus substituted for individuals should, to the extent of their corporate funds, be co-extensive with that imposed by the general law on the owners of similar works. If, indeed, the legislature has, by express enactment or necessary intendment, enacted that they should not be subject to such a liability, there is an end of the question; and if the legislature had under the Acts now under consideration enacted that none of the revenue of the trustees of the Liverpool Docks should be applied to the purpose of discharging liabilities incurred in consequence of the trustees acting as proprietors of docks and warehouses, it would go far to show that the legislature intended that they should not be so liable. But the appropriation clause in the Acts now under consideration has no such effect. . . .

As we have already intimated, in our opinion the proper rule of construction of such statutes is, that, in the absence of something to show a contrary intention, the legislature intend that the body, the creature of the statute, shall have the same duties, and render its funds subject to the same liabilities as the general law would impose on a private person doing the same things. This rule of construction was not admitted by the defendants. They did not rest their case exclusively, or even mainly, on any special provisions peculiar to their own private legislation, but upon broader grounds, which, if we do not mistake them, were in effect two:

---

[4] (1858) 8 E. & B. 801, 812.   [5] (1864) 5 B. & S. 440

They said that by the general law of this country, bodies such as the present are trustees for public purposes, and that, being such, they are not in their corporate capacity liable to make compensation for damages sustained by individuals from the neglect of their servants and agents to perform the duties imposed on the corporation, or, at all events, that the duty of such a corporation was limited to that of exercising due care in the choice of their officers, and that if they had properly selected their officers, any evil which ensued must be the fault of the officer, and that redress for it must be sought from him alone.

A great many cases were cited at your Lordships' bar as supporting this position, many of which are not really applicable to such a case as the present. [Here his Lordship referred to *Lane* v. *Cotton*,[6] *Whitfield* v. *Le Despencer*[7] and *Nicholson* v. *Mounsey*,[8] which relate to servants of the Crown.]

Another class of cases also cited depends upon the following principle. If the legislature direct or authorise the doing of a particular thing, the doing of it cannot be wrongful; if damage results from the doing of that thing, it is just and proper that compensation should be made for it, and that is generally provided for in the statutes authorising the doing of such things. But no action lies for what is *damnum sine injuria*; the remedy is to apply for compensation under the provision of the statutes legalising what would otherwise be a wrong. This, however, is the case, whether the thing is authorised for a public purpose or for private profit. No action will lie against a railway company for erecting a line of railway authorised by their Acts, so long as they pursue the authority given them, any more than it would lie against the trustees of a turnpike-road for making their road under their Acts, though the one road is made for the profit of the shareholders in the company and the other is not. The principle is that the act is not wrongful, not because it is for a public purpose, but because it is authorised by the legislature—see *The King* v. *Pease*.[9] This, we think, is the point decided in *The Governors of the British Cast Plate Manufacturers* v. *Meredith*,[10] *Sutton* v. *Clarke*,[11] and several other cases, as is well explained by Williams J. in *Whitehouse* v. *Fellowes*.[12] But though the legislature have authorised the execution of the works, they do not thereby exempt those who are authorised to make them from the obligation to use reasonable care that in making them no unnecessary damage be done. In *Brine* v. *Great Western Ry.*,[13] Crompton J. says: "The distinction is now clearly established between damage from works authorised by statutes, where the party generally is to have compensation and the authority is a bar to an action, and damage by reason of the works having been negligently done, as to which the owner's remedy by way of action remains." This distinction is as applicable to works executed for one purpose as for another. . . .

There are, however, authorities that bear the other way upon this part of the case, and it is necessary to examine these authorities in order to contrast them with the others. It will be for your Lordships then to decide on which side the preponderance of authority lies. Those in favour of the defendants are *Hall* v. *Smith*,[14] *Duncan* v. *Findlater*,[15] *Holliday* v. *St. Leonard's, Shoreditch*[16] and *Metcalfe* v. *Hetherington*.[17] [His Lordship then submitted (*inter alia*) that Lord Cottenham's dictum in *Duncan* v. *Findlater, supra*, was wrong] . . .

[6] (1701) 1 Ld.Raym. 646.
[7] (1778) 2 Cowp. 754.
[8] (1812) 15 East 384.
[9] (1832) 4 B. & Ad. 30.
[10] (1792) 4 Term Rep. 794.
[11] (1815) 6 Taunt. 29.
[12] (1861) 10 C.B. 779.
[13] (1862) 2 Best & S. 402.
[14] (1824) 2 Bing. 156.
[15] (1839) 6 Cl. & F. 894.
[16] (1816) 11 C.B.[N.S.] 192.
[17] (1855) 11 Exch.Rep. 257.

LORD CRANWORTH L.C.: . . . In both cases the Exchequer Chamber held that the appellants were liable. In both cases they have appealed; and the ground of appeal is, that they are not a public company deriving benefit, like a railway company, from traffic, but a public body of trustees, constituted by the legislature, for the purpose of maintaining the docks, and for that purpose having authority to collect tolls, to be applied in the maintenance and repair of the docks, then in paying off a large debt, and ultimately in reducing the tolls for the benefit of the public. . . .

Where such a body [as the appellants] is constituted by statute, having the right to levy tolls for their own profit, in consideration of their making and maintaining a dock or a canal, there is no doubt of their liability to make good to the persons using it any damage occasioned by their neglect in not keeping the works in proper repair. This was decided by the Court of Queen's Bench, and their decision was affirmed in the Court of Error in the case of *The Lancaster Canal Company* v. *Parnaby*.[18] The ground on which the Court of Error rested their decision in that case is stated by Tindal C.J. to have been that the company made the canal for their profit, and opened it to the public upon the payment of tolls; and the common law in such a case imposes a duty upon the proprietors to take reasonable care, so long as they keep it open for the public use of all who may choose to navigate it, that they may do so without danger to their lives or property.

The only difference between that case and those now standing for decision by your Lordships is, that here the appellants, in whom the docks are vested, do not collect tolls for their own profit, but merely as trustees for the benefit of the public. I do not, however, think that this makes any difference in principle in respect to their liability. It would be a strange distinction to persons coming with their ships to different ports of this country, that in some ports, if they sustain damage by the negligence of those who have the management of the docks, they will be entitled to compensation, and in others they will not, such a distinction arising not from any visible difference in the docks themselves, but from some municipal difference in the constitution of the bodies by whom the docks are managed.

It cannot be denied that there have been dicta, and perhaps decisions, not capable of being reconciled with the result at which I have arrived; but the whole series of authorities has been so fully brought under review, in the very able and elaborate opinion of the learned judges delivered by Blackburn J., in answer to the questions put to them by your Lordships, that I do not feel myself called on to do more than to express my concurrence in that opinion.

Judgment affirmed in both appeals.

---

[18] (1839) 11 Ad. & E. 223.

Anns v. Merton London Borough Council
[1978] A.C. 728
House of Lords

The plaintiffs (Anns and others) were lessees of certain maisonettes in Wimbledon, some under original leases of 1962 and others by assignments of 1967 and 1968. The owners of the block were the builders, Walcroft Property Co. (first defendants). The local authority at the time of construction was Mitcham Borough Council, but before these proceedings were commenced in 1972 the London Borough of Merton (second defendants) had taken over its duties and liabilities. In 1970 structural movements began to occur in the building, and these resulted *inter alia* in cracks in the walls and sloping of floors.

The claims against the Council were for damages for negligence in allowing the builders to construct the block on foundations that were shallower than those required by the deposited plans, alternatively in failing to carry out the necessary inspections sufficiently carefully or at all. It was alleged that, under the building by-laws made pursuant to the Public Health Act 1936, the Council was under a duty to ensure that the building was constructed in accordance with the plans, and that the building should have been inspected before the foundations were covered.

The Court of Appeal having decided that the claims were not statute barred, the House of Lords granted the Council leave to argue on appeal to that House the preliminary question of law, whether in the circumstances the Council was under any duty of care to the lessees at all. Their Lordships (Lords Wilberforce, Diplock, Simon of Glaisdale, Salmon, and Russell of Killowen), affirming the decision of the Court of Appeal, unanimously decided in favour of the lessees for the reasons given in the following judgments.

Their Lordships took time for consideration.

LORD WILBERFORCE [after explaining the procedural background, continued]:
Through the trilogy of cases in this House—*Donoghue* v. *Stevenson,*[1] *Hedley Byrne & Co. Ltd.* v. *Heller & Partners Ltd.*[2] and *Dorset Yacht Co. Ltd.* v. *Home Office,*[3] the position has now been reached that in order to establish that a duty of care arises in a particular situation, it is not necessary to bring the facts of that situation within those of previous situations in which a duty of care has been held to exist. Rather the question has to be approached in two stages. First one has to ask whether, as between the alleged wrongdoer and the person who has suffered damage there is a sufficient relationship of proximity or neighbourhood such that, in the reasonable contemplation of the former, carelessness on his part may be likely to cause damage to the latter—in which case a prima facie duty of care arises. Secondly, if the first question is answered affirmatively, it is necessary to consider whether there are any considerations which ought to negative, or to reduce or limit the scope of the duty or the class of person to whom it is owed or the damages to which a breach of it may give rise: see *Dorset Yacht* case,*per* Lord Reid at p. 1027. Examples of this are *Hedley Byrne's* case where the class of potential plaintiffs was reduced to those shown to have relied upon the correctness of statements made, and *Weller & Co.* v. *Foot and Mouth Disease Research Institute*[4]; and (I cite these merely as illustrations, without discussion) cases about "economic loss" where, a duty having been held to exist, the nature of the recoverable damages was limited: see *S.C.M. (UnitedKingdom) Ltd.* v. *W. J.*

[1] [1932] A.C. 562.
[2] [1964] A.C. 465.
[3] [1970] A.C. 1004.
[4] [1966] 1 Q.B. 569.

Whittall & Son Ltd.[5] and *Spartan Steel & Alloys Ltd.* v. *Martin & Co. (Contractors) Ltd.*[6]

The factual relationship between the council and owners and occupiers of new dwellings constructed in their area must be considered in the relevant statutory setting—under which the council acts. That was the Public Health Act 1936. I must refer to the relevant provisions. . . .

[His Lordship referred to various sections of the Act and to certain by-laws made thereunder and continued]:

Acting under these by-laws, the builder owner (first defendants) on January 30, 1962, gave notice to the Mitcham Borough Council of their intention to erect a new building (*viz.* the block of maisonettes) in accordance with accompanying plans. The plans showed the base walls and concrete strip foundations of the block and stated, in relation to the depth from ground level to the underside of the concrete foundations, "3 feet or deeper to the approval of local authority." These plans were approved on February 8, 1962. . . .

The builders in fact constructed the foundations to a depth of only 2 feet 6 inches below ground level. It is not, at this stage, established when or whether any inspection was made.

To summarise the statutory position. The Public Health Act 1936, in particular Part II, was enacted in order to provide for the health and safety of owners and occupiers of buildings, including dwelling houses, by *inter alia* setting standards to be complied with in construction, and by enabling local authorities, through building by-laws, to supervise and control the operations of builders. One of the particular matters within the area of local authority supervision is the foundations of buildings—clearly a matter of vital importance, particularly because this part of the building comes to be covered up as building proceeds. Thus any weakness or inadequacy will create a hidden defect which whoever acquires the building has no means of discovering: in legal parlance there is no opportunity for intermediate inspection. So, by the by-laws, a definite standard is set for foundation work (see by-law 18(1)(*b*) referred to above): the builder is under a statutory (*sc.* by-law) duty to notify the local authority before covering up the foundations: the local authority has at this stage the right to inspect and to insist on any correction necessary to bring the work into conformity with the by-laws. It must be in the reasonable contemplation not only of the builder but also of the local authority that failure to comply with the by-laws' requirement as to foundations may give rise to a hidden defect which in the future may cause damage to the building affecting the safety and health of owners and occupiers. And as the building is intended to last, the class of owners and occupiers likely to be affected cannot be limited to those who go in immediately after construction.

What then is the extent of the local authority's duty towards these persons? Although, as I have suggested, a situation of "proximity" existed between the council and owners and occupiers of the houses, I do not think that a description of the council's duty can be based upon the "neighbourhood" principle alone or upon merely any such factual relationship as "control" as suggested by the Court of Appeal. So to base it would be to neglect an essential factor which is that the local authority is a public body, discharging functions under statute: its powers and duties are definable in terms of public not private law. The problem which this type of action creates, is to define the circumstances in which the law should impose, over and above, or perhaps alongside, these public law powers and duties, a duty in private law towards individuals such that they may sue for damages in a civil court. It is in this context that the distinction sought to be drawn between duties and mere powers has to be examined.

Most, indeed probably all, statutes relating to public authorities or public

[5] [1971] 1 Q.B. 337.
[6] [1973] Q.B. 27.

bodies, contain in them a large area of policy. The courts call this "discretion" meaning that the decision is one for the authority or body to make, and not for the courts. Many statutes also prescribe or at least presuppose the practical execution of policy decisions: a convenient description of this is to say that in addition to the area of policy or discretion, there is an operational area. Although this distinction between the policy area and the operational area is convenient, and illuminating, it is probably a distinction of degree; many "operational" powers or duties have in them some element of "discretion." It can safely be said that the more "operational" a power or duty may be, the easier it is to superimpose upon it a common law duty of care.

I do not think that it is right to limit this to a duty to avoid causing extra or additional damage beyond what must be expected to arise from the exercise of the power or duty. That may be correct when the act done under the statute *inherently* must adversely *affect* the interest of individuals. But many other acts can be done without causing any harm to anyone—indeed may be directed to preventing harm from occurring. In these cases the duty is the normal one of taking care to avoid harm to those likely to be affected. . . .

It is said—there are reflections of this in the judgments in *Dutton* v. *Bognor Regis Urban District Council*[7]—that the local authority is under no duty to inspect, and this is used as the foundation for an argument, also found in some of the cases, that if it need not inspect at all, it cannot be liable for negligent inspection: if it were to be held so liable, so it is said, councils would simply decide against inspection. I think that this is too crude an argument. It overlooks the fact that local authorities are public bodies operating under statute with a clear responsibility for public health in their area. They must, and in fact do, make their discretionary decisions responsibly and for reasons which accord with the statutory purpose. . . . If they do not exercise their discretion in this way they can be challenged in the courts. Thus, to say that councils are under no duty to inspect, is not a sufficient statement of the position. They are under a duty to give proper consideration to the question whether they should inspect or not. Their immunity from attack, in the event of failure to inspect, in other words, though great is not absolute. And because it is not absolute, the necessary premise for the proposition "if no duty to inspect, then no duty to take care in inspection" vanishes.

Passing then to the duty as regards inspection, if made. On principle there must surely be a duty to exercise reasonable care. The standard of care must be related to the duty to be performed—namely to ensure compliance with the by-laws. It must be related to the fact that the person responsible for construction in accordance with the by-laws is the builder, and that the inspector's function is supervisory. It must be related to the fact that once the inspector has passed the foundations they will be covered up, with no subsequent opportunity for inspection. But this duty, heavily operational though it may be, is still a duty arising under the statute. There may be a discretionary element in its exercise—discretionary as to the time and manner of inspection, and the techniques to be used. A plaintiff complaining of negligence must prove, the burden being on him, that action taken was not within the limits of a discretion bona fide exercised, before he can begin to rely upon a common law duty of care. But if he can do this, he should, in principle, be able to sue.

Is there, then, authority against the existence of any such duty or any reason to restrict it? It is said that there is an absolute distinction in the law between statutory duty and statutory power—the former giving rise to possible liability, the latter not, or at least not doing so unless the exercise of the power involves some positive act creating some fresh or additional damage.

My Lords, I do not believe that any such absolute rule exists: or perhaps, more accurately, that such rules as exist in relation to powers and duties existing under

---

[7] [1972] 1 Q.B. 373.

particular statutes, provide sufficient definition of the rights of individuals affected by their exercise, or indeed their non-exercise, unless they take account of the possibility that, parallel with public law duties there may coexist those duties which persons—private or public—are under at common law to avoid causing damage to others in sufficient proximity to them. This is, I think, the key to understanding of the main authority relied upon by the appellants—*East Suffolk Rivers Catchment Board* v. *Kent*.[8]

The statutory provisions in that case were contained in the Land Drainage Act 1930 and were in the form of a power to repair drainage works including walls or banks. The facts are well known: there was a very high tide which burst the banks protecting the respondent's land. The Catchment Board, requested to take action, did so with an allocation of manpower and resources (graphically described by MacKinnon L.J. [1940] 1 K.B. 319 at p. 330) which was hopelessly inadequate and which resulted in the respondent's land being flooded for much longer than it need have been. There was a considerable difference of judicial opinion. Hilbery J. [1939] 2 All E.R. 207 who tried the case, held the board liable for the damage caused by the extended flooding and his decision was upheld by a majority of the Court of Appeal [1940] 1 K.B. 319. This House, by majority of four to one, reached the opposite conclusion [1941] A.C. 74. The speeches of their Lordships contain discussion of earlier authorities, which well illustrate the different types of statutory enactment under which these cases may arise. There are private Acts conferring powers—necessarily—to interfere with the rights of individuals: in such cases, an action in respect of damage caused by the exercise of the powers generally does not lie, but it may do so "for doing that which the legislature has authorised, if it be done negligently": see *Geddis* v. *Bann Reservoir Proprietors*[9] per Lord Blackburn. Then there are cases where a statutory power is conferred, but the scale on which it is exercised is left to a local authority: *Sheppard* v. *Glossop Corporation*.[10] That concerned a power to light streets and the corporation decided, for economy reasons, to extinguish the lighting on Christmas night. Clearly this was within the discretion of the authority but Scrutton L.J. in the Court of Appeal, at p. 146, contrasted this situation with one where "an option is given by statute to an authority to do or not to do a thing and it elects to do the thing and does it negligently." (Compare *Indian Towing Co. Inc.* v. *United States*,[11] which makes just this distinction between a discretion to provide a lighthouse, and at operational level, a duty, if one is provided, to use due care to keep the light in working order.) Other illustrations are given.

My Lords, a number of reasons were suggested for distinguishing the *East Suffolk* case [1941]A.C. 74—apart from the relevant fact that it was concerned with a different Act, indeed type of Act. It was said to be a decision on causation: I think that this is true of at least two of their Lordships (Viscount Simon L.C. and Lord Thankerton). It was said that the damage was already there before the board came on the scene: so it was but the board's action or inaction undoubtedly prolonged it, and the action was in respect of the prolongation. I should not think it right to put the case aside on such arguments. To me the two significant points about the case are, first, that it is an example, and a good one, where operational activity—at the breach in the wall—was still well within a discretionary area, so that the plaintiff's task in contending for a duty of care was a difficult one. This is clearly the basis on which Lord Romer, whose speech is often quoted as a proposition of law, proceeded. Secondly, although the case was decided in 1940, only one of their Lordships considered it in relation to a duty of care at common law. It need cause no surprise that this was Lord Atkin. His speech starts with this passage, at

[8] [1941] A.C. 74.
[9] (1878) 3 App.Cas. 430 at p. 456.
[10] [1921] 3 K.B. 132.
[11] (1955) 350 U.S. 61.

p. 88: "On the first point" [*sc.* whether there was a duty owed to the plaintiff and what was its nature] "I cannot help thinking that the argument did not sufficiently distinguish between two kinds of duties: (1) A statutory duty to do or abstain from doing something. (2) A common law duty to conduct yourself with reasonable care so as not to injure persons liable to be affected by your conduct." And later he refers to *Donoghue* v. *Stevenson*[12] I think it fair to say that Lord Thankerton (who decided the case on causation) in his formulation of the duty must have been thinking in terms of that case. My Lords, I believe that the conception of a general duty of care, not limited to particular accepted situations, but extending generally over all relations of sufficient proximity, and even pervading the sphere of statutory functions of public bodies, had not at that time become fully recognised. Indeed it may well be that full recognition of the impact of *Donoghue* v. *Stevenson* in the latter sphere only came with the decision of this House in *Dorset Yacht Co. Ltd.* v. *Home Office*.[13] . . .

My noble and learned friend [Lord Diplock] points out that the accepted principles which are applicable to powers conferred by a private Act of Parliament, as laid down in *Geddis* v. *Bann Reservoir Proprietors*,[14] cannot automatically be applied to public statutes which confer a large measure of discretion upon public authorities. As regards the latter, for a civil action based on negligence at common law to succeed, there must be acts or omissions taken outside the limits of the delegated discretion: in such a case "Its actionability falls to be determined by the civil law principles of negligence": see [1970] A.C. 1004, 1068.

It is for this reason that the law, as stated in some of the speeches in *East Suffolk Rivers Catchment Board* v. *Kent*,[15] but not in those of Lord Atkin or Lord Thankerton, requires at the present time to be understood and applied with the recognition that, quite apart from such consequences as may flow from an examination of the duties laid down by the particular statute, there may be room, once one is outside the area of legitimate discretion or policy, for a duty of care at common law. It is irrelevant to the existence of this duty of care whether what is created by the statute is a duty or a power: the duty of care may exist in either case. The difference between the two lies in this, that, in the case of a power, liability cannot exist unless the act complained of lies outside the ambit of the power. In *Dorset Yacht Co. Ltd.* v. *Home Office*[16] the officers may (on the assumed facts) have acted outside any discretion delegated to them and having disgarded their instructions as to the precautions which they should take to prevent the trainees from escaping: see *per* Lord Diplock, at p. 1069. So in the present case, the allegations made are consistent with the council or its inspector having acted outside any delegated discretion either as to the making of an inspection, or as to the manner in which an inspection was made. Whether they did so must be determined at the trial. In the event of a positive determination, and only so, can a duty of care arise. I respectfully think that Lord Denning M.R. in *Dutton* v. *Bognor Regis Urban District Council*[17] puts the duty too high.

To whom the duty is owed. There is, in my opinion, no difficulty about this. A reasonable man in the position of the inspector must realise that if the foundations are covered in without adequate depth or strength as required by the by-laws, injury to safety or health may be suffered by owners or occupiers of the house. The duty is owned to them—not of course to a negligent building owner, the source of his own loss. I would leave open the case of users, who might themselves have a remedy against the occupier under the Occupiers' Liability Act 1957. A right of action can only be conferred upon an owner or occupier, who is such

[12] [1932] A.C. 562.
[13] [1970] A.C. 1004.
[14] 3 App.Cas. 430.
[15] [1941] A.C. 74.
[16] [1970] A.C. 1004.
[17] [1972] 1 Q.B. 373 at p. 392.

when the damage occurs (see below). This disposes of the possible objection that an endless, indeterminate class of potential plaintiffs may be called into existence.

The nature of the duty. This must be related closely to the purpose for which powers of inspection are granted, namely, to secure compliance with the by-laws. The duty is to take reasonable care, no more, no less, to secure that the builder does not cover in foundations which do not comply with by-law requirements. The allegations in the statements of claim, in so far as they are based upon non-compliance with the plans, are misconceived. ... The appeal should be dismissed.

[Lord Diplock, Lord Simon of Glaisdale and Lord Russell of Killowen concurred with Lord Wilberforce.]

LORD SALMON: ... I must now refer to the *East Suffolk Rivers Catchment Board* v. *Kent*[18] upon which the council strongly relied in an attempt to negative any duty of care on their part if and when they inspected the foundations. The *East Suffolk* case, which is not very satisfactory, is certainly a very different case from the present. Here, at the time the council elected to inspect the foundations in the exercise of its statutory powers, no damage had occurred nor could thereafter have occurred if the building inspector had noticed the inadequacy of the foundations. ...

In my opinion a negligent inspection for which the council is vicariously liable coupled with subsequent inaction by the council would amount to an implicit approval of the foundations by the council and would have occasioned the damage which ensued. ...

It is, in my view, impossible to say that because in one set of circumstances a body acting under statutory powers may not owe any duty to exercise reasonable care and skill, therefore another body acting under statutory powers in totally different circumstances cannot owe such a duty. I confess that I am not at all sure what point of law the *East Suffolk* case [1941] A.C. 74 is said to decide. Viscount Simon L.C. seems to have based his decision against the plaintiff on the ground that the Catchment Board did not cause the damage: see his speech at pp. 87, 88. Lord Thankerton undoubtedly based his decision on that ground alone: see his speech at p. 96. ...

Lords Romer and Porter seem to have considered that, on the facts of the case which they were deciding, no negligence could be attributed to the Catchment Board. ...

Lord Porter also referred, at pp. 104–105, to the celebrated passage in the speech of Lord Blackburn in *Geddis* v. *Bann Reservoir Proprietors*,[19] a most lucid passage which has been explained so often that I fear its true meaning is in some danger of being explained away. Lord Blackburn said: " ... it is now thoroughly well established that no action will lie for doing that which the legislature has authorised, if it be done without negligence, although it does occasion damage ... but an action does lie for doing that which the legislature has authorised, if it be done negligently."

If, which I doubt, Lords Romer and Porter intended to lay down that because a local authority or other body endowed with statutory powers, owes no one any duty to exercise those powers in a particular case, it cannot in circumstances such as exist in the instant case, owe anyone a duty when it does exercise the powers to exercise them with reasonable care and skill, then I cannot agree with them.

Personally, I respectfully agree with the dissenting decision of Lord Atkin in the *East Suffolk* case. His views as to the duty of care owed by anyone exercising statutory powers did not differ from those of Lord Thankerton nor I think from those of Viscount Simon L.C. and I have some doubt whether they differed from

[18] [1941] A.C. 74.
[19] 3 App.Cas. 430, 455–456.

the views of Lords Romer and Porter which seem to have turned largely on the facts of that particular case. Lord Atkin said, at p. 89: "every person whether discharging a public duty or not is under a common law obligation to some persons in some circumstances to conduct himself with reasonable care so as not to injure those persons likely to be affected by his want of care. This duty exists whether a person is performing a public duty, or *merely exercising a power which he possesses either* under statutory authority or in pursuance of his ordinary rights as a citizen." [The italics are mine].
Appeal dismissed.

Note
The recognition of the principle that a public body may be liable in negligence as a result of loss caused by the way it carried out (or failed to carry out) its statutory powers or duties does not avoid the need in each particular case to inquire whether a duty of care was owed to the individual plaintiff with regard to the type of injury or harm suffered. The duty of the police, for example, to suppress crime is a general duty owed to the public, not to individual members of the public: Hill v. Chief Constable of West Yorkshire [1987] 2 W.L.R. 1126 (C.A.) (The Yorkshire Ripper case). A body empowered to make grants to cover the cost of improvements to houses does not owe a duty of care to subsequent purchasers that such improvements had been carried out free from defect: Curran v. Northern Ireland Co-ownership Housing Association Ltd. [1987] 2 W.L.R. 1043 (H.L.). An official charged with the duty of registering deposit-taking companies on the condition that they are "fit and proper" bodies to be registered does not owe a duty of care to depositors who, in reliance on a company being registered, deposit money with it and later suffer loss, even if the official knew or ought to have known that the company's affairs were being conducted fraudulently: Yuen Kun Yeu v. Attorney-General of Hong Kong [1987] 3 W.L.R. 776 (P.C.).

In Rowling v. Takaro Properties Ltd. [1988] 2 W.L.R. 418, the appellant claimed to have suffered loss as a result of a minister negligently misinterpreting the terms of a statute as a result of which he thought himself entitled to refuse consent to a proposed arrangement between the appellant and a Japanese company. The Privy Council concluded that even if a duty of care was owed, the minister had not been negligent: his view of the meaning of the statute was a reasonable one and he had referred the matter to a cabinet committee, attended by appropriate civil servants. Lord Keith of Kinkel, delivering the opinion of the Board, referred to the need—in cases where it was relevant—to take care in concluding that a duty of care exists. The question is "of an intensely pragmatic character, well suited for gradual development but requiring most careful analysis" (p. 172).

The House of Lords in Curran and the Privy Council in Yuen Kun Yen and Rowling have expressed the need for caution in reading the speech of Lord Wilberforce in Anns v. Merton London Borough Council [1978] A.C. 728 both with regard to his general two stage approach to the existence of a duty of care and the distinction he drew between "policy" decisions and "operational" decisions: a distinction which Lord Wilberforce recognised was "convenient" and one "of degree."[20] See, too, Jones v. Department of the Employment [1988] 2 W.L.R. 493 (C.A.).

[20] See Rigby v. Chief Constable of Northamptonshire [1985] 1 W.L.R. 1242 for reliance on distinction.

Nuisance

Metropolitan Asylum District (Managers) v. Hill
(1881) 6 App.Cas. 193
House of Lords

The Managers of the Metropolitan Asylum District, constituted by and purporting to act under the authority of the Metropolitan Poor Act 1867, built and maintained a smallpox hospital at Hampstead. Hill, and other Hampstead residents, brought an action for damages for nuisance and for an injunction. The jury found that the hospital was a nuisance *per se*. The defendants argued (*inter alia*) that they had acted only in execution of a duty cast upon them by statute. Pollock B. gave judgment for the plaintiffs, and granted an injunction against using the hospital in such a manner as to create a nuisance to the plaintiffs. The defendants appealed to the Court of Appeal, who affirmed the judgment of Pollock B.

The District Managers now appealed to the House of Lords. Their Lordships (Lord Selborne L.C., Lord Blackburn and Lord Watson) dismissed the appeal.

Lord Selborne L.C.: ... The statute when examined is found to confer in general terms powers extending over a rather wide range of subjects. So far as it relates to a hospital or asylum of this particular kind, there is nothing in it mandatory or imperative. Everything which it necessarily requires may be done, though no such hospital should ever or anywhere be established. The fifth section says, that "asylums to be supported and managed according to this Act may be provided under this Act for reception and relief of the sick, insane, or inform or other class or classes of the poor chargeable in unions or parishes in the metropolis." The sixth section authorises the formation of districts, and the seventh requires that in each district so formed "there shall be an asylum or asylums as the Poor Law Board from time to time by order direct," leaving the class of poor persons for whom any such asylum may be provided entirely open. The fifteenth section enables the Poor Law Board from time to time by order to direct the managers "to purchase, or hire, or to build, and (in either case) to fit up a building or buildings for the asylum of such nature and size, and according to such plan and in such manner as the Poor Law Board think fit"; and the managers are required to carry such directions into execution. Subsequent clauses put the arrangements and conduct of any such asylum under the superintendence of the Poor Law Board. No compulsory power is given to acquire land or any interest in land for any asylum purposes. The Lands Clauses Acts are indeed incorporated by section 52, but section 53 expressly provides that so much of those Acts as relates to the purchase of land, otherwise than by agreement, shall not be put in force except for certain purposes not including these asylums. It appears incidentally from section 69 (which provides for the repayment of certain expenses therein specified out of the Common Poor Fund) that asylums might be "specially provided under this Act for patients suffering from fever or smallpox," but except in that way and from the fact that the general category of "sick" necessarily includes patients suffering from any kind of disease, there is no provision in the Act as to contagious or infectious disorders. If express words or necessary implication and intendment must be shown in order to authorise the Poor Law Board or any managers of an asylum to create a nuisance in the exercise of the discretionary powers given to them, I can find none in the statute.

The result is, first, that this Act does not necessarily require anything to be done under it which might not be done without causing a nuisance; secondly, that as to those things which may or may not be done under it, there is no evidence on the face of the Act that the legislature supposed it to be impossible for any of them to be done (if they were done at all) somewhere and under some circumstances without creating a nuisance; and, thirdly, that the legislature has manifested no intention that any of these optional powers as to asylums should be exercised at the expense of, or so as to interfere with, any man's private rights. The only sense in which the legislature can be properly said to have authorised these things to be done is, that it has enabled the Poor Law Board to order and the managers to do them, if and when and where they can obtain by free bargain and contract the means of doing so.

If the legislature had authorised some compulsory interference with private rights of property within local limits which it might have thought fit to define for the purpose of establishing this asylum, to be used for the reception of patients suffering from smallpox or other infectious disorders, and had provided for compensation to those who might be thereby injuriously affected (in such cases and under such conditions as it might have prescribed), the present case might have been like *The King* v. *Pease*[1] and *The Hammersmith Ry.* v. *Brand*.[2] No person outside the statutory line of compensation, even if the use of the asylum in the manner authorised by the statute had been productive of serious damage to him, could then have obtained any relief or remedy upon the footing that what the statute authorised was a legal nuisance to himself or an actionable wrong. But the case is different when (as here) no interference at all with any private rights is authorised, and no place or limit of space is defined, within which the establishment of such an asylum is made lawful. Neither the Poor Law Board nor the managers could for this purpose have taken a single foot of ground or have interfered with any the most insignificant easement against the will of the plaintiffs, or of any other person to whom such land or easement might belong. No line is here drawn by the legislature between interests which are and interests which are not proper subjects for compensation. Under these circumstances, I am clearly of opinion that the Poor Law Board and the managers had no statutory authority to do anything which might be a nuisance to the plaintiffs without their consent. I therefore move your Lordships to affirm the judgment of the court below and dismiss this appeal.

LORD BLACKBURN: ... I think that the case of *The Hammersmith Ry.* v. *Brand*, in your Lordships' House, settles beyond controversy that where the legislature directs that a thing shall at all events be done, the doing of which, if not authorised by the legislature, would entitle anyone to an action, the right of action is taken away. ... The legislature has very often interfered with the rights of private persons, but in modern times it has generally given compensation to those injured; and if no compensation is given it affords a reason, though not a conclusive one, for thinking that the intention of the legislature was not that the thing should be done at all events, but only that it should be done if it could be done without injury to others. What was the intention of the legislature in any particular Act is a question of the construction of the Act. ...

It is clear that the burthen lies on those who seek to establish that the legislature intended to take away the private rights of individuals to show that by express words or by necessary implication such an intention appears. There are no express words in this Act, and I think the weight of argument is rather against than in favour of such an implication. ...

LORD WATSON: ... The judgment of this House in *The Hammersmith Ry.* v. *Brand* determines that where Parliament has given express powers to construct certain buildings or works according to plans and specifications upon a particular site and for a specific purpose, the use of those works or buildings in the manner contemplated and sanctioned by the Act cannot, except in so far as negligent, be restrained by injunction, although such use constitutes a nuisance at common

[1] (1832) 4 B. & Ad. 30.
[2] (1869) 4 H.L.Cas. 171.

law, and that no compensation is due in respect of injury to private rights unless the Act provides for such compensation being made. . . .

I see no reason to doubt that whenever it can be shown to be a matter of plain and necessary implication from the language of a statute that the legislature did intend to confer the specific powers which I have above referred to, the result in law will be precisely the same as if those powers had been given in express terms. . . .

. . . I do not think that the legislature can be held to have sanctioned that which is a nuisance at common law, except in the case where they have authorised a certain use of a specific building in a specified position, which cannot be so used without occasioning nuisance, or in the case where the particular plan or locality not being prescribed they have imperatively directed that a building shall be provided within a certain area and so used, it being an obvious or established fact that nuisance must be the result. In the latter case the onus in proving that the creation of a nuisance will be the inevitable result of carrying out the directions of the legislature depends upon their making good these two propositions: in the first place that they are bound to obey the imperative order of the legislature; and in the second place that they cannot possibly do so without infringing private rights. If the order of the legislature can be executed without nuisance, they cannot, in my opinion, plead the protection of the statute; and, on the other hand, it is insufficient for their protection that what is contemplated by the statute cannot be done without nuisance, unless they are also able to show that the legislature has directed it to be done. Where the terms of the statute are not imperative but permissive, when it is left to the discretion of the persons empowered to determine whether the general powers committed to them shall be put into execution or not, I think the fair inference is that the legislature intended that discretion to be exercised in strict conformity with private rights, and did not intend to confer licence to commit nuisance in any place which might be selected for the purpose. . . .

Judgment appealed against affirmed, and appeal dismissed with costs.

III. REMEDIES

Public Law and Order 53

O'Reilly v. Mackman
[1983] 2 A.C. 237
House of Lords

A number of prisoners sought by writ (or originating summons, in one case) to challenge the validity of decisions of the Board of Visitors of Hull prison on the ground that they were in breach of the rules of natural justice. In the High Court, Peter Pain J. refused an application of the Board to strike out the proceedings as an abuse of the process of the court. The application was, however, allowed by the Court of Appeal (Lord Denning M.R., Ackner and O'Connor L.JJ.) The prisoners appealed to the House of Lords (Lord Diplock, Lord Fraser of Tullybelton, Lord Keith of Kinkel, Lord Bridge of Harwich and Lord Brightman).

LORD DIPLOCK: . . . My Lords, it is not contested that if the allegations set out in the originating summons or statements of claim are true each of the appellants would have had a remedy obtainable by the procedure of an application for judicial review under R.S.C., Ord. 53; but to obtain that remedy, whether it took the form of an order of certiorari to quash the board's award or a declaration of its nullity, would have required the leave of the court under R.S.C., Ord. 53, r. 3. That judicial review lies against an award of the board of visitors of a prison made in the exercise of their disciplinary functions was established by the judgment of the Court of Appeal (overruling a Divisional Court) in *Reg.* v. *Board of Visitors of Hull Prison, Ex parte St. Germain* [1979] Q.B. 425: a decision that was, in my view, clearly right and has not been challenged in the instant appeals by the respondents.

In the *St. Germain* case, the only remedy that had been sought was certiorari to quash the decision of the board of visitors; but the alternative remedy of a declaration of nullity if the court considered it to be just and convenient would also have been available upon an application for judicial review under R.S.C., Ord. 53 after the replacement of the old rule by the new rule in 1977. In the instant cases, which were commenced after the new rule came into effect (but before the coming into force of section 31 of the Supreme Court Act 1981), certiorari would unquestionably have been the more appropriate remedy, since rule 5(4) of the Prison Rules 1964, which provides for remission of sentence up to a maximum of one-third, stipulates that the "rule shall have effect subject to any disciplinary award of forfeiture. ... " Prison rule 56, however, expressly empowers the Secretary of State to remit a disciplinary award and, since he would presumably do so in the case of a disciplinary award that had been declared by the High Court to be a nullity, such a declaration would achieve, though less directly, the same result in practice as quashing the award by *certiorari*.

So no question arises as to the "jurisdiction" of the High Court to grant to each of the appellants relief by way of a declaration in the terms sought, if they succeeded in establishing the facts alleged in their respective sentence of claim or originating summons and the court considered a declaration to be an appropriate remedy. All that is at issue in the instant appeal is the procedure by which such relief ought to be sought. Put in a single statement the question for your Lordships is: whether in 1980 after R.S.C., Ord. 53 in its new form, adopted in 1977, had come into operation it was an abuse of the process of the court to apply for such declarations by using the procedure laid down in the Rules for proceedings begun by writ or by originating summons instead of using the procedure laid down by Ord. 53 for an application for judicial review of the awards of forfeiture of remission of sentence made against them by the board which the appellants are seeking to impugn?

In their respective actions, the appellants claim only declaratory relief. . . . The only claim was for a form of relief which it lies within the discretion of the court to grant or to withhold. So the first thing to be noted is that the relief sought in the action is discretionary only.

It is not, and it could not be, contended that the decision of the board awarding him forfeiture of remission had infringed or threatened to infringe any right of the appellant derived from private law, whether a common law right or one created by a statute. Under the Prison Rules remission of sentence is not a matter of right but of indulgence. So far as private law is concerned all that each appellant had was a legitimate expectation, based upon his knowledge of what is the general practice, that he would be granted the maximum remission, permitted by rule 5(2) of the Prison Rules, of one third of his sentence if by that time no disciplinary award of forfeiture of remission had been made against him. So the second thing to be noted is that none of the appellants had any remedy in private law.

In public law, as distinguished from private law, however, such legitimate expectation gave to each appellant a sufficient interest to challenge the legality of the adverse disciplinary award made against him by the board on the ground that in one way or another the board in reaching its decision had acted outwith the powers conferred upon it by the legislation under which it was acting; and such grounds would include the board's failure to observe the rules of natural justice: which means no more than to act fairly towards him in carrying out their decision-making process, and I prefer so to put it.

The power of boards of visitors of a prison to make disciplinary awards is conferred upon them by subordinate legislation: the Prison Rules 1964 made by the Secretary of State under sections 6 and 47 of the Prison Act 1952. The charges against the appellants were of grave offences against discipline falling within rule 51. They were referred by the governor of the prison to the board under rule 51(1). It thereupon became the duty of the board under rule 51(3) to inquire into the charge and decide whether it was proved and if so to award what the board considered to be the appropriate punishment. Rule 49(2) is applicable to such inquiry by the board. It lays down expressly that the prisoner "shall be given a full opportunity of hearing what is alleged against him and of presenting his own case." In exercising their functions under rule 51 members of the board are acting as a statutory tribunal, as contrasted with a domestic tribunal upon which powers are conferred by contract between those who agree to submit to its jurisdiction. Where the legislation which confers upon a statutory tribunal its decision-making powers also provides expressly for the procedure it shall follow in the course of reaching its decision, it is a question of construction of the relevant legislation, to be decided by the court in which the decision is challenged, whether a particular procedural provision is mandatory, so that its non-observance in the process of reaching the decision makes the decision itself a nullity, or whether it is merely directory, so that the statutory tribunal has a discretion not to comply with it if, in its opinion, the exceptional circumstances of a particular case justify departing from it. But the requirement that a person who is charged with having done something which, if proved to the satisfaction of a statutory tribunal, has consequences that will, or may, affect him adversely, should be given a fair opportunity of hearing what is alleged against him and of presenting his own case, is so fundamental to any civilised legal system that it is to be presumed that Parliament intended that a failure to observe it should render null and void any decision reached in breach of this requirement. What is alleged by the appellants would amount to an infringement of the express rule 49; but even if there were no such express provision a requirement to observe it would be a necessary implication from the nature of the disciplinary functions of the board. In the absence of express provision to the contrary Parliament, whenever it provides for the creation of a statutory tribunal, must be presumed not to have intended that the tribunal should be authorised to act in contravention of one of the fundamental rules of natural justice or fairness: audi alteram partem.

.	.	.	.	.

My Lords, the power of the High Court to make declaratory judgments is conferred by what is now R.S.C., Ord. 15, r. 16. The language of the rule which was first made in 1883 has never been altered, though the numbering of the rule has from time to time been changed. It provides:

> "No action or other proceeding shall be open to objection on the ground that a merely declaratory judgment or order is sought thereby, and the court may make binding declarations of right whether or not any consequential relief is or could be claimed."

This rule, which is in two parts separated by "and," has been very liberally interpreted in the course of its long history, wherever it appeared to the court that the justice of the case required the grant of declaratory relief in the particular action before it. Since "action" is defined so as to have included since 1938 an originating motion applying for prerogative orders, Ord. 15, r. 16 says nothing as to the appropriate procedure by which declarations of different kinds ought to be sought. Nor does it draw any distinction between declarations that relate to rights and obligations under private law and those that relate to rights and obligations under public law. Indeed the appreciation of the distinction in substantive law between what is private law and what is public law has itself been a latecomer to the English legal system. It is a consequence of the development that has taken place in the last 30 years of the procedures available for judicial control of administrative action. This development started with the expansion of the grounds upon which orders of certiorari could be obtained as a result of the decision of the Court of Appeal in *Rex* v. *Northumberland Compensation Appeal Tribunal, Ex parte Shaw* [1952] 1 K.B. 338; it was accelerated by the passing of the Tribunals and Inquiries Act 1958, and culminated in the substitution in 1977 of the new form of R.S.C., Ord. 53 which has since been given statutory confirmation in section 31 of the Supreme Court Act 1981.

The importance of *Rex* v. *Northumberland Compensation Appeal Tribunal, Ex parte Shaw* is that it re-established, largely as a result of the historical erudition of Lord Goddard C.J. displayed in the judgment of the Divisional Court ([1951] 1 K.B. 711) a matter that had long been forgotten by practitioners and had been overlooked as recently as 1944 in a judgment, *Racecourse Betting Control Board* v. *Secretary for Air* [1944] Ch. 114, given per incuriam by a Court of Appeal of which Lord Goddard had himself been a member. What was there re-discovered was that the High Court had power to quash by an order of certiorari a decision of any body of persons having legal authority (not derived from contract only) to determine questions affecting the rights of subjects, not only on the ground that it had acted outwith its jurisdiction but also on the grounds that it was apparent upon the face of its written determination that it had made a mistake as to the applicable law.

However, this re-discovered ground on which relief by an order of certiorari to quash the decision as erroneous in law could be obtained, was available only when there was an error of law apparent "on the face of the record" and so was liable to be defeated by the decision-making body if it gave no reasons for its determination.

In 1958 this lacuna, so far as statutory tribunals were concerned, was largely filled by the passing of the first Tribunals and Inquiries Act, now replaced by the Tribunals and Inquiries Act 1971. This Act required the giving of reasons for their determinations by the great majority of statutory tribunals from which there is no express statutory provision for an appeal to the Supreme Court on a point of law. But boards of visitors of prisons have never been included among those tribunals that are covered by that Act. The Act also in effect repealed, with two exceptions, what had become to be called generically "no certiorari" clauses in all previous statutes, by providing in section 14(1) as follows:

"As respects England and Wales ... any provision in an Act passed before [the commencement of this Act] that any order or determination shall not be called into question in any court, or any provision in such an Act which by similar words excludes any of the powers of the High Court, shall not have effect so as to prevent the removal of proceedings into the High Court by order of certiorari or to prejudice the powers of the High Court to make orders of mandamus: ... "

The subsection, it is to be observed, says nothing about any right to bring civil actions for declarations of nullity of orders or determinations of statutory bodies where an earlier Act of Parliament contains a provision that such order or determination"shall not be called into question in any court." Since actions begun by writ seeking such declarations were already coming into common use in the High Court so as to provide an alternative remedy to orders of certiorari, the section suggests a parliamentary preference in favour of making the latter remedy available rather than the former. I will defer consideration of the reasons for this preference until later.

Fortunately for the development of public law in England, section 14(3) contained express provision that the section should not apply to any order or determination of the Foreign Compensation Commission, a statutory body established under the Foreign Compensation Act 1950, which Act provided by section 4(4) an express provision: "The determination by the commission of any application made to them under this Act shall not be called in question in any court of law." It was this provision that provided the occasion for the landmark decision of this House in *Anisminic Ltd.* v. *Foreign Compensation Commission* [1969] 2 A.C. 147, and particularly the leading speech of Lord Reid, which has liberated English public law from the fetters that the courts had theretofore imposed upon themselves so far as determinations of inferior courts and statutory tribunals were concerned, by drawing esoteric distinctions between errors of law committed by such tribunals that went to their jurisdiction, and errors of law committed by them within their jurisdiction. The breakthrough that the *Anisminic* case made was the recognition by the majority of this House that if a tribunal whose jurisdiction was limited by statute or subordinate legislation mistook the law applicable to the facts as it had found them, it must have asked itself the wrong question, *i.e.*, one into which it was not empowered to inquire and so had no jurisdiction to determine. Its purported "determination," not being a "determination" within the meaning of the empowering legislation, was accordingly a nullity.

[Lord Diplock then traced the development of modern administrative law and explained how the new Order 53, introduced in 1977 freed applicants for prerogative remedies from the handicaps under which they formerly suffered and allowed applications for a declaration or injunction to be included in an application for judicial review].

So Order 53 since 1977 has provided a procedure by which every type of remedy for infringement of the rights of individuals that are entitled to protection in public law can be obtained in one and the same proceeding by way of an application for judicial review, and whichever remedy is found to be the most appropriate in the light of what has emerged upon the hearing of the application, can be granted to him. If what should emerge is that his complaint is not of an infringement of any of his rights that are entitled to protection in public law, but may be an infringement of his rights in private law and thus not a proper subject for judicial review, the court has power under rule 9(5), instead of refusing the application, to order the proceedings to continue as if they had begun by writ. There is no such converse power under the R.S.C. to permit an action begun by writ to continue as if it were an application for judicial review.

.   .   .   .   .

My Lords, Order 53 does not expressly provide that procedure by application for judicial review shall be the exclusive procedure available by which the remedy of a declaration or injunction may be obtained for infringement of rights that are entitled to protection under public law; nor does section 31 of the Supreme Court Act 1981. There is great variation between individual cases that fall within Order 53 and the Rules Committee and subsequently the legislature were, I think, for this reason content to rely upon the express and the inherent power of the High Court, exercised upon a case to case basis, to prevent abuse of its process whatever might be the form taken by that abuse. Accordingly, I do not think that your Lordships would be wise to use this as an occasion to lay down categories of cases in which it would necessarily always be an abuse to seek in an action begun by writ or originating summons a remedy against infringement of rights of the individual that are entitled to protection in public law.

The position of applicants for judicial review has been drastically ameliorated by the new Order 53. It has removed all those disadvantages, particularly in relation to discovery, that were manifestly unfair to them and had, in many cases, made applications for prerogative orders an inadequate remedy if justice was to be done. This it was that justified the courts in not treating as an abuse of their powers resort to an alternative procedure by way of action for a declaration or injunction (not then obtainable on an application under Order 53), despite the fact that this procedure had the effect of depriving the defendants of the protection to statutory tribunals and public authorities for which for public policy reasons Order 53 provided.

Now that those disadvantages to applicants have been removed and all remedies for infringements of rights protected by public law can be obtained upon an application for judicial review, as can also remedies for infringements of rights under private law if such infringements should also be involved, it would in my view as a general rule be contrary to public policy, and as such an abuse of the process of the court, to permit a person seeking to establish that a decision of a public authority infringed rights to which he was entitled to protection under public law to proceed by way of an ordinary action and by this means to evade the provisions of Order 53 for the protection of such authorities.

My Lords, I have described this as a general rule; for though it may normally be appropriate to apply it by the summary process of striking out the action, there may be exceptions, particularly where the invalidity of the decision arises as a collateral issue in a claim for infringement of a right of the plaintiff arising under private law, or where none of the parties objects to the adoption of the procedure by writ or originating summons. Whether there should be other exceptions should, in my view, at this stage in the development of procedural public law, be left to be decided on a case to case basis—a process that your Lordships will be continuing in the next case in which judgment is to be delivered today [*Cocks* v. *Thanet District Council* [1983] 2 A.C. 286].

In the instant cases where the only relief sought is a declaration of nullity of the decisions of a statutory tribunal, the Board of Visitors of Hull Prison, as in any other case in which a similar declaration of nullity in public law is the only relief claimed, I have no hesitation, in agreement with the Court of Appeal, in holding that to allow the actions to proceed would be an abuse of the process of the court. They are blatant attempts to avoid the protections for the defendants for which Order 53 provides.

I would dismiss these appeals.
Lord Fraser of Tullybelton, Lord Keith of Kinkel, Lord Bridge of Harwich and Lord Brightman concurred.
Appeal dismissed.

Note

Lord Denning M.R.'s judgment in the Court of Appeal is a *tour de force* even by his standards: [1983] 2 A.C. 250. Lord Diplock referred to development of the law on a case to case basis. The following cases illustrate that process. Whether a question is one of public law or private law is often difficult to determine. For a survey of earlier decisions see *R.* v. *Secretary of State for the Home Department Ex parte Dew* [1987] 2 All E.R. 1049.

PRIVATE LAW REMEDIES

Davy v. Spelthorne Borough Council
[1984] A.C. 262
House of Lords

Davy, the owner of certain premises, alleged that on or about November 6, 1979 he entered into an agreement with the council whereby he undertook not to appeal against an enforcement notice to be served by the council upon him in respect of the use of the premises, provided that the notice would not be enforced by the council for a period of three years from the date of its service. The council served an enforcement notice on October 15, 1980, which, Davy alleged was in accordance with that agreement. The enforcement notice stated that the Council required Davy, within three years of the date when the notice took effect, to cease using the land for the manufacture of concrete products and to remove from it all buildings and works. Davy did not appeal against the enforcement notice and the time for so doing had long since expired. Davy alleged that he refrained from appealing against the enforcement notice in pursuance of the agreement of November 6, 1979 and that he entered into that agreement on the advice of officers of the Council.

On August 24, 1982 Davy issued a writ. He claimed damages from the Council on the ground that the Council, or their officers, had purported to advise him as to his rights under the Town and Country Planning Act 1971, and that their advice had been negligent. The Council denied that there was any legally enforceable agreement between Davy and themselves. They also denied that they, or their officers, purported to advise him on his rights, and they said that, if they did give any such advice, it was not given negligently. Davy also sought an injunction ordering the appellants not to implement the enforcement notice and an order that the enforcement notice be set aside.

The Council applied to the High Court to have the writ struck out. Its claim was rejected in a judgment delivered by Sir Robert Megarry V.-C. before the decision of the House of Lords in *O'Reilly* v. *Mackman* [1983] 2 A.C. 237. The Court of Appeal (Cumming-Bruce and Fox L.JJ. and Bush J.) in the light of *O'Reilly* v. *Mackman* ordered that the claims relating to the injunction and setting aside the notice raised questions of public law and could only be pursued by way of judicial review under Order 53. The Court of Appeal refused to strike out the claim in negligence and against that decision the council appealed to the House of Lords (Lord Fraser of Tullybelton, Lord Wilberforce, Lord Roskill, Lord Brandon of Oakbrook and Lord Brightman).

LORD FRASER OF TULLYBELTON: ... The present proceedings, so far as they consist of a claim for damages for negligence, appear to me to be simply an ordinary action for tort. They do not raise any issue of public law as a live issue. I cannot improve upon the words of Fox L.J. in the Court of Appeal when he said (1983) 81 L.G.R. 580, 596:

"I do not think that the negligence claim is concerned with 'the infringement of rights to which [the plaintiff] was entitled to protection under public law' to use Lord Diplock's words in *O'Reilly* v. *Mackman* [1983] 2 A.C. 237, 285. The claim, in my opinion, is concerned with the alleged infringement of the plaintiff's rights at common law. Those rights are not even peripheral to a public law claim. They are the essence of the entire claim, so far as negligence is concerned."

It follows that in my opinion they do not fall within the scope of the general rule laid down in *O'Reilly* v. *Mackman*. The present proceedings may be contrasted with *Cocks* v. *Thanet District Council* [1983] 2 A.C. 286, which was decided in this House on the same day as *O'Reilly* v. *Mackman*. In *Cocks* v. *Thanet District Council*, the House held that the general rule stated in *O'Reilly* v. *Mackman* applied (and I quote the headnote) "where a plaintiff was obliged to impugn a public authority's determination as a condition precedent to enforcing a statutory private law right." In that case, the plaintiff had to impugn a decision of the housing authority, to the effect that he was intentionally homeless, as a condition precedent to establishing the existence of a private law right to be provided with accommodation. It is quite clear from the speech of Lord Bridge of Harwich, with which all the other members of the House agreed, that the plaintiff was asserting a present right to impugn or overturn the decision—see p. 294D: "the decision of the public authority *which the litigant wishes to overturn.*" (Emphasis added.) In the present case, on the other hand, the respondent does not impugn or wish to overturn the enforcement notice. His whole case on negligence depends on the fact that he has lost his chance to impugn it. In my opinion therefore the general rule stated in *O'Reilly* v. *Mackman* is inapplicable. The circumstances in which the procedure under Order 53 is appropriate were described in some detail by Lord Diplock in *O'Reilly* v. *Mackman*. At p. 275B he mentioned the fact that in that case no claim for damages would lie against the defendants, and that the only relief sought was for a declaration, a form of relief that is discretionary only. At p. 281B he explained that one of the reasons why the procedure under Order 53 is appropriate in certain cases is that it provides

"a very speedy means, available in urgent cases within a matter of days rather than months, for determining whether a disputed decision was valid in law or not."

The importance of obtaining a speedy decision is (see pp. 280–281) that:

"The public interest in good administration requires that public authorities and third parties should not be kept in suspense as to the legal validity of a decision the authority has reached in purported exercise of decision-making powers for any longer period than is absolutely necessary in fairness to the person affected by the decision."

That explanation points the contrast with the present case, where the validity of the enforcement notice is not now challenged, and no public authority or third party is being kept in suspense on that matter. Procedure under Order 53 would in my view be entirely inappropriate in this case.

A further consideration is that if the claim based on negligence, which is the only one of the original three claims now surviving, were to be struck out, the blow to the respondent's chances of recovering damages might well be mortal. The court has no power to order the proceedings for damages to continue as if they had been made under Order 53. The converse power under Ord. 53, r. 9 operates in one direction only—see *O'Reilly* v. *Mackman*, at p. 284A-B. So, if the present appeal were to succeed, the respondent's only chance of bringing his claim for damages before the court would be by obtaining leave to start proceedings for judicial review (now long out of time) and then by relying on Ord. 53, r. 7 to attach a claim for damages to his claim for judicial review. That would be an awkward and uncertain process to which the respondent ought not to be subjected unless it is required by statute: see *Pyx Granite Co. Ltd.* v. *Ministry of Housing and Local Government* [1960] A.C. 260, 286, *per* Viscount Simonds. In my view it is not.

LORD WILBERFORCE: . . . As pleaded (and for the purpose of this appeal we are only concerned with the pleading and not with its substance or merits) [the claim] is that the appellant council owed to the respondent plaintiff a duty of care in, through its officers, advising him as to his planning application; that the council was negligent in so advising him; that by reason of this negligence he suffered damage, namely the loss of a chance of successfully appealing against the enforcement notice served upon him by the council. Though this was initially one of several claims, it now stands on its own, and should be judged as an independent and separate action.

To say that such a claim, so formulated, ought to be, or indeed can be, struck out as an abuse of the process of the court seems on the face of it a remarkable proposition. There is no doubt that, side by side with their statutory duties, local authorities may in certain limited circumstances become liable for negligence at common law in the performance of their duties: see for example *Dorset Yacht Co. Ltd.* v. *Home Office* [1970] A.C. 1004, *Anns* v. *Merton London Borough Council* [1978] A.C. 728, 756, 758). In what circumstances then can it be said to be an abuse of process to sue them for negligence in the common law courts?

It is said that, in this case, the right should be denied because the claim involves consideration of a question not of "private law" but of "public law"—namely whether the respondent had or would have had a defence against the enforcement notice; that this consideration cannot take place in an ordinary action but can only take place in a proceeding of what is now called "judicial review" under the provisions of R.S.C., Ord. 53.

The expressions "private law" and "public law" have recently been imported into the law of England from countries which, unlike our own, have separate systems concerning public law and private law. No doubt they are convenient expressions for descriptive purposes. In this country they must be used with caution, for, typically, English law fastens, not upon principles but upon remedies. The principle remains intact that public authorities and public servants are, unless clearly exempted, answerable in the ordinary courts for wrongs done to individuals. But by an extension of remedies and a flexible procedure it can be said that something resembling a system of public law is being developed. Before the expression "public law" can be used to deny a subject a right of action in the court of his choice it must be related to a positive prescription of law, by statute or by statutory rules. We have not yet reached the point at which mere characterisation of a claim as a claim in public law is sufficient to exclude it from consideration by the ordinary courts: to permit this would be to create a dual system of law with the rigidity and procedural hardship for plaintiffs which it was the purpose of the recent reforms to remove.

Appeal dismissed.

Wandsworth London Borough Council v. Winder
[1985] A.C. 461
House of Lords

Winder was the tenant of a flat of which Wandsworth Council was the landlord. The Council increased the rent of the flat to a level which the tenant claimed was unreasonable. He paid the original rent and a sum to cover what he regarded as a reasonable increase. The Council commenced proceedings for arrears of rent due and possession of the flat. The tenant defended the action on the ground that the decision to increase the rent was void for unreasonableness. The Council sought to strike out the tenant's defence on the ground that any challenge to the validity of its decision must be made by way of application for judicial review. In the County Court the Council's application was successful. The Court of Appeal (Robert Goff and Parker L.JJ., Ackner L.J. dissenting) allowed an appeal by the tenant. The Council appealed to the House of Lords (Lord Fraser of Tullybelton, Lord Scarman, Lord Keith of Kinkel, Lord Roskill and Lord Brandon of Oakbrook).

LORD FRASER OF TULLYBELTON: . . . The respondent seeks to show in the course of his defence in these proceedings that the appellants' decisions to increase the rent were such as no reasonable man could consider justifiable. But your Lordships are not concerned in this appeal to decide whether that contention is right or wrong. The only issue at this stage is whether the respondent is entitled to put forward the contention as a defence in the present proceedings. The appellants say that he is not because the only procedure by which their decision could have been challenged was by judicial review under R.S.C., Ord. 53. The respondent was refused leave to apply for judicial review out of time and (say the appellants) he has lost the opportunity to challenge the decisions. The appellants rely on the decisions of this House in O'Reilly v. Mackman [1983] 2 A.C. 237 and Cocks v. Thanet District Council [1983] 2 A.C. 286. The respondent accepts that judicial review would have been an appropriate procedure for the purpose, but he maintains that it is not the only procedure open to him, and that he was entitled to wait until he was sued by the appellants and then to defend the proceedings, as he has done.

In order to deal with these contentions, it is necessary to consider what was decided by the House in those two cases. The question raised in O'Reilly [1983] 2 A.C. 237 was the same as that in the present case, although, of course, the circumstances were different.

. . . There are two important differences between the facts in O'Reilly and those in the present case. First, the plaintiffs in O'Reilly had not suffered any infringement of their rights in private law; their complaint was that they had been ordered to forfeit part of their remission of sentence but they had no right in private law to such a remission, which was granted only as a matter of indulgence. Consequently, even if the board of visitors had acted contrary to the rules of natural justice when making the award, the members of the board would not have been liable in damages to the prisoners. In the present case what the respondent complains of is the infringement of a contractual right in private law. Secondly, in O'Reilly the prisoners had initiated the proceedings, and Lord Diplock, throughout in his speech, treated the question only as one affecting a claim for infringing a right of the plaintiff while in the present case the respondent is the defendant. The decision on O'Reilly is therefore not directly in point in the present case, but the appellates rely particularly on a passage in a speech of Lord Diplock, with whose speech the other members of the Appellate Committee agreed, at p. 285:

"Now that those disadvantages to applicants [for judicial review] have been removed and all remedies for infringements of rights protected by public law can be obtained upon an application for judicial review, as can also remedies for infringements of rights under private law if such infringements should also be involved, it would in my view as a general rule be contrary to public policy, and as such an abuse of the process of the court, to permit a person seeking to establish that a decision of a public authority infringed rights to which he was entitled to protection under public law to proceed by way of an ordinary action and by this means to evade the provisions of Order 53 for the protection of such authorities.

"My Lords, I have described this as a general rule; for though it may normally be appropriate to apply it by the summary process of striking out the action, there may be exceptions, particularly where the invalidity of the decision arises as a collateral issue in a claim for infringement of a right of the plaintiff arising under private law, or where none of the parties objects to the adoption of the procedure by writ or originating summons. Whether there should be other exceptions should, in my view, at this stage in the development of procedural public law, be left to be decided on a case to case basis—a process that your Lordships will be continuing in the next case in which judgment is to be delivered today [*Cocks* v. *Thanet District Council* [1983] 2 A.C. 286]."

The last paragraph in that quotation shows that Lord Diplock was careful to emphasise that the general rule which he had stated in the previous paragraph might well be subject to exceptions. The question for your Lordships is whether the instant appeal is an exception to the general rule. It might be possible to treat this case as falling within one of the exceptions suggested by Lord Diplock, if the question of the invalidity of the appellants' decision had arisen as a collateral issue in a claim by the respondent (as defendant) for infringement of his right arising under private law to continue to occupy the flat. But I do not consider that the question of invalidity is truly collateral to the issue between the parties. Although it is not mentioned in the appellants' statement of claim, it is the whole basis of the respondent's defence and it is the central issue which has to be decided. The case does not therefore fall within any of the exceptions specifically suggested in *O'Reilly* v. *Mackman* [1983] 2 A.C. 237.

Immediately after the decision in *O'Reilly*, the House applied the general rule in the case of *Cocks* [1983] 2 A.C. 286. The proceedings in *O'Reilly* had begun before the Supreme Court Act 1981 (especially section 31) was passed. The proceedings in *Cocks* were begun after that Act was passed, but for the present purpose nothing turns on that distinction. *Cocks* was an action by a homeless person claiming that the local housing authority had a duty to provide permanent accommodation for him. The council resolved that the plaintiff had become homeless "intentionally" in the sense of the Housing (Homeless Persons) Act 1977. Consequently the plaintiff had no right in private law to be provided with permanent housing accommodation by the authority. The plaintiff raised an action in the county court claiming, inter alia, a declaration that the council were in breach of their duty to him in not having provided him with permanent accommodation. In order to proceed in his action he had to show as a condition precedent that the council's decision was invalid. This House held that the plaintiff was not entitled to impugn the council's decision in public law otherwise than by judicial review, notwithstanding that the effect of the decision was to prevent him from "establishing a necessary condition precedent to the statutory private law right which he [was seeking] to enforce": see *per* my noble and learned friend, Lord Bridge of Harwich, at p. 249E. The essential difference between that case and the present is that the impugned decision of the local authority did not deprive the plaintiff of pre-existing private law right; it prevented him from establishing a new private law right. There is also the same distinction as in *O'Reilly* [1983] 2 A.C. 237, namely, that the party complaining of the decision was the plaintiff.

Although neither *O'Reilly* nor *Cocks* [1983] 2 A.C. 286 is an authority which directly applies to the facts of the instant appeal, it is said on behalf of the appellants that the principle underlying those decisions applies here, and that, if the respondent is successful, he will be evading that principle. My Lords, I cannot agree. The principle underlying those decisions, as Lord Diplock explained in *O'Reilly* [1983] 2 A.C. 237, 284, is that there is a "need, in the interests of good administration and of third parties who may be indirectly affected by the decision, for speedy certainty as to whether it has the effect of a decision that is valid in public law." The main argument urged on behalf of the appellants was that this is a typical case where there is a need for speedy certainty in the public interest. I accept, of course, that the decision in this appeal will indirectly affect many third parties including many of the appellants' tenants, and perhaps most if not all of their ratepayers because if the appellants' impugned decisions are held to be invalid, the basis of their financial administration since 1981 will be upset. That would be highly inconvenient from the point of view of the appellants, and of their ratepayers, and it would be a great advantage to them if persons such as the respondent who seek to challenge their decision were limited to doing so by procedure under Order 53. Such procedure is speedy and avoids prolonged uncertainty about the validity of decisions. An intending applicant for judicial review under Order 53 has to obtain leave to apply, so that unmeritorious applications can be dismissed in limine and an application must normally be made within a limited period of three months after the decision which has impugned, unless the court allows an extension of time in any particular case. Procedure under Order 53 also affords protection to public authorities in other ways, which are explained in *O'Reilly* and which I need not elaborate here. It may well be that such protection to public authorities tends to promote good administration. But there may be other ways of obtaining speedy decisions; for example in some cases it may be possible for a public authority itself to initiate proceedings for judicial review. In any event, the arguments for protecting public authorities against unmeritorious or dilatory challenges to their decisions have to be set against the arguments for preserving the ordinary rights of private citizens to defend themselves against unfounded claims.

It would in my opinion be a very strange use of language to describe the respondent's behaviour in relation to this litigation as an abuse or misuse by him of the process of the court. He did not select the procedure to be adopted. He is merely seeking to defend proceedings brought against him by the appellants. In so doing he is seeking only to exercise the ordinary right of any individual to defend an action against him on the ground that he is not liable for the whole sum claimed by the plaintiff. Moreover he puts forward his defence as a matter of right, whereas in an application for judicial review, success would require an exercise of the court's discretion in his favour. Apart from the provisions of Order 53 and section 31 of the Supreme Court Act 1981, he would certainly be entitled to defend the action on the ground that the plaintiff's claim arises from a resolution which (on his view) is invalid: see for example *Cannock Chase District Council* v. *Kelly* [1978] 1 W.L.R. 1, which was decided in July 1977, a few months before Order 53 came into force (as it did in December 1977). I find it impossible to accept that the right to challenge the decision of a local authority in course of defending an action for non-payment can have been swept away by Order 53, which was directed to introducing a procedural reform. As my noble and learned friend Lord Scarman said in *Reg.* v. *Inland Revenue Commissioners, Ex parte Federation of Self Employed and Small Businesses Ltd.* [1982] A.C. 617, 647G "The new R.S.C., Ord. 53 is a procedural reform of great importance in the field of public law, but it does not—indeed, cannot—either extend or diminish the substantive law. Its function is limited to ensuring 'ubi jus, ibi remedium.' " Lord Wilberforce spoke to the same effect at p. 631A. Nor, in my opinion, did section 31 of the Supreme Court Act 1981 which refers only to "an application" for judicial review have the effect of limiting the rights of a defendant sub silentio. I would adopt the words of Viscount Simonds in

Pyx Granite Co. Ltd. v. *Ministry of Housing and Local Government* [1960] A.C. 260, 286 as follows:

> "It is a principle not by any means to be whittled down that the subject's recourse to Her Majesty's courts for the determination of his rights is not to be excluded except by clear words."

The argument of the appellants in the present case would be directly in conflict with that observation.

If the public interest requires that persons should not be entitled to defend actions brought against them by public authorities, where the defence rests on a challenge to a decision by the public authority, then it is for Parliament to change the law.

I would dismiss the appeal.

Lord Scarman, Lord Keith of Kinkel, Lord Roskill and Lord Brandon of Oakbrook concurred.

Appeal dismissed.

Note

Differing news about the desirability of the decision in *Wandsworth L.B.C.* v. *Winder* have been expressed. In "Public Law—Private Law: Why the Divide? A Personal View," [1986] P.L. 221, 227, Woolf L.J. said:

Another area in which there is a fundamental difference between the public law system and the private law system is as to the procedure by which relief is obtained from the courts. While on the whole academic lawyers have been enthusiastic about the role that the courts have played in developing the public law system (which is not altogether surprising, since this to a remarkable degree is due to their influence), recent decision of the courts and in particular the House of Lords as to the procedure which has to be adopted in order to obtain relief against public bodies have been less popular and subject to very stringent academic criticism. Indeed, Sir Patrick Neill, Q.C., when surveying judicial review in the sixth Child Lecture last year, compared the progress of the courts as being rather like a game of snakes and ladders.[1] For him, the longest and most fearsome snake was the decision of *O'Reilly* v. *Mackman*[2] in which Lord Diplock, in a speech with which all the other members of the House agreed, established the principle that a person seeking to challenge a decision of a public authority under public law must, as a general rule, proceed by way of an application under the new procedure of judicial review established in 1977 by Order 53 of the Rules of the Supreme Court. From my side of the board, or should I say the Bench, that decision, far from being a snake, is a ladder which (so far as procedure is concerned) reaches almost to the winning post. For me, the snake is the decision of the House of Lords last year in *Wandsworth London Borough Council* v. *Winder*[3] which distinguished *O'Reilly* v. *Mackman* and held that is was permissible to raise as a defence in an ordinary action an allegation that a decision of a public body was unlawful without having to comply with any of the restrictions applicable to judicial review.

In *Waverley B.C.* v. *Hilden* [1988] 1 W.L.R. 246 Scott I. distinguished *Winder's* case. The Council sought an injunction to restrain the defendant gypsies from parking their caravans on land, contrary to the law. The defendants sought by way of defence to the action to challenge the validity of the Council's resolution to apply for the injunction. Scott J. held that such challenge could only be made by way of judicial review:

"The situation which pertained in *Bristol District Council* v. *Clark* [1975] 1 W.L.R. 1443, *Cannock Chase District Council* v. *Kelly* [1978] 1 W.L.R. 1 and *Wandsworth London Borough Council* v. *Winder* [1985] A.C. 461 was quite different. In each of those cases the invalidity of the relevant council's decision would, if established, constitute a substantive defence to the action being brought. In the present case the alleged invalidity in the council's decision to commence the action is relied on as a defence. But it is, in my view, not a defence in the true sense. It is, on analysis, an assertion that the action was commenced and is being prosecuted without proper authority.

Mr. Hornby has relied on the two passages from Ralph Gibson L.J.'s judgment in *West Glamorgan County Council* v. *Rafferty* [1987] W.L.R. 457 as authority for the proposition that if

---

[1] *Administrative Law: Ladders and Snakes*, March 12, 1985 (Child & Co., 1986).
[2] [1983] 2 A.C. 237.   [3] [1985] A.C. 461.

the invalidity be established the action would have to be struck out. I do not think that that is right. It is not uncommon for actions by corporations to be commenced and for there then to be a challenge to the issue of the writ on the ground of lack of authority. If it is clear that the writ was issued without proper authority and that the proper authority would not be forthcoming, the action will be struck out. But if there is a dispute as to whether there was or was not proper authority, or if there is ground for supposing that the issue of the writ would be ratified by those entitled to do so, then the usual practice would be to stay the action in order to allow the issue of authority to be settled.

The proper method of challenge to the decision of a local authority to commence an action, whether for the enforcement of its own property rights, as in the *West Glamorgan* case [1987] 1 W.L.R. 457, or whether for the enforcement of public rights, as in the present case, is, in my view, by judicial review. That is what was done in *West Glamorgan* case. It was held in *Wandsworth London Borough Council* v. *Winder* [1985] A.C. 461 that the invalidity of an administrative decision can be raised by a defendant as a defence to the action without resorting to judicial review procedure. But that assumes that the invalidity of the decision would, if established, constitute a substantive defence to the action. That was the position in the *Winder* case and also in the two Housing Act cases, *Bristol District Council* v. *Clark* [1975] 1 W.L.R. 1443 and *Cannock Chase District Council* v. *Kelly* [1987] 1 W.L.R 1. But that is not, in my judgment, the case where the decision under attack is a decision to commence the action.

In the present case the council's decision to institute and prosecute this action in its own name is open to challenge. But the defendants' allegation that the decision was unreasonable in a *Wednesbury* sense is not an allegation of a defence to the action. It is an allegation first that the action was commenced without proper authority and, second, that the council lacks locus standi to bring the action in its own name. An attack of this nature ought, in my view, to be conducted by means of judicial review procedure."

See further *Avon County Council* v. *Buscott* [1988] 1 All E.R. 841 (C.A.).

STATUTORY REMEDIES

Pasmore and Others v. Oswaldtwistle
Urban District Council
[1988] A.C. 387
House of Lords

The owner of a paper factory obtained from Charles J. a mandamus directing the Oswaldtwistle Urban District Council (the local sewerage authority) to cause to be made such sewers as might be necessary for effectually draining their district, and in particular the plaintiff's premises, in accordance with the Public Health Act 1875, s.15. Section 299 of the Act provided for complaints to be made to the Local Government Board if a local authority made default in furnishing their district with sufficient sewers; and it went on to provide that if the local authority did not perform their duty within the time limit prescribed by an order of the Board made after inquiry, such order might be enforced by writ of mandamus or the Board might appoint some person to perform such duty. The Court of Appeal allowed the District Council's appeal against the issue of the mandamus, on the ground that it does not lie where Parliament has provided a specific remedy.

Pasmore and others, the representatives of the deceased owner, now appealed to the House of Lords. Their Lordships (Earl of Halsbury L.C., Lord Macnaghten, Lord Morris and Lord James of Hereford) dismissed the appeal.

EARL OF HALSBURY L.C.: The question on this appeal is whether a mandamus which was ordered to issue by Charles J. can be supported. According to that learned judge's view it was a mandamus "commanding the defendants to cause to be made such sewers as may be necessary for effectively draining their district under the Public Health Act 1875, and in particular the plaintiff's premises." I think it right to call attention to the language the learned judge uses, because I am of opinion that it is the key to what I consider to be the error which the learned judge committed in the course of the judgment he delivered in this case. Your Lordships will observe that the first part of that mandamus, "for effectively draining their district under the Public Health Act 1875," follows the language of the statute. Then he has put in this in addition—"and in particular the plaintiff's premises." In the view I take of the statute, that was a provision which there was no authority to add to the mandamus at all. There is no such provision in the statute, and it appears to me that the whole purview, object, and purpose of the statute is one which would not justify such an addition to the language of the mandamus.

The principle upon which the question arises that where a specific remedy is given, it thereby deprives the person who insists upon a remedy of any other form of remedy than that given by the statute, is one which is very familiar, and which runs through the law. I think Lord Tenterden accurately states that principle in the case of *Rochester (Bishop)* v. *Bridges*.[1] He says: "Where an Act creates an obligation, and enforces the performance in a specified manner, we take it to be a general rule that performance cannot be enforced in any other manner." The words which the learned judge, Lord Tenterden, uses there appear to be strictly applicable to this case. The obligation which is created by this statute is an obligation which is created by the statute, and by the statute alone. . . . There is a specified remedy contained in it, which is an application to the proper government department.

It seems to me that if it were possible to conceive a case in which it would be extremely inconvenient that each suitor in turn should be permitted to apply for a

[1] [1831] 1 B.&Ad. 847.

specific remedy against the body charged with the care of the health of the inhabitants of the district in respect of drainage, it is such a case as this; and it is illustrated by the form of the mandamus. When I called the attention of the learned counsel to the form of the mandamus, he treated the observation as if it were a question of some mistake made in the pleadings which would be remedied as a matter of course in these days. But that was not the object of the observation, nor is it the importance of the observation. It is that the obligation itself is such that the form of the mandamus becomes of the substance of the argument. You cannot get out of the form of the mandamus. I know no other form which could be adopted than that which has been adopted. But then that shows how important it is that the particular jurisdiction to call upon the whole district to reform their mode of dealing with sewage and drainage should not be in the hands, and should not be open to the litigation, of any particular individual, but should be committed to a government department. . . .

Appeal dismissed.

Note

The existence of a statutory remedy is always a relevant factor when a court is considering whether in its discretion to grant relief by way of judicial review: *R.* v. *Inland Revenue Commissioners Ex parte Preston* [1985] A.C. 835, 852 *per* Lord Templeman.

In some cases however, as in *Pasmore*, the courts have held that the statutory remedy is the *only* remedy available. See further *Pyx Granite Co.* v. *Ministry of Housing* [1960] A.C. 260; *R.* v. *Secretary of State for the Environment Ex parte Ward* [1984] 1 W.L.R. 834.

STATUTORY RESTRICTION OF JUDICIAL REVIEW

Ouster of Jurisdiction

Anisminic v. Foreign Compensation Commission

[1969] 2 A.C. 147

House of Lords

The Foreign Compensation Act 1950, s.4(4), provided that: "The determination by the Commission of any application made to them under this Act shall not be called in question in any court of law." Before the Suez Incident and on October 31, 1956, the plaintiffs, an English company, owned property in Egypt which was sequestrated under a proclamation of 1956 by the Egyptian authorities. In 1957 the plaintiffs sold the sequestrated property to an Egyptian organisation, T.E.D.O. In 1959 the plaintiffs, who were named in the Foreign Compensation (Egypt) (Determination and Registration of Claims) Order 1962, applied to the Foreign Compensation Commission claiming that they were persons entitled to participate in the Egyptian Compensation Fund. The Commission's provisional determination was that they had failed to establish a claim under the Order.

The plaintiffs brought an action against the Commission for a declaration that the Commission had misconstrued the Order in finding that T.E.D.O. was their successor in title, and that its determination was a nullity. The Commission contended that under section 4(4) of the Foreign Compensation Act 1950 (*supra*) the court had no jurisdiction to entertain the proceedings.

Browne J. made a declaration that the Commission's determination was made without or in excess of jurisdiction and was a nullity (at p. 223). The Court of Appeal (Sellers, Diplock and Russell L.JJ.) reversed that order. The House of Lords (Lord Reid, Lord Pearce and Lord Wilberforce, Lord Morris of Borth–y–Gest dissenting and Lord Pearson dissenting in part) allowed the plaintiffs' appeal.

LORD REID [after stating the facts said]: The respondent's first argument was that in any event such a declaration could not competently be made. I agree with your Lordships in rejecting that argument. If the appellants succeed on the merits the declarations made by Browne J. should be restored.

The next argument was that, by reason of the provisions of section 4(4) of the 1950 Act, the courts are precluded from considering whether the respondent's determination was a nullity, and therefore it must be treated as valid whether or not inquiry would disclose that it was a nullity. Section 4(4) is in these terms: "The determination by the commission of any application made to them under this Act shall not be called in question in any court of law."

The respondent maintains that these are plain words only capable of having one meaning. Here is a determination which is apparently valid: there is nothing on the face of the document to cast any doubt on its validity. If it is a nullity, that could only be established by raising some kind of proceedings in court. But that would be calling the determination in question, and that is expressly prohibited by the statute. The appellants maintain that that is not the meaning of the words of this provision. They say that "determination" means a real determination and does not include an apparent or purported determination which in the eyes of the law has no existence because it is a nullity. Or, putting it in another way, if you seek to show that a determination is a nullity you are not questioning the purported determination—you are maintaining that it does not exist as a determination. It is one thing to question a determination which does exist: it is quite another thing to say that there is nothing to be questioned.

Let me illustrate the matter by supposing a simple case. A statute provides that a certain order may be made by a person who holds a specified qualification or appointment, and it contains a provision, similar to section 4(4), that such an order made by such a person shall not be called in question in any court of law. A person aggrieved by an order alleges that it is a forgery or that the person who made the order did not hold that qualification or appointment. Does such a provision require the court to treat that order as a valid order? It is a well established principle that a provision ousting the ordinary jurisdiction of the court must be construed strictly—meaning, I think, that, if such a provision is reasonably capable of having two meanings, that meaning shall be taken which preserves the ordinary jurisdiction of the court.

Statutory provisions which seek to limit the ordinary jurisdiction of the court have a long history. No case has been cited in which any other form of words limiting the jurisdiction of the court has been held to protect a nullity. If the draftsman or Parliament had intended to introduce a new kind of ouster clause so as to prevent any inquiry even as to whether the document relied on was a forgery, I would have expected to find something much more specific than the bald statement that a determination shall not be called in question in any court of law. Undoubtedly such a provision protects every determination which is not a nullity. But I do not think that it is necessary or even reasonable to construe the word "determination" as including everything which purports to be a determination but which is in fact no determination at all. And there are no degrees of nullity. There are a number of reasons why the law will hold a purported decision to be a nullity. I do not see how it could be said that such a provision protects some kinds of nullity but not others: if that were intended it would be easy to say so.

The case which gives most difficulty is *Smith* v. *East Elloe Rural District Council*[1] where the form of ouster clause was similar to that in the present case. But I cannot regard it as a very satisfactory case. The plaintiff was aggrieved by a compulsory purchase order. After two unsuccessful actions she tried again after six years. As this case never reached the stage of a statement of claim we do not know whether her case was that the clerk of the council had fraudulently misled the council and the Ministry, or whether it was that the council and the Ministry were parties to the fraud. The result would be quite different, in my view, for it is only if the authority which made the order had itself acted in mala fide that the order would be a nullity. I think that the case which it was intended to present must have been that the fraud was only the fraud of the clerk because almost the whole of the argument was on the question whether a time limit in the Act applied where fraud was alleged; there was no citation of the authorities on the question whether a clause ousting the jurisdiction of the court applied when nullity was in question, and there was little about this matter in the speeches. I do not therefore regard this case as a binding authority on this question. The other authorities are dealt with in the speeches of my noble and learned friends, and it is unnecessary for me to deal with them in detail. I have come without hesitation to the conclusion that in this case we are not prevented from inquiring whether the order of the commission was a nullity.

It has sometimes been said that it is only where a tribunal acts without jurisdiction that its decision is a nullity. But in such cases the word "jurisdiction" has been used in a very wide sense, and I have come to the conclusion that it is better not to use the term except in the narrow and original sense of the tribunal being entitled to enter on the inquiry in question. But there are many cases where, although the tribunal had jurisdiction to enter on the inquiry, it has done or failed to do something in the course of the inquiry which is of such a nature that its decision is a nullity. It may have given its decision in bad faith. It may have made a decision which it had no power to make. It may have failed in the course of the inquiry to comply with the requirements of natural justice. It may in perfect good

[1] [1956] A.C. 736.

faith have misconstrued the provisions giving it power to act so that it failed to deal with the question remitted to it and decided some question which was not remitted to it. It may have refused to take into account something which it was required to take into account. Or it may have based its decision on some matter which, under the provisions setting it up, it had no right to take into account. I do not intend this list to be exhaustive. But if it decides a question remitted to it for decision without committing any of these errors it is as much entitled to decide that question wrongly as it is to decide it rightly. I understand that some confusion has been caused by my having said in *R.* v. *Governor of Brixton Prison, Ex parte Armah*[2] that if a tribunal has jurisdiction to go right it has jurisdiction to go wrong. So it has, if one uses "jurisdiction" in the narrow original sense. If it is entitled to enter on the inquiry and does not do any of those things which I have mentioned in the course of the proceedings, then its decision is equally valid whether it is right or wrong subject only to the power of the court in certain circumstances to correct an error of law. I think that, if these views are correct, the only case cited which was plainly wrongly decided is *Davies* v. *Price.*[3] But in a number of other cases some of the grounds of judgment are questionable.

I can now turn to the provisions of the Order under which the commission acted, and to the way in which the commission reached their decision. It was said in the Court of Appeal that publication of their reasons was unnecessary and perhaps undesirable. Whether or not they could have been required to publish their reasons, I dissent emphatically from the view that publication may have been undesirable. In my view, the commission acted with complete propriety, as one would expect looking to its membership. . . .

The effect of the Order was to confer legal rights on persons who might previously have hoped or expected that in allocating any sums available discretion would be exercised in their favour. . . . [His Lordship then set out the Order, and continued]: The task of the commission was to receive claims and to determine the rights of each applicant. It is enacted that they shall treat a claim as established if the applicant satisfies them of certain matters. About the first there is no difficultly: the appellants' application does relate to property in Egypt referred to in Annex E. But then the difficulty begins. [His Lordship then discussed the meaning of a provision relating to successors in title]: If one uses the word "jurisdiction" in its wider sense, they went beyond their jurisdiction in considering this matter. It was argued that the whole matter of construing the Order was something remitted to the commission for their decision. I cannot accept that argument. I find nothing in the Order to support it. The Order requires the commission to consider whether they are satisified with regard to the prescribed matters. That is all they have to do. It cannot be for the commission to determine the limits of its powers. Of course if one party submits to a tribunal that its powers are wider than in fact they are, then the tribunal must deal with that submission. But if they reach a wrong conclusion as to the width of their powers, the court must be able to correct that—not because the tribunal has made an error of law, but because as a result of making an error of law they have dealt with and based their decision on a matter with which, on a true construction of their powers, they had no right to deal. If they base their decision on some matter which is not prescribed for their adjudication, they are doing something which they have no right to do and, if the view which I expressed earlier is right, their decision is a nullity. So the question is whether on a true construction of the Order the applicants did or did not have to prove anything with regard to successors in title. If the commission were entitled to enter on the inquiry whether the applicants had a successor in title, then their decision as to whether T.E.D.O. was their successor in title would I think be unassailable whether it was right or wrong: it

[2] [1968] A.C. 192 at p. 234.
[3] [1958] 1 W.L.R. 434.

would be a decision on a matter remitted to them for their decision. The question I have to consider is not whether they made a wrong decision but whether they inquired into and decided a matter which they had no right to consider.

I have great difficultly in seeing how in the circumstances there could be a successor in title of a person who is still in existence. This provision is dealing with the period before the Order was made when the original owner had no title to anything: he had nothing but a hope that some day somehow he might get some compensation. The rest of the article makes it clear that the phrase (though inaccurate) must apply to a person who can be regarded as having inherited in some way the hope which a deceased original owner had that he would get some compensation. But "successor in title" must I think mean some person who could come forward and make a claim in his own right. There can only be a successor in title where the title of its original possessor has passed to another person, his successor, so that the original possessor of the title can no longer make a claim, but his successor can make the claim which the original possessor of the title could have made if his title had not passed to his successor. The "successor" of a deceased person can do that. But how could any "successor" do that while the original owner is still in existence? . . . In themselves the words "successor in title" are, in my opinion, inappropriate in the circumstances of this Order to denote any person while the original owner is still in existence, and I think it most improbable that they were ever intended to denote any such person. There is no necessity to stretch them to cover any such person. I would therefore hold that the words "and any person who became successor in title to such person" in article 4(1)(b)(ii) have no applicant to a case where the application is the original owner. It follows that the commission rejected the appellants' claim on a ground which they had no right to take into account and that their decision was a nullity. I would allow this appeal.

Appeal allowed.

Note

Their Lordships held unanimously that, in spite of the restriction of judicial review imposed by the Foreign Compensation Act 1950, the court could interfere on the ground of *ultra vires* if the tribunal exceeded its jurisdiction; and a majority (Lord Morris of Borth-y-Gest dissenting) held that the misconstruction of the relevant Order in Council by the Commission constituted an excess of jurisdiction. By stretching the meaning of "jurisdictional error," the House of Lords was thus able to bring an error of law on the part of the Commission within the control of the court.

The Foreign Compensation Act 1969, s.3, allowed a determination by the Commission to be called in question on the ground that it is contrary to natural justice, or by case stated to the Court of Appeal on a question of law concerning the jurisdiction of the Commission or the interpretation of an Order in Council.

The House of Lords in the *Anisminic* case distinguished *Smith* v. *East Elloe R.D.C.* (in which Lord Reid dissented) rather than expressly overruling it: (see *R.* v. *Secretary of State for the Environment, ex p. Ostler, infra*). In proceedings subsequent to the *East Elloe* case the plaintiff failed to show that the Clerk had in fact fraudulently misled the Council (*Smith* v. *Pywell, The Times*, April 29, 1959); but in any event, as Lord Reid pointed out in *Anisminic*, if the authority itself which made the order had acted in bad faith the order would be a nullity.

See further C.T. Emery and B. Smythe, *Judicial Review* (1986) pp 46–56 and 140–164.

Time Limit for Judicial Review

R. v. Secretary of State for the Environment, Ex parte
Ostler
[1977] Q.B. 122
Court of Appeal

Ostler, a corn merchant, applied in December 1975 for leave to apply for an order of certiorari to quash a stopping-up order made under the Highways Act 1959 and a compulsory purchase order made under the Acquisition of Land (Authorisation Procedure) Act 1946[1] and confirmed by the Secretary of State for the Environment in May 1974. He complained that there had been a breach of natural justice. The Secretary of State made the preliminary objection that, whatever the facts, any legal proceedings to attack the validity of the confirmed orders were barred because the six-week period prescribed by paragraph 2 of Schedule 2 to the Act of 1959 and paragraph 15 of Schedule 1 to the Act of 1946 had expired.

The Divisional Court (Lord Widgery C.J., Bridge L.J. and Park J.) granted the Secretary of State leave to appeal to the Court of Appeal on the preliminary point of law, whether proof that the order was a nullity would be an answer to the kind of exclusionary provision with which the court was concerned in this case. The Court of Appeal (Lord Denning M.R., Goff and Shaw L.JJ.), distinguishing the *Ansisminic* case (*supra*) and applying the *East Elloe* case, unanimously allowed the appeal by the Secretary of State. The House of Lords refused Ostler leave to appeal: [1977] 1 W.L.R.258. The facts appear in Lord Denning's judgment.

LORD DENNING M.R. We are here presented with a nice question. Is *Smith* v. *East Elloe Rural District Council*[2] a good authority or has it been overruled by *Ansisminic* v. *Foreign Compensation Commission?*[3]

Boston is an old port. It has a fine church, with its famous tower — the Boston Stump. The centre of the town has, however, in modern times become so congested with traffic that it has been necessary to make an inner relief road. The plan was launched as far back as 1965, but it was not till 1972 that the local authority took steps to acquire land compulsorily. It was to be done in two stages. First, to acquire the land needed for the trunk road itself. Second, to acquire the land needed for the side roads giving access to the trunk road. In respect of each stage there was a public inquiry to consider objections.

The first inquiry (as to the trunk road itself) was held in September 1973. A firm of wine merchants called George Bateman & Sons Ltd. lodged objection on the ground that it would cut off the access to their yards. Now, in order to overcome that objection, it is alleged that a secret assurance was given to Batemans by an officer of the Department of the Environment. Batemans were assured that at the second stage access would be given for the lorries by means of a lane called Craythorne Lane. This was a narrow lane leading out of the market place. Batemans were assured that at the second stage this lane would be widened so as to take their lorries. On getting that assurance, Batemans withdrew their objection at the first inquiry. That was a secret assurance, not known to the public at large.

Now there was another trader, Mr. Ostler, who was interested. He was a corn merchant. His premises were at a corner of the Market Place where Craythorne Lane led out of it. He had no idea that Craythorne Lane was going to be widened.

---

[1] The relevant legislation is currently the Highways Act 1980 and the Acquisition of Land Act 1981.

[2] [1956] A.C. 736.

[3] [1969] 2 A.C. 147.

If it was to remain a narrow lane (as he thought) his business would not be affected by the proposed road. So he did not lodge any objection to it.

The inquiry was held on September 11 and 12, 1973. The proposed new road was approved. It was followed by an order dated March 28, 1974, under the Highways Act 1959, for the stopping up of highways and constructing new ones: and an order dated May 9, 1974, for the compulsory purchase of property needed in order to construct the proposed new road.

Now Mr. Ostler makes this point. He did not know of the secret agreement with Batemans. If he had, he would have lodged objection at the first stage. But not knowing of it, he made no opposition. So the orders were made in his absence.

Now we come to the next item. In July 1974 the local authority made a supplementary order under which they proposed to widen Craythorne Lane itself. Mr. Ostler did object to this. He thought that the widening of Craythorne Lane would injuriously affect his premises and his business: because they were at the corner of Craythorne Lane.

This second stage was the subject of another inquiry. It was held in December 1974 for four days. Mr. Ostler instructed solicitors to object on his behalf. He gave evidence. He sought to refer to the past history. In particular he wanted to say that he would have objected at the first stage if he had known that the whole project would affect his property. But he was not allowed to go into it. The inspector said: "Mr. Ostler, I can't allow that evidence. We are here to discuss the Craythorne Lane scheme only." So his evidence was excluded on that point. The inspector made his report, recommending the widening of Craythorne Lane. The Minister confirmed the order in July 1975.

Two or three months later Mr. Ostler got to know of the secret agreement with Batemans which had been made before the first inquiry. So in December 1975 he applied to the Queen's Bench Divisional Court to quash, not the latest order in July 1975 about Craythorne Lane, but the earlier orders about the line of the trunk road and the acquisitions in consequence of it. He said that they were invalid. His case is that there was a want of natural justice and, further, that there was a want of good faith because of the secret agreement.

The Divisional Court thought that the authority of *Smith* v. *East Elloe Rural District Council*[4] might have been shaken by the *Anisminic* case.[5] So they thought that there should be further evidence before them, such as evidence about the secret agreement and evidence as to whether or no there had been any lack of good faith or any want of natural justice. The department feel that this taking of evidence would involve delay and hold up the work. So Mr. Woolf [for the Secretary of State] has come to this court by way of appeal.

The earlier orders were made in March and May 1974. Much work has been done in pursuance of them. We are told that 80 per cent. of the land has been acquired and 90 per cent. of the buildings demolished. Nevertheless, Mr. Ostler seeks to say that now, nearly two years later, those orders should be upset and declared to be null and void or set aside.

Now it is clear that if Mr. Ostler had come within six weeks, his complaint could and would have been considered by the court. The relevant provision is contained in Schedule 2 to the Highways Act 1959. Paragraph 2 says: "If a person aggrieved by a scheme or order to which this Schedule applies desires to question the validity thereof, or of any provision contained therein, on the ground that it is not within the powers of this Act or on the ground that any requirement of this Act or of regulations made thereunder has not been complied with in relation thereto, he may, within six weeks from the date on which the notice required by the foregoing paragraph is first published, make an application for the purpose to the High Court."

[4] [1956] A.C. 736.
[5] [1969] 2 A.C. 147.

That is a familiar clause which appears in many statutes or schedules to them. Although the words appear to restrict the clause to cases of *ultra vires* or non-compliance with regulations, nevertheless the courts have interpreted them so as to cover cases of bad faith. On this point the view of Lord Radcliffe has been accepted (which he expressed in *Smith* v. *East Elloe Rural District Council* [1956] A.C. 736, 769). In addition this court has held that under this clause a person aggrieved—who comes within six weeks—can upset a scheme or order if the Minister has taken into account considerations which he ought not to have done, or has failed to take into account considerations which he ought to have done, or has come to his decision without any evidence to support it, or has made a decision which no reasonable person could make. It was so held in *Ashbridge Investments Ltd.* v. *Minister of Housing and Local Government*,[6] and the Minister did not dispute it. It has been repeatedly followed in this court ever since and never disputed by any Minister. So it is the accepted interpretation. But the person aggrieved must come within six weeks. That time limit has always been applied.

That paragraph is succeeded by the next but one paragraph, paragraph 4, which is complementary to it: "Subject to the provisons of the last foregoing paragraph, a scheme or order to which this Schedule applies shall not, either before or after it has been made or confirmed, be questioned in any legal proceedings whatever, and shall become operative on the date on which the notice required by paragraph 1 of this Schedule is first published, or on such later date, if any, as may be specified in the scheme or order."

So those are the strong words, "shall not ... be questioned in any legal proceedings whatever." They were considered by the House of Lords in *Smith* v. *East Elloe Rural District Council*.[7] A lady brought an action to set aside an order for compulsory purchase. The six weeks had long since expired. She said the order was induced by the fraud of the clerk to the local council. The majority of the House held that her claim should be struck out against the council, but they allowed it to go on as against the clerk. Mr. Payton told us that afterwards she even failed to prove any fraud against the clerk. So the decision of the House itself was based on a hypothesis which turned out to be unfounded—just like *Donoghue* v. *Stevenson*.[8] But even so, it is a decision that the paragraph does bar an action to quash an order for compulsory purchase even though it is put on the ground of fraud—if it is brought after the six weeks.

Thirteen years later the House had to consider the *Anisminic* case.[9] It was on a very different provision. The Foreign Compensation Act 1950, section 4(4) said: "The determination by the commission of any application made to them under this Act shall not be called in question in any court of law." The House held that that clause only applied to a real determination. It did not apply to a purported determination. They held that there had been no determination, properly so called, by the commission. So their decision could be called in question.

Some of their Lordships seem to have thrown doubt on *Smith* v. *East Elloe Rural District Council*[10]: see what Lord Reid said at [1969] 2 A.C. 147, 170–171. But others thought it could be explained on the ground on which Browne J. explained it. Lord Pearce said, at p. 201: "I agree with Browne J. that it is not a compelling authority in the present case"; and Lord Wilberforce said, at p. 208: "After the admirable analysis of the authorities made by Browne J. ... no elaborate discussion of authority is needed."

I turn therefore to the judgment of Browne J. His judgment is appended as a note to the case at pp. 223 *et seq.* He put *Smith* v. *East Elloe Rural District Council*, at

[6] [1965] 1 W.L.R. 1320.
[7] [1956] A.C. 736.
[8] [1932] A.C. 562.
[9] [1969] 2 A.C. 147.
[10] [1956] A.C. 736.

p. 224, as one of the "cases in which the inferior tribunal has been guilty of bias, or has acted in bad faith, or has disregarded the principles of natural justice." He said of those cases: "It is not necessary to decide it for the purposesof this case, but I am inclined to think that such decisions are not nullities but are good until quashed (*cf.* the decision of the majority of the House of Lords in *Smith* v. *East Elloe Rural District Council*,[11] that a decision made in bad faith cannot be challenged on the ground that it was made beyond powers and Lord Radcliffe's dissenting speech. . . .)."

In these circumstances, I think that *Smith* v. *East Elloe Rural District Council* must still be regarded as good and binding on this court. It is readily to be distinguished from the *Anisminic* case.[12] The points of difference are these:

First, in the *Anisminic* case the Act ousted the jurisdiction of the court altogether. It precluded the court from entertaining any complaint at any time about the determination. Whereas in the *East Elloe* case the statutory provision has given the court jurisdiction to inquire into complaints so long as the applicant comes within six weeks. The provision is more in the nature of a limitation period than of a complete ouster. That distinction is drawn by Professor Wade, *Administrative Law*, 3rd ed. (1971), pp. 152–153,[13] and by the late Professor S.A. de Smith in the latest edition of *Halsbury's Laws of England*, 4th ed., Vol. 1 (1973), para. 22, note 14.

Second, in the *Anisminic* case, the House was considering a determination by a truly judicial body, the Foreign Compensation Tribunal, whereas in the *East Elloe* case the House was considering an order which was very much in the nature of an administrative decision. That is a distinction which Lord Reid himself drew in *Ridge* v. *Baldwin*.[14] There is a great difference between the two. In making a judicial decision, the tribunal considers the rights of the parties without regard to the public interest. But in an administrative decision (such as a compulsory purchase order) the public interest plays an important part. The question is, to what extent are private interests to be subordinated to the public interest.

Third, in the *Anisminic* case the House had to consider the actual determination of the tribunal, whereas in the *Smith* v. *East Elloe* case the House had to consider the validity of the process by which the decision was reached.

So *Smith* v. *East Elloe Rural District Council*[15] must still be regarded as the law in regard to this provision we have to consider here. I would add this: if this order were to be upset for want of good faith or for lack of natural justice, it would not to my mind be a nullity or void from the beginning. It would only be voidable. And as such, it should be challenged promptly before much has been done under it, as Lord Radcliffe put it forcibly in *Smith* v. *East Elloe Rural District Council*[16]: "But this argument is in reality a play on the meaning of the word nullity. An order,"—and he is speaking of an order such as we have got here—"even if not made in good faith, is still an act capable of legal consequences. It bears no brand of invalidity upon its forehead. Unless the necessary proceedings are taken at law to establish the cause of invalidity and to get it quashed or otherwise upset, it will remain as effective for its ostensible purpose as the most impeccable of orders. And that brings us back to the question that determines this case: Has Parliament allowed the necessary proceedings to be taken?" The answer which he gave was "No." That answer binds us in this court today.

Since the *Anisminic* case the court has considered the position in *Routh* v. *Reading Corporation*, December 2, 1970, Bar Library Transcript No. 472 of 1970. Salmon L.J., supported by Karminski and Cairns L.JJ., held that *Smith* v. *East Elloe*

[11] [1969] 2 A.C. 147.
[12] [1969] 2 A.C. 147.
[13] See now (5th ed, 1982) pp. 613–614.
[14] [1964] A.C. 40 at p. 72.
[15] [1956] A.C. 736.
[16] [1956] A.C. 736 at pp. 769–770.

Rural District Council was of good authority, even after the *Anisminic* case. In Scotland, too, it has been applied, in *Hamilton* v. *Secretary of State for Scotland.*[17]

Looking at it broadly, it seems to me that the policy underlying the statute is that when a compulsory purchase order has been made, then if it has been wrongly obtained or made, a person aggrieved should have a remedy. But he must come promptly. He must come within six weeks. If he does so, the court can and will entertain his complaint. But if the six weeks expire without any application being made, the court cannot entertain it afterwards. The reason is because, as soon as that time has elapsed, the authority will take steps to acquire property, demolish it and so forth. The public interest demands that they should be safe in doing so. Take this very case. The inquiry was held in 1973. The orders made early in 1974. Much work has already been done under them. It would be contrary to the public interest that the demolition should be held up or delayed by further evidence or inquiries. I think we are bound by *Smith* v. *East Elloe Rural District Council*[18] to hold that Mr. Ostler is barred by the statute from now questioning these orders. He ought to be stopped at this moment. I would allow the appeal accordingly.

GOFF L.J. [in the course of his judgment, said]: In my judgment, in *Smith* v. *East Elloe Rural District Council* the majority did definitely decide that those statutory provisions preclude the order from being challenged after the statutory period allowed, then by paragraph 15, and now by paragraph 2, and we are bound by that unless *Anisminic Ltd.* v. *Foreign Compensation Commission*[19] has to cut across it that we are relieved from the duty of following *Smith* v. *East Elloe Rural District Council* and, indeed, bound not to follow it.

That raises a number of problems. With all respect to Lord Denning M.R. and Professor Wade, I do myself find difficulty in distinguishing *Anisminic* on the ground that in that case there was an absolute prohibition against recourse to the court, whereas in the present case there is a qualified power for a limited period, because the majority in the *Smith* case said either that fraud did not come within paragraph 15, so that, in effect, it was an absolute ouster, or that it made no difference to the construction if it did.

Nevertheless, it seems to me that the *Anisminic* case is distinguishable on two grounds. First, the suggestion made by Lord Pearce,[20] that *Anisminic* dealt with a judicial decision, and an administrative or executive decision might be different. I think it is. It is true that the Minister has been said to be acting in a quasi judicial capacity, but he is nevertheless conducting an administrative or executive matter, where questions of policy enter into and must influence his decision.

I would refer in support of that to a passage from the speech of Lord Reid in the well-known case of *Ridge* v. *Baldwin.*[21] I need not read it. It sets out what I have been saying.

Where one is dealing with a matter of that character and where, as Lord Denning M.R. has pointed out, the order is one which must be acted upon promptly, it is, I think, easier for the courts to construe Parliament as meaning exactly what it said—that the matter cannot be questioned in any court, subject to the right given by paragraph 2, where applicable, and where application is made in due time—than where, as in *Anisminic*, one is dealing with a statute setting up a judicial tribunal and defining its powers and the question is whether it has acted within them. I think that is supported by the passage in the speech of Lord Reid in the *Anisminic* case[22] where he said: "But I do not think that it is necessary or even

---

[17] 1972 S.L.T. 233.
[18] [1956] A.C. 736.
[19] [1969] 2 A.C. 147.
[20] *Ibid.* at p. 201.
[21] [1964] A.C. 40 at p. 72.
[22] [1969] 2 A.C. 147 at p. 170.

reasonable to construe the word 'determination' as including everything which purports to be a determination but which is in fact no determination at all."

The second ground of distinction is that the ratio in the *Anisminic* case was that the House was dealing simply with a question of jurisdiction, and not a case where the order is made within jurisdiction, but it is attacked on the ground of fraud or mala fides. There are, I am fully conscious, difficulties in the way of that distinction, because Lord Somervell of Harrow in *Smith* v. *East Elloe Rural District Council,*[23] in his dissenting speech, said that fraud does not make the order voidable but a nullity. Lord Reid said the same in the *Anisminic* case[24]; and at p. 199 Lord Pearce equated want of natural justice with lack of jurisdiction.

Nevertheless, despite those difficulties, I think there is a real distinction between the case with which the House was dealing in *Anisminic* and the case of *Smith* v. *East Elloe Rural District Council* on that ground, that in the one case the determination was a purported determination only, because the tribunal, however eminent, having misconceived the effect of the statute, acted outside its jurisdiction, and indeed without any jurisdiction at all, whereas here one is dealing with an actual decision made within jurisdiction though sought to be challenged.

SHAW L.J.: I agree that this appeal should succeed, and I would respectfully adopt the reasons given by Lord Denning M.R. . . . It seems to me that *Anisminic* v. *Foreign Compensation Commission*[25] can be distinguished on two or perhaps three grounds: first, that the statutory order considered in that case, namely, the Foreign Compensation Commission Order, prescribed the basis on which the Foreign Compensation Commission were to found a determination as to whether the substance of a claim was to be treated as established. This rendered the question of whether or not there had been a valid determination at all open to review in circumstances where it could be shown that the commission proceeded on a wrong view of the law.

Secondly, the determination considered in *Anisminic* could not in any circumstances have been a valid determination so that it was void ab initio, while the order in the present case, as in *East Elloe,*was one which *could* be arrived at as a proper order.

Lastly, in the *East Elloe* case it was the validity of the compulsory purchase order that was in question and not any ultimate question of payment of compensation, which, in the last resort, remains as a means of affording redress to a person who has been dispossessed against his will.

Appeal allowed.
Application for certiorari dismissed.
Leave to appeal refused.

[23] [1956] A.C. 736 at p. 771.
[24] [1969] 2 A.C. 147 at p. 170.
[25] [1969] 2 A.C. 147.

7. CROWN PROCEEDINGS

LIABILITY UNDER THE CROWN PROCEEDINGS ACT 1947

No Tortious liability outside the Act

Trawnik v. Lennox
[1985] 1 W.L.R. 532
Court of Appeal

Germans resident in the British Sector of Berlin sought a declaration that it was not lawful for British forces to use a firing range in such a way as to constitute a nuisance to adjoining landowners. The action was brought in England because German Courts have no jurisdiction over civil cases involving the allied forces without the authority of the Allied Kommandatura or appropriate Sector Commandant. Authority was not given to bring proceedings arising from the facts alleged by the plaintiffs in a German Court. The Military Government Courts which were to be established under the instrument providing for the government of Berlin had never been set up. The Crown moved to strike out the writ on the ground that it related to liability of the Crown otherwise than in respect of Her Majesty's Government in the United Kingdom. The Foreign Secretary issued a certificate to that effect under section 40(3)(a) of the Crown Proceedings Act 1947. Sir Robert Megarry V.-C. refused to strike out the action. He concluded that no claim lay within the terms of the 1947 Act but he thought it arguable that proceedings could be brought outside the Act. The Crown appealed to the Court of Appeal (Lawton and Browne-Wilkinson L. JJ., and Sir David Cairns).

LAWTON L.J. In this appeal this court has to decide the following question: can two residents in the British Sector of Berlin, who are not British subjects, bring against the Attorney-General of England, Wales and Northern Ireland a quia timet action in relation to an anticipated nuisance arising from the construction near their houses of a firing range for use by British troops stationed in Berlin? Sir Robert Megarry V.-C. adjudged on 2 April 1984 (ante, p. 544F-G) that it was arguable that such an action could be brought against the Attorney-General. He ordered that the Attorney-General should be joined as a defendant together with Major-General Gordon Lennox who, at that time, was commanding the British troops in Berlin. The Attorney-General has appealed to this court against that order. Major-General Gordon Lennox has not appealed. He claims to be protected from further proceedings by reason of a certificate issued by Her Majesty's Principal Secretary for Foreign and Commonwealth Affairs pursuant to section 21 of the State Immunity Act 1978. The plaintiffs have obtained leave to apply for judicial review of the issue of that certificate.[1] This court has not been concerned with those proceedings.

The Attorney-General's case is that, assuming every fact pleaded in the plaintiffs' re-amended statement of claim can be established (and this court has to make the same assumption), there is no arguable case against him in either his personal capacity or as representing the Crown. There is clearly no case against him in his personal capacity, nor was it suggested that there was. He has had nothing to do with either the decision to construct a range in the British Sector of Berlin or any plans for its use. In so far as he is being sued as representing the Crown, it was

---

[1] *Post* p.403.

submitted on his behalf that the proceedings are misconceived as they are proceedings in tort, and such proceedings cannot be brought against the Crown otherwise than under and in accordance with the Crown Proceedings Act 1947, and these proceedings are not so brought. Even if they could be, it is submitted that he would not be the proper person to represent the Crown as he is only the Attorney-General by right of the Crown in England, Wales and Northern Ireland. He is not the proper representative of the Crown in respect of a cause of action arising overseas.

On 12 August 1983 the plaintiffs issued a writ against the Ministry of Defence. That Ministry, not being a person or corporation known to the common law, can only be sued pursuant to the Crown Proceedings Act 1947. Section 40(2)(*b*) and (3) is in these terms:

"(2) Except as therein otherwise expressly provided, nothing in this Act shall:— . . . *b*) authorise proceedings to be taken against the Crown under or in accordance with this Act in respect of any alleged liability of the Crown arising otherwise than in respect of His Majesty's Government in the United Kingdom, or affect proceedings against the Crown in respect of any such alleged liability as aforesaid; . . . (3) A certificate of a Secretary of State:—(a) to the effect that any alleged liability of the Crown arises otherwise than in respect of His Majesty's Government in the United Kingdom; . . . shall, for the purposes of this Act, be conclusive as to the matter so certified."

On 3 November 1983 Sir Geoffrey Howe, as one of Her Majesty's Principal Secretaries of State, issued such a certificate under section 40(3) It followed that the Ministry of Defence could not be sued.

Mr. Mummery, on behalf of the Ministry of Defence, applied to Sir Robert Megarry V.-C. to strike out the writ and statement of claim. He put his case on two grounds: first, that the Ministry could not be a party to any proceedings alleging a liability arising otherwise than in respect of Her Majesty's Government in the United Kingdom; and secondly, that, in so far as it was submitted, as it was, that the proceedings were taken outside the Act of 1947, they were proceeding in tort which could not be taken against the Crown otherwise than under and in accordance with that Act. The Vice-Chancellor adjudged that the Ministry of Defence could not be sued; but he declined to strike out the action and decided to hear an application to add the British Military Commandant of Berlin as a defendant. He heard that application on 2 April 1984. In the meantime, the plaintiffs had decided to apply in addition for the Attorney-General to be added as a defendant. The Vice-Chancellor gave leave to add both. He said that he had serious doubts about whether the proceedings against the Attorney-General would succeed but was not satisfied that they would fail. In this court Mr. Mummery, now appearing for the Attorney-General, submitted that they would.

Both [counsel] in this court accepted that these proceedings were not proceedings taken under and in accordance with the Act of 1947 and that it followed that the plaintiffs only had such right to sue the Attorney-General as anyone in their position and making the same kind of claim as they were making would have had at common law.

Since, so it was submitted, nuisance is a tort recognised by the law of Berlin, the plaintiffs can bring an action in this court in respect of such a cause of action against anyone within its jurisdiction. That is so. But it is trite law that the Crown cannot be sued in tort: see a long line of cases starting with *Viscount Canterbury* v. *Attorney-General* (1843) 1Ph. 306, 321 and ending with *Adams* v. *Naylor* [1946] A.C. 543, 549, 551 and 555. If the Attorney-General is being sued as the representative of the Crown and the proceedings are in tort, under the common law rules the claim is bound to fail. In my judgment, these proceedings are in tort. The plaintiffs could not have claimed as against the Crown either damages for, or an injunction to restrain, a nuisance. If they cannot claim in respect of a nuisance which has been committed, it would be odd if they could claim for one which some servant of the Crown has threatened to commit. It makes no difference, as is pleaded in the prayer of the re-amended statement of claim, that the remedy sought is a declaration that the Crown should not itself use or permit others to use land so as to cause a nuisance. Mr. Macdonald, being, as I assume, appreciative of the difficulty caused by the Crown's immunity at common law from proceedings in tort, submitted that the plaintiffs could obtain a declaration that they were entitled, first, to enjoy their land without interference by nuisance originating from land occupied by the Crown and, secondly, that the Crown could not authorise servants to cause a nuisance on land which it occupied. In my judgment, these forms of declaration are nothing more than ingenious attempts to disguise with words what the claim is about, namely that they want the court by means of a declaratory judgment to inhibit the Crown by its servants from committing a nuisance. That they cannot do at common law in proceedings against the Attorney-General as representative of the Crown.

.   .   .   .   .

[Counsel for the Attorney-General] further submitted that, even if these proceedings could be brought against some officer of state representing the Crown, the Attorney-General of England, Wales and Northern Ireland was not the one. This was not an attractive argument but, if it was sound in law, the Attorney-General owed a duty to the court to invite our attention to it since the court has no jurisdiction to give a declaratory judgment in a suit against a party who has no interest in the subject matter of the declaration: see *Buck* v. *Attorney-General* [1965] Ch. 745, 771 *per* Diplock L.J. The Attorney-General of England, Wales and Northern Ireland can represent the Crown in these parts of Her Majesty's Dominions. He has no functions as Attorney-General outside them and, in particular, he has no functions in the British Sector of Berlin. The plaintiffs have been unable to discover from the Treasury Solicitor who in Berlin performs functions similar to those of the Attorney-General of England, Wales and Northern Ireland or who, as a matter of law, can represent the Crown in causes of action arising there. The plaintiffs may be suffering a wrong for which there is no remedy in our courts. This is to be regretted; but sympathy for the plaintiffs is no justification for adding as a defendant an officer of state who, as a matter of law, has no interest in the proceedings. I adjudge that the Attorney-General has no interest in these proceedings. It follows that he should be dismissed from them.

I would allow the appeal.

BROWNE-WILKINSON L.J: ... [Counsel for the plaintiffs submitted that, even before the Act of 1947, such an action as this could have been brought against the Attorney-General for a declaration. He submits, correctly, that, although procedure by way of petition of right has been abolished (Act of 1947, section 13 and Schedule 1), nothing in that Act affects the right to bring an action for declaratory relief against the Crown of the kind exemplified by *Dyson* v. *Attorney-General* [1911] 1 K.B. 410. Then he submits that, although there is no reported case of any such action being brought where the cause of action, as in this case, is based on tort, there is no reason why this action for a declaration should not be brought against the Attorney-General, notwithstanding the fact that, before 1947, the Crown was not liable in tort. He puts his case in two alternative ways.

First, he submits that a finding that soldiers firing their rifles on the land constitutes a nuisance would adversely affect the Crown's interest in that land (whatever it may be) since such finding will interfere with the use of such land by the Crown. He submits (and I accept) that before 1875 the Court of Chancery and the court of Exchequer in its equity jurisdiction always allowed the Attorney-General to be joined as a defendant where the decision in the action might adversely affect the title of the Crown to the property which was the subject matter of the action: see *Hodge* v. *Attorney-General*, 3 Y. & C. Ex. 342 and *Esquimalt and Nanaimo Railway Co.* v. *Wilson* [1920] A.C. 358. In my judgment, it is impossible to bring this case within that principle. Although the Crown's enjoyment of the land might well be affected by a finding against the servant of the Crown that such servant's use of the land for the purposes of employment constitutes a nuisance, such a finding would in no way affect the Crown's title to the land or any interest in it. The principle laid down in those cases is entirely concerned with cases where the title of the Crown may be affected. I have no doubt that the Attorney-General could, if he chose, intervene in such a case on the grounds that the decision might affect the Crown in the exercise of its powers or matters of public policy: see, for example, *In re Westinghouse Electric Corporation Uranium Contract Litigation M.D.L. Docket No.* 235 (*No.* 2) [1978] A.C. 547. But it is quite another matter to say that the Attorney-General, against his wishes, can be forced to be a party to proceedings which do not in any way challenge any legal right or title of the Crown.

The second way in which [Counsel] puts his case is to concentrate on the fact that this is a quia timet action. He points out that the rule that the Crown was not liable in tort was based on the principle "the Crown can do no wrong." The Crown can only act by its servants or agents and, since the Crown can do no wrong, it cannot have authorised its servants or agents so to do. Hence, although the servant or agent was personally liable, the Crown could not be held vicariously liable for his acts: see *Wade, Administrative Law*, 5th ed. (1982), p. 700. But, [he] submits if the action is brought *before* the wrongful act is done by the servant, there is no conflict with the principle that the Crown can do no wrong. No wrong has yet been committed and, if the court makes a declaration that the act when committed would be a wrong, the Crown would, of course, take steps to ensure that its servants or agents did not commit such a wrong.

Quite apart from the practical difficulty that, since relief by interlocutory injunction is not possible against the Crown, what starts off as a quia timet action may, by the date of trial, have become an action for a tort already committed, in my judgment, the submission cannot be correct. To bring a quia timet action, it is necessary to show that the threatened act, if done, would constitute a legal wrong *by the defendant*. The operation of the shooting range cannot be a legal wrong by *the Crown* since, apart from the Crown Proceedings Act 1947, the Crown could not commit a tort. Hence the plaintiffs have no right to bring a quia timet action against the Crown based on a threatened tort by its servants or agents.

Mr. Mummery for the Attorney-General submitted that, in any event, the action could not be brought against the Attorney-General of England. He submitted that the certificate given by the Foreign Secretary shows that the case is not brought against the Crown in right of the Government of the United Kingdom and the Attorney-General of England is not the proper respondent to such proceedings: *Buck* v. *Attorney-General* [1965] Ch. 745, 771. I express no concluded view on this submission since I am not satisfied that it has been demonstrated that the case is brought against the Crown otherwise than in right of the Government of the United Kingdom. The Foreign Secretary's certificate is conclusive for the purposes of the Act of 1947 since section 40(3) so provides. But it is not conclusive for other purposes and I am far from clear how liability for the acts of the British Army (as opposed to the forces of any other part of the Commonwealth) can be said not to arise from the acts of the Crown in respect of the Government of the United Kingdom.

However, for the reasons which I have given earlier, I am reluctantly forced to the conclusion that there is in law no justification for joining the Attorney-General as a party to this action and the appeal should be allowed.

SIR DAVID CAIRNS: I agree with the judgment of Brown-Wilkinson L.J. Appeal allowed with costs.

Conclusive certificates: section 40(3)(a).

R. v. Secretary of State for Foreign and Commonwealth Affairs Ex parte Trawnik
The Times, February 21, 1986
Court of Appeal

Lawton L.J., referred in his judgment above to proceedings brought by the plaintiffs to challenge the certificates issued by the Foreign Secretary under section 40(3)(a) of the Crown Proceedings Act 1947 and section 21 of the State Immunity Act 1978. The Divisional Court (Forbes and Kennedy JJ.) held that it was precluded from examining the validity of the certificates. The applicants appealed to the Court of Appeal (May, Ralph Gibson and Stocker K.JJ.)

May L.J. [His Lordship described the cetificates in question. In the first action against the Ministry of Defence the Foreign Secretary issued a certificate under section 40(3) (a) of the Crown Proceedings Act 1947 which stated that "any liability of the Crown alleged in the [applicants'] action . . . arises otherwise than in respect of Her Majesty's Government in the United Kingdom." Following the decision of the Court of Appeal in *Trawnik* v. *Lennox* the Foreign Secretary issued a second certificate under the State Immunity Act 1978, section 21 which provided that such a certificate was

> "Conclusive evidence on any question (a) whether any . . . territory is a constituent territory of a federal state. . . . or as to the person or persons to be regarded [for the purposes of Part 1 of the Act] as the head or government of a state. . . ."

The certificate stated that Germany was a state and that the persons to be regarded as its government included the Kommandatura of Berlin, including Major General Lennox.

The third certificate, issued on November 1, 1984, was in the same terms as the first, issued under the 1947 Act, except that it referred to the action as amended to include the Attorney General and Major General Lennox.]

In his Lordship's view, the fact that the Divisional Court had reached the correct decision could now be shown merely by reference to the judgments of the Court of Appeal in *R* v. *Registrar of Companies, Ex parte Central Bank of India* [1986] Q.B.1114.

In that case the relevant statutory provision was section 98(2) of the Companies Act 1948, which provided that a certificate issued by the registrar in pursuance of the Act "shall be conclusive evidence that the requirements of this Part of this Act . . . have been complied with."

The ratio of the decision was directly in point in the instant appeal. As a matter of construction, the words "shall . . . be conclusive as to the matter so certified" in section 40(3)(a) were equivalent to a provision that the certificate should be conclusive evidence of the matters certified, whether those were questions of fact or law or of mixed fact and law.

Such words did not preclude an application for judicial review of the certificate but such an application, if based on the proposition that what had been certified was so clearly wrong that the certificate had to be a nullity, would be bound to fail because the evidence which counsel would wish to call to prove that very thing could not be adduced.

So far as the certificate under the State Immunity Act 1978 was concerned, the position was *a fortiori* having regard to the actual wording of section 21 of that Act.

If it were necessary to decide the point, the matters certified in the certificates were "matters of state" relating to questions of recognition arising in the conduct of foreign relations and, once held to be so, were not reviewable by the courts: see *Council of Civil Service Unions* v. *Minister for the Civil Service* [1985] A.C. 374).

It followed that the preliminary issues had to be answered in the secretary of State's favour and the appeal should be dismissed.

Appeal dismissed.

Servant or Agent of the Crown: section 38

Tamlin v. Hannaford

[1950] 1 K.B. 18

Court of Appeal

The plaintiff in 1946 was the tenant of a house in Plymouth owned by the Great Western Railway Co., and he sublet some rooms to the defendant on a weekly tenancy. The house became vested in the British Transport Commission by the Transport Act 1947.[1] In 1946 the plaintiff, having given the defendant notice to quit, brought an action in the Plymouth county court claiming possession, and the defendant relied on the Rent Restriction Acts. The county court judge held that since the passing of the Transport Act 1947 the house must be regarded as "owned by the Crown and administered by the British Transport Commission as Crown agents," and that therefore the Rent Restriction Acts did not apply to the house. He accordingly made an order for possession.

The defendant (subtenant) appealed. The Court of Appeal (Bucknill, Asquith and Denning L.JJ.) allowed the appeal, holding that neither on the interpretation of the Transport Act 1947 as a whole, nor on general principle, was the British Transport Commission to be regarded as a servant or agent of the Crown. The case was therefore remitted to the county court to be dealt with on the basis that the house was within the Rent Restriction Acts. The court did not consider it necessary to decide whether—if the house had been Crown property—the plaintiff, as tenant of the Crown, would have been entitled to rely on the rule that the Rent Restriction Acts do not bind the Crown.

Cur. adv. vult.

DENNING L.J.: read the judgment of the court. [Having stated the facts, he continued]

It is, of course, a settled rule that the Crown is not bound by a statute unless there can be gathered from it an intention that the Crown should be bound; and it has been held that, under this rule, the Crown and its servants and agents are not bound by the Rent Restriction Acts. (See, for instance, *Territorial and Auxiliary Forces Association of the County of London* v. *Nichols*[2]). In considering whether any subordinate body is entitled to this Crown privilege, the question is not so much whether it is an "emanation of the Crown," a phrase which was first used in *Gilbert* v. *Corporation of Trinity House*,[3] but whether it is properly to be regarded as the servant or agent of the Crown. (See *International Ry.* v. *Niagara Parks Commission*[4]) In the case of the British Transport Commission, this depends on the true construction of the Transport Act 1947. We have considered the provisions of that statute and, for the sake of clarity, we propose to state their effect without referring to the various sections in detail.

The Transport Act 1947 brings into being the British Transport Commission, which is a statutory corporation of a kind comparatively new to English law. It has many of the qualities which belong to corporations of other kinds to which we have been accustomed. It has, for instance, defined powers which it cannot exceed; and it is directed by a group of men whose duty it is to see that those

---

[1] The British Transport Commission was dissolved by the Transport Act 1962. The re-organisation of road transport has been continued by further Transport Acts in 1980 and 1985. (The last surviving provisions of the 1947 Act were repealed by the Statute Law (Repeals) Act 1974).
[2] [1949] 1 K.B. 35.
[3] (1886) 17 Q.B.D. 795 at p. 801.
[4] [1941] A.C. 328 at pp. 342–343.

powers are properly used. It may own property, carry on business, borrow and lend money, just as any other corporation may do, so long as it keeps within the bounds which Parliament has set. But the significant difference in this corporation is that there are no shareholders to subscribe the capital or to have any voice in its affairs. The money which the corporation needs is not raised by the issue of shares but by borrowing; and its borrowing is not secured by debentures, but is guaranteed by the Treasury. If it cannot repay, the loss falls on the Consolidated Fund of the United Kingdom; that is to say, on the taxpayer. There are no shareholders to elect the directors or to fix their remuneration. There are no profits to be made or distributed. The duty of the corporation is to make revenue and expenditure balance one another, taking of course, one year with another, but not to make profits. If it should make losses and be unable to pay its debts, its property is liable to execution, but it is not liable to be wound up at the suit of any creditor. The taxpayer would, no doubt, be expected to come to its rescue before the creditors stepped in. Indeed, the taxpayer is the universal guarantor of the corporation. But for him it could not have acquired its business at all, nor could it now continue it for a single day. It is his guarantee that has rendered shares, debentures and suchlike all unnecessary. He is clearly entitled to have his interest protected against extravagance or mismanagement.

There are other persons who have also a vital interest in its affairs. All those who use the services which it provides—and who does not?—and all whose supplies depend on it, in short everyone in the land, is concerned in seeing that it is properly run. The protection of the interests of all these—taxpayer, user and beneficiary—is entrusted by Parliament to the Minister of Transport. He is given powers over this corporation which are as great as those possessed by a man who holds all the shares in a private company, subject, however, as such a man is not, to a duty to account to Parliament for his stewardship. It is the Minister who appoints the directors—the members of the Commission—and fixes their remuneration. They must give him any information he wants; and, less they should not prove amenable to his suggestions as to the policy they should adopt, he is given power to give them directions of a general nature, in matters which appear to him to affect the national interest, as to which he is the sole judge, and they are then bound to obey. These are great powers but still we cannot regard the corporation as being his agent, any more than a company is the agent of the shareholders or even of a sole shareholder. In the eye of the law, the corporation is its own master and is answerable as fully as any other person or corporation. It is not the Crown and has none of the immunities or privileges of the Crown. Its servants are not civil servants, and its property is not Crown property. It is as much bound by Acts of Parliament as any other subject of the King. It is, of course, a public authority and its purpose, no doubt, are public purposes, but it is not a government department nor do its powers fall within the province of government.

The correctness of these views is shown by the way in which the railways have been dealt with. Apart from the special provisions as to the constitution of the Commission, all that has happened is that there has been an amalgamation of the previous railway companies into one concern which is expressly made subject to the same rights and liabilities as were the railway companies, including statutory duties, contractual obligations, and even some customary obligations. This one amalgamated concern is run by a statutory corporation called the Railway Executive, but this corporation is nothing more nor less than the agent of the Commission. So far as third persons are concerned, the Railway Executive is treated as running the railways on its own account. For instance, the officers and servants of the former companies are treated as officers and servants of the Railway Executive and not of the Commission. But in the last resort it is the Commission which is responsible. If a judgment against the Railway Executive is not satisfied, execution can be levied against the property of the Commission. All this seems to be quite inconsistent with the notion that the Commission is itself a government department or an agent of the Crown. Execution is not leviable against a government department, even under the Crown Proceedings Act 1947.

We do not find it very useful to draw analogies from other bodies which are differently constituted and differently controlled and exist for different purposes. The Territorial Forces Association, for instance, are not concerned with commercial matters, but with the defence of the realm, which is essentially the province of government and are therefore to be considered agents of the Crown:*Territorial Forces Association* v. *Philpot*[5]; *Territorial and Auxiliary Forces Association* v. *Nichols.*[6] . . .

The only fact in this case which can be said to make the British Transport Commission a servant or agent of the Crown is the control over it which is exercised by the Minister of Transport; but there is ample authority both in this court and in the House of Lords for saying that such control as he exercises is insufficient for the purpose. (See *Cannon Brewery Co. Ltd.* v. *Central Control Board (Liquor Traffic.)*[7]) When Parliament intends that a new corporation should act on behalf of the Crown, it as a rule says so expressly, as it did in the case of the Central Land Board by the Town and Country Planning Act 1947, which was passed on the very same day as the Transport Act 1947. In the absence of any such express provision, the proper inference, in the case, at any rate, of a commercial corporation, is that it acts on its own behalf, even though it is controlled by a government department.

In our opinion, therefore, the British Transport Commission is not a servant or agent of the Crown and its property is as much subject to the Rent Restriction Acts as the property of any other person. The defendant is therefore entitled to raise the Rent Restriction Acts. Sir Valentine Holmes [counsel for the defendant] mentioned a further point, namely, whether in any case the plaintiff, who was clearly not the servant or agent of the Crown, could avail himself of the rule relating to the Crown; but it was not argued and we express no opinion on it. The appeal is allowed and the case remitted to the county court for the decision of that court in the light of the judgment.

Appeal allowed.

Note

Cf. now, Crown Lessees (Protection of Sub-Tenants) Act 1952.

---

[5] [1947] 2 All E.R. 376.
[6] [1949] 1 K.B. 35.
[7] [1918] 2 Ch. 101 at 113; [1919] A.C. 744 at p. 757.

Bank Voor Handel en Scheepvaart N.V. v. Administrator of Hungarian Property
[1954] A.C. 584
House of Lords

A Dutch banking corporation, which after the German invasion of Holland became an "enemy" within the meaning of the Trading with the Enemy Act 1939, owned certain gold bars in London. These became vested in the Custodian of Enemy Property, who sold them, invested the proceeds and paid tax on the income. The investments were later transferred to the Administrator of Hungarian Property in the mistaken belief that they were the property of a Hungarian national. After the war the Dutch bank obtained judgment for the recovery of the proceeds of sale with interest, and the question then arose whether it was also entitled to recover the amount paid by way of income tax. Devlin J. gave judgment for the Bank on the ground that the income was exempt from tax because it was vested in the Custodian of Enemy Property, a person having "Crown status" or at least receiving the income for a "Crown purpose." The Court of Appeal reversed this decision, holding that the Custodian did not receive the money for a "Crown purpose."

The House of Lords, after taking time for consideration, by a majority of three to two (Lord Reid, Lord Tucker and Lord Asquith of Bishopstone, Lord Morton of Henryton and Lord Keith of Avonholm dissenting) restored the judgment in favour of the Bank. The majority of their Lordships held that the Custodian was a "servant of the Crown" and therefore could have claimed immunity from taxation in respect of the income of property held by him in that capacity. Lord Morton and Lord Keith (dissenting) thought that even if the Custodian was a servant of the Crown this was not sufficient, as it had not been shown that the income was "Crown income" or was received for the purposes of government.

LORD REID [after stating the facts, continued]: It is said that the Income Tax Acts do not bind the Crown, and that is undoubtedly true at least to this extent: tax is not payable in respect of income received by the Sovereign, nor is it payable in respect of Crown income received on behalf of the Crown by a servant of the Crown in the course of his official duties. But the authorities show that it is a difficult matter to determine who is to be regarded as a servant of the Crown in this connection. And it may also be a difficult matter to determine whether a servant of the Crown can plead immunity from tax in respect of all income which it happens to be part of his duty to receive, or whether it is also necessary that the income should in some sense be Crown income, or applicable for Crown purposes.

The starting point of any discussion of these questions must be three decisions of this House: *Mersey Docks and Harbour Board* v. *Cameron*,[1] *Greig* v. *Edinburgh University*[2] and *Coomber* v. *Berkshire Justices*.[3] In the *Mersey Docks* case a non-profit-earning statutory corporation claimed immunity from local rates, in *Greig's* case a similar claim was made by a university, and in *Coomber's* case the justices claimed immunity from income tax under Schedule A. So none of these cases was concerned with a servant of the Crown in any ordinary sense, and in each the immunity claimed was from taxation or rating in respect of the occupation or ownership of land. Though these decisions do not govern this case, speeches in all of them contain statements of principle which may be of decisive importance: but in examining those statement one must always, I think, bear in mind the nature of the issue in these cases.

[1] (1865) 11 H.L.C. 443.
[2] (1868) L.R. 1 Sc. & D. 348.
[3] (1883) 9 App.Cas. 61.

In the *Mersey Docks* case the sole question was whether a corporation not subject to control by the Crown or by a Minister, and whose revenues were not Crown revenues, could claim Crown privilege on the ground that it was performing a public duty. Blackburn J. gave a long opinion for the majority of the consulted judges. He recognised that a long series of cases had established that where property though not in Crown occupation is occupied for the purposes of the government of this country no one is rateable in respect of such occupation, and said[4]: "In these latter cases it is difficult to maintain that the occupants are, strictly speaking, servants of the Sovereign, so as to make the occupation that of Her Majesty: but the purposes are all public purposes, of that kind which, by the constitution of the country, fall within the province of Government, and are committed to the Sovereign, so that the occupiers, though not perhaps strictly servants of the Sovereign, might be considered *in consimili casu*." I have found no indication that he thought that, if immunity is claimed on behalf of the Crown by an actual servants of the Crown, the right to immunity depends on whether the claim is made by a superior or by a subordinate servant of the Crown, or depends on the purpose for which the Crown proposes to use the property. . . .

[His Lordship mentioned *Greig's* case and continued:] In *Coomber's* case it was decided that immunity from income tax under Schedule A is similar to immunity from poor rates. Lord Blackburn said[5] that the Act showed no intention to impose tax on property belonging to the Crown and did not take away "the exemption, by virtue of the prerogative, of property actually occupied or enjoyed by the Crown." He then said[6] that the administration of justice, the preservation of order, and the prevention of crime are functions "that by the constitution of this country . . . do, of common right, belong to the Crown," and after discussing earlier cases he added[7]: "I do not say that the assize courts, maintained by the county for the administration of the Queen's justice in the Queen's court, are quite so clearly occupied by the servant of the Crown as those courts which are maintained by the Woods and Forests out of the general revenue of the country. Nor do I say that the police station, maintained by the county for the maintenance of the police, is quite so clearly occupied by the servants of the Crown as a barrack maintained for soldiers, and paid for out of the general revenues of the country. But I think there is great reason for saying that both are maintained for the purposes of the administration, or those purposes of the Government which are, according to the theory of the constitution, administered by the Sovereign." . . .

In my opinion, there is nothing in these cases which requires us to limit the class of servants of the Crown to Ministers and the like or to exclude subordinate servants of the Crown. Those *in consimili casu* are typically bodies like the justices independant of the Crown asserting Crown privilege not for the benefit of the revenues of the Crown but for the benefit of their own revenues in order that the functions which they are carrying out shall not be prejudiced, and it is easy to see why such independent bodies can only be permitted to claim Crown privilege in respect of a very limited class of functions, and only if the property or money in respect of which immunity is claimed is wholly devoted to those functions. But the case of a subordinate servant of the Crown is very different. If a Minister receives income to be used in the service of the Crown it does not matter whether the purposes for which it is to be used are or are not purposes which if carried out by independent bodies would put them *in consimili casu* with servants of the Crown: in all cases he can claim Crown immunity. And I can see no possible reason why, if a subordinate servant of the Crown receives income to be used in the service of the Crown, he should not be entitled to assert the same privilege.

---

[4] (1865) 11 H.L.C. 443 at p. 465.
[5] (1883) 9 App.Cas. 61 at p. 66.
[6] (1883) 9 App.Cas. 61 at p. 67.
[7] (1883) 9 App.Cas. 61 at pp. 69–70.

Neither the Minister nor the subordinate asserts the privilege on his own behalf: both assert it on behalf of and for the benefit of the Crown. . . .

It was suggested by Devlin J. at one point in his judgment in this case that there is now no such thing as a servant of the Crown in the strict sense. I cannot agree. Ministers are pre-eminently Her Majesty's servants: a purist might find some anomaly in that because by constitutional practice the Sovereign can only act on the advice of a Minister. But no one denies that Ministers come within the category of servants of the Crown for the present purpose. And with regard to others I can see no difficulty at all. The Crown (through or with the advice of a Minister) controls them and directs their activities in a way which to my mind makes the term "servant" quite appropriate.

In my judgment the question whether the custodian is a servant of the Crown depends on the degree of control which the Crown through its Ministers can exercise over him in the performance of his duties. The fact that a statute has authorised his appointment is, I think, immaterial, but the definition in the statute of his rights, duties and obligations is highly important. In the ordinary way a civil servant's duties are not prescribed, though his salary may be fixed in Parliament, and I have no doubt that he is a servant of the Crown. But when a statute creates an office it may give to the holder more or less independence from ministerial control so that the officer has to a greater or less extent a discretion which he alone can exercise, and it may be that the grant of any substantial independent discretion takes the officer out of the category of servants of the Crown for the present purpose. But I cannot find that the custodian has any such independent discretion. . . . [His Lordship referred to the powers of the Board of Trade under s.7 of the Trading with the Enemy Act 1939.]

I therefore hold that the custodian is a servant of the Crown, and it is clear that he received this income in the course of his official duties. The appellant argues that that is enough to establish the right to claim immunity from tax. The respondent, on the other hand, argues that that is not at all conclusive and that what really matters is the character of the income: if the income is Crown income then tax is not due, but if it is not and it is only received by the custodian to be held until the time comes to pay it to some private person, then there is no immunity from tax. I am bound to say that this appears to me to be reasonable and not in conflict with any of the decisions, and I am prepared to assume that if a case arose in which it was the duty of a Crown servant merely to hold property with accruing income for a period and then to pay it to some as yet unascertained private person, it would be held that tax is payable on the income accruing. That would be because in such a case payment of tax could not possibly prejudice any Crown interest or purpose.

While it may be that a Crown servant could not claim Crown immunity in respect of his performance of statutory duties which served no Crown purpose at all, I can find nothing to justify the argument that Crown immunity can only be claimed by the Crown (or its servants on its behalf) if it is required to protect some direct or financial interest of the Crown: and still less can I find any support for the argument that immunity cannot be claimed by the Crown unless the Crown alone is interested in the benefit which it will bring. I have already said that there is, in my view, an essential difference between the immunity of the Crown itself and immunity which may claimed by independent bodies on the ground that they are performing functions of a governmental character. There is every reason for strictly limiting the right of such bodies to claim immunity, but I can see no ground for applying those limits to the Crown itself. If an Act of Parliament does not bind the Crown the the Crown can claim immunity from its provisions whether its interest to obtain immunity in a particular case is large or small or direct or indirect. . . .

LORD ASQUITH OF BISHOPSTONE: My Lords, I agree with the conclusions reached by my noble and learned friends, Lord Reid and Lord Tucker.

The only issue, having regard to the concessions and assumptions on which by agreement the case proceeded, is whether, in respect of the "fruits" of investment of the property in question, the Custodian of Enemy Property could successfully have resisted payment of income tax. He could, *ex concessis*, only have done this if he could have established that he shared the Crown's immunity from income tax.

Unfortunately, the leading decisions of your Lordship's House on "Crown immunity" concern immunity mainly in respect of land or buildings: they concern exemption from liability to rates, or Schedule A of the income tax, and any principles deduced from these decisions can only be applied by an analogical extension to cases such as the present, where what is involved is not the use of premises but the possession or handling of chattels or funds.

The principles applied to the occupation of land and buildings (which must form the starting point) seem to include the following:

1. The Sovereign is personally immune not only from rates and Schedule A but from all direct taxation. This is clear, but irrelevant to the present case.

2. "Servants of the Crown" are immune from rates and Schedule A on premises occupied by them as such. This is the result of two other rules—(a) a servant does not "occupy"; his master "occupies" through him—hence the servant is immune; (b) the master being in this case the Sovereign, and immune as such, no one is liable. The suggestion that this immunity is limited to cases where the servant is the holder of, or the modern successor to, a small group of ancient offices has been sometimes ventilated, but would appear to have no foundation in principle, or in any authority binding on this House. On this point I strongly agree with what has fallen from my noble and learned friend, Lord Reid, who has explored this point in some detail.

3. Persons may enjoy immunity who are not servants of the Crown but occupy premises, such as assize courts, judges' lodgings, policemen's lodgings, and the like, and do so exclusively for the performance of the functions of the executive government. These persons are in some of the cases described as "*in consimili casu*" with servants of the Crown. Persons will tend to be placed in this category if the public functions which they discharge are closely connected with the exercise of the Royal prerogative; *e.g.*, *inter alia*, the administration of justice, the preservation of public order, the making of war and the conclusion of peace. And the courts appear on some of the authorities to have taken these last factors into account as relevant in deciding who is a "servant of the Crown" within the second class.

These principles seem to be most clearly stated in the opinion of Lord Cranworth in *Mersey Docks and Harbour Board Trustees* v. *Cameron*,[8] though they emerge also in *Greig* v. *Edinburgh University*,[9] *Coomber* v. *Berkshire Justices*[10] and *Metropolitan Meat Industry Board* v. *Sheedy*.[11]

For completeness perhaps a fourth principle or rule may be added.

4. The courts will lean against including in any of the exempted categories an aggregation of commercial undertakings brought under some degree of public statutory control, and they will (if the other requirements are satisfied) lean in favour of exemption for persons or bodies who are mere ministerial instruments of the Crown's will, lacking in themselves any discretion or initiative.

To adapt these principles, moulded in large measure for a somewhat different purpose, to the facts of such a case as the present is not easy. But the attempt to do so points to the following features of the present case as relevant, and throws them into relief:

1. The custodian is not a commercial corporation subject to public control.

[8] (1865) 11 H.L.C. 443.
[9] (1868) L.R. 1 Sc. & D. 348.
[10] (1883) 9 App.Cas. 61.
[11] [1927] A.C. 899.

2. He is a public officer appointed and removable by the Crown under statutory powers.

3. He enjoys in substance no discretion of his own. In practically every matter he must do what the Board of Trade (or, in some cases, the Treasury) directs him to do.

4. Subject to their control—the Crown's control—he collects, handles, invests and is intended ultimately to distribute in accordance with treaties to be made by the Crown, the property which comes to him (in which, needless to say, he has no personal interest). As counsel for the respondent put it, every act of his has "O.H.M.S." stamped on it.

5. The decision of Russell J. in *Re Munster*,[12] though made under the Trading with the Enemy (Amendment) Act 1914, seem to me in general an accurate description of the status and functions of the Custodian of Enemy Property and the character assumed by property vested in him under the corresponding Act of 1939. He is not the agent or trustee of the aliens, enemy or friendly, who were owners of the property before it came into his hands. When such property vests in him it ceases thereupon beneficially to belong to its original owners; and though in pursuance of "arrangements to be made at the conclusion of peace" (s.7(1) of the 1939 Act), *viz.* in pursuance of treaties of peace to be negotiated by the Crown, the Crown could re-create a title in the original owners, it could, in my view, equally create such a title in anyone else, including itself. . . .

6. The functions of the custodian are intimately linked with the prerogative powers of the Crown to declare and wage war and to make peace. He is a conduit pipe for the flow and canalisation of these powers.

Taking account of these factors collectively, I am of opinion that the custodian is a "servant of the Crown" within the second exempted class, and immune from income tax as regards funds coming into his hands in his capacity as such. I do not think it is a prerequisite to this immunity that those funds must be "Crown income" in the sense of being payable solely and immediately to the central fiscus, or that the immunity is defeated the moment it is shown that the Crown has power to divert them in part or in whole to some other destination. The Crown has in effect an unlimited power of disposition over his property. The case of *Administrator of Austrian Property* v. *Russian Bank for Foreign Trade*,[13] which in my view was rightly decided, seems to me fatal to the contrary view, and I agree with my noble and learned friend, Lord Tucker, that the attempt to distinguish that case from the present case fails.

I am of opinion that the appeal should be allowed.
Appeal allowed.

Note

Both the above cases also illustrate the rule that the Crown is not bound by a statute unless by express words or necessary implication: C. & A.L. p. 276. An unsuccessful attempt to limit the scope of the rule was made in *Department of Transport* v. *Egoroff, The Times*, May 6, 1986. CC.A.) PARKER L.J. said that in his defence and counterclaim the tenant had averred that sections 32 and 33 of the Housing Act 1961 applied to his monthly tenancy, and had alleged various breaches by the landlords of their obligations to repair.

The landlords being a department of the Crown, the crucial question was whether the Crown was bound by sections 32 and 33 of the 1961 Act.[14]

It was common ground that no statute could bind the Crown save by express words or necessary implication. The tenant conceded that there were no words in the 1961 Act expressly stating that the Crown was bound or creating any necessary implication to that effect. Instead, he relied on the proposition founded on the *Magdalene College, Cambridge* case ((1616) 11 Co Rep 66), that there were some classes of statute which always bound the

---

[12] [1920] 1 Ch. 268.
[13] (1931) 48 T.L.R. 37.
[14] See now Landlord and Tenant Act 1985, ss 11–16.

Crown, one of which was a statute made to suppress a wrong. The Housing Act 1961, he argued, was made to suppress a wrong. But that classification in the *Magdalene College* case was too wide to be of general assistance and had been wholly disposed of as a reliable guide by *Province of Bombay* v. *Bombay City Municipal Corporation* ([1947] AC 59). Even if the classification still stood, there was no doubt that sections 32 and 33 of the 1961 Act did not come within it. There was no valid distinction between the Housing Act 1961 and the Rent Restriction Acts 1920 and 1923 which in *Clark* v. *Downes* ((1931) 145 LT 20) were held not to bind the Crown. In the light of the *Bombay* case the test had to be either an examination of the wording of the Act or in exceptional cases a demonstration that the purposes of the Act would be wholly frustrated unless the Crown were bound.

Sir George Waller agreed.

The scope of the rule in favour of the Crown may, however, be curtailed by the operation of the presumption that a statute in the absence of clear words is not to be construed to take away the property of a subject without compensation: *Attorney-General* v. *De Keyser's Royal Hotel* [1920] A.C. 508, 542 *per* Lord Atkinson; *Manitoba Fisheries Ltd* v. *The Queen* (1978) 88 D.L.R. (3d) 462.

An allied privilege of the Crown is to be entitled to claim the benefit of a statute, although not bound by its terms.

Both privileges survive the Crown Proceedings Act 1947: see s.40(2)(f) and s.31(1).

Liability in Contract: Section 1

Thomas v. The Queen

(1875) L.R. 10 Q.B. 31

Queens Bench

Thomas, an engineer, brought a petition of right claiming an award and his expenses in connection with an artillery invention, in accordance with an agreement with the Secretary of State for War. The Attorney-General (Sir Henry James) argued on a demurrer that (1) a petition of right would not lie for any other object than specified land or chattels, and (2) it would not lie for breach of contract or to recover money claimed either by way of debt or damages.

The Court (Blackburn, Quain and Archibald JJ.) gave judgment for Thomas.

BLACKBURN J. [delivering the judgment of the court, said]: . . . Contracts can be made on behalf of Her Majesty with subjects, and the Attorney-General suing on her behalf can enforce those contracts against the subject, and if the subject has no means of enforcing the contract on his part there is certainly a want of reciprocity in such cases. But it is quite settled that on account of her dignity no action can be brought against the Queen; the redress, if any, must be by petition of right, which is now regulated by the 23 & 24 Vict. c. 34.[1] If the suppliant ultimately recovers, he obtains under section 9 a judgment of the court that he is entitled to such relief as the court shall think just. And this form of judgment would be applicable to a case in which it appeared to the court that the plaintiff was entitled to be paid damages for the non-fulfilment of a contract.

It appears that at the time of the passing of the Act there was a general impression that a petition of right was maintainable for a debt due or a breach of contract by the Crown. . . . Indeed, the framers of the Act appear to have considered its chief utility to consist in the applicability of its improved procedure to petitions on contracts between subjects and the various public departments of the Government, so vastly on the increase in recent years, both in number and importance, whilst petitions of right in respect of specific lands or chattels must for the future be exceedingly rare.

But the seventh section of the Act expressly provides that "nothing in this statute shall be construed to give to the subject any remedy against the Crown in any case in which he would not have been entitled to such remedy before the passing of this Act." We are, therefore, called upon to determine the correctness of the general impression referred to, and whether before the statute a petition of right lay in respect of the non-fulfilment of a contract made by the authorised agent of the Sovereign. . . .

As our judgment proceeds mainly on the authority of the *Bankers Case*,[2] we think it right to state that case somewhat at length. Charles II had by Letters Patent under the Great Seal granted to the bankers who had been deprived of their money by shutting of the Exchequer, and to their creditors, annuities in fee, at the rate of 6 per cent., on the moneys thus obtained. These annuities were charged on the hereditary revenue of the excise. No pains had been spared to make the Letters Patent as binding as possible. They contained, *inter alia*, a covenant from the King himself, his heirs and successors, under the Great Seal, that due payment should be made, and that if there was any defect in the Letters Patent the King, his heirs and successors would make a further grant. And the Treasurer, etc., were commanded to give to the patentees tallies and to pay them. The annuities were paid for four years, and then the further payment ceased. During

---

[1] Petitions of Right Act 1860.
[2] (1699) 14 St.Tr. 1; 5 Mod. 29.

the reigns of Charles II and James II the bankers took no steps at law to enforce their claims, but in the first year of William and Mary (1689) when, as Lord Somers suggests, it had become safe to sue the Crown, they commenced proceedings. . . .

Lord Somer's very elaborate argument is entirely directed to establishing that there was no power in the Barons of the Exchequer to order the Treasurer and Chamberlains to make these payments. And as a step, and an important step, in his reasoning, he sets himself to prove that there was a remedy by petition of right which was, as he maintained, the only remedy. He denies Holt's position that *monstrans de droit* was at common law. And he says[3]: "Indeed I take it to be generally true that in all cases where the subject is in the nature of a plaint to recover anything from the King, his only remedy at common law is to sue by petition to the person of the King. I say where the subject comes as a plaint. For, as I said before, when on a title found for the King by office, the subject comes in to traverse the King's title or to show his own right, he comes in the nature of a defendant, and is admitted to interplead in the case with the King in defence of his title which otherwise would be defeated by finding the office. And to show that this was so, I would take notice of several instances. That in the case of debts owing to the Crown, the subject's remedy was by petition appears by *Aynsham's Case*,[4] which is a petition for £19 due for work done at Carnarvon," and he cites many other entries in Parliament from *Ryley*. Whether Lord Somers was right or not in thinking that the entries in *Ryley* are petitions of right, there can be no question that he here expresses a distinct and considered judgment, that a petition of right would lie against the Crown for a simple contract debt, such as that for wages. And unless we overrule this judgment of his which is not opposed to Holt's reasoning [in the *Bankers Case*], and cannot therefore be considered as necessarily overruled by the House of Lords, we must, in this case, give judgment for the suppliant.

And we do not find that this opinion of Lord Somers has been questioned since, but rather the contrary. In Comyn's *Digest*, Prerogative, D. 78, it is said that petition lies, if the King "does not pay a debt, wages," etc. Lord Somers's argument and Chief Baron Comyn's express no doubt as to the soundness of the doctrine thus cited by him. It appears in *Macbeath v. Haldimand*[5] that Lord Thurlow[6] and Buller L. (both *obiter* it is true) expressed an opinion that a petition of right lay against the Crown on a contract. And a similar opinion seems to have been expressed by the Barons of the Exchequer in *Oldham v. The Lords of the Treasury*.[7] And in *The Baron De Bode's Case*,[8] in which the point was raised though not decided, Lord Denman declares "an unconquerable repugnance to the suggestion that the door ought to be closed against all redress or remedy," a doctrine much resembling what Lord Somers calls Lord Holt's "popular opinion," that if there be a right there must be a remedy.

In *The Viscount Canterbury v. The Attorney-General*[9] it was decided that the Sovereign could not be sued by petition of right for negligence; and in *Tobin v. The Queen*,[10] that the Sovereign could not be sued in petition of right for a wrong. But in neither case was any opinion expressed that a petition of right will not lie for a contract, Erle C.J. expressly saying p. 355 that claims founded on contracts and grants made on behalf of the Crown "are within a class legally distinct from wrongs"; and in *Feather v. The Queen*[11] it is assumed in the judgment that it does lie

[3] 14 St.Tr. 83.
[4] Ryley 251.
[5] (1786) 1 Term Rep. 172.
[6] The reference should be to Lord Mansfield.
[7] (*circa* 1800–1827) cited in (1833) 6 Sim. 220.
[8] (1845) 8 Q.B. Rep. 208.
[9] (1842) 12 L.J.Ch. 281; 1 Phil. 306.
[10] (1864) 16 C.B. (N.S.) 310; 33 L.J.C.P. 199.
[11] (1865) 6 B. & S. 257; 35 L.J.Q.B. 200.

"where the claim arises out of a contract as for goods supplied to the Crown on a public service."

We think, therefore, that we are bound by the *Bankers Case* to hold that the judgment on this demurrer should be for the suppliant.

Judgment for the suppliant.

Note

It is still necessary to know when a petition of right lay before 1948—a matter not entirely free from doubt—for the Crown Proceedings Act 1947, s.1, provides that:

"Where any person has a claim against the Crown after the commencement of this Act, and, if this Act had not been passed, the claim might have been enforced subject to the grant of His Majesty's fiat, by petition of right, . . . then, subject to the provisions of this Act, the claim may be enforced as of right, and without the fiat of His Majesty, by proceedings taken against the Crown for that purpose in accordance with the provisions of this Act."

For a petition of right against the Crown in respect of Southern Rhodesia in pre-1860 form, see *Franklin* v. *Att.-Gen.* [1974] Q.B. 185 (Lawson J.).

Liability in Tort: Section 2

Home Office v. Dorset Yacht Co.

[1970] A.C. 1004

House of Lords

Seven Borstal boys, who were working on an island under the control and supervision of three officers, left the island at night and boarded, cast adrift and damaged the plaintiffs' yacht which was moored offshore. The plaintiffs brought an action for damages against the Home Office alleging negligence. On the trial of the preliminary issue whether the Home Office owed any duty of care to the plaintiffs capable of giving rise to liability in damages, Thesiger J. answered the question in the affirmative.

The Court of Appeal (Lord Denning M.R., Edmund Davies and Phillimore L.JJ.) dismissed the appeal by the Home Office. The House of Lords (Lord Reid, Lord Morris of Borth-y-Gest, Lord Pearson and Lord Diplock, Viscount Dilhorne dissenting) confirmed their decision.

LORD REID: My Lords, on September 21, 1962, a party of Borstal trainees were working on Brownsea Island in Poole Harbour under the supervision and control of three Borstal officers. During that night seven of them escaped and went abroad a yacht which they found nearby. They set this yacht in motion and collided with the respondents' yacht which was moored in the vicinity. Then they boarded the respondents' yacht. Much damage was done to this yacht by the collision and some by the subsequent conduct of these trainees. The respondents sue the appellants, the Home Office, for the amount of this damage.

The case comes before your Lordships on a preliminary issue whether the Home Office or these Borstal officers owed any duty of care to the respondents capable of giving rise to a liability in damages. So it must be assumed that the respondents can prove all that they could prove on the pleadings if the case goes to trial. The question then is whether on that assumption the Home Office would be liable in damages. It is admitted that the Home Office would be vicariously liable if an action would lie against any of these Borstal officers.

The facts which I think we must assume are that this party of trainees were in the lawful custody of the governor of the Portland Borstal institution and were sent by him to Brownsea Island on a training exercise in the custody and under the control of the three officers with instructions to keep them in custody and under control. But in breach of their instructions these officers simply went to bed leaving the trainees to their own devices. If they had obeyed their instructions they could and would have prevented these trainees from escaping. They would therefore be guilty of the disciplinary offences of contribution by carelessness of neglect to the except of a prisoner and to the occurrence of loss, damage or injury to any person or property. All the escaping trainees had criminal records and five of them had a record of previous escapes from Borstal institutions. The three officers knew or ought to have known that these trainees would probably try to escape during the night, would take some vessel to make good their escape and would probably cause damage to it or some other vessel. There were numerous vessels moored in the harbour, and the trainees could readily board one of them. So it was a likely consequence of their neglect of duty that the respondents' yacht would suffer damage.

The case for the Home Office is that under no circumstances can Borstal officers owe any duty to any member of the public to take care to prevent trainees under their control or supervision from injuring him or his property. If that is the law, then inquiry into the facts of this case would be a waste of time and money because whatever the facts may be the respondents must lose. That case is based on three main arguments. First it is said that there is virtually no authority for imposing a duty of this kind. Secondly, it is said that no person can be liable for a wrong done by another who is of full age and capacity and who is not the servant or acting on behalf of that person. And thirdly it is said that public policy (or the policy of the relevant legislation) requires that these officers should be immune from any such liability.

The first would at one time have been a strong argument. About the beginning of this century most eminent lawyers thought that there were a number of separate torts involving negligence, each with its own rules, and they were most unwilling to add more. They were of course aware from a number of leading cases that in the past the courts had from time to time recognised new duties and new grounds of action. But the heroic age was over; it was time to cultivate certainty and security in the law; the categories of negligence were virtually closed. The Attorney-General invited us to return to those halcyon days, but, attractive though it may be, I cannot accede to his invitation.

In later years there has been a steady trend towards regarding the law of negligence as depending on principle so that, when a new point emerges, one should ask not whether it is covered by authority but whether recognised principles apply to it. . . .

[His Lordship referred to *Donoghue* v. *Stevenson*[1]; *Hedley Byrne & Co. Ltd.* v. *Heller & Partners Ltd.*[2] *Overseas Tankship (U.K.) Ltd.* v. *Morts Dock and Engineering Co. Ltd.* (*The Wagon Mound*) (*No. 1*)[3]; *The Oropesa*[4]; *Haynes* v. *Harwood*[5]; and *Scott's Trustees* v. *Moss*,[6] and continued:] These cases show that, where human action forms one of the links between the original wrongdoing of the defendant and the loss suffered by the plaintiff, that action must at least have been something very likely to happen if it is not to be regarded as novus actus interveniens breaking the chain of causation. I do not think that a mere foreseeable action possibility is or should be sufficient, for then the intervening human action can more properly be regarded as a new cause than as a consequence of the original wrongdoing. But if the intervening action was likely to happen I do not think that it can matter whether that action was innocent or tortious or criminal. Unfortunately, tortiuous or criminal action by a third party is often the "very kind of thing" which is likely to happen as a result of the wrongful or careless act of the defendant. And in the present case, on the facts which we must assume at this stage, I think that the taking of a boat by the escaping trainees and their unskilful navigation leading to damage to another vessel were the very kind of thing that these Borstal officers ought to have seen to be likely.

There was an attempt to draw a distinction between loss caused to the plaintiffs by failure to control an adult of full capacity and loss caused by failure to control a child or mental defective. As regards causation, no doubt it is easier to infer novus actus interveniens in the case of an adult but that seems to me to be the only distinction. In the present case on the assumed facts there would in my view be no novus actus when the trainees damaged the respondents' property and I would therefore hold that damage to have been caused by the Borstal officers' negligence.

If the carelessness of the Borstal officers was the cause of the plaintiffs' loss, what justification is there for holding that they had no duty to take care? The first argument was that their right and power to control the trainees was purely statutory and that any duty to exercise the right and power was only a statutory

[1] [1932] A.C. 562.
[2] [1964] A.C. 465.
[3] [1961] A.C. 388.
[4] [1943] P. 32.
[5] [1935] 1 K.B. 146.
[6] (1889) 17 R.(Ct. of Sess.) 32.

duty owed to the Crown. I would agree, but there is very good authority for the proposition that if a person performs a statutory duty carelessly so that he causes damage to a member of the public which would not have happened if he had performed his duty properly he may be liable. In *Geddis* v. *Proprietors of Bann Reservoir*[7] Lord Blackburn said, "For I take it, without citing cases, that it is now thoroughly well established that no action will lie for doing that which the legislature has authorised, if it be done without negligence, although it does occasion damage to anyone; but an action does lie for doing that which the legislature has authorised, if it be done negligently." The reason for this is, I think, that Parliament deems it to be in the public interest that things otherwise unjustifiable should be done, and that those who do such things with due care should be immune from liability to persons who may suffer thereby. But Parliament cannot reasonably be supposed to have licensed those who do such things to act negligently in disregard of the interests of others so as to cause them needless damage.

Where Parliament confers a discretion the position is not the same. Then there may, and almost certainly will, be errors of judgment in exercising such a discretion and Parliament cannot have intended that members of the public should be entitled to sue in respect of such errors. But there must come a stage when the discretion is exercised so carelessly or unreasonably that there has been no real exercise of the discretion which Parliament has conferred. The person purporting to exercise his discretion has acted in abuse or excess of his power. Parliament cannot be supposed to have granted immunity to persons who do that. The present case does not raise this issue because no discretion was given to these Borstal officers. They were given orders which they negligently failed to carry out. But the county court case of *Greenwell* v. *Prison Commissioners*[8] was relied on and I must deal with it.

Some 290 trainees were held in custody in an open Borstal institution. During the previous year there had been no less than 172 escapes. Two trainees escaped and took and damaged the plaintiff's motor truck; one of these trainees had escaped on three previous occasions from this institution. For three months since his past escape the question of his removal to a more secure institution had been under consideration but no decision had been reached. The learned judge held that the authorities there had been negligent. In my view, this decision could only be upheld if it could be said that the failure of those authorities to deal with the situation was so unreasonable as to show that they had been guilty of a breach of their statutory duty and that that had caused the loss suffered by the plaintiff.

Governors of these institutions and other responsible authorities have a difficult and delicate task. There was some argument as to whether the present system was fully authorised by the relevant statutes, but I shall assume that it is. This system is based on the belief that it assists the rehabilitation of trainees to give them as much freedom and responsibility as possible. So the responsible authorities must weigh on the one hand the public interest of protecting neighbours and their property from the depredations of escaping trainees and on the other hand the public interest of promoting rehabilitation. Obviously there is much room here for differences of opinion and errors of judgment. In my view there can be no liability if the discretion is exercised with due care. There could only be liability if the person entrusted with discretion either unreasonably failed to carry out his duty to consider the matter or reached a conclusion so unreasonable as again to show failure to do his duty.

It was suggested that these trainees might have been deliberately released at the time when they escaped and that there could have been no liability. I do not agree. Presumably when trainees are released either temporarily or permanently some care is taken to see that there is no need for them to resort to crime to get food or

---

[7] (1878) 3 App.Cas. 430 at pp. 455–456.
[8] (1951) 101 L.J. 486.

transport. I could not imagine any more unreasonable exercise of discretion than to release trainees on an island in the middle of the night without making any provision for their future welfare.

We were also referred to *Holgate* v. *Lancashire Mental Hospitals Board*,[9] where the alleged fault was in releasing a mental patient. For similar reasons I think that this decision could only be supported if it could be said that the release was authorised so carelessly that there had been no real exercise of discretion.

If the appellants were right in saying that there can never be a right in a private individual to complain of negligent exercise of a duty to keep a prisoner under control, I do not see how *Ellis* v. *Home Office*[10] can be correct. The plaintiff was in prison, and on one occasion, as he alleged, owing to inadequate control by warders another prisoner assaulted and injured him. It was assumed that he had a right of action, and the Attorney-General did not challenge this. But when the other prisoner assaulted Ellis he was not in fact under control or he would not have been permitted to carry out the assault. It would be very odd if the only persons entitled to complain of negligent performance of the statutory duty to control prisoners were other prisoners. If the main argument for the appellants were right I think that it would necessarily involve holding that *Ellis* was wrong.

It was suggested that a decision against the Home Office would have very far-reaching effects; it was, indeed, suggested in the Court of Appeal that it would make the Home Office liable for the loss occasioned by a burglary committed by a trainee on parole or a prisoner permitted to go out to attend a funeral. But there are two reasons why in the vast majority of cases that would not be so. In the first place it would have to be shown that the decision to allow any such release was so unreasonable that it could not be regarded as a real exercise of discretion by the responsible officer who authorised the release. And secondly it would have to be shown that the commission of the offence was the natural and probable, as distinct from merely a foreseeable, result of the release—that there was no novus actus interveniens. *Greenwell's* case[11] received a good deal of publicity at the time; it was commented on in the *Law Quarterly Review*, Vol. 68 (1952), p. 18. But it has not been followed by a series of claims. I think that the fears of the appellants are unfounded: I cannot believe that negligence or dereliction of duty is widespread among prison or Borstal officers.

Finally I must deal with public policy. It is argued that it would be contrary to public policy to hold the Home Office or its officers liable to a member of the public for this carelessness—or, indeed, any failure of duty on their part. The basic question is: who shall bear the loss caused by that carelessness—the innocent respondents or the Home Office, who are vicariously liable for the conduct of there careless officers? I do not think that the argument for the Home Office can be put better than it was put by the Court of Appeals of New York in *Williams* v. *State of New York*.[12] "... public policy also requires that the State be not held liable. To hold otherwise would impose a heavy responsibility upon the State, or dissuade the wardens and principal keepers of our prison system from continued experimentation with 'minimum security' work details—which provide a means for encouraging better-risk prisoners to exercise their senses of responsibility and honor and so prepare themselves for their eventual return to society. Since 1917, the legislature has expressly provided for out-of-prison work, Correction Law, §182, and its intention should be respected without fostering the reluctance of prison officials to assign eligible men to minimum security work, lest they thereby give rise to costly claims against the State, or indeed inducing the State itself to terminate this 'salutary procedure' looking toward rehabilitation." It may be that

[9] [1937] 4 All E.R. 19.
[10] [1953] 2 All E.R. 149.
[11] 101 L.J. 486.
[12] (1955) 127 N.E. 2d 545 at p. 550.

public servants of the State of New York are so apprehensive, easily dissuaded from doing their duty and intent on preserving public funds from costly claims that they could be influenced in this way. But my experience leads me to believe that Her Majesty's servants are made of sterner stuff. So I have no hesitation in rejecting this argument. I can see no good ground in public policy for giving this immunity to a government department. I would dismiss this appeal.
Appeal dismissed with costs.

The Armed Forces

Crown Proceedings (Armed Forces) Act 1987

c. 25

An Act to repeal section 10 of the Crown Proceedings Act 1947 and to provide for the revival of that section in certain circumstances.

[15 May 1987]

1. Subject to section 2 below, section 10 of the Crown Proceedings Act 1947 (exclusions from liability in tort in cases involving the armed forces) shall cease to have effect except in relation to anything suffered by a person in consequence of an act or omission committed before the date on which this Act is passed.

2.—(1) Subject to the following provisions of this section, the Secretary of State may, at any time after the coming into force of section 1 above, by order—

    (a) revive the effect of section 10 of the Crown Proceedings Act 1947 either for all purposes or for such purposes as may be described in the order; or

    (b) where that section has effect for the time being in pursuance of an order made by virtue of paragraph (a) above, provide for that section to cease to have effect either for all of the purposes for which it so has effect or for such of them as may be so described.

(2) The Secretary of State shall not make an order reviving the effect of the said section 10 for any purposes unless it appears to him necessary or expedient to do so—

    (a) by reason of any imminent national danger or of any great emergency that has arisen; or

    (b) for the purposes of any warlike operations in any part of the world outside the United Kingdom or of any other operations which are or are to be carried out in connection with the warlike activity of any persons in any such part of the world.

(3) Subject to subsection (4) below, an order under this section describing purposes for which the effect of the said section 10 is to be revived, or for which that section is to cease to have effect, may describe those purposes by reference to any matter whatever and may make different provision for different cases, circumstances or persons.

(4) Nothing in any order under this section shall revive the effect of the said section 10, or provide for that section to cease to have effect, in relation to anything suffered by a person in consequence of an act or omission committed before the date on which the order comes into force.

(5) The power to make an order under this section shall be exercisable by statutory instrument subject to annulment in pursuance of a resolution of either House of Parliament.

3.—Except in so far as an order under section 2 above otherwise provides, any reference to section 10 of the Crown Proceedings Act 1947 in any Act passed, or subordinate legislation made, before the passing of this Act shall be construed as a reference to that section as it from time to time has effect by virtue of this Act.

(2) Subsection (1) above shall apply, as it applies to express references to the said section 10—

    (a) to the references to that section which are comprised in the references in the said Act of 1947 to or to the provisions of that Act itself; and

    (b) to any other references to the said section 10 which are comprised in references to that Act, in references to enactments generally or in references to any description of enactments.

(3) In this section "subordinate legislation" has the same meaning as in the Interpretation Act 1978.

4. There shall be paid out of money provided by Parliament any expenses incurred by a Minister of the Crown or Government department in consequence of the provisions of this Act.

5.—(1) This Act may be cited as the Crown Proceedings (Armed Forces) Act 1987.

(2) For the purposes of the application of any provision of this Act in relation to subsection (2) of section 10 of the Crown Proceedings Act 1947 references in this Act to anything suffered by any person in consequence of an act or omission committed before a particular date shall include references to anything which—

(a) would not, apart from this subsection, be regarded as suffered in consequence of an act or omission; but

(b) is suffered in consequence of the nature or condition at a time before that date of any land, premises, ship, aircraft, hovercraft, or vehicle or of any equipment or supplies.

(3) This Act shall extend to Northern Ireland.

Note

For a detailed commentary, see Current Law Statutes Annotated. Since that commentary was written the decision of Caulfield J. in *Pearce* v. *Secretary of State for Defence* has been upheld by the Court of Appeal and the House of Lords ([1988] 2 W.L.R. 144 and 1027) on the ground that rights of action which might have accrued against the Atomic Energy Authority were not retrospectively affected by the transfer of liability to the Secretary of State under the Atomic Energy (Weapons Group) Act 1973. The Court of Appeal and House of Lords, however, went on to consider the meaning of section 10(2) of the Crown Proceedings Act 1947. Section 10(2) provides:

(2) No proceedings in tort shall lie against the Crown for death or personal injury due to anything suffered by a member of the armed forces of the Crown if—

(a) that thing is suffered by him in consequence of the nature or condition of any such land, premises, ship, aircraft or vehicle as aforesaid, or in consequence of the nature or condition of any equipment or supplies used for the purposes of those forces; and

(b) the [Secretary of State] certifies as mentioned in the preceding subsection;

nor shall any act of omission of an officer of the Crown subject him to liability in tort for death or personal injury, in so far as the death or personal injury is due to anything suffered by a member of the armed forces of the Crown being a thing as to which the conditions aforesaid are satisfied.

The Court unanimously distinguished *Bell* v. *Secretary of State for Defence* [1986] Q.B. 322 on the ground that (i) it had been decided *per incuriam* and (ii) as a decision on the meaning of subsection (1) it was not a binding authority on the meaning of subsection (2). In the view of the court in *Pearce* the "thing suffered" (or "anything suffered") must refer to the act causing the death or injury, *e.g.* the exploding grenade; the phrase, particularly in subsection (2), is not apt to refer to some earlier continuing negligent omission., *Bell* was decided *per incuriam* because the Court of Appeal in that earlier case had only considered whether the "thing suffered could be the continuing allegedly negligent omission of the British military doctors. The Court had overlooked that the misdiagnosis at the German civil hospital could constitute the "thing suffered." In *Pearce* the Court concluded that the misdiagnosis *was* the "thing suffered," which occurred outside the limits of subsection (1) so that as Neill L.J. (who gave judgment in *Bell*, said "The actual decision in that case was correct but as I am now satisfied was reached by the wrong route."

In the House of Lords, Lord Brandon of Oakbrook, who delivered the only speech, expressed his complete agreement that

"in relation to the meaning of the expressions "anything suffered" or a "thing" being "suffered" in section 10(1) of the Act of 1947, *Bell's* case was wrongly decided. It follows that I agree with the unanimous view of the Court of Appeal in the present case that, if it were necessary to answer question (2), it should be answered in the affirmative."

REMEDIES AGAINST THE CROWN

Declaration

Dyson v. Attorney-General
[1911] 1 K.B. 410
Court of Appeal

Dyson brought an action against the Attorney-General claiming a declaration that he was under no obligation to comply with the requirements of a form issued to him by the Commissioners of Inland Revenue under the Finance Act 1910. He contended that the commissioners had no power under the Act to require him to answer certain of the questions put. He further complained that he was given several days less than the Act allowed in which to make the return, and that the return was to be made to the village blacksmith instead of (as the Act required) to the commissioners. The form stated that he would be liable to a penalty not exceeding £50 if he failed to deliver the return within the period specified. Lush J., sitting in chambers, held that the action would not lie.

Dyson now appealed to the Court of Appeal (Cozens-Hardy M.R. and Fletcher Moulton and Farwell L.JJ.), who allowed the appeal.

COZENS-HARDY M.R.: . . . It has been settled for centuries that in the Court of Chancery the Attorney-General might in some cases be sued as a defendant as representing the Crown, and that in such a suit relief could be given against the Crown. *Pawlett* v. *Att.-Gen.*[1] is a very early authority on this point. *Laragoity* v. *Att.-Gen.*[2] is a case where this matter was a good deal discussed. In *Deare* v. *Att.-Gen.*[3] the Attorney-General demurred to such a bill. Lord Lyndhurst, at p. 208, says: "I apprehend that the Crown always appears by the Attorney-General in a court of justice, especially in a court of equity, where the interest of the Crown is concerned. Therefore a practice has arisen of filing a bill against the Attorney-General, or of making him a party to a bill, where the interest of the Crown is concerned"; and the demurrer was overruled. But it is said that these authorities have no application except in cases in which the Crown rights are only incidentally concerned, and that where the rights of the Crown are the immediate and sole object of the suit the application must be by petition of right—see Mitford's *Pleadings*, p. 30. I do not think the distinction thus suggested is supported by authority, nor do I think the distinction would avail at the Attorney-General in the present case. The case of *Hodges* v. *Att.-Gen.*[4] is an important decision. I have examined the record, which fully bears out the report with one exception. The plaintiffs were equitable mortgagees by deposit of the title deeds of certain leasehold premises. George Bailey, who had deposited the deeds, was convicted of felony, the result of which was that the legal title was vested in the Crown. The plaintiffs filed their bill in the Exchequer making the Attorney-General sole defendant. It came on before Baron Alderson, "sitting in equity," as he himself stated. The court declared the plaintiffs entitled to an equitable mortgage, or lien, and referred it to the Master to take an account of what was due to the plaintiffs for principal, interest, and costs; and the decree proceeded to order, "By consent of her Majesty's Attorney-General," that the plaintiffs should hold certain premises until they should be fully satisfied what the Master should find to be due to them, and the tenants were directed to attorn. This seems to me a distinct authority that the court has jurisdiction to maintain an action against the Attorney-General as

---

[1] (1677) 3 Hardr. 465.
[2] (1816) 2 Price 172.
[3] (1835) 1 Y. & C. Ex. 197.
[4] (1839) 3 Y. & C. Ex. 342.

representing the Crown, although the immediate and sole object of the suit is to affect the rights of the Crown in favour of the plaintiffs. The only doubt raised in argument was due to the circumstance that the Crown had the legal estate, and that the Crown could not be compelled to convey that legal estate. But Baron Alderson in a considered judgment expressly held that he had jurisdiction to make a declaration and to direct an account, and also to decree that the plaintiffs should hold possession until they were repaid, although it is true that in the decree itself the last part of the relief, but not the earlier parts, was by the consent of the Attorney-General. So far as I can discover, the authority of *Hodges* v. *Att.-Gen.* has never been challenged, and I think it ought to be followed. It was suggested that there was something peculiar in the jurisdiction of the old Court of Exchequer which might account for such a decision. I cannot adopt this view. No doubt the Court of Exchequer on the Revenue side had peculiar functions which are not transferred by the Judicature Act to all branches of the High Court, but its equity jurisdiction had nothing peculiar, as distinguished from the Court of Chancery, to which by statute this jurisdiction was transferred. What the old Court of Chancery could do can now be done by both Divisions of the High Court.

But then it is urged that in the present action no relief is sought except by declaration, and that no such relief ought to be granted against the Crown, there being no precedent for any such action. The absence of any precedent does not trouble me. The power to make declaratory decrees was first granted to the Court of Chancery in 1852 by section 50 of 15 & 16 Vict. c.86. . . . The jurisdiction is, however, now enlarged, for by Order 25, r. 5, "No action or proceeding shall be open to objection, on the ground that a merely declaratory judgment or order is sought thereby, and the court may make binding declarations of right whether any consequential relief is or could be claimed or not."[5] I can see no reason why this section should not apply to an action in which the Attorney-General, as representing the Crown, is a party. The court is not bound to make a mere declaratory judgment, and in the exercise of its discretion will have regard to all the circumstances of the case. I can, however, conceive many cases in which a declaratory judgment may be highly convenient and I am disposed to think, if all other objections are removed, this is a case to which rule 5 might with advantage be applied. But I desire to guard myself against the supposition that I hold that a person who expects to be made defendant, and who prefers to be plaintiff, can, as a matter of right, attain his object by commencing an action to obtain a declaration that his opponent has no good cause of action against him. The court may well say: Wait until you are attacked and then raise your defence, and may dismiss the action with costs. This may be the result in the present case. That, however, is not a matter to be dealt with on an interlocutory application. It is pre-eminently a matter for the trial. In my opinion the plaintiff may assert his rights in an action against the Attorney-General, and is not bound to proceed by petition of right. It is needless to say that I have not expressed, nor have I formed, any opinion as to the substance of the case alleged by the plaintiff. I have dealt only with the question of form. In my opinion the appeal must be allowed and the order discharged. . . .

Appeal allowed.

[5] See now Order 15, r.16. See further *Malone* v. *Metropolitan Police Commissioner* [1979] Ch.344; *ante* p. 209.

R. v. Inland Revenue Commissioners Ex parte Rossminster
[1980] A.C. 952
House of Lords

The facts are set out, *supra* p. 250. The extracts following deal with the second issue before the House of Lords, whether a declaration should have been granted that the seizure of the documents was unlawful.

LORD WILBERFORCE: ... The second matter, on which the intervention of the court may be called for, arises under section 20C(3). This confers a statutory power independent of any authority in the warrant to seize and remove. Like all statutory powers conferred on executive officers it is subject to supervision by the courts exercising their classic and traditional powers of judicial review. It is undisputed that the words "has reasonable cause to believe" are open to examination in spite of their subjective form: see *Nakkuda Ali* v. *Jayaratne* [1951] A.C. 66 et al. The existence of this reasonable cause and of the belief founded upon it is ultimately a question of fact to be tried on evidence.

So far as regards these appeals the issue is complicated in three ways. First, it has been raised at an interlocutory stage, and at the very beginning of the investigation, upon affidavit evidence. Secondly, the revenue have refused, so far, to disclose their reasonable grounds, claiming immunity from so doing, on the grounds stated above. Thirdly, the defendants being, in effect, the Crown or Crown servants, an interlocutory injunction cannot be granted (section 21 of the Crown Proceedings Act 1947).

The Court of Appeal sought to meet this situation by granting a declaration: and recognising, rightly in my opinion, that an interim declaration could not be granted, gave a final declaration in effect that the revenue had exceeded their powers. I regret that I cannot agree that this was correct. It is to me apparent that there was a substantial conflict of evidence as to the manner in which the searches were carried out, the respondents broadly contending that the officers gave no real consideration to the question whether individual documents might be required as evidence: the revenue asserting that they had detailed instructions what to look for and seize and that these were complied with. I shall not further analyse this issue which was fully and satisfactorily treated by the Divisional Court, for I am satisfied that even if, which I doubt, there might have been enough evidence to justify the granting of interlocutory relief, this fell very far short of supporting a final declaration. I believe that the Court of Appeal was itself really of this opinion. The final declaration granted must clearly be set aside.

Two remarks in conclusion. First I would wish to make it clear that the failure of the respondents at this stage is not necessarily the end of the matter. They can proceed with an action against the revenue for, in effect, excess of power and for trespass and any aggravation can be taken into account. At some stage, which cannot be particularised now with precision but which broadly would be when criminal proceedings are over, or, within a reasonable time, are not taken, the immunity which exists at the stage of initial investigation will lapse. Then the revenue will have to make good and specify the existence and cause of their belief that things removed might be required as evidence for the purpose of "tax fraud" proceedings and the issue will be tried in a normal manner. Secondly, I must express reservations as to the suggestion that the law ought to be changed so as to allow interim declarations to be granted. As regards persons other than the Crown, I see no need for this head of relief, given the power to grant interim injunctions. As regards the Crown I can see that there may be formidable objections against allowing, on incomplete evidence, a form of relief which in effect, may have much the same effect as an injunction. As I have already commented in another context, sensible limits have to be set upon the courts' powers of judicial review of administrative action: these I think, as at present advised, are satis-factorily set by the law as it stands.

LORD DIPLOCK: ...
The final declaration
There was a clear conflict of affidavit evidence of relevant facts before the Court of Appeal as to the time spend by officers in examining individual documents and files before deciding to seize them. The respondents contend the time spent on examining at any rate some of the documents seized was too short to enable the officer concerned to consider whether or not there was reasonable cause to believe that the documents might be required as evidence in criminal proceedings; the appellants deny this. Clearly there are issues of fact to be resolved which cannot with justice be disposed of on the existing affidavit evidence.

The Court of Appeal were of opinion, which I do not share, that on the affidavit evidence before them the respondents had made out a prima facie case that all the documents had been seized unlawfully, and ought to be delivered up to the respondents. But for the fact that the appellants were officers of the Crown against whom there was no jurisdiction to grant injunctive relief, it would appear that the Court of Appeal would have thought it appropriate to grant an interloc-utory injunction only, leaving the question of whether the respondents were entitled to a final injunction to be decided on full oral evidence at the trial. However, section 21 of the Crown Proceedings Act 1947 permits only a declaration of the rights of the parties in lieu of an injunction against officers of the Crown and it has been held, in my continued view correctly, that this does not empower the court to grant interlocutory declarations which would be a contradiction in terms: *International General Electric Co. of New York Ltd.* v. *Customs and Excise Commissioners* [1962] Ch. 784. Faced with this dilemma the Court of Appeal made a final declaration instead.

In so far as this declaration was based upon the quashing of the search warrant only it may be that a final declaration was appropriate, though I express no concluded view on that; but in so far as it was based in the alternative upon the court's prima facie view only, formed upon conflicting affidavit evidence, that even if the warrant were valid the actual seizure of documents by the officers of the board was unlawful, it was, in my view, clearly wrong to make a final declaration which would have the effect of making this hotly disputed issue res judicata between the parties without any proper trial.

My Lords, this serves once again to draw attention to what, for my part, I regard as a serious procedural defect in the English system of administrative law: it provides no means of obtaining interlocutory relief against the Crown and its officers. The useful reforms effected by the amendment to the Rules of the Court by substituting the new Order 53 for the old system of prerogative orders, could not overcome this procedural defect, which would require primary legislation. Such legislation has been recommended in the Report of the Law Commission on which the revision of Order 53 was based. It is greatly to be hoped that the recommendation will not continue to fall upon deaf parliamentary ears.
Appeal allowed.

Note
In *Clarke* v. *Chadburn* [1985] 1 W.L.R. 78 Sir Robert Megarry V.-C. granted a final declaration in interlocutory proceedings. Despite a court order to the contrary a meeting of the National Union of Miners passed resolutions purporting to alter its rules. The plaintiffs sought a declaration that the new rules were void and an injunction to restrain the union from acting upon them.

SIR ROBERT MEGARRY V.-C. .... I need not cite authority for the proposition that it is of high importance that orders of the court should be obeyed. Wilful disobedi-ence to an order of the court is punishable as a contempt of court and I feel no

doubt that such disobedience may properly be described as being illegal. If by such disobedience the persons enjoined claim that they have validly effected some change in the rights and liabilities of others, I cannot see why it should be said that although they are liable to penalties for contempt of court for doing what they did, nevertheless those acts were validly done. Of course, if an act is done, it is not undone merely by pointing out that it was done in breach of the law. If a meeting is held in breach of an injunction, it cannot be said that the meeting has not been held. But the legal consequences of what has been done in breach of the law may plainly be very much affected by the illegality. It seems to me on principle that those who defy a prohibition ought not to be able to claim that the fruits of their defiance are good, and not tainted by the illegality that produced them . . .
. . . the resolution of the N.U.M. changing their rules at their conference held on 11 and 12 July are void for illegality. . . .

The question, then, is whether the court can properly make the declaration sought by the plaintiffs on this motion. Mr. Burton was not satisfied with an injunction against enforcing the new rule about discipline because that would require application to the court to enforce it, whereas a declaration did not. One difficulty is that in modern practice there appears to be no such thing as an interim declaration: but Mr. Burton said that what he wanted was a final declaration, and not an interim declaration. For this, he relied on *International General Electric Company of New York Ltd.* v. *Customs and Excise Commissioners* [1962] Ch. 784. There, Upjohn L.J., with the concurrence of Diplock L.J., rejected the concept of an interim declaration, but envisaged the possibility that in certain cases it might be proper to make a declaration of rights in interlocutory proceedings, though this jurisdiction would be infrequently and sparingly exercised. Such a declaration would finally determine the point, and would not operate only as a declaration for the interim. This statement, I think, was plainly made obiter. Even if one accepts to the full that it correctly states the law, as I do, there is still the question whether the case before me is one which justifies me in exercising this jurisdiction. I also bear in mind that although this motion is inter partes, all five defendants have chosen to be absent and unrepresented, the first and second for good reason, and so I have been deprived of the advantage of hearing what could be said on the other side.

After some hesitation I have come to the conclusion that the circumstances of this case are such that I ought to make the declaration sought. I need not expand on the bitter divisions that now exist in the coal mining industry, on the acts of violence that are common knowledge, or on the attempts made by the majority to intimidate the minority and to prevent them voting. If the N.U.M. chooses to conduct itself fairly and properly in accordance with its own rules, then of course the proposed changes in the rules could be made and would be upheld by the courts. But as long as it disregards its own rules and democratic process for which the rules provide, it must not be surprised if it finds that any changes of rules made by these means are struck with invalidity.

Injunction

R. v. Secretary of State for The Home Department Ex parte Herbage
[1986] 3 W.L.R. 504
Queen's Bench Division

The facts are set out in the judgment of Hodgson J.

HODGSON J.: . . . In these proceedings the applicant seeks interlocutory relief against the respondents. The form of relief sought is an interlocutory interim injunction. The respondents are the Secretary of State for the Home Department and the Governor of Pentonville Prison. The relief sought is an injunction which in its mandatory from reads:

"A mandatory injunction . . . directing that they take all necessary steps forthwith to ensure that, subject only to the proper application of the Prison Rules 1964, the applicant is granted the same opportunities of association with fellow prisoners as are accorded generally to unconvicted prisoners."

The applicant is detained in Pentonville Prison. He is in custody awaiting an extradition warrant for surrender to the United States of America in respect of 25 charges of dishonesty, Those proceedings the applicant is seeking to impugn in habeas corpus proceedings.

In his affidavit the applicant complains of the conditions under which he is detained. There are many complaints. . . .

Very briefly, the applicant's argument in the substantive application can be summarised. The Bill of Rights 1688 is a statute. It prohibits the infliction of "cruell and unusuall punishment." A breach of the provisions of the Bill of Rights can itself ground an application for judicial review. *Attorney-General* v. *Wilts United Dairies Ltd.* (1921) 37 T.L.R. 884, 886, and *Congreve* v. *Home Office* [1976] Q.B. 629, 652, are cited. Specific statutory duties are placed upon the Secretary of State by sections 1, 4(2) and 12 of The Prison Act 1952. Both the Prison Act 1952 and the Prison Rules 1964 made thereunder must be interpreted and exercised so as to give effect to rights recognised by the Bill of Rights and the European Convention on Human Rights. *Reg.* v. *Secretary of State for the Home Department, Ex parte Phansopkar* [1976] Q.B. 606, 626, is cited. Illegality in the performance of statutory powers and duties by the Secretary of State and by the governor are reviewable, and failure to have regard to the Prison Rules 1964 can be taken into account. *Reg.* v. *Secretary of State for the Home Department, Ex parte McAvoy* [1984] 1 W.L.R. 1408 is cited

On the basis of the applicant's affidavit and also certain medical evidence exhibited to an affidavit sworn by the applicant's solicitor. I granted the applicant leave to move for judicial review by way of mandamus directed to the respondents. Since then the respondents have filed evidence in the form of a full and detailed affidavit from the governor. It puts in issue practically everything contained in the applicant's affidavit. The medical evidence may also be in issue. . . .

In opposing this application, Mr. Laws submits that it fails in limine because an interim injunction does not lie against an officer of the Crown and both the Secretary of State and the governor are such officers.

I turn first therefore to consider the question whether on a proper construction of the relevant legislation there is jurisdiction in this court to grant an interim injunction against an officer of the Crown.

The immunity of the Crown and its officers from injunctive relief is to be found in section 21 of the Crown Proceedings Act 1947. Prior to the Act of 1947 the remedy in private law matters against the Crown was by way of petition of right in the High Court. It was confined to four cases, debt due under contract or statute, unliquidated sums due by statute, damages for breach of contract, and recovery of property. Proceedings on the Crown side of the King's Bench Division consisted and consisted only of habeas corpus, mandamus, prohibition, certiorari, and injunction in the nature of quo warranto. These procedures have escaped the procedural reform of the 19th century, although they have been slightly modernised by the alteration of title from writ to order by the Administration of Justice (Miscellaneous Provisions) Act 1938. There was no remedy by way of injunction available on the Crown side of the King's Bench Division, nor was any interim relief available.

Section 21 of the Crown Proceedings Act 1947 provides:

"(1) In any civil proceedings by or against the Crown the court shall, subject to the provisions of this Act, have power to make all such orders as it has power to make in proceedings between subjects, and otherwise to give such appropriate relief as the case may require: Provided that:—(a) where in any proceedings against the Crown any such relief is sought as might in proceedings between subjects be granted by way of injunction for specific performance, the court shall not grant an injunction or make an order for specific performance, but may in lieu thereof make an order declaratory of the rights of the parties: ... (2) The court shall not in any civil proceedings grant any injunction or make any order against an officer of the Crown if the effect of granting the injunction or making the order would be to give any relief against the Crown which could not have been obtained in proceedings against the Crown."

By Section 38(2) it is provided:

" 'Civil proceedings includes proceedings in the High Court or the county court for the recovery of fines or penalties, but does not include proceedings on the Crown side of the King's Bench Division."

It follows that section 21(1) does not apply to Crown side proceedings. The proviso is a proviso to section 21(1).

Mr. Laws submits that because the word used is "proceedings," not "civil proceedings," it has a wider implication and effectively prevents any injunction lying in Crown side proceedings against the Home Secretary. This, with respect, seems to me to be reading far more into that subsection than it can possibly bear. To begin with it applies to the Crown, not its servants. Section 21(2) deals with officers of the Crown. Secondly, prerogative remedies do not in any event lie against the Crown. The only proceedings that can be brought against the Crown are those brought by writ or originating summons under the Act of 1947. There was no need to repeat the word "civil" in the proviso.

Of course the prerogative orders lie against officers of the Crown including ministers, save where the Crown's servant is merely the instrument selected by the Crown for the discharge of the Crown's own duty: see Wade, Administrative Law, 5th ed. (1982), p. 645, and the cases were cited. But in nearly every case mandamus will lie against a minister or department. "When by statute an officer or servant of the Crown has also a duty towards a member of the public" mandamus will lie at the suit of any member of the public who has a sufficient interest: see Reg. v. Commissioners of Customs and Excise, Ex parte Cook [1970] 1 W.L.R. 450, per Lord Parker C.J.

Put another way, where Parliament imposes a duty on someone acting in a particular capacity, mandamus will lie notwithstanding that he is a servant of the Crown and acting on the Crown's behalf: see Padfield v. Minister of Agriculture, Fisheries and Food [1968] A.C. 997 and Reg. v. Secretary of State for the Home Department, Ex parte Phansopkar [1976] Q.B. 606. The use of mandamus against Crown servants is specifically reserved by section 40(5) of the Act of 1947 which reads:

"This Act shall not operate to limit the discretion of the court to grant relief by way of mandamus in cases in which such relief might have been granted before the commencement of this Act notwithstanding that by reason of the provisions of this Act some other and further remedy is available."

It is clear from that subsection that the Act of 1947 contemplated the use of the new procedure in public law matters.

Section 21(2) deals with injunctions against officers of the Crown. (In section 38 "officer of the Crown" is defined to include a minister of the Crown.) If I had to construe that subsection in the absence of authority, I would read it as preventing the Crown being enjoined by the expedient of enjoining a minister selected by the Crown for the discharge of the Crown's own duty. However, in *Merricks* v. *Heathcoat-Amory* [1955] Ch. 567 a mandatory injunction was sought against the Minister of Agriculture, Fisheries and Food to make him withdraw a draft scheme for potato marketing which had been laid before Parliament and was allegedly ultra vires. Although the Agricultural Marketing Acts 1958 and 1983 provided that it was the minister who was to make such schemes, so that the power resided in him rather than the Crown itself, the court held that any remedy by way of injunction was barred by section 21(2): see also *Harper* v. *Secretary of State for the Home Department* [1955] Ch. 238. It is, however, noticeable that Upjohn J. said [1955] Ch. 567, 575:

"Of course there can be an official representing the Crown, that is plainly this case. But if he were not, it was said that he was a person designated in an official capacity but not representing the Crown. The third suggestion was that his capacity was purely that of an individual. I understand the conception of the first and the third categories, but I confess to finding it difficult to see how the second category can fit into any ordinary scheme.

It seems to me questionable whether that dictum can survive in view of later decisions such as *Padfield* v. *Minister of Agriculture, Fisheries and Food* [1968]A.C. 997.

The decision in *Merricks'* case has been criticised as anomalous by Professor Wade who points out that the minister in those circumstances would be liable to compulsory orders in Crown side proceedings: see *Wade, Administrative Law*, 5th ed., p. 519.

In *Reg.* v. *Secretary of State for the Home Department, Ex parte Kirkwood* [1984] 1 W.L.R. 913; [1984] 1 All E.R. 390 the Secretary of State had issued a warrant under section 11 of the Extradition Act 1870 ordering the applicant to be surrendered to the United States authority. Leave to apply for judicial review was granted and the court directed that the grant of leave should operate as a stay of proceedings on the warrant until the application for judicial review was determined. On the minister's application to discharge the stay Mann J. held, as set out in the headnote [1984] 2 All E.R. 390, 391:

"The stay would be discharged because the court was prohibited by section 21 of the 1947 Act from granting an injunction against an officer of the Crown and the stay was equivalent to an injunction restraining the Secretary of State from exercising his executive function. In any event, when exercising his powers under the [Extradition Act 1870] the Secretary of State was not obliged to consider the provisions of the European Convention on Human Rights since it was not part of the law of the United Kingdom; and accordingly, even if there had been jurisdiction to grant the stay, the court would still have ordered it to be removed because the applicant's chances of success by way of judicial review were negligible ..."

Unfortunately no one drew Mann J.'s attention to section 38 of the Crown Proceedings Act 1947 and, indeed, it was "common ground between the parties that proceedings by way of judicial review are civil proceedings": see. at p.393G. That seems to me to have been plainly wrong, "Civil proceedings" in the Act of

1947 are specifically defined to exclude Crown side proceedings. Mann J. felt himself bound to *Reg.* v. *Secretary of State for the Home Department, Ex parte Mohammed Yaqoob (Note)* [1984] 1 W.L.R. 920, a decision of Dillon L.J. sitting as a single judge in the Court of Appeal, but that was in a case brought by originating summons and so fell squarely within the Act. I note, however, that in referring to subsection (2) Mann J. said [1984] 1 W.L.R. 913, 917:

> "In my judgment the sole purpose of subsection (2) is to prevent the subject from achieving indirectly a result which he could not achieve directly by reason of the provisions of subsection (1)."

It seems clear, however, that since 1947 the courts have construed section 21(2) as excluding injunctive relief against an officer of the Crown even when acting under statutory powers or duties specifically laid upon him. I take leave to doubt whether the courts have been correct in so construing section 21(2) but, as I have been referred to no case where this contrary view has been taken, I must assume, I think, that my doubts are without foundation.

After 1947, therefore, anyone wishing to pursue a public law remedy against an officer of the Crown where Parliament has imposed a specific duty upon that officer had two avenues open to him. He could either proceed by writ or originating summons under the Act of 1947, or he could seek a prerogative order from the Divisional Court. On the construction placed by the courts on section 21(2) he could only obtain declaratory relief under the Act of 1947. An interim declaration being unavailable he could obtain no interim relief under the Act. Interim relief was not available in Crown side proceedings for an order of mandamus (though in certiorari and prohibition proceedings a stay could be ordered).

In 1976 the Law Commission reported on Remedies in Administrative Law (Law Com. No. 73; Cmnd. 6407). Many of its recommendations were adopted and implemented by changes in the Rules of the Supreme court. The new R.S.C. Ord. 53, came into force the following year. The Law Commission had thought that legislation would be necessary to effect the changes it recommended, and statutory backing was somewhat unusually given to the new rules four years later by the Supreme Court Act 1981. Section 31(1) and (2) of the Act of 1981 provides:

> "(1) An application to the High Court for one or more of the following forms of relief, namely—(a) an order of mandamus, prohibition or certiorari; (b) a declaration or injunction under subsection (2); or"—and I omit (c) the quo warranto proviso— "shall be made in accordance with rules of court by a procedure to be known as an application for judicial review. (2) A declaration may be made or an injunction granted under this subsection in any case where an application for judicial review, seeking that relief has been made and the High Court considers that, having regard to—(a) the nature of the matters in respect of which relief may be granted by orders of mandamus, prohibition or certiorari; (b) the nature of the persons and bodies against whom relief may be granted by such orders; and (c) all the circumstances of the case, it would be just and convenient for the declaration to be made or the injunction to be granted, as the case may be."

Subsection (2) is, in all material respects, in precisely the same terms as clause 2 of the draft bill appended to the Law Commission report. The reason why the draft clause was in guideline terms was because the remit to the commission did not include any examination of substantive law, but plainly the object was to ensure that in judicial review proceedings declarations and injunctions would only be granted in public law matters: see paragraph 45 of the report. It is equally clear that where mandamus lies against an officer of the Crown, then a declaration or injunction does also. A final mandatory injunction is not necessary: mandamus achieves the same result.

It is perhaps pertinent here to note that there is nothing in the Supreme Court

Act 1981 which permits judicial review proceedings to be brought against the Crown itself. In those comparatively rare cases therefore, such as *Reg.* v. *Secretary of State for War* [1891] 2 Q.B. 326 and *Reg.* v. *Lords Commissioners of the Treasury* (1872) L.R. 7 Q.B. 387, where a Crown servant is merely the instrument selected by the Crown for the discharge of its own duties, proceedings can only be brought under the Act of 1947. This would seem to constitute an exception to what the House of Lords has laid down in *O'Reilly* v. *Mackman* [1983] 2 A.C. 237.

The Law Commission considered that it was a procedural defect that in proceedings under the Crown Proceedings Act 1947 no interlocutory relief was available. Accordingly it recommended that, in proceedings against the Crown, the court should have power to declare the terms of an interim injunction which would have been granted in proceedings between subjects alone. It recommended that this should be achieved by amendment to the Crown Proceedings Act 1947: see paragraph 51 and clause 3(2) to the draft bill appended to the report.

However, the specific recommendation for interim relief against the Crown and its officers in proceedings under the Act of 1947 was not implemented but a general provision as to interim relief was included in the Rules of the Supreme Court. R.S.C., Ord. 53, r.3(10) reads:

"Where leave to apply for judicial review is granted, then—(*a*) if the relief sought is an order of prohibition or certiorari and the court so directs, the grant shall operate as a stay of the proceedings to which the application relates until the determination of the application or until the court otherwise orders; (*b*) if any other relief is sought, the court may at any time grant in the proceedings such interim relief as could be granted in an action begun by writ."

Mr. Newman suggests that there are two possible meanings to rule 3(10)(*b*): (a) mere enabling power allowing the court to grant to an applicant for judicial review all the interlocutory remedies available in an action begun by writ; or (b) the applicant has to show that in fact he has a possible private law cause of action which he could have commenced by writ. It seems to me that the second of those meanings is quite impossible. If an applicant's cause of action is a private law one he would be in the wrong jurisdiction if seeking judicial review.

Mr. Laws submits a third meaning. He says, if I have understood him correctly, that the court has to do this exercise: first decide what relief is sought and against whom; second see whether against that person interim relief would have been available if the relief had been sought by writ. If interim relief would not have been available, then it is not available in R.S.C., Ord. 53 proceedings.

Applying that construction to the facts of this case the argument is that proceedings against an officer of the Crown can only be brought by writ under the Act of 1947; on the accepted construction of section 21(2) an injunction will not lie against a servant of the Crown. Therefore an interim injunction will not lie either. I find this argument unacceptable. It seems to me that, on its plain meaning, the rule merely makes available to the court the interlocutory remedies available in actions begun by writ. Judicial review proceedings can (subject to the qualification mentioned above) be brought against a minister; so long as the guidelines in section 31(2) are complied with an injunction will therefore lie against a minister, and that being so it seems to me that on its plain meaning Ord. 53, r. 3(10) (*b*) permits an interim injunction to be made. This partially achieves, though by a different route, the Law Commission recommendation that interim relief should be available against an officer of the Crown while retaining the immunity from interim relief of the Crown itself.

There is perhaps another argument which could be deployed by the Secretary of State, though it is not one advanced by Mr. Laws. It could be argued that, as guideline (b) requires the court to have regard in deciding whether to grant an injunction to the nature of the person against whom relief can be granted, it

should not grant one against a Crown servant because such relief in actions begun
by writ is not available. But that argument does not convince me and would be a
construction contrary to what the Law Commission intended which, as I have
pointed out, was to restrict the new power to the public law field.

I conclude therefore that the court has jurisdiction to grant an interim injunction
against an officer of the Crown and that accordingly I would have jurisdiction to
grant the interim relief sought in these proceedings against both respondents.

Even if I am right as to the jurisdiction point, I have no doubt that, in the
exercise of my discretion, I ought not to grant interim relief in this case.

On this aspect of the case most of Mr. Laws' submissions have naturally been
aimed at the merits of the substantive case. In the same way as, at the outset of this
judgment, I outlined the applicant's case, I now outline Mr. Laws' case as I
understand it.

So far as the governor is concerned, the decision of the Court of Appeal in *Reg.*
v. *Deputy Governor of Camphill Prison, Ex parte King* [1985] Q.B. 735 decides that this
court cannot exercise any control over a prison governor in the exercise of his
managerial responsibilities, even if his actions constituted a breach of the provisions of the Bill of Rights.[1] In any event the Bill of Rights cannot now be invoked
against an officer of the Crown; nor can it be used to justify the court in making an
impermissible investigation into the facts. (Incidentally, in my judgment the
governor is an officer of the Crown with specific powers and duties imposed upon
him by Parliament.) So far as the Secretary of State is concerned no proceedings
can be brought against him. No proceedings can be brought against him unless it
is shown that he has been petitioned to exercise his powers of control over the
conduct of the prison and he has failed to do so: see *Ex parte King*. He is
empowered to exercise control over the prison and its staff and must be shown to
have failed in that duty. There is no evidence that he has been relevantly petitioned. In any event the court is entitled to come to the conclusion on the affidavit
evidence that the applicant's case fails on the facts.

Not surprisingly there is no guidance as to the principles which ought to apply
when a court is considering the granting of interim relief against officers of the
Crown. Until today no one thought it could be done. I agree with Mr. Newman
that the principles governing interim injunctions in civil proceedings are not
particularly helpful. Clearly the apparent strengths and weaknesses of the two
opposing cases ought to be considered and, as at present advised and without
deciding anything, the obstacles in the way of the applicant's substantive case
seem to me to be formidable indeed. It seems to me also to be clear that it would be
only in very exceptional circumstances that the court would interim mandatory
relief in respect of the administrative functions of officers of the Crown. I agree
with Mr. Newman that there would have to be shown to be great urgency to
prevent the danger of serious injury or damage occurring. The interim relief
sought in these proceedings relates only to the lack of association, and I am quite
unable to see how it would be a proper exercise of discretion to grant that relief. I
should say that the fact that the relief can be and has been cast in a non-mandatory
fashion in the alternative does not alter my view as to the circumstances which
would be necessary before the court would grant that interim relief. It follows that
this application fails.

Application dismissed.

---

[1] An appeal was dismissed on procedural grounds, but both Purchas L.J. and Sir David
Cairns thought the court could exercise jurisdiction over a prison governor alleged to be
acting in breach of the Bill of Rights: [1987] Q.B. 1077. And see now *Leech* v. *Deputy
Governor of Parkhurst Prison* [1988] 2 W.L.R. R.290.

Note

Damages
In private law actions against the Crown, *e.g.* in contract or tort, damages are available in the normal way, as against a private litigant.

The only remedy for wrongs in the sphere of public law is by way of application for judicial review under Order 53 : *An Bord Bainne Co-operative Ltd.* v. *Milk Marketing Board, The Times*, November 20, 1987 (C.A.), following *Bourgoin S.A.* v. *Minister of Agriculture, Fisheries and Food* [1986] 1 Q.B. 716.

Order 53, r.7 refers to a power to award damages but in circumstances where the applicant does have a private law right of action. See *R.* v. *Liverpool City Council, Ex parte Coade, The Times* October 10, 1986: Simon Brown J. accepted that a claim for outstanding arrears of statutory remuneration fell within Ord. 53, r.7 and issued an order in the form of *mandamus* to pay the outstanding sums. On the otherhand his Lordship thought it was wholly inappropriate to pursue a claim for unquantified damages for distress and inconvenience by judicial review.

The possibility of damages under Ord. 53 may also arise by virtue of the Court's power to award damages in lieu of an injunction under the Supreme Court Act 1981, s.50.

CROWN PRIVILEGE : PUBLIC INTEREST IMMUNITY

Conway v. Rimmer
[1968] A.C. 910: [1968] 2 W.L.R. 1535 (Note)
House of Lords

Conway, a former probationary police constable, began an action for malicious prosecution against Rimmer, his former superintendent. In the course of discovery, the defendant disclosed a list of documents, admittedly relevant to the plaintiff's action, which included four reports made by him about the plaintiff during his period of probation, and a report made by him to his chief constable for transmission to the Director of Public Prosecutions in connection with the prosecution of the plaintiff on indictment for the theft of an electric torch valued at 15s. 3d., on which he was acquitted, and on which his civil action was based. The Home Secretary objected to the production of all five documents on the ground that each fell within a class of documents the production of which would be injurious to the public interest.

The District Registrar made an interlocutory order for the production of the documents. Browne J. (in chambers) reversed his order, and the Court of Appeal (Davies and Russell L.JJ., Lord Denning M.R. dissenting) affirmed his decision. The House of Lords (Lord Reid, Lord Morris of Borth-y-Gest, Lord Hodson, Lord Pearce and Lord Upjohn) unanimously allowed the plaintiff's appeal and reversed the decision of the Court of Appeal.

February 28, 1968. LORD REID stated the facts and continued: My Lords, these documents may be of crucial importance in this action. The appellant has to prove both malice and want of probable cause. If the probationary reports were favourable that may tell strongly in favour of the appellant on the question of malice, if they were unfavourable and were not prepared by the respondent they will tell strongly against the appellant in this issue. The respondent's report to the chief constable may well be decisive in the question of want of probable cause. If the respondent included in the report all relevant facts known to him and if no further relevant facts became known to him between the making of the report and the making of the charge, then advice by the Director of Public Prosecutions that prosecution would be justified would make it practically impossible to establish want of probable cause. But if relevant facts known to the respondent were not included the position would be very different.

[His Lordship set out the affidavit of the Home Secretary and continued:] The question whether such a statement by a Minister of the Crown should be accepted as conclusively preventing any court from ordering production of any of the documents to which it applies is one of very great importance in the administration of justice. If the commonly accepted interpretation of the decision of this House in *Duncan* v. *Cammell, Laird & Co. Ltd.*[1] is to remain authoritative the question admits of only one answer—the Minister's statement is final and conclusive. Normally I would be very slow to question the authority of a unanimous decision of this House only 25 years old which was carefully considered and obviously intended to lay down a general rule. But this decision has several abnormal features.

Lord Simon thought that on this matter the law in Scotland was the same as the law in England and he clearly intended to lay down a rule applicable to the whole of the United Kingdom. But in *Glasgow Corporation* v. *Central Land Board*[2] this House held that that was not so, with the result that today on this question the law is different in the two countries. There are many chapters of the law where for

[1] [1942] A.C. 624; 58 T.L.R. 242; [1942] 1 All E.R. 587 (H.L.).
[2] 1956 S.C. (H.L.) 1.

historical and other reasons it is quite proper that the law should be different in the two countries. But here we are dealing purely with public policy—with the proper relation between the powers of the executive and the powers of the courts—and I can see no rational justification for the law on this matter being different in the two countries.

Secondly, events have proved that the rule supposed to have been laid down in *Duncan's* case[3] is far from satisfactory. In the large number of cases in England and elsewhere which have been citied in argument much dissatisfaction has been expressed and I have not observed even one expression of whole-hearted approval. Moreover a statement made by the Lord Chancellor in 1956 on behalf of the Government, to which I shall return later, makes it clear that that Government did not regard it as consonant with public policy to maintain the rule to the full extent which existing authorities had held to be justifiable.

I have no doubt that the case of *Duncan v. Cammell, Laird & Co. Ltd.*[4] was rightly decided. The plaintiff sought discovery of documents relating to the submarine *Thetis* including a contract for the hull and machinery and plans and specifications. The First Lord of the Admiralty had stated that "it would be injurious to the public interest that any of the said documents should be disclosed to any person." Any of these documents might well have given valuable information, or at least clues, to the skilled eye of an agent of a foreign power. But Lord Simon L.C. took the opportunity to deal with the whole question of the right of the Crown to prevent production of documents in a litigation. Yet a study of his speech leaves me with the strong impression that throughout he had primarily in mind cases where discovery or disclosure would involve a danger of real prejudice to the national interest. I find it difficult to believe that his speech would have been the same if the case had related, as the present case does, to discovery of routine reports on a probationer constable.

Early in his speech Lord Simon quoted with approval[5] the view of Rigby L.J., in *Attorney-General v. Newcastle-upon-Tyne Corporation*[6] that documents are not to be withheld "unless there be some plain overruling principle of public interest concerned which cannot be disregarded." And, summing up towards the end, he said[7]: ". . . the rule that the interest of the state must not be put in jeopardy by producing documents which would injure it is a principle to be observed in administrating justice, quite unconnected with the interests or claims of the particular parties in litigation." Surely it would be grotesque to speak of the interest of the state being put in jeopardy by disclosure of a routine report on a probationer.

Lord Simon did not say very much about objections[8] "based upon the view that the public interest requires a particular class of communications with, or within, a public department to be protected from production on the ground that the candour and completeness of such communications might be prejudiced if they were ever liable to be disclosed in subsequent litigation rather than on the contents of the particular document itself." But at the end[9] he said that a Minister "ought not to take the responsibility of withholding production except in cases where the public interest would otherwise be damnified, for example, where disclosure would be injurious to national defence, or to good diplomatic relations, or where the practice of keeping a class of documents secret is necessary for the proper functioning of the public service." I find it difficult to believe that he would have put these three examples on the same level if he had intended the third to

---

[3] [1942] A.C. 624.
[4] *Ibid.*
[5] [1942] A.C. 624 at p. 633.
[6] [1897] 2 Q.B. 384, 395 (C.A.).
[7] [1942] A.C. 624 at p. 642.
[8] *Ibid.* 635.
[9] *Ibid.* 642.

cover such minor matters as a routine report by a relatively junior officer. And my impression is strengthened by the passage at the very end of the speech[10]: "... the public interest is also the interest of every subject of the realm, and while, in these exceptional cases, the private citizen may seem to be denied what is to his immediate advantage, he, like the rest of us, would suffer if the needs of protecting the interests of the country as a whole were not ranked as a prior obligation." Would he have spoken of "these exceptional cases" or of "the needs of protecting the interests of the country as a whole" if he had intended to include all manner of routine communication? And did he really mean that the protection of such communications is a "prior obligation" in a case where a man's reputation or fortune is at stake and withholding the document makes it impossible for justice to be done

It is universally recognised that here there are two kinds of public interest which may clash. There is the public interest that harm shall not be done to the nation or the public service by disclosure of certain documents, and there is the public interest that the administration of justice shall not be frustrated by the withholding of documents which must be produced if justice is to be done. There are many cases where the nature of the injury which would or might be done to the nation or the public service is of so grave a character that no other interest, public or private, can be allowed to prevail over it. With regard to such cases it would be proper to say, as Lord Simon did, that to order production of the document in question would put the interest of the state in jeopardy. But there are many other cases where the possible injury to the public service is much less and there one would think that it would be proper to balance the public interest involved. I do not believe that Lord Simon really meant that the smallest probability of injury to the public service must always outweigh the gravest frustration of the administration of justice.

It is to be observed that, in a passage which I have already quoted, Lord Simon referred to the practice of keeping a class of documents secret being "*necessary* [my italics] for the proper functioning of the public interest." But the certificate of the Home Secretary in the present case does not go nearly so far as that. It merely says that the production of a document of the classes to which it refers would be "injurious to the public interest": it does not say what degree of injury is to be apprehended. It may be advantageous to the functioning of the public service that reports of this kind should be kept secret—that is the view of the Home Secretary—but I would be very surprised if anyone said that that is necessary.

There are now many large public bodies, such as British Railways and the National Coal Board, the proper and efficient functioning of which, is very necessary for many reasons including the safety of the public. The Attorney-General made it clear that Crown privilege is not and cannot be invoked to prevent disclosure of similar documents made by them or their servants even if it were said that this is required for the proper and efficient functioning of that public service. I find it difficult to see why it should be *necessary* to withhold whole classes of routine "communications with or within a public department" but quite unnecessary to withhold similar communications with or within a public corporation. There the safety of the public may well depend on the candour and completeness of reports made by subordinates whose duty it is to draw attention to defects. But, so far as I know, no one has ever suggested that public safety has been endangered by the candour or completeness of such reports having been inhibited by the fact that they may have to be produced if the interest of the due administration of justice should ever require production at any time.

I must turn now to a statement made by the Lord Chancellor, Lord Kilmuir, in this House on June 6, 1956. When counsel proposed to read this statement your Lordships had doubts, which I shared, as to its admissibility. But we did permit it

[10] [1942] A.C. 624 at p. 643.

to be read, and, as the argument proceeded, its importance emerged. With a minor amendment made on March 8, 1962, it appears still to operate as a direction to, or at least a guide for, Ministers who swear affidavits. So we may assume that in the present case the Home Secretary acted in accordance with the views expressed in Lord Kilmuir's statement.

The statement sets out the grounds on which Crown privilege is to be claimed. Having set out the first ground that disclosure of the contents of the particular document would injure the public interest, it proceeds: "The second ground is that the document falls within a class which the public interest requires to be withheld from production and Lord Simon particularised this head of public interest as "the proper functioning of the public service." There is no reference to Lord Simon's exhortation, which I have already quoted, that a Minister ought not to take the responsibility of withholding production of a class of documents except where the practice of keeping a class of documents secret is necessary for the proper functioning of the public service. Then the statement proceeds: "The reason why the law sanctions the claiming of Crown priviledge on the 'class' ground is the need to secure freedom and candour of communication with and within the public service, so that Government decisions can be taken on the best advice and with the fullest information. In order to secure this it is necessary that the class of document to which privilege applies should be clearly settled, so that the person giving advice or information should know that he is doing so in confidence. Any system whereby a document falling within the class might, as a result of a later decision, be required to be produced in evidence, would destroy that confidence and undermine the whole basis of class privilege, because there would be no certainty at the time of writing that the document would not be disclosed."

But later in the statement the position taken is very different. A number of cases are set out in which Crown privilege should not be claimed. The most important for present purposes is: "We also propose that if medical documents, or indeed other documents, are relevant to the defence in criminal proceedings, Crown privilege should not be claimed." The only exception specifically mentioned is statements by informers. That is a very wide ranging exception, for the Attorney-General stated that it applied at least to all manner of routine communications and even to prosecutions for minor offences. Thus it can no longer be said that the writer of such communications has any "certainty at the time of writing that the document would not be disclosed." So we have the curious result that "freedom and candour of communication" is supposed not to be inhibited by knowledge of the writer that his report may be disclosed in a criminal case, but would still be supposed to be inhibited if he thought that his report might be disclosed in a civil case.

The Attorney-General did not deny that, even where the full contents of a report have already been made public in a criminal case, Crown privilege is still claimed for that report in a later civil case. And he was quite candid about the reason for that. Crown privilege is claimed in the civil case not to protect the document—its contents are already public property—but to protect the writer from civil liability should he be sued for libel or other tort. No doubt the Government have weighed the danger that knowledge of such protection might encourage malicious writers against the advantage that honest reporters shall not be subjected to vexatious actions, and have come to the conclusion that it is an advantage to the public service to afford this protection. But that seems very far removed from the original purpose of Crown privilege.

And the statement, as it has been explained to us, makes clear another point. The Minister who withholds production of a "class" document has no duty to consider the degree of public interest involved in a particular case by frustrating in that way the due administration of justice. If it is in the public interest in his view to withhold document of that class, then it matters not whether the result of withholding a document is merely to deprive a litigant of some evidence on a minor issue in a case of little importance or, on the other hand, is to make it impossible to do justice at all in a case of the greatest importance. I cannot think that it is satisfactory that there should be no means at all of weighing, in any civil case, the public interest involved in withholding the document against the public interest that it should be produced.

So it appears to me that the present position is so unsatisfactory that this House must re-examine the whole question in light of all the authorities.

Two questions will arise: first, whether the court is to have any right to question the finality of a Minister's certificate and, secondly, if it has such a right, how and in what circumstances that right is to be exercised and made effective.

A Minister's certificate may be given on one or other of two grounds: either because it would be against the public interest to disclose the contents of the particular document or documents in question, or because the document belongs to a class of documents which ought to be withheld, whether or not there is anything in the particular document in question disclosure of which would be against the public interest. It does not appear that any serious difficulties have arisen or are likely to arise with regard to the first class. However wide the power of the court may be held to be, cases would be very rare in which it could be proper to question the view of the responsible Minister that it would be contrary to the public interest to make public the contents of a particular document. A question might arise whether it would be possible to separate those parts of a document of which disclosure would be innocuous from those parts which ought not to be made public, but I need not pursue that question now. In the present case your Lordships are directly concerned with the second class of documents. . . .

The last important case before *Duncan's case*[11] was *Robinson* v. *State of South Australia (No. 2)*.[12] The State Government had assumed the function of acquiring and marketing all wheat grown in the state and distributing the proceeds to the growers. A number of actions were brought alleging negligence in carrying out this function. The Australian courts had upheld objections by the state to discovery of a mass of documents in their possession. For reasons into which I need not enter, the Privy Council could not finally decide the matter. What they did[13] was "to remit the case to the Supreme Court of South Australia with a direction that it is one proper for the exercise by that court of its power of itself inspecting the documents for which privilege is set up in order to see whether the claim is justified. Their Lordships have already given reasons for their conclusion that the court is possessed of such a power." This case was of course dealt with in *Duncan's case*[14] but not, I venture to think, in a very satisfactory way. Lord Simon said[15] that "their Lordships' conclusion was partly based on their interpretation of a rule of court." In fact it was not. The passage which I have quoted occurs in the judgment before there is any reference to the rule of court. And beyond that Lord Simon said no more than "I cannot agree with this view." So he thought that, even where discovery is sought in an action against the state arising out of what was in effect a commercial transaction, the view of the Minister is conclusive. But Lord Kilmuir's statement promised a considerable relaxation in contract cases.

I shall not examine the earlier Scottish authorities in detail because the position in Scotland has now been made clear in the *Glasgow Corporation* case[16] where the earlier authorities were fully considered. Lord Simons said[17]: "In the course of the

[11] [1942] A.C. 624.
[12] [1931] A.C. 704; 47 T.L.R. 454 (P.C.).
[13] [1931] A.C. 704 at p. 725.
[14] [1942] A.C. 624.
[15] *Ibid*. at p. 641.
[16] 1956 S.C. (H.L.) 1.
[17] *Ibid*. at p. 11.

present appeal we have had the advantage of an exhaustive examination of the relevant law from the earliest times, and it has left me in no doubt that there always has been and is now in the law of Scotland an inherent power of the court to override the Crown's objection to produce documents on the ground that it would injure the public interest to do so."

Now I must examine the English cases since 1942. [His Lordship referred to *Ellis* v. *Home Office*[18]; *Broome* v. *Broome*[19]; *Whitehall* v. *Whitehall*[20]; and *Gain* v. *Grain*[21] and continued:]

These cases open up a new field which must be kept in view when considering whether a Minister's certificate is to be regarded as conclusive. I do not doubt that it is proper to prevent the use of any document, wherever it comes from, if disclosure of its contents would really injure the national interest, and I do not doubt that it is proper to prevent any witness, whoever he may be, from disclosing facts which in the national interest ought not to be disclosed. Moreover, it is the duty of the court to do this without the intervention of any Minister if possible serious injury to the national interest is readily apparent. But in this field it is more than ever necessary that in a doubtful case the alleged public interest in concealment should be balanced against the public interest that the administration of justice should not be frustrated. If the Minister, who has no duty to balance these conflicting public interests, says no more than that in his opinion the public interest requires concealment, and if that is to be accepted as conclusive in this field as well as with regard to documents in his possession, it seems to me not only that very serious injustice may be done to the parties, but also that the due administration of justice may be gravely impaired for quite inadequate reasons.

It cannot be said that there would be any constitutional impropriety in enabling the court to overrule a Minister's objection. That is already the law in Scotland. In Commonwealth jurisdictions from which there is an appeal to the Privy Council the courts generally follow *Robinson's* case,[22] and where they do not they follow *Duncan's* case[23] with reluctance. . . .

Lord Simon did not say that courts in England have no power to overrule the executive. He said (*Duncan's* case[24]): ". . . the decision ruling out such documents is the decision of the judge. . . . It is the judge who is in control of the trial, not the executive, but the proper ruling for the judge to give is as above expressed." That, is to accept the Minister's view in every case. In my judgment, in considering what it is "proper" for a court to do we must have regard to the need, shown by 25 years' experience since *Duncan's* case,[25] that the courts should balance the public interest in the proper administration of justice against the public interest in withholding any evidence which a Minister considers ought to be withheld.

I would therefore propose that the House ought now to decide that courts have and are entitled to exercise a power and duty to hold a balance between the public interest, as expressed by a Minister, to withhold certain documents or other evidence, and the public interest in ensuring the proper administration of justice. That does not mean that a court would reject a Minister's view: full weight must be given to it in every case, and if the Minister's reasons are of a character which judicial experience is not competent to weigh, then the Minister's view must prevail. But experience has shown that reasons given for withholding whole classes of documents are often not of that character. For example a court is

---

[18] [1953] 2 Q.B. 135; [1953] 3 W.L.R. 105; 2 All E.R. 149 (C.A.).
[19] [1955] P. 190; [1955] 2 W.L.R. 401; [1955] 1 All E.R. 201.
[20] 1957 S.C. 30.
[21] [1961] 1 W.L.R. 1469; [1962] 1 All E.R. 63.
[22] [1931] A.C. 704.
[23] [1942] A.C. 624.
[24] *Ibid.* at p. 642.
[25] [1942] A.C. 624.

perfectly well able to assess the likelihood that, if the writer of a certain class of document knew that there was a chance that his report might be produced in legal proceedings, he would make a less full and candid report than he would otherwise have done.

I do not doubt that there are certain classes of documents which ought not to be disclosed whatever their content may be. Virtually everyone agrees that Cabinet minutes and the like ought not to be disclosed until such time as they are only of historical interest.[26] But I do not think that many people would give as the reason that premature disclosure would prevent candour in the Cabinet. To my mind the most important reason is that such disclosure would create or fan ill-informed or captious public or political criticism. The business of government is difficult enough as it is, and no government could contemplate with equanimity the inner workings of the government machine being exposed to the gaze of those ready to criticise without adequate knowledge of the background and perhaps with some axe to grind. And that must, in my view, also apply to all documents concerned with policy making within departments including, it may be, minutes and the like by quite junior officials and correspondence with outside bodies. Further it may be that deliberations about a particular case require protection as much as deliberations about policy. I do not think that it is possible to limit such documents by any definition. But there seems to me to be a wide difference between such documents and routine reports. There may be special reasons for withholding some kinds of routine documents, but I think that the proper test to be applied is to ask, in the language of Lord Simon in *Duncan's* case,[27] whether the withholding of a document because it belongs to a particular class is really "necessary for the proper functioning of the public service."

It appears to me that, if the Minister's reasons are such that a judge can properly weigh them, he must, on the other hand, consider what is the probable importance in the case before him of the documents or other evidence sought to be withheld. If he decides that on balance the documents probably ought to be produced, I think that it would generally be best that he should see them before ordering production and if he thinks that the Minister's reasons are not clearly expressed he will have to see the documents before ordering production. I can see nothing wrong in the judge seeing documents without their being shown to the parties. Lord Simon said (in *Duncan's* case[28]) that "where the Crown is a party . . . this would amount to communicating with one party to the exclusion of the other." I do not agree. The parties see the Minister's reasons. Where a documents has not been prepared for the information of the judge, it seems to me a misuse of language to say that the judge "communicates with" the holder of the document by reading it. If on reading the document he still thinks that it ought to be produced he will order its production.

But it is important that the Minister should have a right to appeal, before the document is produced. This matter was not fully investigated in the argument before your Lordships. But is does appear that in one way or another there can be an appeal if the document is in the custody of a servant of the Crown or of a person who is willing to co-operate with the Minister. There may be difficulty if it is in the hands of a person who wishes to produce it. But the difficultly could occur today if a witness wishes to give some evidence which the Minister unsuccessfully urges the court to prevent from being given. It may be that this is a matter which deserves further investigation by the Crown authorities.

The documents in this case are in the possession of a police force. The position of the police is peculiar. They are not servants of the Crown and they do not take orders from the Government. But they are carrying out an essential function of

---

[26] But see *Air Canada* v. *Secretary of State for Trade* [1983] 2 A.C. 394; *post, per* Lord Fraser of Tullybelton.

[27] [1942] A.C. 624 at p. 642.

[28] [1942] A.C. 624 at p. 640.

Government, and various Crown rights, privileges and exemptions have been held to apply to them. Their position was explained in *Coomber* v. *Berkshire Justices*[29] and cases there cited. It has never been denied that they are entitled to Crown privilege with regard to documents, and it is essential that they should have it.

The police are carrying on an unending war with criminals many of whom are today highly intelligent. So it is essential that there should be no disclosure of anything which might give any useful information to those who organise criminal activities. And it would generally be wrong to require disclosure in a civil case of anything which might be material in a pending prosecution: but after a verdict has been given or it has been decided to take no proceedings there is not the same need for secrecy. With regard to other documents there seems to be no greater need for protection than in the case of departments of Government.

It appears to me to be most improbable that any harm would be done by disclosure of the probationary reports on the appellant or of the report from the police training centre. With regard to the report which the respondent made to his chief constable with a view to the prosecution of the appellant there could be more doubt, although no suggestion was made in argument that disclosure of its contents would be harmful now that the appellant has been acquitted. And, as I have said, these documents may prove to be of vital importance in this litigation.

In my judgment, this appeal should be allowed and these documents ought now to be required to be produced for inspection. If it is then found that disclosure would not, in your Lordships' view be prejudicial to the public interest, or that any possibility of such prejudice is, in the case of each of the documents, insufficient to justify its being withheld, then disclosure should be ordered.
Appeal allowed.
The documents were accordingly produced.

May 2, 1968. **LORD REID.** My Lords, I have examined the five documents with which the case is concerned. I can find nothing in any of them the disclosure of which would, in my view, be in any way prejudicial to the proper administration of the Cheshire Constabulary or to the general public interest. I am therefore of the opinion that they must be made available in this litigation.

Their Lordships accordingly voted that the order of the District Registrar be restored, "that the defendant do produce for inspection at his solicitor's office to the plaintiff and his advisers on reasonable notice the five documents. ...."

Note
Conway eventually lost his action for malicious prosecution because he failed to prove want of reasonable or probable cause (*The Times*, December 17, 1969).

[29] (1883) 9 App.Cas. 61 (H.L.).

R. v. Lewes Justices, Ex parte Secretary of State for the Home Department (Rogers v. Home Secretary)

[1973] A.C. 388

House of Lords

Rogers, a company director, applied to the Gaming Board for certificates of consent in relation to five bingo clubs, which certificates were refused. He then commenced proceedings for criminal libel in respect of a letter written by the Assistant Chief Constable of Sussex to the Board in reply to their request for certain information about him. The Home Secretary and the Board applied for orders of certiorari to set aside witness summonses directed to the Chief Constable and the secretary of the Board to give evidence and to produce certain documents, including the letter requesting the information and reply. The Divisional Court (Lord Parker C.J., Widgery L.J. and Bridge J.) granted the Home Secretary's application and made no order on the Board's application.

On appeal to the House of Lords (Lord Reid, Lord Morris of Borth-y-Gest, Lord Pearson, Lord Simon of Glaisdale, and Lord Salmon) it was held unanimously, varying the decision of the Divisional Court, that the public interest required that the letters should not be produced either by the Chief Constable or by the Board.

Their Lordships took time for consideration.

LORD REID: My Lords, by 1968 it had become notorious that the control of many gaming establishments was passing into the hands of very undesirable people. The Gaming Act 1968 provides for licensing of premises used for gaming and by section 10 it established the Gaming Board for Great Britain with a special duty to keep under review the extent and character of gaming. One of its duties is to deal with applications for its consent to apply for a gaming licence. No licences can be granted to any applicant unless he has obtained such consent from the Board. The functions and duties of the Board in this regard are set out in Schedule 2 to the Act, paragraph 4. The Board are required to make unusually extensive inquiries not only into the capacity and diligence of all applicants but also into their character, reputation and financial standing and any other circumstances appearing to the Board to be relevant.

Applications were made by a company of which the appellant was a director and by the appellant himself. All were refused after the appellant had been interviewed by the Board.

It is the custom of the Board to obtain confidential information about applicants from the police. The appellant says that there came into his possession from an anonymous source a copy of a letter written about him to the Board by Mr. Ross, Assistant Chief Constable of Sussex. Obviously this letter had been abstracted by improper means from the files of the Board or of the police. The appellant says that this letter contains highly damaging libellous statements about him and that he wishes to take proceedings to clear his reputation. The means he chose for doing that was to seek to prosecute Mr. Ross for criminal libel. To succeed he must prove that the letter was sent, so he applied for witness summonses against representatives of the Board and the Chief Constable requiring them to produce, *inter alia*, this letter. The Attorney-General then sought an order of certiorari to quash the summonses on the ground that the documents called for were the subject of Crown privilege and he succeeded.

The appellant's case may not seem to be very meritorious and there are obvious objections to the means which he has chosen for the vindication of his character. But it would be wrong to seek to dispose of this case on narrow grounds, so I shall proceed on the footing that he is acting in good faith and has a legitimate interest in seeking production of the letter. If production is to be withheld it must be on grounds which have nothing to do with the merits or demerits of the appellant.

The ground put forward has been said to be Crown privilege. I think that that expression is wrong and may be misleading. There is no question of any privilege in the ordinary sense of the word. The real question is whether the public interest requires that the letter shall not be produced and whether that public interest is so strong as to override the ordinary right and interest of a litigant that he shall be able to lay before a court of justice all relevant evidence. A Minister of the Crown is always an appropriate and often the most appropriate person to assert this public interest, and the evidence or advice which he gives to the court is always valuable and may sometimes be indispensable. But, in my view, it must always be open to any person interested to raise the question and there may be cases where the trial judge should himself raise the question if no one else has done so. In the present case the question of public interest was raised by both the Attorney-General and the Gaming Board. In my judgment both were entitled to raise the matter. Indeed I think that in the circumstances it was the duty of the Board to do as they have done.

The claim in the present case is not based on the nature of the contents for this particular letter. It is based on the fact that the Board cannot adequately perform their statutory duty unless they can preserve the confidentiality for all communications to them regarding the character, reputation or antecedents of applicants for their consent.

Claims for "class privilege" were fully considered by this House in *Conway* v. *Rimmer*.[1] It was made clear that there is a heavy burden of proof on any authority which makes such a claim. But the possibility of establishing such a claim was not ruled out. I venture to quote what I said in that case, at p.952: "There may be special reasons for with-holding some kinds of routine documents, but I think that the proper test to be applied is to ask, in the language of Lord Simon in *Duncan* v. *Cammell Laird & Co. Ltd.*,[2] whether the withholding of a document because it belongs to a particular class is really 'necessary for the proper functioning of the public service.'"

I do not think that "the public service" should be construed narrowly. Here the question is whether the withholding of this class of documents is really necessary to enable the Board adequately to perform its statutory duties. If it is, then we are enabling the will of Parliament to be carried out.

There are very unusual features about this case. The Board require the fullest information they can get in order to identify and exclude persons of dubious character and reputation from the privilege of obtaining a licence to conduct a gaming establishment. There is no obligation on anyone to give any information to the Board. No doubt many law-abiding citizens would tell what they know even if there was some risk of their identity becoming known, although many perfectly honourable people do not want to be thought to be mixed up in such affairs. But it is obvious that the best source of information about dubious characters must often be persons of dubious character themselves. It has long been recognised that the identity of police informers must in the public interest be kept secret and the same considerations must apply to those who volunteer information to the Board. Indeed, it is in evidence that many refuse to speak unless assured of absolute secrecy.

The letter called for in this case came from the police. I feel sure that they would not be deterred from giving full information by any fear of consequences to themselves if there were any disclosure. But much of the information which they can give must come from sources which must be protected and they would rightly take this into account. Even if information were given without naming the source, the very nature of the information might, if it were communicated to the person concerned, at least give him a very shrewd idea from whom it had come.

[1] [1968] A.C. 910.
[2] [1942] A.C. 624 at p. 642.

It is possible that some documents coming to the Board could be disclosed without fear of such consequences. But I would think it quite impracticable for the Board or the court to be sure of this. So it appears to me that, if there is not to be very serious danger of the Board being deprived of information essential for the proper performance of their difficult task, there must be a general rule that they are not bound to produce any document which gives information to them about an applicant.

We must then balance that fact against the public interest that the course of justice should not be impeded by the withholding of evidence. We must, I think, take into account that these documents only came into existence because the applicant is asking for a privilege and is submitting his character and reputation to scrutiny. The documents are not used to deprive him of any legal right. The Board have a wide discretion. Not only can they refuse his application on the ground of bad reputation although he may say that he has not deserved that reputation; it is not denied that the Board can also take into account any unfavourable impression which he has made during an interview with the Board.

Natural justice requires that the Board should act in good faith and that they should so far as possible tell him the gist of any grounds on which they propose to refuse his application so that he may show such grounds to be unfounded in fact. But the Board must be trusted to do that; we have been referred to their practice in this matter and I see nothing wrong in it.

In the present case the Board told the appellant nothing about the contents of this letter because they say that they had sufficient grounds for refusing his application without any need to rely on anything in the letter. Their good faith in this matter is not subject to any substantial challenge. If the appellant had not by someone's wrongful act obtained a copy of the letter there was no reason why he should ever have known anything about it.

In my judgment on balance the public interest clearly requires that documents of this kind should not be disclosed, and that public interest is not affected by the fact that by some wrongful means a copy of such a document has been obtained and published by some person. I would therefore dismiss the appellant's appeal.

There is a cross-appeal by the Gaming Board because the Divisional Court refused to make in favour of the Board an order to that which they made in favour of the Home Secretary. The point of law certified was: "Whether the Divisional Court were right in refusing to make an order upholding the claim by the Gaming Board for Great Britain to privilege in respect of the production of the letters of July 7 and September 15, 1969 referred to in the said witness summons."

For the reasons which I have given I do not think that the right to withhold the documents depends on or flows from any privilege. It arises from the public interest and the Board are entitled to assert that public interest. I would therefore allow the cross-appeal. . . .

LORD SIMON OF GLAISDALE: My Lords, "Crown privilege" is a misnomer and apt to be misleading. It refers to the rule that certain evidence is inadmissible on the ground that its adduction would be contrary to the public interest. It is true that the public interest which demands that the evidence be withheld has to be weighed against the public interest in the administration of justice that courts should have the fullest possible access to all relevant material (*R.* v. *Hardy*[3]; *Marks* v. *Beyfus*[4]; *Conway* v. *Rimmer*[5]); but once the former public interest is held to outweigh the latter, the evidence cannot in any circumstances be admitted. It is not a privilege which may be waived by the Crown (see *Marks* v. *Beyfus* at p.500) or

[3] (1794) 24 State Tr. 199 at p. 808.
[4] (1890) 25 Q.B.D. 494.
[5] [1968] A.C. 910.

by anyone else. The Crown has prerogatives, not privilege. The right to procure that admissible evidence be withheld from, or inadmissible evidence adduced to, the courts is not one of the prerogatives of the Crown.

Where the Crown comes into the picture is that some of the matters of public interest which demand that evidence be withheld are peculiarly within the knowledge of servants of the Crown. The evidence, for example, may be of acts of state (see A.L. Smith L.J. in *Chatterton* v. *Secretary of State for India in Council*[6]) or have a bearing on national security. Any litigant or witness may draw attention to the nature of the evidence with a view to its being excluded. The court will proprio motu exclude evidence the production of which it sees is contrary to public interest (see Wills J. in *Hennessy* v. *Wright*[7]; *Chatterton's case*[8]; Viscount Simon L.C. in *Duncan* v. *Cammell Laird & Co. Ltd.*[9])—particularly where it falls into a class the exclusion of which has already received judicial recognition, like sources of police information (*R.* v. *Hardy*[10]; *Hennessy* v. *Wright*[11]; *Marks* v. *Beyfus*[12]). But the evidence may fall into a class which has not previously received judicial recognition; or it may be questionably of a previously recognised class; or it may fall outside any class of evidence which should be excluded in the public interest, yet still itself as an individual item be excluded in the public interest. In all these cases a Minister of the Crown is likely to be in a peculiarly favourable position to form a judgment as to the public prejudice of forensic publication; and the communication of his view is likely to be of assistance to the court in performing its duty of ruling on the admissibility of evidence. Moreover, for the reasons stated by my noble and learned friend, Lord Pearson, there are advantages in processing the matter through the Law Officers' Department; and the Attorney-General is traditionally the person entitled to intervene in a suit where the prerogatives of the Crown are affected (see *Adams* v. *Adams* (*Att.-Gen. intervening*)[13]): although there is no prerogative in itself to exclude evidence, certain evidence may affect the prerogative (*e.g.* of diplomatic relations or as the fount to honour).

In his affidavit of February 11, 1971, Sir Stanley Raymond, chairman of the Gaming Board for Great Britain, affirmed that "the said letter of September 15, 1969, from Patrick Ross . . . refers to a source of information." This was at no time challenged. Sources of police information are a judicially recognised class of evidence excluded on the ground of public policy, unless their production is required to establish innocence in a criminal trial (*R.* v. *Hardy*,[14]; *Hennessy* v. *Wright*,[15]; *Marks* v. *Beyfus*[16]). . . .

I would therefore dismiss the appeal of Mr. Rogers and allow that of the Gaming Board.

LORD SALMON [in the course of his judgment, said]: There can be doubt that the letter of September 15, 1969, was written in confidence. There is equally little doubt that the fact alone does not confer immunity either from production of the letter or the disclosure of its contents—*Wheeler* v. *Le Marchant*,[17] per Sir George

[6] [1895] 2 Q.B. 189 at p. 195.
[7] (1888) 21 Q.B.D. 509 at p. 519.
[8] [1895] 2 Q.B. 189.
[9] [1942] A.C. 624 at p. 642.
[10] 24 State Tr. 199 at p. 808.
[11] 21 Q.B.D. 509 at p. 519.
[12] 25 Q.B.D. 494.
[13] [1971] P. 188 at p. 197.
[14] 24 State Tr. 199 at p. 808.
[15] 21 Q.B.D. 509 at p. 519.
[16] 25 Q.B.D. 494.
[17] (1881) 17 Ch.D. 675 at p. 681.

Jessel M.R.; *Att.-Gen.* v. *Clough*.[18] On the other hand, when it is in the public interest that confidentiality shall be safeguarded, then the party from whom the confidential document or the confidential information is being sought may lawfully refuse it. In such a case the Crown may also intervene to prevent production or disclosure of that which in the public interest ought to be protected. Such an intervention goes under the misleading name of Crown privilege. When a document or information of the kind to which I have referred is in the possession of a government department it is the duty rather than the privilege of the Minister to refuse its disclosure. When such a document or information is in the possession of a third party, again it is the duty rather than the privilege of the executive through the Attorney-General to intervene in the public interest to prevent its disclosure. In either case it is ultimately for the court to decide whether or not it is in the public interest for the document or information to be disclosed. Clearly any evidence by a Minister of State commands the highest respect. If protection is claimed on the ground that disclosure of the contents of a document would imperil the safety of the State or diplomatic relations, then the courts would without question normally allow the claim. These are topics particularly within the province of the executive but of which the courts have little, if any, experience. What might appear innocuous to the uninitiated may in reality reveal important defence secrets or cause diplomatic difficulties. There are also classes of documents and information which for years have been recognised by the law as entitled in the public interest to be immune for disclosure. In such cases the affidavit or certificate of a Minister is hardly necessary. I refer to such documents as Cabinet minutes, minutes of discussions between heads of government departments and dispatches from ambassadors abroad. Although different in nature, any evidence as to the sources from which the police obtain their information has always been recognised by the courts as entitled to the same immunity.

This immunity should not lightly be extended to any other class of document or information, but its boundaries are not to be regarded as immutably fixed. . . .

For the reasons I have explained in this speech there is clearly all the difference in the world between the question whether the public interest requires that mundane communications between all persons in the government service should be immune from discovery and the question whether the public interest requires that communications received by the Gaming Board should be immune from discovery.

My Lords, I would dismiss the appeal by Mr. Rogers and allow the Board's appeal, for in my view both the Crown and the Board were entitled to the orders for which they asked.

Appeal dismissed.
Cross-appeal allowed.

Note

Contrast *Norwich Pharmacal Co.* v. *Customs and Excise Commissioners* [1974] A.C. 133. (Records possessed by Customs and Excise necessary to establish identity of persons importing a substance in breach of Norwich's patent. *Held* Any public interest in protecting such confidentiality as might attach to records outweighed by the interests of justice in disclosure for the purpose of applicants' intended proceedings).

[18] [1963] 1 Q.B. 773.

Science Research Council v. Nasse
[1980] A.C. 1028
House of Lords

In two appeals heard together, employees claimed to be entitled, in proceedings before industrial tribunals alleging discrimination, to obtain discovery of confidential assessments and references in the possession of their employers and relating not only to them but also to other persons, particularly the persons preferred to the appellants. In both cases orders for disclosure of all the documents sought had been confirmed by the Employment Appeal Tribunal (Bristow J. presiding in the first case, Phillips J. in the second). In each case an appeal was allowed by the Court of Appeal (Lord Denning M.R., Lawton and Browne JJ.) which held that discovery should only be ordered after the industrial tribunal had inspected the documents itself of such as were necessary for the fair disposal of the case. The employees appealed to the House of Lords (Lord Wilberforce, Lord Salmon, Lord Edmund-Davis, Lord Fraser of Tullybelton and Lord Scarman.)

LORD SCARMAN: . . . The confidential nature of a documents does not, by itself, confer "public interest immunity" from disclosure. The confidential nature of a document or of evidence is no ground for a refusal to disclose the document or to give evidence, if the court requires it: *Alfred Crompton Amusement Machines Ltd.* v. *Customs and Excise Commissioners (No. 2)* [1974] A.C. 405 and *Attorney-General* v. *Clough* [1963] 1 Q.B. 773.

For myself, I regret the passing of the currently rejected term "Crown privilege." It at least emphasised the very restricted area of public interest immunity. As was pointed out by Mr. Lester Q.C. who presented most helpful submissions on behalf of the two statutory bodies as well as specifically for the appellant, Mr. Vyas, the immunity exists to protect from disclosure only information the secrecy of which is essential to the proper working of the government of the state. Defence, foreign relations, the inner workings of government at the highest levels where ministers and their advisers are formulating national policy, and the prosecution process in its pre–trial stage are the sensitive areas where the Crown must have the immunity if the government of the nation is to be effectually carried on. We are in the realm of public law, not private right. The very special case of *D.* v. *NationalSociety for the Prevention of Cruelty to Children* [1978] A.C. is not to be seen as a departure from this well established principle. Immunity from disclosure existed in that case because the House recognised the special position of the N.S.P.C.C. in the enforcement process of the provisions of the Children Act 1969: a position which the House saw as comparable with that of a prosecuting authority in criminal proceedings. But I would not with respect, go as far as my noble and learned friend, Lord Hailsham of St. Marylebone, when he said in that case, at p. 230E: "The categories of public interest are not closed"[1] nor can I agree with the dictum of my noble and learned friend, Lord Edmund-Davies, at p. 245 that, where a confidential relationship exists and disclosure would be in breach of some ethical or social value involving the public interest, the court may uphold a refusal to disclose relevant evidence, if, on balance, the public interest would be better served by excluding it.

[1] Lord Fraser of Tullybelton said of the same dictum in his speech: "Speaking for myself I fully accept that proposition, but any extension can only be made by adding new categories analogous to those already existing, just as in that case immunity was extended to a new category of informers to the N.S.P.C.C. by analogy with informers to the police who were already entitled to immunity. There is no analogy between the suggested public interest in the present cases and the kinds of public interest that have so far been held to justify immunity from disclosure. Such public interest as there is in withholding the documents from disclosure is not enought to justify the creation of a new head of immunity for a whole class of documents."

I do not find anything in *Conway* v. *Rimmer* [1968] A.C. 910 or the cases therein cited which would extend public interest immunity in this way. On the contrary, the theme of Lord Reid's speech is that the immunity arises only if "disclosure would involve a danger of real prejudice to the national interest" (p. 939A). The public interest protected by the immunity is that "harm shall not be done to the nation or the public service by disclosure": Lord Reid at p. 940D. Whatever may be true generally of the categories of public interest, the "public interest immunity," which prevents documents from being produced or evidence from being given is restricted, and is not, in my judgment, to be extended either by demanding ministers or by the courts. And, though I agree with my noble and learned friend, Lord Edmund-Davies, in believing that a court may refuse to order production of a confidential document if it takes the view that justice does not require its production, I do not see the process of decision as a balancing act. If the document is necessary for fairly disposing of the case, it must be produced, notwithstanding its confidentiality. Only if the document should be protected by public interest immunity, will there be a balancing act. And then the balance will not be between "ethical or social" values of a confidential relationship involving the public interest and the document's relevance in the litigation, but between the public interest represented by the state and its public service, i.e., the executive government, and the public interest in the administration of justice: see Lord Reid. Thus my emphasis would be different from that of my noble and learned friends. "Public interest immunity" is, in my judgment, restricted to what must be kept secret for the protection of government at the highest levels and in the truly sensitive areas of executive responsibility.

The submission, therefore, of the respondents in the *Vyas* case that confidential reports upon other employees, and particularly upon those who succeeded where the applicant failed, are immune from disclosure must be rejected. The question, then, becomes one of the exercise of the court's discretion.

It does not follow that, because we are outside the field of public interest immunity, the confidential nature of documents is to be disregarded by the court in the exercise of its discretionary power to order discovery of documents.

Under the modern practice, discovery is to be ordered in the High Court, the county court, and in an industrial tribunal whenever necessary for fairly disposing of the case or saving costs: R.S.C., Ord. 24, rr. 3, 5 and 8 : County Court Rules, Ord. 14, r. 2 (2): Industrial Tribunals (Labour Relations) Regulations 1974, r. 4, of the Schedule as amended.

In most, but not all, High Court litigation discovery is "automatic"; R.S.C., Ord. 24, r. 2. But the right to object to production of documents as unnecessary remains available to the party who has to make the discovery. In an industrial tribunal (as also in the county court) discovery is not automatic. An order has to be made by the tribunal in the proceedings. An industrial tribunal (but not, I think, a county court) may make an order not only upon a party's application, but on its own motion. And the tribunal (or court) may make either a general order or one limited to specific documents or classes of documents.

How should the discretion of an industrial tribunal (or a county court) be exercised in a discrimination case? . . . The criterion is not relevance alone, nor are general orders for discovery appropriate in this class of litigation. The true test, as formulated by the rules of the court, is whether discovery is necessary either to save costs or for the fair disposal of the case. Where speed and cheapness of legal process are essential as they are in county courts and industrial tribunals, general orders should ordinarily be avoided. And where, as will be frequent in this class of litigation, confidential records about other people are relevant, the court must honour the confidence to this extent: that it will not order production unless the interest of justice requires that they be disclosed. No hard and fast rules can be laid down: but I agree with others of your Lordships in thinking that the Employment Appeal Tribunal gave very useful guidance on the appropriate practice in *British*

Railways Board v. *Natarajan* [1979] I.C.R. 326: see the judgment delivered by Arnold J., particularly at p. 333.

To conclude, I recognise the importance of discovery in discrimination cases. There is no special law protecting confidential documents in such cases. It is for that reason that I have avoided discussing the new "statutory torts" or the investigating powers of the statutory bodies. We are concerned with the litigation of private citizens seeking redress for private wrongs. The only complicating factor is the confidential nature of relevant documents in the possession of the party from whom redress is sought. The production of some of these may be necessary for doing justice to the applicant's case. If production is necessary, they must be produced. The factor of confidence however militates against general orders for discovery and does impose upon the tribunal the duty of satisfying itself, by inspection if need be, that justice requires disclosure. Ordinarily, therefore a tribunal will itself examine documents which are confidential before it orders their disclosure.

I agree therefore that the two appeals should be dismissed. It will be for the industrial tribunal in each case to decide whether, and to what extent, discovery should be ordered. I would expect that the tribunal would decide to inspect the documents for which confidence is claimed and determine whether any, and if so, which, should be produced. The inspection should be before the hearing takes place, so that the applicant may consider any that are produced. But the tribunal retains the power to order the production of further documents at a later stage (including at the hearing itself) if in its judgment it becomes necessary to do so in the interests of justice.

Appeals dismissed.

Air Canada v. Secretary of State for Trade
[1983] 2 A.C. 394
House of Lords

The question in this litigation was when and in what circumstances the court should exercise its power to inspect documents which are relevant to an action, with a view to ordering their production, when their production has been objected to on behalf of the Crown on the ground that they fall within a class of documents the production of which would be injurious to the public interest.

The appellants argued that the British Airports Authority (B.A.A.) had increased charges for the use of Heathrow to an excessive level and with discriminatory effect. They alleged that the increases had followed upon instructions from the Secretary of State which were unlawful. They claimed that the Secretary of State had power to give financial directions to the B.A.A., but only for the purposes of the Act of 1975, and not for other purposes such as reducing the public sector borrowing requirement. They said that, because the Secretary of State's dominant purpose was to reduce the public sector borrowing requirement, his directions were ultra vires and unlawful. In order to investigate what was the Secretary of State's dominant purpose, they wish to refer to documents the production of which was objected to on behalf of the Crown.

Bingham J. ordered production for inspection by himself of certain documents (those in Category A — which is explained below in the speech of Lord Fraser of Tullybelton) but not the remaining documents (Category B). He further directed that the order for production should be stayed pending an appeal by the Secretary of State for which he gave leave in accordance with usual practice in cases where documents are ordered to be produced in spite of a claim to public interest immunity.

The Court of Appeal (Lord Denning M.R., Watkins and Fox L.JJ), unanimously allowed the Secretary of State's appeal from the decision of Bingham J., so far as it ordered production of the documents. The airline companies appealed to the House of Lords (Lord Fraser of Tullybelton, Lord Wilberforce, Lord Edmund-Davies, Lord Scarman and Lord Templeman).

LORD FRASER OF TULLYBELTON: ... The Treasury Solicitor on behalf of the Secretary of State served on the plaintiffs a list of documents, but he objected to production of certain of the documents in the list. The objection was supported by a certificate dated June 26, 1981, by Sir Kenneth Clucas, K.C.B., the then Permanent Secretary to the Department of Trade, claiming immunity for two categories of documents in the list. Category A consist of approximately 100 documents being communications between to and from ministers (including ministers' personal secretaries acting on behalf of ministers) and minutes and briefs for ministers, other documents considered by ministers, drafts for consideration by ministers and memoranda of meetings attended by ministers. The certificate explained that all these documents relate to

"(a) The formulation of the policy of the previous government in relation to the early consideration of the policy of the B.A.A. commencing in 1977 . . . (b) In relation to (sic) formulation of the policy of the present government regarding the limitation of borrowing by the public sector with particular regard to the exercise of the Secretary of State's powers to control the B.A.A.'s borrowing and the effect of B.A.A.'s plans for substantial capital expenditure. (c) In relation to formulation of the policy to be adopted by the present government towards the B.A.A.'s proposal for landing fees for 1980–81 . . . (d) In relation to formulation of the policy to be adopted by the present government in view of representations by Members of Parliament and the various airlines using London Heathrow Airport and their representatives.

"Category B. These consist of communications between, to and from senior officials of the Department of Trade, of the Treasury, of the Foreign and Commonwealth Office and of the Departments of Energy, Industry and Transport . . . relating to the formulation of one or more aspects of the policy described in category A."

The certificate further provided, inter alia:

"It is, in my opinion, necessary for the proper functioning of the public service that the documents in category A and category B should be withheld from production. They are all documents falling within the class of documents relating to the formulation of government policy. Such policy was decided at a high level, involving as it did matters of major economic importance to the United Kingdom. The documents in question cannot properly be described as routine documents. . . ."

The certificate explains further the reasons for objection on lines very similar to the certificate referred to in *Burmah Oil Co. Ltd.* v. *Governor and Company of the Bank of England* [1980] A.C. 1090. It was accepted on behalf of the appellants that the objections were valid, that is to say that the certificate stated grounds which were relevant and persuasive, and that it was in proper form. The reason why it was granted by the Permanent Secretary and not by a minister was that some of the documents related to formulation of a policy of the previous government which, by constitutional practice, are not disclosed to their successors in another government.[1] A supplement certificate was made on September 10, 1981, by Sir Kenneth Clucas in respect of a further document but nothing turns upon it. There were further supplemental certificates by Sir Kenneth Clucas's successor as Permanent Secretary of the Department of Trade and by the Secretary of the Cabinet. These were made after the decision by Bingham J. and no special point arises on them.

[Lord Fraser then referred to *Conway* v. *Rimmer* [1968] AC 910 as deciding that a certificate by a minister stating that production of documents of a certain class would be contrary to the public interest, was not conclusive. He then went on to quote Lord Reid]

"I do not doubt that there are certain classes of documents which ought not to be disclosed whatever their content may be. Virtually everyone agrees that Cabinet minutes and the like ought not to be disclosed until such time as they are only of historical interest."

The latter observation was strictly speaking obiter in *Conway* where the documents in question were reports on a probationer police constable by his superiors.

I do not think that even Cabinet minutes are completely immune from disclosure in a case where, for example, the issue in a litigation involves serious misconduct by a Cabinet Minister. Such cases have occurred in Australia (see *Sankey* v. *Whitlam* (1978) 21 A.L.R. 505) and in the United States (see *United States* v. *Nixon* (1974) 418 U.S. 683) but fortunately not in the United Kingdom: see also the New Zealand case of *Environmental Defence Society Inc.* v. *South Pacific Aluminium Ltd.* (*No.* 2) [1981] 1 N.Z.L.R. 153. But while Cabinet documents do not have complete immunity, they are entitled to a high degree of protection against disclosure. In the present case the documents in category A do not enjoy quite the status of Cabinet minutes, but they approach that level in that they may disclose the reasons for Cabinet decisions and the process by which the decisions were reached. The reasons why such documents should not normally be disclosed until they have become of purely historical interest were considered in *Burmah Oil Co. Ltd.* v. *Governor and Company of the Bank of England* [1980] A.C. 1090, 1112, per Lord Wilberforce . . .

Mr. Stamler, who appeared for the plaintiffs, submitted a persuasive argument to the effect that no harm could be done by a judge inspecting the documents in

---

[1] See C. & A.L. p. 116 and p. 313.

private, and that, as they might be of determinative importance in the decision of the action, the judge should "take a peep" as my noble and learned friend Lord Edmund-Davies put it in *Burmah Oil Co. Ltd.* v. *Governor and Company of the Bank of England* [1980] A.C.1090, 1129D. Mr. Stamler submitted that when the question was whether the court should inspect the document in private, the parties seeking disclosure only had to show that the document were likely to be "very significant" for decision of the case without regard to whether they were likely to assist him or his opponent. But he accepted that when the judge, having inspected the documents, came to the later question or whether to order them to be produced, the question was different and it then became relevant to consider whether disclosure would assist the party seeking it.

My Lords, I do not think it would be possible to state a test in a form which could be applied in all cases. Circumstances vary greatly. The weight of the public interest against disclosure will vary according to the nature of the particular documents in question; for example, it will in general be strong where the documents are Cabinet papers than when they are at a lower level. The weight of the public interest in favour of disclosure will vary even more widely, because it depends upon the probable evidential value to the part seeking disclosure of the particular documents, in almost infinitely variable circumstances of individual cases. The most that can usefully be said is that, in order to persuade the court even to inspect documents for which public interest immunity is claimed, the party seeking disclosure ought at least to satisfy the court that the documents are very likely to contain materials which could give substantial support to his contention on an issue which arises in the case, and that without them he might be "deprived of the means of ... proper presentation" of his case: see *Glasgow Corporation* v. *Central Land Board*, 1956 S.C.(H.L.) 1, 18, *per* Lord Radcliffe.

Applying these considerations to the present appeal, I am of opinion that the case for inspection of the category A documents by the court has not been made out. The appeal proceeds on the basis, expressly accepted for the purpose of the present argument by the Lord Advocate, on behalf of the Secretary of State, that the plaintiffs have a cause of action under the constitutional head of the case. It is abundantly clear that they already have documents to support their case — viz., the White Paper on The Nationalised Industries (Cmnd. 7131) published in March 1978 and a statement by the Secretary of State to the House of Commons on February 26, 1980, Hansard 91980), vol. 979, cols. 499–500 in which he announced that he had set a target of six per cent. per annum on net assets revalued at current cost as a reasonable target for the B.A.A., and referred to the White Paper.

The plaintiffs do not make any case that the Secretary of State's true reasons were different from those which he had publicly announced. In these circumstances it seems to me that any information contained in the category A document would almost certainly tend merely to repeat the information already known to and relied on by the plaintiffs, and published to the world. It is unlikely to add anything material. It is therefore unlikely that access to category A documents would assist the plaintiffs in proving their case.

LORD WILBERFORCE: ... The degree of likelihood (of providing support for the plaintiff's case) may be variously expressed: "likely" was the word used by Lord Edmund-Davies in *Burmah Oil*: a "reasonable probability" by Lord Keith of Kinkel. Both expressions must means something beyond speculation, some concrete ground for belief which takes the case beyond a mere "fishing" expedition. One cannot attain greater precision in stating what must be a matter of estimation. I would accept either formula.

LORD SCARMAN: ... Faced with a properly formulated certificate claiming public interest immunity, the court must first examine the grounds put forward. If it is a "class" objection and the documents (as in *Conway* v. *Rimmer* [1968] A.C.910) are routine in character, the court may inspect so as to ascertain the strength of the public interest in immunity and the needs of justice before deciding whether to order production. If it is a "contents" claim, e.g., a specific national security matter, the court will ordinarily accept the judgment of the minister. But if it is a class claim in which the objection on the face of the certificate is a strong one—as in this case where the documents are minutes and memoranda passing at a high level between ministers and their advisers and concerned with the formulation of policy—the court will pay great regard to the minister's view (or that of the senior official who has signed the certificate). It will not inspect unless there is a likelihood that the documents will be necessary for disposing fairly of the case or saving costs. Certainly, if, like Bingham J. in this case, the court should think that the documents might be "determinative" of the issues in the action to which they relate, the court should inspect: for in such a case there may be grave doubt as to which way the balance of public interest falls: *Burmah Oil Co. Ltd.* v. *Governor and Company of the Bank of England* [1980] A.C. 1090, 1134–5, 1145. But, unless the court is satisfied on the material presented to it that the documents are likely to be necessary for fairly disposing of the case, it will not inspect for the simple reason that unless the likelihood exists there is nothing to set against the public interest in immunity from production.

[Lord Edmund-Davies delivered a speech in which he agreed with the reasons given for dismissing the appeal by Lord Fraser of Tullybelton. Lord Templeman, in his speech expressed his agreement with the views of Lord Fraser of Tullybelton and Lord Scarman].

Appeal dismissed.

Note.

In *Hasselblad Ltd.* v. *Orbinson, supra* p. 164 the Court of Appeal refused to recognise that absolute privilege attached to a letter sent to the European Commission in connection with an investigation into alleged breaches of Article 85. Sir John Donaldson M.R. and O'Connor L.J. held, however, that just as there is a public interest immunity from disclosure, so public interest in the administration of justice can prevent the use of documents which, have, as here, been disclosed. Sir John Donaldson M.R. said that "[the letter's] disclosure to Hasselblad was for a very limited purpose and Hasselblad propose to use it for a very different purpose. The obstacles which will, in future, be in the way of the Commission in investigating breaches of articles 85 and 86 of the Treaty, if Hasselblad can proceed with this action, are obvious. Either the Commission will be unable to make any use of volunteered evidential material; because it dare not disclose it to the alleged infringer, or it will disclose this material in the certain knowledge that if the informer is sued for libel, the supply of information will be severely reduced. Furthermore, it cannot be right that national courts and Community institutions shall both independently weigh the force of particular evidence with the possibility of inconsistent results."

INDEX